WITHDRAWN

The Sea of Learning

Mobility and Identity in Nineteenth-Century Guangzhou

Harvard East Asian Monographs 269

The Sea of Learning

Mobility and Identity in
Nineteenth-Century
Guangzhou

Steven B. Miles

Published by the Harvard University Asia Center
Distributed by Harvard University Press
Cambridge (Massachusetts) and London, 2006

© 2006 by the President and Fellows of Harvard College

Printed in the United States of America

The Harvard University Asia Center publishes a monograph series and, in coordination with the Fairbank Center for East Asian Research, the Korea Institute, the Reischauer Institute of Japanese Studies, and other faculties and institutes, administers research projects designed to further scholarly understanding of China, Japan, Vietnam, Korea, and other Asian countries. The Center also sponsors projects addressing multidisciplinary and regional issues in Asia.

Library of Congress Cataloging-in-Publication Data

Miles, Steven B., 1964–
    Mobility and identity in nineteenth-century Guangzhou / Steven B. Miles.
       p. cm. — (Harvard East Asian monographs ; 269)
    Includes bibliographical references and index.
    ISBN 0-674-02134-7 (cl : alk. paper)
    1. Guangzhou (China)—Intellectual life—19th century. 2. Education—China—Guangzhou—History—19th century. I. Title. II. Series.
    DS797.32.G836M56 2006
    951'.275033—dc22   2006010746

Index by the author

Designed and typeset by Pinnacle Design, New York City

∞ Printed on acid-free paper

Last figure below indicates year of this printing
16 15 14 13 12 11 10 09 08 07 06

ACKNOWLEDGMENTS

Although it is of a much smaller scale than the collaborative anthologies described in its pages, this book has benefited even more immensely from the help of numerous teachers, colleagues, and friends. I owe my greatest debt of gratitude to my advisor at the University of Washington, R. Kent Guy, for his encouragement and advice. I hope that I have done justice to his suggestion to write a history of intellectuals rather than an intellectual history. David Knechtges welcomed me into his courses and devoted a great deal of his time to help me with numerous texts. Thanks are also due to my other teachers in Seattle: Hok-lam Chan, Kenneth Pyle, and John Toews. Stevan Harrell very kindly served as an outside reader, and I learned a great deal from him in a very short time. Through discussions and critical readings I have also learned much from my friends and colleagues in Seattle: James Anderson, Morris Bian, Dai Yingcong, Chris Dakin, Keith Dede, Li Yi, Robin McNeal, Tom Reilly, Jennifer Rudolph, Helen Schneider, Stephen Udry, and Ding Xiang Warner.

Like many of the Cantonese examinees at the Sea of Learning Hall, my intellectual development owes much to scholars trained in a cultural center in the north who later taught children of the nouveaux riches on the southern frontier. During my undergraduate years at Trinity University, Donald N. Clark introduced me to Chinese history and inspired me to become a scholar. At the University of Texas, Edward Rhoads guided me through my first years of graduate study and perhaps subtly planted in my mind the idea of working on Guangzhou. During a brief sojourn in the north, I learned a great deal about the art of reading from Guy Alitto.

Several people have read parts of the manuscript in various stages of completion. Peter Bol, Cynthia Brokaw, Michael Chang, Christine Johnson, Chiu-Mi Lai, Li Cho-ying, Susan Mann, Joanna Handlin Smith, Janice Stockard, Wing-Kai To, Lori Watt, Jonathan Wiesen, and members of the History Department Reading Group at the Massachusetts Institute of Technology kindly read and commented on individual chapters. Jerry Dennerline read the entire manuscript for the Harvard University Asia Center Publications Program and offered very helpful comments. Tobie Meyer-Fong has helped me to refine my manuscript in countless ways; she read individual chapters at various stages, read the entire manuscript as a reviewer for the Asia Center, and kindly offered suggestions in response to numerous queries. I am deeply indebted to her. Du Yongtao, Benjamin Elman, Seth Harter, Robert Hegel, Barry Keenan, Yeewan Koon, Li Xiaorong, Sucheta Mazumdar, and Chi-hung Yim offered useful suggestions. John Carroll and Elisabeth Köll provided wise advice on steering a manuscript through to publication.

At National Taiwan University, my teachers Ho Yu-sen and Hsia Ch'ang-pu provided a thorough grounding in Qing intellectual history. Tim Baker, Dennis Cheng, Ts'ai Ch'ang-lin, and Ho Guong-ru also generously shared their insights. At the Academia Sinica, I was kindly hosted by the Institute of History and Philology. Chiu Peng-sheng and Wang Fan-sen at History and Philology, and Chang So-an at the Institute of Modern History, freely offered their time. My fellow visiting doctoral students at Academia Sinica—David Atwill, Robert Culp, Ruth Mostern, and Hilde De Weerdt—helped me to trim an unmanageable topic into a more focused dissertation. At Sun Yat-sen University (Zhongshan daxue) in Guangzhou, my teachers and friends, in particular Bao Wei, Chen Chunsheng, May-bo Ching, Liu Zhiwei, Sang Bing, and Zhou Xiang, have been very helpful in many ways. They, along with other members of the ever-evolving South China Research group, including David Faure, Ma Muk-chi, and Choi Chi-cheung, warmly welcomed me and set a very high example of scholarship. Jakob Klein offered stimulating company on trips to Jiujiang and other areas in the Pearl River delta.

My year at Harvard University's Fairbank Center gave me the opportunity to revise my manuscript for publication. The center's director, Wilt Idema, created an environment in which I could use my time productively. James Watson kindly allowed me attend his seminar. Peter Bol provided a great deal of inspiration, as did his students. At Harvard, I was also fortunate enough to have had an opportunity to learn once again from David Knechtges, who was a visiting fellow in 2002-3. He again offered help with tricky texts and provided hours of enjoyable conversation over his dangerous martinis.

Support from several institutions made this study possible. A University of Washington Taiwan University Exchange Fellowship, a Fulbright Fellowship, and a Pacific Cultural Foundation Research Grant facilitated research in Taipei in 1995-96. Research in Guangzhou in 1997 was conducted under a Fulbright-Hays Fellowship. A Peking University Fellowship for Advanced Research in Chinese Studies, with the Center for Chinese Studies, University of Hawai'i, allowed me to work on the Xie Lansheng diary in Beijing during the summer of 2000. The East Asia Library at the University of Washington, the Harvard-Yenching Library, the Fu Ssu-nien Library at the Institute of History and Philology, the Beijing Library, and the Kyujang-gak collection at Seoul National University all facilitated my research. In Japan, the staff of the Tōyō bunko and Katayama Tsuyoshi at Osaka University helped me greatly. In Guangzhou, I was aided by the Sun Yat-sen University Library, the Zhongshan Library, and the Zhongshan wenxianguan. The latter in particular has on many return trips since 1997 provided a convenient and comfortable research environment.

Material for "Reshaping the Cultural Landscape: History, Poetry, and Anthology" first appeared in the article "Rewriting the Southern Han (917-971): The Production of Local Culture in Nineteenth-Century Guangzhou," *Harvard Journal of Asiatic Studies* 61, no. 2 (June 2002): 39-75, and is reprinted here with permission of the editors. Material for "Zhu 'Jiujiang': Alternative Identities and the Delta's Critique of the City" first appeared in the article "Creating Zhu 'Jiujiang': Localism in Nineteenth-Century Guangdong," *T'oung Pao International Journal of Chinese Studies* 90, no. 4 (December 2004): 299-340.

My colleagues at the College of William and Mary, Southern Illinois University, and Washington University have offered much advice and encouragement. Washington University provided a wonderful environment for completing the manuscript. Nana Okura taught me to question my assumptions and to think anthropologically.

Finally, I wish to thank my parents, K. Dodd and Barbara B. Miles. I am grateful for their encouragement and support over many years.

S.B.M.

CONTENTS

	Tables and Figures	x
	Introduction	1
1	Cosmopolitanism and Insularity: City and Hinterland in the Pearl River Delta	23
2	Xie Lansheng's City: The Social Itinerary of the Cantonese Cultural Elite, 1810–1830	55
3	The City's New Landmark: Creating the Xuehaitang, 1820–1830	91
4	Reshaping the Cultural Landscape: History, Poetry, and Anthology	127
5	Academy, City, and Delta in Crisis and Reconstruction, 1830–1870	164
6	A "Sojourner from Jiangnan": Chen Li and Han-Song Syncretism in Guangzhou	201
7	Zhu "Jiujiang": Alternative Identities and the Delta's Critique of the City	237
8	Reflections on the Sea of Learning: Mobility and Identity in a Cosmopolitan Family	276

APPENDIXES

A	Xuehaitang Co-Directors, 1826–1863	301
B	*Xuehaitang ji* Table of Contents	304

REFERENCE MATTER

Notes	317
Works Cited	395
Character List	425
Index	437

TABLES AND FIGURES

TABLES

1	Xuehaitang scholars as compilers of local gazetteers	131
2	1834 specialized students	186
3	1866 specialized students	187
4	1888 Xuehaitang examination questions for the third month	188
5	1888 Xuehaitang examination questions for the fourth month	189

FIGURES

1	Xie Lansheng's city: a map of Guangzhou from the 1835 Nanhai gazetteer	26
2	The Pearl River delta	43
3	Zhang Weiping studying the Classics under his father's direction	64
4	The Xuehaitang and Wenlan Pavilion	114
5	Title page for the 1863 edition of Luo Xuepeng's *Guangdong wenxian*	145
6	Lustration festivities at Myrobalan Grove in 1860	179
7	Chen Li's city	192
8	The growing academic complex on Yuexiu Hill	198
9	The Enclosure district	238
10	Wang Zhaoyong in the pose of a Xuehaitang scholar	293

The Sea of Learning

Mobility and Identity in
Nineteenth-Century
Guangzhou

❧ INTRODUCTION ☙

ACCORDING TO AN ANECDOTE circulating in the far southern Chinese city of Guangzhou (Canton) during the nineteenth century, a middle-aged Cantonese literatus named Liang Xuyong went to the 1817 metropolitan examination in the capital, Beijing, hoping to obtain the coveted *jinshi* degree. When the examinee from a neighboring cell asked about one of the questions and Liang promptly answered that it was a reference to the *Han shu* (History of the Han dynasty), a third examinee, from Zhejiang province, mockingly expressed surprise that someone from Guangdong—the province where Guangzhou was located—was able to read the *Han shu* at all.[1] Liang passed the examination and earned the *jinshi* degree, but the Zhejiang examinee's facetious remark grated on his nerves. After returning to his native place outside Guangzhou, Liang established an "association for reciting the Classics from memory" in order to prepare younger generations of Cantonese for competition in future examinations. He often spoke of the 1817 examination to his fellow Cantonese literati, enjoining them to "soak in the ancient through study, so as to avoid being sneered at by flippant youths from Jiangsu and Zhejiang."[2]

In 1855, another Cantonese literatus, Gui Wencan (1823–84), wrote a preface to *Jingxue bocai lu* (Broadly selected record of classical studies), a collection of his observations of the lives and scholarship of outstanding contemporary scholars of the Confucian Classics. Though books celebrating the achievements of classical scholarship during the Qing dynasty (1644–1911) were quite common by the middle of the nineteenth century, there was something novel about Gui Wencan's *Jingxue bocai lu*. Not only was the author Cantonese, but he also included many Cantonese literati among his "broadly selected" scholars. Gui and most of these scholars were closely associated with Guangzhou's pre-eminent academy, the Xuehaitang (Sea of Learning Hall), which Gui boasted of as having attained the highest stage of development in the history of academies (*shuyuan*).³ Whereas the anecdote portrays Liang Xuyong's indignation less than four decades earlier as stemming from a lack of recognition as a Cantonese literatus, Gui Wencan's book exudes an air of confidence in the status of elite culture in Guangzhou.

If taken at face value, the contrast between these two episodes suggests that elite culture in Guangzhou had been transformed in the short span of a generation, raising the status of the city itself from a peripheral outpost to a cultural center. Cantonese literati like Gui Wencan, who celebrated this flourishing of Cantonese elite culture, largely attributed it to the role of the Xuehaitang. This famous academy had been established by Ruan Yuan (1764–1849), a native of the Lower Yangzi River basin, or Jiangnan, who served as governor-general of Guangdong and Guangxi provinces from 1817 to 1826. In addition to founding the Xuehaitang, Ruan Yuan organized the compilation and printing at the academy of the *Huang Qing jingjie* (Qing dynasty exegeses of the Classics), a collectanea of what he judged the most important works of scholarship, produced during the Qing up to that time, on the Classics. Most of the scholars whose works were included were natives of five prefectures in the three provinces—Jiangsu, Zhejiang, and Anhui—that formed the heart of the Jiangnan region. In contrast, the collectanea contained the work of only one native of Guangdong, and he was from Jiaying department, far to the east of Guangzhou, the provincial capital. Gui Wencan wrote his *Jingxue bocai lu* to celebrate the same type of scholarship, but with particular emphasis placed on exegetical texts produced in the thirty years since the compilation of the *Huang Qing jingjie*. By including so many Cantonese, most of them associated with the Xuehaitang, Gui marked Guangzhou as a noteworthy site of cultural production, and he centered Cantonese elite culture at the Xuehaitang.

There is little doubt that much had changed in the elite cultural circles of Guangzhou in the four decades between Liang Xuyong's indignation and Gui Wencan's celebration. This period witnessed an intense flurry of activity, ranging from frequent literary competitions to the construction and renovation of academies to the compilation and printing of numerous texts. It is also certainly the case that the Xuehaitang played a pivotal role in directing these changes. Scholars associated with the Xuehaitang—from its inception in the 1820s through the end of the nineteenth century—regularly touted the transformative impact that the academy had on local elite culture. Whether their focus was on urban Guangzhou, the Pearl River delta hinterland surrounding the city, or even more broadly on the entire province of Guangdong, they proclaimed and celebrated the newfound status of Cantonese elite culture.

Modern scholarship on Qing intellectual and political history has largely incorporated this assessment of the Xuehaitang's importance, both in Guangzhou and more broadly throughout China. Thus, the Xuehaitang has rightly been viewed by historians as one of the most influential academies of the Qing dynasty.[4] At the same time, it is necessary to recognize that the nineteenth-century discourse that portrayed the Xuehaitang as having radically altered literati culture also legitimized the new academy's place in Guangzhou, as well as Guangzhou's place as a cultural center in the empire. Such recognition, though not denying that there was meaningful change, raises questions about who constructed this discourse, and why many, but certainly not all, Cantonese literati found it so compelling. Among the larger circle of social and cultural elites in urban Guangzhou and the surrounding Pearl River delta, what types of people responded to Ruan Yuan's new academy? Conversely, why did some elites whom we might expect to have participated not affiliate themselves with the Xuehaitang?

My efforts to answer these questions have led me away from intellectual history to local social and cultural history, and out of the Xuehaitang into its broader circle of influence—from urban Guangzhou to the Pearl River delta hinterland and beyond. The resulting study is as much about the local social and cultural landscape and what might be called the cultural politics of place as it is about the Xuehaitang itself. Literati like Liang Xuyong and Gui

Wencan—who populated and constantly reshaped the local landscape—moved from one place to another and settled in and identified with particular localities. Various segments of the wider Cantonese elite articulated different identities, promoted contrasting styles of scholarship and literature, and offered competing visions of elite Cantonese culture. Although Ruan Yuan and the Cantonese literati at the Xuehaitang went to great lengths to separate their new academy, both physically and symbolically, from the hubbub of the city, it remained firmly embedded in the urban context, as one of many important urban spaces for the city's social and cultural elite. From the perspective of the delta hinterland, the Xuehaitang was immediately associated with the city, whereas for literati from other parts of the Qing empire, it came to represent the accomplishments of the entire province of Guangdong. The place of the Xuehaitang in Guangzhou, the delta, and the wider cultural world of China was articulated through texts, such as the *Jingxue bocai lu*, that constructed the celebratory discourse about the academy.

I will argue that the Xuehaitang did not simply change elite culture in Guangzhou; rather, it fit into a local social and cultural context already undergoing change—which it subsequently expanded, redirected, and in some ways limited. Furthermore, despite the Xuehaitang's seeming monopoly, it will become clear that there were many other sites of cultural production, both within urban Guangzhou and in the delta hinterland, with which Cantonese literati could identify. Mapping out these alternative sites will help explain the reasons why some segments of the larger Cantonese elite found the celebratory discourse a compelling one and others did not.

TRANSREGIONAL, LOCAL, AND URBAN CONTEXTS

This study seeks to answer the above questions about the Cantonese cultural elite of the early and mid-nineteenth century by examining the interplay between scholarly and literary affiliations, on one hand, and social and geographical identities, on the other. Throughout each of the following chapters, I explore transregional, local, and urban contexts, and analyze the texts produced by the Xuehaitang and by scholars who closely identified themselves with the academy and its agenda, reading these texts as claims to identities based on status, geography, and scholarly or literary affinity. As a place with which some local literati identified, the Xuehaitang can be analyzed in relation to other places on a number of levels, which might be conceived of as a series of concentric arenas within which literati competed for cultural resources. In each arena, an examination of the Xuehaitang highlights the spatial dynamics at play.[5]

Transregional Dynamics: Jiangnan-Lingnan

On the first and broadest level, the Xuehaitang can be viewed in the context of transregional dynamics, primarily between Jiangnan and Lingnan; the latter term technically referred to Guangdong and Guangxi, but in practice most often designated Guangdong alone, or even more narrowly only Guangzhou prefecture or the Pearl River delta. Ruan Yuan was a native of Yangzhou prefecture in central Jiangsu province, and his inclusion of so many Yangzhou natives in the *Huang Qing jingjie* reflects a conscious effort to confirm Yangzhou's status as a major cultural center in Jiangnan.[6] At the same time, the compilation of the collectanea and the creation of the Xuehaitang also represented an attempt to transplant a constellation of scholarly and literary practices mastered by Jiangnan literati to the southernmost extent of the empire, Lingnan.

Although the scholarly endeavors promoted by Ruan Yuan at the Xuehaitang were subsumed under the rubric of *kaozheng* learning, or evidential research, they were applied to a wide variety of practices. From the perspective of most *kaozheng* scholars, the field of primary importance was exegesis of the Confucian Classics. In this endeavor, *kaozheng* scholars emphasized a text-based, philological approach, often drawing a distinction between their approach and that of the Neo-Confucians. In general, Neo-Confucians tended to emphasize the practices of moral self-cultivation and philosophical speculation about the place of humankind in the social and cosmological order. Cheng Yi (1033–1107), Zhu Xi (1130–1200), and other Neo-Confucians of the Song (960–1279) and later dynasties conceived of a moral-cosmological order governed by *li* ("principle" or "coherence"). Hence their philosophical system was also referred to as *lixue* (Learning of Principle). Employing the methods of self-cultivation and lecturing as often as those of textual research, their aim was to fathom "meaning and principle" (*yili*). Such comprehension of ultimate principles was most often something experienced almost intuitively, and often in a sudden burst of enlightenment. This indicated that one had attained sagehood, the ultimate goal for the Neo-Confucian scholar.[7]

Evidential research emerged as a fully coherent scholarly discourse in the eighteenth century. Often representing their scholarly orientation in contrast to Neo-Confucian practice prevalent in the Song and Ming (1368–1644) dynasties, eighteenth-century *kaozheng* scholars sought to attain truth through rigorous textual research on the Confucian Classics. These scholars viewed sagehood as an unrealistic goal; instead, they would seek the certainty and authenticity embodied in the texts of the ancient Classics. *Kaozheng* scholars referred to their scholarly practice as "concrete studies" (*shixue*) or "unadorned learning" (*puxue*), in contrast to what they saw as the philosophical "empty speculation about nature and principle" (*kongtan xingli*) popular with Neo-Confucians. Rather, they strove, through textual analysis of the Classics and Histories, to recover the most ancient rituals in their purest form.[8]

This new regimen of textual research, though adopted by scholars of diverse intellectual loyalties, was often more narrowly identified with what came to be known as the school of Han Learning. In the eighteenth century, *kaozheng* scholars, led by Hui Dong (1679–1758) in Suzhou, argued that Han dynasty (206 BCE–220 CE) Confucians' exegeses of the Classics were more reliable than those of subsequent dynasties—most notably the Song—because the former were closer to the time of the ancient sage-kings and putative authors of the classical texts. In particular, they promoted the classical commentaries of Zheng Xuan (127–200) and other Han Confucians over those of Cheng Yi, Zhu Xi, and the Song Confucians, despite the fact that Cheng-Zhu Confucianism maintained a dominant position in imperial ideology and the civil service examinations.[9]

In addition to classical exegesis, many *kaozheng* scholars applied the tools of evidential research to epigraphy (the study of metal and stone inscriptions), geography, and history. Interest in these topics drew many *kaozheng* scholars out of their libraries and into "the field," where they carried out firsthand investigations of such sites as old tombs and temples, seeking stelae inscriptions and other artifacts that could be used to verify information in written texts. By its nature, this type of scholarship lent itself to local studies, and Ruan Yuan was a strong advocate of this approach. Tobie Meyer-Fong has drawn attention to one example of Ruan Yuan's advocacy: his use of a map from an old gazetteer and interviews with local peasants in order to find, in his native Yangzhou, the tomb of a Sui dynasty (589–618) emperor.[10] Due in no small part to Ruan Yuan's tireless promotion, this practice became a fashionable manifestation of evidential research in the late eighteenth and early nineteenth centuries. This had not always been the case: Gu Yanwu (1613–82), the seventeenth-century scholar commonly seen as a forerunner of the eighteenth-century *kaozheng* advocates, is known for his geographical and epigraphical studies in northwest China, rather than in his native Suzhou; his motivations have often been linked to his loyalty to the Ming and resistance against the Qing.[11] In early nineteenth-century Guangzhou, however, overtly localist applications of epigraphy, geography, and history became as important a component of the *kaozheng* movement as was classical exegesis.

Ruan Yuan also promoted a literary agenda at the Xuehaitang; he was particularly fond of literary forms found in the sixth-century *Wenxuan* anthology. Thus he favored such genres as parallel prose, rhapsodies (*fu*), and old-style poetry, in place of the "ancient prose" (*guwen*) and new-style poetry modeled on the masters of the Tang (618–907) and Song dynasties. Although there was a great deal of overlap among the scholarly and literary preferences of literati during the Qing, by the early nineteenth century many proponents of Han Learning favored pre-Tang literary styles, whereas advocates of Neo-Confucianism tended to favor Tang and Song literary styles. During the seventeenth and eighteenth centuries, several *kaozheng* scholars applied the tools of evidential research in carrying out thorough textual analyses of the *Wenxuan*.[12]

Together, these approaches formed a constellation of scholarly and literary practices that in turn entailed different practices of writing, printing, collecting, and reading.[13] Nevertheless, as late as 1821, when Xuehaitang examinations were initiated, these practices were still part of a regionally delimited discourse associated with the cultural centers of the Qing empire: the capital and especially Jiangnan.[14] Thus, in his study of the eighteenth-century evidential research movement, Benjamin Elman has identified a Jiangnan "academic community" composed of a few urban centers, including Yangzhou and Suzhou in Jiangsu, and Hangzhou in Zhejiang. The capital at Beijing served as a second center of evidential research, as it drew literati from throughout the empire and benefited from imperially sponsored projects such as the compilation of the *Siku quanshu* (Complete library of the four treasuries) collectanea.[15] Though literati from outside Jiangnan or the capital might occasionally emerge to contribute something of importance to the field, they had most likely acquired a taste for this during stints in one of these two centers. Such literati had no indigenous institutions of evidential research to which they could return. Consequently, the acknowledged eighteenth-century masters of the *kaozheng* approach to the study of texts and sites, and the literary genres of parallel prose, rhapsodies, and old-style poetry were almost exclusively natives of either the Jiangnan region or Beijing.

As a charismatic patron and proponent of this constellation of practices, Ruan Yuan established two very influential academies, the Gujing jingshe (Retreat for Glossing the Classics) in Hangzhou and the Xuehaitang. Modern scholars often mention these two academies in tandem, as examples of the new style of academy in the late Qing. Nevertheless, Philip Kuhn and Susan Mann have succinctly summarized important differences between the two: one was located in the economic and cultural center of the empire, the other on the southern periphery; one was staffed by holders of the *jinshi* degree brought in from outside Hangzhou, the other by far less eminent local Cantonese.[16] The present study in fact began as a comparison of the two academies and their host cities but was gradually drawn to focus on the Xuehaitang and Guangzhou because of the unique regional dynamics in this case. As Benjamin Elman has noted, one of the most significant developments of evidential research in the nineteenth century, after it had supposedly reached its eighteenth-century apogee in Jiangnan, was the spread of these practices throughout the empire.[17] One of the chief concerns of this study, then, is to address the question of what happened when the set of practices outlined above was transplanted from a cultural center to a city on the empire's southern frontier.

Among Cantonese literati, even those who utilized the Xuehaitang, one finds both fascination with and resentment of Jiangnan elite culture. Therefore, it will be important to explain how these quite foreign scholarly and literary practices, which were consciously exported from Jiangnan by Ruan Yuan, become the predominant mode of scholarly and literary discourse in Guangzhou by the middle of the nineteenth century. This study is sharply focused on urban Guangzhou and the Pearl River delta, but the transregional networks of Qing literati and the regional identities of Cantonese literati will form a constant backdrop to my discussions. As the academy's founder, Ruan Yuan remained a towering figure in the subsequent history of the Xuehaitang. The large number of Jiangnan literati who accompanied him, as well as the officials and Jiangnan literati who later visited Guangzhou, also facilitated the spread of Jiangnan scholarly and literary practices in nineteenth-century Guangzhou.

Guangzhou City and the Pearl River Delta Hinterland

Although the role of Ruan Yuan and his coterie of Jiangnan literati in initiating the Xuehaitang project can hardly be overestimated, the new academy was not established in a vacuum. Almost all of the scholars identified with the Xuehaitang (a group that I shall refer to as "Xuehaitang scholars") were registered residents of Guangdong.[18] Moreover, though few Cantonese literati had mastered the scholarly and literary practices that were all the rage in Jiangnan, Guangzhou and the Pearl River delta boasted a vibrant culture with at least locally meaningful philosophical and literary discourses. Therefore, the scholarly and literary orientation of the new Xuehaitang academy was inevitably altered as it was embraced in a new environment in the far south. On a second, intermediate level, then, the present study will explore both the ways in which the creation of the Xuehaitang altered the local social and cultural landscape, and the process by which it was adapted to fit the local context. I argue that the creation of the Xuehaitang academy reshaped the dynamics between Guangzhou city and the prosperous counties of Guangzhou prefecture in the surrounding Pearl River delta hinterland.

Despite the fact that the local social and cultural landscape was immensely complicated, a clear pattern emerges: the core group of scholars who chose to identify with the Xuehaitang was largely composed of urbanized families from the delta hinterland and sojourners and in-migrants from outside the area who came to reside in urban Guangzhou. In contrast, the new academy was largely ignored by the scions of the well-established elite lineages, concentrated along the West River (Xijiang) in the Pearl River delta outside Guangzhou. Members of the elite drawn from these ensconced lineages certainly possessed the social, economic, and cultural resources to make their presence felt in the city. Such resources were visibly lacking among the large majority of scholars at the Xuehaitang, many having resided in Guangzhou for no more than two or three generations. This then raises the question of how—in an urban enclave surrounded by a hinterland in which lineages were such a dominant factor in social organization—recent immigrants organized in competition for cultural resources.

Any effort to make sense out of the complex social landscape of the Pearl River delta hinterland is greatly aided by the large amount of anthropological and historical research that has been devoted to South China lineages, especially in the New Territories of Hong Kong and the prosperous townships of the Pearl River delta.[19] These studies have emphasized the importance of claims of settlement and descent and of such institutions as ancestral halls, temples, academies, and guilds, all of which functioned as means of securing economic resources and articulating cultural identities. For the most part, this approach has not been applied to Guangzhou, the delta's most important city.[20] Therefore, throughout the following chapters, I devote a great deal of attention to tracing patterns of settlement among both the urban scholars who associated themselves with the Xuehaitang and the hinterland scholars who typically did not.

This contrast, which will be a recurrent theme in the present study, may initially be illustrated by briefly returning to the two Cantonese literati with whom I opened this discussion, Liang Xuyong and Gui Wencan. Both were registered residents of Nanhai county, one of the two counties that shared jurisdiction of Guangzhou city. But Liang hailed from the Nanhai countryside west of the city, whereas Gui was the grandson of a Zhejiang native who migrated to Guangzhou to work as a private secretary in one of the many officials' offices, or yamen, in the city. By Wencan's generation, the Gui family had registered as residents of Nanhai, but, like other in-migrants, resided in the city or its immediate suburbs.[21] Thus, the transition from Liang Xuyong to Gui Wencan not only represented the notable change brought about by the Xuehaitang but also signaled the rise of a new type of Cantonese literatus, a sojourning or in-migrating urbanite who lacked deep genealogical roots in the delta hinterland.

By embracing the imported scholarly and literary practices espoused by Ruan Yuan at the Xuehaitang, members of this initially marginalized segment of the larger Cantonese literati elite secured for themselves a position in Guangzhou. Likewise, in identifying with the Xuehaitang and extolling its transformative impact upon local Cantonese culture, these urban literati reshaped the relationship between Guangzhou city and its delta hinterland. This fluid but nevertheless important dichotomy between city and hinterland will be a central theme, and Chapter 1 will therefore outline in detail the social landscape it implies; throughout, I will draw on genealogies and family histories to emphasize native-place origins and identities of the Cantonese literati. I hope to highlight new patterns of urban settlement, distinct in many ways from previous patterns identified in the delta hinterland, but similar to the phenomenon of "sojourners" in other late imperial Chinese cities.[22]

The Academy in the Urban Landscape

On the third and most narrowly focused level, I examine the Xuehaitang as an institution in an urban context. In addition to locating the Xuehaitang in urban Guangzhou's system of academies, this examination involves analyzing the Xuehaitang as an urban social space, as other scholars have done for such institutions as merchant guilds and native-place associations, temples and monasteries, garrisons, gardens, and granaries.[23] As an urban institution, the Xuehaitang was an important place in the formation of elite identity, and it acted as a vital social space in the construction of elite status.[24]

The Xuehaitang did not have a dominating physical presence in Guangzhou: there were no dormitories to allow students to reside on academy grounds, and, until the institutionalization of "specialized courses" in the 1860s, there were no regularly scheduled meetings between teachers and students. In contrast to other academies, at which a single director typically was in residence for most of the year, the eight co-directors shared administrative duties on a rotating basis and were not expected to reside at the academy. For much of its existence, in fact, activities sponsored by the Xuehaitang as an institution were limited to quarterly examinations, on which examinees were allowed to work at home, and various printing projects.[25] In addition, the academy grounds occasionally served as a site for refined outings, often hosted by one or more co-directors. Yet the Xuehaitang soon occupied an important position in the hierarchy of Cantonese cultural institutions entirely out of proportion to its physical presence. Through the innovative scholarly and literary ideals that it represented and the charismatic and fashionable personalities with whom it was associated, the Xuehaitang quickly became an important source of prestige in the construction of urban Cantonese elite identity.

Although proponents of the Xuehaitang academy emphasized its uniqueness, and though it was indeed in many respects an innovative institution, it was nevertheless deeply embedded in the local urban milieu. Thus, I have constructed a narrative that seeks to situate the Xuehaitang in an urban network made up of administrative, educational, lineage, religious, commercial, and charitable institutions, as well as popular tourist sites. Scholars at the Xuehaitang also studied and taught in the other academies in Guangzhou, served in bureaus established by local officials for the compilation of gazetteers and other texts, and at various times staffed the numerous granaries, militia bureaus, and other elite-managed institutions of the city. They visited and often resided at the firms or in the gardens of the city's wealthy maritime and salt merchants, and hosted outings to various monasteries, gardens, and ancient ruins in Guangzhou and among the surrounding hills and rivers. In addition, Xuehaitang scholars were involved in informal networks of interpersonal relationships, including marriage alliances, property rentals and sales, and innumerable short-lived poetry clubs and competitions.[26]

An analysis of the family backgrounds of the literati who associated themselves with the Xuehaitang reveals not only that many were recent arrivals in Guangzhou but also that almost all of these urban literati had only recently attained high social status. The term "literati" is used throughout this study to designate those members of the social and cultural elite who were at the same time producers of *wen*—"culture" broadly speaking, but more narrowly the types of texts (local histories, literary collections, and genealogies, to name a few) on which this study is largely based.[27] Whereas the social elite from the dominant lineages of the delta hinterland may more accurately be classified as a landholding "gentry" (and will be described as such, particularly in Chapter 7), most of the urban Cantonese literati at the Xuehaitang were from merchant families or families that specialized in serving as subofficials, clerks, or the more prestigious *muyou*—secretaries to the numerous officials stationed in Guangzhou. Moreover, many of the scholars at the new academy who had attained degrees through the civil service examinations were the first in their families to have done so. Income they derived from the land was more likely to come from rents on urban shops than from rural tenant farmers. Thus, the line between the "gentry" class—whether defined in terms of degree-holding or landholding—and other social groups in urban Guangzhou was perhaps even more porous than in Jiangnan cities.[28]

In tracing the social and regional origins of the nineteenth-century Cantonese elite, a clear dichotomy emerges between urban Guangzhou and the Pearl River delta hinterland. The part of the present study that deals with the delta hinterland largely confirms the notion that gentry families—or, more broadly, local elites—in Ming-Qing China were able to maintain their status over many generations.[29] A somewhat different picture emerges from an examination of urban Guangzhou in the nineteenth century. Here, one witnesses not only the rise of individual families but also the emergence of a new subgroup within the larger Cantonese elite. Whereas the social and cultural elite of Guangzhou prefecture during the sixteenth, seventeenth, and early eighteenth centuries appears to have been composed primarily of literati from surname groups that had formed lineages in the delta hinterland and claimed descent from pre-Ming ancestors, the nineteenth century witnessed the growing influence of literati from urban Guangzhou families, many of which had relocated to Guangdong from outside the province only during the Qing and had initially established themselves in Guangzhou through commerce or administrative and secretarial service. Unlike most literati from the dominant lineages of the delta, the newly emergent elites of urban Guangzhou could not claim descent from any eminent ancestors in recent generations.

What the urban literati lacked in genealogical status, however, the Xuehaitang provided in scholarly and literary credentials. Guangzhou's new academy appealed to these emergent urban literati precisely because they lacked continuity as elites in Cantonese localities. Consequently, sojourning literati and in-migrating and urbanized families responded with the greatest alacrity to the new types of scholarship and literature introduced from outside, as the Xuehaitang became part of a family strategy for regional assimilation and social advancement. Perhaps due in part to anxieties over their own socially diverse backgrounds, many Xuehaitang scholars articulated critiques of the "vulgar" urban commercial culture they found all around them. Here again, with its promotion of more meticulous forms of scholarship and more refined styles of literature, the Xuehaitang provided a means for newly emergent literati to distinguish themselves from the rest of the crowd.[30] The Xuehaitang, in other words, became a tool in the competition for cultural resources and prestige at the local level.[31]

TEXTUAL PRODUCTION: SYNCRETISM AND LOCALISM

In addition to analyzing the Xuehaitang and Guangzhou in terms of spatial dynamics, I examine the types of texts produced by Cantonese literati during the nineteenth century. The competition for local status and cultural resources, together with the introduction of new scholarly tools and literary styles, resulted in the production of a large number of printed texts directed at a literati audience. The present study relies heavily on the texts produced by these scholars, attempting to read them both as historical sources and as "strategic texts."[32] That is, in addition to combing these sources for information about their authors' scholarly stances or literary proclivities, I also seek to ascertain the motivations behind their composition, to consider the particular audiences to which they were directed, and to read them as claims of identity and markers of status. Among the large number of texts produced by scholars associated with the Xuehaitang, I have chosen to focus on two categories of texts that contributed to the construction of two prevalent discourses in nineteenth-century Cantonese literati circles: Han-Song syncretism and Cantonese localism.

Among the many fields of scholarship and literature promoted at the Xuehaitang, as well as at other Guangzhou academies, study of the Confucian Classics was seen as a priority. This was reflected in the arrangement of examination essays and poems that were incorporated into four series of collected writings from the Xuehaitang, printed between 1825 and 1886. In the texts they produced outside of Xuehaitang examinations, scholars also devoted a great deal of attention to debating the proper approach to learning, and the best interpretations of the Classics. This type of text has also received the most attention from modern Chinese, Japanese, and Western scholars who have written about the Xuehaitang, its founder, Ruan Yuan, or its most prominent scholar, Chen Li (1810–82).[33]

A common theme resounding through the writings of Xuehaitang scholars on classical scholarship was Han-Song syncretism, reflecting an attempt to mediate between two approaches toward study of the Classics—Han Learning and Song Learning. By the beginning of the nineteenth century, Han Learning referred to *kaozheng* scholars who favored the Han dynasty exegeses or glosses (*xungu*). They typically upheld Zheng Xuan and Xu Shen (ca. 55–ca. 149), compiler of the *Shuowen* dictionary, as models of meticulous philological and exegetical scholarship. In contrast, proponents of Song Learning favored the Cheng Yi and Zhu Xi interpretations of the Classics and promoted a Neo-Confucian project of moral self-cultivation in the pursuit of sagehood. Though in practice there was a great deal of overlap between these two "schools," in the late eighteenth century some proponents of Song Learning began to articulate critiques of Han Learning, perhaps stemming from resentment of the imperial favor shown to advocates of Han Learning in such projects as the *Siku quanshu*.[34] Polemics between the advocates of Han Learning and those of Song Learning increased in the early nineteenth century, culminating in the production of two texts by sojourning Jiangnan literati who were in Guangzhou with Ruan Yuan when he was establishing the Xuehaitang in the 1820s.

The mutual critiques of Han Learning and Song Learning thus constituted an important part of the context in which the Xuehaitang was established. Despite the fact that the Xuehaitang was created in part for the purpose of spreading Jiangnan evidential research to the far south, Han-Song syncretism also became a trademark approach at the academy. Several scholars have addressed the phenomenon of Han-Song syncretism throughout China during the nineteenth century, and a few have dealt with the Han-Song syncretic stance in the thought of Chen Li; however, in the latter case, it has most often been seen as a brave, solitary critique voiced by Chen.[35] In contrast, I argue that Han-Song syncretism was a widespread discourse among nineteenth-century Cantonese literati, though there remained significant differences in emphasis among them. I dwell on this discourse among scholars associated with the Xuehaitang in the context of the regional dynamics between Lingnan and Jiangnan and the local dynamics between urban Guangzhou and the delta hinterland.

Another category of text consists of "localist" texts, by which I mean to refer not to texts that excluded outsiders or the nonlocal but to texts about a particular area, ranging from local histories to poetic celebrations of the local. This category of text has not received as much attention from modern scholars, despite the fact that the proliferation of such texts is one of the most striking features of nineteenth-century Cantonese cultural history. Numerous literary examinations conducted at the Xuehaitang asked examinees to investigate and extol local culture, including historical sites, natural products, and eminent forerunners. Aside from this, scholars who were intimately associated with the Xuehaitang utilized the *kaozheng* methods of textual reconstruction, epigraphy, geography, and on-site investigation to explore local culture and history, and they employed new literary styles and innovative anthological strategies to reconstruct Cantonese elite culture.

In attempting to explain the proliferation of localist texts using novel scholarly and literary techniques, we must take Ruan Yuan's scholarly proclivities into account. He not only exhibited deep interest in exploring the local history of his native Yangzhou and compiling anthologies of Yangzhou literature but also tirelessly promoted local studies in many of the places where he served as an official. As education commissioner in Shandong province during the 1790s, Ruan helped in the compilation of metal and stone inscriptions in the province, and in the following decade, as education commissioner and then governor of Zhejiang, he organized the compilation of an anthology of Zhejiang poets as well as a record of his efforts to preserve local tombs and temples. Upon taking up the post of governor-general in Guangzhou, Ruan continued this practice by organizing the compilation of a new edition of the Guangdong provincial gazetteer.[36]

Nevertheless, the proliferation of localist texts preceded Ruan Yuan's arrival in Guangzhou and persisted long after his departure, suggesting that Cantonese literati also provided an impetus for the localist project. In his study of Neo-Confucian literati in Zhejiang's Jinhua prefecture during the Song, Yuan (1279–1368), and Ming dynasties, Peter Bol finds that Neo-Confucians rose to prominence in Jinhua by presenting themselves as leaders of local culture.[37] Similar dynamics were at work among urban literati at the Xuehaitang during the nineteenth century. Since most scholars at the Xuehaitang were not tied to longstanding scholarly or literary traditions centered on settled lineages, they could be more flexible in adopting the new scholarly practices and literary styles imported from Jiangnan. Yet those who rose in local cultural circles through mastery of imported scholarly and literary practices were clearly preoccupied with employing these new tools in the study and glorification of local culture. In other words, the application of new scholarly practices and literary styles to the study and celebration of the local made the Xuehaitang agenda meaningful in the Cantonese cultural context.

Through a combination of the credentialing offered by the Xuehaitang and the application of its scholarly and literary tools to the exploration of the local, social upstarts and in-migrants who had no recourse to the economic and cultural resources of the established lineages in the delta hinterland managed to gain a near monopoly over elite Cantonese discourse about the local. This process illustrates the influence of migration, urban sojourning, and competition for status on the construction of local identities in late imperial China. Both geographical and social mobility often stimulated articulations of local identity and celebrations of locality; new forms of learning provided the necessary tools. The maintenance of pre-literati commercial ties among the socially ambitious or of pre-Cantonese native-place ties among in-migrants did not preclude literati, in their new social circles as members of the urban elite, from celebrating the local. Based on her study of Shanghai, Bryna Goodman envisions the construction of urban identity as "a process of accretion of identities" that allows for the accumulation of new identities without the displacement of preexisting ones.[38] In the case of nineteenth-century Guangzhou, the Xuehaitang provided learning to a highly mobile group of people who embraced a sense of Cantonese local identity. A powerful synthesis of commercial wealth, official connections, and scholarly and literary expertise allowed these outsiders to usurp local culture, to control Guangzhou by controlling its representation.[39]

This appropriation of local cultural symbols by scholars associated with the Xuehaitang did not go uncontested. A scholar from a West River lineage who could trace his descent from ancestors who had settled the delta in pre-Ming times and who commanded a large number of economic and cultural resources could justifiably claim that he was a more rightful arbiter of Cantonese literati culture than was the son of a sojourning secretary or merchant in urban Guangzhou. After a series of crises in the middle of the nineteenth century, several delta critics of Xuehaitang scholarship and the cosmopolitan culture of Guangzhou in general began to voice their concerns. As a result, one clearly finds in the nineteenth-century Cantonese cultural context a phenomenon of competing constructions of the local.[40]

The localist texts that Xuehaitang literati produced may be seen as simultaneously directed at two audiences, both local and transregional. By using new scholarly practices and literary styles to reconfigure the local cultural landscape, they placed the Xuehaitang—and, by extension, themselves—at the center of Cantonese culture. But this project was also aimed at a transregional audience, especially literati in Jiangnan. As May-bo Ching has observed, the Xuehaitang was "one of the most determined attempts to put Guangdong on the map of the Chinese empire as a place of culture."[41] Thus, the members of the local cultural elite with the most tenuous links to Guangzhou's cultural past, through the activities and prestige of the Xuehaitang, self-consciously reinvented Cantonese culture as a means simultaneously of earning respect for that culture in Jiangnan and points further north and of placing themselves at the center of this reinvented tradition.

NARRATIVE FRAMEWORK

The narrative that I have constructed in the chapters that follow attempts to answer the basic question of how the Xuehaitang fit into the local social and cultural landscape, by examining how the regional, local, and urban dynamics outlined above are manifested in the types of texts that Cantonese literati were most interested in producing and preserving. The contrast between city and hinterland literati is the central pole around which the resulting narrative framework is structured. Although I want to guard against too rigid a reading of this distinction, my attention has repeatedly been drawn to the fact that many of the Xuehaitang scholars were urbanites, "outsiders," and social upstarts, that they produced many localist texts, and that these texts looked very different from the types of texts produced in the hinterland.[42]

Due to the nature of the questions that inform this study, its focus is directed at the wider urban and delta hinterland contexts as often as at the Xuehaitang itself. This is particularly evident in my first two chapters. Furthermore, although literati remain the central actors in the narrative, such social groups as merchants, monks, and courtesans are also deemed important for understanding the place of the academy in Guangzhou. Similarly, in addition to classical exegeses and Confucian debates, I have drawn heavily on such sources as poems, genealogies, and diaries. Chapter 1 provides a broad overview of the social landscape of Guangzhou and the Pearl River delta. My main purpose here is to illustrate differences in settlement patterns between the city and the delta, because these in turn determined one's access to a particular set of cultural resources. Chapter 2 uses the diary of a Cantonese literatus to focus more narrowly on the urban landscape in the two decades surrounding the establishment of the Xuehaitang. The diary's author, Xie Lansheng (1760–1831), was only tangentially related to the Xuehaitang and therefore represents the last generation of urban Cantonese literati whose cultural world was not largely shaped by the new academy. Using his diary as a guide, we follow Xie's movements through the city as he visits temples, gardens, and academies and mixes with merchants, monks, courtesans, artists, scholars, and officials.

Chapter 3 describes how the Xuehaitang fit into this complex social and cultural landscape through an examination of the social backgrounds of the first generation of Xuehaitang scholars, the innovative scholarly and literary agenda of the new academy, and the commemoration of its establishment. Physical and symbolic landscape are also considered: located on a hill along the northern edge of the city, the Xuehaitang was separated from the encroaching commercial world below, as well as from other academies; it was at the same time inescapably tied to that world. Chapter 4 analyzes three types of localist texts produced by scholars associated with the Xuehaitang: history, poetry, and anthology. The chapter culminates in a comparison of two anthologies that illustrate the contrasting delta hinterland and urban Guangzhou constructions of the Cantonese literary and scholarly canon. Chapter 5 documents the fate of the Xuehaitang during four decades of crisis and reconstruction in the middle of the nineteenth century. Most readers will be familiar with many events during these decades, in particular the First and Second Opium Wars (1839-42 and 1856-60, respectively) and the Red Turban uprising (1854-55). The relative significance of these events emerges in a new light, however, when we consider their impact on the social and cultural elite of urban Guangzhou and the delta hinterland. Marked by the emergence of a new generation of Xuehaitang scholars, the middle decades of the nineteenth century witnessed both a reaffirmation of the academy's importance in local cultural life and its role in the changing urban landscape and the shifting dynamics between city and hinterland.

Chapters 6 and 7 present case studies of the two scholars recognized as the outstanding Cantonese classicists of the nineteenth century, Chen Li and Zhu Ciqi (1807-82). Both Chen and Zhu are often described as espousing some form of Han-Song syncretism, but their scholarly ideals were in fact quite different. Chapter 6 is devoted to Chen Li, the grandson of a Jiangnan native who had moved to Guangzhou to serve as a yamen secretary. Although Chen Li was registered as a Guangzhou resident and offered a critique of exclusivist Han Learning, he in many ways continued to identify with Jiangnan and its *kaozheng* scholarship. In contrast, Zhu Ciqi, the subject of Chapter 7, was a descendant of a well-established lineage from Jiujiang township along the West River. Though invited to the Xuehaitang as both a student and a teacher, Zhu sought instead to identify with his native Jiujiang, refused even to reside in Guangzhou city, and offered a biting criticism of scholarship at the Xuehaitang. The contrast between Chen Li and Zhu Ciqi thus represents the increasing divide between Guangzhou and the delta hinterland resulting from the Xuehaitang's appropriation of local culture.

Chapter 8, which concludes this study, is centered on one of the cosmopolitan families in urban Guangzhou that made use of the Xuehaitang. The chapter opens with a poem authored by Wang Quan (1829–91) shortly before the passing of Chen Li and Zhu Ciqi. Alluding to the flourishing early days of the academy, Wang's poetic sentiments provide a departure for some reflections on the Xuehaitang and the urban Cantonese elite. I end this chapter and the book by tracing the trajectories of two sons of Wang Quan's cousin who lived well into the twentieth century. The oldest son, born in 1861, reinvented himself as a custodian of Cantonese literati culture and of Chen Li's learning in particular. Another son, 22 years younger than the eldest, in his youth followed a pattern quite typical of Wang children in the nineteenth century before turning in surprising new directions in the following century.

THROUGHOUT THIS NARRATIVE, I elucidate the interplay between place and identity. Among the nineteenth-century elite of Guangzhou and the Pearl River delta, one's particular social position and geographical place often had a profound impact on one's scholarly and literary orientation. At the same time, I do not argue that the former absolutely determined the latter; identities and affiliations were both multiple and fluid. As merchants and administrators reinvented themselves as literati, and as sons of the delta hinterland relocated to the city, they embraced new identities and developed new affiliations. Beginning in the 1820s, Ruan Yuan's Sea of Learning Hall provided alternative scholarly and literary affiliations that facilitated geographical and social mobility and, for many, the construction of a new identity.

ONE
Cosmopolitanism and Insularity: City and Hinterland in the Pearl River Delta

At the Duanwu Festival, scholars and maidens clog the ferry crossing;
Confusingly mixed, the dragon boats strike ahead in succession.
Suddenly I hear a neighboring barge singing "Water Melody";[1]
Making out the sound, I realize that they are outsiders.[2]
    —Pan Zhaokeng, "Guangzhou Bamboo Branch Song," 1875

In my leisure I come to the river port, listening to fishermen's songs;
Singing in low voices, for what purpose would they shout?
None of them oar their boats toward the Pearl River;
The Pearl River waters are vast, with dangers of wind and waves.[3]
    —Ziyang shanren, "Jiujiang Bamboo Branch Song," mid-nineteenth century

DESPITE THE FACT that the social and cultural landscape of the Pearl River delta during the nineteenth century was immensely complicated and in constant flux, some features are clearly discernable. Anthropologists and historians working on corporate lineages in delta towns and villages have recently mapped out some of these patterns for the hinterland; urban Guangzhou has received less attention. Yet the places that people occupied in the landscape often determined the types of cultural resources available to them, which in turn shaped their scholarly and literary predilections. Therefore, in order to explain why some educated residents of nineteenth-century Guangdong responded with great alacrity to the Xuehaitang while others did not, it is necessary to gain a general understanding of the local landscape, and in particular the features that distinguished urban Guangzhou from the delta hinterland.

As alluded to in the first poem quoted above, Guangzhou boasted a cosmopolitan culture that largely derived its vibrancy from "outsiders" to the region. Many of the people who contributed to this cosmopolitan air were sojourners or recent descendants of ancestors who had migrated to the city from outside the delta during the Qing. Other residents of urban Guangzhou belonged to families or segments of delta lineages that had relocated to the city. Most literati who would be active at the new Xuehaitang academy were representatives of these diverse groups. In contrast, the dominant lineages in the older parts of the delta hinterland, and especially the powerful lineages from the area defined by the Mulberry Garden Enclosure (Sangyuanwei) along the West River, for the most part did not participate in the new Xuehaitang. By the end of the century, members of this insular Enclosure district articulated critiques of the academy, its scholarly and literary agenda, and the decadence of urban life. They instead proffered alternative constructions of what, in their view, were more legitimate forms of local culture. Another region of the delta hinterland important for the present study—the coastal alluvial fields known as the "sands"—was a critical source of funding for cultural pursuits in both cosmopolitan Guangzhou and the insular Enclosure district, fueling the competition for resources between them.

NEWCOMERS IN COSMOPOLITAN GUANGZHOU

Newcomers, both temporary sojourners and permanent in-migrants, assumed important positions in the commercial and cultural life of many cities in Qing China.[4] In nineteenth-century Guangzhou, the scholars who were associated with the Xuehaitang and their patrons came from several distinct cohorts of newcomers residing in urban Guangzhou, grouped according to the often corresponding determinants of occupation and geographical origin. Guangzhou was an important city for officials, and some of them occasionally sought to leave their stamp on the city's cultural landscape. Aside from the higher officials in Guangdong, who came from almost anywhere outside the province, one can identify several regional cohorts whose members tended to specialize in certain occupations. These included Chinese bannermen from the northeast; retired officials and private secretaries from Jiangsu, Zhejiang, and other provinces; subofficials and salt merchants from northern Zhejiang province; and maritime merchants from Fujian. In-migrants from Fujian had already begun to show up in Cantonese literati circles in the early eighteenth century.[5] Such Fujianese literati continued to be important into the nineteenth century, during which time in-migrants from Zhejiang quickly became a force to contend with among the city's cultural elite.[6] Also, in the early nineteenth century, literati from the Hakka area in northeastern Guangdong frequented elite cultural circles of urban Guangzhou. Finally, members of lineages in the delta hinterland who moved to Guangzhou and prospered in various commercial ventures also served as patrons of cultural production. If their sons or grandsons chose to reside permanently in the city, they might become producers of elite culture as well.

As the regional metropolis serving Lingnan, Guangzhou city was the most important administrative seat in South China, as well as a significant commercial and cultural center. Officials posted in Guangzhou did not constitute a coherent cohort in terms of common regional origin, aside from the fact that, because the Qing law of avoidance prevented officials from serving in their home provinces, they were not native to Guangdong. Nevertheless, as a group, officials had an imposing presence in the city. The yamen, or office, of the governor-general of Guangdong and Guangxi provinces was located close to the shore of the Pearl River, in the sector of Guangzhou known as the New City (see Fig. 1).[7] The yamen of the Guangdong superintendent of customs (known to Western merchants as the "Hoppo") was also in the New City. Most other yamen were concentrated in the very heart of the Old City, including those of the Guangdong governor, the lieutenant-governor, and the Guangzhou prefect, all on Huiai Street, which intersected the Old City from the Main East Gate to the Main West Gate.[8] South of Huiai Street were the yamen of the provincial judge, the educational commissioner, the salt controller, and the grain intendant. Finally, the counties of Nanhai, to the west, and Panyu, to the east, shared jurisdiction over urban Guangzhou, and thus the two county magistrates also had their yamen in the city.

When officials assigned to Guangzhou had both the inclination and the necessary charisma, they could have an impact on the elite

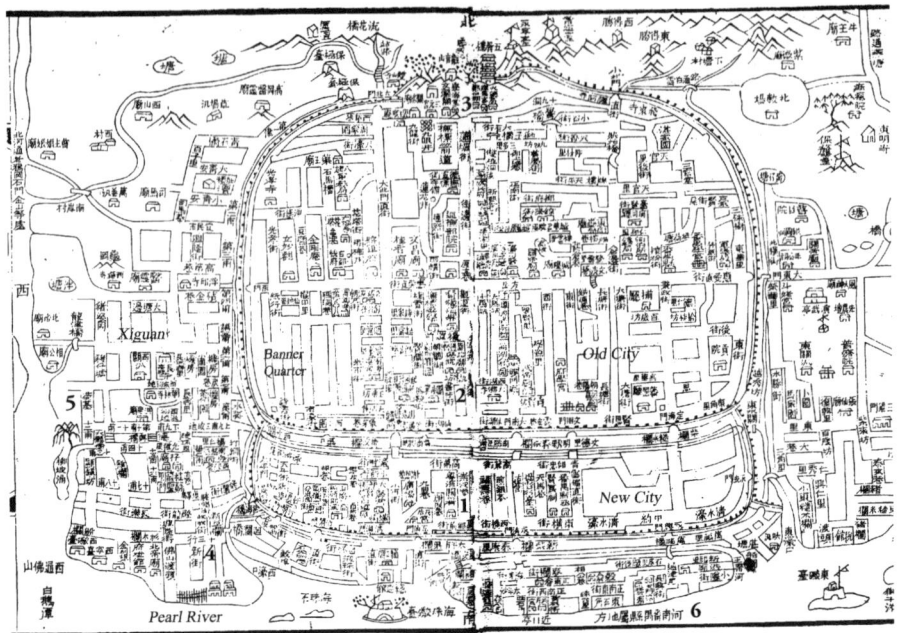

FIG. 1: Xie Lansheng's city: a map of Guangzhou from the 1835 Nanhai gazetteer. Xie was a senior editor but died before the gazetteer was completed. Important locations in relation to Xie's social itinerary include (1) Subo Alley, where the Studio of Constant Awareness was located, (2) Yangcheng Academy (not shown on the map), (3) the Xuehaitang, (4) the maritime merchant firms in Xiguan, (5) the general vicinity of Litchi Cove, and (6) the label indicating Henan, which was part of Panyu county and therefore not shown on the map (SOURCE: *Nanhai xian zhi*, 3.2b–3a).

cultural life of the city, especially in terms of redirecting literary and scholarly trends. One notable example is the Shandong native and poet Wang Shizhen (1634–1711), who in 1685 was dispatched to conduct sacrifices at the God of the South Seas Temple, located east of the city. While in Guangzhou, he mingled with leading local poets, and with his fame helped legitimize the region's growing reputation for poetry.[9] Classical scholarship in Guangzhou was given a brief boost when Suzhou native Hui Shiqi (1671–1741) served as educational commissioner from 1720 to 1726. Hui was an early proponent of Han exegeses; his son, Hui Dong, would be seen as the creator of the Han Learning school. In Guangzhou, Hui Shiqi's approach inspired such students as Nanhai native He Mengyao (1693–1764) and Luo Tianchi (1686–1766), the latter a native of Shunde county south of Guangzhou.[10] The Beijing poet and classicist Weng Fanggang (1733–1818) was another influential educational commissioner.

During his tenure from 1764 to 1771, he helped stimulate local interest in epigraphy by compiling and printing in Guangdong a collection of inscriptions found in the province, the *Yuedong jinshi lue* (Abridged record of metal and stone inscriptions in Guangdong).[11] All these officials created a local stir, but their impact was relatively short-lived because they did not fashion institutions to preserve their legacies. Like his predecessors, Ruan Yuan would inspire a devoted following. It was through the institutional means of his Xuehaitang academy, however, that Ruan's legacy was made a more permanent feature of the local cultural landscape.

Accompanying these numerous officials to their yamen in Guangzhou were large staffs of educated literati from their home regions, many of whom were aspiring officials themselves. Most of these literati served as administrative specialists and private secretaries. Others followed their patrons to this remote southern post to work on various scholarly or literary projects organized in the yamen. This practice became prevalent in Guangzhou during the nineteenth century, largely due to the example set by Ruan Yuan. When Ruan arrived in Guangzhou in 1817 to take up the post of governor-general, he attracted a large entourage of Jiangnan literati and quickly put several of them to work compiling an updated version of the Guangdong provincial gazetteer.

In addition to officials and their staffs, Guangzhou also hosted a large garrison of Eight Banners troops, composed of Manchus and Han Chinese from northeastern China who had early on declared their loyalty to the Qing and been organized into elite military units. Such positions were hereditary, and entire families would be registered as bannermen. After a faulty start disrupted by the Rebellion of the Three Feudatories (1673–81), the Qing state reestablished the Guangzhou banner garrison with three thousand Chinese bannermen selected from the capital. In the middle of the eighteenth century, the number of Chinese bannermen on duty in the Guangzhou garrison was reduced by half, and the rejects replaced by fifteen hundred Manchu bannermen reassigned from the capital. While the official total, which did not include dependents, therefore remained at three thousand, nineteenth-century estimates put the total population of bannermen and their dependents at twenty thousand.[12]

In contrast to most other Chinese cities with banner garrisons, in Guangzhou the Banner Quarter was not walled off from the rest of the city. The western third of the Old City was designated as the garrison compound, and the office of the Manchu garrison general was located on the section of Huiai Street that ran through the Banner Quarter. Though not separated by a wall, the native Cantonese population had been displaced when the garrison was created, and in the nineteenth century the Banner Quarter remained clearly distinguishable from other parts of the city.[13] Relying on fixed incomes established at the beginning of the dynasty, the growing banner population gradually became impoverished in relation to many other residents of the city. One nineteenth-century observer noted that this "part of the city shows a marked contrast to the purely Chinese portion. Their houses are smaller and poorer, and an air of neglect, thrift-lessness, and decay spreads over all."[14] Another simply stated that the "streets are wider here and the population less dense."[15]

Despite the visible differences between the Banner Quarter and the rest of the city, some members of the banner community interacted a great deal with the commercial and cultural elites of Guangzhou. By the nineteenth century, for example, banner families crafted most of the lanterns in Guangzhou's famed lantern market.[16] One Chinese bannerman of the Guangzhou garrison, Liu Qixiong, became wealthy in the salt trade, thus enabling him to donate funds to renovate roads and temples in the banner neighborhoods.[17] A critic noted in 1811 that "within the Guangzhou garrison, Chinese bannermen associate too much with outsiders, scheming for profit."[18] Such intermingling had been one of the motivations for dismissing most of the Chinese bannermen throughout the empire between 1754 and 1779.[19] Guangzhou was the only provincial garrison where Chinese bannermen were retained; they now constituted only half of the official numbers of bannermen in the city, but their dependents must have far outnumbered the newly arrived Manchus. Chinese bannermen who remained in the Beijing garrison became "Manchu," but in Guangzhou a few families began to enter the ranks of Cantonese literati in the early nineteenth century.[20] This was stimulated by the creation, in 1816, of a quota granting degrees to three Guangzhou garrison bannermen in each of the triennial

Guangdong provincial examinations. Among the first group of three was Xu Rong (1792–1855), one of several Chinese bannermen who would play important roles in the cultural life of the city.[21]

Many of the producers of local culture in Guangzhou during the nineteenth century were descendants of recent ancestors who had staffed the numerous yamen in Guangzhou and served throughout Guangdong province as *muyou* (officials' private secretaries), clerks, and subofficials.[22] The vast majority of members of this cohort hailed from "Jiangnan" broadly conceived—that is, southern Jiangsu and northern Zhejiang. Within this group, most came from two prefectures in northern Zhejiang: Shaoxing and Hangzhou. Migrants who relocated from northern Zhejiang and chose to settle in Guangzhou tended to register as residents of Panyu county in order to be eligible for the civil service examinations; only a few registered as Nanhai residents for this purpose. In Qing and Republican editions of the Panyu gazetteer, their ancestors are described as having served as officials or private secretaries in Guangzhou. When reasons are given for their remaining in Guangzhou, this is usually attributed to their having been simply "stuck" in the south, too poor to return home, or orphaned by fathers who served in the city. Genealogies more typically note that the ancestors of local notables served as subofficials or clerks, suggesting that at least some of the ancestors portrayed in gazetteer biographies as officials might more likely have been less prestigious subofficials. The fact that so many came from Hangzhou, and especially Shaoxing, is more than mere coincidence. James Cole has described Shaoxing natives' reputations as legal experts and has documented extensive networks of Shaoxing natives who served as *muyou* and subofficials in disproportionate numbers throughout the empire.[23] Numerous in-migrants who played prominent roles in the cultural life of Guangzhou during the nineteenth century were migrants or descendants of recent migrants from the Shaoxing counties of Shanyin, Guiji, Zhuji, Xiaoshan, and Shangyu, or the two counties that shared jurisdiction of Hangzhou city: Qiantang and Renhe.[24]

Two initial examples should suffice to introduce this pattern of descendants of northern Zhejiang administrative experts settling in Panyu. Shi Shanchang (ca. 1768–1830/31) was a Shanyin native whose father served as a clerk (*li*) in the yamen of the superintendent of customs. When his father died only ten months after Shanchang was born, the boy was raised by his mother and eventually registered as a Panyu resident. As an adult, Shi first pursued a career as a local teacher, then followed his father's example by working as a clerk, and, after his term was up, became a merchant in the foreign trade (*yangshang*). Still not satisfied, he purchased the rank of county magistrate and later served in Jiangxi. His son, Shi Cheng, would become an important scholar and teacher in Guangzhou and, in 1878, would express the family's new Cantonese identity by purchasing land in the city for an ancestral shrine.[25]

The Xu family, by the middle of the nineteenth century residents of the Panyu section of Guangzhou, traced their roots to a surname group residing in Hangzhou's Renhe county since the turn of the sixteenth century. An eighth-generation descendant, lacking an heir, was forced to adopt a son from outside the surname. This adoptive heir became a ninth-generation descendant, named Xu Yong (1762-1819), who came to Guangdong as a *muyou* in the late Qianlong (1736-95) or early Jiaqing (1796-1820) era. Xu Yong's three sons also came south, one after another, and so made their home in the Guangdong provincial capital. After his death, Xu Yong was buried outside Guangzhou and thus was later designated as the First Ancestor (*shizu*) of the branch relocated from Hangzhou. His eldest son, Xu Xuecheng (1783-1854), according to the Xu genealogy also sought a career as a *muyou*, but at first had trouble breaking into the business because those in his profession strictly adhered to cliques.[26] Finally recruited by the magistrate of Xiangshan county in the southern delta, he quickly earned a reputation for his professional skills.[27] The second son, Xu Xuezhou (1789-1826), alternated between careers as a *muyou* and a merchant, often shipping writing supplies from Zhejiang to sell in Guangdong. The family's *muyou* tradition was carried on into the next generation, as Xuecheng's son, Xu Qikang (1811-74), served in the customs yamen and other offices. But the family also began to move into more prestigious literati careers: Xuecheng's second son, Xu Qiyang (1819-72, the adoptive heir of Xuezhou), was a county student who eventually was appointed to be supervisor of one of Guangzhou's academies, the Yangcheng shuyuan. More outstanding scholarly success came with the third son, Xu Qiguang

(1827–84), who earned a *jinshi* degree and became a Hanlin academician and provincial censor.²⁸

Xu Yong and his descendants solidified their position in their new environment through intermarriage, not only with delta natives, but also with people of similar regional and professional backgrounds. Xu Yong's third son, Xu Xuezhu, arranged a marriage between his daughter and Zhang Tingjin (1816–74?), a native of Wu county in Jiangsu who was a private secretary in Dongan county, west of Guangzhou. The *jinshi* Xu Qiguang married the sister of Yang Rongxu (1809–74), a Panyu *juren*, resident of urban Guangzhou, and likely an in-migrant.²⁹

The Xu family also seems to have benefited from maintaining connections with kin who had remained in Hangzhou and retained their Renhe county registration.³⁰ Perhaps one reason that Xu Yong had been able to break into the secretarial business was that many of the Renhe Xu over several generations held important official posts in Guangdong. Other members of the ninth generation, who shared the same great-grandfather with Xu Yong, served in the province: Xu Yue (1719–87) as acting prefect of Guangzhou, and Xu Jun as magistrate of Shunde county from 1774 to 1781. This career track was retraced by Xu Yue's descendants. His son, Xu Xuefan (1772 *jinshi*), had accompanied his father during his service in Guangdong and was even hired to rate Guangzhou prefectural examinations. Xuefan's eldest son, Xu Nailai (1763–1822), held the post of Xiangshan county magistrate for four years at the turn of the nineteenth century, which perhaps explains Xu Xuecheng's first break as a *muyou* coming from that county; Xu Naiji (1777–1839), who later become embroiled in the debate over opium policy in the 1830s, served as Guangdong salt controller in 1832 and 1833 after a term as grain intendant. Xu Naiji further cemented his ties to Guangdong by taking a concubine from Shunde and briefly serving as director of Guangzhou's main academy, the Yuexiu shuyuan, after being appointed by Ruan Yuan in 1817. Finally, Xu Naizhao (1799–1878) was appointed Guangdong educational commissioner in 1849. In fact, even members of the Renhe Xu who did not settle in Guangdong spent so much time there that the 1775 and 1803 editions of the Renhe Xu genealogy were compiled and printed in the southern province.³¹

Like their subofficial and secretarial counterparts, merchants from Shaoxing and Hangzhou had a disproportionate presence in the city, and their descendants would have a great impact on local Cantonese cultural production.[32] The dominant merchants in Guangzhou city were those who controlled the salt and maritime trades; both groups comprised significant numbers of sojourners and migrants. Thus, merchants from Shaoxing and Hangzhou had a pervasive presence in the salt trade. As in other salt distribution centers, such as Yangzhou and Tianjin, it was common for outsiders to dominate Guangzhou's salt trade.[33] Although the salt merchants of Guangzhou have been overshadowed by the city's maritime merchants in modern historical literature, they were seen by their contemporaries as no less important than their maritime counterparts. This fact did not escape one nineteenth-century Western observer who sensed that Guangzhou's salt merchants "in official rank, social position, and wealth enjoyed an importance equal" to the maritime merchants.[34]

The overwhelming presence of Shaoxing and Hangzhou merchants residing in Guangzhou and involved in the commerce in salt can be gleaned from the 1836 edition of the gazetteer of the Guangdong-Guangxi salt trade, *Liang-Guang yanfa zhi*. Because extraprovincial merchants trading in Guangdong were not registered as local residents, their sons were not eligible to sit for the civil service examinations. Accordingly, the Qing government created a special category of sojourning "merchant-registered" (*shangji*) examination candidates, thereby allowing this class limited participation in the county/prefectural and provincial examinations held in Guangzhou. Successful candidates could then proceed to the capital to compete for the highest *jinshi* degree. The *Liang-Guang yanfa zhi* lists three merchant-registered candidates in Guangdong who earned the *jinshi* degree during the Qianlong reign, all of whom were Guiji county natives. In addition, the gazetteer records the names and native counties of twenty candidates who passed Guangdong provincial examinations under merchant registration between 1732 and 1777. Again, all were natives of Hangzhou or Shaoxing: six from Hangzhou prefecture, and, from Shaoxing, eight from Shanyin county and six from Guiji county. After 1777, descendants of salt merchants were formally allowed to register as local residents, almost invariably choosing to register in Panyu county.[35]

The biographical section of the 1871 edition of the Panyu county gazetteer contains numerous examples of local notables whose northern Zhejiang ancestors had come to Guangzhou in the salt trade, registered their sons under *shangji* status for the examinations, and eventually declared Panyu residency. The case of a certain Xu Benyi is typical.[36] Originally a Renhe county native, Xu's father sojourned in Guangdong and had three sons. All attained *shengyuan* (licentiate) status under merchant registration, gained literary reputations, and came to be known as the "Three Xus."[37] Another example is that of the Jin family, which produced several degree holders as well as local poets and scholars and traced its origins back to Shanyin ancestors or, as the Panyu gazetteer more obliquely explains, to "former generations of Zhejiang natives who served as officials in Guangdong" (*xianshi Zheren huan Yue*) earlier in the dynasty. The noted poet and Panyu native Zhang Weiping (1780–1859), who was a close friend of the Jin family and likewise a newcomer from northern Zhejiang, noted that one scion of the family, 1808 *juren* Jin Jingmao, was later burdened with "managing salt duties" (*li cuo wu*).[38] Though gazetteer biographies may have elided a literati family's commercial background, the case of the Jin also demonstrates the diversity of strategies for social advancement pursued by in-migrating, urban families. For the Jin, this strategy seems to have worked well. Writing in the early 1850s, Zhang Weiping described the Jin as a single household that had produced nine holders of examination degrees, a unique accomplishment in nineteenth-century urban Guangzhou.

Other traces of sojourning salt traders from Shaoxing were inscribed upon the urban landscape and appeared in popular literature. A shrine for the Martyred Lady Pan of Shanyin, located on Huiai Street, was dedicated to the daughter of a salt merchant surnamed Pan, from Shanyin county, who had lost his fortune. Because the daughter's fiancé no longer desired to marry her, she committed suicide in despair. The shrine was originally established in 1706 and renovated over a century later in 1819 by descendants of the father.[39] Another vestige of Shaoxing was the Dicang'an (Burial Chapel) outside Guangzhou's Main East Gate. Originally established with funds donated by sojourning Shaoxing merchants, by the nineteenth century the chapel served as a temporary storage facility for the coffins of sojourners who had perished in Guangzhou and whose relatives, if there were any, lacked the means to return the coffin to their native place for burial.[40] Other traces of Shaoxing influence in the Guangzhou salt trade can be found in the novel *Shenlou zhi* (An account of mirages). Putatively set in the Ming Jiajing (1522-66) era, the novel in fact describes a Guangzhou contemporary with the author (approximately the late Jiaqing era). The main character is the son of a wealthy maritime merchant, but the novel also portrays an affluent salt merchant, Wen Zhongweng, as a native of Shaoxing. His sister's husband is also a Shaoxing native in the Guangdong salt trade, and Wen arranges a marriage between his son and the daughter of a subofficial serving in Nanhai county.[41] Thus, northern Zhejiang natives had not only a disproportionate representation in Guangzhou's numerous yamen, but also a pervasive presence among the city's salt merchants; the fictional merchant Wen's Shaoxing origins would thus be familiar to Cantonese readers of an early nineteenth-century novel. Consequently, the cultural elite of Panyu county during the nineteenth century increasingly was composed of Guangzhou city residents who had northern Zhejiang roots.[42]

Just as northern Zhejiang merchants were ubiquitous in the Guangzhou-based salt trade, so the city's most famous officially licensed maritime merchants (the Cohong merchants) traced their origins to central and southern Fujian. And though some of their descendants eventually moved into the cultural elite as bona fide literati, the Fujian merchants were most important as patrons of cultural production. The two most powerful families among the merchants in the maritime trade were both Fujian families that had taken up residence in Guangzhou only during the early Qing.

One of these was the Wu family, originally from central coastal Fujian; during the Kangxi reign (1662-1722) its ancestor, a merchant named Wu Chaofeng (1613-93), had settled in Xiguan, the Guangzhou suburb outside the western portion of the city wall. Wu Chaofeng later had the coffin of his father, Wu Dianbei, transferred from Fujian and interred outside Guangzhou, thus making permanent his status as a new Nanhai resident. As his descendants began to prosper in trade, they built palatial homes and gardens in Xiguan and in the suburb known as Henan, across the Pearl River to the south. In the 1780s, Wu Chaofeng's great-grandson Wu Guoying became the first member of the immigrant family to open up his own business under the maritime monopoly, the Yihe firm. Wu Guoying's third son, Wu Bingjian (1769–1843), in 1801 assumed leadership of the family firm, and during the remainder of the Jiaqing reign became the city's wealthiest maritime merchant, amassing possibly the largest personal fortune in the world.[43]

In the early nineteenth century, the sojourning Wu agnates in Guangzhou began taking steps to recast themselves as a Cantonese lineage. In 1803 Wu Guoying erected a shrine honoring his father, and in 1824 his oldest son, Wu Bingyong, compiled a genealogy. In 1835 the Wus built a shrine devoted to Wu Dianbei, the first ancestor to be interred in Guangdong. In further efforts to establish its legitimacy in Cantonese high society, the family forged marriage ties with such scholar-officials as Wu Rongguang (1773–1843) from Foshan and otherwise used its substantial wealth to legitimize its social standing.[44] Wu Bingjian and another maritime merchant, Lu Wenjin, donated one hundred thousand taels to renovate dikes along the Mulberry Garden Enclosure. Wu's son, Wu Yuansong, made another large donation after floods in 1833 ravaged the same area. In recognition of such contributions, Wu Bingjian and his sons were rewarded with examination degrees and official ranks.[45]

The Pan family, from Tongan county near the southern Fujian port of Quanzhou, was an equally influential maritime merchant family. After gaining experience in the foreign trade in Fujian and Manila, the first in this family to reside in Guangzhou was Pan Zhencheng (1714–88).[46] Pan designated his maritime firm Tongwen: "tong" for Tongan county and "wen" for Wenpu Hill in his home county, "so as not to forget his origins."[47] Pan Zhencheng was in fact buried in Tongan, although he had established opulent residential homes and expansive gardens in Xiguan and Henan. Only with the second generation—of Pan Youwei (1744–1821), Pan Youdu (1755–1820), and five other sons—were members of the Pan family buried in Guangdong.[48] Another branch of the Pan family, stemming from a younger brother of Pan Zhencheng, settled in Guangzhou beginning in the late eighteenth century.[49] The Pan family would be most successful among maritime merchants in entering the ranks of the city's literati.[50]

Aside from the Wu and Pan, at least three other Fujian families edged their way into the elite group of the thirteen officially designated maritime merchants. Of the three, the Xie family appeared most frequently as patrons of elite culture in Guangzhou. The founder, Xie Jiawu (d. 1826), originally hailed from Zhangzhou prefecture in Fujian and, by 1811, was granted a license as a maritime merchant operating the Dongyu firm. Xie Jiawu's sons, Youwen and Youren, when acting as literati rather than merchants, were based in their New City mansion, the Catching Moon Tower.[51] But the Wu, Pan, and Xie were only the most prominent merchants from Fujian; as early as the 1730s at least a thousand other merchants from the two Fujianese cities of Quanzhou and Zhangzhou were trading and residing in Guangzhou.[52] The maritime merchant family patriarch Pan Zhencheng founded an organization for his fellow migrant merchants from Fujian.[53] His son, Pan Youwei, later made mention of a Fujian Street in Henan where there resided "Fujian natives who have grown old with navigating the seas."[54]

Not all of the Fujian families sought their fortunes in the maritime trade; at least one, under the family patriarch Ye Tingxun, established itself in the salt business. The Ye ancestors had at some point moved from Fuqing county, south of Fuzhou, to Tongan, ancestral home of the maritime Pan family. Ye Tingxun's great-grandfather relocated to Nanhai during the early Qing and, in 1815, was enshrined in Xiguan as the family's First Migrant Ancestor. To add luster to the newly completed shrine, Tingxun called upon the visiting Jiangnan prose master Yun Jing (1757–1817) to compose a commemorative inscription. Tingxun and other members of the Ye family made donations for flood relief and other projects during the Jiaqing era, and, like other merchant families, were duly rewarded with ranks and honors. Likewise, Tingxun's family members and succeeding generations of the Ye family began to recast themselves as literati over the course of the nineteenth century.[55]

Sojourning literati from Jiaying department in northeastern Guangdong constituted another important cohort of newcomers operating in the literary and scholarly circles of cosmopolitan Guangzhou during the early nineteenth century. The population of Jiaying was largely composed of Hakkas, a subethnic group in many ways culturally distinct from the Han Chinese who inhabited the delta. Centuries earlier, the Hakkas had settled the mountainous region straddling the provincial borders of Fujian, Jiangxi, and

Guangdong. The most important part of this "Hakka homeland" in far eastern Guangdong was Jiaying department.[56]

Although in administrative terms Jiaying was a component of Guangdong province and thereby fell under the jurisdiction of the numerous provincial officials stationed in Guangzhou, the area may be seen in geographic and economic terms as actually having closer connections to southern Fujian and northeastern Guangdong, including the coastal city of Chaozhou.[57] Unlike most areas in Guangdong that had relatively easy riverine access to Guangzhou, travel from Jiaying to the provincial city was not very convenient. This can be seen in the diary of Weng Xincun (1791–1862), who traveled from his post in Fujian to take up a new assignment as Guangdong educational commissioner in 1825. After passing by Jiaying city, he proceeded upstream along the Han River system through two Hakka counties before his entourage was forced to travel by a land route over a mountain pass linking the Han River system (which runs southeast toward Chaozhou) and the East River system (flowing through the eastern Pearl River delta toward Guangzhou).[58]

Disregarding the hazards of travel between the Hakka homeland and the Pearl River delta, Hakka commoners migrated toward the delta and points further west in increasing numbers after the seventeenth century. By the eighteenth century, as Sow-theng Leong suggests, the Hakka presence in the immediate vicinity of Guangzhou began to be felt, particularly in the more peripheral areas of Guangzhou prefecture outside the low-lying and prosperous counties of Panyu, Nanhai, Shunde, Xinhui, and Xiangshan. In the delta, most of these in-migrating Hakkas worked as tenants for local Cantonese, or Punti, landlords. As the prosperity of the eighteenth century gradually gave way to the growing environmental and economic pressures of the nineteenth, conflicts broke out between Punti and Hakkas, with incidents reported as early as 1802, and culminating in widespread violence by the middle of the century.[59]

Aside from commoners who migrated into the Pearl River delta, Jiaying literati hoping to pass triennial provincial examinations held in Guangzhou also gravitated toward the area. Jiaying consistently placed a high number of successful candidates in these examinations, its success comparable to that of Nanhai, Panyu, and Shunde, the three major counties at the core of the Pearl River delta.[60] Whether they were drawn to Guangzhou to bolster their chances of academic success or were encouraged to remain in the city after having achieved it, many of Jiaying's most prominent literati sojourned in early nineteenth-century Guangzhou for extended periods.[61] In an essay commemorating the departure from Guangzhou of a Jiaying literatus named Xu Qing, the eminent Cantonese painter and poet Xie Lansheng explained that Xu was ridiculed by his fellow Jiaying literati for wishing to return to his native department immediately after failing the provincial examinations.[62] The implication is of course that most Jiaying literati preferred to remain in Guangzhou, and indeed many members of the educated elite from Jiaying had a notable impact in cultural circles of Guangzhou city during the early nineteenth century; a few even settled there permanently. For instance, Qiu Xiande's father moved from Jiaying to Guangzhou as a *muyou* and eventually registered as a Panyu resident.[63] Qiu Xiande went on to earn a *jinshi* degree in 1787 and to serve as director of Guangzhou's main academy, the Yuexiu shuyuan. During his tenure as academy director, Qiu wrote an essay celebrating the construction, between 1807 and 1810, of a clan shrine and hostel in the Old City catering to members of the Qiu surname from counties settled by Hakkas throughout Guangdong province.[64] This gives some indication of the rising importance of eastern Guangdong Hakkas in the cultural life of early nineteenth-century Guangzhou. As we shall see, Jiaying Hakkas also maintained a presence at the Xuehaitang academy in absolute disproportion to their lack of geographical proximity.

Yet as representatives of a subethnic group from a remote corner of the province, Hakkas were not always completely assimilated into Han Chinese society, even in the cosmopolitan atmosphere of Guangzhou. One early nineteenth-century scholar, a Panyu native of northern Zhejiang ancestry, Zhang Biao (1781–1851), in praising his literary companion, the Jiaying poet Li Fuping (1770–1832), revealed his attitude toward most Jiaying Hakkas. A biography of Li noted that Zhang "spoke of Li Fuping's talent as being the most outstanding of the Meizhou poets; and [remarked] that, as for his character, he absolutely lacked the bad habits (*qixi*) of Meizhou commoners and scholars."[65] Nevertheless, in spite of this clear awareness of Hakkas as outsiders, Jiaying scholars and poets found unprecedented opportunities in the competition for local cultural capital in urban Guangzhou during the early nineteenth century.

None of these in-migrating and sojourning cohorts—Chinese bannermen from the northeast, northern Zhejiang subofficials, secretaries, and salt merchants, Fujianese maritime merchants, or Jiaying literati—could claim to have very deep roots in the delta. Whether temporarily sojourning in urban Guangzhou, or having settled there only during the Qing, they were newcomers to the region from the point of view of the delta hinterland. Most of the people who constituted these in-migrating cohorts fall under the category of urban relocation referred to by William Rowe as "sojourning." That is, the people who first relocated to Guangzhou portrayed the move as a temporary one—or at least formally created that impression—and therefore often retained their native-place registration and identity. Banner garrisons never completely rejected the fiction of temporary assignment, and Chinese bannermen were often depicted as natives of the northeast. First-generation migrants from Jiangsu, Zhejiang, and Fujian, whether involved in teaching, administration, or commerce, likewise retained their native-place identities and, even if they died in Guangzhou, were often returned to their native place for burial.[66]

Another cohort with an important presence in both the commercial and elite cultural life of Guangzhou consisted of families who moved permanently from the delta hinterland to the city, a form of relocation Rowe labels "urbanization."[67] Several examples of this can be found among Guangzhou's maritime merchants. Liang Jingguo (1761–1837) was a native of the port of Huangpu (Whampoa), downriver from Guangzhou in Panyu, who managed the Tianbao firm and resided in Xiguan but claimed descent from ancestors who had settled Huangpu in the early Ming.[68] The Li family from Shunde county operated the Xicheng firm. Two other maritime merchants hailed from Xinhui and Heshan counties in the far western portions of the Pearl River delta. Lu Guanheng (d. 1812), who established the Guangli firm in 1792, was one of the most powerful maritime merchants. Natives of Xinhui, the Lu family's ties to Guangzhou were only tangential, as Guanheng's descendants returned to Xinhui after the licensed monopoly was abolished in 1842.[69] Another maritime merchant, Yi Rongzhi (1791–1854), a native of the neighboring county of Heshan, was a latecomer to the maritime trade, only establishing his Futai firm in 1835.[70]

Maritime merchants such as Lu and Yi, although they, too, may be described as sojourners in Guangzhou city, differed from the extraprovincials in significant ways. Whereas the Fujian merchant Wu and Pan families easily established themselves as the two leading private patrons of scholarship and art in cosmopolitan Guangzhou, they had much more difficulty penetrating the social and cultural elites of the delta hinterland outside Guangzhou and Foshan. In contrast, Lu Guanheng and Yi Rongzhi were products of the delta. The Yi genealogy placed Rongzhi in the nineteenth generation of descendants of Heshan (then part of Xinhui) settlers. Moreover, he managed to find wives from among other established lineages of the delta for several of his seventeen sons, thus reaffirming his ties to the delta hinterland through affinal relationships. Yi arranged the marriage of his second son to a daughter of Luo Yuliang (1832 *juren*), of the influential Luo lineage in the Shunde county seat of Daliang. He also married off his first daughter to another Luo of Daliang: Luo Jiabao, a nephew of the 1832 *jinshi* and Hanlin academician Luo Chuanqiu.[71] The ease with which Yi Rongzhi created affinal connections to powerful lineages of the delta hinterland suggests that, in the elite society of Guangzhou and the delta, class affiliations mattered less than regional ones.

Native-place and occupational ties seem to have had some influence on settlement and marriage patterns among the in-migrating cohorts, though perhaps not as rigidly as William Rowe finds for Hankou.[72] Thus, in his depiction of Guangzhou at the end of the nineteenth century, Edward Rhoads suggests that "the division between merchants and gentry could virtually be drawn on a city map" because "most of the commerce and handicrafts, and most of the merchants, were concentrated in the western half of the city, especially the Western Suburb" (Xiguan), whereas the "eastern half of the city, on the other hand, was the stronghold of the gentry."[73] G. William Skinner concurs with this, characterizing the Old City and Eastern Suburb as together constituting the gentry nucleus, and locating the business nucleus in the New City, Xiguan, and the suburb of Henan across the Pearl River to the south.[74] The fact that most *huiguan*, or native-place associations catering to sojourning merchants, were located in the New City and in Xiguan lends credence to this view. These included *huiguan* serving the regional cohorts that have been introduced here, such as the Hangzhou merchants' *huiguan* in the New City. Even more merchant organizations were concentrated in Xiguan, as were the maritime merchant firms, near the famous Thirteen Factories of the European and American traders. The Zhejiang *huiguan* (described as one of the sights of the suburbs), the Fujian *huiguan*, and a Meizhou temple serving Jiaying sojourners, were all located in Xiguan. The salt junks were moored just downstream along the Henan shore.[75]

The location and design of such physical structures as *huiguan* were at times intended to articulate a particular ideological orientation; this would also be reflected in the selection of sites for such literati institutions as the Xuehaitang. Location and design thereby might serve to construct boundaries, as planners took on the pose of pure literati untainted by the city's commercial hubbub. But the people who staffed both commercial and literati institutions flowed freely among various parts of the city. Moreover, as exemplified by the in-migrating cohorts examined here, many families that would produce literati initially gained their foothold in Guangzhou directly through commerce. Others established themselves in the city as minor officials, subofficials, or secretaries who staffed the yamen that regulated the salt and maritime trades. Thus, it is virtually impossible to identify a member of the nineteenth-century, urban Cantonese "gentry"—here defined as holders of civil service degrees—who lacked ties to commerce, whether they were family, marriage, or financial ties.

But a consideration of the regional origins and occupations of various cohorts provides some insight into the physical divisions in the city. As noted by Rhoads and Skinner, civil officials and their staffs were situated in their yamen, most of which were concentrated in the eastern sector of the Old City. Though not walled off from the rest of the city, the Banner Quarter was also visibly distinct. Other regional cohorts also exhibited patterns of settlement in their new urban environment. Descendants of the northern Zhejiang cohort, whether administrative or mercantile, overwhelmingly tended to register as residents of Panyu, and so at least maintained formal residences in Panyu sections of the city such as Henan and the eastern halves of the Old City and New City. Maritime and salt merchants from Fujian typically maintained mansions both in Henan and Xiguan, and might register in Panyu (as did the Pan and Xie) or Nanhai (in the case of the Wu and Ye). In-migrants relocating from the delta—merchant families that often later produced literati—most commonly settled in Xiguan, but also in the New City and Henan.

Viewed from any angle, nineteenth-century Guangzhou appears to have been a city of newcomers, something typical of other large cities in the Qing empire. Kwan Man Bun describes Tianjin, also a major center of the salt trade, as a city with few natives and many settlers.[76] Similarly, William Rowe notes that Hankou was dominated by interregional traders of extraprovincial origin, and thus the city's "connection to its regional hinterland was at best marginal."[77] Antonia Finnane characterizes the community of sojourning merchants in Yangzhou as a "Huizhou colony."[78] Guangzhou likewise was inundated with outsiders who came to dominate local charity, patronage of scholarship and literature, and cultural production itself. Thus, the distinction between merchants and gentry within Guangzhou was less important than that distinguishing in-migrating, sojourning, and urbanized elites in cosmopolitan Guangzhou, on the one hand, from the landholding and commercial elite of the delta hinterland on the other. In contrast to some hinterlands of cities dominated by sojourners, however, the Pearl River delta sustained powerful gentry who commanded a great deal of wealth and prestige.

INSULAR TOWNSHIPS AND OPEN SANDS IN THE DELTA HINTERLAND

From the perspective of the early nineteenth century—before the creation of the Xuehaitang—the center of Cantonese culture lay arguably not in the regional metropolis of Guangzhou city, but rather in the surrounding hinterland of Guangzhou prefecture and parts of Zhaoqing prefecture further west, together forming what today is referred to as the Pearl River delta (see Fig. 2). The older parts of the delta, especially along the West River, were dominated economically, socially, and culturally by well-established lineages that could demonstrate descent from pre-Qing ancestors. Consequently, Cantonese culture here was less easily contested and less readily appropriated by

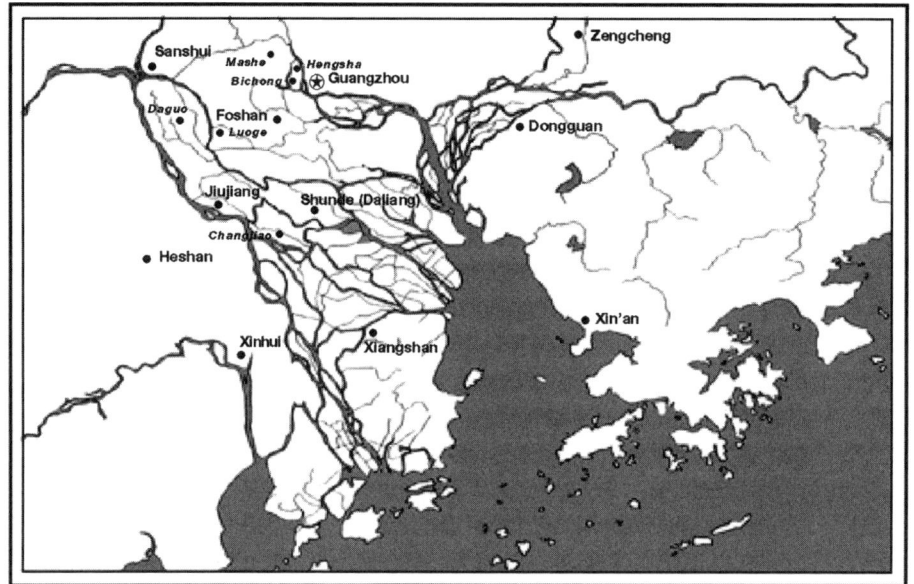

FIG. 2: The Pearl River delta (adapted from Mazumdar, *Sugar and Society*, p. 200).

in-migrating elites. The native social and cultural elite of this region can be seen as another cohort, which, in contrast to the in-migrating cohorts that settled in urban Guangzhou, was based in the hinterland townships and claimed deep genealogical roots in the delta.

In the early nineteenth century, the delta region comprised several distinct areas. It began in the west, where the West and North Rivers joined and then split again in Sanshui county, about ten miles from Guangzhou. Robert Marks points out that the delta was largely manmade, beginning in the Song when wet-rice techniques were brought to the region from Jiangnan. Through water control, irrigation, and land reclamation techniques, the islands and sand bars in Sanshui, Xinhui, Nanhai, and southern Panyu counties were gradually transformed into "enclosed fields" (*weitian*).[79] By 1800, land in these older parts of the delta was intensively farmed by a dense population and was collectively referred to as the "old sands and enclosed fields" (*laosha weitian*). These consisted of polders of rich silt that had matured over a long period, protected by a network of dikes built mainly during the Ming and Qing.[80]

Well-established lineages in the old sands portion of the delta hinterland excelled in cultural production; during the early nineteenth century, however, not all areas of the delta were equally productive.

The county of Dongguan (to the east of Panyu) had produced a number of important figures during the mid- to late Ming flourishing of Cantonese elite culture. Yet, after the bloody Ming-Qing transition, Dongguan never quite regained its former place in delta cultural production.[81] Only the Deng lineage in Dongguan was conspicuous in nineteenth-century literati circles. In contrast, Heshan and Xinhui counties in the western delta, as well as the prefectural city of Zhaoqing beyond them along the West River, continued to produce notable poets and scholars.

In terms of cultural production, however, one particular segment of the delta stood out for the number of degree holders and literati it produced, as well as for the abundant local cultural resources that it generated in the form of subcounty gazetteers, lineage genealogies, and other compilations. This was an area in southern Nanhai and western Shunde counties within and neighboring the Mulberry Garden Enclosure. The Enclosure protected an intensively cultivated area bounded by the West River to the south and west, and by the main branch of the North River to the north and east. Considered a part of the old sands, this area had come by the nineteenth century to specialize in a form of agriculture known as the mulberry embankment and fish pond system.[82] Construction began around 1100 on the dikes that would eventually make up the Mulberry Garden Enclosure. At the height of its sophistication in late imperial times, the connected dikes of the Enclosure stretched a total of 28 miles and protected approximately one hundred thousand acres of land from flood.[83] By the early eighteenth century, Jiujiang township had emerged as the center of this type of agriculture, surrounded by such townships as Shatou and Datong in Nanhai, and Longshan, Longjiang, Ganzhu, and Lelou in Shunde.[84] Toward the end of the century, Jiujiang could be described as a place "without rice fields" and Longshan as a township with less than one hundred *qing* of "village fields," suggesting the extremely high level of commercialization in the district.[85] A late nineteenth-century British traveler through this portion of the hinterland was awed by the density of settlement in the area:

No one who has not passed through this district can have any just conception of the density of the population. Besides the innumerable villages, there are the great towns of Koon-shán [Guanshan], Sha-t'ow [Shatou],

Loong-kong [Longjiang], Loong-shán [Longshan], Kow-kong [Jiujiang], Lak-low [Lelou], and Kom-chook [Ganzhu], all lying close together.[86]

Lacking the fascinated tone of a foreign traveler, the local poet Huang Peifang (1779–1859) described Longshan, one of the major townships in the district, simply as a "giant township."[87]

Although strictly speaking not part of the Enclosure district, two nearby cities greatly contributed to the area's economic and cultural prosperity. Foshan (in Nanhai, just north of the Enclosure) was considered one of the four great towns (*si da zhen*) of the Qing. That is, it was one of four cities in the empire that had emerged as major commercial centers without being at the same time significant centers of political administration. Serving both as a manufacturing center and as the main transshipment point in the Guangxi-Guangdong rice trade, Foshan was second only to Guangzhou in the regional trading hierarchy of Lingnan. Foshan drew almost all its sojourners from the delta hinterland; several of the city's newcomers in Qing times traced their roots to Shunde.[88] To the east of the Enclosure district, Daliang (the county seat of Shunde) may be considered more akin to the West River region than to the city of Guangzhou. Two very influential clusters of lineages dominated here, the Long and the Luo, consistently placing their sons into the civil service. In some cases, the economic interests of the Daliang elite were at odds with those of the Enclosure gentry. For example, both the Luo and the Long of Daliang were heavily involved in the reclamation of alluvial fields along the coast, which tended to cause flooding upstream along the West River.[89]

Nevertheless, in cultural terms, the elites of Foshan, Daliang, and the Enclosure district much more closely resembled one another than they did the in-migrating elites of cosmopolitan Guangzhou. This was especially true of Daliang and the Enclosure district, as the distinctiveness of the area was also reflected in marriage practices. The Enclosure district and most of Shunde largely correspond to the area that Janice Stockard has mapped out and designated as the "delayed transfer marriage area." Here, new brides customarily did not take up residence with their husbands until as long as three years after marriage. Although gentry leaders of Jiujiang and other townships in the area occasionally led campaigns against such practices, the custom did mark off the area from the immediate vicinity of Guangzhou, where major marriage was practiced.[90] Finally, measured in terms of the numbers of degree holders and texts produced, the area along the West River including Foshan, Daliang, and especially the Enclosure district accounted for the bulk of elite cultural production in the Pearl River delta outside of Guangzhou city.

More specifically, economic and cultural production in this West River area was monopolized by the dominant lineages.[91] Unlike the sugarcane cultivation prevalent in Dongguan and Panyu, conversion of rice paddies into mulberry embankments and fish ponds required levels of investment and organizational capacities beyond the means of ordinary peasant households and thus could be managed only by the landed gentry of the district or the lineage corporate estates that they dominated.[92] Another component of economic power not surprisingly dominated by the lineages was control of access to markets in the delta. Thus the Long lineage of Daliang, to name but one example, built up its local economic power through the establishment and control of local markets.[93]

Though Foshan was more cosmopolitan, it was extremely difficult for outsiders, such as Fujian or Zhejiang merchants, to gain a share of the wealth produced in such places as Jiujiang, Longshan, or even Daliang by the middle of the Qing. Sucheta Mazumdar enumerates several restrictions on the free sale of land throughout the delta, but they most accurately apply to the Enclosure district. For example, a lineage estate usually held land in perpetuity, as lineage regulations would forbid the sale of privately owned land in its home village to any person who was not a member of the lineage. Due to the fact that most land in the delta was held by corporate estates such as lineages, land came on the market only in small parcels and this in turn served as a further barrier to capital investment.[94] Mazumdar's argument regarding obstacles to economic penetration of parts of the delta is evocative when applied to the analysis of the cultural interaction between cosmopolitan Guangzhou and the insular Enclosure district. Unable to access the area economically (and perhaps also uninterested in investing there), sojourning elites based in Guangzhou were even less likely to make cultural inroads into the West River heartland of the dominant delta lineages.

The dominant lineages of the Enclosure district and other older areas of the delta hinterland further distinguished themselves from in-migrating upstarts in Guangzhou city in that these lineages could make acceptable claims to descent from Han Chinese ancestors who had arrived in the delta region as early as the Song-Yuan transition. There were a variety of foundation legends that supported such claims to long-standing, delta-based, Han Chinese pedigrees. The most common was the Zhujixiang legend, according to which a concubine of a Song dynasty emperor escaped from the palace and married a merchant of Zhujixiang in the northern Guangdong prefecture of Nanxiong. Fearing the emperor's wrath, residents petitioned the Nanxiong subprefect for permission to migrate to places further south, in what was to become the Pearl River delta, where they registered with local magistrates.[95] These claims of descent were inscribed across the delta landscape in the form of ancestral tombs and shrines.[96] Moreover, the most influential of these lineages could demonstrate descent from degree holders and other members of the delta cultural elite during the Ming, and thereby assert their status as participants in a Cantonese cultural tradition stretching back for at least three centuries. Among the lineages able to distinguish themselves markedly from the newcomers in Guangzhou were the Cai of Longjiang, the Wen of Longshan, the Long and Luo of Daliang and, as we shall see in Chapter 7, the Zhu lineage of Jiujiang.[97]

Though outsiders in the city of Guangzhou tended not to expand their influence into the Enclosure district and other older parts of the delta, the dominant lineages of the delta had more freedom in establishing themselves in the city. Since the middle of the Ming, many successful sons of delta lineages had moved to the provincial city, where they often constructed luxuriant gardens to entertain guests, pursued careers as local teachers, or built academies and ancestral halls catering to lineage members sojourning in the city. The southern branch of the Daliang Luo, for example, maintained the Righteous Reclusion Academy in Guangzhou's Old City, south of Huiai Street. There were also halls that served all members of the same surname group native to Guangzhou prefecture or Guangdong province, such as the Lujiang Academy for the He surname, built between 1808 and 1813.[98]

Nevertheless, the ties of the ensconced West River lineages to cosmopolitan Guangzhou were not as unencumbered as they might initially appear. Mazumdar notes that absentee landlords maintaining no contact with their native villages were less common in Guangdong than in some other regions of the Qing empire because of the fact that tax collection was closely tied to lineage organization.[99] Also, the strategy of controlling markets to build up economic clout for the lineage required a great deal of attention. Furthermore, the primary ancestral temples and rituals of the West River lineages were still centered in the townships. Consequently, the economic and cultural elites of the Enclosure district and surrounding areas tended to remain firmly rooted in the densely populated townships along the West River.

Yet, some members of delta lineages who sojourned in Guangzhou eventually established families or lineage segments that permanently relocated to the city and went on to become important patrons or producers of elite culture there. Like the maritime merchant Lu and Yi families described above, whose ancestral homes were in the western delta, one of the important salt merchant families operating in Guangzhou, the Kong, were natives of the Nanhai countryside. The Kong family was from Luoge township west of Foshan but maintained a lavish residence in the New City. There, they retained their identity as the "Luoge Kong," but also became important patrons and collectors of local art. Likewise, although members of his lineage continued to register as Xiangshan natives, the poet Huang Peifang maintained family mansions and shrines, some putatively dating from the Ming, in the Old Taiquan neighborhood of the Old City. This neighborhood was named after his eminent Ming ancestor, the official and scholar Huang Zuo (*hao* Taiquan, 1490–1566). Not registering as residents of either Nanhai or Panyu—perhaps in order for its sons to sit for less competitive county examinations in Xiangshan—the Huang family balanced its identity between Xiangshan in the delta and urban Guangzhou.[100]

The Kong kept their Luoge choronym and the Huang retained their Xiangshan registration, but other hinterland migrants into Guangzhou and its suburbs branched off from their delta-based kin and articulated urban identities through the production of new genealogies and the construction of migrant ancestral shrines. A good example of this can be seen in the 1848 genealogy of the Chengnan (city-south) Du lineage ("city-south" here referring to the New City south of the Old City). Like most delta lineages, in their genealogy the Chengnan Du claimed descent from ancestors who had migrated to the delta from Zhujixiang in Nanxiong. A descendant of these ancestors was said to have moved during the early Ming from elsewhere in the delta to Daguo township, at Xiqiao Mountain in Nanhai county, and was later designated as the First Ancestor of the Daguo Du when they produced a genealogy. In the Kangxi era, a twelfth-generation member of the Daguo Du moved to Guangzhou's New City and hence came under the jurisdiction of Panyu county; in 1703 his son purchased property in the New City.[101]

Continuing to calculate generations based on the First Ancestor who had moved to Daguo, the relocated segment of the Du began to prosper in Guangzhou with a fifteenth-generation descendant, Du Xian (1708–59), who was able to distribute "no more" than several thousand silver taels to each of his three sons, Du Song (1732–91), Du Yong (1746–1807), and Du Mian (1749–1809), when he divided his property. Less than 30 years later, one of the sons, Du Yong, had accumulated many tens of thousands of taels, enough to provide for a hundred dependents in the extended family and to purchase official rank for himself. Du Yong earned his fortune as a pawn merchant, presumably owning several of the pawnshop towers that dominated the Guangzhou skyline. Capitalizing on his commercial success, he arranged a marriage between his daughter and Pan Zhengheng (亨, 1779–1837), a nephew of the maritime merchant Pan Youdu, and solicited congratulatory essays for family birthdays from among the city's literary elite. In one of these essays, celebrating the eightieth birthday of Du Mian's wife, the renowned Cantonese painter and poet Xie Lansheng described the Du compound in the crowded New City as a complex of numerous houses stretching for an entire *li* (about a third of a mile). He portrayed Du Mian as hosting great banquets where he entertained guests until they were thoroughly satiated, but which also incorporated such literati activities as playing the zither and composing poetry.[102] The next generation began to produce the trappings of an organized lineage. Du Yong's fifth son, Du Renfeng (1787–1835), who served as a salt inspector in Yunnan, set up an ancestral trust and constructed ancestral tombs.

The sixth son, Du You (1795–1853), was a Panyu county student and married the sister of Liu Tianhui (d. 1829), a Nanhai *juren* and future Xuehaitang examinee. Du You compiled the 1848 genealogy, and possessed either the literary connections or the money to convince Zhang Weiping to write the title page in his calligraphy. As a final step in the creation of this new urban Cantonese literary elite family, the Du produced their own *juren* in the next generation.[103]

Though the New City and Henan attracted many urbanized families from the delta, even more eventually settled in Xiguan. For example, the Xiguan Yang's ancestor had moved from Shunde county to Foshan in the late Ming. As a youth, his fifth-generation descendant, Yang Yuanfu (1716–98), relocated from Foshan to Guangzhou's New City, where he was apprenticed in the embroidery business. Over the following two decades he began to establish himself in the trade and make his own money. The family's wealth grew under the guidance of his son, Yang Dalin (1754–1825), who moved the family to Xiguan in 1795. Yang Dalin earned enough of a fortune to support the sixteen sons that he produced with his wife and four concubines, and subsequently used his sons to cultivate affinal relations with the city's commercial elite. These included marriages to daughters of the Nanhai salt merchant Ye Tingxun and the Nanhai Wu and Xinhui Lu maritime merchant families; Dalin's grandson married a daughter of the maritime merchant Pan family.[104] For one of his six daughters, Yang Dalin arranged a match with the son of Qiu Xi, a merchant who hosted the Cantonese literati at a favorite touring site, Litchi Cove (Lizhiwan) in Xiguan.[105] In Yang's case, then, regional origin was less of a concern than was establishing relations with Guangzhou's wealthiest merchants. But the Yang family also intermarried with other Xiguan families that had relocated from Foshan, including the Tan, who would produce two of the Xuehaitang's most famous scholars. When the generation of Yang Dalin's grandsons compiled a genealogy in the early Guangxu era (1875–1908), they proclaimed their urban Cantonese identity by calling themselves the Xiguan Yang.[106]

As illustrated by the cases of the Chengnan Du and Xiguan Yang, segments that had branched off from surname groups in the delta hinterland and relocated to the city made claims of urban identity when they produced genealogies. Some families that migrated from the hinterland to Guangzhou initially continued to identify with their native place and occasionally returned to participate in ritual functions. Once a family produced a genealogy and thereby articulated a connection with a section of the city, it recognized that its close ties to the hinterland had been severed. Identifying themselves as residents of Xiguan or Henan thus entailed a shift of consciousness that affiliated them more closely with newcomers from outside the delta than with their distant kin who remained in the delta.[107] It must also be emphasized that this migration between the delta hinterland and the city was almost exclusively unidirectional; no evidence from genealogies or gazetteers reveals a pattern during the Qing of extraprovincial elites first settling in urban Guangzhou and then relocating to the delta hinterland.

In addition to older parts of the delta hinterland such as Daliang, Foshan, and the Enclosure district, another area known as the "sands" (*shatian* or *shatan*) was important, not for the cohort of literati it produced but rather as a source of financial support for activities of the cohorts we have examined. In contrast to the insular "older sands" of the delta along the Mulberry Garden Enclosure, the newer sands consisted of alluvial fields only in the process of being reclaimed and settled in the nineteenth century. Hence these areas along the coastal portions of Xinhui, Xiangshan, Shunde, Panyu, and Dongguan counties were referred to simply as the "sands" by nineteenth-century inhabitants of the delta. They formed what may be considered the delta's frontier, and indeed exhibited salient characteristics of unsettled frontier culture.[108]

As a frontier, the sands were open to anyone with enough organizational and financial power to reclaim them. Consequently, ownership of newly reclaimed sands most often lay in the hands of corporate estates in Guangzhou, Foshan, and the townships in the older parts of the delta. As one might expect, the dominant lineages of the old sands bordering on the newer sands actually controlled much of the recently reclaimed land in the latter areas. Both the Long and the Luo of Daliang in Shunde organized and financed the reclamation of large tracts of land in the sands; the former controlled the reclaimed sands in a long stretch of coast in Xiangshan county.[109] In the first decade of the nineteenth century, a scion of the Long lineage, Long Tinghuai (1749–1827), utilized his clout as a holder of the *jinshi* degree to urge provincial officials to lighten the tax burden on newly reclaimed sands. Three decades later, an admiring contemporary noted that new sands amounting to "as many as several tens of thousands of *qing*" had been reclaimed due to Long's efforts.[110] In addition to corporate lineages, other corporate estates competing for control of reclaimed sands included academies, charitable institutions, and trade guilds in Guangzhou and the West River townships. According to some scholars, this large-scale reclamation in the newer sands reached its height in the middle decades of the nineteenth century. This is precisely when urban literati in Guangzhou city, centered around the Xuehaitang academy, were appropriating new trends in scholarship and literature in a bid for local cultural supremacy.[111]

The sands were developed by lineages and other corporate trusts based in Guangzhou and the townships of the older sands, with rent collection and day-to-day operations being entrusted to functionaries residing in the sands. As they amassed wealth, these nouveaux riches of the sands accumulated cultural resources for themselves by purchasing or earning academic degrees, compiling genealogies, and erecting ancestral halls.[112] Although these upstarts from the delta frontier nibbled away at the power of the lineages in older parts of the delta, they nevertheless did not have a discernible impact as producers of culture in the arena of urban Guangzhou. This is not to say that the sands had no impact on the city's cultural life. In fact, the sands were crucial as a direct source of funding for many urban institutions, including the Xuehaitang.

Wealth from the sands supported urban cultural pursuits in less direct ways as well. Whereas in-migrating elites of Guangzhou city do not appear to have acquired any economic interests in the older parts of the delta (due to the dominance of entrenched lineages), reclamation in the coastal sands offered wide open opportunities for investment. The influx of capital into Guangzhou in the eighteenth and early nineteenth centuries further accelerated the reclamation of sands, which reached its pre-Republican peak during the years of the Xuehaitang. The upwardly mobile—both of the sands and of the city—were eager to invest their newfound wealth in reclamation of the sands. This was an area in which even in-migrating Fujian and Zhejiang merchants could invest. Thus descendants of Pan

Shicheng, a member of the maritime merchant Pan family who had made his own fortune by moving into the salt trade, are said to have used their wealth and influence to extract even greater riches from the sands.[113] A neighbor of the Pan compound in Henan was Zhang Fenghua, a Guangzhou resident and son of a major tea merchant. In the middle of the nineteenth century, Zhang built upon his father's fortune by purchasing the rights to and organizing the reclamation of extensive sands in southern Panyu and northern Xiangshan counties.[114] Urban merchant families that drew rent from the sands, such as the Pan and Zhang, in turn often supported cultural pursuits in Guangzhou.

In short, strategies of the upwardly mobile elites of the sands mirrored those of the in-migrating elites residing in Guangzhou in that both accumulated cultural capital at the expense of the dominant lineages of the West River region. But whereas the upwardly mobile elites of the sands did not play a significant role in the cultural life of the city, the sands contributed to urban culture by funding numerous scholarly and literary pursuits in Guangzhou, as well as providing an alternative means of investment for city-based mercantile wealth, which in turn lavishly patronized scholarship and the arts in Guangzhou.

CONCLUSION

Depending upon one's perspective, then, in the early nineteenth century the core of Cantonese elite culture could be located either in cosmopolitan Guangzhou or in the insular Enclosure district along the West River. The dichotomy between these two cores, and the competition between them for control over discourse about Cantonese identity, largely frames the analysis in the chapters that follow. A third area of the delta, known as the "sands" to nineteenth-century Cantonese, may be seen as a source for the extraction of wealth by both in-migrating elites in Guangzhou and the dominant lineages of the delta. Wealth derived from the sands fueled the cultural competition between the urban elite of Guangzhou and the corporate lineages of the Enclosure district.

These cohorts, based in urban Guangzhou and the surrounding delta hinterland, would provide potential sources of talent for

Ruan Yuan to recruit when he and his coterie of Jiangnan literati began to assert themselves in the local scholarly and literary world of Guangzhou. As an outsider to the area and a proselytizer of Jiangnan scholarship and literature, Ruan naturally found greater interest in his new academy among the in-migrating cohorts based in urban Guangzhou than among the insular elite of the Enclosure district. These newcomers had the most to gain and the least to lose by assimilating the imported scholarly and literary practices that Ruan sought to promote at the Xuehaitang. Like the new academy's scholarly and literary agenda, many were themselves transplants to the region.

TWO
Xie Lansheng's City: The Social Itinerary of the Cantonese Cultural Elite, 1810–1830

> Two boats carry your poet guests,
> One boat carries the spring wine.
> The tips of our oars make waves as we cross the river;
> Then we tie our boats to a willow on the large levy.
> Along the levy a thousand trees blossom,
> As the warm air steams, turning into rosy clouds.
> Bright reds and light greens reciprocally seek out favors,
> Wanting to compete with Golden Valley for exuberant luxury.
>
> —Xie Lansheng, excerpt from "My Senior Liu Binhua Arranges for Wine at the Halcyon Garden at Huadi and Invites Gao Shizhao, Qi Lin, Zhang Weiping, Lü Xiang, Ye Menglin, and Ye Menglong," 1812 or 1813

THE POEM FROM WHICH the above is excerpted describes refined men gathering to view flowers at Huadi, an area across the Pearl River from Guangzhou and upriver from Henan. A favorite tourist destination for privileged residents of Guangzhou, Huadi delighted visitors with both commercial nurseries and private gardens. The host on this occasion, Liu Binhua (1801 *jinshi*), and the author Xie Lansheng were two of the most prominent members of the Cantonese literary elite, both living in retirement after having held appointments at the Hanlin Academy. We know from a poem written on the same occasion by another participant, Zhang Weiping, that this outing occurred three days after the Lantern Festival of the fifteenth day of the first lunar month—either in 1812 or 1813—and that the peonies had just blossomed.¹ This poem conveys an image of a very exclusive social group of Cantonese men who had achieved the status of literati; however, it also hints at the mingling of different social classes and genders. The presence of Ye Menglong and Ye Menglin, sons of the wealthy salt merchant Ye Tingxun, reminds us of the indispensable role of commercial wealth in creating the world of refined elegance in which the poets dwelled. Likewise, many symbols in the poem, from the flowers and willows to the red and green colors, could be read as clichéd references to courtesans. Among the countless boats that Liu Binhua's guests passed on their brief passage to Huadi from the New City, Xiguan, or Henan would have been many "flower boats" advertising the services of their "famous flowers," or renowned courtesans.

The elegant river life highlighted in Xie Lansheng's poem, as well as the more raucous and confusing world of entertainment that it only partially conceals, was an important part of the local context in which the Xuehaitang was created. When the academy was constructed—a little over a decade after this poem was written—it was intended to alter the cultural landscape of Guangzhou but at the same time inevitably had to adapt to its local environment. Because the current study is largely concerned with understanding the Xuehaitang as an institution embedded in its local context, Chapter 1 presented the geographical cohorts that made up the social and cultural elite of Guangzhou city and the Pearl River delta hinterland in the early nineteenth century. In this chapter, we narrow our spatial focus to the walled city and its immediate suburbs, by examining the important sites, institutions, and associations that composed the social world of Cantonese literati in the early nineteenth century. In addition to such sources as gazetteers, genealogies, and collected writings, this chapter draws heavily on Xie Lansheng's manuscript diary. Covering the years from 1819 to 1829, the diary offers a unique glimpse into the world of the urban Cantonese cultural elite. By revealing the contours of the urban cultural landscape during this period—the significant activities, influential people, and important sites on Xie Lansheng's itinerary—it provides a glimpse into the geographical and social networks that defined elite cultural circles.

With such an understanding, we can then in Chapter 3 assess the ways in which the Xuehaitang expanded, diminished, or otherwise altered the options available to the Cantonese elites and thereby begin to tackle the question of the Xuehaitang's significance in local society. Xie Lansheng in many ways represents the older generation of Cantonese literati that was eventually displaced by the Xuehaitang; he remained active in Guangzhou throughout the 1820s, however, and would even play a supporting role in founding the academy. Thus he was also a link between pre- and post-Xuehaitang Cantonese society.

A detailed analysis of the local context for the Xuehaitang's founding and early years reveals a vibrant urban elite culture. Xie Lansheng and other literati were constantly on the move, meeting and dispersing, crisscrossing from one site to another, enjoying entertainments and cultivating relationships. Guangzhou's merchants were integral components in the network of the city's cultural elite and would continue to be important throughout the nineteenth century. Finally, it will become apparent that Guangzhou was in the midst of a literary revival, in the form of an increased interest in academies and literary societies, when the Xuehaitang was established.

XIE LANSHENG AND GUANGZHOU'S FLOATING WORLD

As a former Hanlin academician and a locally renowned poet, painter, and calligrapher, Xie Lansheng was one of the most important arbiters of taste in urban Guangzhou; his roots, however, lay in the delta. Like the Chengnan Du family in the New City, Xie Lansheng and his closest agnates were among the cohort of families native to the delta hinterland that had relocated to the city during the Qing. The Xie lineage had long resided in the Nanhai county township of Mashe, northwest of Guangzhou. Within Nanhai, however, Mashe was far removed from the most prosperous areas of the county's hinterland, such as Foshan and Jiujiang. Xie Lansheng was the third generation of a branch of the Mashe Xie that had relocated to the city. His maternal grandfather was a Panyu scholar who had studied under Hui Shiqi; a male relative of his paternal grandfather's generation was a senior licentiate by purchase who had a local reputation for calligraphy. Lansheng's father, Xie Jingqing (d. 1806), was a county student, an expert calligrapher, and a competent poet. Attesting to the degree of Xie Jingqing's social standing and cultural prestige, he solicited funds from a Xiangshan county man to print, in 1797 at his Guangzhou studio, a collection of examples of imprints of ancient seals carved in the style of Han dynasty calligraphy, which had been introduced to him by a sojourning literatus from north China. In 1803, Jingqing printed a continuation of this work from imprints that he had collected. He also shared his interest and expertise in Han-style seal carving with the Shunde poet and painter Li Jian (1747–99). Jingqing's younger brother traveled to Yunnan for a year on at least one occasion, suggesting that the family strategy included either long-distance trade or secretarial service.[2]

Xie Lansheng furthered the family's ventures into high society and its claims to literary status. He earned a reputation for poetry in his youth and went on to study under Liu Binhua. Xie eventually found his own academic success, earning a *juren* degree in 1792 and a *jinshi* ten years later. After a brief stint in the capital as a Hanlin Bachelor, Xie announced his decision to forsake an official career in order to care for his aging father. He retired to his Studio of Constant Awareness, just next to the yamen of the superintendent of customs on the Panyu side of the New City (see Fig. 1), and, beginning in 1805, taught at several academies in Guangzhou. Xie Lansheng's older brother, Yunsheng (d. 1823), resided in his father's former studio in Guangzhou; his younger brother, Guansheng (d. 1835), also made his home in the city.[3]

While Xie Lansheng and his immediate relatives were settled in the city, they nevertheless maintained ritual ties with their kin in Mashe. On a fairly regular basis during the 1820s, on the eighth, ninth, or tenth day of the ninth month Xie Lansheng would either go down to the countryside with his brothers to "worship the mountain"—presumably the place where his ancestors were buried—or send his sons and nephews to perform the same task.[4] On at least one occasion Lansheng met in Mashe with Xie lineage elders and representatives of another lineage to mediate disputes. When kin from Mashe visited Guangzhou, they also often called on Lansheng. The generation of Xie Lansheng and his brothers thus seems to have occupied a middle position between hinterland and city, negotiating rural and urban identities even as the latter gradually took precedence over the former. One can imagine that, like the Chengnan Du, Xie Lansheng's descendants would eventually have produced urban-based genealogies and shrines. In any case, Xie Lansheng cultivated relationships with literati from both city and delta. Two of his younger urban associates, Wu Lanxiu (d. 1839) and Xiong Jingxing (1816 *juren*), would be among the first eight co-directors at the Xuehaitang. Even closer to home, Xie's second son, Niangong (ca. 1800–ca. 1840), would be appointed a co-director in 1832. But Xie also maintained friendships with members of dominant lineages of the delta hinterland. For example, he once visited the Jiujiang studio of a scholar from that township's Guan lineage, gracing Guan with a poem and a painting on the theme of the studio. Xie Lansheng's son-in-law, Cai Jinquan (1832 *jinshi*), was a scion of the Cai lineage from Longjiang, next to Jiujiang in the Enclosure district; Jinquan would also participate in early Xuehaitang examinations.[5]

Despite his ties with and occasional visits to the delta hinterland, the locus of Xie Lansheng's activities was narrowly centered on Guangzhou and its immediate environs. Several Buddhist monasteries fell within this sphere, including the Guangxiao (Illuminate Filial Piety) and Liurong (Six Banyan) monasteries in the Banner Quarter, and Changshou (Longevity) Monastery in Xiguan; the most important monastery on Xie Lansheng's itinerary, however, was Haichuang (Sea Banner), located across the Pearl River in Henan.[6] Haichuang Monastery was one of the few places that Westerners were allowed to visit in the first half of nineteenth century, and as a result many Western sources describe the monastery in great detail. These accounts portray Haichuang as the largest Buddhist establishment in the region, occupying in their estimation several acres and housing anywhere from one to two hundred monks. Western visitors noticed the monastery's printing office and library, yet ironically commented that the monks were overwhelmingly illiterate. The monastery was located next to the complex of mansions and gardens owned by the maritime merchant Wu family—another site frequented by Western visitors. Perhaps due to its proximity to the Wu residence, Western observers noted that the Wu family, and the women in particular, were great patrons of the monastery.[7]

Although frequently whisked through the monastery by their merchant hosts, Western visitors were not invited to literati gatherings at Haichuang, which also were often hosted or attended by merchants. Haichuang appears to have occupied as important a space for Cantonese literati in the early nineteenth century as Timothy Brook suggests that monasteries did for the gentry of the late Ming.[8] For example, Haichuang had been one of Li Jian's favorite retreats, and still stored a copy of the *Jin'gangjing* (Diamond sutra) transcribed by Li in 1797.[9] Moreover, contradicting the reports by Western observers, Xie Lansheng describes Haichuang as having many poet-monks. These talented and learned monks, along with the setting, enticed Xie to make frequent trips across the Pearl River to visit Haichuang for vegetarian breakfast and dinner feasts, where he discussed Chan (Zen) philosophy with the monks, engaged in Chan meditation alone, or played chess with monks and fellow literati.[10] A more thorough description of one such outing is preserved in the collected writings of Yun Jing, the Jiangnan writer whom the salt merchant Ye Tingxun had retained to compose an inscription for the Ye family's ancestral shrine. Yun commemorates a gathering at Haichuang in which Cantonese literati hosted him on his sojourns in the late summer of 1815. The Cantonese literati in attendance—described as sporting unlined robes and straw sandals, and clutching palm fans—included Xie Lansheng and his brother Guansheng; the poets Zhang Weiping and Huang Peifang; the scion of a salt merchant family, Huang Qiaosong; the Shunde painter and close friend of Xie Lansheng, Zhang Ruzhi; a future participant in Xuehaitang examinations, Zhong Qishao (1791 *juren*); and the monk Jiangyue. Wu Bingyong, an older brother of the Yihe head merchant Wu Bingjian, also attended the gathering, as did Ye Menglin and Ye Menglong. In Yun's portrayal, the outing began with one participant playing the zither and another the flute, while Yun, perhaps suffering from the oppressive tropical heat, borrowed Jiangyue's couch for a nap. After waking, the visiting Jiangnan prose master played chess with several others. Xie Lansheng saw the scene and suggested painting the group, using the theme of the "Six Gentlemen" from the Yuan dynasty. The participants later composed poems on the theme, thereby extending the prestige gained from interacting with a visiting literatus from Jiangnan.[11]

Other sites and activities on Xie Lansheng's social agenda were associated with particular seasons and festivals. Social calls to various officials, merchants, and literati during the New Year celebrations were followed in the second or third lunar months with tours atop the city wall, beginning at the Main North Gate, to view the bright red kapok (*mumian*) flowers. At the Duanwu Festival in the fifth month, touring boats carrying literati, courtesans, and performers vied for strategic points along the Pearl River, such as the Chigang Pagoda on the Henan shore, to observe dragon boat races.[12] The arrival of the fifth month also meant that litchis were in season, and no spot was more popular for picking and consuming the fruit than Litchi Cove, along the western edge of Xiguan. Here, in the early 1820s, the Nanhai merchant Qiu Xi opened up his Tang Litchi Garden, featuring the Peeling Litchi Pavilion. After Ruan Yuan visited the site and wrote a poem on the garden—to which was appended his son Ruan Fu's essay arguing that cultivation of litchis at this site had begun in the Tang dynasty—the garden quickly became a favorite on the itinerary of Cantonese literati and visiting officials.[13] Whereas on at least one occasion Xie Lansheng brought his wife and other women in the family to Qiu's garden and was personally waited on by the owner, more often he was in the company of fellow literati and anonymous "female companions" when he visited Litchi Cove, where the "flower boats came and went like weaving."[14] The bustling activities of the fifth month were followed by Ullambana, or the Festival of the Hungry Ghosts, in the middle of the seventh month, and the Mid-Autumn Festival in the middle of the eighth. Finally, in the tenth month, Xie Lansheng typically accompanied Haichuang monks or fellow literati on junkets to view chrysanthemums at the numerous gardens and nurseries at Huadi.[15]

In addition to the festivals, Xie Lansheng's annual social calendar was filled with appointments. Despite his fondness for "quiet sitting" at Haichuang, Xie and his companions seem to have been constantly on the move, flowing back and forth between meeting places and sites of interest. During the height of his social activities, Xie often slept at a different place for several nights running, perhaps at his New City studio one night, at a merchant's firm in Xiguan the next, and at Haichuang or a friend's study in Henan the next. Xie Lansheng's Guangzhou was indeed a floating world—both figuratively, in the sense that social boundaries were crossed, and literally, in that many social calls and almost any excursion involved boating.[16] Whether crossing the river to Henan and back, attending banquets or operas on flower boats, or moving up- or downstream to various sites, Xie rarely spent more than a few consecutive days entirely on land.

Indeed, one should not conceive of the Pearl River as a barrier separating Henan from the rest of Guangzhou, but rather imagine how its two shores, as well as popular sites along the river, were connected by the community of boats it supported.[17] Western observers' estimates of the number of boats on the Pearl River in the 1830s and 1840s ranged from forty thousand to over eighty thousand.[18] They were also struck by the variety of boats, from those of the Dan (or "Boat People"), to the salt junks anchored downstream at Henan, to "passage-boats, which daily move to and from neighboring villages and hamlets; ferry boats, which are constantly crossing and re-crossing the river; huge canal-boats, laden with produce from the country; cruisers; [and] pleasure boats."[19]

Though this great variety of craft did not usually appear in the writings of Xie Lansheng and other literati, the flower boats that served as floating brothels attracted the voyeuristic attention of foreign and Chinese visitors alike. One Westerner who visited Guangzhou in 1844 described a passing flower boat: "here, in a large and beautiful green and golden barge, is the sound of music, and between the silken curtains we may descry some of those painted Jezebels."[20] Similar sentiments, minus the Biblical reference, could be found in Li Jun's (1817 *jinshi*) diary, which recorded his tour of service in Guangzhou to administer the provincial examination in 1828. After the papers had been ranked and the results announced, Li crossed the Pearl River to join a banquet at Haichuang to mark his coexaminer's return to the capital. En route, Li caught a glimpse of distant flower boats anchored beneath the shade of trees, with scarlet curtains covering the doorway, and pitied himself for not being able to see the faces of the "pearl maidens" (*zhuniang*) inside.[21] In his famous *Six Records of a Floating Life*, Shen Fu—a Suzhou native who came to Guangzhou for business and pleasure in the 1790s and patronized the "Yangzhou group" of flower boats offering women dressed in Jiangnan fashion—described the wine boats that served them as "broadly spread [across the river] like scattered leaves floating on the water."[22] Yet flower boats were not exclusively used as brothels. In many cases, "flower boat" simply designated an intricately decorated barge, and many such boats were privately owned, as was the flower boat of the Longshan Wen lineage that Xie Lansheng passed on his way to Haichuang one day.²³ On other occasions, Xie boarded flower boats for dim sum or to take in an opera, though often enough in the company of sing-song girls.²⁴

Through all the hustle and bustle, Xie Lansheng and his companions strove to maintain what must have been a porous and constantly negotiated line between what they perceived as the refined and vulgar. The thousands of Dan who lived on boats were so far removed socially that they did not challenge literati prerogatives, and hence a boatman might even make for entertaining conversation on a trip to Mashe in the countryside.²⁵ But social upstarts, likely linked to urban commercial wealth, often threatened to intrude on Xie's sophisticated gatherings. On one rainy day during the fifth month, when Litchi Cove would normally have been deluged with touring boats, Xie found a secluded pavilion at Qiu Xi's Tang Litchi Garden where he enjoyed a chance to finish three small painting scrolls, a wonderful experience that he felt vulgar people could not hope to understand. When a group of revelers suddenly came to destroy the mood, Xie summarily rolled up the paintings and left.²⁶

LITERATI AND THEIR MERCHANT PATRONS

In addition to such sites as Haichuang Monastery and Litchi Cove, the mansions, studios, gardens, and even firms of Guangzhou's commercial elites were major sites on Xie Lansheng's social circuit. The largest and most opulent mansions and gardens were of course those maintained by the city's salt and maritime merchants. A member of the maritime merchant Pan family who moved into the salt trade, Pan Shicheng, constructed the most extravagant of nineteenth-century Guangzhou gardens, the Sea Mountain Immortals' Lodge, next to Litchi Cove in Xiguan. The maritime merchant Pan and Wu families maintained estates in Henan, replete with numerous gardens, residences, and studios. One approving Western visitor described the Pan family complex as being composed of "a series of villas . . . newly decorated with gilt and light-coloured painting, giving it a rich and cheerful appearance, the courtyards being very neatly paved with blocks of well-polished granite."²⁷

FIG. 3: Zhang Weiping studying the Classics under his father's direction on the Pan family estate in Henan (SOURCE: *Huajia xiantan*, 1.1b-2a).

Wealthy and socially ambitious merchant families used their sprawling estates to entertain many of the city's pre-eminent scholars, writers, and artists, but these merchants also housed literati on a more permanent basis. Seeking to have his sons excel in the requisite skills of literati culture, Pan Youdu hired notable local scholars to serve as resident teachers, including Zhang Weiping's father, Zhang Bingwen (1801 *juren*), and Jin Jing'e (1802 *jinshi*), of the aforementioned Panyu Jin family. Jin Jing'e brought with him his younger brother, Jingmao. Thus the younger Zhang and Jin spent much of their youth studying and playing with Pan children at the Yisongyuan (Garden of the Righteous Pines) on the Pan estate (see Fig. 3).[28] In 1804, before Xie Lansheng took up his career as an academy teacher, the Pan family had also hired him as a resident teacher. Subsequently, Xie continued to perform educational services for his former hosts, as indicated one day in late 1822 when he went to the Pan residence ceremonially to begin formal instruction of one of the young Pan sons. The Pan family also made use of its daughters to cultivate ties to the city's cultural elite; Pan Youwei, for example, succeeded in arranging a marriage between one of his daughters and the poetic prodigy Chen Tan (1784–1851) of Panyu.[29]

Not to be outdone, the maritime merchant Wu family hosted an equal number of local literati—typically from native places in the delta hinterland—at its Wansongyuan (Myriad Pines Garden) in Henan, upon which Xie Lansheng bestowed a plaque engraved in his prized calligraphy. In the 1810s, Myriad Pines was frequented by many of the literati regulars at Haichuang: Xie Lansheng and his brother Guansheng; the salt merchant-turned-poet Huang Qiaosong; and Zhong Qishao and Cai Jinquan, both of whom would participate in early Xuehaitang examinations.[30] In the 1820s, both Zhong Qishao and Xiong Jingxing resided at Myriad Pines for several years. Liang Mei (1788–1838), a scholar from Shunde county who for the most part lived in Guangzhou and would become a major Xuehaitang figure, spent two years at the Wu family's Listening to Billows Tower, next to Myriad Pines. One son of the famous Shunde poet Zhang Jinfang (1747–92) also resided at Myriad Pines for many years.[31]

Another maritime merchant with Fujian roots, Xie Youren, was a reliable patron of the local teacher Chen Qikun (1826 *jinshi*) and also hosted literary gatherings attended by Zhang Weiping and other poets.[32] Xie Youren and his older brother Youwen could also compose decent verse, having taken lessons from the renowned poet of Zhaoqing prefecture, Tan Jingzhao (1773–1830). Further demonstrating his scholarly competence, Xie Youren later annotated the complete poems of the famous Jiangnan poet Yuan Mei (1716–98).[33] The maritime merchant from Heshan county in the western delta, Yi Rongzhi, had an extensive library in Guangzhou city that he made available for use by sojourning scholars such as Ruan Rongling of Xinhui.[34] Whereas the Pan family from Fujian tended to patronize recent migrants from outside Guangdong province, Yi Rongzhi was known in the world of scholarship and the arts primarily for his patronage of a sojourning scholar who, like Yi, came from the western delta.

Patronage of scholarship, literature, and art in Guangzhou was not limited to the maritime merchants. Panyu native Huang Qiaosong, whose family had long been in the salt business, supported at least three local poets, all of them future Xuehaitang examinees: Panyu's Zheng Fen, Chen Huang of Shunde, and Li Guangzhao from Jiaying.[35] The scholar-official Kong Jixun (1792–1842) of the Luoge

Kong, the family that had made a fortune in the salt trade, collected over forty thousand *juan* of books at his Haoshang Guanyuxuan (Atop the Moat Studio for Observing Fish) in the New City. The eminent Guangdong poet Feng Minchang (1747–1806) wrote calligraphy for the studio's plaque, and the famous poet and Xiangshan native, Huang Peifang, was in residence there for a few years as well.[36] The Nanhai salt merchant Ye Tingxun also hosted such luminaries as Feng Minchang, who visited the River Tower in 1804 to view the moon at night; in return, Feng bequeathed a plaque to the tower. Ye Tingxun's sons, Menglin and Menglong, invited Zhang Weiping to test their own sons; Zhang lodged at the Ye family school for three years. Their strategy paid off when Menglong's oldest son earned a *juren* degree in 1831.[37] Xie Lansheng described Du Mian, brother of the pawn merchant Du Yong, as a famed host of parties characterized by a mixture of high culture activities and less refined drinking. Another literatus, Wu Yingkui (1795 *juren*), only met Du Mian two years before the latter's death in 1809, but claimed to have known him well. In a lament written for his departed friend, Wu described floating excursions on the Pearl River from which no one returned sober.[38]

As we saw in Chapter 1, the spatial ordering of the city exhibited some distinction between merchants and literati. Whereas the expansive estates owned by successful maritime and salt merchants were located in Xiguan or Henan, several notable literati maintained residences in the Panyu section of the Old City, a sector of Guangzhou typically seen as a stronghold of gentry culture.[39] For example, Chen Tan's Kuang Study was located in the northeastern corner of the Old City. Here Chen could satisfy his fixation on the Cantonese poet Kuang Lu (1604–50), who had also resided in the neighborhood. During the Daoguang era, the Consigned Garden, just inside Minor North Gate, was a popular meeting place for poetry and drinking parties attended by Zhang Weiping, Huang Peifang, Xiong Jingxing, Yang Rongxu, and Du You, who was Du Yong's son and Yang's relative by marriage.[40]

Nevertheless, in the nineteenth century, the "merchant" sectors of the city were increasingly the loci of "gentry" or "literati" activities. To begin with, the educated offspring of successful merchant families who entered the Cantonese cultural elite continued to reside in Xiguan or the New City. Residences in these areas, as well as at Huadi and Henan on the opposite side of the Pearl River, became important sites for libraries, gardens, and poetry clubs. Several of the most famous scholars' studios of the time, mostly built by commercial wealth, were located in the New City: Li Changrong's (b. 1813) Willow Hall, Ding Xi's (ca. 1808–50) River Bright Tower, and, on the edge of Pearl River outside Yongqing Gate, Xu Xiangguang's (1832 *jinshi*) Sleeve Sea Tower.[41] Xie Lansheng's associate Xiong Jingxing established his Auspicious Rams Streamside Lodge in Xiguan.[42] When not sitting for examinations, visiting academies, or calling on officials, Cantonese literati spent their time outside the Old City.

This pattern would continue throughout the Daoguang era. In the early 1840s, Deng Dalin, the son of a popular pharmacist in the New City, constructed his Almond Grove Villa across the Pearl River next to Huadi. There, he pursued his interests in alchemy and played host to such members of the Cantonese cultural elite as Xie Youren, Huang Peifang, Du You, and several Haichuang monks. Deng was eventually able to collect enough poems from eminent visitors to produce two volumes of verse praising his garden.[43] At the same time, the poet Zhang Weiping rented a residence in a section of a garden at Huadi owned by the Pan family. A few years later, in the same area, Zhang Weiping's sons built their father his own Garden for Listening to the Pines.[44] A contemporary account of the salt merchant Pan Shicheng's Sea Mountain Immortals' Lodge revealed the degree to which merchant and gentry elites intermingled in the suburbs of Guangzhou:

Outside the Guangzhou city wall, there is much vacant space on the western stretch of the Pearl River. Rich families and powerful lineages, as well as *shidaifu* [scholar-officials] who have finished their service and returned home, all build broad gardens and manage villas here as places for relaxation and banqueting. The most famous ones are those of Zhang Weiping, Deng Dalin, and Pan Shicheng. Yet Zhang's and Deng's two gardens are not spacious and can be captured in a single gaze. As for the one that is most expansive and monopolizes the advantages of terraces and pavilions, water and stones, everyone mentions the Pan garden.[45]

Aside from the mansions, libraries, and gardens of Guangzhou's salt and maritime merchants, the maritime merchants' firms were also important sites on Xie Lansheng's itinerary. Located in Xiguan near the famous foreign factories, the maritime merchant firms constantly appear in Xie's diary as sites for entertainment or for planning or culminating a day's activities, and thus constituted integral nodes in his social network. Xie's younger brother, Guansheng, his second son, Niangong, and his fifth son all resided at the Wu family's Yihe firm for extended periods of time in the early 1820s.[46] Like Zhang Weiping and Jin Jingmao at the Pan estate in Henan, Xie's sons probably studied together with the Wu children. In any case, the firms were frequent destinations for Xie Lansheng. For example, on several occasions, after an entire afternoon of operas at the Wu shrine in Henan or a great feast at the Yihe firm, Xie would go to spend the night at the Li family's Xicheng firm. Alternatively, Xie might meet a friend for drinking at the Xicheng firm or pass by the Yihe firm to play chess with his fifth son.[47] One afternoon in 1824 Xie accompanied the sojourning Yangzhou painter Wang Pu to the Lu family's Guangli firm to see an opera. That evening he joined the Lu brothers' banquet aboard a flower boat. After the guests dispersed at nine o'clock, Xie returned to the Guangli firm to spend the night.[48] On a previous occasion dating to early January 1822, Xie followed dinner at the Guangli firm by accompanying the Lu family entourage on its trip to the Lu ancestral home in the Xinhui township of Shitou. After a brief visit to the Lu ancestral hall, Xie spent most of his time on board the Lu boat discussing painting with Wang Pu.[49]

Literati such as Xie Lansheng were drawn to the homes and firms of Guangzhou's commercial elite not only by the remuneration received for teaching, but also by the access such sites offered to fine paintings and calligraphy, including commodified specimens produced by previous generations of Cantonese literati, as well as more ancient works. While Xie Lansheng was paying a call on Wu Bingyong in the summer of 1821, for example, Bingjian's son Yuanhua (1801–33) brought out Song and Yuan silk fans and a painting on a small silk scroll.[50] On another visit to Yihe, during the Ullambana festival in 1824, Xie viewed an album of Li Jian's paintings that had been acquired by Wu Bingjian's younger brother, Bingzhen. In the evening the group boarded a flower boat, dining at a banquet hosted by Bingjian and afterward viewing festival displays.[51] Visiting the Wu household after a trip to Haichuang, Xie was dazzled by the "very numerous ancient curios of every kind" that one of the Wu sons had brought back from the capital.[52] Under Pan Zhengwei, the Pan family also built an impressive collection of calligraphy and paintings. These included Tang rubbings, paintings produced by the Yuan master Ni Zan (1301–74) and the early Qing master Shitao (1630–1707), and works by local artists such as Li Jian.[53] Access to such collections enabled Xie Lansheng and other literati not only to see such masterpieces but also to borrow artwork from their merchant patrons. Xie was particularly fond of Shitao's paintings, and so was thrilled to borrow from Wu Yuanhua an album of Shitao paintings that had once belonged to the Shunde painter and poet Zhang Jinfang. He also borrowed landscape albums from the Nanhai Ye family of merchants and collectors.[54]

To the extent that a clear line can be drawn between merchants and literati in early nineteenth-century Guangzhou, there was a mutually beneficial exchange between them. This exchange included gifts sent from merchants to literati such as Xie Lansheng during festivals. For instance, two days before the Duanwu Festival in 1826, Xie received gift assortments from the Dongsheng firm, operated by the Liu family from Anhui province, as well as presents from the Lu Guangli firm and the Xie brothers of the Dongyu firm; Xie carefully noted in his diary that in each case he accepted only four varieties.[55] Monasteries were also involved in this exchange. Haichuang typically sent vegetarian meals to mark Duanwu and congee to observe Laba, the eighth day of the twelfth month.[56]

In return, Xie Lansheng and his fellow literati not only graced merchants' banquets with their refined presence and their expertise in literary and artistic judgment, but also offered up more tangible items to their merchant benefactors; Xie, for example, wrote his calligraphy on an album of paintings by Wu Bingyong and sent a painted fan to Wu Bingjian. Similarly, during a vegetarian repast at Haichuang, Xie favored a monk with a fan sporting his calligraphy before he and Zhong Qishao rushed off to Wu Bingzhen's flower boat. Even deceased patrons continued to enjoy Xie's calligraphy and prestige, as when he paid a visit to the maritime merchant Xie home in Xiguan, in order to dot the "*zhu*" character on the spirit tablet of the recently departed Xie Jiawu. Xie Lansheng and other

Cantonese literati were obliged to pay courtesy calls at the merchants' homes to mark important birthdays, celebrate the conferral of ranks, and to mourn family deaths.[57]

Describing the late Ming, both Craig Clunas and Yü Ying-shih have observed a new attitude among literati toward selling their literary services to wealthy merchants.[58] A similar dynamic was at play in early nineteenth-century Guangzhou, as is manifest in the relationship between Xie Lansheng and his merchant patrons. Xie meticulously recorded his total income for each month in the margins of his diary, and he specifically noted having received remuneration for such services as judging compositions for various academies and literary societies. Xie's younger associates were at times equally blunt about this commercial exchange. Zhang Weiping observed that Xiong Jingxing annually brought in several hundred taels from selling his calligraphy and paintings.[59] In the preface to a jocular poem that he composed on a wine shop in the New City, Zhang asked what harm there would be in spending the price of a picul of rice to buy wine, since "once drunk, there would be poems and calligraphy to take care of the bill."[60] Here, Zhang may have mocked his own complicity in the exchange between literati, on the one hand, and merchants and shop owners, on the other; yet he wrote about it unabashedly. Conversely, when Zhang recalled his youth at the Pan family estate, he portrayed its refined gardens as being a world apart from the hubbub of the wine shop and the market, though he gained access to it by a similar means of exchange.

Not all interaction between literati and merchants was as frivolous as portrayed in Zhang Weiping's poem. Rather, gentry clout and commercial wealth often combined to promote crucial social welfare projects. One such instance took place in 1809, when Xie Lansheng and Qiu Xiande led a group of 37 degree-holding gentry in donating twenty thousand taels for defense against pirate incursions into the Pearl River estuary. Guangzhou's salt merchants contributed an even larger amount.[61] At about the same time, Xie Lansheng and Ye Menglong organized the distribution of famine relief at Hualin Monastery in Xiguan.[62]

Despite the crucial roles played by Guangzhou's maritime and salt merchants—as patrons of cultural pursuits and supporters of social welfare—voices critical toward these merchants could occasionally be heard, whether in playful jibes or more serious admonitions. As an example of the former, the author of the novel *Shenlou zhi* portrays salt merchant Wen's character as rustic, but his gardens and pavilions as refined.[63] In a more somber tone, Du Yong, who had expanded his family's wealth through what he perceived as the legitimate pawn business, warned his sons against moving into the maritime or salt trades, even though he had arranged a marriage between his daughter and a son of Pan Youwei. Du felt that the fortunes of maritime and salt merchants rose and fell too suddenly; he pointed to their extravagance and lack of caution when riding the wave of success, and the disastrous consequences they faced after falling into debt.[64] Writing in his older age, the Panyu literatus Lin Botong (1775–1845), himself from a family of doctors who had practiced their trade in Guangzhou for several generations, remarked:

> When sons of the marketers (*shiren*) and sons of scholar-officials (*shidaifu*) are young, there is no need for them to be too far apart. But after growing up, those on the one side who through practice become familiar with greater and lesser decorum (*wei yi*) are not comfortable when they see the dull and stupid; those on the other side who are dull and lack culture (*wen*) see greater and lesser decorum and believe it difficult to study.[65]

One gathers that this passage shifts from a descriptive to a prescriptive mode as it progresses. Sons of merchants and literati who grew up together continued to interact frequently in adulthood. This was certainly the case with such cultural luminaries as Zhang Weiping and Xie Lansheng.

Nevertheless, anti-merchant rhetoric at times proved to be a compelling discourse among Cantonese literati. In a controversy that swelled up in the decade preceding the establishment of the Xuehaitang, criticism of one maritime merchant family was aired publicly and led to the political mobilization of dozens of literati. This case involved the Shitou Lu of the Guangli firm after the death in 1812 of the family's patriarch, Lu Guangheng. In the spring of 1814, his son, Wenjin, and fellow members of the Shitou Lu lineage mustered up the support of Tan Dajing (1775 *jinshi*) and other Xinhui gentry to petition authorities to allow Guanheng to be entered into the Local Worthies Shrine. Lu and his gentry backers justified their support by pointing to Guanheng's charitable acts and to the fact that he had printed *Zhouyi benyi zhu*, an annotation of Zhu Xi's commentary to the *Yijing* (Classic of change) by a local scholar named Hu Fang (1654–1727). The petition eventually gained the support of provincial officials and was approved in January 1815. To celebrate the entry of his father's tablet into the Local Worthies Shrine early that summer, Lu Wenjin arranged a boisterous ceremony in front of the county school, an event attended by many merchants and complemented by musicians, operas, and a banquet.[66]

Meanwhile, after returning from a failed attempt in the metropolitan examinations, the disgruntled Panyu *juren* Liu Huadong (1773–1836) found out about the affair. Outraged, Liu wrote an essay entitled "Mourning Baisha," in which he suggested that because the great Ming philosopher Chen Xianzhang (1428–1500, known as "Master Baisha") was, like Lu Guanheng, a Xinhui native, the fact that both were honored in the Local Worthies Shrine was tantamount to an ox and a stallion sharing the same trough. Accordingly, Liu sent a letter of protest to the governor-general (Ruan Yuan's predecessor), arguing that merchants should not recklessly be honored in a Confucian temple. But the letter was summarily returned because the governor-general did not wish to grant a private audience to anyone lacking the credentials of office. Liu then revealed his frustration to his close friend, Chen Tan, who colluded with Liu in revising, printing, and privately distributing the letter as a pamphlet. In the pamphlet, Liu pointed out that when Lu Guanheng had printed Hu Fang's annotation of the *Yijing*, he had taken credit for the preface, which in fact had been authored by Tan Dajing. By means of the pamphlet's immense popularity, Liu and Chen were able to mobilize over two hundred followers from among the city's literati. With much fanfare Liu composed a *jiwen* (essay for the dead), led his sympathizers to the prefectural school's Local Worthies Shrine to pay their respects at Chen Xianzhang's tablet, recited the essay, and burned it as an offering. The crowd prostrated and wailed loudly.

Still not satisfied, they went from one yamen to another until they dug up evidence of a 1787 case in which Lu Guanheng had gotten into fisticuffs with an older cousin and uprooted some of the latter's hair. Armed with this new proof of Guanheng's lack of character, they all then signed a petition to the provincial authorities. But the officials reportedly stalled—amidst rumors of having received bribes from Lu Wenjin—and instead took Liu and Chen into custody as their two names appeared first on the petition. Liu spent five months of the ten-month case in the Nanhai jail, where a young Panyu scholar named Yi Kezhong (1796–1838) from time to time daringly visited Liu and brought him porridge.[67] With the case at an impasse, the Qing court sent two imperial envoys to investigate. After more maneuvering between literati and officials, the envoys ruled that Lu Guanheng indeed could not be considered a worthy because he had struck an older cousin and because, not having authored the preface to Hu Fang's annotation, there was no evidence that he had any scholarly accomplishments. Lu's tablet was officially expelled in early 1816; for his role in the protest, Liu Huadong had his *juren* degree revoked.[68]

Though the Lu Guanheng case appears from one angle to have been driven by a desire to maintain status distinctions between literati and merchants, the possibilities of regional bias complicate the picture when the native-place origins of the supporters and opponents are taken into account. In their initial assessment of the case, the two imperial envoys found that only Xinhui natives had backed the original petition in favor of entering Lu Guanheng into the shrine, and no Xinhui natives could be found among the critics. Only later, when the protestors pressured Zhang Yanji (1808 *jinshi*), a Xinhui literatus currently teaching in Guangzhou, into signing the petition against Lu, were officials forced to act.[69]

Ironically, both leaders of the literati who expressed outrage over Lu Wenjin's insult to the Cantonese philosopher Chen Xianzhang were recent arrivals to Guangzhou. Liu's father had migrated to Guangdong from western Fujian to enter the salt trade, and Liu had been the first in the family to register as a Panyu resident. Chen was a descendant of migrants from Fujian's Tongan county; they had only begun to register as Panyu residents with his father. Thus, presaging the subsequent appropriation of Cantonese culture by scholars associated with the Xuehaitang, the Lu case involved in-migrants usurping a local cultural icon—in this case Chen Xianzhang—to legitimize their own standing in local society. Further complicating the picture, Chen's brother-in-law and favorite maternal cousin was none other than Pan Zhengheng (亨), of the maritime merchant Pan family from Tongan.[70] Just a few years after the protest, when Zhengheng's cousin, Pan Zhengheng (衡, 1787–1830), built a studio on the Pan estate to store his large collection of Li Jian paintings, it was not only Xie Lansheng who produced a commemorative work—Chen Tan also composed a poem and Liu Huadong contributed an essay.[71] Thus, though the vociferous critique of Lu Guanheng invoked anti-merchant rhetoric, it was at the same time the result of complicated and shifting alliances among different regional cohorts and status groups, and, like the Cantonese cultural elite in general, cannot be reduced to a simple dichotomy between merchants and literati.[72] In short, as was the case in many late imperial Chinese cities, the line between merchant and gentry or literatus was porous; however, anti-merchant rhetoric could also prove to be a powerfully motivating discourse.

GUANGZHOU'S ACADEMIES AND TEACHERS

Academies in Guangzhou were also important sites on Xie Lansheng's itinerary, as they were for many Cantonese literati. The oldest functioning major academy in the city was Yuexiu shuyuan, where Xie Lansheng had briefly taught in 1805.[73] Though it was named after Yuexiu Hill on the north side of Guangzhou, the name quite literally means "the outstanding talent of Yue (Guangdong)." Located in the central section of the walled Old City, and just south of the yamen of the Guangzhou prefect and the Guangdong lieutenant-governor on Huiai Street, Yuexiu was the quintessential official academy. It had been established in 1710 by provincial officials as an academy serving the entire province of Guangdong, administering civil service examination–style testing for *shengjian* (licentiates and state students) and *tongsheng* (apprentice students). Academy directors (*yuanzhang*) were for the most part holders of the *jinshi* degree, hired from "north of the range"—that is, north of Guangdong, and, in practice, most commonly from Zhejiang, Jiangsu, and Jiangxi. Before the beginning of the nineteenth century, several Guangdong natives filled the post, but usually only temporarily, until another director could be hired.[74]

During the second half of the Jiaqing reign, the academy twice received attention from local officials. First, in 1809, provincial officials and academy director Qiu Xiande increased the student quota and proclaimed a new set of academy regulations. In 1820, Guangzhou prefect Luo Hanzhang (1762–1832) raised a total of 3,600 taels for major repairs of academy buildings and the addition of student dormitories. Over the following decade, Yuexiu faced mounting financial challenges, but provincial officials continued to increase funding for the academy. In 1827 and again in 1829, the Guangdong grain intendant and other officials in Guangzhou donated funds to be deposited with merchants for interest. By that time, the academy annually had at its disposal 4,840 taels to meet its continually increasing costs. The director's annual salary was 500 taels, plus another 6.19 taels per month for food. After the quota was increased in 1809, one hundred "formal students" (*zhengkesheng*) and half as many "outer students" (*waikesheng*), as well as nine separately designated banner students, sat for monthly examinations at the school.[75]

Another major Guangzhou academy benefiting from the attention of officials in the Jiaqing reign was Yuehua shuyuan (Yue Florescence Academy), where Xie Lansheng served as director in the 1810s.[76] Yuehua was unique in Guangzhou in that it was originally designed as an academy catering to the sojourning merchant population of Guangdong. Beginning in 1721, a quota had been established for members of sojourning salt merchant households who wished to sit for civil service examinations in Guangdong but had not been able to do so before because they were still registered as residents of their native provinces. This created a demand for training merchant sons and, in 1755, the Guangdong salt controller responded to requests and donations from the merchant community by establishing Yuehua Academy. By the beginning of the nineteenth century, after descendants of sojourning salt merchants in the early Qing had been allowed to register as students in Guangdong counties (as it happened, almost exclusively Panyu county), Yuehua no longer served the merchant class exclusively but instead functioned in a capacity similar to that of the older Yuexiu academy.[77]

Nevertheless, Yuehua retained its connection to the provincial salt administration and the Guangzhou salt merchant community.[78] The Guangdong salt controller in 1806 led an effort to raise money for restoring the academy, and four years later an acting salt controller increased the student quota. Yet another salt controller in 1814 led Guangzhou merchants in donating 4,000 taels to be deposited for yearly interest to support the academy. Merchants donated funds for repairs in 1820, and in 1828 and 1829 salt controller Geng Weiyou (1802 *jinshi*) twice donated 4,000 taels to help finance the academy, which was suffering from low returns on its interest deposits. By the middle of the Daoguang reign, Yuehua had a yearly income of 3,412 taels. The student quota had been increased over the years from an original 30 "formal students" to 118 "formal students" and 67 "outer students," which included a small quota for residents of the banner garrison. Of these, 30 *shengyuan* were to be weeded out through testing. Most of this increase was due to repeated requests by Xie Lansheng's mentor, Liu Binhua, who served as director from 1813 to 1829 on an annual salary of 320 taels.[79]

As the two main official academies in Guangzhou serving the entire province—a third provincial academy, Duanxi shuyuan, was located in Zhaoqing prefecture to the west—Yuexiu and Yuehua were geared toward preparing students for the civil service examinations, and hence education at the two academies naturally exhibited a predilection for state-sanctioned Cheng-Zhu Confucianism. The original Yuexiu regulations, in accordance with a 1736 edict, were modeled on Zhu Xi's famous regulations for Bailudong (White Deer Grotto) Academy in northern Jiangxi province. In addition, the Bailudong regulations were engraved in Yuexiu's Former Worthies Hall, which contained honorary tablets for the Five Masters of Neo-Confucianism in the Song—Zhou Dunyi (1017–73), Cheng Yi and Cheng Hao (1032–85), Zhang Zai (1020–77), and Zhu Xi—as well as tablets for native Guangdong philosophers and statesmen from the Tang through the Ming. The Former Worthies Shrine at Yuehua likewise was devoted to the Five Masters of the Song.[80]

Although education at Yuexiu and Yuehua was essentially focused upon preparation for the civil service examinations, the type of scholarship promoted at the academies also tended to fluctuate with the intellectual disposition of charismatic directors and provincial officials. Many of them were fervent adherents of Cheng-Zhu Confucianism, *lixue*, or Song Learning.[81] Wang Zhi, a Zhili native who served as Yuexiu director from 1736 to 1742, "throughout his life exclusively pursued Song Learning, attacking [the Han dynasty Confucians] Kong Anguo and Zheng Xuan while honoring [Zhou Dunyi of] Lian and [the Cheng brothers of] Luo."[82] Feng

Chengxiu (1702–96), a Nanhai native who twice served as Yuexiu director (1755, 1781–82) and printed two sets of student examination essays, reminded students that their writing of eight-legged essays would "contain the Way" only by adhering to the learning of the Five Masters.[83] Finally, the native Guangdong poet Feng Minchang (not related to Chengxiu), who served as Yuexiu director sporadically from 1801 to 1806, taught students that "the learning of the sages and worthies essentially consists of seeing one's mind-heart (*jianxin*)," thereby evoking Neo-Confucianism in general and perhaps also betraying an interest in the Cantonese philosophical tradition of the Ming.[84]

Likewise, Yuehua Academy included among its former directors several strong adherents of Cheng-Zhu learning or, more generally, *lixue*. Both Feng Chengxiu and Feng Minchang taught at Yuehua, the latter instructing students in the importance of "abiding in reverence" (*zhujing*), a cornerstone of Cheng-Zhu learning. Liu Binhua served at the academy briefly in 1804–5 and then again in an uninterrupted tenure from 1813 to 1829. He emphasized the priority of moral character by having his students first master the *Zhuzi xuedi*, a collection of Zhu Xi's sayings topically arranged by Guangdong native Qiu Jun (1420–95) and patterned after the *Lunyu* (Analects of Confucius). Yet, in addition to the typical monthly examinations on passages derived from the *Four Books*, Liu required students to participate in annual examinations on classical exegesis and policy questions. He rewarded the outstanding students with books, brushes, and inkstones purchased with his own salary.[85]

Nevertheless, not all Yuexiu and Yuehua directors concentrated exclusively upon Cheng-Zhu Learning and examination preparation; some, in fact, even promoted the scholarly ideals of evidential research and Han Learning that would later be systematically introduced at the Xuehaitang. He Mengyao—who had been a protégé of the Han Learning scholar Hui Shiqi when the latter served as Guangdong educational commissioner—presided over Yuexiu Academy between 1750 and 1752. Xuehaitang scholars in the nineteenth century would point to He, who produced a work on mathematics, as evidence of a nascent tradition of evidential research in Guangdong. Li Fuping, the only Guangdong native whose work would be included in the collection of Qing exegeses on the Classics, the

Huang Qing jingjie, set out as director of Yuehua Academy between 1805 and 1808 to cure academy students of the habit of guessing at meanings, as well as of their inability to draw evidence from the Classics.⁸⁶

Scholars such as He Mengyao and Li Fuping did not long succeed at implanting the practice of evidential research at either academy. Their successors' repeated efforts to broaden the educational horizon at both academies beyond the confining study of the *Four Books* and *Five Classics* for examination preparation suggest that they were fighting an uphill battle to maintain an innovative curriculum. The Yuexiu director in the late 1810s, Guangdong native Chen Changqi (d. 1820), had worked with several of the most famous *kaozheng* scholars on the editorial board of the comprehensive *Siku quanshu* anthology, compiled in the 1770s and 1780s. Though his own scholarship exhibited a bent for evidential research, Chen advocated combining the essentials of Han and Song Learning, because he saw both approaches as transcending the single-minded purpose of his students. In response to Yuexiu students who wished to learn how to improve their examination-style essays, he urged them to put aside thoughts of examination success and rewards from office and instead "to study classical learning to the roots, to forge their minds and nature, and thereby thoroughly to comprehend the principles of things."⁸⁷

The third major official academy operating in Guangzhou on the eve of the founding of the Xuehaitang, Yangcheng shuyuan (City of Rams Academy), would become the most important site on Xie Lansheng' social itinerary when he began teaching there in 1821. Yangcheng was formed in the previous year, when, after having raised money to repair the Yuexiu and Yuehua academies, Guangzhou prefect Luo Hanzhang turned his attention to three small academies and two charitable schools run by the prefecture. Combining the resources of these disparate institutions, Luo created Yangcheng Academy, which was to provide instruction to 110 "formal students" and 60 "outer students" from Guangzhou prefecture. By selling off assets from the defunct schools, raising funds from among the local elite, and securing five thousand taels from the prefect's yamen, Luo was able to amass a deposit substantial enough to provide an annual interest income of three thousand taels for the academy. As director of the new academy, Xie Lansheng earned a yearly salary of four hundred taels.[88]

Having served at various local administrative posts in Guangdong for two decades, Luo Hanzhang saw his new prefectural academy as a vehicle for transforming the base customs he found so prevalent in the province. Prior to creating Yangcheng Academy, Luo had required students at Yuexiu to respond to policy questions on curbing the outrageous extravagance he perceived throughout the Pearl River delta, in addition to addressing such topics as the suppression of secret societies and bandits. He continued this tack at Yangcheng. In a commemorative inscription he composed to mark the establishment of Yangcheng, Luo expressed a desire to train a core of educational officials and yamen secretaries capable of transforming the "extravagant customs and perfidious sentiment" that he believed led to the "deceitful practices and ceaseless litigation" he had encountered in the prefecture. He hoped that those who did not seek administrative posts would return to their local villages and work to decrease the level of violence there.[89] As Xie Lansheng succinctly characterized Luo, the prefect perceived a connection between education and pacification.[90]

But Xie Lansheng and his students were motivated by a set of concerns different from those expressed by Luo Hanzhang. Hired for the post in late 1820, Xie took advantage of Yangcheng's location in the provincial capital to create opportunities not available to prefectural academies outside Guangzhou prefecture. In addition to regular examinations—twice a month under the director, and once under the prefect—Yangcheng students were also tested monthly by provincial officials, beginning with the governor-general in the second lunar month, the governor in the third, and subsequently on down the bureaucratic ladder. Moreover, like their counterparts at the three provincial academies, Yangcheng students could sit for special examinations under the educational commissioner; these examinations, offering them a chance at qualifying for the provincial examinations, afforded a higher rate of success than qualifying examinations through the official county schools. After Luo left Guangzhou for a new post in Shandong in May 1821, educational officials in Panyu and Nanhai petitioned the educational commissioner to discontinue this practice. Since educational officials in these two counties were natives of prefectures outside Guangzhou, they naturally would have resented this new shortcut to the provincial examinations exclusively enjoyed by Yangcheng students, who were registered in Guangzhou prefecture. In response, Xie Lansheng justified this privilege to his students, arguing that the elite of Guangzhou prefecture had donated over half the funds for renovating the provincial examination compound in early 1822. He also sent a letter to Luo Hanzhang, who, fortunately for Xie, returned to Guangzhou in late 1822 as the new governor of Guangdong. With his newfound authority, Luo reinstated the Yangcheng privileges and ensured that they would become precedent.[91]

Although Luo's long career in Guangdong was ended by a transfer just a few months later, Yangcheng maintained its status as one of the major Guangzhou academies until the end of the nineteenth century. One reason for this longevity was the steady course set by Xie Lansheng as the academy's first director from 1820 to 1831. Moreover, not only was there evidently a great demand for new academies in Guangzhou during the 1820s, but the special privileges offered by Yangcheng also attracted a large number of prospective students. For its first term, in February 1821, Yangcheng tested over 2,000 licentiates/state students and apprentice students seeking to fill 170 slots at the new academy. This demand did not drop off over the following decade, as more than 2,000 hopeful students tested in 1824, over 1,500 two years later, and exactly 2,124 showed up for screening in 1829.[92] Students admitted in 1823 were treated, during a two-week stretch in the spring, to a series of lectures by Xie Lansheng on such Neo-Confucian texts as Zhou Dunyi's *Taiji tushuo* (Explanation of the diagram of the supreme ultimate), Zhang Zai's Western Inscription, and Cheng Hao's *Dingxing shu* (Letter on settling nature), a letter in response to Zhang Zai, in many ways complementing Zhou's *Taiji tushuo*.[93]

After initiating Yangcheng classes in 1821, Xie Lansheng spent less time at Haichuang Monastery and the maritime merchants' gardens and firms, and more time interacting with Yuexiu and Yuehua directors and supervisors (*jianyuan*). From his base at Yangcheng, Xie often called on Yuehua head Liu Binhua, Yuexiu supervisor Wu Lanxiu, or one of the several Yuexiu directors during the 1820s, before attending formal banquets hosted by the city's officials. On some occasions, one of the three major academies would itself serve as a site for banquets and operas. But Xie still found time to call on the maritime firms, as in an instance in late 1821, when Liu Binhua and Wu Lanxiu collected Xie at Yangcheng for a tour of the Guang-li, Tongfu, Tongdong, and Tianbao firms.⁹⁴

A fourth academy, Wenlan shuyuan, was somewhat different from the three academies introduced thus far, but nonetheless appears frequently in Xie Lansheng's diary and illustrates the convergence of merchant and literati interests. This multifunctional institution originated in 1810 when the new lieutenant-governor, Zeng Yu (1759–1830), had organized the dredging of the Six Arteries, the major canals running through Guangzhou city. Together with He Taiqing, an 1809 *jinshi* from Shunde then residing in Xiguan, the maritime merchants requested that authorities clear a canal that ran through Xiguan as well. To monitor the canal once dredging was completed, the merchants contributed buildings on property that had been confiscated from a debt-ridden fellow merchant in the 1780s. The remaining merchants had then been required to purchase the property in order to pay off their colleague's debt.⁹⁵

Since the property was in 1810 still jointly managed by the maritime merchants and was furthermore conveniently located along the recently dredged canal, they proposed to use one of the buildings as a "public office" (*gongsuo*) from which the annual clearing of the canal would be coordinated, thereby allowing commercial boats easier access to that area of town. Regulations drawn up in that year were designed to prevent undesirable social elements from encroaching upon the canal. In addition to prohibiting the construction of low bridges that inhibited transport, the regulations forbade nightsoil boats from entering the canal. Wenlan organizers asserted that, on the pretext of collecting nightsoil, these boats anchored behind homes along the canal and not only oppressed residents with their foul odor but also provided their operators with opportunities to steal from incautious homeowners.⁹⁶ These regulations were reinforced in a formal pronouncement issued by Zeng Yu in 1812.⁹⁷

In addition to establishing the *gongsuo*, managers availed themselves of the opportunity to renovate another building on the property to serve as an academy, a place where "literati" (*shizi*) could participate in poetry and prose competitions. Remaining buildings were rented out to provide funding for both maintaining the canal and holding the literary competitions. The academy and its competitions were intended exclusively to serve students from families that had resided and paid taxes in Xiguan for at least 30 years. Thus, Wenlan participants were mostly natives of the Nanhai countryside or Xinhui and Shunde counties who had relocated to Xiguan, but also included extra-provincial migrants such as the Ye family from Fujian. The 1811 covenant establishing Wenlan Academy listed donations from the maritime merchant firms, including those frequented by Xie Lansheng (Yihe, Xicheng, Guangli, and Dongyu) as well as the firms of the Pan family. The four maritime merchant families commonly acknowledged as being the wealthiest—the Lu, Pan, Wu, and Ye—alternated in providing annual funding for the academy. Wenlan was to be managed by a committee of "gentry," but here again the lines distinguishing merchant from gentry were porous. Early "gentry" managers included such literati stalwarts at Wu parties as Zhong Qishao and Zhang Ruzhi, and also Yang Dalin, the rising Xiguan merchant who created ties to Guangzhou's most powerful merchants through an aggressive marriage strategy.[98]

Wenlan Academy had a regular teacher, Wang Jianxin (1837 *juren*), a native of Datong township in the Nanhai portion of the Enclosure district, who "lodged" at the academy for over 50 years. Though Wang might have lectured at the academy, the poems or essays written for the competitions (called *huiwen*, or "association compositions") were to be judged by an outside teacher of proper standing and examination fame, because it was feared that a Xiguan instructor would elicit suspicions of favoritism. Academy regulations from the late nineteenth century noted that prizes, consisting of combinations of such items as silver taels, silk fans, stationery, and foreign cloth, were to be awarded to authors of the best papers. Larger monetary prizes were distributed as rewards for passing the provincial and metropolitan examinations. Other sources describe Wenlan as the site of poetry meetings (*shihui*) for which Xie Lansheng served as a judge of the entries. Evidence of this can be found in the Xie Lansheng diary as well. For example, Xie rated one set of Wenlan *huiwen* in the summer of 1820, another batch in the summer of 1823, and later that year went to the academy to read over poetry papers. Again, in the spring of 1825, Wenlan sent to Xie over six hundred *huiwen* papers, and Xie agreed to finish ranking them by the end of the month. Xie Lansheng was of course paid for his services and, in return, he donated to the academy such items as fans decorated with his calligraphy to be used as prizes.[99]

Some of Guangzhou's more popular teachers operated outside the system of academies, though their style was reminiscent of Cantonese academies in the Ming dynasty. During the Ming, academies in Guangzhou prefecture, whether located in the city or the delta hinterland, tended to be intimately associated with a single, charismatic teacher. As a result, academies often became defunct after the death of the scholar most closely associated with them. Academies that survived nominally might exist only as shrines to the founder or scholar after whom they had been named, but rarely provided instruction to students. When, during the Kangxi reign, the Qing state began to encourage the construction of provincial academies geared toward examination preparation, this pattern began to change in Guangdong. Increasingly, students seeking an intimate relationship with a charismatic teacher often had to look outside the official academies.[100]

The most successful private teachers active in the 1810s and 1820s reportedly drew hundreds of students. Zhang Yanji, the teacher pressured into speaking out against Local Worthy Lu in 1815, is said to have had almost two hundred students in Guangzhou. In the 1820s, Liang Xuyong, the literatus from the Nanhai countryside who had been insulted in the 1817 metropolitan examination, gave up pursuit of an official career and instead opted to take students in Xiguan. Foshan native Lao Tong (1734–1801) was another popular teacher in Guangzhou at the turn of the nineteenth century, reportedly drawing several hundred students. An 1801 *jinshi* from the Guan lineage of Jiujiang township, Guan Shilong, also taught in Guangzhou. In the first decade of the nineteenth century, Guan took students at his temporary residence in the Old City, but became so popular that he had to move to a building with larger capacity. Still there was not enough room; those hoping to hear his lectures but who had not been accepted as formal students listened from outside. Among those formally accepted was He Wenqi (ca. 1780–1855), a native of Zhenyong township in the Enclosure district, who would later become a popular Yuexiu director. Almost all of these private teachers, as well as their students, seem to have been natives of rural Nanhai temporarily living in urban Guangzhou. Both Zhu Ciqi and Kang Youwei (1858–1927), also natives of the Nanhai countryside, would attract similarly devoted followings in the late nineteenth century.[101]

LITERARY SOCIETIES AND COMPETITIONS

In addition to teaching at the Yuexiu, Yuehua, and Yangcheng academies, Xie Lansheng was often called upon to rank *huiwen* for various literary societies. In 1822 alone, Xie recorded having rated *huiwen* for, among other locales, the Xiguan suburb, Longshan township in the Enclosure district, and Xinhui county's Chaolian township. In what was presumably a lineage-based competition, Xie noted having received over twenty pieces from the Li surname, without indicating native place. In the same year, Xie even rated papers for Aofeng Academy in his native Mashe township.[102] Such competitions often imitated the civil service examinations. For example, the owner of the Tang Litchi Garden, Qiu Xi, held a grand competition for essays and poems. Apparently emboldened by the fact that Ruan Yuan had composed a poem and inscribed a plaque for his garden, Qiu invited the governor-general to judge the compositions, though Ruan deputed the task to a youth on his staff. With much fanfare Qiu had the list of successful authors displayed in front of the temple in Xiguan where he resided.[103]

In contrast to many of these ephemeral literary competitions, several of Xie Lansheng's associates organized literary groups that made a more lasting impression on the Cantonese cultural landscape. Three such gatherings are important for our purposes because they represent the ascendancy of a younger generation of literati who would be active at the Xuehaitang. The first of these was organized by Zeng Yu, the lieutenant-governor who had dredged the Six Arteries, to mark the construction of a shrine in honor of the classicist Yu Fan (164–233). Yu was a subject under the Three Kingdoms state of Wu who was banished to Guangzhou. There he is said to have built a garden called Myrobalan Grove, on the remains of a residence of a Southern Yue (204–111 BCE) king, supposedly gathering about him a large following of devoted local students. By the sixth century, the site on which Yu Fan was thought to have built his garden had become a Buddhist institution that eventually evolved into Guangxiao Monastery.[104]

Largely forgotten after his banishment to Guangzhou, Yu Fan was rediscovered by Han Learning enthusiasts in Jiangnan during the eighteenth century. Though not considered a classicist himself, Zeng Yu initiated the dedication in Guangzhou of a new shrine to Yu Fan, on the grounds of Guangxiao Monastery. When the shrine was completed in 1811, Zeng wrote a commemorative essay in his famed parallel prose and invited several prominent local poets to commemorate the shrine. A total of fifteen local and sojourning poets joined the event and displayed their skills to help mark the occasion. The Cantonese poets included Xie Lansheng's mentor, Liu Binhua, his younger colleague, Zhang Weiping, and the poet Huang Peifang. Somewhat younger literati also took part: Chen Tan, who would soon become embroiled in the Local Worthy Lu case; Chen's relative and friend, Pan Zhengheng (亨); and Zheng Haoruo (1813 *bagong*).[105]

A second important group was formed in 1812, when Huang Peifang, Zhang Weiping, Tan Jingzhao, Lin Botong, Kong Jixun, Duan Peilan (1787–1845), Huang Qiaosong, and two Daoist priests formally established a poetry society and resort on White Cloud Mountain north of the city. They transformed a choice location at this popular tourist destination into a private playground that they dubbed Yunquan shanguan (Cloud and Springs Mountain Lodge).[106] Here they built a hall honoring three predecessors on the mountain. The first of these, the great Song dynasty poet Su Shi (1037–1101), had visited the spot during his exile and immortalized the mountain in verse. Cui Yuzhi, one of the only scholar-officials from the delta area to have made a mark in the Song dynasty, was also worshiped in the hall. The third worthy honored was Huang Zuo, the famous scholar-official of the Ming and direct ancestor of Huang Peifang. This new group came to be known as the "poetry circle of the seven masters," naturally excluding the Daoists, who were relegated to the role of maintaining the resort.[107]

Gatherings at Cloud and Springs brought together several people who would be active participants in Xuehaitang scholarly and literary life long after the lodge they constructed in 1812 had fallen into disrepair.[108] Three members of the group, Huang Peifang, Zhang Weiping, and Lin Botong, would eventually be appointed as Xuehaitang co-directors. Several other members were from merchant backgrounds. Huang Qiaosong, the son of a Panyu family grown wealthy in the salt trade and a frequent guest at the Wu family gardens and Haichuang, would become a regular participant in early Xuehaitang examinations. Kong Jixun and Duan Peilan were welcomed into the group as poetry students under Huang because they were from families of some commercial wealth. Kong was a member of the Luoge Kong family of Nanhai, which had earned its fortune in the salt trade. Duan was a Panyu licentiate; however, because he was the son of a concubine, he reportedly received only a "middling person's" share when his father's property was divided. Yet this provided enough for him to contribute, depending upon the source, either two or four thousand taels for landscaping and construction of the mountain lodge's various prospects.[109]

Literati associated with the Xigutang (Longing for the Ancient Hall) formed one final literary group active on the eve of the establishment of the Xuehaitang, but with an even closer evolutionary link to the academy. Like most of the poets who celebrated the Yu Fan shrine and the Cloud and Springs lodge, the literati associated with the Xigutang were younger than Xie Lansheng—one of the members was his son, Niangong—and therefore represent something of a generational shift. More a group of literati than a club based at a particular site, there was in fact no such "hall." Rather, similar to the contemporary poetry and prose competitions at Wenlan Academy, Xigutang activities consisted of literary competitions (*wenke*) at monthly meetings initiated in 1821 and hosted in alternation by two group members at various locations. One indication of the close connection between the Xigutang and the Xuehaitang is the striking overlap of membership. The list of Xigutang participants includes many names that will become familiar through our analysis of the Xuehaitang: Zeng Zhao (d. 1854), Wu Lanxiu, Ma Fuan (1789-1846), Xiong Jingxing, Zhang Biao, Xu Rong, Wu Yingkui, Huang Zigao (1794-1839), Hu Tiaode, Wen Xun (1832 *juren*), Deng Chun (1778-1851), Yang Shiji (1810 *juren*), Liu Tianhui, and Xie Lan-sheng's son, Niangong. In addition, Xigutang members included three veterans of the old Cloud and Springs group who would also have a presence at the Xuehaitang: Lin Botong, Zhang Weiping, and Huang Peifang.[110] Each of these seventeen members would also take part in Xuehaitang examinations; seven of the first eight Xuehaitang codirectors appointed by Ruan Yuan in 1826 were Xigutang members. Finally, the connection between the two groups was made explicit by an editor of a local anthology that contains an essay on the Xigutang written by Zeng Zhao. In a postscript to Zeng's essay, the editor recalled that the group "was formed in 1821 to study ancient-style prose and verse (*guwen ci*)," and that "two years later Ruan Yuan established the Xuehaitang *to expand upon it*, where they combined this with study of classical exegesis and *shi* and *fu* poetry."[111]

Little information exists concerning the literary ideals of the Xigutang group aside from Zeng Zhao's essay and brief references in biographies of group members in county gazetteers. The group is most often described as promoting "ancient-style prose and verse."[112] In his essay, Zeng expresses admiration for Wei Xi (1624–81) and other literati who formed a group of reclusive ancient prose stylists in Jiangxi during the early Qing. Yet he described their prose as being somewhat "thin" as a result of their weakness in classical studies. If Zeng and his cohorts in the Xigutang group could both imitate Wei Xi and bring with them a strong foundation in classical studies, then the Xigutang writing might be "able to parallel the Han and surpass the Tang, not to mention the writers of the Song."[113] Zeng's literary ideals closely resonated with those espoused by Ruan Yuan, who was just then promoting pre-Tang literature through the Xuehaitang examinations. But others in the group did not share all of Zeng's views on literature. Wu Yingkui, an ancient prose stylist of some repute in the delta, particularly admired Wei Xi without acknowledging Wei's "thin" understanding of classical studies. Hu Tiaode was especially fond of the writing of the Eight Masters of the Tang and Song. Ma Fuan upheld as a model Fang Bao (1668–1749), doyen of the Tongcheng ancient prose school. In correspondence exchanged with Zeng Zhao, Ma cautioned Zeng against his fetish for the extraordinary and ancient, which he saw as dangerously close to that of the Seven Masters of the Ming, archaists who called for conscious imitation of Qin and Han prose.[114]

Thus, it is difficult to pin down a specific literary orientation shared by members of the Xigutang group, suggesting that local affinity was what held the group together. Like the "ancient learning" soon to be promoted at the Xuehaitang, "ancient prose" might be variously interpreted, implying either pre-Tang models or the works of the Tang and Song masters. Moreover, though the overlap in membership between the Xigutang and the Xuehaitang is intriguing, it is not exactly clear to what degree Ruan Yuan might have had a hand in directing or, at least, inspiring the Xigutang agenda. The fact that Ruan is not mentioned in any source as the driving force behind the Xigutang suggests that the core group of Xuehaitang scholars that emerged from the Xigutang ancient-prose writers brought with them their own concerns and interests, and that the direction taken by the Xuehaitang may reflect a local Cantonese agenda as much as it does the influence of Ruan Yuan. Indeed, the Xuehaitang curriculum—with its unusually heavy emphasis upon literary exercises in comparison to Ruan's Hangzhou academy, the Gujing jingshe—most likely represents a compromise with this local literary group. Ruan's task, then, was to expand Guangzhou's latest literary circle, and to graft onto it a new emblem that promoted Ruan's agenda, informed by the uniquely Jiangnan fusion of evidential research, Han Learning, and literary styles found in the *Wenxuan* anthology.

CONCLUSION

References to the Xuehaitang in numerous biographies in gazetteers and literary collections written in the late nineteenth and early twentieth centuries credit the academy with bringing about a radical and positive transformation in the practices of Guangzhou's cultural elite. As will become clear in the following chapters, the Xuehaitang did indeed alter the local cultural landscape. But the image of an academically and culturally moribund environment being injected with vibrancy more accurately reflects the assumptions of Ruan Yuan on the one hand and, on the other, the interests of those who, by means of the Xuehaitang, claimed for themselves a place at the top of Cantonese elite society and established their credentials as arbiters of local culture.

Thus, whereas it would be difficult to overstate his role in shaping the direction of the Xuehaitang, Ruan Yuan was not working in a vacuum. The governor-general established his new academy in a local environment of great excitement and growing possibilities. This environment offered an eminent local literatus like Xie Lansheng, as well as more marginal members of the cultural elite, a wide range of options for patronage, literary and scholarly expression, and social advancement. Those with the right credentials, or those with money, could gain access to the important sites on Guangzhou's social circuit. As places like Litchi Cove were inundated by ever increasing numbers of the wealthy and socially ambitious, those above them constantly had to create more refined settings. The social life of Guangzhou's commercial and cultural elites, at times appearing to outsiders such as Ruan Yuan as an intellectual backwater, or considered by cynical local observers to be a vulgar, floating world, was undeniably vibrant.

Moreover, despite the fact that the Xuehaitang would define itself against pre-existing conventional academies in Guangzhou, it also appears, when viewed from the perspective of its local context, to be the culmination of a local literary and academic florescence beginning in the early nineteenth century. This can be seen initially in the various literary competitions held and literary societies formed in the decade or so before the establishment of the Xuehaitang. It may also be observed in the increased attention that local officials, often at the urging of the local elite, paid to renovating academies, increasing their funding, and raising student quotas. Furthermore, during the early decades of the century, academy directorships—posts traditionally filled by famous scholars from outside the province—increasingly went to Guangdong residents. There thus appears to have been what might be described as a "Cantonization" of academy directorships, though in addition to such delta natives as Xie Lansheng, many of these supposedly native Cantonese were in fact drawn from such sojourning and in-migrating cohorts as the Jiaying Hakkas and the northern Zhejiang administrative personnel and salt merchants, a characteristic similarly typical of the Xuehaitang.

In short, the cultural life of the social elite in Guangzhou during the early nineteenth century—on the eve of the founding of the Xuehaitang—exhibited a thirst for cultural capital in the form of education and other accouterments of the literary and scholarly elite. Despite later self-congratulatory assessments of the Xuehaitang's role in spreading learning to Guangzhou, academic life in the city was already flourishing along with its commerce. Understanding this vibrancy and the competition to attain ever higher levels of cultural achievement provides a means of explaining the appeal of the Xuehaitang.

⋇ THREE ⋇
The City's New Landmark: Creating the Xuehaitang, 1820–1830

> On the north wall is the King of Yue Hill,
> Forming a single corner like Penglai.
> The red kapok flowers above
> Illuminate the terrace of study below.
> The Sea of Learning continues former wise ones,
> Ceaselessly netting multitudinous talents.
> Seeking the glosses from substantive facts
> Enables us to connect the essentials of ultimate principle.
> "Nature" and "fate" steeped in empty talk,
> At once are swept away like drifting dust.
> Exerting effort we receive the teacher's transmission,
> In the hope of using it to instruct future generations.
> —Wu Lanxiu, "Sending Off My Teacher, Ruan Yuan, Junior Guardian of the Heir Apparent, to His New Post in Yun-Gui," 1826

BY THE TIME HE ARRIVED in Guangzhou on November 30, 1817, as the new governor-general of Guangdong and Guangxi, Ruan Yuan had already earned a reputation as a patron of scholarly and literary projects and as an advocate of evidential research and Han Learning. He was a native of Yangzhou in Jiangsu, one of the major Jiangnan centers of the eighteenth-century evidential research movement. While serving as commissioner of education in Shandong during the early 1790s, Ruan erected a shrine in honor of the Han dynasty Confucian Zheng Xuan, a scholastic hero to Han Learning enthusiasts in the Qing. As Zhejiang commissioner of education in Hangzhou from 1795 to 1798, Ruan organized the compilation of a dictionary of the Classics, the *Jingji zuangu*. Upon returning to Hangzhou as Zhejiang governor in 1800, Ruan established a new academy, the Gujing jingshe. In contrast to usual practice, Ruan appointed two directors to the academy. Moreover, this was the first academy with an explicit Han Learning orientation. "The glosses of Han dynasty scholars are particularly close to the time of the sages and worthies," Ruan explained in his commemoration of the founding of the Gujing jingshe, and "what is known by those far away never has the substance of those close by."[1] In other words, Han glosses of the Classics were more reliable than those of the Song. Continuing to promote such scholarship as governor of Jiangxi from 1814 to 1816, Ruan organized the reprinting of a definitive edition of the *Shisanjing zhushu* (Commentaries and sub-commentaries to the Thirteen Classics), a collection of Han and Tang classical exegeses, in order to make more widely available pre-Song alternatives to the Cheng-Zhu interpretations of the Classics.

Ruan Yuan continued his patronage of scholarship upon taking up his post as governor-general in Guangzhou. He first organized local scholars in compiling a new edition of the *Guangdong tongzhi* (Guangdong provincial gazetteer). Like the *Jingji zuangu* project in Zhejiang two decades before, this endeavor brought together a group of scholars who would form the nucleus of a new academy. In addition to the sojourning Yangzhou literatus Jiang Fan (1761–1831), the chief editors were drawn from among the province's most eminent older scholars: Chen Changqi, Liu Binhua, and Xie Lansheng. The chief collator was Ye Menglong, son of the salt merchant Ye Tingxun. Several of the section compilers (*fenzuan*) and section collators (*fenjiao*) were scholars familiar from the literary groups discussed in Chapter 2 and would also become prominent figures in the future Xuehaitang. Section compilers included Liu Huadong, who led the protest against Local Worthy Lu; the Xigutang members and future Xuehaitang co-directors Wu Lanxiu, Zeng Zhao, and Wu Yingkui; and three other literati who would participate in early Xuehaitang examinations—Zheng Haoruo, Li Guangzhao, and the old scholar Cui Bi (1801 *juren*). The future co-director, Xiong Jingxing, and a future examinee at the Xuehaitang, Deng Chun, served as section collators. Another future co-director, Yi Kezhong, joined the gazetteer staff in December 1819 to gather material for the section on metal and stone inscriptions.²

Whereas the gazetteer by no means represented a repudiation of Song Learning values, it did furnish an opportunity for Ruan Yuan subtly to introduce his methods and ideals of historical evidential research. Certain sections of the new gazetteer, such as that on metal and stone inscriptions (a popular subject for Ruan Yuan and other *kaozheng* scholars), were especially detailed compared to previous editions and allowed local scholars to hone their skills as researchers.³ During the process of compilation, chief editor Xie Lansheng noted that Yi Kezhong and Zeng Zhao had reported many mistakes in Weng Fanggang's *Yuedong jinshi lue*.⁴ As the compilation of the provincial gazetteer was drawing to a close, and while the Xigutang group was conducting its monthly meetings, Ruan Yuan began to hold the examinations in "ancient learning" (*guxue*) that would eventually coalesce into the Xuehaitang.

The governor-general clearly had come to his Guangzhou post with a scholarly and literary agenda in mind and envisioned the Xuehaitang as a means of transforming the local cultural landscape by introducing the latest trends in scholarship and literature from Jiangnan. Many aspects of the Xuehaitang in fact distinguished it from other local academies. At the same time, Ruan Yuan's academy was inevitably assimilated into the local landscape, even as he sought to alter that landscape. This chapter explores the dynamics of transformation and assimilation in the process of establishing the new academy, from the initiation of the examinations in 1821 to the formation, by the early 1830s, of a coherent group of literati who identified themselves as Xuehaitang scholars. The Xuehaitang offered a curriculum unique to Guangzhou, which attracted particular types of scholars. An overview of the process of selecting a permanent site and constructing the academy also reveals an effort to highlight the academy's uniqueness and raises the question of how the Xuehaitang fit into the social itinerary of the elite described in Chapter 2. Furthermore, in celebrating and commemorating the new academy, scholars associated with the Xuehaitang emphasized the unique place of the academy in Guangzhou through what may be termed a discourse of difference. In all these ways, the group of scholars who responded with the greatest alacrity to the governor-general's examinations differentiated their new Xuehaitang from other Cantonese academies, even as the new academy became part of the local landscape.

THE XUEHAITANG EXAMINATIONS IN ANCIENT LEARNING

In the spring of 1821, Ruan Yuan announced examinations in ancient learning, apparently having harbored this notion for some time. Zhang Weiping explained—in an explanatory note to a poem commemorating a spring banquet, held in 1818 at Ruan Yuan's yamen, and attended by Yuexiu director Xu Naiji, Yuehua director Liu Binhua, and Xie Lansheng—that in addition to discussing the compilation of the provincial gazetteer, the governor-general also mentioned the possibility of compiling an anthology of classical studies and expressed his desire to construct a hall to test scholars in ancient learning and to name it "Xuehai" (Sea of Learning).[5] Preoccupied with security concerns, Ruan apparently delayed his ambitions for a few years, until early 1821.[6] On March 1, Xie Lansheng noted in his diary that the governor-general tested scholars on six topics in ancient learning. Xie ordered his second son, Niangong, to take the examinations. These examinations in ancient learning—the Xuehaitang examinations—that Xie Lansheng noted in his diary began with seasonal examinations held regularly on the temporary premises of Wenlan Academy. Several weeks later, on April 13, Xie Lansheng observed that the list of successful papers in ancient learning was "displayed on the wall of the [Wenlan] academy's Xuehaitang (Sea of Learning Hall)."[7] A permanent site for the Xuehaitang was chosen in 1824, with construction completed early the following year. Ruan Yuan compiled the first collection of Xuehaitang examination essays and poems, *Xuehaitang ji*, in 1825 and appointed eight co-directors in 1826, just before he was transferred out of Guangdong.

In the inaugural Xuehaitang examinations in the spring of 1821, scholars were asked to write analytical postscripts (*shuhou*) to Wang Yinglin's (1223–96) *Kunxue jiwen* (Record of findings from hard-earned scholarship), Gu Yanwu's (1613–82) *Rizhi lu* (Record of knowledge gained day by day), and the *Yangxin lu* (Record of self-renewal) by Qian Daxin (1728–1804).[8] The first of these works, though produced by a Song scholar, was considered in the Qing to be an exemplary forerunner to the type of reading notes so popular among evidential researchers. The *Rizhi lu* was the standard model for this genre throughout the Qing; Qian Daxin's work was the best recent example of this type of scholarship. In their postscripts, Xuehaitang scholars evaluated the authors' relative strengths and weaknesses in accumulating evidence for research in a wide variety of fields, ranging from philology and exegesis to history and epigraphy.[9]

Ruan Yuan's motivation for testing Cantonese scholars in these works may be gleaned from the preface he later wrote for the 1825 *Xuehaitang ji*. Ruan made it clear that the academy curriculum would emphasize evidential research of the Classics over the moral self-cultivation stressed by Song Learning:

> In ancient times, the noble classes all had the method transmitted by the teachers (*shifa*).
> The Duke of Zhou esteemed culture (*wen*), setting norms for it with ritual;
> Confucius discoursed on the Way, complying with it through filial piety.
> For this reason, "restraint under ritual" begins with emphasizing "extensive learning";[10]
> Before "earnest practice of it," one must first avail oneself of "clear discrimination of it."[11]
> The *Poetry* and *Documents* hand down their constant [moral] instructions;
> The biographies and annals relate their standard admonishments (*fayu*).
> Scholars recite and enact them,
> To the end of their lives not exhausting them.
> It is like:
> > Eating requires beans and grains, which cannot be given up for a day;
> > Housing must have beam and roof; this is what people all know
> How [can one] further establish theories to stray from ancient teachings?[12]

Cleverly alluding to passages from the *Lunyu* and *Zhongyong* (Doctrine of the mean) that were intimately familiar to anyone who had spent any time preparing for the civil service examinations, Ruan Yuan sought to show that, even in the *Four Books* arranged by Zhu Xi, one could find proof that the "extensive learning" inherent in evidential research was the necessary step prior to the "earnest practice" emphasized by Cheng-Zhu Learning. Lest future students forget this fundamental approach to learning, Ruan's preface would later be engraved on the walls of the Xuehaitang after it was constructed in 1824 and 1825.

In another early Xuehaitang exercise, Ruan asked examinees to use the methods of evidential research to trace the origins of a term central to the philosophical system developed by Song New-Confucians: "nature" (*xing*). The title of the exercise reads:

> Question: Why do the "Book of Yu" and "Book of Xia" sections of the *Shujing* (Book of documents), the "Sacrificial Odes of Shang" section of the *Shijing* (Book of poetry), and the "Hexagram Judgments" section of the *Yijing* not address nature or even contain the character *xing*? In what text was "nature" first addressed? Does the meaning of "nature" as spoken of by people of the Zhou and Han dynasties match that of Confucius and Mencius or not?[13]

This question reflected Ruan Yuan's own scholarly preoccupations, as exemplified by his recently completed essay, "Ancient Glosses on Nature and Fate" ("Xingming guxun").[14] Reiterating the tone of his commemoration of the Gujing jingshe, Ruan in this essay sought to demonstrate the authentic meanings of "nature" and "fate" in the most ancient classical passages, as explicated by Han Confucian commentaries before these meanings were, in his view, misguidedly reinterpreted by Song Confucians under the influence of Buddhism. Yet in their answers to the question on this subject, the Xuehaitang scholars offered a variety of viewpoints. Lin Botong argued that even though the ancient texts did not mention "nature" by name, they nevertheless still addressed such issues, ones that would be seen as particularly important by Song Confucians.[15] Zeng Zhao echoed this sentiment but then concluded his answer by criticizing Song Confucians for speaking of "recovering original [nature]," a concept seen by *kaozheng* scholars as having been derived from Buddhism.[16]

The divergence in answers to this examination question, and the fact that Lin's essay, rather than Zeng's, was included in the *Xuehaitang ji*, cautions against a simplistic characterization of the Xuehaitang as pushing an exclusive Han Learning agenda. In fact, as exemplified elsewhere in his preface to the *Xuehaitang ji*, Ruan envisioned an eclectic curriculum:

> Now are brought forth many well-known scholars:
> Some practice the Classics and primary annotations,

seeking the meaning of the Song and Qi dynasty commentaries.[17]
Some explicate etymology,
    investigating the glosses in the *Cang* and *Ya*.[18]
Some analyze the Way and principle,
    keeping to the proper transmission of Huian [Zhu Xi].
Some examine the historical annals,
    searching for the school method of Shenning [Wang Yinglin].
Some even take standards from the Han and Jin,
    becoming precisely familiar with Xiao's *Selections*;[19]
or imitate as teachers the Tang and Song [masters],
    each gaining in poetry or utilitarian prose.[20]

Ruan Yuan undoubtedly sought to promote evidential research, Han dynasty classical exegesis, and *Wenxuan* literary models at the new academy. Yet in other areas Ruan was, by 1821, less exclusive in his approach to scholarship and literature than he had been previously. Perhaps sensitive to the strong influence of *lixue* in Guangdong, Ruan affirmed the importance of Zhu Xi in understanding "meaning and principle," even if he paid less respect to Zhu's successors. In fact, Han Learning–Song Learning syncretism was a constant undertone to the Xuehaitang's emphasis on evidential research.[21]

This eclectic approach may in part have been a response to the polemics coming from two of his staff members recruited from Jiangnan, Jiang Fan and Fang Dongshu (1772–1851). Jiang Fan was much closer to Ruan than was Fang and much more deeply immersed in Han Learning. Like Ruan a native of Yangzhou, Jiang later studied in Suzhou with Jiang Sheng (ca. 1721–99), a student of Hui Dong. In the summer of 1818, Jiang Fan made his way down to Guangzhou, where Ruan Yuan employed him as a chief editor of the provincial gazetteer and an assistant in the compilation of the *Huang Qing jingjie*. Jiang remained in Guangzhou until 1825 or 1826, attracting a group of admirers including Wu Lanxiu, Zeng Zhao, and Yi Kezhong. In 1821, Zeng wrote a preface, and Wu Lanxiu a postscript, to Jiang's *Lijingwen*, a study of ancient institutions that would later be included in an anthology compiled by the Xuehaitang scholar Tan Ying (1800–1871). Some Xuehaitang literati maintained contact with Jiang Fan after his return to Yangzhou. Yi Kezhong, for instance, called on Jiang there in 1828 on his travels between Guangzhou and the capital.[22]

Jiang Fan brought with him to Guangzhou a manuscript that he had written entitled *Guochao Hanxue shicheng ji* (Record of the transmissions of the teachers of Han Learning in the present dynasty). In the opening passages, Jiang documented what he saw as the regretful decline of Han dynasty schools of classical exegesis transmitted from teachers to students (the "transmissions of the teachers") during the Southern Dynasties (420–589), the rejection of Zheng Xuan's interpretations in the Tang official commentaries, and the consequent neglect of Han commentaries by Confucians during the Song dynasty.[23] The *Hanxue shicheng ji* celebrated the revival of Han Learning during the current Qing dynasty through both Jiangnan scholarship and imperial sponsorship. Jiang's manuscript consisted of biographies and descriptions of the works of scholars—primarily from Jiangnan—whom he saw as heroes of the Han Learning movement during the Qing. Ruan Yuan arranged for the *Hanxue shicheng ji* to be printed in Guangzhou in 1818 and wrote a preface for it in January 1819.[24]

Fang Dongshu also found himself in Guangzhou at this time, as a rather more disgruntled member of Ruan's coterie. In 1819 and 1820, Fang served in a relatively minor position on the provincial gazetteer editorial staff before heading Haimen Academy on the Lianzhou peninsula in remote southwestern Guangdong. Fang then went back to his native Tongcheng county in Anhui for a few months in 1822, before he was invited by Luo Hanzhang, founder of Guangzhou's Yangcheng Academy, to return to Guangdong. In 1823, Fang headed an academy in the mountainous northern prefecture of Shaozhou until Ruan Yuan hired him to serve as a teacher in the governor-general's yamen in 1824. At this time, Fang wrote a manuscript largely directed against Jiang Fan's *Hanxue shicheng ji*, entitled *Hanxue shangdui* (An exchange with Han Learning), although it was not published until 1831.[25]

Both Jiang Fan and Fang Dongshu took part in rating Xuehaitang examination papers, and the first edition of Xuehaitang writings even included a piece by Fang. But though Fang was not entirely ignored by Ruan Yuan and the circle of scholars at the Xuehaitang, he certainly felt his approach to scholarship and literature was at odds with theirs. As Fang recollected in a prefatory note to another work, *Shulin yangzhi* (Vessel raised amidst a jungle of books), in the spring of 1825 Ruan queried a group of Xuehaitang scholars (Xuehaitang *shi*) at the academy on what books they planned to write. Also present, Fang lamented that in this later age writing books was too easy and frequent an undertaking, tantamount to the condition Confucius described as "doing without knowing."[26] Fang was thus moved to write this book (apparently sensing no irony here) in which he recited a few bequeathed passages from the "bygone wise one," Confucius, as a means of discouraging the production of more useless works by young scholars at the academy. The feeling seems to have been mutual, as one later scholar reported an instance, recounted by Zeng Zhao, in which Ruan Yuan had told his staff members that the learning of Tongcheng men was vacuous and careless (*kongshu*). The author speculated that Fang, certainly having heard rumors of Ruan's comments, wrote the *Hanxue shangdui* and *Shulin yangzhi* in revenge. This report can never be substantiated, but it does reflect the polemical nature and the prominent role of personalities in the Han-Song debate, as well as the proximity of that debate to the Xuehaitang.[27]

Ruan Yuan might have favored Jiang Fan and Han Learning, but he did not take a polemical stance in his role as patron of the Xuehaitang. Rather, he demonstrated eclectic ideals, both in his preface to the *Xuehaitang ji* and in his selection of papers to be included in the collection. Ruan Yuan's eclectic approach to scholarship can also be seen in his acceptance of New Text Confucianism, a school of Confucianism that had recently emerged in Changzhou and which favored versions of classical texts written in the "contemporary-style script" (*jinwen*) popular in the Former Han dynasty. New Text Confucianism had been transmitted by Confucians in the Former Han, but was eventually displaced by the Old Text school during the Later Han. The two schools also favored alternative exegetical traditions of various Classics, with Old Text scholars, for example, favoring the Zuo Commentary to the *Chunqiu* (Spring and autumn annals) and New Text scholars promoting the Gongyang Commentary.[28]

The name of the Xuehaitang, in fact, alludes to an epithet for He Xiu (129–82), a defender of the Confucian New Texts and an adversary of the Old Text scholar Zheng Xuan. In his annotations to one of his father's poems, Ruan Yuan's son, Ruan Fu, asserts that the name was derived from an anecdote about He Xiu in the fourth-century text, *Shiyi ji*, compiled by Wang Jia.[29] In it, Wang describes He Xiu's vast erudition and relates that He wrote a defense of the Gongyang Commentary and a critique of the Zuo Commentary. Wang then mentions that after Zheng Xuan's critique of He Xiu, scholars flocked to He "like small streams flowing toward the great sea," and that Zheng was known in the capital as the Jingshen, or "Classics God," and He as Xuehai, or "Sea of Learning."[30] Several of the writings celebrating the creation of the Xuehaitang explicitly made reference to He Xiu as the inspiration behind the academy's appellation. The most partisan phrase appears in a commemorative poem by Xu Rong:

> We will take the Gongyang learning of the two Han Dynasties,
> Directly sweeping away the empty and embellished to reveal the Old and New [Texts].[31]

Yet this should not be taken as sufficient evidence to argue that the Xuehaitang was an academy primarily devoted to Gongyang or New Text Confucianism. An equal number of commemorative pieces mentioned He Xiu and Zheng Xuan in tandem—as did Ruan Yuan's preface to the *Xuehaitang ji*—or paid homage to the latter alone.[32] Zheng Fen, the Panyu poet and resident at Huang Qiaosong's estate, perhaps wishing to highlight the surname he shared with the Han Confucian, began his poem celebrating the Xuehaitang with a line asserting the authority of Zheng Xuan: "Distinguish clearly the lineage stemming from the honorable Zheng [Xuan's] native place."[33] Several commemorative essays and poems associated "Xuehai" with a phrase from Yang Xiong's (53 BCE–18 CE) *Fayan* (Model sayings), which spoke of a hundred rivers flowing to the sea as if "mimicking the sea."[34] Thus, the academy's name contained a range of meanings, from celebrating its role in transmitting advanced learning to an imperial outpost on the edge of the South Sea, to symbolizing the eclectic breadth of scholarship and literature promoted at the Sea of Learning Academy. Xie Lansheng, the aging Yangcheng director, stretched the limits of eclecticism in a commemorative essay that he wrote, justifying evidential research at the Xuehaitang with an appeal to Wang Yangming's (1472–1529) theory of the unity of knowledge and action and arguing that Buddhists and Daoists pursued the same goals in their approach to scholarship as did Confucians.³⁵ If this last and rarely voiced interpretation leaves open the question of the academy's scholarly ideals, however, annual ceremonies at the Xuehaitang after 1826 reminded students of the scholarly traditions that remained at the core of the curriculum. Xuehaitang scholars might praise He Xiu or study Zhu Xi, but they only observed two birthdays—Ruan Yuan's in the first month of the lunar calendar and Zheng Xuan's in the seventh.³⁶

Most modern scholars who have written about the Xuehaitang have emphasized the promotion of evidential research or, more narrowly, Han Learning at the academy.³⁷ Indeed, Ruan Yuan was an avid patron of evidential research, if not by this time an exclusive Old Text Han Learning advocate, who considered one mission of the new academy to be that of rescuing Guangzhou from what he saw as its stagnant tradition of Ming philosophical speculation. Moreover, many second- and third-generation Xuehaitang scholars suggested that the founding of the academy marked the beginning of "classical and historical scholarship" or "classical studies and ancient learning" in Guangdong. Clearly, propagating the Jiangnan practice of classical scholarship was of primary importance to the academy's founder.

Nevertheless, the Xuehaitang curriculum was not composed entirely of studies in the Classics and Histories. On the contrary, Ruan Yuan's literary agenda at the Xuehaitang becomes apparent upon examining the *Xuehaitang ji*. The way in which exercises are arranged in the collection tells us something about how the editor Ruan Yuan conceived of the curriculum at the academy. Though he does give priority to classical exegesis—placing such exercises as explications (*jie*) and examinations (*kao*) at the beginning, followed by such categories as discourses (*lun*) and historical essays—he devotes many chapters exclusively to literary exercises. The last seven of sixteen chapters contain literary exercises in parallel prose, rhapsodies, and, most prevalently, *shi* poetry.³⁸ Within the category of literature, this arrangement reflects Ruan Yuan's priorities, stressing pre-Tang literary forms found in the sixth-century *Wenxuan* anthology—such as rhapsodies and parallel prose essays—over poetry imitating later Tang and Song masters.³⁹

The most explicit side of Ruan's literary agenda lay within the realm of prose, and it is here that the connection between his classical and literary agenda is most conspicuous. In four essays included in chapter 7, Ruan had students analyze the difference between "literary prose" (*wen*) and "utilitarian prose" (*bi*). This distinction goes back to the Northern and Southern Dynasties, when writers and anthologists began to classify literary genres that contained rhymes as *wen* and all others as *bi*. Ruan Yuan reinterpreted this distinction, asserting that only prose that was parallel and rhymed could be considered truly literary prose; other forms of prose lacked these refined qualities and characterized plain styles used in historical annals. This was a critical issue for Ruan, who preferred the pre-Tang parallel "ancient prose" (*guwen*) contained in the *Wenxuan* to the Tang-Song "ancient prose" popular among *lixue* advocates in the Qing.[40] Awareness of this connection can be seen in a letter to Luo Hanzhang in which Fang Dongshu bemoaned the fact that "famous scholars in the provinces all venerate parallel prose," whereas free prose (*sanwen*) was increasingly neglected.[41] Fang's claims were clearly exaggerated, at least in Guangdong, which could boast of few parallel prose masters. Only through the Xuehaitang examinations did several Cantonese writers earn reputations as masters of this genre, including Liang Guozhen (1840 *jinshi*), Tan Ying, Zheng Haoruo, and the prodigy Yu Bifang.[42]

Numerous accounts of the founding of the Xuehaitang note that the new academy was to test students in "Classics, Histories, poetry, ancient-style prose, and lyric-poetry" (*jing shi shi guwen ci*).[43] Indeed, what is most striking in perusing the *Xuehaitang ji* is that the vast majority of contributors to the collection were included as poets. This suggests that Ruan Yuan meant to push a literary as well as scholarly agenda, but it may also represent a compromise with the local context. In other words, by Jiangnan standards at least, Ruan Yuan found a dearth of competent classicists with whom to work in Guangzhou.[44] Rather, he praised several of the most influential early Xuehaitang scholars for their literary accomplishments in particular. Among the eight original co-directors personally appointed by Ruan in 1826, several were chosen on the basis of their literary expertise. Wu Lanxiu was known as the pre-eminent composer of lyric (*ci*) poems in Guangdong, and Ma Fuan and Wu Yingkui had gained fame for their ancient-style prose. Both Xu Rong and Xiong Jingxing were appointed above all because Ruan appreciated their poetic skills.⁴⁵ Other scholars at the Xuehaitang also gained recognition for their literary talents, including Tan Ying and Yi Kezhong. Cui Bi was a much older Panyu native who took part in early Xuehaitang exercises. After he passed away, Ruan bequeathed an inscription for his tomb honoring "the *poet* Cui Dinglai [Cui Bi]."⁴⁶

A final indication of the importance of literature at the Xuehaitang is the fact that, as far as can be documented, its literary examination topics had a relatively immediate impact on the examinations of at least one of the other local academies. In December 1822, after only two years of Xuehaitang examinations, Xie Lansheng used "Moonlight brightens the isles by night" as a poetry topic for examinations at Yangcheng Academy and noted in his diary that this was derived from a Xuehaitang exercise.⁴⁷ In this exercise, examinees had been required to compose poems based on four-character lines selected from the *Ershisi shipin* (Twenty-four categories of poetry) by Sikong Tu (837–908).⁴⁸ Xie Lansheng similarly incorporated other Xuehaitang poetry examination topics and noted in his diary that he was doing so, in July 1823 and again in October.⁴⁹

Assessing the types of questions posed in Xuehaitang examinations and the answers to those questions that were deemed worthy of inclusion in the *Xuehaitang ji* (see Appendix B), as well as culling Ruan Yuan's appraisals of various Cantonese scholars who studied at the Xuehaitang, can give us some sense of what we may conceive of as the "Xuehaitang curriculum." In the context of academy education in early nineteenth-century Guangzhou, this unique curriculum, promoted by the Xuehaitang examinations, through the publication of model responses, and in the composition of countless poems marking visits to the academy, added a new component to the local cultural milieu.

A COSMOPOLITAN NETWORK OF XUEHAITANG EXAMINEES

The unique curriculum advertised in the Xuehaitang examinations attracted a wide range of scholars, but a survey of those scholars who were most successful in the examinations and who most closely identified themselves with the academy reveals that it drew especially heavily from particular regional cohorts of aspiring literati. Like the imported scholarship and literature promoted at the academy, most of the important participants in the early Xuehaitang examinations were themselves newcomers to urban Guangzhou, and many of them were "outsiders" to the Pearl River delta. The family histories of many Xuehaitang scholars closely resembled those of the inmigrating urban elite described in Chapter 1. In short, cosmopolitan Guangzhou city was much more open to the Xuehaitang agenda than was the insular Enclosure elite.

Two sources provide information on the most successful scholars in the early examinations. The first of these is the *Xuehaitang ji*, a collection, printed in 1825, of essays and poems written in response to questions posed in Xuehaitang examinations. Edited by Ruan Yuan himself, one can safely assume that the scholars whose examination responses appeared in the collection were, if not representative of all who participated, certainly seen by Ruan as having made the greatest contributions. Aside from single essays or poems contributed by Ruan Yuan, his son Ruan Fu, Fang Dongshu, the Guangzhou garrison official Xiukun, and a Zhejiang literatus, the remaining 99 figures whose registration is known and whose works were included in the *Xuehaitang ji* were registered residents of Guangdong counties. In most cases in the collection, authors' names, residential registration, and degree are indicated.[50] This list of scholars in the *Xuehaitang ji* can be supplemented by the *Xuehaitang dinghai keshi lu*, a record of two examinations at the academy that were presided over by educational commissioner Weng Xincun in the spring and winter of 1827. This record consists of lists of top examinees in prose and poetry, providing the name and native-place registration of each examinee and usually a terse comment on the quality of his essay or poem.[51]

Residents of Panyu county constituted one quarter of the scholars included in the *Xuehaitang ji*. Almost all of the Panyu residents were newcomers to the delta, and, of these, a large number were inmigrants from northern Zhejiang. Zhang Weiping's ancestral home, for example, was in Shanyin county. The Zhang family had begun to reside in Guangzhou as sojourners with Zhang's great-grandfather, but continued to associate with other people from northern Zhejiang. His grandfather, Zhang Yuan, married a Shanyin woman; when she died at an early age, he married a woman surnamed Huang whose grandfather had come from Qiantang county to serve as a minor military officer in Guangzhou. Their son, Zhang Bingwen, at first registered in local schools as a son of a sojourning merchant (*shangji*). Bingwen married the daughter of a salt merchant from Hunan, who had become a Panyu resident and had hosted visiting literati at his residence in the New City. Zhang Bingwen later changed his registration to that of a Panyu resident and attained the *juren* degree in 1801.[52] Despite its Zhejiang roots, the family also bolstered its prestige in Guangzhou by claiming descent from the younger brother of the famous poet, official, and Shaozhou native Zhang Jiuling (673–740).[53] Zhang Bingwen's son, Weiping, was the most famous poet who took part in the early Xuehaitang examinations. Although he was in Guangzhou for the earliest Xuehaitang literary competitions, in 1822 Zhang passed the civil service examinations in Beijing and thereafter served for several years as a county magistrate in Hubei.

Two other Panyu residents of Zhejiang origin were Zheng Haoruo and Zhang Biao. Zheng Haoruo's ancestors had migrated from Zhejiang; by the time Zheng was studying at the Xuehaitang in the 1820s, he was known to be from a wealthy family and to have collected a large number of books at his Banyan Studio in Guangzhou's Old City.[54] Zhang Biao was somewhat older than Zheng Haoruo, but was a close friend. Zhang's father was a native of northern Zhejiang who served as a *muyou* to an official in Guangzhou and for some reason never returned to Zhejiang. As a result, Zhang was registered as a Panyu resident. Prior to the beginning of Xuehaitang examinations, Zhang had joined Liu Huadong and Chen Tan in their protests against Local Worthy Lu. He participated in the 1821 Xuehaitang examinations and in the following year Ruan Yuan invited him to teach his son.[55]

Several participants in the early Xuehaitang exercises were descendants of migrants from Fujian. One of the main contributors of essays on the Classics was Lin Botong, an 1801 *juren* who had been a prominent member of both the Cloud and Springs group and the Xigutang group. Having migrated from Fujian to Panyu, Lin's ancestors for a number of generations practiced medicine outside Guangzhou's Main South Gate in the New City. Lin's father was the first in recent family history to devote his life to study of the Classics, and

Lin Botong continued the family's foray into the cultural elite by studying under the Foshan scholar Lao Tong.[56] Likewise, one of the poets included in the *Xuehaitang ji*, Wu Jiashu, was descended from ancestors who had migrated from Fujian and settled in the Panyu countryside north of Guangzhou; they later moved to Xiuyi ward in Xiguan and became known as the Xiuyi Wu, while retaining their Panyu registration. Wu Jiashu's father, Wu Yingchang (1761–1826), was an 1801 *juren* together with Lin Botong. Because Wu Yingchang shared native-place and same-year ties with Lin Botong, Wu Jiashu and his brother later asked Lin to write the funerary inscription for their father.[57] Although he was not included in the *Xuehaitang ji*, another descendant of Fujian ancestors, Ye Tingying, was ranked for his poetry in the spring 1827 examination. Of the same generation as Ye Tingxun, Tingying was a member of the Ye family from Tongan, Fujian, which had settled in Nanhai and entered into the salt trade.[58]

A few prominent Xuehaitang scholars were descended from recent migrants from other provinces. Hou Kang (1798–1837) had only four papers included in the *Xuehaitang ji* but would become the most prominent classicist and historian in the second collection of Xuehaitang writings, published in 1838. Hou's grandfather, Hou Jinxuan, was a native of Wuxi in Jiangsu who had moved to Guangzhou city. By Hou Kang's generation, the family had registered as Panyu residents.[59] The most prolific Panyu poet in the *Xuehaitang ji* was Yi Kezhong, with 38 poems in the collection. According to his biography in the Panyu county gazetteer, Yi's father was a native of Shanxi province who served as an archivist in the Guangdong salt controller's yamen and took a local Panyu woman as a second wife. When the elder Yi died in office, his body was returned to Shanxi; Yi Kezhong's mother remained in Guangzhou and had her son registered as a Panyu resident.[60] Similarly, Qi Lin, a Panyu resident and 1798 *juren* with but a single poem in the *Xuehaitang ji*, was descended from a Jiangxi native who had served as an assistant to a Panyu county magistrate in the late 1690s.[61]

The *Xuehaitang ji* also included the poetry of three Chinese bannermen assigned to the Guangzhou garrison. The most prolific poet among them was Xu Rong, one of the first three bannermen of the Guangzhou garrison to earn the regular civil service *juren* degree in

1816. Fan Feng (1789–1876) was a second Chinese bannerman who participated in early Xuehaitang examinations and who many years later would be made a co-director. Fan's father, Fan Mengjiao, was remembered as having blazed a trail for members of the Guangzhou garrison in the civil service examinations. In appreciation for Mengjiao's teaching his grandsons, the Guangzhou garrison general had donated grain to purchase state student status for Mengjiao. After 1800, when garrison bannermen were first allowed to sit for the county and prefectural civil service examinations, Mengjiao removed himself from state student rolls in order to participate and became a prefectural student a few years later. Fan Feng further fulfilled the family's literary aspirations through his participation in Xuehaitang examinations.[62] A third Chinese bannerman who had a presence in the first decade of the Xuehaitang was Xiukun. Although Xiukun grew up in Guangzhou, where his father was stationed, he was not a member of the local garrison. Consequently, whereas the Xu and Fan families seem to have been working to enhance their image as part of the Chinese (or, more specifically, Cantonese) cultural elite, Xiukun appears to have been moving in the opposite direction, striving to "become Manchu," as Mark Elliott suggests. His original surname was Feng; but, imitating his famous great-uncle Yinglian (1707–83), he adopted the name Xiukun to express his Manchu identity.[63]

Despite the long trip to Guangzhou from Jiaying department in the Hakka homeland, the works of eighteen Jiaying scholars are included in the *Xuehaitang ji*, and they account for 23 percent of the poems included in the collection.[64] Whatever the reason for the large number of scholars from the Hakka area in the early Xuehaitang, they found ways to embed themselves as sojourners in the Guangzhou community. For example, Wu Lanxiu was the subdirector for schools in Panyu county between 1821 and 1822 and also served as a supervisor at Yuexiu Academy in 1819 and again from 1824. Although Wu retained his registration as a Jiaying student, he was clearly a long-term sojourner in Guangzhou and built up a large book collection there, which he stored at Yuexiu.[65] Li Guangzhao and Liao Ji were the most prolific Jiaying poets in the *Xuehaitang ji*. Li had close ties to Guangzhou: his poetry was printed there in 1814, he took part in the compilation of the provincial gazetteer, and he died in the city years later. Similarly, Liao Ji was poor and unable to support his relatives and so, according to his biographer, upon capping went to study in Guangzhou where he gained fame for his poem on the shadow of a plum blossom. This earned Liao an audience with Ruan Yuan, who subsequently invited him to participate in Xuehaitang examinations. Another Jiaying literatus in the early Xuehaitang examinations was He Qijie, who served as supervisor at Yuexiu Academy in 1823 and stayed on as a "vice-supervisor" when Wu Lanxiu returned to Yuexiu in the following year. Zhang Qihan (1797–1865), an 1822 *juren*, had three poems included in the *Xuehaitang ji*. Although not a native of Jiaying, Wen Xun hailed from Changle county in the same Hakka region of eastern Guangdong.[66]

In addition to descendants of extraprovincial sojourners and literati from the Hakka region, several of the most important scholars in the first decade of the Xuehaitang were members of urbanized families that had relocated to Guangzhou from the delta. Within this cohort, the scholar with the greatest presence at the Xuehaitang was Tan Ying, a future co-director for three decades. Tan Ying's First Migrant Ancestor had moved from Xinhui county in the western delta to Foshan in Nanhai county. Tan Jianlong, Tan Ying's father, relocated to Guangzhou's Xiguan, still under the jurisdiction of Nanhai. Attaining the rank of law secretary in the lieutenant-governor's yamen, Jianlong built a villa in Xiguan that attracted literati visitors such as Liu Huadong, who wrote a plaque for the villa. Jianlong was fond of banqueting friends on fine spring and autumn days at various locations in Xiguan, just as the Du family was doing in the New City. He was close to Yang Dalin, the wealthy merchant who, like Tan Jianlong, had also moved from Foshan to Xiguan. In fact, the Tan and the Yang were two of four families in their Xiguan neighborhood that intermarried to maintain social status in the suburb. Like Xie Lansheng's balancing of a New City residence and ritual duties in Mashe, the Tan family maintained a dual identity, sinking new roots in Xiguan social circles yet continuing annually to visit the First Migrant Ancestor's tomb near Foshan.[67]

Liang Mei was another Xuehaitang scholar who was becoming more connected to urban Guangzhou than to his native place in the delta hinterland. A native of rural Shunde county, Liang resided at the Wu estate in Henan for two years. He later built his own studio in Xiguan near Changshou Monastery and married off his only daughter to Tan Ying.⁶⁸ Aside from Tan Ying, the most prolific Nanhai poet in the *Xuehaitang ji* was Xiong Jingxing, a Xigutang member. Like Tan and Liang, Xiong resided in Xiguan, where he maintained his Auspicious Rams Streamside Lodge near the banks of the Pearl River.⁶⁹ As we have seen, Xie Lansheng's second son, Niangong, an 1822 *juren*, also took part in the early Xuehaitang exercises. He had only two poems included in the collection but would eventually be appointed a Xuehaitang co-director.⁷⁰

Other scholars in the early Xuehaitang exercises were sojourners or migrants from the western portions of the delta. Wu Yingkui, a native of Heshan county, across the West River from Nanhai's Jiu-jiang township, spent many years in Guangzhou, including a two-year stay at Liurong Monastery in the Banner Quarter.⁷¹ Zhong Qishao, the scholar from Xinhui county who resided for many years at the Wu estate in Henan, also maintained a studio in Xiguan. A friend of Hou Kang and student of Zhang Biao, Liang Guozhen belonged to a branch of a lineage in the Xinhui township of Chaolian that had moved to Guangzhou city several generations before and currently resided there as Panyu residents.⁷²

In contrast to urban scholars, relatively few literati who resided in the delta hinterland regularly participated in the Xuehaitang examinations, but there were some notable exceptions. For example, Wu Rongguang—official, collector of art and antiques, and Foshan native—proudly proclaimed that several of his brothers and cousins took part in the examinations. They included his brother Wu Miguang (1789-1871) and his lineage cousins Wu Kuiguang and Wu Linguang.⁷³ But Foshan may have been exceptional. Surprisingly few natives of Shunde county—only ten—contributed to the *Xuehaitang ji*. In addition to Liang Mei, who had relocated to Xiguan, three Shunde natives were important in the early Xuehaitang examinations: Zhou Yinqing (ca. 1793-ca. 1875), Zhao Jun (1808 *gongsheng*), and Ma Fuan.⁷⁴ Already a holder of the *juren* degree when the Xuehaitang examinations were first held, however, Ma won the *jinshi* degree in 1829 and thereafter spent most of his time in Beijing.⁷⁵ What is most notable about the Shunde natives in relation to the Xuehaitang examinations is the absence of any representatives of the powerful Luo or Long lineages of Daliang, who practically monopolized the cultural, as well as economic, production of Shunde.

Similarly, only a very few scholars from the Enclosure district in western Shunde and southern Nanhai participated in the early Xuehaitang examinations.[76] The most notable exception to this trend was the Jiujiang native Zeng Zhao. Unlike the Jiujiang gentry to be examined in Chapter 7, Zeng does not seem to have been heavily involved in local Jiujiang affairs. As a youth, he and Liu Tianhui, a fellow Nanhai native with a single essay in the *Xuehaitang ji*, studied the Classics and Histories in Xiguan. Ruan Yuan became aware of Zeng when one of the Jiangnan scholars in his yamen, Ren Zhaolin, came across a copy of Zeng's annotation of the *Zilin* (Forest of characters), a fifth-century work on glosses highly valued by *kaozheng* scholars.[77] Ren showed the annotations to Ruan, who was duly impressed with Zeng's work and invited the Jiujiang native to teach the Classics to his sons, to help compile the provincial gazetteer, and later to join the Xuehaitang examinations. Zeng would become known as the first genuine Han Learning scholar in Guangdong. The authors of Zeng's biography in the 1872 Nanhai gazetteer compare him with Panyu's Lin Botong and Heshan's Wu Yingkui, both of whom were capable in the early Daoguang era of discussing the Classics profoundly; they had also both studied under the local Neo-Confucian Lao Tong, however, and consequently their learning "in the final analysis did not extend beyond the pattern set by the people of the Song."[78] In contrast, the biographer claims, the promotion of pure Han Learning began with Zeng Zhao.

A few poets in the *Xuehaitang ji* were from the area in southern Panyu county bordering on the sands. For example, the collection includes four poems by Cui Bi, a native of Yuangang, as well as one poem by Xie Guangfu, an 1804 *juren* and scion of an influential lineage from Shiqiao in far southern Panyu.[79] But for both Cui and Xie, native-place ties to the sands set them apart from other Panyu residents. Most of the Panyu Xuehaitang scholars were residents of urban Guangzhou and had little connection to the agricultural hinterland. In contrast, despite the wealth that lineages in southern Panyu derived from the sands, few of their sons bothered to participate in Xuehaitang examinations.

From this survey of some of the early Xuehaitang examinees, including all of the scholars most closely identified with the academy, it appears that the academy largely catered to extraprovincial in-migrants, literati sojourners from the Hakka region, and urbanized families relocated from the delta. Whether from the delta or outside Guangdong, most of these literati belonged to socially ambitious families of merchants or subofficials and *muyou*. In this sense, the burgeoning Xuehaitang community mirrored the cosmopolitan society of Guangzhou city, but it certainly was not representative of Guangdong province, or even the delta, as a whole. The dominant lineages of the Enclosure district and other older parts of the delta, as well as scholars from such prosperous prefectures as Huizhou and Chaozhou, were largely absent from the Xuehaitang. The vested interests and cultural concerns of the strong lineages along the West River in southern Nanhai and western Shunde, as well as newly rising lineages of the reclaimed sands in southern Panyu, eastern Shunde, and Xiangshan, were not represented at the academy. Members of old lineages in the Guangzhou hinterland were descendants of the literati who had produced the first flowering of Cantonese scholarship and literature in the Ming. Thus, the "insiders" at the Xuehaitang were really "outsiders" from the perspective of the delta hinterland. As a result, scholars at the Xuehaitang had little interest in preserving lineage scholarly traditions and were therefore open to cosmopolitan intellectual traditions newly imported from Jiangnan by Ruan Yuan. The Xuehaitang provided a means to enhance their cultural status and to reshape the Cantonese cultural landscape by placing themselves directly in the center of it.

MOUNTAIN HALL: CONSTRUCTING THE ACADEMY

In addition to its unique curriculum and the fact that it largely appealed to a cosmopolitan group of urban scholars, the Xuehaitang was further distinguished from the city's other academies by the selection of its site, its construction, and the institutional arrangements that Ruan Yuan made for the academy upon his departure from Guangzhou in 1826. During the first four years of its existence, the physical presence of the Sea of Learning Hall amounted to little more than a signboard suspended at Wenlan Academy in the

Xiguan suburb. Here, Ruan Yuan accepted answers to examination questions, on which students were allowed to work at home, and posted the rankings. Ruan presumably intended to use the Wenlan grounds only as a temporary location for the Xuehaitang, until he could decide on a permanent site.[80]

An 1838 gazetteer of the Xuehaitang academy, *Xuehaitang zhi*, describes the process of selecting that site. Although the discovery of an ideal place on Yuexiu Hill is presented as being somewhat fortuitous, it is significant that the reasons for not choosing some sites are so clearly articulated in the gazetteer. For instance, Ruan first thought of building the new academy at the site of the old Southern Garden in the New City—where famous local poets, the Former and Later Five Masters of the Southern Garden, had gathered during the Ming—but felt it was "too damp and narrow." Next, the reader is told, Ruan planned to construct the Xuehaitang next to Wenlan Academy in Xiguan, but decided against it because the place "did not have much scenery."[81] Ruan was also likely dissuaded from turning the Wenlan grounds into a permanent home for the Xuehaitang after a horrendous fire that began in the evening of November 1, 1822. The worst fire disaster in anyone's memory, the blaze destroyed, by various estimates, between 10,000 and 17,600 homes and shops in Xiguan.[82] Next, according to the Xuehaitang gazetteer, Ruan Yuan contemplated using some buildings near one of Xie Lansheng's favorite leisure destinations, Haichuang Monastery.[83] The attraction for Ruan lay in the monastery's proximity to the supposed site of the former residence of the first-century BCE scholar Yang Fu, which Ruan Yuan intended to "renovate." This plan also fell through; Ruan ruled out this location because he "disliked its proximity to the market" (*xian jin shi*).[84] Unfortunately, it is not clear what Ruan meant by this, as all three of the sites he had considered thus far—in the New City, Xiguan, and Henan—were in the most highly commercialized areas of the city and were filled with numerous markets of all kinds. Conceivably, Ruan was referring to the "furniture shops, tea hongs, and large matting factories" that one Western observer noticed in Henan.[85] Along the southern bank of the Pearl River in Henan one could also find docked the Yangzhou group of flower boats and, further downstream, the salt junks. Most likely, Ruan meant the lavish buildings and gardens of the Wu family of maritime merchants that dominated the neighborhood around Haichuang Monastery.

Finally, in the fall of 1824, as Ruan Yuan was inspecting repairs on the northern side of the city wall that ran over the top of Yuexiu Hill, he found a spot near the base of the hill a short distance inside the wall that he felt would make an ideal permanent location for the Xuehaitang.[86] He placed Wu Lanxiu and Zhao Jun in charge of supervising construction of the academy. Work began in the ninth lunar month of 1824 and was completed in the winter, probably in January of 1825, when Xie Lansheng wrote his commemoration of the establishment of the academy and visited the site.[87] On the twentieth day of the first lunar month (March 9, 1825), Ruan carried on a private tradition of avoiding guests and making tea on his birthday, but this year he chose the Xuehaitang as his refuge. Two days later, the governor-general invited Xie Lansheng and other literati to a banquet at the academy.[88] In the fall, Ruan and the Cantonese gentry met to discuss construction of the adjacent Wenlan Pavilion (Wenlan'ge), where the *Huang Qing jingjie* was to be stored, and celebrated its completion the following year.[89]

Just as the academy's curriculum distinguished it from the type of education provided by conventional academies, so the location and construction of the Xuehaitang symbolically set it apart from other institutions. In his preface to the *Xuehaitang ji*, Ruan referred to the academy as a "mountain hall" (*shantang*), which would become a common trope in subsequent writings about the academy.[90] In its new location—on Yuexiu Hill, overlooking Guangzhou to the south and beyond it, the Pearl River—the new academy stood above and looked down over the rest of the city. In their many essays and poems celebrating the academy's completion, as well as in Huang Peifang's drawing for the Xuehaitang gazetteer (see Fig. 4), Xuehaitang scholars portrayed their new academy as dominating the cityscape, atop the "visual hierarchy" of buildings in the city.[91] In the image projected by the gazetteer, the Xuehaitang looked out over the tiles and smoke of the city—erasing the towering pawnshops—to "connect" with the Liurong Monastery's Flowery Pagoda and the Chigang Pagoda, and beyond them with the distant hills and "seas" (the numerous rivers crisscrossing the delta).[92] Nevertheless, it is not certain that the Xuehaitang was situated and designed for the

FIG. 4: The Xuehaitang and Wenlan Pavilion. In this drawing by Huang Peifang, the academy dwarfs the city below (SOURCE: *Xuehaitang zhi*, facing page 1a).

purpose of imparting this impression to people outside the Cantonese literati class. The often detailed Western accounts of Guangzhou and Yuexiu Hill produced in the mid- and late nineteenth century did not mention the Xuehaitang, in part because other buildings on Yuexiu Hill attracted the attention of Westerners and non-elite Chinese. The five-story Zhenhai Tower, which was perched atop the city wall that ran over Yuexiu Hill, impressed everyone who saw it. Guanyin Temple, on an adjacent hill to the west, regularly attracted female devotees, and a mix of commoners thronged the heights on festival days.[93]

Though to a certain extent the Xuehaitang appropriated a section of the contested space on Yuexiu Hill, the site of the academy also offered a secluded alternative to the more hotly contested spaces in the city below.[94] The Yuexiu, Yuehua, and Yangcheng academies were all located near the center of the walled Old City, where they not only neighbored numerous provincial and subprovincial yamens but also increasingly felt the pressure of a bustling urban culture. Feng Minchang, in the early years of the nineteenth century, had lamented the fact that an enormous restaurant was opened adjacent to the Yuexiu building that housed that academy's collection of imperially bestowed books.[95] In contrast to these truly urban institutions, early Xuehaitang scholars saw their academy as removed from the vulgarity below. Wu Lanxiu appreciated the Xuehaitang's location on Yuexiu Hill as "a place separated from the mundane world, wherein scholars make no distinction between host and guest."[96] In his poem cited at the outset of this chapter, Wu likened the Xuehaitang to the immortals' island retreat of Penglai. Firmly planted on the slope of Yuexiu Hill, the Xuehaitang thereby "elevated" Cantonese high society, redirecting its attention away from the raucous life of the river, where the sexes and classes mixed freely in a "floating world," toward the solidly grounded heights on the opposite side of the city. In his study of Ming gardens, Craig Clunas reminds us that height was equated with enlightenment and the "lofty" pursuits of the cultured elite. Describing the perspective of the elite in depictions of gardens, Clunas writes that "the vulgar mass is 'down there,' and the gentleman is physically elevated."[97] Similarly, in constructing the Xuehaitang, Ruan Yuan and his Cantonese literati cordoned off an area that could serve as a sanctuary for the more refined members of the male elite. Accordingly, contact with representatives of the common, vulgar, and feminine world beneath them was limited. Academy regulations graciously afforded the "short-sleeved and bare-footed" masses the opportunity to peer into the academy grounds from outside the gate; otherwise, access was denied to the unrefined.[98]

Although the Xuehaitang was not imposing enough to appear in Western descriptions of Guangzhou, essays and poems commemorating its construction called attention to its unique design. One term often associated with evidential research was "unadorned learning" (*puxue*). Advocates of *puxue* during the Qing described their own methods of careful and painstaking research, solidly grounded in textual exegesis, as "unadorned" in contrast to other areas of intellectual pursuit they considered "ornate" or "embellished" (*hua*). In the writings of literati associated with the Xuehaitang, the latter term sometimes referred to the type of philosophical speculation common to *lixue*, but more often designated what the authors perceived as the artificially formalistic or "embellished" style of examination essays and poetry. Instead, learning at the Xuehaitang was to represent a return to the essential and unadorned learning of the ancient past, through a curriculum grounded in the Classics, early Histories, and forms of literature prevalent before the Tang and Song. This approach was to be reflected in the very design of the academy. Wu Lanxiu and Zhao Jun, the two scholars charged with supervising construction, ensured that the framework of the hall would be left unengraved, and that the layers of steps would remain unpolished, advising workers "not to favor elegance, but only to adopt the unadorned and plain."[99] This of course stood in marked contrast to the intricately carved and brightly painted homes, temples, guild halls, and ancestral halls found throughout Guangzhou, not to mention the ornately decorated flower boats. Another scholar, Wu Yue, reiterated this notion in his celebratory essay:

> The honorable [Ruan] constructed the hall and study,
> With rafters dense and plinths uniform;
> Its unadorned [style] is like [his] learning,
> [Toward which] many scholars will be able to ascend.[100]

Yuexiu Hill also struck Ruan Yuan as an ideal location for the Xuehaitang because of its historical relics and the symbolism of its flora. He observed that, because remains of Han and Five Dynasties (907–60) sites could be traced on the hill, it was an ideal space for Cantonese literati to observe their ancient past.[101] These remains supposedly included the Yue King Terrace of the Southern Yue Kingdom, a local regime that had flourished in the second century BCE. In addition, the hill was full of distinctively Cantonese flora, such as the kapok tree with its bright red flowers, whose color was often associated with the hot climate of the region, or "southern fires."[102] Wu Lanxiu and Xiukun oversaw the planting of dozens of "red" plum and a hundred "jade" plum trees. In addition to the kapoks and plums, Xuehaitang scholars took advantage of the banyans, pines, chrysanthemums, and other foliage to generate countless poems on the respite offered by the hill. One section of the small Xuehaitang gazetteer was even devoted to flowers and trees on Yuexiu Hill.[103]

Chen Li, who would later become the most famous scholarly product of the academy, noted that the Xuehaitang grounds were the only true garden within the city walls of Guangzhou.[104]

In her study of Southern Song academies, Linda Walton demonstrates that Zhu Xi and other founders of academies paid a great deal of attention to the physical environment surrounding potential academy sites, because "the process of moral self-cultivation was dependent both on the historical 'sediment' of those who had gone before, preserved in the ecology of a particular locale, and on acquiring knowledge and understanding of nature in order to comprehend universal principle."[105] Some of the same dynamics were at work with Ruan Yuan and the Xuehaitang, as both "ancient traces" and native flora were important attractions of Yuexiu Hill as a site.[106] In other respects, the choice and design of landscape seem unique to early nineteenth-century Guangzhou. Rather than serving as aids to moral self-cultivation, the archeological sites and native flora offered both practice in on-site investigation and inspiration for literary composition. In his record of planting plums, Wu Lanxiu observed that the academy's surroundings were "truly sufficient to verify the Southern Han [917–71] and supplement exegeses of the *Erya*," a compendium of glosses dating from approximately the third century BCE, and included as one of the *Thirteen Classics*.[107] Locating the Xuehaitang among these Cantonese symbols also firmly centered the academy in its local context and thereby legitimized it as a place of Cantonese culture. In this manner, the group of scholars most closely identified with the Xuehaitang, many of whom had very shallow Cantonese roots, in a sense appropriated the most meaningful local cultural symbols as their own. At the same time, the location provided for unambiguous spatial and symbolic separation of the refined world of the new academy from the ignoble world below.

A final mark of difference between the Xuehaitang and the other academies of urban Guangzhou was its institutional design. The name itself advertised the academy's uniqueness; it was not a conventional academy, or *shuyuan*, but rather a "hall" (*tang*).[108] Likewise, Ruan Yuan's institutional innovations for the Xuehaitang distinguished it from other academies. In the summer of 1826, when he was transferred to the governor-generalship of Yunnan and

Guizhou, Ruan Yuan took steps to ensure the continued existence of the Xuehaitang after his departure. Numerous commemorative essays and poems that compared the Gujing jingshe and the Xuehaitang must have reminded Ruan that his first academy had not fared well: lectures at the Gujing jingshe had been suspended after he left Hangzhou in 1809, the academy's dilapidated buildings had to be repaired in 1824, and testing would be resumed at the academy only in 1833.[109] Whereas Wu Lanxiu and Xiukun symbolically secured the longevity of the Xuehaitang by planting plum trees, Ruan Yuan took more concrete measures to ensure the academy's survival.[110] Unlike most academies, which had a single director, or the Gujing jingshe, which had two, the Xuehaitang was to have eight co-directors (*xuezhang*, literally "learned elders" or "directors of learning"). Ruan appointed the first eight in 1826: Lin Botong, Ma Fuan, Wu Lanxiu, Wu Yingkui, Xiong Jingxing, Xu Rong, Zeng Zhao, and Zhao Jun. All of these first eight co-directors, as well as subsequent ones, were registered residents of Guangdong; yet, as we have seen, many were relatively recent arrivals to the region. None of the original eight held the *jinshi* degree at the time of their appointment. Moreover, each co-director received what was in relative terms a very meager salary of 36 taels per year, compared to 300–500 taels for directors of other major academies. Forced to find other sources of income in Guangzhou, they typically worked as advisors of provincial officials, managed granaries and other institutions, and compiled county and prefectural gazetteers. This unprecedented system of eight teachers had the advantage of helping to maintain the scholarly and literary legacy of the academy's founder. Bringing together a group of literati with a wide range of scholarly and literary preoccupations, the system of co-directors also institutionalized the eclectic ideals expressed by Ruan in his preface to the *Xuehaitang ji*.

Like the co-directors' salaries, the overall income and expenditures of the Xuehaitang were also modest in comparison to other Guangzhou academies. The 1838 Xuehaitang gazetteer records a total annual income of 1,511.982 taels, with expenses totaling slightly less than that, at 1,259.44 taels.[111] Yet the Xuehaitang did not require a large budget. The practice of allowing students to take examinations at home precluded the necessity of maintaining dormitories, and the smaller number of students, combined with less frequent quarterly examinations, meant less expenditure for student stipends. A Xuehaitang scholar writing later, in the 1870s, commented that the academy did not provide student stipends at all, in contrast to the standard provincial academies.[112] Academy income was derived from rent on shops in the New City and from reclaimed "sands" in Panyu and Nanhai, as well as interest earned on money Ruan Yuan had donated and deposited with merchants. The latter fund was managed by Wu Bingjian and other maritime merchants through Wenlan Academy.[113]

A DISCOURSE OF DIFFERENCE: CELEBRATING THE XUEHAITANG

Wu Lanxiu, in the poem he composed on the occasion of Ruan Yuan's departure from Guangzhou (quoted at the outset of this chapter), praises the role of the Xuehaitang in "sweeping away like drifting dust" the "empty talk" of Neo-Confucian philosophical speculation. Similarly, in numerous writings, spanning diverse genres, that commemorate the establishment of the academy and are included in the *Xuehaitang ji*, Wu and other Xuehaitang scholars were adamant in distinguishing the new academy from others geared toward preparation for the civil service examinations. Such portrayals often required acknowledging the heretofore underdeveloped status of classical studies in Guangdong, as in a commemorative essay by the aged Panyu scholar Cui Bi:

The scholarly class of Guangnan [Guangdong] in the current dynasty is not as good as that in Jiang[su] and Zhe[jiang]. . . . Aside from the examinations, if one seeks those who thoroughly comprehend the notes and commentaries of the various Classics as well as the assorted Histories, [they are so few that] one can count them with one's fingers. This is even more true [if one attempts to enumerate] those who have collected books numbering as many as 10,000 *juan*. Thus the department and prefectural academies merely assess students in examination essays and poetry.[114]

Fan Feng went further in contrasting Cantonese scholarship, which he saw as mired in the Ming philosophical past, with more modern learning (*jin zhi xue*):

Modern learning traces [matters] from beginning to end and arrives at deep profundity. Yet the Cantonese are [still] imbued with the vestiges of Wang Yangming, tracing their intellectual descent from his theory of innate knowledge of the good (*liangzhi*) and thereby denying Kangcheng [Zheng Xuan] and Huian [Zhu Xi]. They see the Six Classics as disconnected and belittle glossing and careful examination as only a secondary duty. In a moment releasing their grip on the writing brush, they talk loftily and discuss ingeniously. Any books they do not see with their own eyes they point out as spurious volumes. Fathers have admonished their children and teachers have instructed their followers, so that [the Cantonese] have become unshakeable [in their beliefs]. [Their scholarship becoming] vacuous and coarse, flaws have accumulated for three centuries. How could the honorable [Ruan Yuan's] founding of this hall be likened to a department or prefecture renovating an academy, increasing endowments for student stipends, and thereby making an empty claim to cultivating talent?[115]

By "modern learning," Fan Feng means the latest trends in *kaozheng* scholarship then being imported from Jiangnan and promoted at the Xuehaitang as a more authentic "ancient learning" than was popular in the Ming. A critique of Wang Yangming and Ming philosophical speculation written in early nineteenth-century Guangzhou would have implicated Chen Xianzhang, the Ming-era Cantonese philosopher who was often mentioned in tandem with Wang. Yet, though visitors to Guangzhou, such as Ruan Yuan, immediately associated Cantonese scholarship with Chen Xianzhang, few contemporary Cantonese scholars were avid practitioners of the fifteenth-century philosopher's learning. Aside from scholars in Xinhui, Chen Xianzhang's native county, Cantonese Confucians in the Qing were much more likely to have been followers of Zhu Xi.[116] Chen Xianzhang did remain an important icon among Cantonese scholars, as was demonstrated in the case of Local Worthy Lu, but his learning was not prevalent in the delta outside Xinhui. Nevertheless, for scholars at the Xuehaitang who wished to promote a new brand of learning, the association of native Cantonese scholarship with "empty" Ming philosophical speculation made for a convenient contrast and provided a raison d'être for succeeding generations of Xuehaitang scholars. Perhaps it is no surprise that someone such as Fan Feng, a Chinese bannerman who had no ancestors steeped in the Ming philosophical tradition, could readily make this critique.

Although these essays by Cui Bi, Fan Feng, and others, which form the final chapter of the *Xuehaitang ji*, would never mention specific examples of other academies against which the Xuehaitang was defined, the "department and prefectural academies" in Cui's and Fan's essays euphemistically designated all official academies, or at least those outside the provincial capital, that stressed examination-style writing in their curricula. Moreover, the Xuehaitang was established just at a time when local officials, most notably Luo Hanzhang, boasted of cultivating talent by renovating academies and increasing student stipends. In representing the Xuehaitang as an alternative to academies that merely drilled students for the examinations, authors echoed claims made by founders of academies in the Southern Song and Ming dynasties, who defined their institutions in contrast to government schools.[117] These critiques of conventional academies by Xuehaitang scholars thus delegitimized competing claims to cultural pre-eminence.

Examinations at the Xuehaitang were indeed different from those at the other premier academies in the city. At Yangcheng Academy, for example, examinations under Xie Lansheng consisted of civil service examination–style essays and poems. For the former, students were simply provided a passage from one of the Four Books on which they were expected to elaborate. Typical examples from 1821 and 1822 are two passages from the *Lunyu*: "Zhonggong, being chief minister to the head of the Ji family," and "The superior man, having obtained their confidence, may then impose labors upon his people."[118] In contrast, when he administered examinations at the Xuehaitang in 1827, Weng Xincun asked students to produce examinations or explications of terms in passages in the Classics, praises (*song*) or commemorative essays (*ji*) on historical topics in parallel or free prose, and rhapsodies and *shi* poems. Commenting on the classical exegesis of Liu Huadong's son, Liu Zechang, Weng praised his minute detail (*xiangmiao*). Similarly, Weng regarded Hou Kang's exegesis as a "close examination substantiated by a great deal of evidence" (*qie kao ji you genju*). Among the literary papers, Weng remarked on the elegance of Liang Mei's parallel prose record of Litchi Cove and his rhapsody on the same theme.[119]

The unique nature of the Xuehaitang was reinforced with Ruan Yuan's initiation of the compilation of the *Huang Qing jingjie*. Compiled between 1825 and 1829, this fourteen hundred-*juan* collectanea celebrated the Jiangnan production of evidential research in the Qing dynasty. Over 90 percent of the scholars whose works were incorporated into the collectanea were natives of five prefectures in the three provinces that constituted Jiangnan: Jiangsu, Zhejiang, and Anhui.[120] Several works collected in the *Huang Qing jingjie* were previously still in manuscript form, and Cantonese scholars had certainly never laid eyes upon such pathbreaking examples of Jiangnan scholarship. For example, Ruan brought with him a detailed *Erya* commentary recently written by Hao Yixing (1757–1825), allowing Lin Botong and Zeng Zhao to examine it.[121] The printing of the *Huang Qing jingjie* in Guangzhou and the storage of its printing blocks in the specially constructed Wenlan Pavilion adjacent to the Xuehaitang announced to Cantonese scholars that evidential research had now arrived in the southernmost part of the empire. From Ruan Yuan's perspective, the academy and the collectanea were part of the same strategy. The collectanea simultaneously glorified the advanced state of scholarship in Ruan's native Jiangnan and provided a standard of erudition for novices in Guangzhou to follow. As Ruan exclaimed in his preface to the *Xuehaitang ji*, "the cultured rule of the Great Qing [has spread] from the north to the south."[122]

Just as the printing of the *Huang Qing jingjie* represented an importation of Jiangnan scholarship into Guangdong, so Xuehaitang scholars commemorating the establishment of the new academy evoked the legacy of Hangzhou's famous Gujing jingshe, portraying it as a sister institution to the Xuehaitang. Ruan Yuan's assertion in his commemoration of the Gujing jingshe of the superiority of Han classical interpretations resonated in a second essay by Fan Feng commemorating the Xuehaitang:

People of the Han were not far removed from ancient times and were still able to get what was passed on by the disciples of Confucius. Thus Xu [Shen's] and Zheng [Xuan's] glosses of the Classics involved no more than following the text to establish the gloss. They merely sought to illuminate in detail the passages and sentences.[123]

Identifying with Ruan Yuan's first academy, established in Jiangnan, served further to distinguish the Xuehaitang from other academies in Guangdong. Moreover, this act lent credence to the Xuehaitang as the legitimate guardian of the newly imported methods of evidential research and convictions of Han Learning.

Because celebratory essays and poems sought to emphasize the uniqueness of Guangzhou's new academy, they leave the impression that the Xuehaitang was radically separated from the other academies. Yet such claims masked some very tangible connections between the Xuehaitang and contemporary Guangzhou academies. A functional analysis of the Xuehaitang in its local context reveals that it was quickly assimilated into a system of urban academies. First, Ruan Yuan did not ignore education at the conventional academies. In 1822, he appointed to the Yuexiu Academy directorship He Nanyu, a Huizhou (Guangdong) native who had acquired the *jinshi* degree in 1799, when Ruan helped administer the metropolitan examinations in Beijing. Ruan then wrote a preface to the 1824 collection of Yuexiu student examination essays and poetry, compiled by He.[124] Later Ruan asked He to choose, from over one hundred literary pieces commemorating the establishment of the Xuehaitang, the most outstanding representatives of each genre for inclusion in the *Xuehaitang ji*. Moreover, three of the four chief editors selected by Ruan to compile the provincial gazetteer were older scholars, such as Xie Lansheng, who had a great deal of experience teaching in Cantonese academies. Similarly, Ruan hired Li Fuping, who had introduced evidential research to Yuehua students in 1805, to help evaluate responses to Xuehaitang examinations.[125]

The fact remains that Ruan Yuan chose not to appoint directors of the established academies to head the new Xuehaitang; yet, the first generation of teachers there was naturally closely connected to the older academies. Two of the early co-directors of the Xuehaitang, Zhang Weiping and Wu Lanxiu, served as supervisors at Yuexiu Academy; Zhang filled the post in 1817, with Wu following in 1819 and again for several years after 1824. At least four future Xuehaitang co-directors, Zhang, Xiong Jingxing, Zeng Zhao, and Huang Peifang, registered as Yuexiu students at different times between 1804 and 1822. Yangcheng director Xie Lansheng's son, Niangong, was also a key figure in the early days of the Xuehaitang. Likewise, the second generation of Xuehaitang teachers emerged from the older academies, as exemplified by Chen Li's education.

Born in 1810, Chen studied under Xie Lansheng at Yangcheng in 1825 and registered as a Yuexiu student two years later while also sitting for the 1827 winter examination at the Xuehaitang. Later, Chen was a member of the outstanding Yuehua class of 1832, which also produced future co-director Tan Ying, before being selected as a Xuehaitang "specialized student" in 1834 and co-director in 1840.[126] The 1835 Nanhai gazetteer, in fact, describes the Xuehaitang as a "public place" (*gongsuo*) at which seasonal examinations were held for students from the Duanxi, Yuexiu, Yuehua, and Yangcheng academies, although not all participants in the Xuehaitang examinations were registered as students at these four academies.[127] All of this is perhaps to state the obvious: Xuehaitang scholars did not ignore examination preparation despite simultaneously seeking more "refined" alternatives. Yet it is important in understanding the relationship between the old and new Guangzhou academies to remember that they were more closely connected, through the movement of teachers and students between academies, than the self-differentiating statements of the Xuehaitang founders would suggest.

CONCLUSION

The new Xuehaitang reshaped the cultural geography of Guangzhou in tangible ways, and, as the following chapter will demonstrate, scholars associated with the Xuehaitang produced new constructions of Cantonese elite culture. Nevertheless, the discourse of difference employed in commemorations and celebrations of the founding of the Xuehaitang obscured the extent to which the new academy was incorporated into local society. According to Xuehaitang regulations, any "refined person," whatever his intellectual proclivities, was allowed to visit the academy on outings to Yuexiu Hill.[128] It quickly became a regular stop on the social itinerary of Xie Lansheng and other elderly Cantonese literati. In addition to attending banquets hosted by Ruan Yuan before his departure to Yunnan, Xie Lansheng accompanied such academy stalwarts as Wu Lanxiu and Wu Yingkui on occasional excursions to the Xuehaitang. The academy offered an ideal vantage point for viewing the moon at the Mid-Autumn festival and other times.[129] From this perspective, then, it appears as if the academy was simply assimilated into the local landscape.

Ruan Yuan's vision for the academy was perhaps best captured in a poem by his wife, Kong Luhua (1777–1833), writing from the governor-general's yamen: "Not for the sake of leisurely tours did he build this hall / But for transmitting learned enterprise and testing in composition."[130] Though Xie Lansheng was quite happy to make use of the Xuehaitang for better views of the moon, Ruan Yuan's academy was primarily aimed at a younger, more malleable generation of Cantonese literati. With Xie's death in 1831, one such young literatus, Tan Ying, lamented that "in the South, the older generation has completely withered away."[131] But by this time Tan and other urban Cantonese literati had come to see themselves as part of an identifiable group of scholars associated with the Xuehaitang, replacing the generation of scholars represented by Xie Lansheng. In poems to one another, scholars associated with the Xuehaitang spoke of "our like-minded associates at the Xuehaitang" (*Xuehaitang tongren*) or "the various gentlemen of the Xuehaitang" (*Xuehaitang zhuren*).[132] At this point, the Xuehaitang had become the focal point of cultural identity for a growing number of Cantonese literati. And in this sense the academy was not simply another feature assimilated into the local landscape. Rather, it significantly shifted the focus—away from the river, the monasteries, and the confusing commercial world below—toward the new mountain hall.

From a wider perspective, the Xuehaitang also diverted attention away from the delta hinterland and toward Guangzhou. Benjamin Elman has emphasized the importance of kinship ties and cultural resources mustered by corporate lineages in maintaining scholarly and literary traditions over several generations in Jiangnan. Examples include the Hui family and Han Learning in Suzhou, the Zhuang family and New Text Confucianism in Changzhou, and Fang Dongshu's Fang lineage and *guwen* prose in Tongcheng.[133] Although the powerful lineages of the Pearl River delta hinterland did not produce schools of scholarship or literature that had much influence outside Guangdong, they did control enough economic and cultural resources to create and pass on scholarly and literary practices within a given lineage or locale. This can be seen, for example, in the case of Xinhui county, where descendants of Chen Xianzhang and his students continued to adhere to the teachings of the Ming philosopher. But the in-migrating, sojourning, and urbanized elites who congregated in Guangzhou city lacked local roots deep enough to make this strategy feasible. Though some urban institutions, such as Yuehua Academy, were designed to cater to a segment of the sojourning population, they lacked a unique scholarly or literary identity.

In the Xuehaitang, Ruan Yuan created an institution that could be employed to construct just such an identity. It allowed the diverse group of relocated and rising elites, many of whom might have been seen as marginal from the point of view of the delta, to make a place for themselves in Cantonese high society. Many aspects of the new scholarly and literary creed promoted at the Xuehaitang were unambiguously foreign, representing a conscious effort to transplant Jiangnan practices of evidential research and styles of literature to a peripheral region of the empire. Urban Guangzhou's community of sojourners and upstarts responded enthusiastically to the new academy, quickly making it their own and relying on it to increase their own status in Cantonese cultural circles. Evidential research, and Han Learning in particular, with its emphasis on "transmission of the teachers" (*shicheng*) and the "schools method" (*jiafa*), created a genealogy for the motley group of scholars at the Xuehaitang; they could now claim scholarly descent within hoary and revered traditions. Similarly, the Xuehaitang provided a space for sons of migrants, merchants, and subofficials to become local literati. This first generation of Xuehaitang scholars quickly came to dominate the construction of Cantonese cultural identity.

⊰{ FOUR }⊱
Reshaping the Cultural Landscape: History, Poetry, and Anthology

> How magnificent! Letters are flourishing in our dynasty;
> The *Four Treasuries* has made available the great norms of antiquity.
> In the repositories of the inner court these precious editions were stored;
> Bestowing sets to Jiangsu and Zhejiang, they were transmitted to the frontier.
> But Yue is located in the South, situated amidst the southern fires;
> Man vapors and Dan rains spread across this land of weeds and beasts.[1]
> The literary circle of Qujiang ushered in a formal beginning;
> Former and Later Masters of the Southern Garden followed in succession.
> The winds of culture rushed forward, advancing daily;
> Strings and song were heard in neighboring households, all in tranquility.
> The craftsmanship of Guangzhou is regarded as the most ingenious;
> The water clocks of the Western Oceans allow one to see this skill.
> Even if discussing wood-block artisans, ours are also extremely good,
> And essentially able to compete with other places in boasting of rare talent.
> —Li Yingzhong, excerpt from "Poem on Woodblock Printers," 1820s

FOR ONE OF HIS Xuehaitang examinations in ancient learning, Ruan Yuan had asked students to compose poems on the theme of woodblock book printers. The lines quoted above are an excerpt from one poem and attest to the importance attached to printing and the pride with which Cantonese scholars in the Daoguang era glorified the flourishing of printing in their city. A Cantonese scholar would not likely have written such a poem before the 1810s. Although the Pearl River delta generated a great deal of wealth during the eighteenth century, Guangzhou was not known for its library collections or printing houses, at least among discriminating bibliophiles.[2] But beginning in the early nineteenth century, even before the creation of the Xuehaitang, Guangzhou witnessed an unprecedented expansion in the compilation and printing of the types of books deemed worthy of eulogizing in the eyes of literati.

Driving this boom in printing was the emergence of several large private libraries, a trend led by such merchant families as the Pan, Wu, Ye, and Kong. In addition, several literati associated with the Xuehaitang built sizable private collections of their own, some of which could even compare to respectable private collections of Jiangnan literati. Starting his collection in 1808, Zeng Zhao eventually acquired a library containing several tens of thousands of *juan* (chapters). Wu Lanxiu claimed that his family's library was even more extensive, but did not contain as many rare Song and Yuan works as did Zeng's collection. Tan Ying and Zhang Weiping could also boast of respectable collections.[3] These Cantonese bibliophiles of the early nineteenth century had to stock their libraries, often at great cost, with books printed outside the region. They were especially eager to acquire books from Jiangnan and Beijing, often visiting bookshops on trips to the capital to sit for the metropolitan examinations. *Sushu*, or books imported from Suzhou, were sold in Guangzhou bookshops at exorbitant prices. One Xuehaitang scholar, Liang Mei, went to great lengths—if, indeed, somewhat circuitously—to build up his respectable Spring Hall library in Xiguan. In a ritualized act of filial piety, Liang had shaved off a sliver of his thigh to make a medicinal stew for his ailing mother. Healed, his mother in turn pawned off her precious hairpins and earrings to help Liang accumulate a respectable collection. Liang, his son-in-law Tan Ying, and other Cantonese literati later commemorated these mutual acts of sacrifice through a painting of the Spring Hall library and poems recounting its origin.[4]

This interest in collecting in turn fed a great upsurge in the compilation, collation, and printing of texts in Guangzhou and the delta during the nineteenth century. Amid this proliferation of texts, a great deal of attention was paid to local, Cantonese culture. In the first place, this is evident in the Xuehaitang curriculum, as reflected in numerous essays and poems on local themes contained in the four collections of examination writings. Beyond the academy's curriculum itself, Xuehaitang scholars working individually, in collaboration with one another, or under the sponsorship of officials or merchants, wrote, compiled, and printed a large number of localist texts. As a result, though the production of such texts was initiated before the creation of the Xuehaitang, over the course of the nineteenth century the academy and its scholars came to dominate this process. Thus, the center of what is often viewed as a great nineteenth-century flourishing of Cantonese culture shifted from the delta hinterland to urban Guangzhou, as Xuehaitang scholars employed new scholarly approaches and literary styles to produce these texts. This chapter will examine three exemplary ways in which literati associated with the Xuehaitang reshaped the local cultural landscape through the production of texts: the writing of local history, the composition of poetry on the local, and the compilation of local anthologies.

LOCAL HISTORY

History was an important component of the Xuehaitang curriculum; after questions about classical exegesis, examinees were typically asked to address topics drawn from the earliest dynastic histories (see Appendix B). In addition to this, scholars associated with the Xuehaitang devoted a great deal of attention to producing local historical texts and, in the process, rewrote local history. Several of them had participated in the compilation of the provincial gazetteer, and this experience in turn provided impetus for the proliferation of local histories by bringing to light previously overlooked historical figures and sites. As we have seen, Ruan Yuan's emphasis, in the tradition of Gu Yanwu, on the importance of on-the-spot investigation of sites and artifacts, made of the provincial gazetteer a model for conducting a certain kind of historical study.

Aside from the ubiquitous presence of Xuehaitang scholars on the staffs of county, prefectural, and provincial gazetteer compilation bureaus (see Table 1), two antiquarian historians associated with the Xuehaitang turned their attention to more ancient local history. Working separately in the Daoguang era, Wu Lanxiu and Liang Tingnan (1796–1861) produced studies of a short-lived but notorious local regime. One of the Ten Kingdoms that ruled various regions of the former Tang empire in the tenth century, the Southern Han was founded by a regional satrap named Liu Yan, who declared himself emperor and established his capital in Guangzhou.

Though he was capable enough to gain control of most of Guangdong and Guangxi, Liu Yan earned a reputation for cruelty. He was succeeded by rulers depicted as equally cruel, less competent, and more extravagant, culminating in the last Southern Han ruler, Liu Chang, who saw his regime destroyed and himself taken captive by invading armies of the Northern Song.[5]

The earliest accounts of the Southern Han were written by southerners, such as the *Liushi xingwang lu* (Record of the rise and fall of the Liu house) by Hu Binwang (1000 *jinshi*). Although Hu's work had been available to Ming scholars, it was lost by the nineteenth century. After the survivors of the Southern Han passed from the scene, almost all historical accounts of the southern kingdom, such as dynastic histories of the Five Dynasties and Ten Kingdoms, were subsequently written by northerners. In the sixteenth and seventeenth centuries, a few Cantonese scholars began to take an interest in the Southern Han. For example, Qu Dajun (1630–96) incorporated anecdotes about the Southern Han in his Guangdong encyclopedia, *Guangdong xinyu*. These included descriptions of the Liu Yan and Liu Chang tombs and the inscriptions from the Eastern and Western Iron Stupas (two stupas produced by the Southern Han regime and housed in Guangxiao Monastery).[6] Reflecting the judgments proffered by northern historians, Qu offered a harsh critique of the Southern Han, but he focused attention on consequences for local inhabitants.[7] At about the same time, outside Guangzhou, the Southern Han did receive some attention in the *Shiguo chunqiu* (Annals of the Ten Kingdoms), compiled by Wu Renchen (1628–89), a native of Hangzhou. None of these references to the Southern Han, however, represented a sustained or systematic study of the local regime.

The early nineteenth-century revival of interest in the Southern Han was due in part to the agenda set by officials serving in Guangzhou. Through his promotion of the Yu Fan Shrine, Zeng Yu had drawn attention to Guangxiao Monastery, where such Southern Han artifacts as the Western and Eastern Stupas could be found. Similarly, compiling the provincial gazetteer under Ruan Yuan reminded local scholars of the importance of on-site examination of inscriptions in writing local history. Wu Lanxiu and Liang Tingnan emerged from this milieu as the two major local historians of the Southern Han.

Table 1
Xuehaitang Scholars as Compilers of Local Gazetteers

Gazetteer (date)	Chief editor(s)	Section compiler(s)	Map-maker(s)
Guangdong tongzhi (1822)	Xie Lansheng Jiang Fan	Wu Lanxiu Zeng Zhao Cui Bi Liu Huadong Zheng Haoruo Wu Yingkui Li Guangzhao	
Xiangshan xian zhi (1827)	Huang Peifang	Zeng Zhao Li Guangzhou	
Zhaoqing fu zhi (1833)	Huang Peifang Jiang Fan		
Nanhai xian zhi (1835)	Xie Lansheng Tan Ying	Xiong Jingxing Zeng Zhao Zhang Le Hu Tiaode	
Heshan xian zhi (1836)	Wu Yingkui		
Xinhui xian zhi (1840)	Huang Peifang Zeng Zhao	Ruan Rongling	
Changle xian zhi (Daoguang era?)	Wen Xun		
Longmen xian zhi (1851)	Zhang Weiping		
Shunde xian zhi (1853)	Liang Tingnan		
Panyu xian zhi (1871)		Chen Li Chen Pu Jin Xiling	
Nanhai xian zhi (1872)		Tan Ying Li Zhengwei Zou Boqi	Luo Zhaocang Kong Jifan
Guangzhou fu zhi (1879)	Li Guangting	Zhou Yinqing Tan Ying Chen Pu Jin Xiling Tan Zongjun Li Zhengwei	Chen Li
Xianshan xian zhi (1873/1880*)	Chen Li		Luo Zhaocang
Xinning xian zhi (1891)	Lin Guogeng		

*The title page of this edition of the Xiangshan gazetteer is dated 1873, but the preface, authored by Chen Li, is dated 1880.

At the time of the early Xuehaitang examinations, Wu Lanxiu began a decade of research, preparing copious notes for three historical works on the Southern Han: *Nan-Han ji* (Annals of the Southern Han), *Nan-Han dili zhi* (Gazetteer of Southern Han geography), and *Nan-Han jinshi zhi* (Gazetteer of Southern Han inscriptions). The *Nan-Han ji* was modeled upon Xun Yue's (148–209) *Han ji*, which in turn was an abstract of Ban Gu's (32–92) *Han shu*. In contrast to the *Han shu*, the material in Xun's work was arranged in strictly chronological order, with passages from Ban Gu's treatises and biographies inserted into the chronological annals.[8] Wu Lanxiu likewise gave all of his information in chronological order, but, consulting various sources, he incorporated materials that were normally excluded from standard dynastic histories. Unlike Xun Yue's work—but true to Xuehaitang scholarly practice—Wu used extensive interlinear commentary to list sources of information, to offer explanatory quotes from other sources and comments, and to provide variant readings of characters or passages. Wu drew on a wide array of textual sources, but, more importantly, he also made frequent reference throughout the *Nan-Han ji* to the information on inscriptions contained in his *Nan-Han jinshi zhi*.

It seems that Wu Lanxiu's main purpose, rather than that of condemning what many judged to be an immoral or incompetent regime, was to gather reliable information documenting the Southern Han experience. Unlike some historians writing during the Song, Wu used Southern Han reign titles and dates rather than those of the "legitimate" northern dynasties. Conversely, he referred to each Southern Han leader—from Liu Yan to Liu Chang—as the "Han ruler" (*Han zhu*) rather than "emperor." Jiang Fan, who had worked with Wu Lanxiu on the provincial gazetteer staff, wrote a postscript for the *Nan-Han ji* in which he emphasized Wu's accomplishments in evidential research. According to Jiang, because Wu Lanxiu was meticulous in citing sources, his work was far superior to Wu Renchen's *Shiguo chunqiu*.[9] Wu Lanxiu's colleague at the Xuehaitang, Tan Ying, also praised his work. Tan asserted that the *Nan-Han ji* "is the best among books that record the affairs of the Ten Kingdoms," implying that the outstanding history of any regime of the Five Dynasties and Ten Kingdoms period was a history of the Guangdong regime written by a Guangdong native.[10]

The other major historian of the Southern Han working during the 1820s was Liang Tingnan.[11] A Shunde native, Liang had deeper genealogical roots in the Pearl River delta than did Wu Lanxiu, but his interest in the Southern Han stemmed from time spent in the city. In the preface to his *Nan-Han shu* (History of the Southern Han), written in the winter of 1829–1830, Liang noted that he was inspired to study Southern Han history because of an experience in his youth. When residing at Guangxiao Monastery, he made rubbings of inscriptions on the Western and Eastern Iron Stupas forged in the Southern Han. Reading the inscriptions, Liang noticed inconsistencies with Wu Renchen's *Shiguo chunqiu*.[12] Here, Liang reiterated one of the most important scholarly creeds articulated by Ruan Yuan: one needed to gain access to local history through on-site investigations of metal and stone inscriptions and other materials. The implication of this was that a native, or at least a long-term resident in the Pearl River delta, was in the best position to do this and thereby more likely to produce a complete and accurate picture of the Southern Han.

Modeled on Ban Gu's *Han shu*, the *Nan-Han shu* consists of imperial annals (*benji*) and biographies (*liezhuan*), though it lacks the tables and treatises found in most standard histories. Like Wu Lanxiu's *Nan-Han ji*, Liang Tingnan's history includes in the main texts of his annals information drawn from a wide variety of sources, most importantly stele inscriptions, not found in previous studies of the Southern Han. For example, one learns from his annals of Liu Chang that in 964 a copper bell was cast by imperial order for the Longevity Monastery in Xingwang superior prefecture (the prefecture where the Southern Han capital was located, the area around modern-day Guangzhou city). He also mentions in the annals when rhapsodies (*fu*) were composed by Southern Han literati to celebrate the construction of various palaces.[13] Instead of providing variant readings of characters in interlinear notes, Liang compiled a companion volume of such notes entitled *Nan-Han shu kaoyi* (Variant readings in the *Nan-Han shu*).

These two major studies of the Southern Han by Wu Lanxiu and Liang Tingnan called attention to a local history that predated the late Northern Song, when, according to claims of the most common foundation legends, migrant ancestors of the dominant lineages of the delta hinterland first settled the region. Seemingly, this was a history without much tangible connection to nineteenth-century residents. Nevertheless, the new popularity of textual and inscriptional studies gave Xuehaitang scholars the tools and motivation for re-examining the remote history of Guangzhou and the delta. If Wu Lanxiu and Liang Tingnan did not entirely reverse previous historical judgments of the Southern Han, their studies at least reappropriated the history of this local regime as their own and thereby opened up new possibilities in the study of local history.

POETRY ABOUT THE LOCAL

Composition of poetry based on local themes also thrived as a product of the Xuehaitang, but this type of cultural production exhibited a more celebratory tone than did histories of the Southern Han. In general, poetry is an aspect of academy education in late imperial China that has received very little attention. Yet it was a regular part of examinations at academies such as Yuexiu and Yuehua, because of the mid-eighteenth-century reintroduction of poetry questions into the civil service examinations.[14] The facts that the vast majority of contributors to the *Xuehaitang ji* were included as poets and that poetry exercises occupied the largest portions of all four series of Xuehaitang collected writing attest to the importance of poetry in the new academy's curriculum. Moreover, themes common to Xuehaitang poetry exercises in turn were imitated at other academies in Guangzhou and also appeared in verse composed by Cantonese poets at outings throughout the city.

Ruan Yuan's literary agenda is evident in the poetry exercises conducted at the Xuehaitang, as seen in the prevalence of such pre-Tang literary forms as rhapsodies and old-style poetry (*guti shi*). Tang poetry was also an important component of the literary exercises, as Du Fu (712–70) was often presented as a model for imitation; yet the popular Tang-style quatrains (*jueju*) are noticeably absent from the *Xuehaitang ji*. The most striking aspect of the poetry collected in the *Xuehaitang ji* is not its stylistic characteristics but rather its thematic content: the overwhelming majority of poems in the collection can be characterized as "localist" poetry. Such poetry exercises ask students to categorize, describe, or glorify local peoples, products, scenery, or literary accomplishments. These include (to name a few examples in addition to the ones described below): adaptations of Du Fu's "Wandering in the Hilly Woods of General He" to scenes in the Guangzhou suburbs; an imitation of "Observing the Moon While Longing for the Remote," a poem by the pioneer of Cantonese poetry in the Tang, Zhang Jiuling; and a set of five exercises describing the scenery of White Cloud Mountain, site of the old Cloud and Springs Mountain Lodge.[15] Such exercises were certainly common in late imperial China; imitating outstanding examples of verse by altering original themes to suit local environments was a natural method of training young poets. Nevertheless, when compared to the curriculum at Ruan Yuan's Gujing jingshe in Hangzhou, poetry exercises were much more important at the Guangzhou academy. Of the poetry contained in the first editions of collected writings from the two academies, both compiled under the direction of Ruan Yuan, local themes are noticeably more prevalent in the Xuehaitang collection.[16]

The centerpiece of the poetry included in the *Xuehaitang ji*—an exercise in which examinees were asked to match "Hundred Chants on the South Sea Region"—occupies a full two *juan* and begins the *shi* poetry section of the collection. The original "Hundred Chants" had been written by a Fujian native, Fang Xinru (1177-1222), who served as an official in Guangdong. In this set of poems, Fang described one hundred natural and historical sites in and around Guangzhou and prefaced each poem with a detailed note on the location, origin, or vicissitudes of the site depicted in verse. Whereas Fang composed these poems in quatrains, Xuehaitang poets kept with the academy's literary agenda, matching the original themes using tetrasyllabic old-style poetry. Fang's original prefaces were included in the collection; several of the new poems contained supplemental interlinear notes added by the Xuehaitang authors. Over thirty examinees who participated in this exercise had at least one poem selected for inclusion in the *Xuehaitang ji*. Yi Kezhong had the most selected (36 in all) and was said to have completed them in a single night, impressing Ruan Yuan with this display of talent.[17]

As Ruan Yuan left no preface to this or any other set of poems in the *Xuehaitang ji*, it is difficult to assess the motivation behind this exercise. It is nevertheless clear that Jiang Fan, one of many Jiangnan literati attracted by Ruan to Guangzhou, contributed to the circulation of Fang Xinru's text among Cantonese scholarly circles in 1821. In the summer of that year, Wu Lanxiu wrote a postscript to an edition of the text that he was hoping to print, in which he noted that he had prepared the text from a manuscript edition that he had borrowed from Jiang Fan.[18] This suggests that the text was not widely available in Guangzhou before Jiang Fan brought it there. In his postscript, Wu Lanxiu praised the collection not only for its elegant verse but also for its evidential research, which provides a clue as to the motivation behind the central place that the "Hundred Chants" occupied in the *Xuehaitang ji*.[19] Many of the poems in this set and elsewhere in the collection were exercises in the application of evidential research methods to archaeological, epigraphical, and historical investigations. Fang Xinru's detailed prefaces provided both models to follow and assertions to confirm or disprove in the supplemental notes inserted by the Xuehaitang poets. The *kaozheng* tone at times even appeared in the poetry itself, as in a couplet from Li Guangzhao's poem on Yu Hill:

> By the ancient glosses, the characters for *Yu* and *yu* are interchangeable;[20]
> That is to say, Yu Hill used to be connected to the city's
>   southern corner.[21]

In an interlinear note, Li pointed out an example of this interchangeable usage from the *Shanhai jing* (Classic of mountains and seas).

Another thing that stands out about the "Hundred Chants" exercise is that the subject of these investigations was local history. Fang's original poems dealt with numerous remains and relics from the Southern Han regime and, to a lesser extent, the earlier Southern Yue kingdom. Most Xuehaitang poets, following the judgments of the standard histories, characterized the Southern Han regime as illegitimate and its rulers as audacious. A typical example is the following excerpt from one poem on the "Bronze Images of the Lius," referring to bronze engravings of the Southern Han ruler Liu Chang and his two sons:

> Travelers all remarked upon the skill of [Southern Han] artisans,
>   But did not know that
> The [images] were completed with the blood of these artisans.

From that time, once a summons for an image went out,
The hundred artisans dared not come to Southern Yue.[22]

The poets could not, however, ignore the significant ways in which the regime had left its mark upon the local landscape. These included, in addition to building temples, walls, and other structures, such feats as flattening mountains and dredging lakes. Vestiges of the Southern Han thus appeared in poem after poem. Moreover, poetry and historical scholarship reinforced one another—Wu Lanxiu, author of the *Nan-Han ji*, contributed six "Hundred Chants" pieces.

In short, this largest set of poems included in the *Xuehaitang ji* was as much an exercise in the application of the tools of evidential research as it was training in the composition of verse. Furthermore, both the verse and the often extensive interlinear notes depicted local history and, if not always glorifying such regimes as the Southern Han, certainly made readers aware of their impact; this in turn served to portray the circle of poets gathered at the Xuehaitang as the custodians of early Cantonese culture. This exercise also stimulated the production of similar poems outside the Xuehaitang. Xie Lansheng used two "Hundred Chants" poems—"Elixir Islet" and "Brush-Bequeathed Study"—as a Yangcheng Academy test topic in late 1821.[23] In the 1840s, Fan Feng wrote a continuation of the "Hundred Chants," adding even more painstakingly detailed notes about various sites not mentioned in the original work.[24]

Next to the "Hundred Chants," the largest set of poems in the *Xuehaitang ji* extolled the virtues of Guangdong's most famous fruit, the litchi. Like the "Hundred Chants," the "Lingnan Litchi Songs" were replete with detailed notes on local phenomena, pointing out very specialized varieties of litchi and methods of cultivation unique to a certain county or village. Reminiscent of "bamboo branch songs" (*zhuzhi ci*), the "Litchi Songs" were written in quatrains that imitated popular language and incorporated some local dialect. Though such a topic might strike some readers as frivolous, local products were perceived as important regional symbols, as meaningful as were historical artifacts from local kingdoms of the past. In comparing native produce to that of other regions, the Xuehaitang poets pointed to the injustices and parochialism inherent in previous rankings of litchi varieties by natives of Fujian and

Sichuan. In particular, they took aim at a series of litchi handbooks authored by Fujianese literati: Cai Xiang (1012–67), Xu Bo (1570–1642), and Deng Qingcai (fl. 1620s).[25] This can be seen in parts of the set of 60 poems authored by Tan Ying and so admired by Ruan Yuan:

#55

> Up to now there has been no universally accepted critique of superior and inferior [litchi varieties];
> Yet who will still contest the quality [of litchi varieties] in the south?
> Zhu Yizun[26] naturally was a predecessor who discerned fairly;
> In demoting the purple and rewarding the red, his judgments were the most balanced.[27]

In an explanatory note to this poem, Tan observed:

> Zhu Yizun states, "Among litchis, the ultimate is the 'chess green' [variety] produced in Guangdong. Fine varieties from Fuzhou still cannot match [even] the 'black leaf' variety of Lingnan. When Cai asserts in his *Handbook* that 'the most exquisite varieties of Guangnan only compare to lower varieties from Eastern Fujian,' he is merely expressing local bias."[28]

#59

> Litchi handbooks; everyone says their arguments are hackneyed;
> "Bright achievements" drawn in red, the ink resplendent and fresh.
> Accomplished elders in the modern day grieve for the withered and fallen;
> Admonishing Cai and refuting Xu must await Guangdong natives.[29]

Again, Tan adds an explanatory note:

> I have heard that Wen Rugua wrote a *Lingnan Litchi Handbook*.[30] [Lu You's] *Random Notes from the Old Scholar's Cottage* states, "Yu Shen quit government and resided in Fuzhou. In the mansion was a litchi tree that was absolutely huge and beautiful. It was called the 'bright achievement.' 'Red bright achievement' was the name of an imperially bestowed library in Yu Shen's home." The preface to Deng Qingcai's *Litchi Handbook* does not dare to admonish Xu or remonstrate with Cai.[31]

Tan and the Xuehaitang poets were referring to more than the agricultural products of Guangdong; in another poem Tan made explicit the connection between litchis on the one hand and literature about the litchi on the other. The literati tradition of writing about the litchi began, at least in the minds of Xuehaitang poets, with the great progenitor of Lingnan poetry, Zhang Jiuling, and his "Rhapsody on the Litchi." In his preface to the rhapsody, Zhang had bemoaned the fact that northern literati paid no attention to the luscious southern fruit.[32] In addition to Zhang's rhapsody, the Xuehaitang poets also frequently alluded to Su Shi's *shi* poems on the litchi, most often the second of two poems entitled "Eating Litchis." In this poem, Su claimed that, since he (with the help of his staff?) daily ingested three hundred litchis, there would be no harm in long remaining a resident of Lingnan.[33] Conveniently overlooking the fact that Su was a native of Sichuan *banished* to Guangdong, Tan and the Xuehaitang poets appropriated his poem for the literary canon of the Cantonese litchi:

#54

Both the Sichuan painting and Fujian handbooks investigated
   the unusual;[34]
Yet this rustic fellow [Tan] still lays claim to producing exquisite verse.
Who will raise his hand for Eastern Yue literary compositions?
After Zhang Jiuling's rhapsody, there was Su Shi's poem.[35]

Another Xuehaitang poet, Li Rumei of Jiaying, incorporates the final line of Su Shi's poem in the last of his three "Lingnan Litchi Songs." Yet by altering the context of the line, Li strengthens even further its affirmation of Su's supposed desire to reside in Lingnan:

Vermilion clouds in the center of the sky dissipate into fragrant dust;
The mountains and rivers of the Hundred Yue are renewed in
   clustered brocade.[36]
Little wonder that Yuju Supervisor Su Shi from Emei[37]
Only thought of becoming a long-term Lingnan resident.[38]

Going further, Liang Mei plays with Su Shi's line in describing his own status as a native of Lingnan:

Since birth I have been fortunate enough to be a Lingnan resident
On summer outings and spring outings, with no concern for poverty.
Day after day in succession eating three hundred,
My official title should be declared the "litchi person."[39]

Finally, Lin Botong abandoned all allusion and made explicit the connection between the litchis of Lingnan and the talented scholars of Guangdong, who he felt had largely been ignored outside of the province:

> South-facing branches of the Great Yu Range include the ancient plum;[40]
> Yet among the fruits the fragrant litchi also contends for greatness.
> It is comparable to recommending scholars, seeking a generation of renowned ones;
> From the distant past South of Heaven has never lacked talents.[41]

In interlinear commentary, Lin explained the analogy between comparing fruits and recommending scholars: "According to the *Guoshi bu*, [the Tang official] Li Zhifang once ranked fruit names as if recommending scholars. Someone recommended the litchi. He said, 'We should pass it in the top position.'"[42]

It was not uncommon for Cantonese scholars to praise their esteemed companions by comparing them to the celebrated fruit of the region; in an 1819 lyric poem marking an outing to Litchi Cove, Yi Kezhong had described his companion Wu Lanxiu as "Guangdong's precious fruit."[43] Now employing this literary device in the Xuehaitang exercise on the litchi, the Xuehaitang poets intimated that the cultural, as well as the agricultural, products of Guangdong had not gained their deserved recognition throughout the empire. If the Cantonese poets at the Xuehaitang ultimately meant to refer to native literary and scholarly talent, then Ruan Yuan did not necessarily share their high assessment of Cantonese literature and scholarship. In 1823, precisely during the span of five years in which the *Xuehaitang ji* poetry exercises were being conducted, Ruan composed a poem on the star fruit (*yangtao*) of his native Jiangnan, contrasting it with the Lingnan litchi. Here Ruan characterized the litchi of Lingnan as piquant but rated the fruit—and by implication, the elite culture—of Jiangnan as more subtle and ultimately of higher value. His poem reads:

> The litchi is produced in Lingnan;
> Its fame was already great in the Han and Tang.
> Its flavor is voluptuous and its nature fiery;
> How can such an exceptional thing not be harmful?
> Who would have expected that the "five-corner peach"[44]

With its clear and subtle taste would in the end be better?
But if we try asking someone who understands flavors,
We will discover that true flavor lies beyond merely the sour or sweet.[45]

Praising the litchi was nothing new among Cantonese poets; the Xuehaitang poets, however, did so in a very novel way. They employed the tools of evidential research, newly promoted at the Xuehaitang, to produce a large corpus of writing about the litchi. In doing so, they enhanced their legitimacy as the most capable arbiters of local Cantonese culture.

ANTHOLOGIES I: LUO XUEPENG AND THE *GUANGDONG WENXIAN*

In addition to works of history and poetry, a large number of anthologies of prose and poetry by previous or contemporary Cantonese writers were produced in Guangzhou during the nineteenth century. Several anthologies of Cantonese literature had been compiled during the late Ming and very early Qing dynasties. According to David Faure, the sixteenth century witnessed a cultural coming of age for the elite of the Pearl River delta. An important element in this process was the scholarly elite's representation of literati culture in Guangdong as being centered in the delta.[46] The few notable scholars and statesmen that Guangdong produced before the Ming—such as Zhang Jiuling of the Tang and Yu Jing (1000–1064) of the Song—had typically been natives of the far northern prefecture of Shaozhou, bordering on Nanxiong. The Ming elite claimed them as their own cultural forebears and at the same time shifted the cultural core of Guangdong southward toward the delta. This can be seen, for example, in the 32-*juan Lingnan wenxian*, which assembled the writings of 260 scholars, from Zhang Jiuling through delta-based scholars in the Wanli reign (1573–1619).[47] Printing of Ou Huairui's *Jiaoya*, a collection of over 500 poets, was never completed; it still circulated among early Qing scholars in manuscript form.[48] This initial boom in the production of local anthologies culminated in Qu Dajun's 1687 *Guangdong wenxuan*, a collection of prose and poetry in 39 *juan*. These early anthologies of Cantonese literature typically began with Zhang Jiuling, who was considered to be the cultural progenitor in Guangdong; the works of anyone before Zhang were thought irretrievable or irrelevant.

During the eighteenth century, there were few such attempts to create comprehensive Cantonese anthologies, but a second phase of such compilations began early in the next century, with several anthologies predating the establishment of the Xuehaitang.[49] Wen Runeng (1748–1811), a scholar from the Wen lineage in Longshan, relied on his own resources to print a pair of compilations of Lingnan prose, the 66-*juan Yuedong wenhai*, and poetry, the *Yuedong shihai* in 100 *juan*. Two other collections were first printed in 1813 and featured contemporary poets: the *Guochao Linghai shichao*, edited by Ling Yangzao of Panyu, and the *Lingnan qunya*, compiled by Yuehua Academy director Liu Binhua. Also in the last decade of the Jiaqing reign, Luo Xuepeng printed the first installment of an ambitious anthology of writings of moral exemplars from Guangdong's past. In the early Daoguang reign, Chen Zaiqian collected eighteen recent and contemporary writers of *guwen* prose—including many members of the Xigutang group—in his *Guochao Lingnan wenchao*.[50]

In their various constructions of Cantonese culture, anthology editors brought with them their own preferences and agendas, working to depict to a particular audience a version of tradition that suited their particular needs. Nevertheless, anthologies produced in the delta hinterland before the establishment of the Xuehaitang shared many elements, in contrast to anthologies later collaboratively produced by the Xuehaitang scholar Tan Ying and the maritime merchant Wu Chongyao. Through the efforts of Tan and others, Xuehaitang scholars took over the initiative in the production of local anthologies and, in the process, redirected the focus of Cantonese high culture from the delta to the city. This contrast can be illustrated by a comparison of a typical pre-Xuehaitang, delta-based anthology, Luo Xuepeng's *Guangdong wenxian*, with one of several anthologies produced by the Xuehaitang scholar Tan Ying.

A native of Daliang in Shunde, Luo Xuepeng was not a major figure in the scholarly world of urban Guangzhou, but he belonged to a prestigious and powerful lineage. The Daliang Luo—comprising two separate lineages, one northern and one southern—produced a number of scholars during the Qing who earned distinction in the civil service examinations, including Luo Dunyan (1814–74), who would serve as president of the Board of Personnel in the 1870s. Luo Xuepeng's only noteworthy direct relative, his great-grandfather Luo Lianghui, gained a place in gazetteers for his acts of filial piety in the face of pirates during the Kangxi era.[51] Likewise, Luo Xuepeng did not achieve great success in the examinations. He spent some years in the capital as a state student, but returned to his native Shunde after several failed attempts in the examinations. Between 1808 and 1810, Shunde and other coastal districts were plagued by pirates roaming the complicated network of waterways, this time under the notorious Zhang Bao.[52] This initiated a new phase of increased violence in Guangdong that would last for several decades. Luo Xuepeng responded by presenting a memorial on the problem to the Guangdong-Guangxi governor-general; Luo later submitted to his successor policy proposals on coastal security and the purchase of imported rice. Despite the fact that the two governors-general are said to have adopted some of his proposals, Luo was never in a position to realize any far-reaching administrative ambitions.[53]

Aside from pursuing these aspirations, Luo had throughout his life transcribed selections from *wenji* (literary collections) of past Guangdong scholars when he happened upon them. After becoming frustrated with the examinations, he began in 1805 to pursue this hobby in earnest. Biographies of Luo claim that he initiated the process of compiling the *Guangdong wenxian* when he was "old and poor." In fact, Luo must have commanded substantial financial resources to have considered compiling such an anthology; it was to be printed in several installments at his Spring Radiance Thatched Hall (Chunhui caotang), outside Daliang's east gate.[54] Luo printed his own poetry collection, *Chunhui caotang shiji*, there as well. Nevertheless, financing the project did become a burden. He was compelled to sell property and could finish printing only the first installment before his death in December 1817. His two sons carried on the project, but at one point were also forced, due to insufficient funding, to discontinue printing the second and third installments. These were eventually completed, and another Shunde native, Pan Shichang, helped in the editing of the fourth installment. Installments two through four included long lists of proofreaders—literati from Shunde and a few from other counties, only one of whom ever appeared in Xuehaitang records.⁵⁵ The *Guangdong wenxian* is recorded in the 1822 provincial gazetteer as a four-installment collection in 18, 9, 18, and 26 *juan*, a tally consistent with later versions of the collection.⁵⁶ A planned fifth installment was never produced, although the first four installments were reprinted in 1863.

Despite having begun his work as an individual project, Luo felt compelled to seek the advice of more eminent colleagues. He availed himself of a fellow Shunde native to present an early draft to Ruan Yuan's predecessor as governor-general, who appreciated the work and prepared some comments but was transferred out of Guangdong before Luo could request that he contribute a preface.⁵⁷ Luo also showed his work to a fellow Shunde scholar, Feng Longguan. Feng was a member of a lineage with a strong *lixue* tradition, but his own interests leaned toward evidential research: he was a noted book collector who excelled in research on geography and metal and stone inscriptions.⁵⁸ Feng felt the compilation to be incomplete and to contain some errors; he did, however, later write a eulogy of Luo that was included in later editions at the beginning of the first installment.

Although Luo Xuepeng might have been plagued with uncertainties about the organization of the *Guangdong wenxian*, the prefaces and editorial standards construct for the reader a coherent, organic Cantonese literary tradition. The format and design of printed editions of the anthology also convey the normative purpose of the *Guangdong wenxian* and suggest the wide audience to which it was directed. For example, a banner at the top of the title page of the 1863 edition, also printed at the Luo studio in Daliang, reads, "Lingnan personages of the first order"—that is, figures who can serve as moral exemplars for Cantonese in particular (see Fig. 5). The paratext of the *Guangdong wenxian*, ranging from the title page to the long lists of proofreaders, more closely resembles that of a commercially produced book than a literary collection aimed at a selective audience.⁵⁹

The beginning of Luo's 1814 preface to the first installment anticipates the tone of the poem quoted at the outset of the chapter in its recognition that Guangdong is too remote a region to have benefited from the imperial bestowal of three *Siku quanshu* copies to the Jiangnan region.⁶⁰ Guangdong deserved a repository of its own,

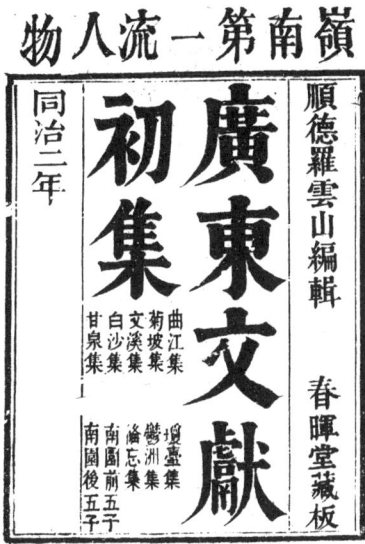

FIG. 5: Title page for the 1863 edition of Luo Xuepeng's *Guangdong wenxian*. The line across the top of the page reads: "Lingnan personages of the first order."

Luo argues, but required one dedicated only to the essential works, unlike the overly comprehensive *Siku quanshu*. Luo then explains his standards in assessing what works should be included in this category:

> In discussing the ancients, great moral fortitude is of primary concern, not just their speech and writings. Thus what is recorded in this humble selection consistently and carefully sticks to this purpose. In general, it includes the necessary as opposed to the detailed and values the essential as opposed to the numerous.... Moreover, if one wants books to circulate widely, they must be simple and convenient. If [this anthology were so massive as to] sweat an ox and stuff a cart, then its circulation would become stagnant and difficult to carry out.[61]

Such a view at first seems at odds with the goals of a compiler attempting to rescue a local cultural tradition from sinking into oblivion. Yet, considered in the context of the growing availability of printed literature in Guangdong at this time, Luo in his preface implies that the tradition he seeks to preserve runs the risk of being lost in a deluge of books. At the same time, Luo argues in his editorial principles that parochialism has inhibited the circulation of crucial literary and historical texts of the Cantonese canon. As Luo describes it, "The Zhang lineage will not glance at a collection of Li writings, and the Li lineage will not glance at a Zhang collection."[62] Luo's aims as a compiler, then, work in cross directions: he wishes not only to present an inclusive Cantonese literary canon but also to limit the parameters of that canon to what he sees as its essentials.

These parameters become evident in the organizational principles of the compilation. Luo portrays the figures included in the first installment as residing at the pinnacle of the Cantonese literary canon. As with the late Ming compilations, the *Guangdong wenxian* begins with the literary collection of the Tang poet and statesman Zhang Jiuling. This is followed by the *Jinjian lu*, a series of admonitions in ten topics that Zhang presented to the Tang emperor Xuanzong (r. 712–55) on the occasion of the emperor's birthday. Many of Luo Xuepeng's contemporaries believed extant versions of the *Jinjian lu* to be Song and Ming forgeries, but Luo defended the text's veracity. Next, Luo includes selected writings of two Song statesmen from Guangdong: Cui Yuzhi, one of the icons honored by the Cloud and Springs group, and Li Maoying (1201–57). They are followed by Chen Xianzhang and Zhan Ruoshui (1466–1560), creators of the Cantonese school of *lixue* during the Ming. Luo follows these with selected works of three political figures in the Ming: Qiu Jun, a grand secretary and author of the *Zhuzi xuedi* so emphasized by Liu Binhua at Yuehua Academy; Liang Chu (1453–1527), also a grand secretary and a fellow native of Shunde; and Hai Rui (1514–87), the county magistrate hailed as an upright defender of the common people.[63] Luo rounded out the first installment with selected poetry of the Former and Later Five Masters of the Southern Garden. The Former Five Masters, led by Sun Fen (1337–93), formed a literary society in Guangzhou during the early years of the Ming. The Later Five Masters recreated their tradition in the Jiajing reign. In the editorial principles, Luo explains that these most exemplary Cantonese forebears are arranged in chronological order by dynasty. Within the same dynasty they are arranged categorically in declining order of importance, from *lixue* philosophers, to officials, and finally to men of letters.[64]

Although Luo differentiates among these three categories, he conceives of all of the figures in the first installment as embodying, in different ways, the spirit of *lixue*. He draws upon a passage in the Zuo Commentary to the *Chunqiu* that explains three accomplishments by which one can be remembered after death. The first, virtue, is of the highest meaning. It is followed by achievements of deed and, in turn, by achievements of word.[65] Luo relates these to accomplishments in moral philosophy, government service, and literature:

Our eminent predecessors in Yue all produced great achievements from flourishing virtue and produced fine words from moral conduct. As examples, there are: the *Jinjian lu* preceding Han Yu in critiquing Buddha and Laozi and preceding Cheng [Yi] and Zhu [Xi] in promoting the *Doctrine of the Mean*; Cui Yuzhi's notion that "if none are not reverent then inner reverence will be constantly preserved, and if thoughts have no wickedness, then it will be difficult for external wickedness to enter . . ."; Li Maoying's idea that "the inner is important, the outer is not"; Sun Fen's maxim to "investigate until reaching the principle of nature and fate of Heaven and Man"; Qiu Jun's work, *Zhuzi xuedi*; and Hai Rui's desiring to learn to be a sage or worthy from the time he began study.[66] None of these [achievements in deed or word] did not proceed from *xin* (mind/heart) and *xing* (nature). Indeed, not only Chen [Xianzhang] and Zhan [Ruoshui] were famous practitioners of *lixue*.[67]

In Luo's conceptualization, the common thread that linked the diverse achievements of all these great philosophers, statesmen, and poets of the Cantonese past was their practice of *lixue*. Luo suggested that the reader could see in these moral exemplars the spirit of the Northern Song Neo-Confucian Cheng Yi and, beyond him, that of Confucius and Mencius as well. Yet the spirit embodied in their achievement was at the same time unique to Guangdong. The lofty moral fortitude (*gaofeng*) of Zhang Jiuling and Cui Yuzhi or the integrity of direct remonstrance (*zhijie*) in Hai Rui was seen as representative of "our Yue." Luo asked the reader, "Who says Southerners are [morally] feeble?!"[68]

In the second installment, Luo continues to use themes of moral achievement as a means of organizing his selection. He wishes to recognize here outstanding examples of determined integrity that were not completely covered in the first installment.[69] A large portion of the second installment is devoted to four late Ming figures who "sacrificed themselves for their lord" and whose "loyalty and righteousness" are expressed in the compositions they wrote. All of these moral exemplars were Ming loyalists, three of them martyrs.[70] Luo points out that, although Chen Bangyan (1603–47), Kuang Lu, Li Suiqiu (1602–46), and Han Shanggui (1572–1644) came from different counties—Nanhai, Panyu and Shunde—their native townships or villages all lay within a hundred-*li* area at the confluence of these three counties. Their self-sacrifice, then, can be attributed only to the "brilliance of spirit of the mountains and rivers" in their native place.[71] Luo also included in the second installment two collected biographies of former worthies; one of these was *Record of Famous Worthies Arranged by Prefecture*, a work compiled by his great-grandfather, Luo Lianghui.

The third installment of the *Guangdong wenxian* is dedicated to the Ming-era followers of Chen Xianzhang who embodied the principles of *lixue* in their scholarship. There seems to be less coherence to the fourth installment than to the previous three, but it appears to be a celebration of lineage and group literary traditions. For example, Luo includes, with local pride, a section devoted to the Five Masters of the Phoenix City (Daliang). Unlike other groups of Cantonese poets during the Qing, Luo points out that these five Shunde poets shared a common native county as well as a common poetics.[72] This installment is the first in the collection to contain works by Qing scholars, with the exception of the *Record of Famous Worthies* in the second installment; Luo Lianghui's work, however, only collected biographies of people who had lived in the Ming and earlier.

Moreover, none of the Qing poets included in the fourth installment were contemporaries of Luo. The most recent writings were those of Pan Wenyin, grandfather of the fourth installment's collator, Pan Shichang. It is conceivable, but difficult to demonstrate, that the planned fifth installment would have been devoted to contemporary figures. Significantly, Luo seems to have been unable to find great philosophers or statesmen to represent the Qing; thus the fourth installment is composed entirely of poets. Poetry was indeed a strength of Cantonese literati during the early and mid-Qing. Yet, in Luo's view, accomplishments in literature—though commendable and hence worthy of inclusion in such a compilation as this—were somehow of a lower order than achievements in statesmanship or moral philosophy. This dearth of statesmen and *lixue* philosophers could not have been lost on Luo. Hence, one wonders whether Luo saw his anthology as preserving a vibrant tradition, or as commemorating one in the process of vanishing.

ANTHOLOGIES II: TAN YING AND THE *LINGNAN YISHU*

In contrast to Luo Xuepeng's project, the most important anthologies produced in Guangzhou prefecture during the middle of the nineteenth century benefited from the sponsorship of wealthy urban merchants and the editorial expertise of a community of scholars who had been building book collections of their own. In particular, several important compilations emerged from a collaborative effort between the maritime merchant Wu Chongyao and the Xuehaitang scholar Tan Ying. The largest of these was the *Yueyatang congshu* (Collectanea from the Hall of Yue Refinement), a collection of nearly two hundred rare works from the Tang through the Qing, irrespective of the native-place origin of the authors.[73] Three other Wu-Tan collaborations resulted in anthologies of Cantonese writers: the *Chuting qijiu yishi*, a collection of recent and contemporary poets; the *Yue shisanjia ji*, a collective publication of thirteen rare *wenji* of Ming and Qing scholars; and the *Lingnan yishu* (Surviving works from Lingnan), the focus of the following discussion. Tan also helped in the printing of the salt merchant Pan Shicheng's *Haishan xianguan congshu* (Collectanea from the Sea Mountain Immortals' Lodge).[74] This cooperation between merchant capital and scholarly expertise enabled compilation and printing on a scale unprecedented in Guangzhou. At the same time, it provided an opportunity to put forth a new scholarly agenda, which in turn offered alternative constructions of the Cantonese cultural canon.

The financial patron and nominal editor of the *Lingnan yishu* was Wu Chongyao. A scion of the Yihe firm's Wu family, and younger brother of Wu Yuansong, Wu Chongyao had continued the family's strategy of making large donations for public causes, for which the state had conferred upon him a *juren* degree.[75] The younger Wu assumed the head of the family firm in 1833, after his older brother, Wu Yuanhua, was forced to resign due to accusations of involvement in the contraband opium trade. Despite the dissolution, with the conclusion of the Opium War, of the maritime merchants' Cohong monopoly on foreign trade, Wu Chongyao continued to play a leading role in public affairs, negotiating with foreigners in the 1840s and 1850s and raising funds for the defense against a rebel siege of Guangzhou in 1854. The family fortune was maintained into the Tongzhi reign (1862–74), and Wu Chongyao's generation went even further in realizing the family's aspirations of attaining literati status.[76] Wu had studied under the family's resident scholar, Zhong Qishao, whose poetry he printed. Both Chongyao and a cousin, Wu Yuankui, also printed collections of their own poetry. As an adult, Chongyao hired the noted prose stylist and Xuehaitang scholar Xu Yubin to teach the Wu children at Myriad Pines in Henan.[77] Zou Boqi (1819–69), the mathematics expert at the Xuehaitang, in 1861 was a long-term guest at the Wu family's Xiguan residence, where he had access to Western astronomical texts.[78]

Just as his father and uncles had lured Xie Lansheng and other literati with access to calligraphy and painting, Wu Chongyao enticed members of the scholarly community with opportunities to contribute to large anthologies. The Cantonese literatus hired by Wu to assess and compile the rare books in his library collection was the Xiguan resident and Xuehaitang scholar Tan Ying, who had won the appreciation of Ruan Yuan for his expertise in parallel prose as well as his cycle of "Lingnan Litchi Songs."[79] When not serving as a county educational official or at an academy, Tan spent his time in Guangzhou exploring his interest in surveying the literary and scholarly heritage of his native region. Thus, when Tan was invited to move from his modest "scholar's vegetable patch" to Wu Chongyao's magnificent "ink estate" to edit Wu's anthologies, he gladly accepted.[80] In compiling the *Lingnan yishu* between 1831 and 1863, Tan Ying brought together a total of 61 texts, printed in six installments. As with the other anthologies Tan Ying compiled for Wu Chongyao, the Xuehaitang scholar wrote postscripts signed in Wu's name for almost every text. After Wu Chongyao died in 1863, his son, Shaotang, continued to cooperate with Tan in printing other anthologies.

In hiring Tan Ying, Chongyao and Shaotang obtained more than a single editor, for Tan was linked into a network of book collectors and *kaozheng* scholars based at the Xuehaitang. Zeng Zhao, Wu Lanxiu, and Wu Yingkui, three of the first eight Xuehaitang co-directors (appointed in 1826), and Huang Zigao (appointed in 1830), all contributed rare editions that Tan incorporated into the collection. These scholars were introduced to the methods and scholarly ideals of evidential research not only through Ruan Yuan's Xuehaitang examinations, but also through interaction with Ruan's coterie of Jiangnan scholars, including Jiang Fan and Jiang Yuan (1767–1838).[81] Like their colleagues from Jiangnan, Cantonese literati had become avid book collectors, and they saw in the anthologies sponsored by Wu Chongyao an opportunity to realize their own printing ambitions. For example, in 1866, when Xuehaitang co-director Li Guangting (1812–80) was teaching at Duanxi Academy in Zhaoqing and ran across the rare works of a local scholar he deemed printworthy, he wrote to Tan and asked him to mention it to Wu Shaotang. Tan had already printed the work. Although Li was too late in this instance, one can imagine that a large number of texts discovered in the Pearl River delta during the mid-nineteenth century came to Tan's attention in this manner.[82]

Accordingly, many of the texts in the *Lingnan yishu* were introduced to Tan Ying by fellow Xuehaitang co-directors and Jiangnan sojourners. Tan copied several of the texts from Huang Zigao's library, including *Lixue jianyan*—a work written by the Song scholar Ou Shiheng (1217–77) and arranged by a descendant of his in 1586—and an original early Ming edition of Chen Lian's (1369–1453) *Gazetteer of Luofu Mountain*.[83] From Wu Lanxiu, Tan acquired a manuscript copy of another Ming work, Huang Zuo's *Record of the Hanlin Academy*. Wu borrowed Jiang Fan's hand copy of Huang Zhong's (1496 *jinshi*) work on Siam and Malacca, the *Haiyu*, and collated it with a version of the work in the *Xuejin taoyuan*, a collectanea compiled and printed by the Jiangnan bibliophile Zhang Haipeng (1755–1811); then he delivered it to Tan for inclusion in the anthology. Jiang Fan was also instrumental in contributing a literary collection of the Tang scholar Liu Ke that he came across while working on the provincial gazetteer. In 1823, Zeng Zhao transcribed a borrowed copy of He Mengyao's *Suandi*, a work on mathematics. He then got help from Jiang Yuan in collating two of the chapters. Together with Wu Lanxiu, Zeng hoped to raise funds to print the work himself, but was unsuccessful; it was later included in the *Lingnan yishu*. Zeng also transcribed, from the sojourning Zhejiang scholar Hong Yixuan (1765–1837), a Ming-era work on the *Chunqiu*. Some texts, such as Huang Zuo's gloss to Zhu Xi's *Xiaoxue*, Tan transcribed from his own library; others he stumbled across while compiling the Nanhai gazetteer in 1830, such as the memorials of the Ming official Guo Shangbin (1604 *jinshi*). Thus, the *Lingnan yishu* was essentially a collaborative project, growing out of the shared interests and expertise of a group of urban Cantonese scholars associated with the Xuehaitang and benefiting from their interaction with Jiangnan literati who were drawn to Guangzhou by Ruan Yuan.[84]

In a commemoration of Wu Chongyao's library, where he carried out much of the editorial work, Tan Ying explicitly and favorably compared the anthologies compiled under Wu's patronage to those put together by Wen Runeng and Luo Xuepeng.[85] Indeed, several characteristics of the *Lingnan yishu* immediately set it apart from previous Cantonese anthologies. The title of the collection reflected the nature of the work that went into compiling it: this was a bibliophile's anthology. Whereas previous collections sought to provide a comprehensive overview of the Cantonese poetic, prose, or written canon, this collection would offer only a selection of rare works. Therefore, in contrast to the coherent hierarchy of significance implied in the organization of the *Guangdong wenxian*, the ordering of texts in the *Lingnan yishu* had a random appearance. Tan Ying's 1831 preface to the collection further indicated the unique nature of this new anthology. Written in very ornate parallel prose, it was unlike anything else previously produced in Guangdong. The preface was a display of both erudition and literary skill—parallel prose was a trademark of Tan Ying, and symbolic as well of the literary ideals espoused at the Xuehaitang. Combining the careful scrutiny of a *kaozheng* bibliophile and the embellishment of a parallel prose master, Tan Ying applauded his own diligence in searching for lost works:

I have
>covered completely the yellow silken [volumes]
>collected and perused historical editions

> supplemented deficiencies and mended remnants
> drawn together the lost and gathered the missing.
> Those that have become
> buried in confusion for many years
> rotten from soot and cut by moths,
> how could they be displayed in markets?
> They are only kept in secret tents.
> I persistently wished to
> mend them and put them in order by hand,
> personally adding titles and labels;
> and submit them to the carver's awls,
> [so that] they would forever be in circulation.[86]

Consisting of texts assembled from private libraries, the purpose of the compilation was to make sure that rare manuscripts did not vanish with the dissolution of a single family's collection. Tan next extols the earliest textual production of his native province, but then mourns its loss:

> Alas! since
> prose began with Duo Jiao[87]
> songs originated with Zhang Mai[88]
> Chen Qin expounded the learning of the Zuo Commentary[89]
> Yang Fu compiled a book on *Southern Tribes*[90]
> Shi Xie wrote annotations to the *Spring and Autumn Annals*[91]
> Wang Fan wrote notes and accounts for the Jiao-Guang region[92]
> a forest of scholars devoted themselves to the *Change*'s commentaries,
>   but are only recorded in the *Liang History*[93]
> the name of the literary collection by the Commander who Pacifies Yue,
>   is only appended to the *Sui Treatise*[94]
> ... Qujiang's[95] poetry is extant, but the *Shijian* was previously lost[96]
> The Attendant Censor's prose survives, but his *Nianli* is long gone.[97]
> Even if one happens to collect [these works] from amongst tiny fragments,
> There still would be no way to arrange them in order.[98]

These Cantonese cultural artifacts from the Han through the Tang have been lost or scattered. The line mentioning Zhang Jiuling's *Shijian* is especially noteworthy because it projects the *kaozheng* scholar's skepticism as the attitude underlying this anthology. Though Luo Xuepeng had defended the veracity of the edition of this text that he had included in his *Guangdong wenxian*, here Tan indicates his judgment that the extant copy of the *Jinjian lu* was a spurious edition. In fact, during the 1820s, the *Jinjian lu* had been the subject of an examination topic at the Xuehaitang; essays by Tan and Huang Zigao were included in the *Xuehaitang ji*.⁹⁹ In one examination essay not included in the *Xuehaitang ji*, Zhou Yinqing directly quoted and then refuted Luo Xuepeng's assessment of Zhang's text in the *Guangdong wenxian*: "Some say 'The *Jinjian lu* preceded Han Yu in critiquing Buddha and Laozi and preceded Cheng [Yi] and Zhu [Xi] in promoting the *Doctrine of the Mean*.' But they do not realize that these were practices found only in Song, Yuan, and later times."¹⁰⁰ Zhou then quoted several passages from the extant *Jinjian lu* to lend weight to his argument that it was a spurious post-Tang text.

Tan Ying continues his preface by alluding to the cultural production of more recent dynasties:

There were
    Hu Binwang, who recorded completely the rise and fall¹⁰¹
    Li Daxing, who investigated questions about previous institutions¹⁰²
    Gu Yashi, who once edited the commentary to the *Change*¹⁰³
    Yu Andao, who again printed the *Han History*¹⁰⁴
    Chen Yongzhuo's discussions of the zither¹⁰⁵
    Huang Yizhi's instruction in archery¹⁰⁶
    Suiru's old *Odes*,
        which Li Fanxie once recorded in his book¹⁰⁷
    Yuzi's bequeathed works,
        which Ji Cangwei alone preserved in his collection¹⁰⁸
    Zhang Mengqi's miscellaneous compositions,
    with its name plagiarized as Zhuowu¹⁰⁹
    and Ou Qitu's new edition,
    with its title the same as that of Haixue's [collection].¹¹⁰
For some of these, there are no leads by which to seek and inquire;
with others, one hopes to be able to ponder and search.
Some from beginning to end are lost and scattered;
with others, the bamboo slips and book sacks are in disarray.¹¹¹
This is that over which our people collectively sigh,
and that about which knowledgeable ones are deeply distressed.¹¹²

Even these products of the Song and Ming dynasties were in danger of being lost. The goal of the current compilation therefore was to preserve as many texts as possible. It was not necessary to print again here what could easily be found elsewhere:

As for
> Wenzhuang's supplemental work to the *Yanyi*[113]
> Ganquan's comprehensive work on *gewu*,[114]

they are already
> as bright as the Sun and stars
> as marked as the Song and Hua [mountains].[115]

As for works that have circulated widely for a long time, they have been otherwise noted and I will not bother with them.[116]

Although only fragments of the Cantonese literary past were to be preserved in this anthology, they were of great value:

> A single scale of a fish also contains a spectrum of nine colors;
> a broken piece of shell truly becomes a hundred treasures.[117]

In contrast to the *Guangdong wenxian*, the *Lingnan yishu* was not meant to be a comprehensive yet concise introduction to the Cantonese cultural canon. Tan Ying's anthology both called for a different practice of reading and announced that a new scholarly community in Guangzhou had come into its own. The compilation was a testament to the rare book collections and new approaches to scholarship that had emerged in the city during the previous few decades. It was compiled by and for a select group of scholars, book collectors, and patrons of scholarship. The style and erudition of the preface indicated the limited size of the audience to which the *Lingnan yishu* was addressed, signaling to the reader that the image of Cantonese elite culture put forth in the *Lingnan yishu* would differ from that presented in previous anthologies.

One way in which that image differed from earlier ones was a result of temporally expanding the parameters of Cantonese high culture to include earlier cultural forebears. Previous comprehensive anthologies invariably began with the Tang poet-statesman Zhang Jiuling, who was seen as the forefather of Cantonese literature. In contrast, the fifth installment of the *Lingnan yishu* opens with three pre-Tang texts reconstructed by Zeng Zhao. Zeng pieced together Yang Fu's *Yiwu zhi*, from the *Taiping yulan* (an encyclopedia compiled in 984), Li Shan's (d. 689) annotation of the *Wenxuan*, Huang Zuo's 1561 edition of the Guangdong provincial gazetteer, and other sources. A description of tribes and customs in Guangdong written in the Later Han, Yang Fu's work contained rhyming appraisals (*zan*) and, allowing for a loose definition of poetry, was touted by some scholars as the first example of Cantonese verse. Zeng reconstructed two other early texts in a similar manner. The *Jiaozhou ji* by Liu Xinqi records the affairs of an early administrative region incorporating parts of modern-day Guangdong and Guangxi. Zeng judged this text to be a product of the Jin dynasty (265–420). A similar work by Wang Shaozhi (d. 443), the *Shixing ji*, was a record of a commandery corresponding to Qujiang county in northern Guangdong. Though the name of Yang Fu's *Yiwu zhi* had been familiar to Cantonese literati since the Ming, the work was considered irretrievable. Even Tan Ying's 1831 preface alluded to its loss. The 1822 provincial gazetteer, of which Zeng was a section editor, listed both the *Yiwu zhi* and the *Shixing ji* as lost works, even though Zeng was working on the reconstructions in 1821.[118]

Tan also included in the fifth installment the *Yueshi souyi*, a four-*juan* collection of rare Cantonese poetry assembled by Huang Zigao. In his 1839 preface to the collection, Huang pointed out that previous anthologies of Cantonese poetry, such as Wen Runeng's *Yuedong shihai*, all "take widely gathering and glorifying former philosophers as their main aim. Thus, they all start with Zhang Jiuling, as if there were no poetry before Zhang."[119] In contrast, Huang begins the collection with poems of Liu Shan, a Nanhai native who lived during the Chen dynasty (557–88). Although this first section was composed of only nine of Liu's poems, lifted from the seventh-century compendium, *Yiwen leiju*, it nonetheless suggested to Huang's contemporaries that they would have to look further back, beyond Zhang Jiuling, for the origins of Cantonese poetry. In addition, Huang included rare selections of Song and Yuan poetry, which he felt had been edited out of the Cantonese poetic canon by Ming scholars, in their overzealous devotion to Tang poetry. Though prefaces to previous Cantonese anthologies might evoke an early tradition, the collections themselves almost always began with Zhang Jiuling.[120] With the textual reconstructions by Zeng Zhao and Huang Zigao, the *Lingnan yishu* pushed back in time the beginning of the extant literary canon.

Aside from temporally expanding the Cantonese canon, the *Lingnan yishu* also extended its scope to include alternative voices to those of the most popular icons, as in Huang Zigao's efforts to call attention to Song and Yuan poetry. Similarly, the second installment begins with the collected writings of Liu Ke, a Tang-era native of Qujiang. Scholars in Guangzhou were not unaware of Liu's existence; Qu Dajun, for example, had devoted a section to Liu in his late seventeenth-century *Guangdong xinyu*.[121] Yet Jiangnan officials and scholars in Guangzhou played a large role in elevating Liu's status among nineteenth-century Cantonese literati. In 1820, while working on the provincial gazetteer, Jiang Fan came across a one-*juan* edition of Liu's writings that had been culled together in the recently compiled compendium of Tang writing, the *Quan Tang wen*. Believing that the works of Liu Ke should be put on an equal standing with those of Zhang Jiuling, Ruan Yuan had Liu's writings printed as a separate book, though the plates were later lost. In addition, Ruan's son, Ruan Fu, compiled a biography of Liu that was included in the provincial gazetteer. The collection of Liu's writings that appeared in the *Lingnan yishu* was based upon a version recently printed in Qujiang and was collated against Mao Qiling's *Lushan zhi* (Lu Mountain gazetteer) and a stone rubbing in Wu Yingkui's library. In a preface written for the Ruan Yuan edition of Liu's collection, Jiang Fan judged Liu to be second only to Han Yu as a Tang prose stylist. Although his writing was not as free and unrestrained as Han's, Jiang asserted, Liu's prose surpassed that of the great master in rigor. In other words, Han's prose suffered because his scholarship was inclined toward "empty talk" and was thus a precursor to Song Learning—without, however, the Song scholars' ability in detailed analysis. Liu, in contrast, exerted much effort in studies of the *Chunqiu* and *Mengzi* (Mencius), yet he avoided bringing in Chan (Zen) language.[122] Whereas Luo Xuepeng had made the dubious claim that Zhang Jiuling was somehow a predecessor to the *lixue* tradition, here Jiang Fan and his admirers in Guangzhou were equally anachronistically presenting Liu as an alternative to that tradition. Thus, editors sought to organize the Cantonese literary past in ways that legitimized the scholarly preoccupations of the moment.

In fact, much of the previous scholarship included in the *Lingnan yishu* mirrored the type of evidential research conducted at the Xuehaitang. Taken together, it implied that there had existed a nascent tradition of evidential research in Guangdong before the establishment of the academy in the 1820s. Physically the largest text in the anthology, the *Suandi* was a work on mathematics by He Mengyao, who would have been better known to readers of the fourth installment of the *Guangdong wenxian* as a poet, rather than as a mathematician.[123] But He had studied closely under Hui Shiqi when the latter served as Guangdong educational commissioner in the 1720s. A century later, when Jiang Fan came to Guangzhou, he had hoped to find He's work. Jiang was at first unsuccessful, until Zeng Zhao traced a copy from another friend in 1821. The edition incorporated in the *Lingnan yishu* was collated by the Xuehaitang's own mathematical expert, Zou Boqi.[124]

Another potential representative of a nascent tradition of evidential research was Chen Changqi. Having served as an editor on the staff of the *Siku quanshu*, Chen certainly had the necessary credentials. Three of Chen's works were included in the fifth installment: an astronomical treatise, an annotation of the *Lüshi chunqiu* (Master Lü's spring and autumn annals), and a study of rhyme in the *Chuci* (Songs of Chu) poems. In the postscript to the work on astronomy, Tan Ying quoted the biography of Chen written by the Xuehaitang scholar Wen Xun, in which Wen listed Chen's close friends in the *kaozheng* movement: Dai Zhen (1724–77), Qian Daxin, Zhu Yun (1729–81), Wang Niansun (1744–1832), and Ren Dachun. According to Wen Xun, Chen equaled them in skill and breadth of learning.[125] Before he died in 1820, Chen was selected by Ruan Yuan as one of the chief editors of the provincial gazetteer. There he worked with Jiang Fan and served as an inspiration to younger members of the staff such as Zeng Zhao, who made these three works by Chen available to Tan Ying.

The third installment included another work that foreshadowed the critique of certain Song Learning notions that the most famous Xuehaitang scholar, Chen Li, would offer in the late nineteenth century. This was the *Zhengxue xu* (Extension of proper learning) by the Xinning county scholar Chen Yufu (1690 *juren*).[126] In his own preface to the work, Chen Yufu explained his motivation:

As a youth, I often read Song and Ming scholars' criticisms of Han and Tang exegeses. In my heart I doubted [these criticisms]. I thought that if the Way of the sages and worthies like the Sun and Moon were connected to Heaven, and if the bequeathed Classics were all extant, then how could it be true that from the Han to the Tang there were only one or two people who . . . were able to get the intent of the sages and worthies?¹²⁷

In other words, Chen Yufu was calling into question the notion of *Daotong*, advanced by some Neo-Confucian scholars in the Song, which claimed that no one after Mencius—until the Song—had truly grasped the Dao. Chen believed that the *Rulin zhuan* (Biographies of Confucian scholars) sections of Han and Tang histories, by focusing exclusively upon their glosses of the Classics, inadvertently confirmed the notion that scholars of those dynasties had failed to grasp the moral big picture. Thus Chen set about to gather biographical information from other sections of the histories, in order to demonstrate that these scholars were also moral exemplars who understood something of the larger meaning of the Classics. Illustrating this approach is his assessment of Zheng Xuan, who came to symbolize the school of Han Learning in the Qing; here, Chen stressed the debt that later Confucians owed the Han and Tang scholars for their pioneering exegeses of the Classics. Chen accepted that Song interpretations were superior to those of the Han and Tang. But he compared the role of the Song scholars to that of improving the taste of a recipe; they should not deny the fundamental Han and Tang contributions of fire and cooking.¹²⁸ In his attempt to recast the classical scholars of the Han and Tang as grasping the larger "meaning and principles" of the Classics, Chen Yufu anticipated the Han-Song syncretism of the Xuehaitang.

The Xuehaitang's Han-Song syncretic approach surfaced in other places within the *Lingnan yishu* anthology. For example, the fourth installment opens with the annotation, by the early Qing scholar Hu Fang, of Zhu Xi's commentary to the *Yijing*. There was a great deal of irony in the inclusion of this work. In 1814, supporters of the maritime merchant Lu Wenjin's bid to have his father, Lu Guanheng, recognized as a local worthy had pointed to the fact that Guanheng had printed Hu Fang's text. But Liu Huadong and other critics complained that the preface, though attributed to Lu Guanheng, had in fact been written by the literatus Tan Dajing. Now, in the late 1840s, no one protested when a maritime merchant took credit for a postscript, also authored by a hired scholar surnamed Tan, introducing the very same book. (One wonders what had happened to literati outrage at pretentious merchants.) Tan Ying's postscript struck up a Han-Song syncretic tone, applauding Hui Shiqi's praise of Hu Fang's transmission of *lixue*, even though Hui's own studies of the *Yijing* favored Han interpretations.[129]

Most of the postscripts, however, focus upon textual histories of the works included in the collection. Almost all of the postscripts for earlier texts refer to assessments of those works in the *Siku quanshu*. In other places, Tan provides references to the texts, regarding questions of veracity or multiple editions, in the works of other Qing scholars. In addition, he is careful to note from whose library a given text was obtained. This was not an unusual practice in Daoguang China; in comparison to other Cantonese anthologies, however, the *Lingnan yishu* was unique in the amount of attention it devoted to such matters. Whereas prefaces, introductory biographies, or postscripts in such anthologies as the *Guangdong wenxian* most often emphasized the morality or deeds of the author of a given text, postscripts in the *Lingnan yishu* were more inclined to note the progeny of the text itself. In other words, the latter anthology represented a shift of focus from author to text.

Finally, the *Lingnan yishu* celebrated the scholarship produced by the scholarly elite associated with the Xuehaitang. The fifth and sixth installments included the works of six early co-directors, thereby serving to confirm the stature of the new academy. Only one contemporary scholar, Ling Yangzao, appeared in the anthology without having been formally associated with the Xuehaitang. It also indicated that Guangzhou was entering a new period of cultural florescence that might at last be on equal footing with that of the Ming. Part of the new canon included the classical scholarship of Hou Kang, Lin Botong, and Zeng Zhao, but the *Lingnan yishu* also contained works by Xuehaitang scholars on local Cantonese history and culture, such as Wu Lanxiu's three studies of the Southern Han, as well as his *Duanxi yanshi*, a survey of the famously high-quality inkstones of Zhaoqing. A work in a similar vein is Wu Yingkui's *Lingnan lizhi pu*, a handbook of the Guangdong litchi. As Wu relates in his 1826 preface, he and his friends were led to assemble this handbook during an excursion to Litchi Cove to avoid the summer heat.[130] In this careful compilation, Wu classifies previous references to the quintessential southern fruit into such categories as "cultivation" and "varieties" of litchi. In a tone similar to the Lingnan litchi poems by Tan Ying and others, Wu intended this handbook to correct the biased compilations of the Fujianese litchi handbooks. As Tan Ying adamantly notes in his editorial postscript, reflecting the opinion he first articulated in his litchi songs, "Lingnan litchis are the best in the empire!"[131]

Although both the *Guangdong wenxian* and the *Lingnan yishu* claimed to represent Cantonese elite culture, the editor of each anthology appropriated local cultural icons and shaped the cultural landscape to fit his own scholarly, literary, and moral vision. The anthologies were also aimed at different audiences. Though one can catch a glimpse of Shunde chauvinism in the fourth installment of the *Guangdong wenxian*, this anthology nevertheless seems directed at a broad spectrum of the educated elite throughout the Pearl River delta. Luo Xuepeng can take for granted that his audience is already familiar with the authors in the collection; he strives merely to remind readers of what is important and to move them with these paragons of morality. The *Lingnan yishu* appeals to a much narrower, urbanized segment of the delta elite, primarily composed of the group of scholars who were responsible for its compilation. It serves as a self-congratulatory testament to the flourishing community of book collectors and evidential researchers among Guangzhou's nouveaux riches. In a radically different tone from that of Luo Xuepeng, Tan Ying, in his parallel prose preface to the collection, attempts to impress the reader with his breadth of knowledge of the obscure. At the same time, the *Lingnan yishu* appealed to a much broader audience outside of Guangdong. Jiangnan scholars sojourning in Guangzhou had aided in gathering several of the texts later included in the anthology, and the anthology in turn indicated that Guangzhou could participate in the scholarly trends emanating from Jiangnan.

CONCLUSION

In his study of the Jiangnan "academic community," Benjamin Elman demonstrates the connection between the expansion of printing and libraries and the flourishing of *kaozheng* scholarship in that region during the eighteenth century.[132] Similarly, beginning in the early nineteenth century, Guangzhou and the Pearl River delta witnessed an unprecedented proliferation of printed texts and libraries. Like their counterparts in Jiangnan, Cantonese literati developed a great interest in collecting rare books. The circulation of these texts among Cantonese scholars and bibliophiles facilitated and inspired the further production of texts. Whereas the expansion of printing in Jiangnan was most closely linked to classical scholarship, in Guangzhou a noticeably large number of the newly produced texts were specifically devoted to local, Cantonese culture. This chapter has introduced three categories of "localist" texts: histories, works of poetry, and anthologies. These texts were initially conceived and largely produced between 1810 and 1850, revealing the high level of energy that was invested in exploring the local during this period.

Though this trend predated the Xuehaitang by a decade—as evidenced by the anthologies of Wen Runeng and Luo Xuepeng—by the middle of the nineteenth century this exploration of the local was almost entirely dominated by the circle of scholars associated with the Xuehaitang. This raises the question of why so much energy came to be directed toward local culture. As envisioned by Ruan Yuan, the principal function of the Xuehaitang was to spread the methods and ideals of evidential research, before this time a scholarly practice essentially limited to Jiangnan and the capital, to more remote regions of the empire. In this sense, the brand of classical scholarship offered at the Xuehaitang was an imported, relatively unfamiliar, practice. Local Cantonese discourses and practices of philosophical and classical scholarship were for the most part slighted by Ruan Yuan and the circle of scholars at the Xuehaitang. The heavy emphasis upon the local among Xuehaitang scholars therefore might be read as representing an accommodation with the local environment. Ruan Yuan certainly was a proponent of investigation and celebration of the local, yet the degree to which Xuehaitang scholars emphasized the local is nonetheless remarkable. By employing their newly acquired tools—*kaozheng* methodology and "ancient" literary styles—to explore, preserve, and celebrate local culture, they demonstrated the relevance of the Xuehaitang approach and thereby justified the importation of these tools.

But a local culture can never simply be preserved; rather, it is both reclaimed and reconstructed in the very act of "preservation" and celebration. Whether exploring local historical traces, celebrating the local fruit, or lionizing cultural icons of the past, scholars associated with the Xuehaitang enhanced their position among the larger local elite. Moreover, through writing about Cantonese culture, they reshaped the local cultural landscape by portraying it in new ways. This resulted in a local culture that, though still recognizably Cantonese, also appeared in a different guise. Previously neglected symbols of Cantonese culture were emphasized, and traditionally popular symbols were elided or portrayed in a new light. Most important, elite Cantonese culture, as reconstituted by Xuehaitang scholars in the nineteenth century, was now more centered in urban Guangzhou, and appeared to be culminating in activities organized by the literati associated with the academy.

Viewed from a distance, localist texts produced by nineteenth-century Cantonese literati (whether they were associated with the Xuehaitang or not) seem to represent a unified, newly confident Cantonese elite culture asserting itself vis-à-vis other regions of the empire. This comes across clearly in "Lingnan Litchi Songs" by Tan Ying and Lin Botong, and defiantly in the prefaces and editorial principles Luo Xuepeng composed for his anthology; one can also find subtle hints of it in the Southern Han histories authored by Wu Lanxiu and Liang Tingnan. When viewed from a closer perspective, fissures appear in this façade of local pride. Such writing about the local—in histories, verse, and especially anthologies—was an arena of contention, in which scholars centered at the Xuehaitang in cosmopolitan Guangzhou city were pitted against the literati of old lineages established along the West River in the delta hinterland. Thus, anthologies produced by maritime merchant capital and Xuehaitang scholarly expertise looked very different from those compiled by delta-based lineages such as the Longshan Wen and the Daliang Luo. This suggests that the nineteenth century's great proliferation of localist texts was in part driven by this competition over defining what it meant to be "Cantonese." Over the course of the nineteenth century, and through the efforts of the Xuehaitang, an urban-centered construction of local elite culture gradually prevailed.[133]

⸤ FIVE ⸥
Academy, City, and Delta in Crisis and Reconstruction, 1830–1870

> The mountain hall, its countenance transformed, rises up again;
> People, resembling frightened ducks, scatter and once more return.
> Never expecting to ascend it for a view with this day's wine,
> The green reflection in our eyes is the mountain of a bygone time.
> For ten years cultured letters have met with the passing of the *kalpa*;
> Yet the hundred trees of plum blossoms have not been completely cut down.
> Thrice observing Penglai, its waters are still clear and limpid;
> Whistling winds have ceased, but the hair on my temples is speckled gray.
> —Chen Pu, "On a Winter Day in 1863 the Renovation of the Xuehaitang is Completed. County Magistrate Zhou Yinqing, County School Directors Tan Ying, Chen Li, Chen Liangyu, and Li Guangting, *Juren* Jin Xiling, and I Toast One Another. I Make a Painting, Writing a Poem upon It. The Various Gentlemen All Have [Matching] Poems."

IN THE MIDDLE DECADES of the nineteenth century, Guangzhou and the delta faced a succession of serious problems, beginning with massive flooding in the 1830s. Though floods typically were more of a concern for the Enclosure lineages than for Guangzhou's urban elite, the city itself suffered a tremendous deluge in 1833, which inundated neighborhoods even in the northern parts of the Old City, toppling the shabby homes of the poor. With much of Guangzhou under water for weeks, the city's population naturally took refuge on Yuexiu Hill, certainly ruining any plans for refined outings on the grounds of the Xuehaitang that summer.[1] The 1833 flood augured ill for Guangzhou; though some segments of Cantonese society continued to prosper throughout the nineteenth century, historians have documented not only a mounting ecological crisis but also rising levels of violence in the Pearl River delta, the latter ranging from banditry among secret societies to pitched battles between Cantonese (Punti) and Hakkas to British incursions during the Opium War.[2] The crises escalated in the 1850s, when the city's residents found themselves threatened first by a massive rebellion in 1854 and then by a four-year foreign occupation beginning in 1857. During the ensuing reconstruction of the 1860s, however, many of Guangzhou's institutions, including its academies, quickly recovered and even expanded the scope of their operations.

This chapter considers the question of how these mid-century crises, and the subsequent reconstruction, affected both the place of the Xuehaitang in urban Guangzhou and, more broadly, the dynamics between the city and its delta hinterland. Conventional wisdom, considering the Qing empire as a whole, has concluded that the evidential research associated with the Xuehaitang faced burgeoning criticism, entering into a precipitous decline by mid-century.[3] Nevertheless, in the intense competition for resources during the reconstruction of the 1860s, a new generation at the Xuehaitang reaffirmed and even enhanced the influence of the academy, its agenda, and the urban scholars associated with it. Ruan Yuan's scholarly vision became institutionalized in the Xuehaitang curriculum, and his academy remained firmly rooted in Guangzhou's expanding system of academies.

We will begin with an examination of the new generation of Xuehaitang scholars, followed by a description of their encounter with the delta hinterland during rebellion and occupation. Next, we shall turn to various aspects of the reassertion of urban literati culture and the reconstruction and expansion of urban institutions, paying particular attention to the relationships between academy and city and between city and hinterland. Chapters 6 and 7 will elaborate on these themes through case studies of the two most famous Cantonese scholars commonly associated with the Xuehaitang, Chen Li and Zhu Ciqi.

CONTINUITY IN THE NEW GENERATION

There was a high degree of continuity in both the leadership and the scholarly and literary agenda of the Xuehaitang throughout the mid-century crises and reconstruction. Despite a high turnover of co-directors, those appointed during this period closely resembled—in terms of their native place and social origins, as well as their scholarly and literary predilections—their predecessors among the first generation of co-directors. In his study of the events preceding and during the Opium War, James Polachek notes a significant number of co-directors appointed in a short period—six between 1837 and 1840. This was more than at any other time, aside from the appointment of the original eight co-directors in 1826.[4] But part of what Polachek sees as a "frantic juggling" of co-directors was due to the deaths of many members of the first generation of Xuehaitang scholars. A poem by Xu Rong, written when Tan Ying, returning from a failed attempt at the metropolitan examinations, visited him at his post in Hangzhou, refers to their numerous mutual friends who had recently died. Most of them were closely associated with the Xuehaitang and had died within a few years of one another: Wu Lanxiu (1839), Yi Kezhong (1838), Liang Mei (1838), Wu Yingkui (?), Xie Niangong (ca. 1840), Xie Niandian (?), Huang Zigao (1839), Hou Kang (1837), and Lin Botong (1845), as well as the Pan family scion Pan Zhengheng (亨, 1837).[5] Xu Rong himself died a few years later, in 1855, when Taiping forces overran Zhejiang. Thus, the high rate of turnover among the Xuehaitang co-directorate between 1837 and 1840 was primarily a result of the passing of the first generation of scholars associated with the academy.[6]

The continuity in Xuehaitang co-director appointments comes into sharper focus when we take a step back from the turnover in the late 1830s and look at the broader generational transformation, in which new co-directors and other scholars closely identified themselves with the Xuehaitang during the period of crisis and reconstruction. Some among the older generation of Xuehaitang scholars witnessed the beginning of the mid-century crises, and a few even survived long enough to help celebrate early efforts at reconstruction. Both Xiong Jingxing and Zeng Zhao survived into the Xianfeng reign (1851–61), the latter passing away in 1854. The poets Zhang Weiping and Huang Peifang lived to see the defeat of the Red Turbans, but both died in 1859, before the Xuehaitang was rebuilt. A few scholars, such as Tan Ying and Fan Feng, spanned the generations. Tan was the only scholar to have his writings included in all four collections of Xuehaitang examination papers, and Fan

Feng lived just long enough to be appointed a co-director in 1875. Many among the new generation of Xuehaitang scholars, born in the 1810s and 1820s, had studied at the academy and were thus shaped by its curriculum. Those from this generation who became co-directors took up the post during two decades of instability, the 1840s and 1850s, and a decade of reconstruction in the 1860s.

As with the first generation of Xuehaitang scholars, many in this new generation were newcomers to the region or had only tentative ties to the delta hinterland. A few of the second-generation co-directors came from families that could claim long-term residence in the delta hinterland, but, as in the case of Xie Lansheng, their lives were increasingly centered in urban Guangzhou. Both Chen Pu (1820–87), named a co-director in 1861, and Li Guangting, appointed in 1863, were natives of Panyu county. The Chen family claimed descent from pre-Song ancestors who had settled in the remote Panyu countryside, but whose descendants later relocated to Henan near the Chigang Pagoda.[7] Chen Pu's grandfather was a doctor; his father made a living as a shop owner in Guangzhou.[8] Li Guangting was from the Panyu countryside further downstream along the Pearl River, but had lived in the city since his youth.[9] Similarly, co-directors Liang Tingnan and Zhou Yinqing, appointed in 1840 and 1863, were both from Shunde; the Xuehaitang expert in mathematics, Zou Boqi (appointed in 1857), was a native of Bichong township in Nanhai, just west of the city.[10]

In addition to attracting urbanized delta natives, the Xuehaitang also continued to serve as an important cultural resource for scholars from several of the in-migrating cohorts surveyed in Chapter 1. For example, Chinese bannermen from the Guangzhou garrison maintained a small but visible presence at the academy. In addition to the aged Fan Feng, Chen Liangyu (1814–81) was made a co-director in 1858.[11] Scions of merchant families from Fujian also regularly took Xuehaitang examinations. Examples include two sons of Pan Zhengheng (衡), Pan Shu (1810–65) and Pan Dinggui (1811–40).[12] The most notable difference in the types of scholars closely associated with the Xuehaitang is the decreasing presence of Hakka literati from Jiaying. One of the few Jiaying Hakkas who played an important role at the academy in the second half of the nineteenth century was Zhang Qizeng (1840 *juren*), appointed co-director in 1885.[13]

To an even greater extent than at the time of its founding, however, the Xuehaitang facilitated the ascendancy of urban literati from families with roots in the northern Zhejiang prefectures of Hangzhou and Shaoxing. Xu Qiguang (1850 *jinshi*), a co-director from 1877, was the most successful scholar produced by the Xu (許) family, which, as we saw in Chapter 1, had moved from Hangzhou's Renhe county to Guangzhou, where family members specialized in the *muyou* business. Xu Hao (1810–79), a devoted student under Chen Li at the Xuehaitang, belonged to a family that devised a similar strategy. This Xu (徐) family hailed from Qiantang county, also in Hangzhou, and specialized in serving as legal secretaries. Xu Hao's father pursued this trade in Guangzhou, Zhaoqing, and Shaozhou prefectures and registered his sons as Panyu residents. Both Xu Hao and his brother carried on the family specialty; Xu Hao would go on to serve several of Guangzhou's top provincial officials during reconstruction.[14] Jin Xiling (1811–92), designated as a co-director in 1853, belonged to the Panyu Jin family, which had migrated from Shanyin county.[15] Shen Shiliang (1823–60), appointed co-director in 1858, also had Shanyin roots. His grandfather and father had traveled to Guangzhou and had been "unable" to return to Zhejiang; thus Shen was registered as a Panyu resident.[16]

Another Shanyin family, surnamed Wang, illustrates the continuing northern Zhejiang connection and the ways in which study at the Xuehaitang became part of an in-migrating family's strategy for accumulating cultural capital in its new surroundings.[17] After Wang Lunzhi (d. 1769) capped off a career as a minor official with a brief stint in Guangdong, subsequent generations of the Shanyin Wang, like the Renhe Xu and Qiantang Xu, pursued a specialized strategy of serving as *muyou* in the province. Based on the Wang genealogy, no fewer than eleven of Lunzhi's sons, grandsons, great-grandsons, and great-great-grandsons subsequently worked as *muyou* in Guangdong. Others were clerks and minor officials in Guangdong or visited their relatives living and working in the province.[18] One of Lunzhi's grandsons, Wang Ding, was a *muyou* in Shunde and other counties in Guangdong and was buried in the province when he died. Wang Ding had brought along his family, including his young son, Wang Quan, who—together with his cousin Wang Chu (1824–97), later a *muyou* in Guangdong for four decades—received a classical education in Guangzhou. Clearly possessing a knack for literary composition, Wang Quan won many of the poetry and prose competitions around town. Nevertheless, in order to support his father, who was "too poor to return" to Shanyin, Wang Quan worked as a *muyou* under both county- and provincial-level officials, never again setting foot outside Guangdong.[19] Like other members of the Wang family living in Guangzhou, he eventually registered as a Panyu resident.

In addition to earning income as a *muyou*, Wang Quan took advantage of the cultural prestige offered by the Xuehaitang. The Wang genealogy proudly proclaims that, in the 1850s and 1860s, Wang Quan was "admired by" Zhang Weiping, Tan Ying, Chen Liangyu, Shen Shiliang, and Chen Li, all closely associated with the Xuehaitang. Moreover, Wang Quan and his son, Zhaoquan (1859–1929), studied at the Xuehaitang, as did Wang Chu's two sons, Zhaoyong (1861–1939) and Zhaohong (1878–1902).[20] Furthermore, the Shanyin Wangs intermarried with Shaoxing and local families whose sons were Xuehaitang examinees or students. For example, Zhu Qilian (1853–99), a scholar from Xiaoshan county who later registered as a Panyu resident, married Wang Quan's daughter.[21] For his son Zhaoquan, who registered as a Panyu resident and earned a *juren* degree, he arranged a marriage with a daughter of the Nanhai merchant and scholar Liao Zhen. Liao's son, Liao Tingxiang (1844–98), would become a Xuehaitang co-director.[22] Evidently, the Xuehaitang continued to attract many students from cosmopolitan Guangzhou's sojourning, in-migrating, and socially ascending families.[23] It still drew some scholars from the delta hinterland, but, for them, the urban academy was a less essential cultural resource.

Furthermore, offspring of the first- and second-generation scholars maintained a strong presence at the academy. For example, two of Zhang Weiping's sons had their works included in the third collection of Xuehaitang examination essays and poems, the *Xuehaitang sanji*, printed in 1859. Similarly, the works of three of Jin Xiling's sons appear in the fourth collection, the 1886 *Xuehaitang siji* (an inclusion that was perhaps facilitated by the fact that Jin edited this last collection). Jin also put into the collection one poem by Shen Zetang (d. 1926), son of Shen Shiliang. Lin Shixian, an 1869 "specialized student" at the Xuehaitang, was the grandson of Lin Botong. Chen Li's son, Zongkan (1846–?), had two essays in the

Xuehaitang siji, and his grandson, Qinghe, was an 1888 specialized student. Zhang Qizeng, the Jiaying Hakka appointed co-director in 1885, was a younger brother of Zhang Qihan, who had taken Xuehaitang examinations in the 1820s. Specialized students in the 1890s included Chen Pu's son, Yanxu, and Chen Liangyu's grandson, Shoutong.[24] Ye Renlan (1843–1905), who had an essay included in the *Xuehaitang siji*, was the son of Ye Tingying, an 1827 examinee at the Xuehaitang and a cousin of the salt merchant Ye Tingxun.[25]

Among second- and third-generation members of these Xuehaitang families, the most promising scholar was Tan Zongjun (1846–88). He was the second son of Tan Ying; his mother was the only daughter of Liang Mei.[26] As a young man in the late 1860s—before placing second in the 1874 metropolitan examinations and being appointed a Xuehaitang co-director in 1880—Zongjun was closely associated with other youthful urban literati who studied at the Xuehaitang. Tan recalled in a poem that, in a manner reminiscent of the young Zhang Weiping and his friends, who hawked their literary talents to keep themselves well supplied with drinks, whenever he had extra income from the writings he had sold, he and his friends would pool their money for drinks at a wine shop inside the Main South Gate separating the Old City and New City. In his explanation of the poem, Tan listed seven friends by their literary names. All five of those who can be positively identified had examination papers included in the *Xuehaitang siji*: Deng Weisen, Chen Zongkan, Liao Tingxiang, Zheng Quan (1888 *juren*), and Liang Qi (1885 *juren*), son of a Xuehaitang examinee who married Xiong Jingxing's daughter.[27]

Sons of some delta lineages occasionally took Xuehaitang examinations and might even be selected as co-directors, but for the urban elite of Guangzhou city, affiliation with the Xuehaitang became a means of perpetuating family status in the absence of the kinds of resources mustered by the dominant lineages of the delta hinterland. Similarly, most members of the Cantonese urban elite could not draw on the types of resources provided by family traditions of learning, which spanned generations in such Jiangnan cities as Suzhou and Changzhou.[28] Therefore, as it had from the outset, the Xuehaitang continued to appeal to the urbanized, in-migrating, and socially rising elite of Guangzhou city. Aside from the decreasing presence of the Jiaying Hakkas, the group of literati identifying themselves with the academy after the late 1830s closely resembled their predecessors who had studied at the academy under Ruan Yuan.

ENCOUNTERING THE HINTERLAND

Much of the preceding analysis has highlighted the differences between urban literati in Guangzhou and literati from the dominant lineages of the delta hinterland. But when they were faced in the 1850s with the turmoil of domestic rebellion and foreign occupation, urban and rural literati relied upon one another and emphasized their common interests. During the 1854-1855 Red Turban uprising, refugee gentry streamed into Guangzhou, seeking the protection offered by its walls, and hoping to receive succor from official troops or to raise money for their own militias. When British and French forces occupied Guangzhou in 1857, this flow was reversed, as urban literati sought refuge in the homes of kin and associates in the countryside. Once both threats had subsided, however, urban and delta-based elites sought to create or consolidate control over their institutions, leading to competition for scarce resources during reconstruction.

The Red Turban uprising, which had been brewing for a few years, erupted in the spring of 1854, with the rebels capturing numerous cities and townships throughout Guangdong. The uprising came to the Pearl River delta in June, when rebels sacked the county seat of Dongguan, to the east of Guangzhou. Foshan fell to rebels in early July, and Daliang several weeks later. Meanwhile, another rebel army laid siege to Guangzhou itself, making initial assaults on the North Gate on July 13. A week later, a full-scale Red Turban attack on Guangzhou was beaten back on the northern reaches of Xiguan, but the rebels maintained their stranglehold on the city. Throughout the siege, Governor-General Ye Mingchen (1807-59) observed operations from the Zhenhai Tower on the north wall along Yuexiu Hill, just above the Xuehaitang. The rebels' grip on the city was loosened only on September 7, when government troops and militias surged out of the East Gate to disperse a large rebel camp in the Eastern Suburb. By early November, government forces had driven away rebels north of the city. Across the Pearl River, in Henan, they eliminated the last of the insurgents surrounding Guangzhou in March 1855. When Daliang was recovered in May, the rebel threat to Guangzhou was entirely removed.[29]

For the urban literati associated with the Xuehaitang, the rebellion represented an intense encounter with the countryside, a stark reminder of the existence of peripheral regions beyond the delta, hitherto experienced only on tours of scenic spots or during stints of service as educational officials in counties outside the delta. During the siege, the in-migrating urban literati were largely confined to Guangzhou, while many members of the delta elite were driven into the city, at least temporarily, to beseech officials for aid and to cooperate with other refugee gentry in organizing and financing militias. For example, having grown up in the city but maintaining ties to his native place in the Panyu countryside, Li Guangting returned home at the first hint of trouble, to raise funds for a local militia from among neighboring wealthy families. When rebels occupied nearby areas, Li fled back into the city and sought aid from officials, but they were preoccupied with the defense of the city itself. So Li and other refugee gentry from the township established a bureau to coordinate units of local braves. Li then led his militia force in driving rebels from the area and remained in the countryside for several years to head the township bureau.[30] Most scholars at the Xuehaitang, lacking these connections to the hinterland, could only nervously wait out the crisis.

Not long after the city's elite celebrated the defeat of the Red Turbans, Guangzhou was again threatened, this time by the British and French. In what came to be known as the Arrow, or Second Opium, War (1856-60), Guangzhou once more made an easy target for foreign troops. Yet this second conflict was much more disruptive of city life than had been the First Opium War (1839-42). An initial British bombardment of Guangzhou began in late October 1856. Over the following two days, the British destroyed parts of the city wall and burned down houses in the crowded streets of the New City. In early November, the British aimed their cannon at government offices in the Old City, inevitably demolishing homes and shops as well. British forces withdrew in December while conducting negotiations with the Qing. Yet the situation remained tense; one foreign observer caustically remarked the following summer that in Guangzhou "the rich are flying while the poor are starving."³¹

Once these negotiations had broken down and the British and French had prepared their forces, they resumed their attack on Guangzhou, beginning with the occupation of Henan and subsequent bombardment of Guangzhou in December 1857. Shells reached halfway up Yuexiu Hill, and caused fires in several places throughout the city.³² Rather than withdrawing after this initial shelling, the foreign army this time completely occupied Guangzhou, beginning on December 29. Unfortunately for the Xuehaitang, the British and French appreciated the strategic advantages afforded by Yuexiu Hill, rather than the ancient traces and native flora so admired by Ruan Yuan. Consequently, once they had scaled the city walls, they fought their way up to the Zhenhai Tower and occupied the Guanyin Temple and other institutions on the hill. In early January, the invading forces made their way into the city, capturing Ye Mingchen. Throughout the occupation, the British and French continued to station troops on Yuexiu Hill, as the entire city was at the mercy of whoever commanded this location.³³

According to at least one foreign observer, commercial life in the city returned to its bustling normality within several weeks, but the occupation had a more disruptive impact on the academic elite. Numerous temples and other buildings on Yuexiu Hill, including both the Xuehaitang and Wenlan Pavilion, were damaged, destroyed, or converted into barracks. Co-directors frantically hired coolies to remove the original *Huang Qing jingjie* printing blocks that were stored in the pavilion, but many were lost. The surviving plates were transferred by boat to the ancestral hall of Zou Boqi's lineage, in Bichong township, for safekeeping. Other urban sites of academic importance were also damaged in the bombardment. When the British began their attack, the Panyu elite had been in the process of compiling a new edition of the county gazetteer. Shells struck the gazetteer bureau at the county school on Huiai Street, incinerating volumes of rare books by past Panyu scholars that had been assembled in preparation for compiling the gazetteer. As a result, many writings by Lin Botong, Yi Kezhong, Hou Kang, and other early Xuehaitang scholars perished in the flames. Many of the bookshops inside the Main South Gate were also destroyed, as was the Jin family study in the New City.³⁴ Xuehaitang examinations were not resumed until 1860, and then only at a temporary site until the academy could be repaired.³⁵

Though most literati fled Guangzhou during the barrage, the aging Huang Peifang stayed behind, unwilling to leave his family home and studio in the Old City neighborhood named after his ancestor, Huang Zuo. Somehow, although neighboring houses were demolished, Huang and his studio remained unscathed. Huang was well into his seventies and must have been quite feeble; his refusal to leave illustrates his attachment to urban Guangzhou despite the fact that he was registered as a Xiangshan county resident.³⁶ In contrast to Huang Peifang, however, most urban literati abandoned the city in 1857. Xiguan initially provided a safe haven, but several of the urban scholars associated with the Xuehaitang chose to move further away and thus found themselves living in the delta countryside for the first time. Because they either had never had ancestral homes in the delta or, if originally from the delta, had since lost contact with their kin, urban literati availed themselves of scholarly or business connections with delta natives. Chen Pu fled Guangzhou on the day that Yuexiu Hill was first occupied, painfully but imaginatively recalling "the wild deer rambling across the Yue Terrace."³⁷ Perhaps because his ancestral home in Henan was too close for comfort, Chen Pu first sought refuge with the Zhao lineage in Hengsha village, in Nanhai just west of the city, but then took up Zou Boqi's invitation to reside at the Zou estate in nearby Bichong, where the remaining *Huang Qing jingjie* printing blocks were being stored.³⁸

Several urban literati expressed dismay in verse written during their initial flight from the city, but they soon produced other poems that exhibited a romantic fascination with the countryside. Toward the end of 1856, Tan Ying and his son Zongjun avoided the British bombardment by residing at Litchi Cove (an ideal place for the author of the "Lingnan Litchi Songs"!) and villages on the western borders of Xiguan. Two years later, rather than calling on their distant kin in Foshan, the Tans spent half a year at the He family garden at Heshun, just northeast of Xie Lansheng's native Mashe township in Nanhai.³⁹ Both father and son expressed their interest in the lifestyle of their hosts: Tan Ying wrote of "village pestles and neighbors' fires, in a cycle with the stars and frost / the grain cheap, the harvest bountiful, I dream and sleep in peace," and Zongjun described Heshun as a place where, "with sails and masts merchants gather at the crossing / with panpipes and drums they honor the *she* god," and where the dust of warfare could not reach the small abode that was their paradise.[40]

In his youth, Shen Shiliang, one of the many Xuehaitang scholars with Shanyin roots, had studied under Li Ruwei (1811–86), a native of Changjiao township in southern Shunde county who previously had taught students in the New City and had also taken Xuehaitang examinations.[41] Now, in the face of foreign occupation, Shen abandoned his New City home, heading first for Xiguan, then down to Changjiao—with his most precious Song and Ming editions in tow—to enjoy the safe haven offered by his old teacher. Shen's collected poetry contains a series of 30 poems, replete with explanatory notes, portraying his refuge with the Li lineage. After an opening poem documenting at first hand the difficulties endured by refugees from the city, almost all of the subsequent poems show his admiration for the local resources of the Changjiao Li. Shen describes fish ponds and mulberry cultivation, praises the abundance of food, and notes with approval the lineage-wide tax collection methods in place since the Yongzheng era (1723–35).[42]

Rebellion from the countryside and foreign occupation of their provincial city, then, provoked urban and rural Cantonese literati to find common cause. Though urban or delta identities, as well as scholarly and literary affiliations, were important markers of distinction among various components of the local elite, the boundaries separating one group from another were never hard and fast. Cantonese literati negotiated among various "factions" of the cultural elite, finding common interests and intellectual or artistic consonance as the situation demanded. It is thus important to keep in mind the complexity of the social landscape, even among the minority of the population that formed the Cantonese social and cultural elite. Urban and rural literati did not hesitate to cooperate when faced with threats to their way of life, even if subtle tensions always lurked beneath the surface. And when competition for economic and cultural resources intensified in the 1860s, members of the urban elite often found that their interests were at odds with those of the powerful lineages in the delta hinterland.

REASSERTING URBAN LITERATI CULTURE

By the time the British and French occupation ended, in October 1861, Cantonese literati had suffered through more than two decades of intermittent disturbances. Yuexiu Hill had been overrun by Guangzhou's "barefooted" masses, nearly taken by Red Turbans, and finally desecrated by foreign troops. Although urban literati like Tan Ying and Shen Shiliang wrote fondly—and perhaps also somewhat patronizingly—of their experiences in the countryside, they returned to the city as soon as they felt it was safe to do so. In the poem quoted at the outset of this chapter, Chen Pu aptly characterized the coterie of urban scholars at the Xuehaitang, representing them as frightened ducks, flying away at the first sign of danger and gradually returning to reclaim Yuexiu Hill. As Chen and his associates reassembled after rural rebellion and urban occupation, they set themselves to the task of reasserting their place in Guangzhou. An important element of this, discussed below, was the restoration of academies and other institutions, the organization of printing projects, and the curricular development at the Xuehaitang in the 1860s. Yet, even before this, Xuehaitang scholars led the urban elite in celebrating the restoration of literati culture, as can be seen in two literary gatherings reminiscent of those in the decade preceding the establishment of the academy.

In the first case, Guangzhou's urban elite gathered to celebrate one of the city's saviors from the Red Turban menace. Huang Xianbiao, a Panyu native, was at the time a sublieutenant in charge of a military post on the northern edge of Xiguan. When Red Turbans attacked Guangzhou from the northwest on July 20, 1854, Huang led a small force of regular troops and militia to cut off a column of thousands of rebels and is said personally to have killed dozens of them in the ensuing melee. Guangdong governor Bogui (d. 1859), observing the heroism of Huang's detachment from the safety of Zhenhai Tower, had him promoted to lieutenant. The next year, after the rebel threat had dissipated entirely, Guangzhou's literary elite, especially those who resided in Xiguan, met to compose verse praising Huang's heroics, and published the poems in a collection entitled *Huang Shenzhi shourong jigong lu* (Commemoration of the achievements of Lieutenant Huang Xianbiao). The collection, prefaced by Zhang Weiping and others in 1855, contained laudatory poems by over 80 authors, as well as a record of the events written by Liang Tingnan. Among the poets were the former maritime merchants Wu Chongyao, Xie Youren, and Liang Lunshu (1790–1877), and such Xuehaitang scholars as Huang Peifang, Fan Feng, Xiong Jingxing, Tan Ying, and Zhang Weiping's star student of poetry, Li Changrong.[43] This celebratory collection represents an expression of gratitude on the part of a relieved urban elite and served to reassure Guangzhou's urban literati that the rule of letters had in the end prevailed.

In 1860, while Guangzhou remained under British and French occupation but was otherwise essentially peaceful, a more select group of urban literati organized a series of poetic outings, in a second example of the reassertion of literati rule. This occasion consisted of several meetings to observe the lustration (*xi*) festival, a ceremony with a long history among China's poetic elite, but which was also symbolic of a particular aesthetic. Originally held on the first *si*-day (the sixth day in a twelve-day cycle) of the third lunar month, the festival had since the Han dynasty perennially been observed on the third day of the third lunar month. In later dynasties, the elite typically wrote poems and drank wine by streams and rivers to mark the occasion. But the ceremony was most closely associated with Wang Xizhi (321–79), who hosted a famous lustration celebration in 353 in Shaoxing.[44] More recently, and also in the context of a return to stability and a reaffirmation of literati values, Wang Shizhen had presided over lustration ceremonies at Red Bridge in Yangzhou in the 1660s.[45]

In their 1860 celebrations, the poets made frequent reference to both Wang Xizhi and Wang Shizhen, but their lustration observances also evoked specifically Cantonese meanings. Local scholars believed that the Southern Yue ruler Zhao Tuo had built the Yue King Terrace on Yuexiu Hill as a place for holding lustration festivities.[46] Moreover, the group of poets who met in 1860 consciously sought to reconstitute what had become a local fad in recent decades of celebrating the festival. Through repeated references, authors placed their 1860 ceremonies in the context of previous gatherings, beginning with a lustration festival ceremony in 1815 at Changshou Monastery in Xiguan, hosted by Lieutenant-Governor Zeng Yu.[47]

During the early years of the Xuehaitang, Ruan Yuan had greatly admired Tan Ying's parallel prose essay modeled on the topic of a lustration festival ceremony.[48] But the ceremony seems to have become especially popular among Cantonese literati in the aftermath of troubled times. For example, in a parallel prose essay, Zhang Weiping commemorates an 1843 lustration gathering, on the Pearl River at Huadi, of a group of twenty Cantonese literati—including the Xuehaitang scholars Zhang, Huang Peifang, Tan Ying, Chen Li, Shen Shiliang, and Xu Hao, as well as Chen Qikun, a local teacher from a Shanyin family of *muyou*. Referring to British incursions during the Opium War, Zhang symbolically reclaims this urban space: "Previously the rebellious foreigners were not pacified and disturbed the immortal city; now the coastal disorders are settled, and this kingly path is again respected."[49]

The lustration ceremony subsequently became a popular pastime among a select group of urban Cantonese literati. In 1845, 1853, and 1857, Li Changrong hosted observances at his Willow Hall in the New City; attendees included such local luminaries as Zhang Weiping, Huang Peifang, Tan Ying, and Su Liupeng (1796–1862), a renowned painter whose grandson would study at the Xuehaitang in 1890.[50] Deng Dalin's Almond Grove Villa near Huadi was also a popular site. Du You, Shen Shiliang, and Xu Yubin attended a lustration ceremony there in 1848; in 1854 a former Xuehaitang examinee named Li Yingtian (1852 *jinshi*) invited Zhang Weiping, Shen Shiliang, Xu Yubin, and others to Almond Grove Villa before moving on to a wine shop near the Pan estate in Henan, where they observed the lustration ceremony.[51]

The year 1860 was a special one for lustration devotees because most urban literati had just returned from their refuge in the countryside and this year happened to have an intercalary third month, which allowed for multiple celebrations. As a result, this group gathered on several occasions throughout the year. They began their observances with two separate meetings on the third day of the third month. Li Changrong invited Fan Feng, Xu Hao, Tan Ying, and Tan's student at the Xuehaitang, Chen Qirong, to the Willow Hall. Meanwhile, a Xinhui native named Luo Tianchi, who resided for years at Yingyuan Temple below Yuexiu Hill, hosted Xuehaitang co-directors Chen Li and Chen Liangyu, as well as Yan Xun and

FIG. 6: Lustration festivities at Myrobalan Grove in 1860 (SOURCE: *Gengshen xiuxi lu*).

Liang Yusen (two Xuehaitang poets), at Changshou Monastery. On the first day of the intercalary third month, Li Changrong, Wang Quan, Yan Xun, and other urban literati gathered at Guangxiao Monastery's Myrobalan Grove for a preparatory celebration, and two days later Fan Feng, Xu Hao, Pan Shu, and others assembled at the Almond Grove Villa. In all, various combinations of these poets met a total of nine times at six sites in and around Guangzhou over the course of 1860, culminating in "autumn lustration" ceremonies in the middle of the seventh month and the first *si*-day of the eighth month.[52]

More important, in contrast to previous years, the poets who met in 1860 edited a commemorative volume of the year's observances, entitled *Gengshen xiuxi ji* (Literary collection from the 1860 lustration celebrations). In addition to prefaces and postscripts by Li Changrong, Chen Qirong, and the Cantonese parallel prose master Tan Ying, the text is composed of poems written on each occasion and drawings of each site (see Fig. 6). In the poems and prefaces, the authors emphasize continuity with the lustration "tradition" by paying homage to the original "Shanyin gathering" under Wang

Xizhi, Wang Shizhen's ceremonies at Red Bridge, and Zeng Yu's Changshou Monastery gathering; they also repeatedly refer to the series of crises that had disrupted more recent celebrations. Several poems note the destruction in 1857 of the Rong family's Consigned Garden, at the base of Yuexiu Hill, where Zhang Weiping, Tan Ying, and Chen Qikun had organized lustration observances before the British and French occupation.[53] Other poems remark on the passing of the previous generation of literati. In his first poem on the 1860 ceremony at Willow Hall, for example, Li Changrong observes that several attendees of the 1853 event—Zhang Weiping, Huang Peifang, and Du You—were all deceased.[54] Li's second poem expresses protonationalistic sentiments, proclaiming that he was "not moved by [Wang] Xizhi alone," but also by the crises facing the dynasty.[55]

Literary outings that resulted in the printing of two collections of poetry—one in honor of Lieutenant Huang and the other celebrating the 1860 lustration observances—marked a crucial step in the reassertion of urban elite culture. Both collections were primarily products of Guangzhou's community of urban literati, who had only weak ties to the delta hinterland. When they saw their city defended by an obscure sublieutenant surnamed Huang, they made sure to recognize his contribution. In 1860, many of these same literati celebrated the reconstruction of urban elite culture in Guangzhou, despite the continued foreign occupation, by repeatedly reenacting and rewriting an elite cultural ritual, with symbolic connections both to Jiangnan literary culture and to the local Cantonese environment. As second-generation Xuehaitang scholars sought to ensure a favorable allocation of reconstruction funding, these literary events served to reestablish their cultural legitimacy as part of the urban elite.

RECONSTRUCTION STRATEGIES IN CITY AND HINTERLAND

In addition to celebrating the defense of their city and recreating the pre-crisis lifestyle, urban Cantonese literati took steps to ensure that their academic institutions and literary projects were securely funded, despite the intense competition for resources during the reconstruction of the 1860s. Though the larger, "national" project of reconstruction, known as the Tongzhi Restoration, has been portrayed by some historians as little more than the last gasp of the *ancien régime*, more recent studies have emphasized the benefits that local elites derived from new sources of funding and innovative "elite-managed" institutions.[56] In Guangzhou and the Pearl River delta, various segments of the elite scrambled for a piece of this reconstruction pie. Elite members of the dominant lineages of the Enclosure district, Daliang, and other prosperous areas of the delta hinterland utilized the militias formed in response to foreign incursions and the Red Turban uprisings to consolidate their hold on local resources and expand their control further into the sands. In Guangzhou city, the scholarly elite associated with the Xuehaitang asserted itself as well, by managing urban granaries and other institutions, and securing funding from sympathetic officials for their scholarly projects. The amount of energy that they devoted to ensuring the survival of the Xuehaitang and the projects associated with it indicates the academy's importance as a local cultural resource.

In Chapter 7 we will examine in detail the creation of Rulin Academy, a corporate institution controlled by the elite of Jiujiang township, in the Enclosure district. The elite of Daliang likewise consolidated its power during crisis and reconstruction, a process that illustrates the strategies pursued in the delta hinterland as opposed to those employed by urban literati. Two members of the dominant Daliang lineages, Long Yuanxi (1810–84) and Luo Dunyan, took advantage of the pacification of the Red Turbans to augment their power. After government troops recovered Daliang in May 1855, Long Yuanxi organized the Shunde Central Militia Bureau (Shunde tuanlian zongju). This bureau in turn became a vehicle that allowed representatives of Shunde's most powerful lineages, including the Changjiao Li as well as the Long and Luo of Daliang, virtually to rule much of the county for the rest of the century. Long Yuanxi and Luo Dunyan mobilized the militia again in 1858, in an effort to oust the British and French from Guangzhou city. Although this attempt ended in a fiasco, and though the symbolism of a hinterland army laying siege to the city must not have resonated well with the urban elite, Long and Luo were undeterred in asserting their control over the countryside. In 1859, the Shunde bureau took control of a stretch of sands on the border of Xiangshan and Shunde, known as the Sixteen Sands of the Eastern Sea (Donghai shiliu sha). By the middle of the 1860s, new provincial officials were being warned about the power of the Daliang Long and Luo, demonstrating that these dominant lineages of the delta had profited nicely in the reconstruction.[57]

As some dominant lineages of the delta augmented their power through the control of local taxes and militia, they increasingly came into conflict with provincial officials in Guangzhou. Strong provincial officials who attempted to reassert government control over taxation in the delta hinterland often met with stiff opposition there, but were supported by urban literati who benefited from officials' efforts to siphon funds from the hinterland into the city. Thus, when Guo Songtao (1818–91), who served as governor from 1863 to 1866, established a government bureau to carry out a survey of unregistered sands, the dominant lineages that controlled these sands resisted. Two decades later, Governor-General Zhang Zhidong (1837–1909) created a Central Sands Bureau (Shatian zongju) to conduct a new survey, but again met with much resistance.[58] When Zhang succeeded in forcing an elite-managed tax-farming organization in Dongguan county, the notorious Mingluntang, to remit taxes to the provincial government, he used some of this money to support urban printing projects. Likewise, the urban elite centered at the Xuehaitang offered critiques of the militia organized by the delta lineages. Fan Feng, retaining some of the martial heritage of his Chinese banner background, derided the various schemes presented by "green students and useless gentry" (qingjin feishen) to provincial officials during the Opium War.[59] Similarly, Chen Li privately observed that the rural militia was not only useless but also the main source of bandits and rebels in the disturbances of the 1850s.[60]

Provincial authorities and urban literati shared an interest in gaining control over income derived from the sands, potentially at the expense of established lineages in townships bordering on the sands.[61] Just as the delta elite was creating increasingly sophisticated corporate institutions in the hinterland during the middle decades of the nineteenth century, so the urban elite asserted its role in managing local affairs. Although they were at times critical of the methods used by delta elites to augment their power, the urban elite associated with the Xuehaitang devised similar strategies in Guangzhou—the one exception being, of course, that the urban elite did so under the patronage of provincial officials rather than in defiance of them. The fact that many members of Guangzhou's in-migrating elite served as *muyou* on county, prefectural, and provincial staffs must have predisposed officials to support urban projects. Moreover, urban literati, particularly those associated with the Xuehaitang, were employed in various ad hoc projects sponsored by provincial officials. In one such project, a newly established map bureau was given the task of drawing detailed maps of Guangdong province, and the major scholars on its staff included Chen Li, Zou Boqi, and Gui Wencan.[62]

The most important institution under the control of Guangzhou's urban elite (and in particular several Xuehaitang scholars) was a preexisting elite-managed granary that was used to fund urban scholarly projects during reconstruction in the 1860s. This institution, known as the Kind Relief Granary (Huiji cang), had formally been proposed by group of gentry in the 1830s. Ou Yuzhang (1808 *jinshi*), a high-ranking gentry from the Nanhai section of the Enclosure district, headed the list of gentry sponsors. Ou's name most likely appeared at the top only because of his status as a former Hanlin academician and current Yuexiu director, as he does not seem to have been heavily involved in subsequent granary operations. Other sources give credit to Xuehaitang co-directors Lin Botong and Yi Kezhong, or to Chen Qikun, for conceiving the granary and lobbying officials.[63] In any case, in 1837 the project won the approval of Governor-General Deng Tingzhen and Governor Qi Gong (1777-1844). When it was completed in the following year, there were in fact two components, an East Granary and a West Granary, both located on Westlake Street in the southern part of the Old City. The project was funded by donations from the city's elite, including the maritime merchants. Significantly, Deng and Qi explicitly acknowledged that the new granary was to be managed by those who had supported its creation, rather than by supposedly corrupt yamen underlings. Among others, Huang Peifang was an early manager. The granary was initially set up with an endowment of 124,982 taels, of which 110,000 remained after meeting the costs of construction. Of this, 40 percent was to be used to purchase grain, and the remaining 60 percent was deposited in interest-earning accounts. Though it is not mentioned in accounts of the granary's founding, other sources indicate that it also derived rent from land under its control.[64]

Although it was established in order to ameliorate such disasters as the 1833 floods that had sent city residents scrambling up Yuexiu Hill, the granary's assets were put to creative use by the Guangzhou elite during the reconstruction era. In 1862, Governor-General Lao Chongguang (1802–67) ordered that 240 taels of annual rents derived from lands under the granary's control be diverted to help meet Xuehaitang expenses. Though it is unclear who initiated this idea, two years later the granary manager was Shi Cheng, the current Yuexiu director and grandson of a Shanyin *muyou*. Taking advantage of high grain prices, Shi sold the granary reserves, set aside a sufficient portion for an emergency, and used the surplus to fund the reprinting of Ruan Yuan's provincial gazetteer, as the original printing blocks had been destroyed during the 1857 shelling of Guangzhou. A decade later, Chen Li and Wenlan Academy director Wang Jianxin shared management of the granary. Under their control, the granary acquired several tens of acres of sands in Xiangshan and Panyu, from which they derived rent and interest. In this case, at least, Guangzhou's urban, in-migrating elite vied with the elite members of the dominant lineages in the delta for access to wealth offered by the sands. Where the latter had at its disposal large amounts of land and newly formed militias controlled by such corporate entities as ancestral halls and academies, the former utilized official patronage. Such cooperation with city-based officials allowed the urban literati to invest in cultural resources, such as the reconstruction of the Xuehaitang and a further elaboration of Ruan Yuan's curricular ideals.[65]

DEVELOPING THE XUEHAITANG IN RECONSTRUCTION

In glorifying the establishment of the Xuehaitang, Ruan Yuan and the first generation of scholars who studied there had sought to differentiate the new academy from older academies in Guangdong, by extolling an eclectic blend of novel and imported scholarly and literary ideals, ranging from evidential research to *Wenxuan* literary models. Yet despite the unique content of the Xuehaitang examinations and the popularity of the academy grounds as a site for "refined gatherings," co-directors and examinees did not regularly meet at the academy in their roles as teachers and students. A new experiment in 1834 resulted in the creation of a system of "specialized courses" (*zhuanke*), in which "specialized students" (*zhuanke sheng*) were allowed to concentrate in a particular field and study closely with one of the eight co-directors. After 1834, the specialized courses were discontinued due to a lack of funding, but urban literati availed themselves of the opportunities afforded by reconstruction in the 1860s to revive and institutionalize the specialized courses, marking a real departure from the conventional education in Qing academies. The institutional innovation of specialized courses at the Xuehaitang sought to realize in practice the claims to uniqueness advanced by early supporters of the academy.

Two followers of Ruan Yuan, Lu Kun (1772–1835) and Qian Yiji (1783–1850), are credited with creating the system of specialized students. Lu, who had been transferred to the Guangdong-Guangxi governor-generalship in 1832, was a member of the famed 1799 *jinshi* class, for which Ruan had served as an examiner. Zhejiang native Qian Yiji followed Lu to his new post in Guangzhou to compile a gazetteer of the Guangdong salt monopoly. Noting that Xuehaitang examinees did not necessarily even visit the co-directors, Lu feared that, in the absence of the founder's charisma, pedagogical practice at the academy lacked vitality. Thus, upon Qian's completion of the gazetteer, Lu retained him to lecture students in an informal capacity and to help alleviate the threat of complacency at the Xuehaitang. Together with Lin Botong, Wu Lanxiu, and Zeng Zhao—three original co-directors still at the academy—Qian devised a method for testing students specializing in a single Classic. He then brought their suggestions to Lu Kun, who instituted the system and ordered that the first class of ten specialized students be selected in 1834.[66]

It is unclear to what extent Ruan Yuan, who was still governor-general of Yunnan and Guizhou in 1834, had a hand in creating the specialized courses; he did certainly communicate with Xuehaitang scholars after leaving Guangzhou, bestowing on the academy a stone-engraved depiction of Yunnan's Lake Erhai.[67] Regardless of how direct a role Ruan played in 1834, the specialized courses closely corresponded to the curricular ideals of the academy imagined by Ruan in the 1820s. In his preface to the *Xuehaitang ji*, Ruan had presented a vision of the specialized courses in embryonic form, describing students specializing in pre-Song classical exegeses, ety-

Table 2
1834 Specialized Students

Student	Text
Chen Li	Guliang commentary to *Chunqiu*?
Zhang Qizeng	*Hanshu*
Wu Wenqi	*Da Dai Liji* (Elder Dai's Record of Rites)
Zhu Ciqi	(declined appointment)
Li Nengding[a]	*Chunqiu*
Hou Du[b]	*Liji* (Record of Rites)
Wu Ping	Gongyang commentary to *Chunqiu*
Pan Jili	*Shijing*?
Jin Xiling	*Shijing*
Xu Yubin[c]	*Wenxuan*

NOTES: I list the names in the order in which they are listed in the *Xuehaitang zhi*. Unfortunately, neither the *Xuehaitang zhi* nor the *Xuehaitang zhuanke zhangcheng* lists the fields of this first class of specialized students. This table is based on Qian Yiji's evaluation of specialized students' exercises. See Qian Yiji, *Kanshi zhai jishi xugao*, 10:36a–40b. Qian does not include evaluations of Chen Li's and Zhu Ciqi's work. The latter in fact declined his appointment as a specialized student; however, it is my impression that Zhu was selected to specialize in the works of Zhu Xi. We know from other sources that Chen Li in 1834 studied the *Guliang zhuan*, and so I assume that this was his specialty in the Xuehaitang specialized course. See Chen Li, "Guliang lizheng xu," in his *Dongshu ji*, 3.12b.

[a]Li Nengding belonged to a family of sojourners from Shaanxi who registered as Panyu residents. *Panyu xian xu zhi*, 20.16a.

[b]Hou Du was Hou Kang's younger brother. *Panyu xian zhi*, 48.4a.

[c]Xu Yubin was likely an in-migrant because he was registered as an urban—or *bushu* 補屬 (added)—resident of Panyu. A student of Wu Lanxiu, Xu was also a nephew of Liang Mei (Xu's mother was Liang's younger sister). The 1871 Panyu gazetteer records Liang Mei's sister's act of cutting her flesh to provide blood for medicine for her ailing husband (Yubin's father), just as Liang Mei used his own flesh in a soup to cure their mother. Xu Yubin, *Dongrongguan yigao*, 6.1a; *Panyu xian zhi*, 51.30a; *Panyu xian xu zhi*, 19.26b.

mology, the works of Zhu Xi, historical studies, *Wenxuan*-style literature, and Tang-Song poetry and utilitarian prose.[68] Specialized students in 1834 in fact chose from much the same fields as these. Each of the ten students nominated by the co-directors was to select one text in which he was interested, from among any of the Thirteen Classics (with Han and Tang commentaries and subcommentaries), the first four Standard Histories (*Shiji*, *Hanshu*, *Hou Hanshu*, and *Sanguo zhi*), the *Wenxuan*, Du Fu's poetry, Han Yu's prose, and the collected works of Zhu Xi. A student would keep daily records of his progress, which would be appraised quarterly by the co-direc-

Table 3
1866 Specialized Students

Student	Text
Gui Wenchi	*Shiji*
Pan Naicheng[a]	Mao recension of the *Shijing*
Liang Qi[b]	Han Yu's collected writings
Kong Jifan	*Suanjing shishu* (Ten mathematics classics)
Gao Xueyao	*Liji*
Chen Qingxiu[c]	*Zhouli* (Rites of Zhou)
Cui Yanwen	Zhu Xi's complete works
Wang Guorui	*Erya*
Zhou Guo	*Yili* (Rites and ceremonies)
Wu Xuezao	Zuo commentary to *Chunqiu*

[a]Pan Naicheng was the son of Pan Jili, one of the first ten students selected in 1834.
[b]Liang Qi appears in the *Xuehaitang zhi*, 27a, under his original name, Liang Yitang 梁以瑭.
[c]Chen Qingxiu was a grandson of Chen Li's brother. Wang Zongyan, "Chen Dongshu xiansheng nianpu," p. 55.
SOURCE: *Xuehaitang zhi*, 27a–b.

tor whose expertise most closely matched the student's interest.[69] This first class of specialized students and the texts in which they specialized are indicated in Table 2. Five of these first ten specialized students would later become Xuehaitang co-directors: Chen Li in 1840, Jin Xiling in 1853, Li Nengding in 1858, Zhu Ciqi in 1859, and Zhang Qizeng in 1885. Despite this prestigious first group, however, specialized courses were discontinued after only a single term. The courses had no permanent source of funding, and after Lu Kun died in office in October 1835, no provincial officials demonstrated the will to resume them.

After a hiatus of 30 years, specialized courses were revived as part of the general reconstruction of the Xuehaitang. Despite the use of the academy grounds as barracks by the occupying forces from 1857 on, Xuehaitang co-director appointments were still made in 1858 and 1859, a third collection of examination papers was printed in 1859, and examinations were resumed in 1860. The mountain hall itself was repaired two years later, collapsed soon thereafter in a typhoon, and was again rebuilt in 1863. In addition, Governor-General Lao Chongguang organized the reprinting of the *Huang Qing jingjie*, Ruan Yuan's *Yanjingshi ji* (Collected writings from the

Table 4
1888 Xuehaitang Examination Questions for the Third Month

Examine the differences and similarities between *Shujing* and *Shijing* [references to] the Xi and Ju.*ᵃ*

Address the theory that the *Shijing* and the *Liji* represent the inner and outer aspects of the same phenomenon. (This is Wang Yinglin's theory. Try expanding upon it.)

Explicate "Proclaiming the *shi*" in the Marriage Ritual section of the *Yili*.

Explain the theory of new meaning in the *Chunqiu*. (This phrase comes from Du Yu's preface.)

Of the six types of characters, phonetic compounds are the most common. [In describing sounds], in addition to stating that a certain component of a character is phonetic, the *Shuowen* also uses such phrases as "both are phonetic," "is also phonetic," and "omits the phonetic." What do these phrases mean? Try distinguishing among them.

Address the theory that Chu Shaosun supplemented the *Shiji*.*ᵇ*

Interpret [the concept of] reverence.

Explain the method of dividing a circle with eight secants.

Imitate Fu Liang's "Instruction for Building the Zhang Liang Temple, Written for the Duke of Song."*ᶜ*

Expand Cai Yong's "Rhapsody on the Writing Brush" (ancient style).*ᵈ*

Match Han Yu's "Three Poems on Setting Out on the Southern Stream."

Match Du Fu's poem, "Righteous Bird."

NOTES: One can note similarities between the two sets of examination questions translated here and a set from December 1868 included in the "Xuehaitang kao," and translated by Benjamin Elman. See Rong Zhaozu, "Xuehaitang kao," opposite p. 1; Elman, *From Philosophy to Philology*, pp. 127–28.

*ᵃ*Xi 漆 and Ju 沮 are the names of two streams that appear in these two Classics. See Legge, *The Chinese Classics*, 3: 123 and 4: 291, 588.

*ᵇ*Chu Shaosun 褚少孫 (104?–30? BCE) added supplemental passages to Sima Qian's *Shiji*. Loewe, *Early Chinese Texts*, p. 406.

*ᶜ*Fu Liang 傅亮 lived during the earlier Song dynasty (420–78). Xiao Tong, *Wenxuan*, 36: 5a–6b.

*ᵈ*Cai Yong 蔡邕 (133–92) was a rhapsody master during the Later Han.

SOURCE: *Xuehaitang keti*, unpaginated.

Classics Research Study), and the first two series of Xuehaitang collected writings. The first project was initiated in the late spring of 1860, on the grounds of Changshou Monastery, with the Xuehaitang co-directors Chen Li and Tan Ying both involved in the compilation.[70] During this phase of reconstruction, Chen Li found in Guo Songtao a provincial official willing to support his plan to revive the specialized courses. As restored under Guo's patronage in 1865, the

Table 5
1888 Xuehaitang Examination Questions for the Fourth Month

Write an analytical postscript to Yuan Mei's "Identifying the Metal Bound [Coffer]."[a]
Explicate the terms "feast," "honor," and "pledge" in the "Crimson Bow" Poem [of the *Shijing*].[b]
Explicate the passage "Guests stand atop the western steps" in the District Symposium section of the *Yili*.
Explicate Jiao and Xia in the *Zuo Commentary*.[c]
Address the theory that the ten heavenly stems are all images of human form.
Explain the differentiation between Daoists and Supernatural Beings (*shenxian*) in the Bibliographic Treatise of the *Hanshu*.
Write an analytical postscript to Zhu Xi's "Commemoration of the Classics and Histories Pavilion at the Fuzhou Prefectural School."
Use the continual proportion method to find differences in pipe pitch.
Write a preface for a reprint edition of the *Wenxuan*.
Continue the "Rhapsody on Printing Books" (ancient style).
Write a poem on this theme: Ascending the Six Banyan Temple Pagoda. (Use the rhyme scheme of Du Fu's "Ascending Kind Grace Temple Pagoda.")

[a] This metal bound coffer 金縢 appears in a chapter of that title in the *Book of Zhou* section of the *Shujing*. See Legge, *The Chinese Classics*, 3: 356.
[b] See Legge, *The Chinese Classics*, 4: 278–79.
[c] "Jiao" 焦 and "Xia" 瑕 were two cities/districts in the state of Jin 晉 during the Chunqiu era. See Legge, *The Chinese Classics*, 5: 217, 694.

specialized courses followed the format of the original system, with the addition of one new field, mathematics. Also, Guo designated a three-year term of study for the new specialized courses, with the first group to begin study in 1866. The 1866 class and their texts are listed in Table 3.

Although the governor provided funding for the new group of specialized students to stay at the academy for three years, he made no provisions to guard against the possibility that the system might be discontinued as it had been in the 1830s. The Xuehaitang co-directors then created an opportunity to ensure the longevity of the specialized courses. Beginning in 1866, tenants on one of the plots of land originally set aside to support the academy "agreed" to have their original rent of 450 taels doubled. In 1869, co-director Zhou Yinqing suggested to Governor Li Futai (1807–71) that this additional income be used to provide for twenty specialized students' stipends and related expenses. Zhou requested the same funding for two more classes of twenty specialized students each, for 1872 and 1875. By this time, a precedent had been set, and new classes of specialized students were created with increasing frequency through 1897, under the enthusiastic patronage of such provincial officials as Zhang Zhidong in the 1880s.[71]

Through the initiative of Chen Li and Zhou Yinqing, then, the long-defunct specialized courses were revived and institutionalized in the Xuehaitang curriculum. This system had only been a vague ideal in Ruan Yuan's preface to the *Xuehaitang ji*. Lu Kun and Qian Yiji created specialized courses in 1834 but did not provide a mechanism capable of perpetuating them. This might have been the fate of the 1866 class as well, had it not been for the opportunism of Zhou Yinqing, who, in the scramble for funding during the reconstruction of Guangzhou, managed to secure a reliable source of financial support for specialized courses.

While creating the innovative specialized courses, the Xuehaitang continued to hold examinations for the much larger group of regular examinees at the academy. Examination topics show a remarkable amount of consistency, both from one month to the next, and when juxtaposed with the scholarly and literary ideals of the founder. Typical sets of questions are those for the third and fourth lunar months of 1888, as shown in Tables 4 and 5. The first four questions for each month ask students for exegeses of classical passages in the form of explications (*jie*), examinations (*kao*), and explanations/theories (*shuo*). These are typically followed by one question each on philology, early (usually Han) history, *lixue*, and mathematics. Finally, students are required to comment on or imitate pre-Tang rhapsody or parallel prose pieces, and a Tang-Song poet, most often Du Fu.

Though extant sets of examination questions from 1888 to 1896 demonstrate scholarly and literary content that is remarkably consistent with Ruan Yuan's vision, the way in which these regular examinations were conducted suggests a very distant relationship between co-directors and regular students. Examination questions were publicized monthly from the second through eleventh months of the lunar calendar.[72] They instructed students to submit their answers after fifteen days to a designated site in Guangzhou. Sites used for the collection of examination papers included the Yuexiu, Yuehua, and Yangcheng academies, as well as the Kind Relief Granary, a Panyu county academy, and, only on occasion, the Xuehaitang itself. Beginning in the eleventh month of 1888, students were reminded that their stipends would be revoked if they missed more than three of the monthly examinations. This is hardly what one would expect from a city's academic elite. Such a remote and perfunctory relationship between the academy and the regular examinees suggests that education at the Xuehaitang did not always live up to the transformative experience imagined by those who celebrated the academy in writing.

Nevertheless, the Xuehaitang continued to attract Cantonese and sojourning literati seeking a refined setting for their outings. For example, in a "Record of Viewing the Moon at the Mountain Hall," Chen Li describes spending two days and nights at the Xuehaitang in the middle of the tenth month of 1866, studying, drinking, viewing the full moon, and talking to Wang Quan.[73] A decade later, Wen Tingshi (1856–1905), a young literatus from Jiangxi sojourning in Guangzhou and studying under Chen Li, noted in his diary for June 8, 1876, that he and Yu Shimei (1859–1915), an 1876 specialized student, climbed up to the Xuehaitang in order to escape the summer heat and to enjoy a few rounds of chess. The following day, Wen declined an invitation from Chen Zongkan and others for a meal at the Xuehaitang.[74] From this perspective, the Xuehaitang maintained its dominant presence in the local cultural landscape and continued to be an important site on the social itinerary of Guangzhou's urban elite.

THE XUEHAITANG IN THE EVOLVING SYSTEM OF ACADEMIES

The rebuilding of the Xuehaitang and the revival and formalization of its specialized courses were part of a larger reconstruction of institutions in Guangzhou following the series of crises that culminated in the foreign occupation of the city. Despite the competition for resources, the system of academies in Guangzhou actually expanded during the subsequent period of reconstruction. Older academies continued to play an important role in Cantonese academic life, and

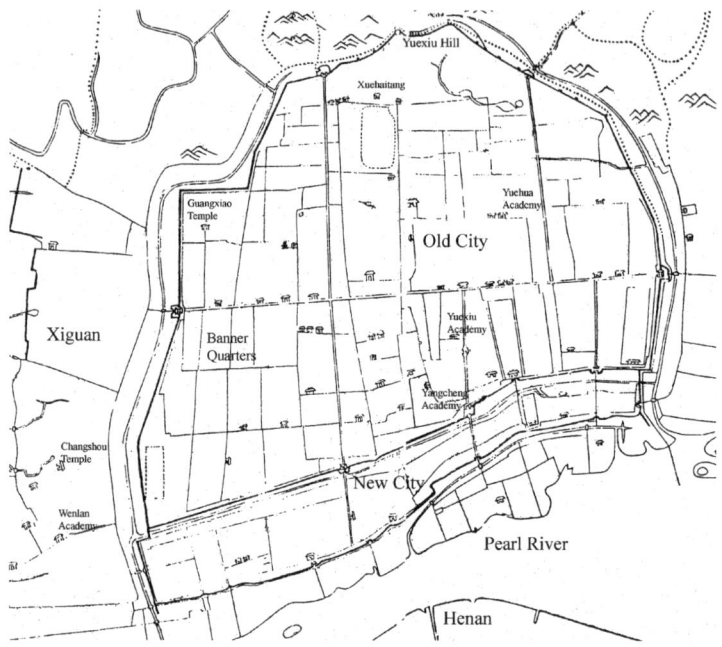

FIG. 7: Chen Li's city. This is adapted from a map of Guangzhou drawn by Chen Li for the 1879 Guangzhou prefectural gazetteer. The gazetteer was compiled and printed at Yuexiu Academy (SOURCE: *Guangzhou fu zhi*, 8.3b–4a).

two new academies were established on Yuexiu Hill alongside the Xuehaitang (see Fig. 7). The fervent renovation of older academies and founding of new ones in Guangzhou during the Tongzhi reconstruction reflects a pattern throughout Guangdong and in other parts of the Qing empire. For Guangdong, Liu Boji shows that, during the Qing, the Tongzhi period had the highest annual rate of construction of new academies in Guangdong province.[75] Barry Keenan and Mary Rankin have documented a similar jump in rates of academy construction in Jiangsu and Zhejiang.[76]

The oldest official academy in Guangzhou, Yuexiu, continued to function in a stable manner throughout the nineteenth century, under several Cantonese directors. In contrast to the eighteenth-century practice of hiring northerners to fill the post, Ou Yuzhang, the literatus from the Enclosure district who had headed the list of gentry supporting the establishment of the Kind Relief Granary, held the post for a decade from 1832 to 1842. Ou was followed by another literatus from the Nanhai section of the Enclosure district, He Wenqi, who taught at Yuexiu for almost a decade.[77] After these two teachers from the Enclosure district, Shi Cheng, manager of the Kind Relief Granary, headed the academy for 23 years beginning late in the Xianfeng reign. During his long tenure at Yuexiu, he secured funding from provincial officials for major renovations at the academy.[78]

Somewhat less is known about the other two major Guangzhou *shuyuan*, aside from the fact that they, too, continued to operate. Writing in 1841, the author of the Yuehua gazetteer, Liang Tingnan, stated that the academy was commandeered as a temporary yamen several times after 1830. The most famous instance of this was, of course, when Imperial Commissioner Lin Zexu conducted his 1839 anti-opium campaign from the academy. According to Liang, not only was instruction at Yuehua interrupted, but the physical complexion of the academy was altered as well.[79] Liang, hastily compiling the gazetteer while taking refuge outside the city during the first Opium War, certainly regarded the situation as bleak, but education at Yuehua was resumed after the crisis, as life in the city returned to normal. For example, a refugee Guangxi scholar close to Chen Li, Zheng Xianfu (1801–72), briefly headed Yuehua in 1860, and Liang Zhaohuang (1827–86), a nephew of the maritime merchant Liang Lunshu, served as director and printed Yuehua student examination papers covering the years 1874–78.[80] Finally, Yangcheng Academy continued to thrive under a series of successors to the academy's first director, Xie Lansheng. Chen Qikun, from a family of Shanyin *muyou*, taught at the academy in the 1830s and 1840s. He was followed after 1849 by Deng Shixian (1802 *jinshi*), a Hanlin academician from the Nanhai portion of the Enclosure district, and Luo Jiaqin of the Daliang Luo lineage, who headed Yangcheng for a decade in the 1850s and 1860s.[81] Thus, directorships of the three main conventional academies in Guangzhou alternated between literati from powerful Daliang and Enclosure district lineages, on the one hand, and sojourners and in-migrants in Guangzhou, on the other.[82]

These three older academies continued to thrive because the wider Cantonese elite, including the academic elite at the Xuehaitang, recognized a shared interest in training their sons for the civil service examinations. As a result, education at the older academies continued to emphasize training in the *Four Books* and the composition of civil service examination essays and poetry. Yuexiu director He Wenqi was in high demand among the Cantonese elite for his expertise in examination-style writing. His students even included Chen Pu, who became a Xuehaitang co-director in 1861. He Wenqi's successor, Shi Cheng, noted with pride that more than ten Yuexiu students over the years had won top honors in the provincial examinations—under his direction, one Yuexiu student placed first in the 1865 metropolitan examinations, another became the 1871 *zhuangyuan* (first place in the palace examination), and yet another the 1874 *bangyan* (second place in the palace examination).[83]

Guangzhou's urbanized and in-migrating families—the main source of Xuehaitang examinees, specialized students, and co-directors—also took full advantage of the opportunities afforded by the conventional academies. The Shi family discussed in Chapter 1 is a case in point. Shi Cheng was a longtime Yuexiu director, and his brother, Shi Duan, took Xuehaitang examinations frequently enough to place ten poems in the *Xuehaitang sanji*. Shi Cheng's grandson and another Shi who appears to be of the same generation were specialized students in the 1890s. Wu Feng, another literatus with Shanyin roots, was both a Yuehua Academy student and a frequent Xuehaitang examinee. Tan Zongjun, a future Xuehaitang examinee and co-director, studied at Yuexiu in the 1850s and the early 1860s. Tan's friend Liao Tingxiang served both as a Xuehaitang co-director and later as director of Yangcheng.[84]

Not only did urban Cantonese students not perceive any contradiction in studying at both the Xuehaitang and the more conventional academies, but tangible evidence of the Xuehaitang's continued high standing among the older academies may be found in the dissemination of books. As of the 1840s, copies of the *Huang Qing jingjie* could be found in both the Yuehua and Yuexiu academy libraries. The former academy's collection also included two other staples of the Xuehaitang curriculum: the *Wenxuan* and the Thirteen Classics with Han and Tang commentaries and subcommentaries. The Yuexiu library housed a copy of the *Gujing jingshe wenji*, the collected student writings from Ruan Yuan's Hangzhou academy. By the 1890s, Duanxi, the old official academy in Zhaoqing, had accumulated, among other items, the *Huang Qing jingjie*, all four editions of Xuehaitang examination essays and poems, a work by Zeng Zhao on the *Zhouli*, Chen Li's *Dongshu dushuji*, and several other texts by Xuehaitang scholars.[85]

During the Tongzhi-era reconstruction of Guangzhou, two new academies were established on Yuexiu Hill, next to the Xuehaitang. The future site for the first of these, the Jupo jingshe (Jupo Retreat), originated as the center of a park between the Xuehaitang and the old Daoist Yingyuan Temple, and was opened in the Daoguang era by Guangzhou's garrison general. During the 1850s, Governor-General Ye Mingchen transformed the park into the Eternal Spring Immortals' Lodge, a personal playground for his sojourning father. When foreign troops occupied Guangzhou, Ye was captured and the lodge damaged, although a British observer noted in 1858 that "Yeh's House" was "the only house in Canton city which an English gentleman would think inhabitable."[86] Perhaps in an effort to provide a counterexample to Ye's perceived frivolity in the face of disaster, Governor Jiang Yili (1833–74) and salt controller Fang Junyi (1815–89) in the mid-1860s suggested using the site to establish a new academy. Fang supervised the academy's construction and appointed Chen Li as its first director. In order to lend the location a new air of respect, the academy was dubbed the Jupo jingshe, referring to Cui Yuzhi (whose literary name was "Jupo"), the statesman and poet of the Song, who had studied on Yuexiu Hill and been honored as a local worthy by the Cloud and Springs group. After the Jupo jingshe's initial income was diverted to fund the new Yingyuan Academy in 1869, Fang's successor donated 22,000 taels for an interest-earning deposit with pawn merchants to support Jupo.[87]

The Jupo jingshe essentially became the personal academy of Chen Li, the subject of the following chapter. Chen suggested modeling the new academy upon the Xuehaitang; students would be tested in Classics, Histories, literary prose, and utilitarian prose. In addition, Chen continued the Xuehaitang ideal of specialized courses, expecting Jupo students to master one text toward which their natures were inclined. In addition to adopting the Xuehaitang curriculum largely unchanged, however, Chen sought a much closer relationship between himself and the approximately 40 Jupo students selected. Thus, Chen required 30 examinations over the course of a year, in contrast to quarterly (and later monthly) tests at the Xuehaitang. Finally, he organized several large-scale printing projects at the new academy. After Chen Li's death in 1882, his students established a system of four co-directors, erected a shrine in honor of Chen, and stuck closely to the precedents he had originally derived from the Xuehaitang.[88]

Unlike the Jupo jingshe, the second new academy established on Yuexiu Hill during reconstruction bore no obvious resemblance to the Xuehaitang. This was the Yingyuan shuyuan, established in 1869 by Guangdong lieutenant-governor Wang Kaitai (1823–75). Founded adjacent to the old Yingyuan Temple, Wang intended the academy to serve as a training ground for Guangdong natives who had achieved *juren* status. Whereas students in most cases left academies after becoming *juren*, the sole purpose of Yingyuan Academy was to prepare and support this level of degree-holders in taking the metropolitan examinations. Thus, in addition to providing a stipend and testing students in examination-style writing, the academy also financed students' travel to the capital, gave rewards to candidates who placed first in metropolitan and palace examinations, and granted subsidies to successful candidates assigned to posts in any of the Six Boards or the Hanlin Academy. An annual income of 5,760 taels supported the above expenses for a hundred students, as well as a salary of 600 taels plus amenities for a single director.[89]

In his commemoration of Yingyuan Academy, Wang Kaitai makes very little pretense about either instilling Song Learning ideals of moral cultivation or following Han Learning standards of textual research; rather, he unabashedly celebrates his aims of producing examination and official talent, proudly naming a studio on the academy grounds after that of his fifth-generation ancestor, the 1703 *huiyuan* and *zhuangyuan*.[90] Similarly, Wang notes that it would be coincidentally appropriate to retain the name of the old temple, Yingyuan, for such an academy as this. He advocates, however, downplaying the Daoist meaning (which could be translated as "Temple of Meeting the Origin") in favor of an interpretation that better reflected the aspirations of the new institution: "Academy for Placing First" in the metropolitan and palace examinations. Students who achieved this goal would have stele inscriptions erected at the academy in their honor.[91] Another commemoration of the academy,

CRISIS AND RECONSTRUCTION, 1830–1870   197

by Gui Wenchi, Wencan's younger brother and one of the 1866 specialized students at the Xuehaitang, is equally outspoken in its affirmation of examination success as a goal of learning:

As for the Yingyuan Academy, it is indeed sufficient to:
  Compete for brilliance with the Two Zhe [Zhejiang],
  Match the excellence of the Eight Min [Fujian]⁹²
(Original note: Both Zhejiang and Fujian have established academies for *juren*.)⁹³

After acknowledging a Cantonese classical tradition stretching back to the Han (which indeed requires quite a mental stretch), as well as a tradition of statesmanship beginning with the Tang, Gui proceeds to praise the examination success of Cantonese scholars:

If [one] discusses the record of examination fame,
[There have been] in the past many fabulous and extraordinary talents.
Mo Xuanqing abruptly rose up from the Duan river,
  capping [his] family and given names in the first position;⁹⁴
Lun Yugang in turn ascended in Nanhai,
  Combining fathers and sons [to produce] four *yuan* [top examinees].⁹⁵
The Imperial influence in the Kangxi reign widely spread;
The human culture of Lingnan luxuriantly arose.⁹⁶

Yet Gui's commemoration of Yingyuan Academy is significant less for what it says than for the manner in which it was presented to Cantonese readers. It appeared in the 1886 *Xuehaitang siji*, alongside similar commemorations of the creation of the Jupo jingshe and the reconstruction of the Xuehaitang. The Yingyuan, and with it, education exclusively designed to produce examination talent, appeared as having attained a status equal to that of the Jupo jingshe and the exalted Xuehaitang. Ruan Yuan's academy no longer stood alone on Yuexiu Hill, looking down on the mundane world below; rather, it was part of an academic complex composed of three specialized academies and a library at the Wenlan Pavilion (see Fig. 8). The Yingyuan Academy was, in Gui's imagery, one leg of a tripod:

Close by, it neighbors the [Jupo] retreat,
Further on, it is next to the mountain hall,
As if constituting the form of a tripod standing erect,
Making even brighter the image of Southern perspicacity.⁹⁷

FIG. 8: The growing academic complex on Yuexiu Hill. Points of interest include (1) the entrance to Yingyuan Academy, (2) the entrance to the Jupo jingshe, (3) the Dragon King Temple, (4) the Xuehaitang, and (5) Wenlan Pavilion (SOURCE: *Yingyuan shuyuan zhilue*, 1b–2a).

It is conceivable that some Xuehaitang scholars grimaced at the idea of an explicitly examination-oriented academy encroaching upon the noble preserve of the Xuehaitang, but there is no evidence that they did. No less a figure than Chen Li—who, having made seven unsuccessful attempts at the *jinshi* degree, and thereby recognizing the need for such an academy—bestowed upon it a congratulatory tablet. Xuehaitang co-director Chen Pu was designated the first "elite manager" (*shendong*) at Yingyuan.[98]

Several points emerge from this brief survey of Guangzhou academies during the Tongzhi reign. Most noteworthy is the fact that the community of academies continued to expand, despite stiff competition for resources during reconstruction. Even the older or more conventional Yuexiu, Yuehua, and Yangcheng academies persevered until the end of the century. Directed by resident Cantonese who remained at their posts for unprecedented lengths of time, these institutions retained a niche in the evolving system of academies. At the same time, the previously solitary Xuehaitang was joined during the process of reconstruction by the Jupo Retreat and Yingyuan Academy. The Xuehaitang had from its inception been closely tied to the conventional academies in Guangzhou—proclamations of its uniqueness notwithstanding. What early Xuehaitang scholars had presented as a scholarly and literary rift between their academy and the others had, by the end of the Tongzhi reign, been acknowledged as a functional division among the academies. Nevertheless, the prestige of the Xuehaitang had not been diminished. Thus, Wang Kaitai celebrated his affinity with fellow Yangzhou native Ruan Yuan by noting in a couplet that his Yingyuan Academy neighbored the Xuehaitang. In establishing the examination-oriented Yingyuan Academy, Wang professed to be continuing Ruan's tradition, or, literally, "transmitting his heart/mind."[99] Thus, though the Xuehaitang no longer stood alone on Yuexiu Hill, Ruan Yuan's academy continued to be a source of prestige and maintained its status as the pre-eminent academy until the creation of the Guangya shuyuan (Broad Refinement Academy) in 1887.[100]

CONCLUSION

This chapter began by raising the question of how the series of crises and subsequent reconstruction in the middle four decades of the nineteenth century affected both the place of the Xuehaitang in the elite cultural world of Guangzhou and the dynamics between Guangzhou and its delta hinterland. Despite the high rate of turnover among Xuehaitang co-directors between 1838 and 1840, I have presented an image of continuity in its leadership and in the academy's place within the hierarchy of Cantonese academies. This image of continuity becomes apparent when examining long-term trends over the entire mid-nineteenth century. Moreover, in contrast to intellectual historians, who tend to focus on the thought of a few avant-garde thinkers, my focus on educational institutions suggests that, far from having lost its appeal by the mid-nineteenth century, the curriculum originally designed by Ruan Yuan in the 1820s was reaffirmed and reached its fullest institutional development only in the second half of the nineteenth century. The Xuehaitang—never as radically separated from conventional academies as its devotees claimed—was even more firmly embedded in urban Guangzhou's system of academies after reconstruction; its high status within that system, however, was not radically altered.

This emphasis on continuity is not meant to suggest a lack of change; even the institutionalization and routinization of a curriculum originally envisioned in the 1820s certainly marks a significant transformation. Additionally, the Xuehaitang played an increasingly important role in the evolving dynamics between city and hinterland, surviving the mid-century crises, thriving during reconstruction, and benefiting the urban elite associated with it. Ruan Yuan's academy had always held a special attraction for Guangzhou's sojourning, urbanized, and in-migrating families. This was even more the case in the late nineteenth century. As educated members of dominant lineages in the delta were turning their attention to bureaus and militias near their hinterland homes, the in-migrating urban elite in Guangzhou increasingly exploited the cultural resources offered by the Xuehaitang. Even more so than before the mid-century crises and reconstruction, the Xuehaitang was an institution that served the urban elite. As second and third generations of urban elite families chose to associate themselves with the academy, they constructed local scholarly and literary lineages, as well as genealogical ones. Finally, though resentment of the Xuehaitang began to be voiced by both urban and rural scholars—as we shall see in the following two chapters—it was from the delta hinterland, rather than from urban Guangzhou, that the loudest and most consistent criticisms would be articulated.

⊰ SIX ⊱
A "Sojourner from Jiangnan": Chen Li and Han-Song Syncretism in Guangzhou

> Even before my capping,
> I first met Zhang Weiping.
> Seeking to inquire about his method of study,
> I begged him to state the details.
> He answered, "For the *Four Treasuries*,
> The *Annotated Catalog* raises the chief points.
> A thousand gates combining ten thousand doors,
> It is truly like the ancient Jianzhang Palace.[1]
> From this you'll come to recognize the gates and paths,
> And gradually be able to ascend its halls."
>
> —Chen Li, excerpt from "Moved by My Old Teachers," 1852/53

HAVING RECOVERED FROM a near-fatal illness in the spring of 1871, Chen Li decided to set the record straight on his scholarly vision in the event that he would not survive a recurrence. In his "Self-Narration" ("Zishu"), the eminent Xuehaitang co-director recounted the intellectual journey that conducted him from youthful, "reckless" forays into evidential research to a newfound appreciation, in middle age, of the Han-dynasty Confucian Zheng Xuan and the Song-dynasty Neo-Confucian Zhu Xi.[2] Indeed, Chen Li experienced a mid-life crisis of sorts, one that entailed a re-evaluation of the scholarly ideals of the Xuehaitang. Yet he by no means turned his back on evidential research in favor of the Neo-Confucian quest for sagehood. He lived for another decade after writing his "Self-Narration" and, during these years, worked feverishly to develop pedagogical and printing projects essential to the *kaozheng* enterprise.

This chapter and the one that follows examine the two most influential classicists associated with the Xuehaitang, and arguably the most important Cantonese scholars in the middle of the nineteenth century: Chen Li and Zhu Ciqi.³ These two scholars not only had a tremendous influence on local scholarship but also present ideal case studies to illustrate the place of the Xuehaitang in the local cultural landscape. Chen Li and Zhu Ciqi were similar in many ways. In addition to the fact that later scholars have often associated them together with the Xuehaitang, both articulated versions of the most widespread trend in nineteenth-century Confucian scholarship, Han-Song syncretism. As participants in an empire-wide discourse of Han-Song syncretism, the statements of one are often easily recognizable in the other. Moreover, they both offered critiques of the Xuehaitang and its scholarly agenda.

Despite their similarities, Chen Li and Zhu Ciqi inhabited different spaces within the wider Cantonese cultural landscape. Zhu Ciqi, the subject of Chapter 7, belonged to the most productive branch of a dominant lineage in Jiujiang township, in the heart of the Enclosure district; Chen Li was the grandson of an immigrant from Jiangnan who had settled in urban Guangzhou. Furthermore, in contrast to Zhu Ciqi, Chen Li's imagination was preoccupied by Jiangnan and the scholarly practice of evidential research that it had spawned, and his particular mediation of Han Learning and Song Learning reflected this. By drawing a contrast between Chen Li and Zhu Ciqi, I do not intend to suggest an absolute dichotomy between city and delta determining the scholarly or literary priorities of scholars resident in either place. Rather, I will argue that the cultural landscape of urban Guangzhou overlapped but was not entirely congruous with that of the delta hinterland. That is to say, despite their shared Cantonese identities, literati in the city and hinterland had access to different combinations of cultural resources. Consequently, they approached Han-Song syncretism from opposite directions and articulated distinct versions of Cantonese elite identity. Ultimately, the Xuehaitang had a much greater presence among the geographically and socially mobile urban elite, represented by Chen Li, than it did among literati from the delta hinterland such as Zhu Ciqi.

EXPERIMENTS IN EVIDENTIAL RESEARCH

Chen Li's roots lay in Jiangnan. Like most Xuehaitang scholars resident in Panyu county, he came from a family of merchant and secretarial sojourners in Guangzhou city. Furthermore, like many families in nineteenth-century Guangzhou, Chen Li's family traced its roots to Shaoxing prefecture in northern Zhejiang. In the early Ming, an ancestor moved from Shaoxing to Nanjing, then still the Ming capital. When this ancestor died, he was buried on Zhong Hill (Zhongshan) on the outskirts of Nanjing, and his descendants were registered as residents of Jiangning, one of the two counties that shared jurisdiction of Nanjing.[4]

In the eighteenth century, Chen Li's grandfather, Chen Shiqi, was the first in the family to move to Guangzhou, where he relied on his maternal uncle (surnamed Han and a Jiangning native as well) to help him establish himself. Soon, his developing prosperity allowed him to purchase the rank of law secretary (*liwen*) in the lieutenant-governor's yamen. When he died, he was buried outside Guangzhou's East Gate; his two sons, including Chen Li's father, Chen Dajing, remained in Guangzhou. As a nonresident sojourner, Dajing was ineligible for the civil service examinations. Nevertheless, he received a classical education from Wei Jilian, a Shanyin county native who had attained *shengyuan* (licentiate) status as a merchant-registered student in Panyu during the Qianlong reign.[5] Despite this early classical education, Chen Dajing served for a time as a yamen clerk and then became a merchant. Chen Dajing must have gained a fair amount of influence in the city before his death in 1819, as he was close to the maritime merchant Liang Jingguo and had been encouraged by Governor-General Jiqing (d. 1802) to purchase the rank of county magistrate. He and his brother, both residing in the New City, were also influential or wealthy enough to call on the Panyu poet Lü Jian to write a preface for the family's manuscript genealogy.[6]

Like many families of in-migrants, the Chen family initially established itself in its new home by maintaining ties to fellow sojourners. Chen Dajing's principal wife, for instance, was the daughter of a Guiji man who also purchased the rank of law secretary in the lieutenant-governor's yamen.[7] Chen Li's older sister married the son of a Renhe county family, surnamed Tang, that was involved in the salt trade in Guangzhou. Chen Li later recalled that when he visited his sister at the Tang home as a young child, his sister would wake up early in the morning, make herself up in front of a large European mirror, and then take him out into the Tang family garden, where they would "climb a small tower to look at the artificial mountains, observe red fish, and play with parrots."[8] As with most in-migrating families connected to commercial wealth, the Chens did not neglect education. Chen Li was the first in his immediate family to register as a Panyu resident, and his family wasted little time in preparing him for the examinations. In 1815, at six *sui*, Chen began reading his cousin's examination essays. Two years later, Chen Dajing hired his old teacher Wei Jilian to take over his son's education. That a sojourning merchant would hire a sojourning merchant–registered *shengyuan* to teach his son perhaps represents the dominance of this group over Guangzhou city culture and, at the same time, indicates a propensity of sojourning merchant elites in the city to stick together.[9]

After receiving instruction from Wei Jilian and several other private teachers, Chen Li began to pursue an education in Guangzhou's academies, an encounter that would last a lifetime.[10] He entered Yangcheng Academy in 1825, developing, under the guidance of Xie Lansheng, an early interest in poetry. In August of the following year, educational commissioner Weng Xincun passed Chen in the Panyu county examinations. Chen took Xuehaitang examinations in 1826 under the eight newly appointed co-directors, and in 1827 under Weng Xincun. Among the first generation of Xuehaitang co-directors, it was Zhang Weiping and Hou Kang to whom Chen remained close. Zhang Weiping naturally taught poetry, but, as Chen recalls in the poem that opens this chapter, Zhang also introduced Chen to the hallmark of eighteenth-century evidential research, the *Siku quanshu*. Himself a student of Lin Botong, Hou Kang taught Chen Li the Classics, beginning with the *Yijing*. Chen's Guangzhou home was not far from that of Hou Kang and his brother, Hou Du. Also in 1827, Chen began studies at Yuexiu Academy, where he met two men who would become lifelong friends—Yang Rongxu, a future Xuehaitang co-director, and Gui Wenyao (ca. 1807–54), of the Nanhai Gui family.[11] Chen moved in 1832 from Yuexiu to Yuehua Academy—under director Chen Hongchi (1805 *jinshi*), a Zhejiang literatus—and there joined an outstanding group of students that included Tan Ying, Liang Mei, and Hou Kang. Eminent Xuehaitang co-directors, such as Wu Lanxiu and Zeng Zhao, also paid visits to Yuehua. In the same year, Chen Li also began reading the *Yugong zhuizhi* (A modest approach to the "Tributes of Yu") by Hu Wei (1633–1714), a seminal work in *kaozheng* geographical studies included in the *Huang Qing jingjie*. By 1832, then, the 23-*sui* Chen Li was already a promising young member of Guangzhou's cultural elite. In addition to the standard education preparing him for the examinations, Chen was already dabbling in the evidential research and literary pursuits promoted at the Xuehaitang. His ties to the Xuehaitang were solidified in 1834, when he was selected as one of ten members of the first class of specialized students.[12]

Chen combined his examination preparation and *kaozheng* studies in the fall of 1832, when he passed the provincial examinations. Cheng Enze (1785–1837), the chief examiner for this Guangdong provincial examination, was a native of Anhui's Huizhou prefecture, which had produced several of the most important *kaozheng* scholars in the late eighteenth and early nineteenth centuries, including the most famous eighteenth-century scholar, Dai Zhen. Cheng himself had impeccable *kaozheng* credentials. His father had pursued "Zheng Xuan learning," and Cheng Enze studied under his fellow townsman and ritual specialist Ling Tingkan (1757–1809). Moreover, Cheng Enze specialized in mathematics, geography, etymology, and seal calligraphy—all fields central to the *kaozheng* project. Most important from the perspective of the Xuehaitang scholars, he was also an intimate friend of Ruan Yuan.[13]

When Cheng arrived in Guangzhou, he determined to pass students based on their mastery of substantive learning (*shixue*), a hopeful sign for Xuehaitang scholars eager to earn the *juren* degree. Accordingly, he used the third-day policy questions to query students in astronomy, geography, and mathematics. This last subject sufficed to stump Hou Kang, who was caught wholly unprepared for a question on mathematics. Determined to redeem himself, Hou and his brother Hou Du began a mathematics study group at a local temple. Meanwhile, Cheng Enze also regretted not having had an opportunity to pass Zeng Zhao in the provincial examination, as he admired Zeng's lengthy essay in the *Xuehaitang ji* analyzing the similarities and differences in the Mao recension and Zheng commentary to the *Shijing*.[14] Much to Cheng's disappointment, Zeng declined to take the examination because he was in mourning. Nevertheless, Cheng did discover other Cantonese students capable of substantive learning. Zhang Biao's student at the Xuehaitang, Liang Guozhen, impressed Cheng with his use of the Zheng commentary on the *Shijing*. Xuehaitang co-director Yi Kezhong, Wen Xun, and the young Chen Li also demonstrated enough expertise in substantive learning to pass the examination. Chen Li's newly won *juren* degree catapulted him into the higher echelons of Guangzhou's cultural elite, thereby making him an attractive marriage prospect for the maritime merchant Pan family. Thus, in November 1833, Chen married a daughter of Pan Youdu, reinforcing his ties to the commercial elite of the city.[15]

In the ensuing two decades, Chen Li began to produce his early works in evidential research; four projects initiated in the 1830s are particularly noteworthy. In his *Santongshu xiangshuo*, Chen elaborated upon Qian Daxin's study of the ancient Xia, Shang, and Zhou dynasty calendars. Perhaps inspired by Cheng Enze's 1832 policy question in mathematics, Chen also started a work on geometry entitled *Husanjiao pingshi fa*. Also, between 1838 and 1840, Chen produced a study of the *Shuowen* entitled *Shuowen shengtong* (he later changed the name to *Shuowen shengbiao*).[16]

The most influential work begun by Chen in the 1830s, however, was his pioneering study of Lu Fanyan's 601 dictionary of Chinese characters, the *Qieyun*. Chen's study—initiated in 1838 and given the title *Qieyun kao* (An examination of the *Qieyun*)—sought to reconstruct the sounds of the pre-Song Chinese language, based upon the *Qieyun*'s classification of characters into rhyme groups according to a method by which pronunciation was indicated by syllabic transcription. In his 1842 preface, Chen reiterated the *kaozheng* scholar's faith that philology was the key to recapturing China's ancient past. Therefore, only through an understanding of the pre-Song system of syllabic transcription could one really get at the authentic pronunciation of the words of the ancients preserved in the Classics. In a concluding "General Discourse" to the *Qieyun kao*, Chen Li explained that rhyme tables (*dengyun tu*) of the Song dynasty were clearly influenced by a phonological method of Indian, or Buddhist, origins. The *Qieyun*, so Chen thought, represented authentic, indigenous Chinese pronunciations. Furthermore, he sought to trace the origins of the *Qieyun*'s method to followers of Zheng Xuan, the Later Han icon of Qing dynasty *kaozheng* scholars. Throughout the *Qieyun kao*, Chen drew all of his inspiration from Jiangnan scholars, and his study seemed to be aimed at a Jiangnan audience. Not only was Chen Li's work pioneering in the sense that it opened up a new subfield of philology, but it also represented one of the earliest Cantonese contributions to Qing evidential research.[17]

Chen Li continued his "substantive studies" in the 1840s, with a collection of maps and explanations of the waterways in the geographical treatise section of the *Han shu*. This was meant as a supplement to the work of the Zhejiang scholar Qi Shaonan (1706–68). In a similar cartographic project, the *Kaozheng Hushi Yugong tu*, Chen made use of the Qing set of maps, *Neifu ditu* (Palace Treasury edition maps), as well as an updated version of the *Shuijing zhu* (Notes to the *Classic of Waterways*), to clarify Hu Wei's *Yugong zhuizhi*. In 1849, Chen printed many of these early forays into evidential research together, under the title *Dongshu leigao* (Classified manuscripts from the Eastern Study). The vision driving these scholarly projects was reminiscent of Ruan Yuan's emphasis on the importance of on-site investigation, as it was recently put into practice by Liang Tingnan in his study of Southern Han history. Zhang Weiping wrote an 1851 poem for Chen, explicitly praising the latter's application of this scholarly creed: "Ban and Li were both northerners / they never personally visited southern rivers."[18] That is, as a resident of the south who could personally observe the local geography, Chen Li had access to information that had not been available to *Han shu* author Ban Gu or *Shuijing* annotator Li Daoyuan (d. 526).[19]

BALANCING JIANGNAN AND CANTONESE IDENTITIES

In addition to this early production of scholarship, Chen Li devoted his time to building his reputation as a teacher in Guangzhou and traveling to the capital for the metropolitan examinations. Chen began taking students as early as 1837, initially as a tutor in the home of Zhang Weiping, and subsequently at a Chan Buddhist monastery in the New City.²⁰ Finally, in the fall of 1840, Chen became the youngest Xuehaitang co-director, a position he would retain for several decades.²¹

Meanwhile, Chen Li made a total of seven unsuccessful attempts at the *jinshi* degree. These repeated disappointments were not entirely uncompensated, however, for Chen was able to recreate his Jiangnan roots as he passed through the region a total of fourteen times on his way to and from the capital. He often took advantage of these trips to check on his ancestral graves outside Nanjing, and thereby to reaffirm his identity as a native of Jiangnan. Returning from the capital at the end of 1844, Chen augmented his usual itinerary, touring such famous Nanjing sites as the Rain Flower Terrace.²² On another return from the capital, this time in 1850, he inspected the ancestral graves and then paid a visit to his old friend from Yuexiu Academy days, Gui Wenyao. Gui, who was serving as Huai-Hai military-administrative *daotai*, agreed to charge the Jiangning county magistrate with the task of issuing a proclamation prohibiting the destruction of the Chen gravesites. On his next visit, in 1852, Chen attempted to have the magistrate's proclamation engraved in stone before his various ancestral tombs. He was prevented from doing so by local agnates, who asserted that a geomancer would not allow it. Thus Chen had to settle for having the proclamation inscribed on a single stone in front of the grave of his grandfather's mother, surnamed Han. Though his interest in honoring his ancestors did not always coincide with that of his distant agnates in Jiangning, Chen Li was able to consult Jiangning genealogies to verify and supplement the copy maintained by the Panyu branch.²³

Chen also took advantage of his trips through Jiangnan to solidify his scholarly affiliation with the region. He twice visited the aging Ruan Yuan in Yangzhou—in 1841, on his way to the capital, and again in the summer of 1844, after his fifth failure at the examination. During this latter visit, Ruan bestowed upon Chen a copy of his *Yanjingshi zai xuji* (A further continuation of collected writings from the Classics Research Study), which Chen meticulously punctuated.²⁴ In addition, Chen requested Ruan's calligraphy for a signboard to hang over his study in Guangzhou, the Yi Jiangnan guan (Remember Jiangnan Lodge)—essentially advertising Chen's native-place identity. After 1853, when Hong Xiuquan's (1813–64) Taiping army conquered Nanjing, Chen named a collection of lyric poetry after the Remember Jiangnan Lodge. In addition, Chen chose *Zhongshan ji* (Zhong Hill collection) as the name of one of the numerous permutations of his collected writings. Chen notes that he was inspired to choose this name after reading the *Hou Han shu* biography of Zhao Qi (d. 201), the famous annotator of the *Mengzi*, who had changed his own name in order to demonstrate his determination not to forget his native place.[25] In 1869, several years after Nanjing was retaken from the Taipings, Chen reiterated his identity with Jiangnan in a poem he composed for the Guangdong salt controller, Fang Junyi, upon his transfer to a new post in Jiangnan as the Liang-Huai salt controller. Although he often privately loathed being asked to write such occasional pieces, he chose here to emphasize his native place and to implore Fang to look after the Chen ancestral graves:

> With poems and wine, upright minds admired;[26]
> Our departing songs, so suddenly finished.
> An Imperial summons arrives outside the fiery peaks,
> Transferring you to atop the clear Huai.
> I am just a sojourner from Jiangnan,
> Again disappointed and vexed when facing the wind.
> Not able to bind my leggings for travel,
> Accompanying one another following the officials' boat.
> My family at Rain Flower Terrace,
> Has graves and tombs of previous generations.
> With wars and campaigns now for several years,
> How could the pine and catalpa not have been affected?[27]
> Now, Sir, you go to serve at Jinling,[28]
> Our banners to watch one another from afar.
> I still belong to the commoner class
> But you on the Yangzi and I in Yue still rely on each other.
> I beg you, Sir, to consider my poor clan,
> Sending down orders to search and inquire.
> Have them repair the horse-mane tumuli;
> With provisions respectfully bequeathed by Shushi.[29]
> When your thoughts reach my ancestors,
> For generations we [descendants] will never forget.[30]

Yet Chen Li did not always emphasize his Jiangnan identity, choosing on some occasions to exhibit the same consciousness of local Cantonese culture as did his colleague at the Xuehaitang, Tan Ying. An essay entitled "On the Cantonese Dialect" ("Guangzhou yin shuo") is the best example of this. Here, Chen utilizes his considerable expertise in phonology to argue that Cantonese is the Chinese dialect that most closely resembles the language of the *Qieyun*.[31] Elsewhere, in a tactic similar to the one employed by Tan Ying in the *Lingnan yishu* anthology, Chen digs up a biography of a Wanli-era (1573–1619) native of Sanshui county who defended the glosses of Han-dynasty Confucians because they were closer to the sages of antiquity.[32] On other occasions, however, Chen Li and his associates at the Xuehaitang enacted Jiangnan identities. Thus, in a letter to his student, Gui Wencan (then residing in the capital), Chen compared Gui to the eminent *kaozheng* scholar Dai Zhen and himself to Jiang Yong (1681–1762), Dai's teacher who remained behind in his native Anhui.[33] But Chen was also wary of rebuke from Jiangnan contemporaries, cautioning Gui against telling "outsiders" of his having made this comparison. In the same letter, Chen informed Gui that he had sent a copy of Lin Botong's recently published work to the capital with Li Nengding and Jin Xiling; he again cautioned Gui against sharing the work with outsiders (*waisheng ren*), because the overly ambitious title of *Maoshi tongkao* (Comprehensive examination of the Mao recension of the *Shijing*) might easily invite sharp scrutiny and criticism.[34]

By the beginning of the Xianfeng reign in 1851, then, Chen Li had firmly established himself as one of Guangzhou's most productive scholars. He was quite typical of the city's cultural elite in the nineteenth century. Like many in the generation of Xuehaitang scholars that preceded him, Chen did not have deep roots in Guangzhou. His grandfather had moved from Nanjing and the family only registered as Panyu residents beginning with Chen Li. Despite the shallowness of this connection to the delta, Chen nevertheless established some roots in the city, widely linking circles of future merchant benefactors, officials on assignment in the city, and urban literati. Finally, like many others in Guangzhou, Chen at times chose to emphasize his alien origins. He described himself in poetry as a "sojourner from Jiangnan" and re-established this identity on his frequent visits to and from the capital. In addition to emphasizing his ancestral ties to Jiangnan, Chen Li devoted his energy to mastering the new learning that was imported from Jiangnan and promoted at the Xuehaitang. In stark contrast to the direction he would have received in Guangzhou two or three decades earlier, teachers such as Zhang Weiping advised Chen to begin with the *Annotated Catalogue* of the *Siku quanshu* compendium. In his early scholarly works on phonology, geography, and mathematics, Chen sought to supplement or complete research projects carried out by Qing predecessors in Jiangnan. If these works did not gain a Jiangnan audience, Chen at least made sure that his local audience would be awed by his command of Jiangnan scholarly discourse.

TRANSITIONS: CHEN LI'S CRITIQUE OF EVIDENTIAL RESEARCH

As mentioned at the outset of this chapter, Chen Li, in his 1871 "Self-Narration," portrayed himself as having undergone an intellectual transition in which he rejected frivolous youthful experiments with literature and evidential research, instead contemplating the larger meanings of the Classics, explicated in the works of Zheng Xuan and Zhu Xi. He further explained his position a few years later, in a letter to the leading *Lunyu* scholar in Jiangnan, Liu Gongmian (1824–83). Chen recalled that "before I reached middle age, in studying the Classics, every time I had a doubt about the meaning [of a specific passage], I would explicate (*jie*) and examine (*kao*) it [incessantly]. Later I suddenly changed, realizing that I could never explicate and examine [each passage] satisfactorily. Instead I sought subtle words and larger meanings."[35]

Chinese intellectual historians in the twentieth century emphasized the radical nature of Chen's mid-life transition from a pure Han Learning stance to one of Han-Song syncretism. Qian Mu, for example, saw this transformation as the key to understanding Chen's scholarly ideals, depicting it as one instance of an empire-wide rejection, after the Jiaqing reign, of Han Learning and evidential research.[36] Similarly, Hu Chusheng noted a critical turning point in Chen's thought, in which he "entered the domain of Song Learning."[37] Both Qian and Hu located this transition in 1844, citing a passage from Chen Li's manuscripts quoted in the chronological biography and included in a 1931 issue of the journal *Lingnan xuebao* (in which selected passages from the manuscripts were arranged topically). In this passage, written in the mid-1860s, Chen claimed that his intellectual development as a young man had been impeded by contemporary scholarly trends. His relative progress over the previous two decades had been entirely due to an 1844 argument with Li Nengding, one of the ten specialized students of 1834 and a future Xuehaitang co-director. Eighteen forty-four was also the year in which Chen Li visited Ruan Yuan for a second time, an event that the modern scholar He Yousen views as a key to understanding Chen's transition.[38]

If Chen Li first began to doubt the Han Learning agenda in 1844, these doubts were confirmed only gradually by his experiences in the following years. In 1850, after a sixth failure at the *jinshi* degree, Chen was appointed subdirector of the Heyuan county school in eastern Guangdong. Arriving at his post in late December, he found the county's bandits threatening and its officials apathetic and summarily resigned early in 1852. In the 1854 Red Turban attack on Guangzhou, Chen fled with his family to a village some sixty *li* east of the city, where he sought shelter with the family of Zhong Fengqing (b. 1775), another member of the 1832 *juren* class. Similar to Shen Shiliang's reaction when staying with the Changjiao Li, Chen was enthralled with—and perhaps somewhat envious of—the rustic tranquility afforded by the Zhong lineage organization, in contrast to the provincial city.[39] Chen and his family again fled Guangzhou during the 1857 occupation of the city by the English and French. This time, he was hosted by the Zhao lineage in Hengsha. In addition to seeking out one of the Zhao sons who had studied at the Xuehaitang, Chen Li recalled looking out toward Yuexiu Hill from a building in the Zhao garden, wondering what remained of the mountain hall. He returned to his old Guangzhou home in September 1859, when the Xuehaitang was still dilapidated, and then headed for the countryside once more in the spring of 1860, this time to serve as director of Longxi Academy (Longxi shuyuan) in Dongguan county. Less than a month after arriving, however, Chen was drawn back to the city to head a compilation project.[40]

It is not clear to what extent the events of the 1840s and 1850s contributed to Chen Li's doubts about the *kaozheng* project, but he did begin a serious rereading of the collected works of Zhu Xi in 1844. Over the next decade, Chen also began to read the *Zhuzi yulei* (Conversations with Master Zhu, arranged topically), marking what he felt to be the most critical passages. While the family was residing in Hengsha to avoid the foreign occupation, Chen's eldest and most promising son, Chen Zongyi (1839–59), transcribed the marked passages into a single volume. After his son suddenly died on October 10, 1859, Chen Li determined to publish the volume as *Zhuzi yulei richao* (Daily transcriptions from the *Zhuzi yulei*). In a November 1861 preface, Chen Li lamented, "Alas! Amid the chaos of war and refugees, alone taking up a tradition of learning ignored by the present age, a father and son discussed and recited it together at the edge of a deserted river."[41]

With the death of his son, Chen Li perhaps saw himself as an isolated figure in the scholarly world of urban Guangzhou, alone willing to advocate a reconsideration of Zhu Xi. As we shall see, Chen was hardly exceptional in promoting a mediation between Han and Song learning; nevertheless he increasingly depicted himself as a solitary figure. Throughout his copious manuscripts and the reading notes that survive from the last three decades of his life, Chen repeatedly expresses his dissatisfaction not only with current scholarly trends throughout the empire but also with a narrow focus on classical exegesis at the Xuehaitang itself. Though he periodically revealed his critique in his printed notes and correspondence, Chen usually left his most biting criticisms in manuscript form. There, he occasionally bemoaned the proliferation of books in his day, in a tone reminiscent of Luo Xuepeng and Fang Dongshu, and of Zhu Xi several centuries before—yet in remarkable contrast to the "Poem on Woodblock Printers" celebrating the spread of print culture to Guangzhou (quoted at the outset of Chapter 4). Such passages represented more rhetorical strategy than deep commitment, for Chen Li headed numerous printing projects in the Xianfeng and Tongzhi reigns; however, Chen's notes reveal that he did have an ax to grind, his points often illustrated with excerpts from the Classics or passages from contemporary writings. On the proliferation of books, for instance, Chen quotes with approval his

1832 examiner, Cheng Enze: "Writing has almost reached the point at which every person grasps a pearl and every family embraces a gem; yet rarely does one see a book that provides a gateway to the sages and worthies."[42]

This raises the question of why a scholar would lament the unprecedented variety and accessibility of books in the 1860s, at the same time that Guangzhou's once-bustling book market, inside the South Gate, was already showing signs of decline.[43] Chen Li wished to emphasize the point that current fads, of evidential research in particular, tended only to obscure the fundamental purpose of study: knowing the ancients. In a manuscript he prepared for publication shortly before his death, Chen explained that scholars "should strive to know what the ancients *already* knew rather than striving to know what the ancients had not yet known."[44] That is to say, since the knowledge of the ancients could be found in the Classics, and since the great majority of passages in the Classics had been adequately explained by the Han and Tang commentaries and subcommentaries, as well as by some of the commentaries of Zhu Xi, it made much more sense to devote one's energy to mastering the knowledge contained in such passages. Instead, Chen perceived that most of his contemporaries were focusing entirely upon the small number of classical passages that had not been adequately explained by previous exegeses. In the most egregious cases, Chen averred, bookish dilettantes focused on isolated passages or characters without ever taking the time to read a Classic from cover to cover. In trying to convey what he saw as a misguided approach to learning, Chen made use of a medical analogy:

Those people of today who often [pursue] the fragmentary in classical studies, never once looking at a single set of [Han and Tang] commentaries and subcommentaries, are like someone who, not knowing medicine, consults the [pharmacopoeia] *Bencao* for a few prescriptions and speaks only of these. Is it acceptable to refer to someone like this as knowledgeable in medicine? Likewise, is it acceptable to refer to someone like this as knowledgeable in the Classics?[45]

Chen occasionally illustrated the problems he perceived in scholarship by citing a passage from Xu Gan's (170–217) *Zhong lun* (Balanced discourses):

In learning, larger meanings are of foremost importance, and the names of things are secondary. When the larger meanings are revealed, the names of things follow thereafter. Yet the broad learning of debased literati strives after the names of things, is meticulous about utensils and weapons, and is painstaking in glossing. They select sections and sentences (*zhangju*) for commentary but cannot connect them with the ultimate larger meanings in order to capture the mind-hearts of the former kings. They are no different from female scholars reciting poetry or junior eunuchs transmitting orders. As a result, scholars put effort into contemplation without knowing the Dao, wasting days and months with no achievement. Thus a gentleman should choose well in selecting a teacher.[46]

In one instance in which he cited the *Zhong lun* passage, Chen added: "When I read these lines as a youth, I was greatly displeased. Looking back on it now, I only disliked that they struck at me. Now I understand that these lines in truth acutely pinpoint the malady of modern scholars."[47]

Chen Li wished to make a distinction between thoroughly reading the Classics (*dujing*) and merely explicating them (*jiejing*), the type of exercise that was given priority in the Xuehaitang examinations.[48] Merely explicating single passages leads nowhere, as Chen stressed in his letter to Liu Gongmian. In another instance, Chen elaborated:

What is the reason for explicating the Classics? Is it not because we desire to read them to illuminate their meaning? If so, then once one has explicated [a passage], then one must *read* it. If one merely explicates it without reading it, then what is the point in explicating it in the first place? If I do not read again what the ancients have already explicated, then how can I hope that later generations will read what I explicate?[49]

Reading thus entailed comprehension on a deeper level than merely explaining the words of a passage. Though philology was still absolutely essential in interpreting the words of a text, Chen urged readers to contemplate the underlying "larger meaning" (*dayi*) of the most important Classics; individual passages could be understood only in the context of the entire text in which they appeared. Furthermore, borrowing language from the *Zhuzi yulei*, Chen argued that "reading" entailed "masticating" (*ju, jue*)—searching out the "flavor" (*wei*) of a passage in order to comprehend the intent of the sage-authors.[50] In terms of reading practices, then, Chen Li favored the Song Learning emphasis on reflective comprehension over the Han Learning practice of philological analysis.

The objects of Chen Li's ire were mostly Jiangnan scholars. He particularly disapproved of Hui Dong—the father of Han Learning narrowly defined—and Wang Niansun (1744–1832) and his son Wang Yinzhi (1766–1834). Of the Wang father and son, Chen felt that they typified the readiness of *kaozheng* scholars to change the readings of characters in the Classics, entirely disregarding established interpretations. The Wangs were renowned for their *Jingyi shuwen* (Narrative of things learned about meanings in the Classics), a work prominently featured in the *Huang Qing jingjie*. In it they show a propensity to argue that given characters in the Classics were "borrowed" (*jiajie*) characters and hence should be replaced with what the Wangs demonstrated should be the original characters. Such things, Chen thought, should not be done so lightly.[51]

According to Chen Li, the haste with which the Wangs and others overturned previously accepted readings of given classical passages reflected a fundamentally irreverent attitude toward the learning of the sages and the commentaries of Han, Tang, and Song Confucians. This repelled Chen far more than any particular instance of mistaken exegesis:

> The Wangs exclusively pursued glossing, putting forth their own interpretations to change the explanatory notes of ancient Confucians. If scholars do not read their book [the *Jingyi shuwen*] carefully, then they will think that refuting ancient Confucians and changing to new interpretations is a permissible feat. Furthermore, the Wangs make plenty of mistakes; it is just that the evidence they cite is detailed and extensive and the style of their writing is sharp and precise, carrying the reader away every time.[52]

In his youth, Chen Li had himself perhaps been mesmerized by the dizzying array of evidence that the Wangs and other Jiangnan *kaozheng* scholars were able to amass for purposes of explicating in minute detail a single line or character. Indeed, Chen's critique of *kaozheng* masters seems interlaced with envy, as he admits elsewhere in his manuscripts that his memory is weak, allowing him only to lecture on the learning of meaning and principle (*yili zhi xue*).[53] At the same time, because he could not possibly manipulate such large amounts of evidence and thus chose not to employ such a reading strategy, Chen felt that he was able to perceive things that others could not. He looked askance at exegesis conducted merely for the sake of self-promotion, at the expense of Confucian predecessors. This type of classical scholarship, Chen once commented to Zou Boqi, his closest friend among the Xuehaitang co-directors of the Tongzhi era, no longer deserved the name "unadorned learning." It was every bit as "flowery" as the examination-style essays against which evidential research had been contrasted when the Xuehaitang was first established.[54]

In portions of his private notes that he presumably never intended for publication, Chen Li directed his criticisms toward his own colleagues at the Xuehaitang. In one instance, Chen recalled a conversation he had had with Zeng Zhao, who was, aside from Fan Feng, the most partisan Han Learning advocate among the first generation of Xuehaitang scholars. Zeng suggested that local teachers should use the Huang Kan (488–545) commentary (*Lunyu yishu*) to instruct children in the *Lunyu*, rather than the commonly used ones—presumably those of He Yan (190–249) and Zhu Xi. Chen thought Zeng's desire to foist his fetish for obscure commentaries upon mere children was inexplicable.[55] In another case, Chen reacted to a passage from the "Record of Learning" ("Xueji") section of the *Liji*. He copied one passage from the text of the Classic: "the teachers of today, . . . teach without any sincerity" (今之教者, . . . 使人不由其誠).[56] He then recorded Zheng Xuan's commentary, "'*You* (由) here means 'use/proceed from.' [Teachers] make the students recite it, but in interpreting it do not use/proceed from their sincerity." Applying the passage and commentary to his own time, Chen added, "Today, teachers of examination-style writing (*shiwen*) are just like this. And the Xuehaitang putting out exegetical [questions] (*jingjie*) is like this as well."[57] For Chen, then, exercises in exegesis at the Xuehaitang had degenerated to the point where they were no longer distinguishable in practice from exercises in examination writing conducted at other academies. In making this comparison, Chen emphasized less the continuity of content than the similarly perfunctory and formalistic performance of examination and exegetical exercises. Just as students who sat for the civil service examinations rarely did so in hopes of better understanding Zhu Xi and the other Song masters, so Xuehaitang scholars and students competed to dazzle one another with inventive philological and hermeneutic devices newly imported from Jiangnan, rather than expressing a sincere desire to reveal ancient truths. In other words, sons of ambitious urban Cantonese families saw both the civil service examinations and the Xuehaitang examinations primarily as means of social advancement.

Thus, by the beginning of the Tongzhi era, Chen Li had come to reassess the value of the scholarly practices in which he had been trained. Evidential research, as Chen saw it, represented not so much a quest for certainty as a potentially misguided project capable of casting doubt upon the very certainty contained in the Classics. Nevertheless, Chen was no "anti-intellectualist."[58] Such scholars as Qian Mu argue that Chen Li restrained his published criticisms of Han Leaning or evidential research lest his contemporaries deride him, but Chen Li himself explains his motivations in different terms. He feared that a wholesale rejection of evidential research could lead to the same type of "empty learning" that had supposedly provoked the downfall of the Ming dynasty. This so frightened Chen that he made notes to himself to be cautious in his critique of Han Learning.[59] After citing the eighteenth-century *kaozheng* scholar Duan Yucai's (1735–1815) criticism of contemporary scholars who ignored the Song masters, Chen made explicit his concerns:

At the time when Han Learning was at its height, only one or two out of a hundred among the class of scholars (*shidaifu*) read books. Now Han Learning is already in decline, and only one or two in a thousand read books. The rest do not even know what a Classic is. If someone attacks Han Learning in the present age so that everyone follows him, then there will be no one in the entire realm who reads books.[60]

Likewise, despite his avowed interest in Zhu Xi, Chen Li did not accept all of the characteristics that his contemporaries often associated with Song Learning or Neo-Confucianism more generally. In fact, many of Chen Li's concerns about Song Learning echoed the criticisms raised by Han Learning scholars in eighteenth-century Jiangnan. First, Chen rejected the pursuit of sagehood; he saw this as pretentious and impractical. In addition, he did not accept the notion of *Daotong*—the idea that the Way of the sages had been transmitted from the ancient sage-kings to Confucius, had passed down through Confucius' immediate disciples to Mencius, and then had been lost for over a thousand years before somehow being retrieved by, depending upon what one wished to claim, Han Yu, Zhou Dunyi, or Cheng Yi.[61] *Daotong* and the ideal of sagehood both struck Chen Li as implausible, but, more important, as intolerably arrogant and irreverent. Moreover, Chen paid little heed to Neo-Confucian concerns about such metaphysical problems as the relationship between principle (*li*) and material force (*qi*), or the distinction between feelings that have not yet issued forth (*weifa*) and those that have issued forth (*yifa*). Because he did not regard such issues as urgent, they are conspicuously absent from the passages that Chen and his son distilled from the *Zhuzi yulei* into *Zhuzi yulei richao*. One wonders, then, what Chen Li found appealing in a Zhu Xi devoid of such notions. Like many of his contemporaries who had been dazzled by evidential research as youths but at mid-century found themselves holding the Zhu Xi banner, Chen promoted Zhu Xi and Song Learning primarily as a corrective to what he saw as the narrowness of Han Learning. Consequently, nineteenth-century "Song Learning" or Neo-Confucianism looked quite different from Song and Ming versions.[62]

"MASTER ZHU WAS FOND OF EVIDENTIAL RESEARCH"

Han-Song syncretism (*Han-Song tiaohe*)—the attempt to combine the respective strengths of Han Learning and Song Learning, while expurgating the "flaws" of each—constituted the most prevalent new intellectual movement among nineteenth-century Chinese Confucians before the Sino-Japanese War (1894–95), New Text Confucianism and Western Learning notwithstanding. Chen Li was certainly one of the most persistent and lucid exponents of Han-Song syncretism, but despite his self-portrayal as a solitary figure, he was far from alone. This was particularly true in Guangzhou, where Han Learning had very shallow roots from the outset, and where a discourse of Han-Song syncretism had been articulated at the Xuehaitang. As a result, Chen Li's promotion of Han-Song syncretism in the Xianfeng era was not particularly new; yet in the texts he produced, he offered a more systematic attempt at mediation than any of his contemporaries in Guangzhou.[63]

In the decades after Jiang Fan and Fang Dongshu initiated the Han-Song debate in Guangzhou, neither side lacked zealous advocates, which were in some respects organized around a correlation between residence and scholarship. Some exceptions can be found, but staunch defenders of Neo-Confucianism, whether of the Song or Ming variety, were more likely to reside outside Guangzhou city in delta townships or villages, whereas zealous advocates of Han Learning were largely confined to the city. For example, in Daliang, Luo Dunyan and Huang Jing (1844 *jinshi*), both Hanlin academicians, were fond of studying "principle" and the "mind-heart" together.[64] There is no record of any Daliang Luo, in fact, ever taking Xuehaitang examinations. Similarly, a scion of the Xian lineage in Foshan, Xian Yi, had taken some Xuehaitang examinations but then gave up on them in disgust over what he saw as the academy's bias against Song Learning.[65] Several urban scholars trained at the Xuehaitang, such as Xu Hao, were at times equally adamant in their espousal of Han Learning. Xu, who was a correspondent of Chen Li, surely elicited the latter's consternation by acknowledging in an 1854 preface to his collection of classical exegesis that he was entirely enamored of Wang Niansun and son.[66] Wu Wenqi, one of the ten 1834 specialized students, is another example. Although a native of Heshan county in the western reaches of the delta, Wu resided in Henan and "throughout his life took Han Learning as his basic aim."[67]

Nevertheless, despite these examples of rather polemical scholarly stances, espousal of Han-Song syncretism in various degrees of balance was much more common in nineteenth-century Guangzhou prefecture. The doyen among Guangdong scholars when Ruan Yuan arrived at his Guangzhou post in 1817 was Chen Changqi. Appointed to the commission in charge of compiling the *Siku quanshu* in 1773, Chen had run with the likes of such Jiangnan *kaozheng* luminaries as Dai Zhen, Qian Daxin, and Wang Niansun and could therefore claim stronger credentials in Han Learning than any other Guangdong resident of his day. Yet in his biography of Chen, Wen Xun describes his teacher's overarching scholarly ideal as that of not wishing to differentiate between Han and Song.[68] Similarly, in an essay entitled "Discourse on Han Learning and Song Learning," Huang Peifang stressed that neither the glosses (*xungu*) of Han Learning nor the "meaning and principle" of Song Learning may be abandoned. In his own day, however, Huang feared that the practical benefits offered only by Song Learning were being ignored amid the clamor of Han Learning advocates.[69] Among the first eight Xuehaitang co-directors, Lin Botong was the most vocal participant in the discourse of Han-Song syncretism. Lin's student Jin Xiling portrayed him as "following Han Confucian standards (*zong*) in scholarship and Song Confucian methods in daily practice."[70]

Though this discourse of Han-Song syncretism was not entirely an outgrowth of the Xuehaitang curriculum, Ruan Yuan's eclectic scholarly orientation certainly facilitated its development. To begin with, Ruan's preface to the first collection of student writings legitimized "analyzing the Way and principle" in the Zhu Xi tradition as a field of study at the academy. The discourse of Han-Song syncretism continued to gain acceptance at the Xuehaitang after Ruan Yuan left Guangzhou. In 1836, Xuehaitang examinations asked scholars to write an essay on the theme, "Master Zhu did not reject the ancient glosses." In his essay on the topic (a topic that he himself quite likely formulated), Lin Botong argued that Zhu Xi was alone among the Song Confucians in applying the methods of evidential research to the ancient glosses of Han and Tang Confucians, thereby avoiding the "empty words" typical of his contemporaries.[71] Another Xuehaitang scholar, and one of the numerous Jiaying Hakkas at the academy, Li Zhongpei was so inspired by this topic that he expanded his essay into a sixteen-*juan* discourse, published in 1843 and enumerating 153 examples in which Zhu Xi addresses or incorporates Han commentaries. Li begins by arguing, in the first *juan*, that when it came to the names of things, Zhu Xi followed the ancient glosses nine times out of ten; he suggests, in the last *juan*, that when it came to larger meanings and subtle words (*dayi weiyan*), Zhu's commentaries were superior to the ancient ones nine times out of ten.[72]

Among the Xuehaitang co-directors contemporary with Chen Li, Jin Xiling was the most consistent exponent of syncretism. A member of the immigrant Jin family in Panyu, Jin Xiling began classical studies under Lin Botong in 1828, and soon became his most devoted student. Aside from receiving training in Duan Yucai's *Maoshi guxun zhuan*—a study of ancient glosses to the Mao recension of the *Shijing* and a characteristic product of Jiangnan evidential research—Jin naturally also picked up Lin's syncretism. In a letter presented to

Lin and preserved in Jin's collected writings, Jin responds to his teacher's instructions that he weigh the advantages and disadvantages of Han and Song Learning.[73] Later, in *Lixue yongyan* (Trite comments on *Lixue*), Jin Xiling discussed the major philosophical ideas of Zhu Xi. Throughout the work, Jin pointed out instances in which Song Confucian interpretations were not at odds with those of the Han Confucians.[74]

Even many Cantonese scholars exhibiting a clear bias toward either Han Learning or Song Learning commonly framed their views in syncretic discourse. Xu Hao, noted above for his zealous support of evidential research, commented in an essay entitled "On Evidential Research" ("Kaozheng lun") that he had never seen a case in which one might abandon meaning and principle to speak of evidential research alone.[75] Chen Changqi's student, Wen Xun, began an essay entitled "Scholarship" ("Xueshu") by paying equal homage to Zheng Xuan and Zhu Xi. Soon, however, he revealed a Song Learning bent by reinterpreting Dai Zhen's comment that "Han Confucians got the institutions and numbers; Song Confucians got the meaning and principle" to mean "the various Confucians of the Han and Tang got the rudimentary (*cu*) elements, while the various masters of the Song got the precise (*jing*) elements and put them into practice."[76] It seems that Fang Dongshu had his sympathizers in Guangzhou, for Wen closed his essay by expressing admiration for the vocal critic of Han Learning advocates. What is most important for the current argument, though, is that Wen felt compelled to cloak his views in the language of Han-Song syncretism.

The point of all this is to suggest that Chen Li was anything but "poles apart from the popular scholarly trends of his time," as one modern scholar characterizes his Han-Song syncretic stance.[77] Rather, Chen operated in an environment in which the discourse of Han-Song syncretism was quite prevalent, even among scholars with a preference for one approach over the other. Chen Li had pursued classical learning from one of Lin Botong's star pupils, Hou Kang, and thus was clearly situated in a scholarly lineage of Han-Song syncretism. Moreover, Chen himself acknowledged the influence of this discourse upon his own intellectual development. In a eulogy written for his 1826 examiner, Weng Xincun, Chen recalled an analogy Weng had used to explain the importance of combining

Han and Song. "Han Learning," in Weng's words, "is like selecting rice; Song Learning is like cooking it."[78] In light of this, Chen Li's mid-life scholarly transformation more accurately reflected an acknowledgment of the Han-Song syncretism current in Guangzhou than a radical rupture with the intellectual environment in which he worked.

Though Chen Li's Han-Song syncretism was hardly unique in the context of nineteenth-century Guangzhou, he directed more scholarly energy toward mediating between the two exegetical traditions than did many of his contemporaries. Chen's early efforts at mediation resulted in the publication of *Hanru tongyi* (Comprehensive meanings of the Han Confucians). In his 1856 preface to the work, Chen defended Confucian masters of the Han dynasty against the charge, leveled at them by Song Neo-Confucians, that they had stressed glossing to the neglect of meaning and principle (*yili*) (concepts most often identified with Song Learning). Advocates of Han Learning in the Qing had similarly ignored Han Confucian contributions in the area of meaning and principle. Therefore, Chen hoped to show both the modern standard-bearers and the critics of Han Learning that "Han Confucians' theories of meaning and principle were pure, solid, precise, and extensive."[79] Chen Li faced a major stumbling block, of course, in that Han Confucians for the most part had left behind no works in such common Neo-Confucian genres as the *yulu* (recorded conversations), or even *wenji* (collected writings). Consequently, Chen suggests, one had to look elsewhere to find Han Confucian discussions of meaning and principle, namely, in their classical exegeses. Whether enthusiasts or detractors, those who failed to acknowledge the unavailability of such genres as the *yulu* in the Han and thereby assumed that Han Confucians were simply unconcerned with the issues that Song Confucians addressed in such genres lacked a proper historical understanding.[80] In the *Hanru tongyi*, then, Chen would facilitate the discovery of meaning and principle in Han Confucian classical commentaries by selecting passages from these commentaries and arranging them into such Song Confucian philosophical categories as *li* (principle), *xin* (mind-heart), and *xing* (nature). A majority of the passages were lifted from the commentaries of Zheng Xuan; others were taken from Zhao Qi's commentary to the *Mengzi* and the *Chunqiu fanlu* by the second-century BCE Confucian Dong Zhongshu. The end product of this enterprise thus resembled something like Zhu Xi's *Jinsi lu* (Reflections on things at hand), except that it incorporated Han Confucian commentaries rather than Northern Song Neo-Confucian metaphysical ruminations.[81]

Chen Li planned to follow up the *Hanru tongyi* with a much more ambitious project, in which he would discuss the larger meanings of each Classic and then proceed to a chronological appraisal of classical hermeneutics. Starting his project during the 1850s, Chen left it incomplete at the time of his death in 1882.[82] The title Chen chose for his planned magnum opus, *Xuesi lu* (A record of study and contemplation), reflected his syncretic agenda, alluding to a passage in the *Lunyu* in which Confucius warns of the dangers of failing to maintain a balance between study and contemplation.[83] This passage is often cited in the discourse of Han-Song syncretism; here, "study" is meant to refer to the textual research of Han Learning, and "contemplation" to the moral self-reflection of Song Learning. Chen described the project, in an 1862 letter to his old friend and former Xuehaitang co-director Yang Rongxu, as a "philosophical" (*zi*) book that sought to analyze Confucianism through the ages. He portrayed it as his life's work, having already spent a decade at it.[84] Elsewhere, Chen compared his book to Huang Zhen's (1213–80) *Huangshi richao* (Mr. Huang's daily transcriptions), compiled at the end of the Southern Song. Just as Huang supposedly had intended his work to rescue Song Learning from certain "insubstantial" tendencies of the age, so Chen Li implied that the *Xuesi lu* would do the same for Han Learning in the Qing—preserving what was useful in it rather than rejecting it outright.[85]

The ultimate aim of the *Xuesi lu* was to obtain a satisfactory mediation between Han and Song Learning, and Chen Li employed a variety of strategies with this goal in mind. One was to argue for resemblance—that is, to suggest that Zhu Xi really never rejected the Han glosses, or that Han Confucians such as Zheng Xuan never ignored meaning and principle. Both the 1836 Xuehaitang examination topic and Chen's 1856 *Hanru tongyi* utilized this strategy. An alternative strategy consisted of emphasizing complementary correspondence, as seen in the title of the *Xuesi lu*. Here, Han and Song learning would be portrayed as two contrasting, yet mutually dependent, fields of personal (both intellectual and moral) cultivation. Arguments employing complementary correspondence were often presented in a parallel style. So, most typically, Han Learning was associated with glosses and Song Learning with meaning and principle, with both seen as necessary to complete fulfillment. Chen employed both strategies throughout the various permutations of the *Xuesi lu*, often intertwined with a third, synecdochic strategy of representing Han and Song Learning by Zheng Xuan and Zhu Xi. For example, in one passage of his manuscript reading notes, Chen Li compared his two scholarly heroes using parallelism:

> Lord Zheng pulled together the *Three Rituals*
>   to form the unified ritual of the Duke of Zhou;
> Master Zhu pulled together the *Four Books*
>   to form the unified learning of Confucius.[86]

Though these comparisons may strike the modern reader as forced, they came naturally to authors of poetry and parallel prose and conveniently highlighted instances of resemblance and complementarity between Zheng and Zhu.[87]

After surviving illness in 1871, Chen Li quickly went about editing portions of the *Xuesi lu* for publication as the *Dongshu dushu ji* (Reading notes from the Eastern Study). By the time of his death, Chen had completed, in addition to chapters on each of the major Classics, one chapter each devoted to Zheng Xuan and Zhu Xi. In the Zheng Xuan chapter, Chen Li praises the Later Han classicist first and foremost for emphasizing the importance of maintaining a foundation of learning in the study of the Classics. As with most of his eighteenth-century Han Learning predecessors in Jiangnan, Chen Li also associates Zheng Xuan with ritual studies. Zheng was best known in the Qing, after all, for his commentaries on the three classical ritual texts: *Zhouli*, *Yili*, and *Liji*. Beyond this, Chen Li most admired Zheng Xuan's *jiafa*—"schools method," or scholarly methodology. Chen Li describes Zheng's *jiafa* as "having a scholarly lineage (*you zongzhu*) while simultaneously recognizing alternative [interpretations] (*yi you butong*)."[88] In other words, Zheng Xuan would primarily follow one exegetical tradition for a given Classic, without hesitating to incorporate interpretations from another exegetical tradition or to provide his own if necessary, all the while noting variant readings. It is in this respect that Chen privileges Zheng Xuan over such Later Han contemporaries as He Xiu, the patron saint of New Text studies in the Qing, who too rigidly adhered to a single exegetical tradition. Wang Su (195–256), viewed by Chen as having purposely sought out errors in Zheng Xuan commentaries, is an even worse culprit. Only Zheng Xuan was able to sustain a proper balance between upholding a particular school of classical exegesis and remaining open to alternative or even new interpretations.[89] Those Han Learning advocates in the Qing who purported to be followers of Zheng Xuan struck Chen Li as having completely missed the fundamental essence of the Zheng method. Wang Niansun and Wang Yinzhi in particular reminded Chen Li of Wang Su, finding fault in their predecessors merely for the sake of gaining scholarly repute.[90] Chen was outraged by the fact that Jiang Fan, a dogmatically partisan Han Learning champion, had dared to take as his sobriquet, the "Zheng [Xuan] Hall."[91]

Just as he had attempted to demonstrate, in *Hanru tongyi*, that Zheng Xuan and the Han Confucians were actually quite concerned with discovering meaning and principle, so in the Zhu Xi chapter of the *Dongshu dushu ji* Chen Li seeks to remake the Song philosopher into a ritualist and evidential researcher. In the opening passages of the chapter, Chen Li points to instances—primarily drawn from the *Zhuzi yulei*—in which Zhu Xi emphasizes the importance of the Han and Tang classical commentaries and subcommentaries, appreciates glossing, and addresses an imperial succession crisis in the Song by quoting Zheng Xuan on rituals. He even cites a case in which Zhu Xi is concerned with printing a new edition of Xu Shen's *Shuowen* dictionary. Although not averse to exposing flaws in its scholarly method, "Master Zhu," in Chen Li's view, "was fond of evidential research."[92] In contrast, as in the collected transcriptions from the *Zhuzi yulei* that Chen Li and his son had compiled, common Neo-Confucian metaphysical concepts are noticeably absent from the Zhu Xi chapter of the *Dongshu dushu ji*.

Constructions such as the ones presented above were common parlance in the discourse of Han-Song syncretism in nineteenth-century Guangzhou, of which Chen Li was the chief spokesman. In contributing to the discourse of syncretism, Chen Li redefined Han Learning and Song Learning in order to make them more compatible. Zheng Xuan and other laudable Han Confucians became, in Chen's hands, seekers of meaning and principle, as well as paragons of Confucian virtue. Chen stressed the moral practice of Han Confucians he thought had been ignored. Conversely, through his portrayal of Zhu Xi, he downplayed the Song Neo-Confucians' interest in metaphysical questions and their quest for sagehood. In place of these, Chen described Zhu Xi as a balanced ritualist and moralist who was fond of evidential research.

RECONSTRUCTION GUANGZHOU AND THE *KAOZHENG* PROJECT

In the aftermath of the crises of the Xianfeng era, Chen Li not only articulated his mediation of Han and Song Learning but also remained intensely active in local scholarly projects. Chen took advantage of the unprecedented availability of private and public donations during the period of feverish reconstruction activity to further his academic endeavors, which included the development of academy education, the facilitation of printing projects, and the distribution of specialized research projects to his students. To fund this revival of the academic enterprise in Guangzhou, Chen vigilantly flattered provincial officials eager to add cultural credentials to their already proven military records. Throughout it all, Chen maintained a keen interest in scholarly goings on in Jiangnan. An analysis of the kinds of projects he pursued during reconstruction reveals that although Chen Li called into question many practices and attitudes of Han Learning and the larger evidential research enterprise—even among his colleagues at the Xuehaitang—he nevertheless remained fundamentally grounded in the *kaozheng* project.

To begin with, Chen Li's proclaimed dissatisfaction with his youthful forays into evidential research did not prevent him in his later years from revising, supplementing, and preparing for publication several of his early texts. In 1857, Chen prefaced his early work on geometry, *Husanjiao pingshi fa*. He devoted four months of the same year to producing a work on music theory entitled *Shenglü tongkao*. Basing his study on passages in the *Zhouli* and *Liji*, Chen sought to do for ancient music what many eighteenth-century Jiangnan *kaozheng* scholars had done for ancient ritual. Hereafter, Chen

Li hoped that discussions of music theory could avoid "empty talk," a charge commonly leveled at works in the Song Learning vein.[93] Like his phonological research on the *Qieyun*, this work remained a standard for students of Chinese music well into the twentieth century. A few years later, in 1863, Chen wrote a preface on the occasion of printing his *Kaozheng Hushi Yugong tu*. Toward the end of his life, Chen arranged for publication a supplement to his work on the *Qieyun*. Entitled *Qieyun kao waipian*, prefaced in 1879, and printed in 1880, it traces the development of pre-Song syllabic transcription into the 36 phonetic initials (*zimu*) used in the rhyme tables of the Song dynasty.[94] Finally realizing that he could never finish all of the projects he conceived, Chen Li recorded titles of planned works in the hope that successors would be inspired to write them. The titles reflect both Chen Li's grounding in evidential research and the nineteenth-century trend toward syncretism. These included, for example, *Maoshi Zheng-Zhu hechao* (Combined transcriptions of Zheng Xuan and Zhu Xi annotations of the Mao recension of the *Shijing*), *Yili sanjia hechao* (Combined transcriptions of the three schools of *Yili* exegesis), and *Chunqiu sanzhuan yitong ping* (Critique of similarities and differences of the three commentaries of the *Chunqiu*).[95]

Occasionally in his notes and correspondence from the last two decades of his life, Chen Li strikes the pose of the eremitic poet Tao Yuanming (365–427), who bemoaned, after the death of his most promising son, the absence of anyone with whom he could converse about learning. In one instance, Chen resolved to keep his mouth shut and to take only flora as his companions, noting this as his reason for planting flowers and trees on the Xuehaitang grounds during reconstruction.[96] These occasional lamentations notwithstanding, Chen Li remained quite active during the 1860s, both at the Xuehaitang and at the new Jupo jingshe. He was instrumental in reviving the long-defunct Xuehaitang system of specialized students, which involved cultivating close relationships with provincial officials. Fortunately, Chen Li found one such official who he believed truly understood him, Governor Guo Songtao.[97] Guo seems to have held Chen in relatively high regard, despite the governor's generally dim view of the Cantonese.[98] Although Chen Li declined to serve on Guo's secretarial staff, he was usually present when the governor invited the Xuehaitang co-directors on an outing or to his yamen. Little wonder then, that Guo was the chief official sponsor of the revived specialized courses. After presiding over the March 1866 matriculation ceremony at the academy, Guo appointed Chen Li, along with Chen Pu, Jin Xiling, and Zou Boqi, to supervise the curriculum. When Guo left office later that summer, Chen and the Xuehaitang scholars hosted him at Pan Shicheng's Sea Mountain Immortals' Lodge in Xiguan before seeing him off two days later.[99]

Chen Li not only smoothed the way for Guo Songtao's sponsorship of the specialized courses but was also largely responsible for designing the revived program. In a commemoration of the Xuehaitang's newly constructed Punctuating Classics and Determining Ambition Studio (Lijing bianzhi zhai)—where the specialized studies would be conducted—Chen emphasized that classical studies should begin with textual analysis and with the selection of a single Classic in which to specialize, as was the practice during the Han. But then Chen added a caveat: after this initial stage, a student risked becoming nothing more than a pedantic scholar if he did not go further toward realizing the ancient ideal of a thoroughly comprehending and morally complete literatus (*shi*).[100] This perhaps signaled a veiled attack on narrow exegetical exercises. Yet the fact remains that Chen Li was at the very center of Xuehaitang activities even as he raised doubts about the evidential research enterprise. In the same year that Guo Songtao, Zhou Yinqing, and Chen Li orchestrated the revival of the specialized courses, Chen updated and reprinted the 1838 Xuehaitang gazetteer compiled by Lin Botong. In the last years of his life, Chen also busied himself editing the fourth series of Xuehaitang examination essays and poems, *Xuehaitang siji*, which was completed by Jin Xiling in 1886, after Chen's death.

As was the case with the restoration of the Xuehaitang specialized courses, the creation of the Jupo jingshe resulted from cultivating connections with provincial officials—in this case, salt controller Fang Junyi and Guo Songtao's replacement as governor, Jiang Yili. Yet the Jupo jingshe provided Chen Li with an opportunity to embody his particular scholarly vision. In a commemoration of the academy's construction, Chen emphasized differences from the Xuehaitang, pointing out that Jupo tested students 30 times per year, as opposed to the traditional quarterly examinations at the Xuehaitang. On the walls of the front studio of the Jupo jingshe, Chen inscribed a line most often associated with the early Qing scholar Gu Yanwu, which for nineteenth-century Confucians evoked the Han-Song syncretic balance of moral cultivation and textual studies: "Conduct yourself with a sense of shame; extensively study the [classical] texts."[101] Chen later elaborated on his pedagogical ideals in a lecture to Jupo students:

> In classical studies, it is essential to recognize meaning and principle rather than exclusively pursuing glosses and searching for evidence. As for meaning and principle in the works of Zhu Xi, I have the *Zhuzi yulei richao* in five *juan*; for the meaning and principle in the classical commentaries of the Han Confucians, I have the *Hanru tongyi* in seven *juan*. These can serve as an initial guide.[102]

Thus, at his new academy, Chen Li incorporated his critique of misguided evidential research into the curriculum and yet left the basic elements of the Xuehaitang agenda unchanged. The format of a collection of Jupo student writings compiled by Chen is remarkably similar to the four collections of Xuehaitang examination writings. As in the Xuehaitang collections, the *Jupo jingshe ji* begins with exercises in classical exegesis. These are followed by various discourses, colophons, and prose and poetic literary pieces. Upon closer inspection, however, the Jupo collection reveals the influence upon the students of Chen's critique. As with the Xuehaitang collections, the *Jupo jingshe ji* begins with explications (*shi*) of given characters, but the content reflects Chen Li's particular concerns. For example, in an explication of the character *bo* ("extensive" or "broad," as in "extensive learning" or *boxue*), a student distinguishes between "broad learning" properly understood and the aimless extensive learning of the present day. He refers to the same passage in the *Hanshi waizhuan* (Han Ying's illustrations of the didactic application of the *Book of Poetry*) that Chen Li had cited in his commemoration of the academy: "from loving one thing comes breadth, from breadth precision" (*hao yi ze bo, bo ze jing*).[103] Closely following Chen Li's line of argument, the student in his explication asserts that one's learning cannot be considered truly broad unless it is rooted in concentrated specialization.[104] In another exercise, one student writes a colophon to Wang Yinzhi's *Jingyi shuwen* in which he admires the precision of Wang's work but then proceeds to point out numerous instances of forced interpretations. In a "discourse," another student reiterates Chen Li's distinction between the *jiafa* of Zheng Xuan and the stubborn adherence to a single school of thought characteristic of He Xiu.[105] Nevertheless, the curriculum of the Jupo jingshe remained firmly grounded in the pedagogical practice of the Xuehaitang, as exemplified by another examination question in the Jupo collected writings: "In his annotation of the *Lunyu*, Master Zhu used He Yan's commentary as the basis. Did He Yan base his commentary on that of Zhang Yu, that of Zheng Xuan, or did he devise it himself? Illuminate this with a detailed examination of the [*Jingdian*] *Shiwen* and the *Jiaokanji*."[106]

In addition to curricular development at both the Xuehaitang and the Jupo jingshe, Chen Li vigorously organized numerous large-scale compilation and printing projects during the reconstruction period. Once again, the titles of books that Chen had a hand in printing reflect his intellectual priorities. After heading the Longxi Academy in Dongguan for a brief few weeks in 1860, Chen packed up and left for Guangzhou, when Governor-General Lao Chongguang hired him as chief editor of a new edition of the *Huang Qing jingjie*. Roughly half of the original plates for this collection of Qing exegeses of the Classics had been lost when the Xuehaitang was destroyed in the foreign occupation. Though Chen was already beginning to have doubts about the direction in which evidential research was headed, he jumped at the chance to reprint the Qing exegeses, and the project was completed in 1862. Two years later, Chen Li supervised a new printing of Ruan Yuan's 1822 Guangdong provincial gazetteer.[107] During this same year, Chen Li joined his Xuehaitang protégés Gui Wencan, Zhao Qiying (1826–65), and Zou Boqi on the bureau in charge of drawing detailed maps of Guangdong province, with explanatory notes for which he devised the editorial guidelines.[108]

Chen Li took on the burden of printing essential works with increasing urgency, and surely relish, when Wu Chongyao passed away in 1863. Unsure as to whether or not Wu's son would continue in his father's footsteps, Chen sought to relocate the center of Cantonese elite cultural publication from merchant patrons to the academies, thereby allowing Chen to determine exactly what should be printed.[109] In April 1868, at a printing bureau (*shuju*) established by Fang Junyi, Chen began printing the *Siku quanshu zongmu tiyao* (Annotated general catalog of the *Siku quanshu*), demonstrating that he had not forgotten the instructions of his teacher, Zhang Weiping.[110] In 1871, the prominent official Zeng Guofan (1811–72) sent a letter to the current governor-general, Ruilin (d. 1774), urging him to establish a bureau to reprint the Thirteen Classics with Han and Tang commentaries and subcommentaries.[111] When Chen printed, at the Jupo jingshe in 1872, a collection of primarily Song classical exegeses originally compiled in the early Qing (*Tongzhitang jingjie*), urban Cantonese scholars had at their disposal the major works of classical exegesis from the Han through Qing dynasties. Furthermore, Chen printed the *Jingdian shiwen* in 1870 and later compiled and printed a collection of relatively obscure Han works, entitled *Gu jingjie huihan* (Collected ancient classical exegeses). This collectanea contained a total of sixteen works, including a reconstruction of Zheng Xuan's annotation of the *Yijing*, Dong Zhongshu's *Chunqiu fanlu*, and the *Hanshi waizhuan*. In a similar compilation, *Xiaoxue huihan* (Collected philological texts), Chen Li combined such crucial tools of philological research as *Shuowen*, *Fangyan*, and a Northern Song text, *Guangyun*.[112]

Aside from completing, arranging, and publishing his early studies in evidential research, promoting curricular development, and organizing ambitious compilation and printing projects, Chen Li also distributed among his students a wide assortment of specialized (*zhuan*) tasks that reflected his scholarly preoccupations. According to Chen, a student needed to concentrate upon a single Classic, using the Han and Tang commentaries and subcommentaries as a guide and gradually branching out from there. Since scholars could not possibly master every field, they must specialize in their own while communicating with specialists in other fields. Only in this way could one become a comprehensive scholar (*tongru*). This was Chen's view of the Zheng Xuan method, as well as his remedy to what he saw as the tendency of evidential research scholars to dabble in one Classic one day and another the next, without a comprehensive sense of purpose. When Guo Songtao supported Chen in re-establishing specialized classes at the Xuehaitang, Chen saw this as a chance to realize his dream of reviving the Han Confucian method of specialization.[113]

Accordingly, Chen urged each of his colleagues and students to specialize in a given field. Thus his correspondence and manuscript notes are interspersed with references to their specialties or to projects he designed specifically for them. In a letter to Gui Wencan, Chen suggests that "substantive learning" can be preserved if Gui sticks to ritual and Chen to music, while Zou Boqi specializes in astronomy and mathematics and Chen's student Zhao Qiying in geography.[114] Similarly, in his manuscript notes on the topic of Zheng Xuan commentaries, Chen divides tasks among his students: "Zhao [Qiying?] on the *Shangshu dazhuan* annotation, Gao [Xueyao?] on the *Yijing* commentary, Feng [Zuoxun?] on the *Zheng zhi*, etc."[115] Expressing the desire that his students would continue his unfinished work, Chen writes, "Modern Interpretation of the *Zhouli*—Gui Wencan."[116] These plans divulge a strong commitment to preserving and developing the fundamental textual basis of evidential research, and, in this sense, should be seen as an affirmation of the Xuehaitang enterprise. Moreover, as Benjamin Elman has suggested, specialization into discrete disciplinary fields was a natural outgrowth of the eighteenth-century evidential research movement.[117] Chen Li, despite his transformation, was seemingly still very much steeped in *kaozheng* practice.

Finally, although Chen Li did not pass through the region again after failing the metropolitan examinations for a seventh time in 1852, Jiangnan nevertheless loomed large in Chen's imagination throughout the period in which he pursued the scholarship, pedagogy, and editing described above. Chen maintained contact with several of the most prominent nineteenth-century Jiangnan successors to the eighteenth-century *kaozheng* movement. During his 1844 visit to Ruan Yuan, Chen had learned of Liu Xing'en's (1832 *juren*) research on the Guliang commentary of the *Chunqiu*. Chen later corresponded with Liu and wrote a preface for Liu's important study of the commentary. In his manuscript notes, Chen Li recalls paying a visit to Suzhou to inquire of Chen Huan (1786–1863), an expert on the Mao recension of the *Shijing*, about the state of classical studies in Jiangnan.[118] Well into the 1870s, Chen Li corresponded closely with Jiangnan's pre-eminent interpreter of the *Lunyu*, Liu Gongmian, as well as with Dai Wang (1837–73), a maverick student of the great Gujing jingshe director Yu Yue (1821–1907).[119] In addition, one finds in the manuscript notes detailed descriptions of where various Jiangnan scholars resided. So, for instance, of the expert on the Zuo commentary of the *Chunqiu*, Liu Wenqi (1789–1856), and his son, Liu Yusong (1818–67), Chen records, "style-name Mengzhan, an Yizheng county native, 1819 senior licentiate of the third class; son Liu Yusong, style-name Boshan, sobriquet Songya, 1840 senior licentiate of the third class; their residence is in Yangzhou east of the salt controller's yamen, west of the Sanzhu Chapel Bridge."[120]

CONCLUSION

What should one conclude about such jottings, in which Chen Li notes precisely where the famous scholars of Jiangnan may be found? In the 1871 "Self-Narration," with which this chapter begins, Chen declares that he has changed course intellectually. Rather than continuing his aimless youthful experiments in evidential research, Chen proclaims, he had determined after middle age to seek for "larger meanings" in the Classics, rediscovering Zhu Xi in the process. Yet the jottings in Chen's notebook are part of a large body of evidence suggesting that he never fully uprooted himself from the context in which he had carried out his youthful experiments.

For Chen Li, as for other Xuehaitang scholars, the evidential research movement and Jiangnan were inextricably linked. A second-generation Xuehaitang scholar, Chen Li was typical of many in the previous generation, in that he was part of the large community of sojourners and in-migrants who dominated academy life. Chen tried at times to straddle the two worlds of Jiangnan and Guangzhou; his focus, however, remained fixed on Jiangnan. He re-enacted his connection to Jiangnan in the filial practice of visiting ancestral tombs, expressed it in verse, and inscribed it above his Guangzhou study. When he was no longer able to travel through Jiangnan, he continued correspondence with the outstanding Jiangnan classicists of his day.

Likewise, Chen Li never completely separated himself from the *kaozheng* agenda that was imported from Jiangnan and promoted at the Xuehaitang academy. Despite dissatisfaction with classical exegetical practice at the Xuehaitang, and with partisan Han Learning more generally, Chen remained fundamentally entrenched in that very agenda. His marked concern later in life with revising, supplementing, and publishing his youthful studies in phonology, geography, and mathematics is one indication of this. In addition, Chen was instrumental in channeling reconstruction funds into recreating an institutional environment in which serious evidential research was possible. His efforts in reprinting the essential reference tools of the *kaozheng* enterprise reveal with perhaps greater clarity exactly where Chen Li's priorities lay. This is seen as well in Chen's ability to secure the patronage of provincial officials for the projects of resurrecting the long-defunct specialized classes at the Xuehaitang and of establishing the Jupo jingshe, a new academy closely patterned after the Xuehaitang but modified by Chen.

Finally, Chen Li's mediation of Han Learning and Song Learning similarly reveals an emphasis upon the evidential research enterprise initially created in eighteenth-century Jiangnan. Though Chen's forced efforts at mediation reinvented both Han Confucians and Song Neo-Confucians, it seems that Song Learning is stretched further. Zhu Xi comes across in Chen's portrayal as philologist and ritualist; the moral and metaphysical aspects of Zhu Xi's thought are downplayed and dismissed. Song Learning for Chen was a corrective meant to rid Qing *kaozheng* scholars of their fetishes; it was not intended as a replacement.

Chen Li's particular mediation of Han and Song Learning was also part of a larger discourse of Han-Song syncretism that was, over the course of the nineteenth century, increasingly prevalent throughout the empire and especially resonant in Guangzhou. In this sense, Chen Li was inextricably embedded in local scholarly discourse. Chen was not, as he bemoans in moments of self-pity (and as some modern scholars have suggested), absolutely alienated, worlds apart from his contemporaries. Rather, Han-Song syncretism was an integral component of the Xuehaitang experience, a consequence of Ruan Yuan's particular preoccupations in the 1820s, as well as the fact that syncretism made evidential research more palatable in a region steeped in Neo-Confucian learning but lacking experience in evidential research. The discourse of Han-Song syncretism, despite a certain amount of sloganeering, was flexible enough to accommodate a variety of intellectual loyalties. Thus Wen Xun, who was partial to Song Learning, and Xu Hao, evincing a bias for evidential research, both felt obliged to frame their views in syncretic discourse. Likewise, Chen Li, who was oriented toward Jiangnan and evidential research, and Zhu Ciqi, who was intensely focused upon the delta and highly critical of Ruan Yuan, earned reputations through their explorations of Han-Song syncretism as the greatest of nineteenth-century Cantonese scholars. Chen and Zhu in many respects led parallel lives, but, as we shall see in Chapter 7, Zhu Ciqi in fact rejected Han Learning much more completely and embraced a Neo-Confucian identity to a much greater degree than did Chen Li.

⁂ SEVEN ⁂
Zhu "Jiujiang": Alternative Identities and the Delta's Critique of the City

> The walled city has much dust and din,
> All the more so near the urban magnates.
> Turning my head southward, looking to my native place,
> For one hundred *li* the azure clouds are high.
>
> —Zhu Ciqi, excerpt from "Another Poem Sent to Tingguang from the Walled City," Guangzhou, 1835

IN THE FALL OF 1881, the ailing septuagenarian Zhu Ciqi refused to receive any more guests, exclusively devoting his time to ordering his manuscripts for publication. Two months later, realizing that he could never finish the work, he incinerated all the manuscripts he could find. Titles of the lost manuscripts reveal the once ambitious designs of the author: *Guochao mingchen yanxing lu* (Record of words and deeds of famous officials of the present dynasty), *Guochao yimin zhuan* (Biographies of former [Ming] subjects), *Xingxue yuanliu* (Origins and development of the Learning of Nature), and *Wushi shizheng lu*, a collection of historical events from the Song, Liao (907–1125), Jin (1115–1234), Yuan, and Ming dynasties that Zhu deemed relevant for the current age. After Zhu died on February 7, 1882, his most devoted students pieced together what writings had been missed by their teacher and printed them together under the title *Fenyu ji* (Collection remaining from the fire).[1]

Zhu Ciqi was a native of Jiujiang township (*bao*) in the southern part of Nanhai. He became recognized, along with Chen Li, as one of the two greatest Cantonese scholars in the middle of the nine-

FIG. 9: The Enclosure district. This is adapted from a map of the Sangyuanwei (Mulberry Garden Enclosure) drawn by Chen Li for the 1879 Guangzhou prefectural gazetteer (SOURCE: *Guangzhou fu zhi*, 8.38b–39a).

teenth century. The two are also commonly grouped together as the two most prominent nineteenth-century Cantonese exponents of Han-Song syncretism. Outside Guangdong, Zhu is remembered as the teacher of Kang Youwei, though little else is known about him.[2] Within his native province, Zhu had students who were important locally—such as Jian Chaoliang (1851-1933)—and who were far more faithful to his teachings than was Kang. Nevertheless, it has been quite difficult to get a grasp of Zhu Ciqi's learning due to the dearth of extant materials.

This does not leave the historian at a complete loss, however, for Zhu Ciqi left unscathed three compilations—of lineage and local history and literature—in which he had played a significant editorial role. The *Zhushi chuanfang ji*, edited by Zhu in 1861, is an anthology of writings authored by members of the Jiujiang Zhu lineage. Zhu Ciqi also set guidelines for the 1869 Zhu lineage genealogy and promoted the revision of the local Jiujiang gazetteer, which was printed in 1883, shortly after his death. Taken together, these three texts demonstrate an intense interest in a very local cultural arena.

Furthermore, seen in the context of the increasing autonomy of Jiujiang's gentry leaders, Zhu's critique of Xuehaitang scholarship, and his decision to teach in Jiujiang, they represent part of a basic cultural reconfiguration, centering Cantonese culture on the subcounty level in the Pearl River delta, rather than in urban Guangzhou.

It is possible to ascertain—by examining the materials that Zhu Ciqi refrained from, or perhaps was constrained from, burning—which cultural resources he deemed important; such examination furthermore reveals a great deal about how Cantonese literati in the delta differed from their urban counterparts. In contrast to much of the preceding narrative, which is devoted to the pre-eminent urban Cantonese academy, the Xuehaitang, this chapter shifts focus from city to hinterland, contextualizing Zhu Ciqi's motives by introducing another academy, the township where it was located, and the native literati who established it. Although Jiujiang's academy was created during the same decade as the Xuehaitang, it served different functions. Emerging out of this context, Zhu Ciqi voiced a critique of urban Guangzhou and the Xuehaitang and articulated an alternative identity for the Cantonese elite native to the delta hinterland.

JIUJIANG TOWNSHIP

Located 140 *li* southwest of Guangzhou, Jiujiang was one of several prosperous Nanhai and Shunde townships within the Mulberry Garden Enclosure that relied on the fish pond and mulberry embankment economy (see Fig. 9). In the ponds, residents raised several different but compatible species of carp—bottom-dwellers recycling the waste of top-dwellers—harvested from the West River. On the embankments separating ponds, farmers grew mulberry bushes to feed silkworms and various grasses for feeding the fish. Silkworms, pigs, and humans provided excrement that could be used as fertilizer for the fish ponds. Commercial aquaculture and sericulture brought great wealth to the district, but it also meant that there were few cultivable fields in Jiujiang and neighboring Enclosure townships; residents accordingly had to import rice.[3]

Among these townships, Jiujiang stood out as the nucleus of the Enclosure economy. A subcounty official, the Nanhai registrar (*zhubu*), had his yamen located in Jiujiang and was responsible for overseeing Jiujiang, Datong, Shatou, Heqing, and Zhenyong.[4] Jiujiang's Great Market straddled the arterial canal that ran through the center of the township and formed the confluence of the four sectors (Northside, Southside, Eastside, and Westside) into which Jiujiang was divided. Running along either side of the canal, the market was, by 1883, composed of over fifteen hundred shops along 26 lanes. The market was officially open on the third, sixth, and ninth days of the ten-day cycle, though it is described as never being completely empty.[5] Jiujiang's importance in comparison to that of other Enclosure district townships was evident to B. C. Henry, the Western traveler who visited the area in the late nineteenth century:

> Kow-kong [Jiujiang] is the largest, and forms a little kingdom in itself. It is said that during the war at the close of the Taiping rebellion, a census was taken with a view to estimating the fighting strength of the people, and it was found that Kow-kong alone could furnish the 300,000 able-bodied men as soldiers. The limits of this town lie within a space five miles wide and seven or eight long. The town is composed of coteries of villages around the main centre of trade.[6]

As was the case with other places in the Pearl River delta, it was only in the Ming that Jiujiang emerged as an important commercial center fostering a gentry culture. Despite the foundation legends of Jiujiang's lineages, and aside from a single stone inscription uncovered in the 1810s, Jiujiang could point to few historical records predating the Ming. In fact, compilers of a 1657 Jiujiang gazetteer recognized that during Tang-Song and earlier times the area that would eventually constitute the Enclosure district consisted only of sparsely populated islands.[7]

The origins of Jiujiang as a settled and prosperous community are reflected in two legendary events that claim for Jiujiang the legitimacy of imperial favor: construction of the Enclosure and acquisition of fishing rights upstream along the West River. According to legend, the dikes constituting the Enclosure had first been constructed by two officials during the Northern Song, who continued to be honored in a temple along the dike. The historical record becomes clearer in the early Ming, though it is still described in legendary terms. An important upriver section of the Enclosure ruptured in 1395, resulting in severe flooding. In response, a wealthy commoner of Jiujiang, Chen Bomin, is said to have presented plans for extensive renovation of the West River dikes to the Hongwu court in Nanjing, which granted its approval and placed Chen in charge of the project. When the project was completed in 1397, Jiujiang supporters of Chen had a literatus from neighboring Xinhui county write a record of the event and a praise (*song*) of Chen. Chen was also later worshiped in numerous shrines along the Enclosure, the most important of which was maintained by his descendants in Jiujiang. This event is important in the formation of a collective identity among the educated elite of the Enclosure district. In contrast to the legend of the Enclosure's origins, this account of Chen Bomin's efforts in the early Ming makes local residents, rather than officials of the state, the active agents in maintenance of the Enclosure dikes, and places Jiujiang at the very center of Enclosure activities.[8]

A second legendary event to which Jiujiang traced its prosperity was the township's capture of monopoly fishing rights on the West River. Eggs laid by mature carp in Guangxi tributaries produced hatchlings that would accumulate in bends of the West River in Guangdong. Jiujiang fishermen referred to them as "fish sprouts" (*yumiao*) or "fish flowers" (*yuhua*), because they resembled flowers amidst the algae. All along the West River—but especially along the stretch from Changzhou island in the eastern Guangxi county of Cangwu to the prefectural city of Zhaoqing in Guangdong—Jiujiang natives operated fishing stations (*bu*), where a team of fishermen would set up camp to scoop the fry into baskets tied to scaffolds in the water.[9] Once the "fish flowers" were harvested, they were quickly transported to Jiujiang, where they were sorted according to species and then deposited in fish ponds. There, they were often reared for a month before being sold to other pisciculturalists in the Enclosure district, who would raise them to maturity. Households throughout the Enclosure district that specialized in the fish pond and mulberry embankment economy had to purchase "fish flowers" from Jiujiang. Alternatively, the fry would be allowed to mature until the following spring, when thousands of Jiujiang merchants transported the fish live—in specially outfitted boats that allowed for the circulation of fresh river water—to destinations throughout the Lingnan region and beyond.[10] Typically, Jiujiang boats would return from selling the fish bearing shipments of rice to supply Jiujiang and other Enclosure townships. This annual cycle of harvesting, rearing, and marketing fish fry and fingerlings was a unique and central feature of the Jiujiang economy. By the late seventeenth century, Jiujiang had earned such a reputation for dominating the West River fish industry that Qu Dajun extensively quoted relevant passages from the 1657 Jiujiang gazetteer in his *Guangdong xinyu*.[11]

Both the 1657 and the 1883 gazetteers claim that the rights to harvest West River "fish flowers" were taken over, along with the duty to pay various fishing levies (*yuxiang*), from the Dan in 1501. According to the legend establishing these rights, in that year, "Dan households of each river" absconded, leaving behind a tax responsibility of several thousand *shi* of rice. On the recommendation of Governor-General Liu Daxia (1436–1516), an edict was issued granting "Jiujiang commoners" the rights to operate fishing stations all along the West River, but also obligating them to pay taxes for the use of these stations. Over the course of the sixteenth century, Jiujiang natives were granted further rights, along with further tax obligations, to harvest fish fry on the West River and to market live fish throughout Guangdong.[12] Regardless of how the fishing rights and tax obligations were acquired, they continued to be associated with the Dan. Expertise in predicting the arrival of different species of fish fry from the various West River tributaries was a skill specifically attributed to the Dan, even by editors of the Jiujiang gazetteers. More recently, a 1932 survey of the West River fish fry industry found that most harvesters were indeed Dan. As members of the Jiujiang elite sought to convert fishing industry wealth into cultural capital, however, they stubbornly defended Jiujiang fishing and marketing rights while adamantly distinguishing themselves from the Dan.[13]

Jiujiang was thus a community that simultaneously looked inward and outward. The "Enclosure" that surrounded Jiujiang and neighboring townships protected the delicately balanced fish pond and mulberry embankment economy. But these ponds were stocked with fish fry harvested all along the West River, and the fish that the ponds produced were marketed by Jiujiang natives throughout South China. The influence of Jiujiang natives along the West River, all the way into Guangxi, is reflected in the number of Jiujiang elite who had visible connections to the western province. There is also evidence of Jiujiang merchants traveling as far afield as Vietnam.[14] Thus, in a local manifestation of the traditional gender division of labor—in which "men plow, women weave"—editors of the 1883 gazetteer portrayed the local men as selling fish flowers and the women feeding silkworms. At the same time, the editors depicted Jiujiang as a place where residents came together in lineages and rarely sojourned outside the township.[15] Yet this image was belied by the gazetteer's descriptions of the township's economy. The composite picture that emerges, then, is one in which Jiujiang natives traveled extensively outside the Enclosure district, often in an economically exploitative manner, but closely guarded their own township from infiltration by in-migrating peoples. This closure against in-migration was affected through the efforts of an elite group of gentry who controlled Jiujiang's dominant lineages.

THE JIUJIANG LINEAGES

In addition to securing economic benefits, Jiujiang began to produce recognizable gentry and lineages from the middle Ming. The first Jiujiang *juren* was from the Guan surname in 1438; he was followed by the township's first *jinshi*, a Huang, in 1457.[16] In the ensuing decades, Jiujiang replicated these early successes, producing a total of 60 *juren* between 1438 and 1642, and eleven *jinshi* between 1457 and 1640. And this success was monopolized by a few descent-groups— the Guan, Huang, Zhu, Zeng, and Chen being the most successful. Most important during the Ming and early Qing was the Guan, which produced the greatest number of degree-holders well into the eighteenth century. By the end of the Ming, these descent-groups formed lineages through the construction of ancestral shrines and lineage halls dominated by the same surnames.[17]

Characteristic of most lineages in the delta during late imperial times, Jiujiang lineages asserted claims of descent from ancestors who had migrated from Nanxiong in northern Guangdong in the 1270s. The Guan claimed descent from an ancestor mythically named Guan Nanxiong, whose bones were taken by his sons from Nanxiong for burial in Jiujiang after they moved there in the Xianchun era (1265–74).[18] The descendants of Chen Bomin, who initiated dike construction in the early Ming, also professed Nanxiong origins. In an epitaph written for Chen, a Hanlin academician from Jiujiang, Guan Shangjin (1721 *jinshi*), asserted that Chen's great-grandfather had come from Nanxiong to settle in Jiujiang, thus becoming the Chen lineage's migrant ancestor.[19] However tenuous, these claims of descent from Nanxiong ancestors provided the educated elite of Jiujiang and the entire delta hinterland with a great deal of genealogical prestige, a local cultural resource not available to most of the urban elite in Guangzhou.

Despite the acquisition of gentry status by Jiujiang's most successful families, they were never entirely separated from the township's commercial interests in fish and silk, both within Jiujiang and beyond. One can find traces of the projection of Jiujiang economic concerns outside the township in the surprisingly large number of Jiujiang literati who earned *shengyuan* status or *juren* degrees as registered students of other Guangdong counties. The number of Jiujiang literati who earned degrees as Guangxi students is even more noteworthy, as this perhaps indicates the extent of Jiujiang fishing and commercial interests in that province. Most of these were students registered in Cangwu county, just across the border from Guangdong on the West River.[20] Likewise, within Jiujiang, gentry leaders of the dominant lineages asserted control over local economic organization. Four members of Jiujiang's dominant lineages who earned *jinshi* degrees between 1508 and 1619 are recorded as having taken initiative in moving or renovating the Great Market and thereby establishing their authority.[21]

By the nineteenth century, two other lineages that had been less influential in township affairs began to assert themselves: the Feng and the Ming. Although three ancestral shrines are listed for the Feng in the 1657 gazetteer, the only Jiujiang Feng recorded as having made a mark in the Ming was Feng Yushun, a 1636 *juren*, who had studied under Zhu Guangyun, a 1615 *juren*. Beginning in the eighteenth century, a few Feng, all from Tiejiao neighborhood on the Northside of Jiujiang, managed to pass provincial examinations, either in Guangdong or Guangxi. By 1800, one of these Feng *juren* commemorated the completion of a pagoda at the Feng shrine in Tiejiao, a project financed by well over a hundred Feng. Finally, the Tiejiao Feng produced an impressive five *jinshi* between 1829 and 1868.[22]

The rise of the Ming of Shajiao neighborhood in Jiujiang's Eastside was equally spectacular, if only because of their more obscure origins. Only one Ming shrine, located in Shajiao, is noted in the 1657 gazetteer. Sometime in the eighteenth century, an elderly ninth-generation Jiujiang Ming with no sons, Ming Jingran, was dissuaded by a lineage elder from adopting a non-Ming as heir. Instead, he acquired a concubine who bore him three sons. Before he died at 96 *sui*, Jingran was able to embrace his great-grandson, Ming Lizhao, a future 1821 *juren* who would have a lot of clout in Jiujiang affairs. The Ming had especially close ties to Cangwu county in Guangxi, and nineteenth-century gazetteers of both Nanhai and Cangwu claimed Shajiao Ming *juren* as their own.[23] Nevertheless, the Shajiao Ming worked closely with the Feng and the Zhu in ruling Jiujiang after the 1820s.[24]

In contrast to the Feng and Ming, Zhu Ciqi's lineage had enjoyed a more prestigious place in the early development of Jiujiang. According to the Zhu lineage genealogy, Zhu's First Migrant Ancestor (*shiqianzu*), Zhu Yuanlong, settled in Jiujiang's Shangsha village in 1274. As was the case with other Jiujiang lineages, the Zhu asserted descent from ancestors who had moved from Nanxiong.[25] Yuanlong's son, Zhu Ziyi, was the first Zhu registered as a Nanhai resident and thus became the First Ancestor (*shizu*) of the Jiujiang Zhu ancestral cult. Tales of Zhu Ziyi relate that when he first settled in the village, supposedly in the late Yuan, influential residents ignored him. Only after a long time did he gradually win them over through his refined conduct, with the result that "the *shidaifu* [gentry] in the village came to see him as one of their own."[26] Of course, there were no *shidaifu* in Jiujiang at that time—if by that term we mean holders of higher-level degrees—but this account nevertheless serves the purpose of establishing the gentry credentials of the Zhu.

Another component of the Jiujiang Zhu foundation legend relates that, after winning over his influential neighbors, Zhu Ziyi married the daughter of a wealthy Shangsha man surnamed Guan, who lacked a son of his own.[27] Ziyi and his Guan wife produced three sons, who in turn became the focal ancestors of three branches of Jiujiang Zhu, organized into the Yongguan Hall, the Cunzhu Hall, and the Yisi Hall. The Yisi ancestor, Zhu Shuida, is said to have first settled in the Taiping neighborhood on Jiujiang's Westside. This branch produced Zhu Ciqi and the largest number of other important Jiujiang Zhu in the nineteenth century.[28]

By the middle of the sixteenth century (thus somewhat later than the Guan, Huang, and Zeng), a few segments of the Jiujiang Zhu began to produce degree-holders. Success began with Zhu Wenjin of the Yisi branch's fifth generation, who was a *gongsheng* of 1525. The Zhu soon produced more examination successes, with a 1552 *juren* (Zhu Mo, d. 1580) and a 1574 *jinshi* (Zhu Rang, d. 1604) in the seventh generation, a 1585 *juren* (Zhu Lingxiao) in the eighth generation, and four more in the tenth generation. This examination success on the part of the Jiujiang Zhu further stimulated lineage-building efforts and cultivation of marriage alliances. The 1869 Zhu genealogy claims that an ancestral shrine in honor of Zhu Ziyi was constructed during the Jiajing reign under the direction of Zhu Rang. Ancestral shrines multiplied well into the nineteenth century, the most important being the three lineage branch halls. The first recorded Zhu genealogy was compiled in 1577, though it was never printed. A genealogical chart of the Yongguan Hall Zhu was compiled in 1691, and a genealogy of the entire lineage again put together in 1716.[29]

As symbolized in the foundation legend, the Zhu had strong affinal relations with the Jiujiang Guan, a special relationship that continued well into the nineteenth century, as Jiujiang Zhu showed a marked preference for marriages with the Guan.[30] The Zhu also forged marriage alliances with other important Jiujiang literati. For instance, the 1525 *gongsheng* Wenjin took advantage of his success by pursuing an aggressive marriage strategy, arranging weddings for one of his daughters with a Guan 1591 *juren* and for another with a Zeng 1585 *juren*, who was in turn the son of a 1543 *juren*. Likewise, 1585 *juren* Zhu Lingxiao married a granddaughter of the 1516 Zeng *juren*; the couple's son, Guangyun, earned a *juren* in 1615. Further solidifying their affinal ties, many Zhu and Guan maintained teacher-student or patron-client relationships. In the early Qing, for example, the future Hanlin academician Guan Shangjin was spotted as a promising talent by a local teacher, Zhu Guocai (d. 1689).[31]

Despite the development of strong ties to Jiujiang by the end of the sixteenth century, the attractions of the big city were enticing, at times threatening to lure the most promising native sons of the late

Ming away from Jiujiang to Guangzhou. After becoming the first Zhu to pass the provincial examinations in 1552, Zhu Mo and his sons built a resort outside Guangzhou's North Gate—where they entertained that city's poetic elite—and a mansion in the provincial city, where his sons and grandsons would also reside.[32] This family of the Zhu lineage, not unlike Huang Peifang and other descendants of Xiangshan's Huang Zuo, thus came close to establishing a de facto permanent residence in the city.[33] But Zhu Mo and his sons were unwilling to cut their Jiujiang ties completely, retaining their original residence there. This served Zhu Mo's sons and grandsons well, as they were able to seek refuge in Jiujiang during the chaotic years of the Ming-Qing transition. Afterward, it was rare for Jiujiang Zhu to relocate permanently to Guangzhou. This reorientation of focus from city to township is reflected in the 1869 Zhu genealogy, which attributes the survival of Zhu Mo's descendants to his decision to retain his "humble cottage" in Jiujiang.[34]

Thus, despite the unique economy that supported their activities and sent Jiujiang natives throughout South China and even into Vietnam, the gentry leaders of Jiujiang's dominant lineages, including the Zhu, increasingly made Jiujiang township, rather than Guangzhou city, the focus of their cultural self-representations after the Ming-Qing transition. This, of course, did not preclude members of the Jiujiang elite from pursuing cultural matters in Guangzhou. For example, in the eighteenth century, Zhu Jizhao (1736 *juren*) established an academy in Guangzhou for Zhu clan members from throughout the province.[35] But this institution primarily functioned to unify Zhu when they gathered in Guangzhou for examinations, rather than as a permanent city residence exclusively for Jiujiang Zhu. For the most part, Jiujiang became their central concern.

If the Qing Jiujiang gentry's vision of the fundamental economic, social, or cultural unit extended any further beyond the township, it was only to encompass as allies the elites of other Enclosure district townships. The most influential lineages in neighboring townships were the Wen of Longshan, who generated an astounding eleven *juren* between 1779 and 1813, and the Cai of Longjiang.[36] The elite of this area was wealthy and locally conscientious enough to produce most of the subcounty gazetteers compiled in Qing-dynasty Guangdong. There are gazetteers of both Longjiang and Longshan, the latter compiled in 1805 by Wen Runeng. Jiujiang literati compiled two gazetteers for their township during the Qing. Only the town of Foshan, lying between this area and the prefectural seat of Guangzhou, produced more subcounty gazetteers. Literary societies and scholarly circles, occasionally organized exclusively among the Jiujiang elite, at times also included literati from among the Enclosure gentry. One such literary society for the composition of occasional poems included Jiujiang literati from the Zeng, Feng, and Guan lineages, as well as a Cai from Longjiang and the anthologist from Longshan, Wen Runeng.[37] The Enclosure elite thus conceived of this area as a culturally coherent unit distinct from both the Nanhai county seat in Guangzhou and the Shunde county seat, Daliang. Zhu Ciqi in the middle of the nineteenth century would continue to limit most of his scholarly and literary communication to fellow Enclosure gentry. His extant writings contain numerous letters and poems to Zhu, Feng, Ming, and Guan—and few to anyone else. In other words, the main participants in the Zhu Ciqi movement were, as we shall see, other members of dominant lineages of the Enclosure district.

The point of this account of settlement in Jiujiang is to explore how elite members of the Zhu and other Jiujiang lineages, in part through their genealogical claims, produced a unique set of cultural resources. Thus, though an urban literatus such as Chen Li clearly shared certain cultural resources with delta literati such as Zhu Ciqi, other resources—such as claims of Nanxiong descent and genealogical ties to the Ming Cantonese elite—were possessed by Zhu alone. But Jiujiang literati also faced a unique set of problems and developed novel institutions for managing them.

AUTONOMOUS GENTRY RULE AT RULIN ACADEMY

Over the course of the century leading up to the compilation of the 1883 township gazetteer, the Jiujiang elite increasingly felt itself threatened by a variety of outside forces—including encroachment on Jiujiang fishing rights, flooding, and banditry—as well as such perceived moral vices as gambling, prostitution, and marriage resistance among women. Such threats to prosperity stimulated, or served as pretexts for, the consolidation of gentry power within Jiujiang and the projection of Jiujiang power throughout South China. As the gentry created institutions for consolidating authority locally, they enforced a Neo-Confucian morality within Jiujiang and exhibited a unique Jiujiang identity throughout the delta. Managing this multifaceted project was Rulin Academy (Rulin shuyuan), a corporation controlled by a small group of literati and gentry managers from among Jiujiang's dominant lineages.

Although Jiujiang gained commercial wealth through control of the West River fishing industry, the township's exclusive rights to the harvesting of fish fry and marketing of fish fingerlings were challenged almost from the beginning. Editors of the 1657 gazetteer complained about Jiujiang boats being held for "inspection" by yamen underlings in Longchuan in northeastern Guangdong until fees were paid.[38] Similar instances occurred wherever Jiujiang boats plied. The fundamental problem was that it was difficult to maintain a monopoly on fishing rights and technology when the harvesting and marketing operations were extended over such a wide geographical range; when Jiujiang natives migrated to other places, their loyalties to home lineages faded. Jiujiang leaders were well aware of this. For instance, Changzhou in Guangxi's Cangwu county had been the site of Jiujiang fishing stations as early as the seventeenth century. By the 1880s, editors of the Jiujiang gazetteer lamented that Jiujiang descendants residing in Changzhou, though they were intimately familiar with the affairs of Jiujiang, had lost any feelings for their native land, and, as a result, fry-rearing technologies were being transferred to "outsiders." This in turn threatened to lower the price that Jiujiang natives could get on the market. Other "outsiders" sought to make money by more nefarious means. With increasing frequency over the course of the eighteenth century, Jiujiang natives were forced to pay fees for unobstructed passage of boats to harvesting or marketing sites. Moreover, the methods that others used to intimidate Jiujiang boats became increasingly rough, from destroying the fish fry by planting poison upstream to burning down the sheds erected by fishermen at the fish stations.[39]

Jiujiang natives responded by repeatedly petitioning local and provincial authorities to issue pronouncements against interfering with the free navigation of Jiujiang boats. In their petitions, Jiujiang natives were often at pains to distinguish themselves from the Dan, an indication that this was a difficult image to shake. Nevertheless, judging from the number of petitions that survived, incorporated in official proclamations and inscribed on stone tablets, authorities seem to have responded favorably to them. For example, in 1774 a Jiujiang petition convinced the Guangdong grain intendant to issue a prohibition on interference with Jiujiang boats; the proclamation was distributed with names of the Guangzhou and Zhaoqing prefects, as well as their subordinate county magistrates. This covered all of the West River within Guangdong province. A few years later, Guangxi provincial officials responded to Jiujiang requests to repeat this prohibition in Wuzhou and Xunzhou prefectures, thereby extending coverage to practically the entire West River basin.[40] Before the nineteenth century, the names of Jiujiang natives that appear on such petitions cannot be identified as belonging to the degree-holding gentry. Nevertheless, the influence of Jiujiang's landholding (or pond-holding) gentry was impressive. Though the petitions were meant to portray the fragility of the fish fry industry, the heavy burden of the various levies, and the degree to which Jiujiang monopoly rights were being challenged, the stone inscriptions they resulted in revealed the impressive reach of Jiujiang power. Through stone inscriptions erected in counties all along the West River basin—stretching from the township far into the neighboring province of Guangxi—Jiujiang asserted its claim to control an entire industry.

Another problem threatening Jiujiang prosperity was an even older one. Flooding in the late Qianlong reign culminated in a massive 1794 deluge that broke the Enclosure in several places. The Enclosure gentry, led by Wen Rugua of Longshan, pushed the provincial authorities for a general reconstruction of the Enclosure, a pattern that was repeated throughout the nineteenth century. The construction was finished four years later under the direction of the registrar Ji Huijia.[41] Despite these efforts, the Enclosure broke again in 1813 and in 1817. Wen Rugua, with the support of several Jiujiang literati, once again pressed provincial officials to find a lasting solution, this time in the form of a permanent fund for yearly dike repairs. The new governor-general, Ruan Yuan, responded by requesting in a memorial to borrow eighty thousand taels from the provincial treasury to deposit for interest with Nanhai and Shunde pawn merchants.⁴² In 1819, and again a decade later, local officials exhorted the Nanhai Wu and Xinhui Lu maritime merchant families to donate enormous sums of money to replace earthen with stone dikes along the Enclosure.⁴³

Floods plagued the Enclosure district yet again in the 1830s and in 1844. In the first instance, a long list of Enclosure gentry—including Feng Rutang (1831 *juren*), Zeng Zhao, Ming Lun, and Hu Tiaode—solicited funds for dike construction; in the latter case, Jiujiang *juren* Ming Lun and Longshan *juren* Feng Fengchu called upon officials to disburse huge amounts of money for repair.⁴⁴ In 1841, a local official suggested dismantling Enclosure dikes and casting the stones into the Pearl River in order to impede the passage of British naval vessels; the "people inside the Enclosure" (*weinei ren*) nervously resisted this, and some residents of Shatou went so far as to take turns guarding the Enclosure dikes.⁴⁵ In 1853, another Jiujiang Ming—Zhu Ciqi's friend and Ming Lizhao's son, Ming Zhigang—"together with the Enclosure gentry (*weishen*)"—repeatedly submitted petitions for a yearly Enclosure repair fund.⁴⁶ Clearly, elite representatives of the dominant lineages along the Enclosure perceived a shared interest in the face of threats from outsiders. After completion of an Enclosure maintenance project in the 1860s, Ming Zhigang brought together previous gazetteers commemorating dike repairs from 1794 to 1867 to form a comprehensive gazetteer of the Mulberry Garden Enclosure. Such compilations presented the Enclosure gentry as a coherent and unified elite that shared common interests. The central place given to Chen Bomin in the Enclosure's history, and to Ming himself as compiler, portrayed Jiujiang as the heart of the Enclosure district.⁴⁷

A third threat to the prosperity of Jiujiang and its Enclosure neighbors was the increasing incidence of banditry, beginning in the late Qianlong era. In fact, in 1780 Jiujiang narrowly escaped a massacre; it was, however, not at the hands of bandits, but rather at those of an overzealous official determined to end their presence in the township. The new governor, Li Hu, had discovered that bandits near Panyu county's Shawan township had been harbored by local military units, and unfortunately many Shawan residents were killed as a result of Li's bandit suppression campaign there. Aware of growing imperial suspicions of his predecessors' lack of vigilance,

Li was determined to wipe out any other bandits under his jurisdiction. He next turned his attention to Jiujiang, where a similar group of brigands was known to have been hiding. As Li was about to set out with his forces for Jiujiang, the Nanhai county magistrate interceded on behalf of the township. Securing the governor's agreement to postpone the campaign, the magistrate rushed to Jiujiang for negotiations with 1777 *juren* Hu Ting and other representatives of the Jiujiang elite. Hu, himself a student of an eminent member of the Zhu lineage, succeeded in mobilizing the gentry to suppress the bandits, thereby saving Jiujiang from a disaster.[48] Yet Jiujiang's bandit troubles were only beginning. In June 1809, a pirate gang under the notorious Zhang Bao attempted to pillage Jiujiang. The pirates withdrew after a full day of fighting, inflicting only minor damage along the edge of the West River. Two leaders of Jiujiang's defense, Zhu Chengwan (d. 1823) and Chen Lüheng (1819 *juren*), had earlier organized a Jiujiang literary society with a third native son, Guan Shiang (1792 *juren*). Thus literary societies both in Jiujiang and within the Enclosure district as a whole could also function as means of mobilizing the elite in emergency responses to flooding and banditry.[49]

After the initial threats, in the late Qianlong and early Jiaqing periods, of fishing competition, flooding, and banditry, Jiujiang's dominant lineages took steps to provide for more complete control of the township's affairs. By the middle of the nineteenth century, the fruits of their labor had gradually ripened into Rulin Academy, through which they virtually ruled the township. The roots of the academy lay deep in Jiujiang's Ming past, when the township's nascent elite customarily met at the Buddhist Zhengjue Monastery. Almost any literatus of standing in late Ming Jiujiang—including Zhu Bolian (1634 *jinshi*) and Zhu Shilian (1621 *juren*), the most distinguished ninth-generation members of the Jiujiang Zhu—bequeathed poems written on excursions to the site.[50] The temple was renovated in the Qianlong era, as Jiujiang's Confucian elite completely displaced the Buddhist monks.

Ironically, the April 1786 creation of the Jiujiang registrar post (which represented the authority of the imperially appointed Nanhai county magistrate) in fact provoked the next stage in the development of a Jiujiang government managed by local elites. Likely a response to Jiujiang's bandit problems in 1780, the new subcounty official was in charge of Jiujiang and the four neighboring Nanhai townships of Datong, Shatou, Heqing, and Zhenyong. The new yamen, completed in 1789, was constructed on the site of a former Jiujiang academy.[51] On the pretext of having lost one local meeting place, the Jiujiang elite in 1784 determined to expand the Zhengjue Monastery temple complex, giving it a new, unambiguously Confucian name: the Old Forest of Scholars Temple (Rulin gumiao). Two years later, construction was completed on halls in honor of such deities as Wenchang, Beidi, Guandi, and Guanyin. In addition, the elite managers established at the same site a temple for the God of Wealth (Caishen) and revived another old academy, Elephant Hill Academy. Here, the Jiujiang elite gathered on the third day of the second month, as their predecessors had in the Ming, in a meeting known as the Kuiwen hui (loosely translated as "association for examination success").[52] Soon, Rulin Academy would supersede the Old Rulin Temple complex, but the temple remained important as a secondary focal point for the Jiujiang elite and was duly renovated in 1823 and again during 1869 and 1870.[53]

The next stage in the creation of a permanent elite-managed local government occurred a little over a decade later, with the establishment of the Rulin Literary Society Silk Market (Rulin wenshe sixu). In 1799, Jiujiang gentry leaders Hu Ting (the hero who had suppressed bandits and negotiated with county officials in 1780), Huang Shixian, and Ming Bingzhang convinced county authorities to allow them to consolidate several dispersed and impermanent silk markets into a single permanent location in the heart of the Great Market. Rent from the market would be used to support preparation for the civil service examinations. County authorities approved this scheme in 1802, and construction of the Silk Market was completed a few weeks later. Income from rent was distributed every other year, during the Kuiwen meetings at the recently established Old Rulin Temple. This operation funded the education and examination success of an alliance of elite members of dominant Jiujiang lineages, not to mention some of their other business ventures.[54]

Finally, in the 1820s, just as the Xuehaitang was being established, the small circle of Jiujiang leaders moved to establish Rulin Academy. The new institution was designed to serve as headquarters for their expanding interests and, according to the 1883 gazetteer, began as a Ming-Feng joint venture to put Jiujiang on equal standing with Foshan to the north. The impetus came from Ming Lizhao, who in 1825 pointed out to Feng Yunzheng that Jiujiang needed an academy after the registrar's 1789 usurpation of the old one. Smitten with the idea, Feng supervised construction of the new academy, which, financed by funds donated in the names of lineage elders by the Chen and other dominant Jiujiang lineages, was completed in 1827. On either side of the new academy, Jiujiang elite managers erected shrines honoring local worthies and meritorious officials. In the latter, they paid homage to such officials as the Nanhai county magistrate who in 1780 had interceded on the township's behalf with Governor Li Hu, and the registrar who had supported Enclosure repairs in the 1790s.[55]

Despite the homage paid to selected local officials, Jiujiang's new academy functioned in a manner somewhat autonomous from the underlings and soldiers who enforced state authority. Jiujiang's elite gained independence from intrusive representatives of the state through intelligent appeals to the calligraphic and literary tastes of the current governor-general, Xuehaitang founder Ruan Yuan. One Jiujiang Zeng was none other than Ruan's protégé at the Xuehaitang, Zeng Zhao. Zeng requested his teacher to write a large-character signboard for the new academy in Han clerical script. How could Ruan refuse? His most devoted follower at the Xuehaitang had asked him to promote his "stele school" of calligraphy for a new academy named "Rulin," the title of the section of dynastic history that was devoted to biographies of classical scholars, and which happened to be another of Ruan's projects. When the Jiujiang lineage leaders received their new signboard on July 16, 1826, Ming Lizhao arranged for the other Jiujiang literatus with Xuehaitang connections, Hu Tiaode, to write a letter of thanks in parallel prose, an important component of Ruan's literary agenda. When Ming and Hu presented the letter to Ruan at his yamen, explaining that they wished to pursue their scholarly interests at the new academy with greater freedom from annoying underlings, Ruan was obliged to issue a proclamation effectively barring police, county agents, and—most important—tax collectors from the academy grounds. Ming Lizhao and Feng Yunzheng had orchestrated events perfectly, with only two days to spare before Ruan left, on July 30, for his new post in Yunnan.⁵⁶

Freed from interference by yamen subordinates, Feng, Ming, and other Jiujiang gentry leaders quickly set to organizing collection of local taxes through Rulin Academy. Under this reorganization, Jiujiang natives who marketed fish fingerlings outside the township were required to pay the old fish levy at the academy, in exchange for a license, before their boats would be allowed to proceed upriver. Ostensibly preventing state retribution by ensuring that lineage members paid their taxes, Jiujiang lineage leaders had in effect inserted themselves into the tax collection process. And it is no coincidence that the Jiujiang gentry now began to appear, in full force and with all their symbolic capital, on official proclamations prohibiting competitors' interference with the Jiujiang fishing trade.

Though a portion of the money derived from control of fishing taxation presumably was forwarded to the state, some income from such taxes was combined with rent from the Silk Market and used to support the lineages' literary elites in their pursuit of examination success—a strategy that the editors of the 1883 gazetteer made explicit in their account of the role Ming Lizhao and Feng Yunzheng played in creating the academy. They noted that Yunzheng's son, Feng Xiyong, passed the provincial examination in 1828 and proceeded to earn a *jinshi* degree the following year. In the ensuing 40 years, seven more Jiujiang sons won *jinshi* degrees. Compared to only four *jinshi* produced throughout the Qing up to this point (all of them Guan), Jiujiang seemed on the verge of surpassing its late Ming accomplishments. In addition to Feng Xiyong, two other Tiejiao Feng of the same generation earned *jinshi* degrees, in 1863 and 1868. Two of Feng Xiyong's sons, Feng Jinglue and Feng Shizong, passed in 1860 and 1865. Ming Lizhao's son, Ming Zhigang, accomplished the same feat in 1852. Chen Xinmin, son of Chen Lüheng (who had organized the township's defense against Zhang Bao in 1809), became an 1836 *jinshi*. Feng Yunzheng's and Ming Lizhao's work seems to have paid off, especially for the Feng and Ming. The eighth and most famous example of Jiujiang's sudden resurgence of examination success was Zhu Ciqi, who won his *jinshi* degree in 1847.⁵⁷

ZHU CIQI'S GUANGZHOU EDUCATION AND JIUJIANG ACTIVISM

The examination successes of Zhu Ciqi and other Jiujiang Zhu of his generation coincided with the emergence of Rulin Academy. Several lineage members, in particular his brother Zhu Shiqi (ca. 1795–1856), were intimately involved in developing strategies for dealing with threats to Jiujiang and Enclosure district prosperity. At the same time, Zhu Ciqi came of age with Guangzhou's Xuehaitang. At two key junctures, Zhu was presented with opportunities to enter the elite core of Xuehaitang scholars in Guangzhou, but ultimately he opted to identify himself with Jiujiang. This was not predetermined, however, for in his early years Zhu divided his time between Guangzhou and Jiujiang, pursuing an education and participating in elite management of local affairs.

Like most of his eminent predecessors in the late Ming, Zhu Ciqi was a member of the Yisi Branch of the lineage from the Westside neighborhood of Taiping; however, Zhu Ciqi was not their direct descendant and his immediate ancestors were more obscure. His father, Zhu Chengfa (ca. 1762–1829), became wealthy as a merchant, traveling as far away as Wu county, in Jiangsu, on business presumably related to the silk or fish trade. Chengfa earned enough money to establish a Zhu lineage charitable estate on the Westside, near Elephant Hill. The 1883 gazetteer biographers mention little about Zhu Chengfa, aside from recounting cases of his charity and his interest in reading the *Capital Gazette*.[58] In contrast, his principal wife—the mother of Zhu Ciqi and a daughter of the Jiujiang Zhang—seems to have been well educated and willing to advise Zhu lineage leaders on local affairs before her death in 1821.[59]

Zhu Ciqi and his brothers were fifteenth-generation lineage members. His eldest brother, Zhu Shiqi, was deeply concerned with the dual threats of banditry and flooding. In response to the threat of banditry, no doubt with the 1809 incursions of pirates into the Enclosure district in mind, Zhu Shiqi wrote a proposal for mutual defense among eleven Nanhai and Shunde townships in the district. In it, he argued for elite-managed defense, as opposed to relying on the state. After massive flooding in the district in 1829, Zhu Shiqi wrote a letter to provincial officials asserting that repairing the

Enclosure would not get to the root of the problem. Instead, officials should restrict construction of "sands" downstream, in Xinhui and Xiangshan counties, that blocked the natural flow of the West River. Zeng Zhao echoed Shiqi's argument four years later in his own letter to the Guangdong grain intendant on the flooding problem. As evidence, Zeng pointed to Zhu Shiqi's *Xijiang dahai tu* (Map of West River passages to the sea). In dealing with issues of flooding and banditry, then, Zhu Shiqi focused his attention upon the unique concerns of Jiujiang and the Enclosure district, at times in competition with elites in other parts of the Pearl River delta.[60]

The second of Zhu Chengfa's sons, Zhu Bingqi, receives very little attention from editors of both the Zhu genealogy and the 1883 gazetteer. Most likely, he carried on his father's trade, as he made at least one trip to Vietnam.[61] Zhu Ciqi was the third son. The youngest was Zhu Zongqi, a prefectural student who gave up on the provincial examinations after three failed attempts. Thereafter, he involved himself in Jiujiang affairs, including the compilation of the Zhu genealogy and Jiujiang gazetteer.[62]

Although Zhu Ciqi began his education at five *sui* under a fourteenth-generation Zhu in Jiujiang, he was soon sent to Guangzhou in pursuit of further studies. In 1819, when Zeng Zhao introduced him to Ruan Yuan, the precocious Zhu dazzled the governor-general with a poem written at his command.[63] Starting in 1824, Zhu studied under Xie Lansheng at Yangcheng Academy, where Chen Li began his academy education a year later. In 1828, both Zhu and a fellow Jiujiang student, a Guan, caught the attention of educational commissioner Weng Xincun and were granted *shengyuan* status. In 1832, Zhu moved to Yuehua Academy, where Chen Li was also studying at the time.[64]

Soon, two key players in establishing the specialized students at the Xuehaitang became familiar with Zhu Ciqi. Governor-General Lu Kun recognized young Zhu as a dignified scholar (*zhuangshi*) whose talent and moral capacity were unmatched. Qian Yiji, in Guangzhou as part of Lu's entourage and an occasional judge of county students' papers, consistently placed Zhu at the head of his class. Zeng Zhao and Li Fuping arranged for the aged Qian to meet Zhu. In 1835, when Lu and Qian, at Ruan Yuan's behest, moved to select the first class of specialized students, Zhu Ciqi was among the ten chosen ones. Yet Zhu declined on the pretext of illness.[65]

Zhu Ciqi spent the next few years shuttling back and forth between Guangzhou city and the delta countryside. In 1836, he resided in Guangzhou's Liurong Monastery. Three years later, Jiujiang natives scored a victory in the provincial examinations, as Zhu Ciqi and Zhu Shiqi passed in Guangdong, and Ming Zhigang and another Jiujiang Zhu, Zhu Wenbin, passed in Guangxi.[66] After receiving the degree, Zhu Ciqi worked as a private tutor in southern Panyu, despite exhortations to teach in Guangzhou where he could earn more money. Zhu won a *jinshi* in 1847 and then was assigned to Shanxi, where he spent seven years waiting for an appointment and serving as a county magistrate.[67]

Except when he was actively seeking education in Guangzhou, Zhu Ciqi was immersed during the 1830s and 1840s in the continually expanding operations of Jiujiang's lineage leaders centered at Rulin Academy. At times, he resided for long periods in Jiujiang, as in 1845, when he stayed at the old Zhengjue Monastery on Elephant Hill. Following the precedent of his Ming ancestors, Zhu wrote a set of poems taking the temple as a theme. Like his brother Shiqi, Zhu Ciqi worked with other Jiujiang lineage leaders in mobilizing repair of the Enclosure against the threat of flooding, a danger that was realized in 1833 and 1834, when high waters broke through Enclosure dikes. When the West River again rose to dangerously high levels in 1839, Zhu Ciqi, Ming Lun, and Feng Rutang (a Feng of the same generation as Feng Yunzheng), cajoled Jiujiang commoners into shoring up the dikes.[68]

Zhu Ciqi played a less direct role in the next major Rulin Academy project, the creation of a Grain Wharf in 1843, although he was in the delta region at the time. Putatively established by the "entire township," Feng Xiyong took the lead in this project, joining with Feng Rutang and Liao Xiongguang, two of Zhu Ciqi's closest correspondents, to have a canal on Jiujiang's Southside dredged. Twenty *mu* of sands were donated from the Guan Shimei Hall (one of the six Guan branches in Jiujiang); the income was used to set up shops and granaries. Other expenses were met with donations from each of the lineages. Another local, 1835 *juren* Li Guochen, supervised the construction and daily operations of the new Grain Wharf, for which Zhu Ciqi was said to have praised his honesty. The wharf project was clearly a branch operation of Rulin Academy, based on the people involved and the fact that the creation of the wharf was commemorated on a Rulin Academy stele. Feng justified this move as a means of facilitating rice imports into grain-deficient Jiujiang, a situation exacerbated by Foshan's command of the delta rice trade. A decade earlier Zhu Ciqi himself had promoted the creation of a charitable granary to alleviate this problem. Quite likely, this too fell under the control of the academy.[69]

Rulin Academy leaders also took steps in the 1830s and 1840s to ensure their control over the fish levy and to prevent encroachment upon Jiujiang fishing rights by outsiders. The latter were muscling their way into the fish fry harvest by demanding fees at various stations along the West River. "Township Regulations" (*xianggui*) posted at the academy detailed the amounts of taxes to be collected. Beyond this, Rulin Academy leaders used the prestige gained from their newly won degrees to pressure local authorities to prevent increasingly violent abuses by outsiders against Jiujiang fishermen and sellers who were being driven out of the business. This naturally deprived lineage leaders at the academy of extra tax income. Their efforts came to fruition on July 2, 1843, when Governor-General Qi Gong issued a proclamation against "private" (that is, outside Rulin Academy control) selling in the industry. The proclamation incorporated the original petition signed by dozens of Jiujiang gentry, including the *juren* Feng Rutang, Ming Lun, Ming Zhigang, Zhu Shiqi, and Zhu Ciqi; commoners' names do not appear.[70]

While taking control of the township's finances, lineage leaders at Rulin Academy simultaneously attempted to impose on Jiujiang commoners their own particular version of Confucian morality. In 1837, they moved against gambling in the township. When one gambling den was discovered in that year, authorities learned upon interrogation of a certain Yu Yabao that the operation had been protected by a military *juren* by the name of Yu Binggang. The Yu were a relatively minor lineage in Jiujiang, boasting a single hall listed in the 1883 gazetteer and producing only a single civilian *juren*; most other notable Yu were military men. When few dared speak out against the Yu gambling operation, Zhu Ciqi and Chen Xinmin (Chen Lüheng's son and a leader of the academy) initiated the crackdown. Other lineage leaders followed suit. One curmudgeon among the Guan, an 1821 *juren* named Guan Jiaju, would flail his folding fan at players and pieces alike whenever he stumbled across a gambling game in the Great Market. In contrast to some of its more liberal Enclosure neighbors, Jiujiang soon earned a reputation as a gambling-free township.[71]

Other targets of Rulin Academy moralism were prostitution and marriage resistance. Editors of the 1883 gazetteer proudly claim that "Jiujiang maintains the greatest distinction between the sexes," pointing to the absence in their township of traveling prostitutes' pleasure boats.[72] An 1833 Nanhai county magistrate's proclamation against women and girls worshiping in temples was inscribed on a Rulin Academy stele, as was an 1842 prohibition against women and girls committing suicide as a form of marriage resistance. The close associate of Zhu Ciqi and leader of the academy, Feng Rutang, initiated a personal crusade against this practice. If a new wife committed suicide in protest, academy leaders allowed the husband's family to bury the dead bride in a grave only hastily covered with straw; the girl's family had no right to give her a proper burial. Marriage resistance is said to have dissipated as a result of Feng's efforts.[73]

Thus, by 1849, when Zhu Ciqi began his official career as a county magistrate in Shanxi, Rulin Academy had almost reached maturity as well. Lineage leaders based at the academy had managed to corner the Jiujiang market in silk and fish, to translate this income into cultural production, and to begin imposing new standards of morality upon the township community. Zhu Ciqi, though not personally involved in every academy project, certainly was part of the inner circle. Editors of the 1910 Nanhai gazetteer quote an 1899 memorial by Governor-General Li Hongzhang (1823–1901), which, after extolling the amazing self-control of Jiujiang residents in regard to gambling, attributes this rare phenomenon in the delta to the teaching of Zhu Ciqi.[74] One suspects that this "self-control" was more a product of Rulin Academy enforcement than of Zhu Ciqi's teaching. The township's reputation by the middle of the nineteenth century was not lost even upon foreign travelers through the region. Describing Jiujiang (Kow-kong), one observer offers a telling description of the township and academy:

ZHU "JIUJIANG" ▶ 261

They have one of the finest schools in the empire, the Ue-lam Shü-uen [Rulin shuyuan]. Its students everywhere take high rank, and several of the leading gentry of the place have won the highest literary honours. The corporation controls all the town affairs, not allowing Government officials to have authority except in rare cases. Gambling, prostitution, and other evils are forbidden, and the laws, in most cases, are rigidly enforced. It is said that a man may take his daughters to any place of entertainment in the town without exciting suspicious remarks.[75]

Anyone in Jiujiang looking for a good time, however, did not need to go very far:

The tide of wickedness thrown back from the gates of Kow-kong finds ready admission through the open doors of Loong-kong [Longjiang], the adjoining town. There gambling and all forms of vicious amusement flourish under the especial patronage of the gentry. The Kow-kong swarm the streets of the neighboring town, and pour their money into the coffers of the Loong-kong people.[76]

During Zhu Ciqi's seven-year tenure as a county magistrate, his cohorts at Rulin Academy added a final component to the academy power structure. This last piece was largely in response to the Red Turban rebels, who overran Jiujiang and other Enclosure townships, as well as Daliang and Foshan, in the summer of 1854. Feng Xiyong and Ming Zhigang made quick escapes to Guangzhou, where they used their resources to fund and organize militia. In late November or early December 1854, Feng and Ming established the Tongan Militia Bureau, in cooperation with exiled elites from the Enclosure townships of Datong and Heqing.[77] When government troops recovered Jiujiang in May 1855, the Tongan Bureau was commissioned to oversee the rounding up of rebels in the township, and established a temporary headquarters in a Zeng lineage hall. Zhu Zongqi and Zhu Wenbin helped first official troops and then the Bureau's militia in distinguishing the "good" from "bad" elements, over two thousand of whom were killed.[78] Under Feng Xiyong, Ming Zhigang, and Guan Zhongyang, Jiujiang split with Datong and Heqing to establish an enduring township bureau, retaining the name Tongan. Feng and Ming later moved the Jiujiang bureau from its temporary headquarters at the Zeng lineage hall to Rulin Academy. Henceforth, Jiujiang lineage leaders maintained a permanent patrol of a hundred men, with enough money set aside to pull together a force of a thousand in an emergency.[79]

When, at mid-century, the elite of Jiujiang felt its prosperity was being threatened, lineage leaders responded by taking government into their own hands. Under the rubric of Rulin Academy they created an institution that dominated Jiujiang affairs: collecting taxes, funding education, enforcing morality, and maintaining local security. Because Zhu Ciqi was a Jiujiang native who had been an important member of the Rulin Academy circle before winning his *jinshi* degree, when he returned from his service in Shanxi he had strong connections in Jiujiang, but few in Guangzhou.

ZHU "JIUJIANG" AND THE CRITIQUE OF URBAN GUANGZHOU

Returning south in 1855, Zhu Ciqi taught Zhu lineage members and other old acquaintances at the Nanhai county school in Guangzhou for a year before moving to Jiujiang. Back in his native township, Zhu Ciqi did not participate as avidly in Rulin Academy affairs as he had before entering the service, but he remained closely tied to the academy leaders and intensely devoted to lineage affairs and, as we shall see, lineage and local history. In 1860, Zhu convinced two sons of Zhu Tinggui, a wealthier lineage member who had made his fortune trading in Vietnam, to donate thirty thousand taels to establish a charitable estate for the Jiujiang Zhu. Combining this with other donations, Zhu Ciqi secured official approval for the project, portraying the new corporate estate as properly based upon the model developed by Fan Zhongyan (989–1052). In the following year, Zhu took measures to ensure that lineage members observed the correct Confucian burial rituals, even if these ran counter to township custom.[80]

Zhu Ciqi's main vocation, however, was scholarship and teaching. Beginning in 1857, he resumed taking students, supported at first by an affluent member of the Guan lineage.[81] Zhu conducted lectures on Ritual Hill on Jiujiang's Southside, where he gathered a large and devoted following over the subsequent 25 years. Most of his students were sons of Enclosure gentry who could proffer claims of descent from ancestors who had settled the delta from Nanxiong during the Song. These included Zhu's son-in-law, Liang Yaochen, one of three brothers from nearby Guanghua in Shunde, who all studied under Zhu.[82] Another of the three brothers, Liang Yaoshu, won top honors in the 1871 metropolitan examinations, which brought much acclaim to his teacher. In later years, Jian Chaoliang and Kang Youwei became known as the two most famous students of Zhu Ciqi. Jian, a Shunde native whose father had moved to Foshan, was the devoted disciple, who most closely preserved his master's learning by compiling Zhu's surviving writings and a chronological biography. Kang, in contrast, was an impetuous prodigy who left Ritual Hill in frustration in 1879, only later to look back fondly upon his years there.[83] But Jian and Kang shared with their teacher an identity anchored in the delta hinterland; in contrast, Guangzhou urbanites did not study under Zhu Ciqi.[84]

At first glance, Zhu Ciqi's decision to retire to Jiujiang as a local teacher is not particularly remarkable—previous scholars from Jiujiang had quietly negotiated between "retirement" in Jiujiang and activity in Guangzhou. But Zhu made an ideological stance out of his decision to live in Jiujiang. Partly, Zhu was a product of changed times; he stressed subcounty activism just as Jiujiang lineage leaders at Rulin Academy were asserting the township's independence from county authority. Moreover, a few years earlier, another Enclosure district literatus had made a very public statement by retiring to his native place. In the winter of 1851–52, He Wenqi, the popular teacher who had headed Yuexiu Academy since 1844, resigned his position after a dispute with the governor-general and retired to his native Zhenyong township. His biographer was Zhu Ciqi's student Jian Chaoliang, who later drew attention both to He Wenqi's retirement in the 1850s and his earlier recommendation of the young Zhu Ciqi to a provincial official inspecting the Mulberry Garden Enclosure in the 1830s.[85]

Whereas He Wenqi offered a recent precedent of righteous retirement for Enclosure literati, Zhu Ciqi went a step further by taking on a local identity. After 1857, he came to be referred to by the name of his native township, thus quite literally being identified with "Jiujiang." In this manner, he evoked the tradition of the two famous Ming philosophers of the delta, Chen "Baisha" (Chen Xianzhang) and Zhan "Ganquan" (Zhan Ruoshui)—if not reflecting the substance of their learning, certainly calling to mind their charisma and rootedness in the delta. Both Chen and Zhan were instantly associated with physical places in the delta hinterland, a form of identity not available to most urban Guangzhou scholars associated with the Xuehaitang.[86] Moreover, Zhu "Jiujiang" never again set foot in the provincial capital, as his biographers loudly proclaim. In 1859, when Zhu was invited to serve as a co-director of the Xuehaitang, he declined, although a position was left open for him for two decades.[87]

Zhu rearticulated his position in an exchange of letters with Guo Songtao, governor of Guangdong and patron of the Xuehaitang. On December 12, 1863—the very day that Gui Wencan introduced to Guo the names of current Xuehaitang co-directors—Guo rushed a letter to Zhu via a special Nanhai county messenger. Guo had hoped to have a chance to meet with Zhu, as the two both earned the *jinshi* degree in 1847. Instead, Guo received a polite refusal a week later, in which Zhu declined on the pretext of a chronic illness; despite his disappointment, Guo deemed superb the "style and reasoning" of Zhu's response. Guo tried to lure Zhu out of seclusion at least once more, but to no avail. Throughout the remainder of his term as governor (that is, until the summer of 1866), Guo occasionally found time to pay visits to the Xuehaitang or to host such academy stalwarts as Chen Li, Jin Xiling, and Chen Pu at his yamen. In contrast, Zhu Ciqi stood firm in his refusal to set foot in Guangzhou, take up his post at the Xuehaitang, or meet with the likes of Guo Songtao.[88]

Chen Pu, one of Guo's favorites at the Xuehaitang, derided what he saw as Zhu's sanctimonious eremitism:

[You, Guo,] invited for audiences such Guangdong scholars as Zou Boqi, Chen Li, and Jin Xiling, all of whom are pure Confucians who do not recklessly seek audiences.... After returning from service in Jiangxi, I was invited for an audience. I accepted with the utmost sincerity, not daring to play the role of recluse. Only Zhu Ciqi, having retired and living in his home village, was invited by you, Guo, several times for an audience but in the end never went.[89]

Chen Pu put forth this critique of Zhu Ciqi's reclusive stance in a farewell essay for Guo Songtao, who had provided the funding that enabled the Xuehaitang to revive its previously discontinued system of specialized students. The fact that almost the entire essay is concerned with the Zhu incident indicates how important an issue it must have been to Guo, as well as for Chen.

Chen Pu perceived quite vividly that Zhu Ciqi's decision to retire to Jiujiang was not a fortuitous one; rather, Zhu "Jiujiang" was making an ideological statement. Unlike his predecessor Zeng Zhao, Zhu chose to distance himself from the intellectual world of Guangzhou. In other words, Zhu intended his adamant refusal to set foot in Guangzhou to serve as an unspoken, but very loud, "text," in which he communicated his critique of Guangzhou and its academy. His actions conveyed his critique clearly, obviating the need for any written text. Hence nothing of his fundamental convictions was lost—not on Chen Pu in 1866, nor when he burned his manuscripts nearly two decades later. Zhu's disciples made sure that his message would last, in the form of fanciful tales they disseminated, recounting their teacher's tribulations in Guangzhou and honorable reclusion in Jiujiang. In the pithiest of these, found in a manuscript account of Zhu Ciqi's life, the author describes an 1812 incident in which Guangzhou crooks snatched a six-*sui* Ciqi who had accompanied his father to the city. On the following day, a group of youths, impressed with the child's bearing, dutifully brought little Ciqi back unharmed to the distressed father.[90] Though the author's intent is to illustrate Zhu's charisma, the subtext is not lost either: Guangzhou is a dangerous place that can be transformed only by a Jiujiang sage, even if the sage is but a mere child.

As was the case with other natives of Jiujiang and the Enclosure district, Zhu Ciqi was exposed to a variety of scholarly orientations. Like most places in the delta outside Xinhui county, the Ming Guangdong philosophical approach associated with Chen Xianzhang and Zhan Ruoshui had fallen out of favor in the Qing. But devout practitioners of Cheng-Zhu Neo-Confucianism were abundant throughout the delta and in Jiujiang as well. In the generation of Zhu Ciqi's father, Jiujiang native Guan Shilong was a Cheng-Zhu expert who took students in Guangzhou. One of the leaders of the Shajiao Ming lineage, Ming Yong, earned a reputation as an avid devotee of the *Four Books* arranged by Zhu Xi.[91]

In the early decades of the nineteenth century, other Jiujiang natives offered an alternative to Cheng-Zhu learning. Discussing Zeng Zhao, the 1883 Jiujiang gazetteer notes that "the fact that recently rural scholars know that in addition to eight-legged essays there are [other types of] composition, that aside from examination poetry there are lyric poems and rhapsodies, and that aside from the *Four Books* there are the Classics and Histories, is largely due to Zeng's efforts."[92] Zeng Zhao was somewhat of an anomaly: an Enclosure literatus open to the Xuehaitang and its imported scholarly orientation. Perhaps this is because Zeng, despite bearing a Jiujiang surname that had been powerful in the Ming, does not seem to have been a central figure in the Jiujiang power structure at Rulin Academy. The academy leaders needed Zeng only when they wanted to curry favor with Ruan Yuan in 1826. Zeng nevertheless managed to gather a few followers from among fellow members of the Enclosure elite. Hu Tiaode was another Jiujiang examinee in the early days of the Xuehaitang, who "exerted effort in learning the Han Confucians' glosses" and achieved recognition for his skill writing prose patterned after Han dynasty models. Pan Jili, a native of Heqing township, west of Jiujiang, who had previously studied in Guangzhou under Zeng Zhao, was one of the first ten specialized students at the Xuehaitang in 1834.[93]

Therefore, Zhu Ciqi inhabited a cultural landscape rich with models of both Han Learning and Song Learning, though the former was clearly much more firmly entrenched in Guangzhou city than in the Enclosure district. Like his counterpart, Chen Li, Zhu Ciqi sought to combine the strengths of Han and Song, though the two scholars differed in their interpretations of what those strengths were. For an intellectual tradition that put so much emphasis on "transmission of the teachers" (*shicheng*) in a scholarly lineage, it is unclear exactly where Zhu Ciqi picked up his skills in evidential research. Zeng Zhao introduced him to Ruan Yuan, but Zhu never referred to either man as "teacher." Nevertheless, Zhu Ciqi's students, in the manuscript account of his life, portray the youthful Zhu beating his Xuehaitang *kaozheng* contemporaries at their own game. One of several such instances concerns the Kind Relief Granary, managed by the urban elite of Guangzhou, for which Yi Kezhong had won Qi Gong's approval in the 1830s. Zhu Ciqi, however, found a passage in the *Song shi* (History of the Song dynasty) in which "Kind Relief Storehouse" had referred to a funeral home for scholar-officials who had died in Guangdong; hence, it would not make an auspicious name for a granary. Similarly, Hou Kang is portrayed as seeking comment on his compositions from Zhu, when the latter was a student at Yuehua Academy in 1832.[94] Aside from these exchanges with Xuehaitang scholars, and other episodes in which he received the attention of Ruan Yuan (in 1819) and of Qian Yiji (in 1834), Zhu had very little interaction with famous *kaozheng* masters of his day. This stands in stark contrast to Chen Li, who maintained close correspondence with Jiangnan's leading scholars. The only exception is when Zhu met the aged Wang Yun (1784–1854) when both were serving as county magistrates in Shanxi. A native of Shandong province, Wang was an expert in *Shuowen* studies.[95]

In an 1853 letter to Wang Yun, Zhu Ciqi revealed his plans to compile a history of Qing Confucians, modeled after Huang Zongxi's (1610–95) *Mingru xuean*; here he stressed that he did not wish to draw a distinction between Han and Song Learning, as Jiang Fan had done in the *Hanxue shicheng ji*.[96] This is Zhu Ciqi's earliest extant statement on Han-Song syncretism. As was the case with Chen Li, Zhu valued Han Confucians as much for their upright actions as for their correct glosses.[97] Zhu Ciqi encapsulated his brand of Han-Song syncretism in what his students recorded as the "four substantive" aspects of self-cultivation and the "five substantive" components of book learning. The former included "sincerely enacting filial and brotherly feeling" (*dunxing xiaodi*), "honoring name and integrity" (*chongshang mingjie*), "transforming psychophysical endowment" (*bianhua qizhi*), and "regulating deportment" (*jianshe weiyi*). The five components of learning consisted of training in the Classics, Histories, dynastic institutions, nature and principle, and literary composition. Kang Youwei's curriculum under Zhu Ciqi reflected this eclectic approach; he recalled studying subjects ranging from the writings of Song Confucians to parallel prose. Nevertheless, in contrast to Chen Li, Zhu Ciqi does not appear to have urged his students to produce specialized studies in mathematics, phonology, geography, or other such fields.[98]

Furthermore, Zhu Ciqi was clearly disgruntled with the type of institutionalized evidential research represented by the Xuehaitang.

Jian Chaoliang preserved in his chronological biography what he described as the essentials of Zhu's critique of Xuehaitang evidential research and Han Learning. Zhu directed particular ire at the academy's founder and scholarly icon, Ruan Yuan. Free from the constraints of Guangzhou and the Xuehaitang, Zhu Ciqi was able to offer a more direct criticism of the academy and its founder than was Chen Li. Zhu unflinchingly derided what he saw as Ruan Yuan's biased compilation of the *Huang Qing jingjie*: "The anthology purports to be about 'our dynasty.' Not all of the scholars of this era have been Han Learning advocates; yet it does not mention one word about such scholars as Fang Bao."[99] In another instance, Zhu bemoaned the fact that the most brilliant scholars in the preceding century had been limited by the confines of Han Learning, and he saw Ruan Yuan as the rear guard of this school.[100] Of Han Learning scholars in general, pursuing their overly precise research as civilization crumbled around them, Zhu remarked, "Those Han Learning scholars fail to see the western wall for looking east."[101] The author of an annotated edition of Zhu's extant writings, who refers to himself as a second-generation disciple of the master, elaborates upon a passage in the chronological biography in which Zhu comments on the inherited flaws of Wang Yangming's thought. Just as the fall of the Ming may be attributed to the flaws of Wang Yangming, so the author cites with approval Zuo Zongtang's (1812–85) condemnation of evidential research for inviting disaster upon the empire.[102] When read in light of his continual rebuffs of the Xuehaitang and Guo Songtao, Zhu's rejection of evidential research, as portrayed by his students, contained an implicit critique of Guangzhou cosmopolitan culture as well.

Zeng Zhao's 1819 introduction of Zhu Ciqi to his intellectual patron had backfired. After deciding to reside in Jiujiang, Zhu clearly wished to dissociate himself from the scholarship of the Xuehaitang founder. Whereas the academy offered the training, as well as the library and printing facilities, necessary for evidential research, Zhu sought an alternative in Jiujiang. In a fashion more reminiscent of Song and Ming ideals of sagehood, Zhu came to be regarded by the disciples gathered around him on Ritual Hill as a *zhiyi zhi shi*, or a "scholar of moral purpose." In embracing an alternative identity, culminating in the act of burning his manuscripts, Zhu clearly set himself apart from the bookish Xuehaitang scholars.[103]

WRITING THE LOCAL: GENEALOGY, ANTHOLOGY, AND HISTORY

Nevertheless, Zhu Ciqi did not exactly put to flame every manuscript he had had a hand in composing. The dramatic nature of his act belies the great amount of effort he devoted toward preserving lineage and local history. During his quarter century of "retirement" in Jiujiang, Zhu Ciqi busily organized three ambitious compilation projects. Not coincidentally, the Jiujiang Zhu lineage was expanding its corporate holdings during this same time. In a spurt of activity over the decade following Zhi Ciqi's retirement to Jiujiang, the Jiujiang Zhu renovated lineage halls, purchased land for lineage estates, and printed a new lineage genealogy. This momentum carried over into the compilation of a lineage anthology and the 1883 Jiujiang gazetteer.

Shortly after his retirement to Jiujiang, Zhu Ciqi began drawing up editorial standards for compilation of the *Zhushi chuanfang ji*. He assigned editorial tasks to his younger brother Zongqi and other lineage members. The final product consisted of an "inner collection" of writings by Zhu lineage ancestors, and an "outer collection" that included eulogies, biographies, and poems about Zhu lineage members authored by eminent contemporaries (mostly delta natives of the seventeenth century). Though Chen Li was solicited to write the title page in his prized seal calligraphy, the 1861 preface was written by someone closer to home: Zhu's student Liang Yaoshu. Zhu Ciqi's editorial principles provided readers with a narrative structure in which the Jiujiang Zhu began to produce literary texts in the mid-sixteenth century, suffered the loss of most of these texts when Zhu Mo's Guangzhou mansion was destroyed in the Qing occupation, and saw the destruction of many remaining texts with the failed defense of Jiujiang itself.[104]

Aside from this, two Zhus stand out in the anthology. The first is Zhu Shilian, the 1621 *juren* who was sacrificed in the anti-Qing resistance. The collection enhances his identity as a Ming loyalist by incorporating essays and poems by other local martyrs such as Chen

Zizhuang (1596–1647). Chen had grown up in Jiujiang because his father had moved there from elsewhere in Nanhai county after marrying a daughter of Zhu Rang, the first Jiujiang Zhu *jinshi*. Chen Zizhuang placed third in the 1619 metropolitan examination before falling out of favor with the eunuch Wei Zhongxian (1568–1627). Thereafter, Chen Zizhuang's brother and son both became ardent members of the Restoration Society (Fushe). Throwing one's lot in with the Restoration Society in the Ming-Qing transition was dangerous business, however—the society's members excelled in Ming loyalism and martyrdom but not in warfare. Chen Zizhuang, his son, and Zhu Shilian all perished in the anti-Manchu resistance. Whereas the Zhu lineage had reached a zenith in the Jiajing reign, and again in the last two decades of the Ming, Zhu Shilian's martyrdom marked a decline in lineage fortunes—measured in terms of examination degrees won—from which it never fully recovered.[105]

The *Zhushi chuanfang ji* also highlights lineage members' local activism in the nineteenth century. The most prolific writer in the collection is Zhu Shiqi, the recently deceased older brother of Zhu Ciqi. Moreover, emphasis is placed upon those writings of Zhu Shiqi that deal with local issues. Perhaps the central piece in the collection is his letter to the governor-general about West River flooding. Zhu argued that the sources of flooding were the stone embankments and reclaimed sands in areas along the coast downriver.[106] None of his proposals were enacted, though Ming Zhigang reiterated his concerns in an 1869 petition to provincial authorities.

Meanwhile, in the spring of 1859, Zhu Ciqi and Zhu Zongqi led lineage members in setting up a bureau for a new compilation of the Jiujiang Zhu genealogy. Though they originally planned to finish printing by January 1862, the project took over ten years to complete. Two sons of Zhu Tinggui, the lineage member who had made a fortune trading in Vietnam, donated over seventeen hundred taels to compile the genealogy—a sum that met the costs of salaries and printing—and other members donated smaller amounts. A comprehensive work in twelve *juan*, the compilation included, in addition to genealogical charts, sections devoted to biographies, shrines, tombs, and writings of Zhu lineage members. As with the *Zhushi chuanfang ji*, Zhu Zongqi is credited with the role of chief editor, and Zhu Ciqi is listed as the "supervisor." Yet the Jiujiang gazetteer biography of Zhu Ciqi suggests that he actually performed the task of compiling the work.[107]

Even more clearly than in the *Chuanfang ji*, the new genealogy presents a narrative of prosperity and cultural connections to Guangzhou in the mid-Ming, martyrdom and disaster in the Ming-Qing transition, and local Jiujiang activism in more recent times. Zhu Shilian emerges once again as the tragic hero of the Ming-Qing transition. His biography describes the roles he and Chen Zizhuang played in raising troops in Jiujiang and then in joining Chen Bangyan, another Restoration Society member, in a futile attempt to recapture Qing-occupied Guangzhou city in 1647. After being repulsed, Zhu led his troops back to Jiujiang. Later he was put in charge of defending nearby Gaoming county. When Qing forces threatened, Zhu bit his finger, wrote a suicide poem in blood, and led two thousand men to their deaths in battle. His two sons had to hide from the authorities for several years, until restrictions were lifted. In 1822, when Zhu Ciqi was sixteen *sui*, lineage elders erected a Shrine of Teaching Loyalty in honor of Zhu Shilian.[108]

The Zhu lineage anthology and genealogy reflect the scope of Zhu Ciqi's vision, which was sharply focused on the township and lineage. Yet these two works reveal the surprising extent to which the preoccupations of evidential research had seeped down even to Jiujiang. Kai-wing Chow suggests that one aspect of evidential research often overlooked by modern scholars is its emphasis upon ritual, in particular as it pertained to the lineage.[109] This was one "useful" pursuit in which Zhu Ciqi felt confident employing evidential research. As he explained in the preface and editorial principles of the genealogy, the biographical chapters were to be modeled on Ruan Yuan's draft "Rulin" biographies of Confucian scholars for the dynastic history. Moreover, in delineating lines of descent, Zhu carefully employed the minute genealogical distinctions outlined in Qin Huitian's (1702–64) *Wuli tongkao* (Comprehensive study of the classics of rites).[110] The scholarly practices promoted at the Xuehaitang, then, were laudable when applied toward the lineage; they only became a target of attack when urban Guangzhou literati with few legitimate ties to Cantonese culture hoisted it as their scholarly banner.

The final compilation project in which Zhu Ciqi was involved resulted in the 1883 edition of the township gazetteer, the *Jiujiang Rulin xiangzhi*. Zhu, along with the leading Rulin Academy activists Ming Zhigang and Feng Rutang, took the initiative in promoting compilation of the new gazetteer. Zhu had discussed the project with Ming as early as 1874. As this Zhu-Ming-Feng triumvirate was full of prestige but sorely lacking in energy in the late 1870s, Feng Xiyong's son, Feng Shizong, supervised the business side of the project. Zhu Ciqi himself died on February 7, 1882. Li Xun (1864 *juren*), son of the Grain Wharf manager and Rulin Academy activist Li Guochen, took over as chief editor in 1882. Chapter compilers included Zhu Zongqi and Zeng Zhao's son, Zeng Zhongli, both of whom died before the compilation was completed.[111]

The 1657 edition of the gazetteer had remained in manuscript form, though it circulated widely enough to have been quoted by Qu Dajun. The manuscript was finally printed in 1874, which surely provided Zhu Ciqi with the spark to compile a new edition.[112] Whereas the old gazetteer was simply titled *Jiujiang xiangzhi* (Gazetteer of Jiujiang township), the new edition added the name "Rulin" for the administrative unit (*xiang*) to which Jiujiang *bao* belonged. This title change also connoted a close link to the township's new effective governing body, Rulin Academy, and boasted of Jiujiang's recent successes in the civil service examinations.

For the new gazetteer, Zhu Ciqi had personally outlined the editorial principles and assigned various tasks to local scholars. One of the original motivations behind the project had been to provide a more detailed description of Jiujiang and its elite than was possible in prefectural and county gazetteers. But the new chief editor, Li Xun, decided after Zhu Ciqi's death in 1882 to incorporate passages from previous county gazetteers wherever expedient. As a result, it is unclear to what extent the revised edition, as it appeared in 1883, reflected the project as the Zhu brothers had envisioned it.[113]

Some chapters nonetheless are attributed to Zhu Zongqi. If these chapters in turn reflect his brother's vision, then Ciqi evidently meant to distinguish Jiujiang from other parts of Nanhai, particularly Guangzhou city. For example, the third chapter contains matching passages on climate and customs. The one on climate reads:

Jiujiang's climate is of one accord with the climate of Nanhai; yet the water and soil differ therein. Jiujiang is a rural part of Nanhai, distinct from the [provincial] capital. . . . The [provincial] capital's rivers flow in four directions. . . . The water's flavor is salty, its people are big-bellied and fair skinned. In the countryside, the river flows long and clear. Its flavor is subtle. Its people are lean and dark. This is how the water of the two places is different.[114]

Similarly, the passage on customs reads:

Jiujiang's customs are of one accord with those of Nanhai; yet there is also a distinction between the countryside and the [provincial] capital. The capital has a surplus of *wen* [refinement], the disadvantage of which is occasional corruption. The countryside has a surfeit of *zhi* [substance, simplicity], the disadvantage of which is occasional rusticity.[115]

Taken together, the lineage anthology, lineage genealogy, and local history produced by Zhu Ciqi and his Jiujiang associates were components of a coherent project with specific purposes. Both the Zhu genealogy and the Jiujiang history made strategic claims of identity.[116] All three texts presented the Zhu and other Jiujiang elites as distant descendants of Han Chinese ancestors from Nanxiong and, more recently, of Ming loyalists and loudly denied any relationship to the Dan, with which Jiujiang fishermen apparently were often confused. Through its celebration of Zhu literary production, the anthology sought to associate the Zhu lineage with the state-sanctioned gentry culture by demonstrating mastery of elite cultural forms.[117]

Nevertheless, these texts also constructed an identity of Jiujiang uniqueness, as editors emphasized distinctions between Jiujiang and Guangzhou. Though the Zhu genealogy constructed a cultural identity encompassing other delta lineages that could claim descent from Nanxiong ancestors and Ming martyrs, it also distinguished the delta lineages from more recent arrivals to the region—in particular the urban cultural elite of Guangzhou city. The Jiujiang gazetteer also drew attention to Jiujiang uniqueness in a way that county and prefectural gazetteers did not. Whereas almost all counties and prefectures had produced local histories, subcounty gazetteers were rare in Guangdong before the twentieth century. By producing two,

Jiujiang elevated itself to an elite class—together with Foshan and Longshan—within the Pearl River delta.

CONCLUSION

Although he portrayed himself as a recluse and burned his writings, Zhu Ciqi was intensively involved in textual production. When he retired to Jiujiang and began teaching in 1857, he gathered about him a group of devoted students. Over the following two decades, Zhu organized the compilation of a lineage genealogy, a collection of lineage writings, and a revision of the local Jiujiang gazetteer. Moreover, in the detailed editorial principles he devised for these compilations, Zhu exhibited a great deal of concern for following legitimate precedents of proper form and style.[118] Genealogies and anthologies of lineage writings were certainly not unusual in Qing China. Subcounty gazetteers were much less common during the Qing, at least in Guangdong, but several Enclosure district townships, as well as Foshan, had managed to print a number of local histories. Nevertheless, the amount of effort Zhu Ciqi put into these three compilations in the twenty years after his withdrawal to Jiujiang is significant.

Furthermore, the compilation of these three texts must be considered in the context of the relationship between Guangzhou and its hinterland, the latter as represented by Jiujiang. The narrative of the Jiujiang Zhu lineage presents a macrocosm of Zhu Ciqi's own life; it is a narrative that begins with examination success and cultural links to Guangzhou and ends in local Jiujiang activism. Where his older brother Zhu Shiqi had expressed the demands of Jiujiang and its Enclosure neighbors in terms of local defense and flood control, Zhu Ciqi constructed the area in elite cultural terms. And if sojourning urban scholars based at the Xuehaitang had appropriated Cantonese culture for themselves, Zhu Ciqi sought to reclaim cultural significance for the delta lineage and locale. The image presented in his records of lineage and local history was one of selfless martyrdom and local activism, and it reflected more the ideals of Song Learning than those of Han Learning. In other words, the cultural ideals voiced in these compilations were much closer in tone to those of Luo Xuepeng's *Guangdong wenxian*, with the exception that, in place of statesmanship, the former stressed the ideal of local activism. Through these compilations, the hinterland appeared as culturally more authentic than the putative center of that culture, Guangzhou. The true essence of delta elite culture, according to the Jiujiang Zhu lineage, lay neither in the reclaimed sands along the coast, nor in the city of Guangzhou; rather, it was best exemplified by the martyrs and local activists whose ancestors had settled and thrived along the West River in the Enclosure district.

Aside from the lineage and local compilations, Zhu Ciqi's actions made another type of statement to his students and admirers in the delta. Zhu's withdrawal to Jiujiang, as well as his repeated rebuffs of invitations from Guangzhou's elite academy and provincial officials, spoke to his delta audience in no uncertain terms. Moreover, though Zhu Ciqi may not have written texts to interpret his actions and preserve his memory, his students did. This perhaps sheds some light on Zhu Ciqi's last meaningful act, the incineration of his unfinished manuscripts. He was not the first Cantonese literatus to burn his own writings in old age. The 1835 Nanhai gazetteer biography of Xie Lansheng, in addition to recording Xie's printed works, states that toward the end of his life he burned some of his manuscripts, saying they were only good for catching profit and rank and hence should not be transmitted.[119] Zhu Ciqi appears to have been more thorough, and his biographers make the burning of his manuscripts an action much more central to his persona. For Zhu and his followers, meaning lay both in the act itself and in what was preserved. Whereas Chen Li in Guangzhou lamented the proliferation of books yet feverishly went about printing more, Zhu Ciqi presented himself as a model for others through his actions. Zhu had no need to worry about his legacy; he had ensured the memory of the Jiujiang Zhu by printing books, and of Zhu "Jiujiang" by burning them.

EIGHT
Reflections on the Sea of Learning: Mobility and Identity in a Cosmopolitan Family

> Beneath Sir Ruan's shrine the path winds round;
> People in the lecture hall are few, the old trees sparse.
> Suddenly I recall the hundred poems on the litchi;
> When Guangzhou was most resplendent, in the early Daoguang.
> —Wang Quan, "Six Miscellaneous Poems Written on a Summer Day," 1879

WANG QUAN COMPOSED THIS QUAINT poem shortly before the deaths of the prominent Cantonese Confucians Chen Li and Zhu Ciqi. Though not particularly elaborate, Wang's poem is typical of sentiments expressed in verse by the literati who associated themselves with the Xuehaitang in the early Guangxu reign, and it touches on a number of the important themes stressed throughout the preceding chapters. Read as the product of an age in which China was on the cusp of a radical transformation, Wang's musings on the Sea of Learning Academy and its founder, Ruan Yuan, set an appropriate tone for some final reflections—on the academy's place in the local Cantonese landscape and on how the interplay of mobility and identity in nineteenth-century Guangzhou compares with this phenomenon in other cities in late imperial and modern China. Accordingly, Wang Quan, his short poem, and the experiences of some younger members of the Wang family will provide a framework for bringing the present study to an end.

Wang's poem hints at the role of urban institutions as conduits for social mobility and the articulation of local identities among geographically mobile, cosmopolitan elites. Wang himself belonged to one of the in-migrating cohorts that played such a dominant role at the Xuehaitang, and more generally in Cantonese elite culture, during the nineteenth century, as described in Chapters 1 and 5. His recollection of Tan Ying's songs on the litchi reminds the reader of the prominence of localist texts in the flourishing high-end publishing industry, funded by merchant wealth and fed by Xuehaitang scholarship, as examined in Chapter 4. Projects ranging from Wang Quan's short poem to the ambitious collaborative anthologies of Wu Chongyao and Tan Ying enabled in-migrating urban literati and merchants largely to control the articulation of Cantonese local identity at the elite level. Finally, like the later generations of Xuehaitang scholars, Wang Quan had no personal experience of the academy's early days under Ruan Yuan. He bemoans the loss of its resplendence—yet the academy, its founder, and the literature produced there were still powerfully relevant to urban Cantonese literati of Wang's generation. Beginning in the 1890s, and increasingly in the first decade of the twentieth century, however, younger members of the Wang family and the urban Cantonese elite more generally were provided with new opportunities that took them far beyond the Xuehaitang and Guangzhou. Tracing the life trajectories of two Wang brothers who lived well into the twentieth century, we will see that one brother found new means of mobility and new sources of identity, whereas another reinvented himself as a faithful custodian of the cultural production associated with the academy.

MOBILITY AND THE URBAN ELITE

Scholars researching urban elites in late imperial China have long noted links between geographical mobility and social mobility—that is, the way in which migration can serve as a means of acquiring elite status. Studies have examined localities that specialized in exporting migrants and sojourners, as well as places that attracted many in-migrants. In English-language scholarship on late imperial China, G. William Skinner was one of the first scholars to point to several areas that exported cultivated talent as a strategy of social mobility.[1] This was followed by more specialized studies. Though not focusing on migration, Harriet Zurndorfer offers a detailed local history of Huizhou prefecture in Anhui province, which would become a major exporter of sojourning merchant families, especially in the salt trade.[2] James Cole draws attention to the numerous Shaoxing natives who worked as subofficials and legal secretaries throughout China.[3] Our "Cantonese" poet, Wang Quan, illustrates the importance of these two talent-exporting areas. Wang's family claimed descent from an ancestor who had moved during the late Yuan dynasty from Wuyuan county, in Huizhou prefecture, to settle in Shaoxing prefecture's Shanyin county. Wang was a prominent surname in Huizhou, and this particular Wang family joined what Antonia Finnane has called the "Huizhou diaspora."[4] Like his father, uncles, and cousins, Wang Quan sought employment as a secretary, or *muyou*, in counties and prefectures across Guangdong, taking advantage of the Shaoxing network described by Cole.

Other studies, including the present one, focus on areas that imported talent, and emphasize the degree to which sojourners or in-migrants were able to climb the social ladder. For example, in his study of the Jiangnan county of Jiading in the seventeenth century, Jerry Dennerline observes that "one pattern of elite mobility . . . began with in-migration."[5] William Rowe has shown that sojourning salt merchants came to dominate the social and cultural life of Hankou by the late Ming and, after having suffered terrible setbacks during the Ming-Qing transition, rose again by the late eighteenth century.[6] More recently, Finnane has vividly described how families of sojourning Huizhou merchants became the leading figures in eighteenth-century Yangzhou high society through construction of gardens and the patronage of painting.[7] Similarly, this study, concerned with urban Guangzhou, has revealed the importance of the inwardly and upwardly mobile in Cantonese high cultural circles during the nineteenth century.

The present study differs from earlier studies in that it focuses on one particular institution that facilitated the acquisition of elite status for in-migrating or urbanizing families. The Xuehaitang served primarily as a status-granting and identity-constructing institution in one of the most important Chinese cities in late imperial and modern times. Wang Quan is representative of the geographically and socially mobile urban Cantonese families that accumulated status in large part through success in Xuehaitang examinations and more generally by associating with the academy through urban touring, socializing, and literary production. In other words, members of the most mobile segment—urbanized families, sojourners, and socially rising families—of the larger Cantonese cultural elite embraced the Xuehaitang agenda as a strategy for social mobility; in the process they constructed both elite and Cantonese identities. The Xuehaitang and its learning thus stood at the nexus of geographic and social mobility, on one hand, and the construction of elite cultural identity, on the other.

Therefore, rather than emphasizing the place of the Xuehaitang in the intellectual history of China, I have situated the academy in its urban Cantonese context, as an institution functioning in ways similar not only to other academies but also to such institutions as clan halls, gardens, monasteries, and temples. Such an approach reveals similarities with other urban institutions in other late imperial Chinese cities. Though not emphasizing sojourners or in-migrants in particular, Susan Naquin's description of the role of Beijing temples "in the creation and demonstration of status, the formation of communities and collectives, and the expression of local identities" well applies to the function of many other urban institutions and sites in late imperial Chinese cities.[8] Furthermore, the Xuehaitang, though open to all "refined" men, held out particular appeal to urban Cantonese literati, mostly either sojourners or members of recent migrant or urbanized families. In this sense, the Xuehaitang also functioned in a manner similar to other institutions in late imperial metropolises, in that it was primarily directed toward a migrant community. One obvious example of such institutions is the native-place association, or *huiguan*.[9] But many other urban institutions and sites catered to urban sojourners and in-migrants, ranging from shrines and temples (which were often connected to *huiguan*) to academies offering training to sons of sojourning salt merchants, such as Guangzhou's Yuehua Academy. Such institutions not only provided comfort and succor to uprooted travelers but also facilitated social mobility for migrant families in their new urban environment. Thus, sojourning in large regional metropolises provided more opportunities for social mobility than was usually the case in late imperial China. For a small but potentially significant minority of the urban population, geographical mobility was closely linked to social mobility.

The greatest patrons of elite culture in nineteenth-century Guangzhou, aside from officials such as Ruan Yuan, were maritime merchant families from Fujian and salt merchant families of rather more diverse origin. The latter included some urbanized families from the Pearl River delta, such as the Kongs, but also many families from northern Zhejiang, and at least one from Fujian. Many of these families, such as the Pan family of maritime merchants, eventually produced sons who become producers as well as patrons of culture. Other members of the literary elite rose from slightly more humble origins. Like so many prominent families in the western suburb of Guangzhou, Tan Ying's family had relocated from Foshan only in his father's generation. Most such families were involved in commerce. A few Han bannermen from the Guangzhou garrison reinvented themselves as Cantonese literati and made significant contributions to local elite culture. Hakka-speaking literati from Jiaying were also important figures in urban Cantonese elite culture, though this was more often the case in the early nineteenth century than in the middle decades. Meanwhile, families from northern Zhejiang became increasingly prominent in urban Guangzhou during the nineteenth century. If not originally involved in the salt trade, these families specialized in working as subofficials or *muyou*, marketing their administrative expertise.

The Wang family exemplifies the growing importance of this northern Zhejiang cohort. As we saw in Chapter 5, the Wangs were a highly mobile extended family from Shanyin. From the late eighteenth century and throughout most of the nineteenth century, generations of Wangs served as administrative experts—occasionally as magistrates, but more often as *muyou*, particularly in matters of law and taxation. Many Wangs spent a large part of their lives moving from one yamen to another throughout Guangdong province, either renting or purchasing more permanent homes in Guangzhou to which they periodically returned. When working as *muyou* away from Guangzhou, they were sometimes clearly distinct from literati; Wang Quan and his cousin Wang Chu told their successors that they rarely had a chance to interact with local gentry (*qi di shishen*) in the counties where they served.[10] Rather, their social support initially came from making connections to other sojourning families. Both Wang Quan and Wang Chu married daughters of northern

Zhejiang families that had relocated to Guangzhou.[11] Yet, through success in either the civil service examinations or the Xuehaitang examinations, some members of the Wang family were able to join the refined outings of the Guangzhou elite and reinvent themselves as Cantonese literati. Thus, as he gained a literary reputation in the early 1850s, Wang Quan was introduced to such Xuehaitang luminaries as Chen Li, Shen Shiliang, Chen Liangyu, and Chen Pu. As late as 1860, he still identified himself as a Shanyin resident, but in later poems and prefaces to poems he articulated a sense of identity with his "new" home: "I have long resided in Guangzhou and view it as my old native place."[12] Appearing in his published collection of poems, these sentiments claimed for Wang not only the identity of a Guangzhou resident but also the status of a resident Cantonese literatus.

In contrast to the cosmopolitan Wang family, many literati who belonged to powerful lineages based in the Pearl River delta hinterland could draw upon resources unavailable to their urban counterparts. To borrow a phrase from Timothy Brook's analysis of gentry culture in the late Ming, one can visualize the Cantonese cultural elite inhabiting a "polarized cultural landscape."[13] In contrast to Brook's usage, however, I have argued that there was a great deal of correspondence between the cultural and physical landscapes in which urban and delta literati dwelled. David Faure asserts that, until the Ming, urban Guangzhou was culturally divorced from its hinterland. During the Ming, elite members of what would emerge as the great lineages in the West River basin asserted Han Chinese culture in a region previously populated by non-Han aboriginal peoples. What resulted from this marriage between Guangzhou and its hinterland was the first flourishing of a distinct Cantonese culture that was at the same time unambiguously Han Chinese and "Confucian."[14] From the point of view of the nineteenth-century Cantonese elites examined here, the city of Guangzhou was becoming culturally less embedded in the hinterland, as urban and delta literati articulated competing constructions of Cantonese elite identity. Whereas in terms of trade or "popular" culture, urban Guangzhou may have remained deeply entrenched in its surroundings, this examination of social and cultural elites reveals between the two areas different settlement patterns, contrasting claims of identity, and access to distinct combinations of cultural symbols and practices. There was, however, some overlap between these sets of symbols and practices, which created an area of contested cultural space between the two poles. Delta elites proudly proclaimed descent from Zhujixiang ancestors, and urban elites touted their mastery of evidential research or parallel prose; both groups claimed a central place in Cantonese elite culture.

TEXTUAL PRODUCTION AND LOCAL IDENTITY

In recalling the hundred litchi poems, Wang Quan's short piece draws attention to another theme prominently featured in the current study: the proliferation of literature and scholarship celebrating the local. Wang explains in a note that Ruan Yuan once used litchi songs as a Xuehaitang examination topic, that Tan Ying composed one hundred quatrains on the theme, and that Ruan expressed his great appreciation of the poems by incorporating them into the academy's collection of model essays and poems, the *Xuehaitang ji*. The litchi poems were produced during the height of interest in the local, judging by the large number of localist texts produced by Cantonese literati in the late Jiaqing and Daoguang eras.

This emphasis on the Cantonese local between 1810 and 1850 mirrors other instances of localism in both space and time. Several historians have identified recurring cycles of "localist turns" in other parts of China. Increased local activism in some contexts has sought to articulate identity through the production of localist texts such as gazetteers and literary anthologies.[15] Thus, Robert Hymes, Peter Bol, and others have noted an increase in elite local activism in the late eleventh and twelfth centuries, and again in the sixteenth century, corresponding to the Southern Song and late Ming.[16] Another cycle of localism occurred in the nineteenth century, or late Qing. Though several historians have written important works on the gentry appropriation of power and activism by local elites during the nineteenth century, the proliferation of localist texts, particularly in the early part of the century, has only recently begun to be explored.[17] In the twentieth century, the local has been celebrated in scholarship and literature both during the Republican period and in the post-Mao era.[18]

Cycles of localism in Guangzhou and the delta have largely matched this pattern. Though literati culture here was not firmly enough established to have taken part in the Southern Song "localist turn," this area certainly fits into the broader late Ming trend of a proliferation in the articulation of local identity. In the mid- and late Ming, Guangdong first produced a significant number of scholars, poets, and officials who had an impact in the cultural centers of the empire to the north, in Jiangnan and the capital. These successful and well-connected Cantonese literati were also largely responsible for the first flourishing of Cantonese elite culture through the production of localist texts—beginning with Huang Zuo's local histories, in the middle of the sixteenth century, and culminating in Qu Dajun's *Guangdong xinyu*, printed in 1700. Measured by the production of localist texts (documented in Chapter 4), another high point was marked in the early and mid-nineteenth century, after more than a century in which very few localist texts were produced. This trend ebbed somewhat in the late nineteenth century, but was revived early in the following century. In fact, many of the authors and compilers of localist texts produced in the 1930s and 1940s belonged to the genealogy of Xuehaitang scholars and urban Cantonese literati described throughout this study. These early twentieth-century producers of localist texts included a relative of Huang Peifang, a nephew of Xu Hao, and, as we shall see below, one of the Wangs.[19] Most recently, a new cluster of such texts appeared in the 1990s, when Guangdong presses produced several series of modern editions of Ming, Qing, and Republican works.[20] Many of the basic sources used in this study were drawn from these two periods of increased production of localist texts during the twentieth century. This most recent revival of localism was not limited to textual production, but was also inscribed in the rapidly changing delta landscape: on an elementary schoolyard in Jiujiang in the late 1990s, one could find a recently built Zhu Ciqi memorial hall.[21]

These recurring cycles of localism, in radically different temporal and spatial contexts, indicate not only the appeal of the local but also the flexibility of conceptions of local identity. In nineteenth-century Guangzhou, urban "Cantonese" local identity differed from that of the delta in several ways. Throughout the nineteenth century, newcomers to the city quickly adopted native cultural icons whenever it suited their interests or purposes, just as Wang Quan made use of the Ruan Yuan shrine (itself an "imported" cultural icon) and the litchi in his short poem. Yet newcomers' appropriation of local cultural symbols or embrace of local identities did not necessarily entail the displacement of pre-existing identities articulated by delta elites. Rather, competition between urban and delta elites through the production of localist texts reflects two different ways in which mobility and identity interacted. William Rowe emphasizes the ease with which sojourners in Hankou embraced local identity through philanthropic activities, a strategy akin to the scholarly activities of the urban historians, poets, and anthologists described in Chapter 4 of the present study.[22] In contrast, Antonia Finnane explains the proliferation of localist literature in early nineteenth-century Yangzhou as an attempt to distinguish local, or native, culture from immigrant culture.[23] This explanation seems to mesh more with the localist projects of Zhu Ciqi and the Jiujiang gentry than with the newcomers who utilized the Xuehaitang. Though there was naturally a great deal of overlap between natives' and newcomers' constructions of local culture, these constructions could nonetheless be deployed for strikingly different purposes and directed at distinct audiences.

This flexibility in the construction and deployment of local culture and identity should caution us against equating a new cycle of local cultural production with a separation of the local from the center, at least in cultural terms. To begin with, an increasing celebration of the local does not necessarily entail a rejection of the extralocal, nor does it necessarily present an obstacle to the construction of larger communities of identity. For example, in her research on native-place associations in early twentieth-century Shanghai, Bryna Goodman demonstrates that "native-place networks institutionalized in sojourner associations played a formative role in . . . state-building nationalisms."[24] Likewise, in his recent study of Manchukuo, Prasenjit Duara suggests that the local was often seen as a repository for the authentic values of larger collectivities such as the nation.[25]

The fact that many of the people who celebrated the Xuehaitang as a success, and who spearheaded the production of localist texts, were nonlocals indicates the importance of extralocal or transregional networks in constructing the local.[26] The Xuehaitang and all of its affiliated activities were created and sustained by a geographically and socially diverse group of people. Most important, at least initially, were the charismatic official, Ruan Yuan, who wanted to proselytize evidential research and *Wenxuan* literature, and the Jiangnan literati accompanying him to Guangzhou. A group of very wealthy merchants from in-migrating families, equipped with the inclination to exchange money for cultural resources, not only funded the academy but also sponsored numerous activities by Xuehaitang scholars. A diverse but socially ambitious array of in-migrating families lacking local cultural resources, along with urbanized families from the delta, came together to administer and take Xuehaitang examinations and to socialize at the academy. For all of these reasons, the Xuehaitang was both a local and a cosmopolitan institution.

My purpose in drawing a contrast between cosmopolitan Guangzhou and the insular Enclosure district of the delta hinterland in Chapter 1 was to emphasize the cultural resources exclusively available to the delta elite and the extent to which this area of the delta was closed to urbanites. Nevertheless, it is important to keep in mind that the delta elite was not isolated; remembering the lengths to which Jiujiang literati went to protect the widespread economic interests of their township should quickly dispel such a notion. The most successful delta literati—people like Zhu Ciqi—not only had access to urban Guangzhou, but could also, if they advanced enough in the examination and bureaucratic hierarchy, cultivate significant transregional relationships. Throughout the nineteenth century, several powerful delta lineages in Daliang, Foshan, and the Enclosure district produced some high-ranking officials with important connections at court. Such ties were probably not essential for maintaining a sense of local identity—as John Dardess finds for the elites of Taihe county during the Ming—yet many nineteenth-century delta literati were involved in what he calls a "national matrix."[27] Rather than conceiving of a single national network, however, I would suggest that both the urban and delta elites had ties to overlapping but nonidentical national networks.

In addressing the important question of what tied the periphery (Guangzhou and the delta) to the political and cultural centers of the empire (Beijing and Jiangnan), it is necessary to avoid imagining a zero-sum contest between local gentry and the state. That is, one of the benefits of a locally focused study is the realization that different segments of any broadly conceived "local elite" cultivated and maintained numerous links both with the state and with counterparts in other regions of the empire and beyond. In terms of elite culture, the proliferation of localist texts and the Cantonization of academy directorships in the nineteenth century do not necessarily imply that Guangdong somehow became unhinged from the rest of China.[28] Rather, the Xuehaitang was sustained by a highly mobile group of cosmopolitan literati, officials, and merchants who maintained kinship, native-place, professional, and scholarly and literary ties with various elites in other localities throughout the empire. Few families exemplify this better than the Wangs of Shanyin and Panyu. Though the central government may have declined as a driving force in shaping literati cultural identity, Guangzhou was *more* closely linked to other cultural centers after the Xuehaitang was constructed and the localist texts printed, even as the city grew *less* connected to the delta hinterland.

MOBILITY AND IDENTITY IN A NEW AGE

In contrast to Gui Wencan's confident celebration of the Xuehaitang and Cantonese elite culture in his 1855 *Jingxue bocai lu*, Wang Quan's poem written a quarter of a century later gives a sense of the passage of time, of decline from the glory days of the Xuehaitang's founding in the 1820s. For Wang Quan, at least, associating the Xuehaitang with stillness and decline was not an aberration. Wang echoes this theme in the first lines of another poem written very soon after, in the late autumn of 1880, on accompanying a friend on a visit to the Xuehaitang:

> Entering the gate we see autumn hues;
> The setting sun shines through sparse trees.
> The bamboo is thick, the mountain studio quiet;
> The moss is uncultivated, the stone path deep.[29]

It was quite appropriate for Wang to voice feelings associated with autumn—this was a common trope in Chinese poetry, Wang was well into middle age when he wrote the poem, and Chinese literati of his time had suffered through the mid-century crises and sensed impending changes. Nevertheless, there is some irony in the poem's depiction of decline, when it is read in the context of the early Guangxu period. Born in 1828, Wang had not witnessed the supposed height of the Xuehaitang in the early Daoguang era and consequently had no personal experience of its presumed decline. Moreover, though the academy's scholarly and literary agenda may have lacked novelty in Wang's time, the Xuehaitang as an institution was, in 1880, experiencing a period of unparalleled stability and growth. In addition to increasingly frequent regular examinations, new groups of specialized students were added throughout the following two decades, culminating in one group of twenty students named in 1896, and another group of ten in the following year. Classes of specialized students in the 1880s had included Wang Quan's son, Wang Zhaoquan, and Zhaoquan's second cousin Zhaoyong. The Xuehaitang was not disbanded until 1903, by which time Guangzhou's conventional academies were also closed, in favor of the new schools, or *xuetang*.[30]

What is most interesting about Wang Quan's poem, then, is the extent to which the collective memory of a glorious founding decade maintained its hold on the imagination of new generations of urban Cantonese literati. Nostalgia aside, there also seems to be something very practical about Wang's panegyric for the Xuehaitang. Wang and his relatives had made their way to Guangzhou in order to profit from administrative service. It seems unlikely that Wang would have praised the glory days of the Xuehaitang if he, his son, and other family members were not continuing to avail themselves of the status that Xuehaitang credentials could offer in the late nineteenth century. The images that he produced in verse—of Ruan Yuan, litchi poems, and a quiet urban academy surrounded by trees and bamboo—had deep contemporary relevance for people like Wang Quan.

Nevertheless, circumstances began to change rapidly in the late 1890s, as old institutions such as the Xuehaitang disappeared, making way for new institutions that offered alternative means of social mobility and new cultural resources for claims of identity. Several of the families that had previously utilized the Xuehaitang successfully adapted to these new institutions and continued to make a place for themselves in Guangzhou and beyond. These new opportunities, as well as nostalgia for the old institution and the cultural achievements associated with it, can be seen by briefly tracing the life trajectories of members of the next generation of Wangs. Fortunately, extant *nianpu* (chronological biographies or autobiographies) allow us to do this with two sons, born over twenty years apart, of Wang Quan's cousin, Wang Chu. Their early lives, through the end of the nineteenth century, follow similar trajectories—and familiar ones for members of the Wang family.

When Wang Chu's eldest son, Zhaoyong, was born in 1861 at the family's temporary residence in the Old City, his father was serving in Dianbai county in southwestern Guangdong. After infancy, Zhaoyong spent most of his youth moving with his father between family residences in Guangzhou and yamen in counties throughout Guangdong. A listing of some of these postings gives us a sense of how mobile this professional strategy required the family to be. At four *sui*, in 1864, Zhaoyong accompanied his father by sea to Maoming county, near Dianbai. Between 1865 and 1867, Zhaoyong lived with his father in Xinyi county, just north of Maoming. In 1867, he followed his father back to Guangzhou, but then after several days they went to Zengcheng county, east of Guangzhou, suggesting that Wang Chu was able to find employment very quickly. Wang Chu also took Zhaoyong to his new posting in Kaiping county, on the western edge of the delta, in 1868. In the following year, Zhaoyong resided in Guangzhou while his father worked in the independent subprefecture of Chixi, carved out of Xinning county in the aftermath of the Hakka-Punti conflicts.[31] In 1870, now ten *sui*, Zhaoyong went with his father to Lufeng county in southeastern Guangdong; they returned to Guangzhou the next year. Early in 1872, father and son went to Deqing department on the West River near the Guangxi border. In 1873, they came back to Guangzhou, but in the following year again went to Zengcheng county, and the year after that to Leizhou prefecture in the southwest. Zhaoyong and his father returned to Guangzhou in 1877, where they resided in the New City; later that year, however, Zhaoyong followed his father to a new posting in Boluo, the county just east of Zengcheng.[32]

Despite its peripatetic lifestyle, the Wang family devised flexible and diversified strategies to ensure the education of its sons. This included primary education, preparation for the civil service examinations, and training to carry on the family practice. Like matrons of scholar-official families in Jiangnan and elsewhere, Zhaoyong's mother was educated, and she oversaw his studies in the evenings.³³ In the winter of 1865–66, Wang Chu's eldest brother, Shilin (1811–78), brought his son from Shaoxing to Xinyi, where Wang Chu was working. Shilin then became Zhaoyong's primary instructor, following Wang Chu and Zhaoyong from one place to another until 1877.³⁴ After his uncle left in that year to be with his son (who was then working in another Guangdong yamen), Zhaoyong's education began to expand in some new directions. Zhaoyong and Wang Quan's son, Zhaoquan, began studies under Zheng Quan, a member of the 1869 class of specialized students at the Xuehaitang. Taking Zhaoyong to his new posting in Zengcheng later in the year, Wang Chu hired a local scholar to prepare his son for the civil service examinations. But soon Wang Quan sent a letter to his cousin arguing that it was most beneficial to study in the provincial capital, where Zhaoyong could be exposed to a wide circle of teachers and colleagues. Convinced by this logic, Wang Chu ordered Zhaoyong to return to Guangzhou, reside at Wang Quan's residence, and resume his studies, together with Zhaoquan, under Zheng Quan. They were joined by Tao Shaoxue (1863–1908), another young Panyu student from a sojourning Zhejiang family. Zhaoyong was also personally instructed by the family's most promising literatus, Wang Quan.³⁵

Wang Zhaoyong's transition into adulthood exemplifies the Wang family's increasing ties to Guangzhou during the nineteenth century, and the opportunities for some of these sojourning Shanyin professionals to reinvent themselves as Cantonese literati. At 17 *sui* (in 1877) he was married to a woman from Shunde county, and in the following year he began to take county and prefectural examinations as a registered Panyu resident. Zhaoyong made an unsuccessful attempt at the provincial examinations in 1882, a year in which he also studied composition under another Panyu Tao of northern Zhejiang descent, the Xuehaitang co-director Tao Fuxiang. Two years later, at 24 *sui*, Zhaoyong was selected as a specialized student at the Xuehaitang. His second cousin, Zhaoquan, had been in the previous class of specialized students and would later serve as a co-director at Chen Li's academy, the Jupo Retreat. Finally, Zhaoyong won a *juren* degree in 1889, but failed in the metropolitan examinations the following year.³⁶

From Wang Chu's point of view, however, sending his son into the *muyou* business was always an attractive alternative to repeated efforts at winning a *jinshi* degree—if successful, Zhaoyong could conceivably be saddled with the weighty responsibilities of a county magistrate. Thus, working as a *muyou* in Sanshui county in 1882, Wang Chu ordered Zhaoyong to accompany him and study the Qing statutes and substatutes. Four years later, this time serving in Yingde, north of Guangzhou, Wang Chu decided that working as a *muyou* was indeed the easiest route to a secure future for his son; he had Zhaoyong review legal procedures, learning how to handle official communications (*picheng*). These studies, and perhaps his father's connections, paid off for Zhaoyong, as the magistrate of the neighboring Wengyuan county hired him to manage punishments and finances. In 1890 and 1891, Zhaoyong managed the staff in Chixi, where he had lived with his father two decades before. Zhaoyong subsequently made one more attempt at the metropolitan examinations and attended his ailing father at posts in Sihui and Lufeng counties, alternately further studying administrative procedures and teaching at a local academy.[37]

After failing in a third attempt, in 1894, to win a *jinshi* degree, Wang Zhaoyong seems to have resigned himself to following in his father's footsteps. He managed judicial cases and taxation in remote Suixi county before landing a position in the yamen of wealthy Shunde county in 1896, pulling in a monthly stipend of one hundred taels. In 1898, Zhaoyong took up a low-ranking post in the salt administration, supervising a distribution center in Lechang county in far northern Guangdong. Finding his new duties relatively light and his income favorable, Zhaoyong stayed at his Lechang post for several years. He was at times joined by family members, including a concubine to replace his recently deceased wife. This woman was a former servant, presented to Wang by Shen Shiliang's son, Zetang. Zhaoyong also maintained the family's ties to Guangzhou, using his growing income to purchase a home in the New City.[38]

Wang Chu's youngest son, Zhaoming, was born over two decades after his eldest brother, yet his childhood was remarkably similar to Zhaoyong's early life. Zhaoming spent the first nine years of his life in the county offices of five different Guangdong counties where his father was working.[39] Toward the end of that period, when most of the family was residing with Wang Chu in Sihui, Zhaoming began to learn the family practice from Zhaoyong. In 1892, Zhaoming returned with his father to Guangzhou and began to receive instruction in the Classics under private teachers. After his mother died in 1895, and his father followed a year after, he accompanied, in 1898, his older brother Zhaoyong to his salt administration post in Lechang. While in Lechang, Zhaoming began studying under a Panyu native and former Chen Li student, who happened to be the father-in-law of another of Zhaoming's older brothers. Zhaoming returned from Lechang to Guangzhou in 1901, began taking examinations at a local county-level academy, and soon took the civil service examinations as well.[40]

If Wang Zhaoming had been on such a trajectory just a decade earlier, he almost certainly would eventually have taken Xuehaitang examinations, like his older brother Zhaoyong and other Wangs. But times had changed, and Zhaoming's trajectory turned in startling directions. In 1903, he was selected by the provincial government to study in Japan at the Tokyo College of Law and Administration, a fitting choice in light of the Wang family practice.[41] While in Japan, Zhaoming was exposed to radically new ideas; he joined Sun Yat-sen's (1866–1925) newly formed Revolutionary Alliance, which sought to overthrow the Qing dynasty and establish a Chinese republic. Zhaoming sent a letter to his eldest brother back in Guangzhou explaining that, since he had become a revolutionary, he was severing relations with the family and breaking off his engagement to a local woman, presumably chosen by Zhaoyong as the family head. Traveling with Sun Yat-sen in Southeast Asia, Zhaoming met and eventually married the daughter of an overseas Chinese family. After attempting to assassinate the Manchu regent in 1910 and spending more than a year in jail, Zhaoming won acclaim as a revolutionary hero under his better-known sobriquet, Wang Jingwei (1883–1944). He went on to become an influential member of Sun Yat-sen's revamped party, the Guomindang, served as president of the Executive Yuan in the mid-1930s, and eventually became notorious as a Japanese collaborator.[42]

Though the 1911 Revolution was a triumph for the young Wang Jingwei, it was a transition of a different sort for Wang Zhaoyong. As he tells it in his chronological autobiography, the rhythm of

Zhaoyong's movements changed; retiring from his post in Lechang when that county fell to revolutionaries, he took on the identity of an *yimin*—a "leftover person" from the previous dynasty. Zhaoyong was about the same age in 1911 as Wang Quan was when he authored the poem that starts this chapter. As an experienced administrator with blood ties to a leading revolutionary, Zhaoyong must have been attractive to the new revolutionary and local regimes that replaced the Qing. The new provincial governor, Wang Jingwei's former classmate at Tokyo College of Law and Administration, Hu Hanmin (1879–1936), offered him a post, but Zhaoyong declined. He also refused to head the reconstituted provincial salt administration. In the first year of the new Chinese Republic, 1912, Wang Jingwei re-established ties with the family in Guangzhou, whereas Wang Zhaoyong vowed never again to serve the state. Zhaoyong spent most of the next two and a half decades shuttling back and forth between Guangzhou and Macao, seeking refuge in the Portuguese colony whenever a new contender for power seized the provincial capital. Ironically, at times Zhaoyong fled Guangzhou to avoid the very forces that allowed Wang Jingwei and his companions in the fledgling Guomindang back into Guangzhou to establish a revolutionary base, as in 1920 and 1921, when the military leader Chen Jiongming (1878–1933) seized Guangzhou and temporarily allied himself with Sun Yat-sen. Zhaoyong last left Guangzhou for Macao in 1937 to avoid Japanese air strikes, a few years before Jingwei would accept the Japanese offer to head a new puppet regime in Nanjing.[43]

During his years as an *yimin*, Wang Zhaoyong became a custodian of nineteenth-century Cantonese literati culture, particularly as it had been embodied in the Xuehaitang. No longer an administrator, he began to recreate himself in the image of the nineteenth-century Cantonese literati who had so inspired Wang Quan (see Fig. 10). Not unlike Chen Li and Zhu Ciqi in their declining years, Zhaoyong began to write, compile, edit, and publish with a passion. This began in 1911, shortly before the revolution, when Zhaoyong printed Wu Lanxiu's collection of lyric poetry. In 1914, he started compiling a collection of biographies and assessments of Qing-era Cantonese painters, entitled *Lingnan hua zhenglue*, an ambitious endeavor that would be completed only in 1927 and sent to the

FIG. 10: Wang Zhaoyong in the pose of a Xuehaitang scholar. A portrait of Wang Zhaoyong (*right*) at seventy-six *sui* in 1937 closely resembles a drawing of the early Xuehaitang co-director Yi Kezhong (*left*). The Yi Kezhong drawing comes from a collection of drawings of Qing-era Confucian scholars first produced by Ye Yanlan 葉衍蘭 (1856 *jinshi*) and printed in 1929 by his grandson, Ye Gongchuo 葉恭綽 (1880–1968). Like the Wang family, the Ye family also consisted of sojourners from northern Zhejiang. Yanlan was descended from natives of Yuyao county who worked as *muyou* in Guangdong in the late Qianlong era and eventually registered as Panyu residents. The Wang Zhaoyong portrait appears at the front of his chronological autobiography. Both likenesses suggest the aesthetic imagination of Qing-era Confucians among their cultural descendants in the Republican era (sources: Ye Gongchuo, *Qingdai xuezhe xiangzhuan*, p. 365; Wang Zhaoyong, *Weishang laoren ziding nianpu*, front page; Ye Gongchuo, *Ye Xiaan huigao*, "Ye Xiaan xiansheng nianpu," p. 1).

printers in the following year. Wang also played an important role in compiling a new edition of the Panyu gazetteer, begun in 1918 but not completed until 1931. Unlike some other Republican-era gazetteers of Pearl River delta counties, the new Panyu gazetteer did not record information about the post-Qing years. Whether or not Wang had a hand in making this editorial decision, it certainly tallied with his *yimin* identity. Shortly before beginning work on the Panyu gazetteer, Wang had compiled a record of Cantonese *yimin* from the Yuan dynasty. In it, he explained that other collections had paid sufficient tribute to Cantonese *yimin* from the Song and Ming dynasties, but had neglected the Yuan, which, surely not coincidentally, was, like the Qing, a conquest dynasty.⁴⁴

In these years, Wang Zhaoyong proved to be an especially avid promoter of Chen Li, printing his old teacher's literary works—but doing so only after Chen's sons had died, as they had insisted on honoring their father's wishes never to publish these peripheral writings. Such works included Chen Li's *Lyric Poems from Remember Jiangnan Lodge*, printed in 1914, and the *Bequeathed* Shi *Poems of the Master of the Eastern Study*, edited and printed in 1931.⁴⁵ In addition to publishing his teacher's writings, Wang Zhaoyong organized ceremonies and erected shrines in Chen Li's honor. A Chen Li shrine had originally been established at the Jupo Retreat after his death. The shrine survived Jupo's conversion into a new school in 1903 but was destroyed during the 1911 Revolution. Zhaoyong decided to erect a new Chen Li shrine next to the Panyu Library that one of his sons had established in his position as head of Panyu county. On Chen Li's birthday in April 1923, Wang Zhaoyong gathered other former Chen Li students, as well as his students' students, to conduct a proper ceremony. Seven years later, Wang solicited the services of an artist to engrave Chen Li's image in stone and then installed it on a wall of the shrine.⁴⁶

The most poignant image of Wang Zhaoyong as a man of the old dynasty living in a new age comes from an account of his activities during the years of the May Fourth Movement, in which many younger educated Cantonese embraced iconoclasm. In contrast, Wang Zhaoyong played the antiquarian. Zhaoyong notes in his chronological autobiography that, when the Guangzhou city walls were finally completely demolished between 1918 and 1920, he and a colleague searched through the rubble and found some very old bricks with characters inscribed on them. At first, the workmen were surprised at the aged scholars' interest in discarded bricks. When they realized there were profits to be had, however, Zhaoyong and his friend faced stiff competition in their search. The few worthwhile artifacts that they managed to gather became the basis for a small book assembled by Wang, which described in detail the characters on each brick and indicated the age in which it must have been produced. In Wang's judgment, some of these bricks were well over a thousand years old. Though some of the reader's sympathy is lost upon learning that it was actually Wang's servants who were made to rummage through the debris, the title of his short work—*A Record of Remnant Bricks from the Guangzhou Wall*—aptly conveys the futility of preserving Cantonese literati culture in the face of the municipal government's modernizing schemes.[47] It portrays a sense of loss much more convincingly than does Wang Quan's poem written four decades earlier.

One event from Wang Zhaoyong's life after 1911 that also testifies to the irrecoverable loss of a bygone era in fact began as a renaissance. Early in 1920, under the sponsorship of the Guangxi clique of militarists then controlling Guangzhou, the old Xuehaitang examinations were revived.[48] Because the former site of the Xuehaitang, long since demolished, had been occupied by military units, it was off limits. Accordingly, the organizers borrowed library space in the center of town as a temporary location and hired a group of co-directors with civil service and academy credentials from the old dynasty, including the second cousins and former Xuehaitang specialized students, Wang Zhaoquan and Zhaoyong.[49] The co-directors followed Ruan Yuan's practice of quarterly examinations in Classics, Histories, free and parallel prose, and new- and old-style poetry. The new Xuehaitang examinations persisted for a short while, through the vicissitudes of warlord and revolutionary Guangzhou, but were abandoned after the winter examination in 1921. By then, Wang Zhaoyong no longer held his position, having fled to Macao when Chen Jiongming's army occupied Guangzhou in October 1920. When Zhaoyong received news in Macao of the official closure of the Xuehaitang, he expressed relief in his diary, remarking that he had long since been retired and that now it would be easier to avoid social entanglements.[50]

Nevertheless, Wang Zhaoyong did note a few years later, in 1924, that the best essays and poems from the briefly revived Xuehaitang examinations had been printed in a collection entitled *Xuehaitang keyi*.[51] This collection in three *juan* reveals that the examinations of 1920 and 1921 were in many ways faithful recreations of nineteenth-century models. The first section is devoted to classical exegesis. In this category, the top essay discusses the "Tribute of Yu" section of the *Shangshu*, citing the work of Chen Li, among others. Essays in the second *juan* address historical issues, including assessments of the learning of postclassical Confucians such as Cheng Yi and Chen Xianzhang. Nostalgia for the glory days of the Xuehaitang comes across most clearly in the third *juan*, which contains literary essays and poems. There are songs on the Southern Han iron posts, imitating those composed by Yi Kezhong and others a century before. In one exercise, which was perhaps designed by the *Lingnan hua zhenglue* author Wang Zhaoyong, examinees wrote poems on Cantonese painters such as Xie Lansheng and Chen Pu.[52]

The most striking literary pieces are the ones that open the third *juan*: prefaces to poems celebrating observances of Ruan Yuan's birthday on the twentieth day of the first lunar month in 1921. On this day—February 27 on the Western calendar—these latter-day Xuehaitang scholars held a poetry competition at the academy site, though in reality they were forced to meet at an alternative site on the south side of the city, since Yuexiu Hill was occupied. The author of one preface, Tan Zuqiang, expresses nostalgia for the Guangzhou of Ruan Yuan's time: "Reflecting on the period between Jiaqing and Daoguang, waves were calm and the dust settled, harvests were bountiful and people at peace, sticks and drums of war were not heard, while strings and singing voices responded in harmony."[53] Tan's Republican-era preface resonates with Wang Quan's early Guangxu poem, but the sense of a lost resplendence of Cantonese literati culture feels much more genuine now. Another preface, by Huang Rongkang (1876–1945) of Sanshui, draws a stark contrast to the glory days of Ruan Yuan's time by bemoaning the vanishing sites of the past, favorite stops on the itineraries of nineteenth-century urban Cantonese literati from Xie Lansheng to Wang Quan: the northern wall that ran over Yuexiu Hill, the Southern Garden site in the New City, the Pearl River, and Yuexiu Hill, also called Jade

Mountain.⁵⁴ Traces of these refined sites of bygone times, celebrated in countless essays and poems by nineteenth-century Xuehaitang scholars, were vanishing, due not only to the military, industrial, and administrative exigencies of a new age but also to simple neglect. Heirs to the prestigious literati of the past were now powerless to reclaim space that they had once dominated:

> Today, this single remaining mountain, how many times has it faced catastrophe? The Sea of Learning Hall is also near dilapidation. The reds of the kapoks on the northern wall have been turned to a place where the setting sun shines on abandoned ramparts; the greens of grass at the Southern Garden have become a paradise for calling frogs in the gathering rains. The Pearl River has been completely dredged and turned to sand for the battle dead; since Jade Mountain is dark, who will make a space for literary gatherings?⁵⁵

APPENDIXES

APPENDIX A
Xuehaitang Co-Directors, 1826–1863

This is a tentative table culled from various materials. Some explanations and sources of information are listed below:

The *Xuehaitang zhi*, 20a–appended 34b, lists the co-directors from 1826 to 1882, as well as the lunar month and year of each appointment. Unfortunately, it does not state the duration of each co-director's tenure at the academy. When no evidence exists that a co-director left his post, I have assumed that his appointment continued.

Xuehaitang zhi, 34b, includes an 1828 inscription listing Ruan Yuan's "students" (clearly referring to the co-directors) at the Xuehaitang as Zhang Biao, Wu Yingkui, Lin Botong, Wu Lanxiu, Zeng Zhao, Ma Fuan, Xiong Jingxing, and Xu Rong.

Xuehaitang zhi, 35b, includes an 1835 inscription listing Ruan Yuan's "students" at the Xuehaitang as Zhang Biao, Huang Zigao, Lin Botong, Wu Lanxiu, Zeng Zhao, Xie Niangong, Xiong Jingxing, and Yi Kezhong.

In an 1847 preface to the *Yuexiu shuyuan zhi*, Liang Tingnan notes that Zhang Weiping and Huang Peifang are "currently" serving as Xuehaitang co-directors. Elsewhere he notes that Tan Ying and Chen Li are both currently Xuehaitang co-directors. *Yuexiu shuyuan zhi*, 13.14a–b, 13.32a.

In a diary entry for December 12, 1863, Guo Songtao lists the Xuehaitang co-directors as Zou Boqi, Chen Li, Jin Xiling, Zhou Yinqing, Zhu Ciqi, Chen Pu, Li Guangting, and Tan Ying. Guo Songtao, *Guo Songtao riji*, p. 137.

Although Zhang Biao did not die until 1851, he suffered from an eye ailment that led to blindness. Therefore, I am assuming that Zhang Weiping took his position in 1838. Zhang Qizeng, *Bianzhen liangshi wenchao*, 2.7b; Zeng Zhao, *Miangchenglou jichao*, 4.16a.

Zhu Ciqi never took up his appointment at the Xuehaitang, but his position was left open for him for several years. *Xuehaitang zhi*, 23b; Rong Zhaozu, "Xuehaitang kao," p. 46.

Year					Co-directors				
	Zhao Jun Zhao Biao	Wu Yingkui	Lin Botong	Wu Lanxiu	Zeng Zhao	Ma Fuan	Xiong Jingxing	Xu Rong	
1826									
1827									
1828									
1829		Huang Zigao							
1830									
1831						Zhang Weiping			
1832									
1833						Xie Niangong			
1834								Yi Kezhong	
1835									
1836									
1837				Hou Kang				Tan Ying	
1838	Zhang Weiping			Huang Peifang					
1839									
1840		Chen Li							
1841						Liang Tingnan			
1842									
1843									
1844									
1845			Yang Rongxu						
1846									
1847									
1848									

Year	Co-directors					
1849						
1850						
1851						
1852						
1853		Jin Xiling				
1854						
1855						
1856						
1857						
1858			Li Nengding	Zou Boqi	Chen Liangyu	Shen Shiliang
1859	Zhu Ciqi					
1860						
1861			Zhou Yinqing		Li Guangting	Chen Pu
1862						
1863						

APPENDIX B
Xuehaitang ji Table of Contents

Juan	Exercise	Author(s)
1	Explication of *Tuan* (judgments) in the *Yijing* (Book of Change)	Ruan Yuan Wu Lanxiu Zheng Haoruo
	Explication of instructions in the *Shujing* (Book of Documents)	Zhang Biao Wu Lanxiu Xiong Jingxing
	Explication of *ya* (Minor and Major Odes in the *Shijing*) (Book of Poetry)	Liang Guozhen Li Yingqi Zheng Haoruo
	Explication of records of *Yili* (Ceremony and Rites) chapters	Liang Guozhen
	Explication of commentaries to the *Chunqiu* (Spring and Autumn Annals)	Zhang Biao
	Explication of records and commentaries in the *Yili* and commentaries to the *Chunqiu*	Zhang Weiping
2	Question: Regarding interpretations of palaces in the *Yili*, whose interpretation is precise and correct?	Lin Botong
	Question: Why do the "Book of Yu" and "Book of Xia" sections of the *Shujing*, the "Sacrificial Odes of Shang" section of the *Shijing*, and the "Hexagram Judgments" section of the *Yijing* not address nature or even contain the character *xing*? In what book was nature first addressed? Does the meaning of "nature" as spoken of by people of the Zhou and Han dynasties match that of Confucius and Mencius or not?	Lin Botong Yi Kezhong

APPENDIX B: *XUEHAITANG JI* TABLE OF CONTENTS

Juan	Exercise	Author(s)
	Question: From the Yuanfeng period (1078–85), several people have produced commentaries to the *Zizhi tongjian* (Comprehensive mirror for aid in government). How would you assess each commentator?	Lin Botong Yi Kezhong
	Interpretation of the Character "*Guang*" (broad)	Zeng Zhao
3	Similarities and differences in the Mao recension and Zheng commentary of the *Shijing*, Part I	Zeng Zhao
4	Similarities and differences in the Mao recension and Zheng commentary of the *Shijing*, Part II	Zeng Zhao
5	Compose a postscript for Chen Jian's *Xuebu tongbian* (Comprehensively discerning the weeds of learning)	Wu Yue Lin Botong Ruan Yuan
6	Theory that Chen Xianzhang's learning developed out of Zhou Dunyi	Wu Yingkui Deng Chun Zheng Haoruo
	Postscript to Wang Yinglin's *Kunxue jiwen* (Record of findings from hard-earned scholarship)	Zhang Biao Wu Yingkui Lin Botong Zheng Haoruo
	Postscript to Gu Yanwu's *Rizhi lu* (Record of knowledge gained day by day)	Zhang Biao Wu Lanxiu Lin Botong Wen Xun
	Postscript to Qian Daxin's *Shijiazhai Yangxin lu* (Record of self-renewal from the Ten Yokes Study)	Zhang Biao Wu Lanxiu Lin Botong Zeng Zhao Zheng Haoruo
7	Postscript to Wei Shou's *Weishu* (History of the Wei dynasty)	Wu Lanxiu Yang Maojian Liang Guozhen
	Postscript to *Yiqie jing yinyi* (Pronunciation and meanings in all sutras)	Huang Zigao
	Theory of the *Appended Words* [of the *Yijing*]	Zeng Zhao
	Investigation into *wen* (literary prose) and *bi* (utilitarian prose)	Liu Tianhui Liang Guozhen Hou Kang Liang Guangzhao
	Investigation of the *Wenxuan* Annotation	Huang Zigao
	Annotation of Xiao Tong's Preface to the *Wenxuan*	Zhang Biao Deng Chun

Juan	Exercise	Author(s)
8	Investigation into origin and development of examination writing	Zheng Haoruo Liang Jie Yang Maojian Zhou Yinqing Hou Kang
	Preface to *Reflections on Examination Writing*	Ruan Yuan
9	Investigation of Honorary Names in the Han and Jin Dynasties	Zeng Zhao Fang Dongshu
10	Rhapsody on the Inkstones of Duanxi	Chen Tong Liang Mei Huang Zigao Liu Ying
	Rhapsody on Peacocks	Ju Huang Liang Jian Tan Ying Liang Mei Liu Guangju
	Inscription on the Stone House in Duanzhou	Li Qinghua Yan Li Liu Ying
	Postscript to a record of respectfully reading the *Siku quanshu* catalogue	Ju Huang
	Imitation of Yu Xin's *Teng wang ji* Preface	Hou Kang (2)
	Imitation of "Essay on Observing the Lustration Festival at Reed Stream on the Third Day of the Third Month"	Tan Ying
11	Match Fang Xinru's "Hundred Chants on the South Sea Region":	
	Pan Hill	Li Guangzhao
	Yu Hill	Li Guangzhao Yi Kezhong
	Ren Xiao City Wall	Zhao Jun
	Three Cities	Yi Kezhong
	Clear Sea Military Tower	Zhao Jun
	Temple of the Five Genii	Yi Kezhong
	Broadly Pacifying Hall	Chen Mengzhao
	Stone Screen Hall	Lin Botong Yao Jinguang
	Ten Worthies' Shrine	Yi Kezhong
	Iron Posts	Li Guangzhao Yi Kezhong Wu Kuiguang
	Elixir Islet	Wu Lanxiu

APPENDIX B: *XUEHAITANG JI* TABLE OF CONTENTS ✤ 307

Juan	Exercise	Author(s)
	Nine Sun Stones	Wu Lanxiu
		Zhao Jun
	Yue Tower	Yi Kezhong
	South Moat	Cui Bi
		Wu Yingkui
		Tan Ying
		Liang Mei
	Buddha-Nature Monastery	Yi Kezhong
	Breeze or Banner Hall	Yi Kezhong
	Brush Bequeathing Study	Cui Bi
	Bodhi Tree	Wu Yingkui
	Ren Xiao Tomb	Wu Yingkui
	Jinghui Monastery Thousand-Buddha Pagoda	Wu Yingkui
	Multitudinous Wonders Hall	Li Guangzhao
		Qi Lin
	Bronze Images of the Lius	Huang Yu
		Huang Zigao
	The Double Watchtower of the Lius	Xiong Jingxing
		Li Guangzhao
	Foreign Pagoda	Wu Yingkui
	Sea Mountain Tower	Su Yingheng
		He Qijie
	Yue Well Ridge	Yi Kezhong
	Yue Terrace Well	Yi Kezhong
	Xilan Mountain Guangguo Monastery	Yi Kezhong
	The Seven Eastern Monasteries	Li Guangzhao
	The Seven Western Monasteries	Li Guangzhao
	The Seven Southern Monasteries	Li Guangzhao
	The Seven Northern Monasteries	Li Guangzhao
	Floating Mound Mountain	Li Guangzhao
	Coral Well	Li Guoguang
	Courting Han Terrace	Luo Rizhang
	The Suburban Altar of the Lius	Yi Kezhong
	Flower Parapet of the Liu King	Li Guangzhao
		Xiong Jingxing
	Foreigners' Mound	Yang Shiji
	Flower Fields	Wu Lanxiu
	Stone Gate	Yi Kezhong
	The Springs of Greed	Wu Yingkui
	Deep Fragrance Shores	Wu Yingkui
	Jiankong Pavilion	Xie Niangong
	Luminous Islet	Yi Kezhong

308 APPENDIX B: *XUEHAITANG JI* TABLE OF CONTENTS

Juan	Exercise	Author(s)
11, cont.		
	Sweet Stream	Xiong Jingxing
		Li Guangzhao
	Majiao Mountain	Zhang Qihan
	Thunder Grotto	Wu Kuiguang
	Reed Stream	Li Guangzhao
		Zhang Qihan
12	Dripping Water Cliff	Xiong Jingxing
		Yang Shiji
		Xu Qing
	Calamus Temple and Juezhen Monastery	Yi Kezhong
	Flowing Cup Pond	Yi Kezhong
	Old Immortal Ge's Alchemy Stone	Yi Kezhong
	Lady Bao Well	Yi Kezhong
	Suspended Bell	Li Youqi
	The Tomb Suspected to Be That of Zhao Tuo	Yi Kezhong
	Baoxiang Peak Shengyin Monastery	Yi Kezhong
	Tiger Running Springs	Li Guangzhao
	Moving Rock	Tan Ying
		Cai Ruping
	White Cloud Grotto	He Qijie
		Yi Kezhong
	Three Teachings Palace	Li Guangzhao
	Crane Stretching Terrace	Li Guangzhao
		Liang Jiagui
	Grotto of the Greater and Lesser Waterfalls	Li Guoguang
	Tigerhead Cliff	Yi Kezhong
	Jingtai Mountain Seven Immortals' Temple	Yi Kezhong
	Zhuoxi Springs	Li Guangzhao
	Obedience Chapel	Yi Kezhong
	Tumulus Mountain	Wu Lanxiu
	Horse Bridle Mountain	Yi Kezhong
	Pipa Islet	Wu Lanxiu
	Mutually Facing Ridges	Yan Sizong
	South Sea Temple	Shi Huaibi
		Ruan Fu
	Bathing Day Pavilion	Li Guangzhao
		Shi Huaibi
	Copper Drum	Li Zhongpei
		Li Guoguang
		Liang Guochen
	Boluo Secret Fruit	Li Guangzhao
		Wu Yingkui

APPENDIX B: *XUEHAITANG JI* TABLE OF CONTENTS ❦ 309

Juan	Exercise	Author(s)
	King Ascending Islet	Yi Kezhong
	Luminous Transformation Temple	Yi Kezhong
	Walking Pearl Stone	Shao Yong
	Lu Xun's Old City in Henan	Yi Kezhong
	Datong Monastery	Yi Kezhong
	Embracing Flag Mountain	Yi Kezhong
	Flower Mountain Monastery	Yao Jinguang
	Yellow Den Cliff	Wu Yingkui
		Li Yingzhong
	Golden Sesame Cliff	Xiong Jingxing
	Qingyuan Gorge	Shao Yong
	Gorge Mountain Guangqing Monastery	Xiong Jingxing
	Flying Over Palace	Shao Yong
	Dharma Stone	Yi Kezhong
	Fishing Terrace	Yi Kezhong
	Harmonious Radiance Grotto	Li Youqi
	Drowning Rhinoceros Pool	Yi Kezhong
	Dragons' Horn-grinding Stone	Yi Kezhong
	Old Man Pine	Yi Kezhong
	Zifu Monastery Arhat Pavilion	Li Youqi
	Phoenix Terrace	Li Guangzhao
	Meeting Immortals Temple	Li Guangzhao
		Xiong Jingxing
	Dragon Cave	Shao Yong
	Golden Ox Mountain	Yi Kezhong
	Immortals' Fountain Mountain	Xu Qing
	Meichuan City	Wu Lanxiu
		Wu Yingkui
	Liu Mountain	Xiong Jingxing
	Continuation of matching Fang Xinru's "Hundred Chants on the South Sea Region"	Liao Ji (20 pieces)
13	Visiting the site of the Southern Garden on a spring day	Chen Tong
		Tao Kechang
		Liang Mei
	Four praises of [items in a] studio in early summer: Bamboo silk curtain	Zhang Weiping
		Xiong Jingxing
		Chen Tong
		Ma Fuan
		Lin Botong
		Li Yu
		Tao Kechang

Juan	Exercise	Author(s)
13, cont.		
	(Bamboo silk curtain)	Liu Ying
		Cai Ruping
		Huang Yinglin
		Li Youqi
	Palm-leaf fan	Zhang Weiping
		Xiong Jingxing
		Yang Shiji
		Liang Mei
		Li Youqi
		Cai Jinquan
	Rush grass mat	Zhang Weiping
		Xiong Jingxing
		Chen Tong
		Yang Shiji
		Ma Fuan
		Xie Niangong
		Li Guoguang
		Wu Yingshao
	Bamboo awning	Zhang Weiping
		Xiong Jingxing
		Chen Tong
		Ma Fuan
		Xu Rong
		Liang Mei
		Tao Kechang
		Li Fengxiu
		Guo Pei
	Imitate Zhang Hua's "Exhorting Determination" poem	Lin Botong
		Cui Bi
		Zhong Qishao
		Li Guoguang
	On the ninth day ascending White Cloud Mountain to look out at White Clouds over the Sea	Liang Mei
		Zhang Weiping
		Wu Lanxiu
		Yi Kezhong
		Li Youqi
14	Poems based upon phrases in Sikong Tu's *Twenty-four Categories of Poetry*	Liang Mei (9)
		Tan Ying (4)
		He Yinghan (3)
		Xu Rong (12)
		Xiong Jingxing (3)

APPENDIX B: *XUEHAITANG JI* TABLE OF CONTENTS ▸ 311

Juan	Exercise	Author(s)
		Liu Rudi (1)
		Zhou Yongfu (1)
		Fan Feng (1)
		Shi Fengtai (1)
	Imitations of Yuan-era poets' poems on ten terraces to Chant on ten terraces in Guangdong:	
	Yue King Terrace	Xu Rong
		Ju Huang
	Crane Stretching Terrace	Xu Rong
	Loitering Terrace	Xu Rong
	Lofty Terrace	Xu Rong
		Xiukun
	Fishing Terrace	Xu Rong
		Fan Jun
	Stone Screen Terrace	Xu Rong
	Wondrous Lofty Terrace	Xu Rong
		Liang Jian
		Huang Qiaosong
	Treasure Moon Terrace	Xu Rong
		Ju Huang
		Zhang Yingfeng
	Observing Mist Terrace	Xu Rong
		Huang Yu
	Observing Sun Terrace	Xu Rong
	Song on the Tower of the Thirty-six Rivers	Liang Guanghuai
	Song of the Lotus Whisker Pavilion and the Yellow Peony Poems	Liang Guanghuai
		Liang Mei
		Qian Kun
	Poem on Woodblock Printers	Li Yingzhong
		He Huizu
		Liang Jian
	Passing by Reed Stream Picking Reeds, Nurture Them	Li Qinghua
		Liu Ying
	Imitate Zhang Jiuling's "Observing the Moon While Longing for the Remote"	Li Yingzhong
		Tan Ying
	Wandering through the various hilly woods gardens outside of Guangzhou on a summer day, using the rhyme scheme of Du Fu's "Wandering in the Hilly Woods of General He"	Zhao Jun (2)
		Liang Boxian
		Huang Zigao (2)
		Shi Bing (2)
		Liang Mei
		Zhang Daxiang (2)
	Shadows of Sails	Yang Shiji

Juan	Exercise	Author(s)
14, cont.		
	(Shadows of Sails)	Ye Qiying
		Yi Kezhong
		Wu Linguang
		Xu Zhichao
	Shadow of a Pagoda	Zhao Jun
		Yi Kezhong
	Reading Du Fu's "Autumn Interests"	Zhou Wenwei
		Wu Miguang
		Xiukun
	Reading Xie Huilian's "Autumn Longings"	Zheng Qiaosong
15	Lingnan Litchi Songs	Tan Ying (60)
		Yang Shiji (3)
		Li Rumei (3)
		Liang Guozhen
		Wu Meixiu (4)
		Huang Guangzong (3)
		Li Guoguang (2)
		Xie Guangfu
		Zhang Zongzhang
		Xu Zhichao
		Zhao Jun (3)
		Li Fengxiu (3)
		Liang Mei (10)
		Huang Qiaosong (2)
		Li Yu
		Yan Sizong (2)
		Li Xie
		Wu Jiashu
		Li Rufu (2)
		Li Zhongkai
		Zhang Qihan (2)
		Cui Bi (2)
		Lin Botong (2)
		Wu Yingkui (3)
		Luo Rizhang
		Xiong Jingxing (2)
		Huang Weiqing (3)
		Cui Shuliang (6)
		Ruan Fu (4)
16	Commemoration of the Establishment of Yuexiu Hill's Xuehaitang	Zhao Jun

APPENDIX B: *XUEHAITANG JI* TABLE OF CONTENTS 313

Juan	Exercise	Author(s)
	Stele Commemorating the Establishment of Yuexiu Hill's Xuehaitang	Wu Yue Tan Ying
	List of Names and Commemoration of the Establishment of Yuexiu's Xuehaitang	Fan Feng
	Inscription on Yuexiu Hill's Newly Established Xuehaitang, with Preface	Fan Feng
	Preface to Poems on the Newly Established Yuexiu Hill Xuehaitang	Ju Huang Xie Niangong
	Commemoration of the Establishment of Yuexiu Hill's Xuehaitang	Cui Bi
	Script for a Rafter in the Newly Established Xuehaitang on Yuexiu Hill	Tan Ying
	Commemoration of Planting Plums at the Xuehaitang	Wu Lanxiu
	Poems on the Newly Established Xuehaitang	Xu Rong (6) Zheng Fen (4)

REFERENCE MATTER

NOTES

INTRODUCTION

1. To be more specific, an examinee in a neighboring cell from Shanxi province (*lin hao Shanyou xiaolian* 鄰號山右孝廉) asked Liang Xuyong about the poetry question (*shiti* 詩題), which was on the theme of *tongsheng maoyu* 桐生茂豫 (Anne Birrell translates this line as "Makes all living things strengthen and be glad"). Liang responded that this four-character phrase could be found in the *Han shu* Treatise on Suburban Sacrifices, or seasonal sacrifices at the bounds (*jiaosi zhi* 郊祀志). Relying on computer databases rather than on memory, we can see that this in fact comes from the nineteen hymns composed for the Suburban Sacrifices by the Bureau of Music and included in the Treatise on Rites and Music (*liyue zhi* 禮樂志), rather than from the Treatise on Suburban Sacrifices. Since students were assigned to examination cells and alleys according to province, it is unclear precisely when during the examinations an exchange between Liang Xuyong and examinees from different provinces might have taken place. See *Han shu*, pp. 1045, 1052, 1055; Anne Birrell, *Popular Songs and Ballads of Han China*, pp. 33–38; Benjamin A. Elman, *A Cultural History of Civil Examinations in Late Imperial China*, pp. 185, 553–54; Michael Loewe, *Crisis and Conflict in Han China, 104 BC to AD 9*, pp. 197–99; Angela Zito, *Of Body & Brush: Grand Sacrifice as Text/Performance in Eighteenth-Century China*, p. 43.

2. Tan Zongjun, *Licun suibi*, 13a–b. Tan gives an approximate idea of Liang Xuyong's age by noting that he was already beyond the age of 40 *sui* (*nian guo buhuo* 年過不惑, alluding to the Confucian *Analects*) and that Liang was 30 years older than Tan's father, Tan Ying (1800–1871). Since Tan Ying was born in 1800, Liang must have been born approximately in

1770. This would make him slightly above the average age of successful *jinshi*. See Elman, *A Cultural History of Civil Examinations in Late Imperial China*, pp. 290, 705–6.

3. Gui Wencan, *Jingxue bocai lu*, 4.1b. In his book, Gui includes a brief biography of Liang Xuyong but does not mention the incident at the 1817 examination. Gui Wencan, *Jingxue bocai lu*, 8.8b–9a.

4. Chinese historians of education and academies during the Qing see the Xuehaitang as representative of a new style of academy, emphasizing rigorous training in the Classics, Histories, and literature and going beyond an exclusive focus on preparing students for civil service examinations. See, for example, Chen Dongyuan, "Qingdai shuyuan fengqi zhi bianqian," p. 17; Chen Dongyuan, *Zhongguo jiaoyu shi*, pp. 454–55; Sheng Langxi, *Zhongguo shuyuan zhidu*, pp. 157–59; Xie Guozhen, *Jindai shuyuan xuexiao zhidu bianqian kao*, p. 2; and Zhang Zhengfan, *Zhongguo shuyuan zhidu kaolue*, p. 37. More recently, Li Xubai has incorporated this celebratory tone in his study of "unadorned learning" (evidential research) in Guangdong. See his *Qingdai Guangdong puxue yanjiu*, pp. 1, 9. Among Western historians, Benjamin Elman has characterized the Xuehaitang as a center both of "New Text" Confucianism and Han-Song syncretism. See his "The Hsueh-hai t'ang and the Rise of New Text Scholarship in Canton," and *From Philosophy to Philology: Intellectual and Social Aspects of Change in Late Imperial China*, p. 246.

5. On the concept of geographical and functional arenas in explaining local elites in China, see Joseph W. Esherick and Mary Backus Rankin, eds., *Chinese Local Elites and Patterns of Dominance*, pp. 10–11.

6. As Tobie Meyer-Fong has recently pointed out, Yangzhou, located north of the Yangzi River, only began to be recast as a Jiangnan (literally, "south of the river") city in the seventeenth century. Meyer-Fong, *Building Culture in Early Qing Yangzhou*, pp. 26–28. Meyer-Fong's discussion of the shifting relationship between Yangzhou and Jiangnan problematizes the notion of "Jiangnan" as a regional unit. From the perspective of nineteenth-century Cantonese literati, dwelling in a city too far removed ever to be considered a part of Jiangnan, the notion of Jiangnan itself is not called into question. As we shall see in Chapter 6, however, some Cantonese literati were deeply concerned with the question of the position of Lingnan vis-à-vis Jiangnan in the cultural hierarchy of places.

7. Peter K. Bol, "Neo-Confucianism and Local Society, Twelfth to Sixteenth Century: A Case Study," p. 247.

8. Elman, *From Philosophy to Philology*, pp. 3, 27; R. Kent Guy, *The Emperor's Four Treasuries: Scholars and the State in the Late Ch'ien-lung Era*, p. 155. More recent scholarship has added to our understanding of the evi-

dential research movement by emphasizing the purist and ritualist aspects of this new discourse. See Kai-wing Chow, *The Rise of Confucian Ritualism in Late Imperial China*; Zhang Shouan, *Yi li dai li: Ling Tingkan yu Qing zhongye ruxue sixiang zhi zhuanbian*; Zito, *Of Body & Brush*.

9. Elman, *A Cultural History of Civil Examinations in Late Imperial China*, pp. 440–43.

10. Meyer-Fong, *Building Culture in Early Qing Yangzhou*, pp. 118–19.

11. Elman, *From Philosophy to Philology*, pp. 189–90.

12. David R. Knechtges, *Wen xuan, or, Selections of Refined Literature*, pp. 58–63; Ma Jigao, *Qingdai xueshu sixiang de bianqian yu wenxue*, pp. 99–110.

13. Though it is not a central focus of the present study, this set of practices also included calligraphy, with *kaozheng* scholars exhibiting a fondness for the seal and clerical scripts. See Bai Qianshan, *Fu Shan's World: The Transformation of Chinese Calligraphy in the Seventeenth Century*, pp. 167, 258–60; Elman, *From Philosophy to Philology*, pp. 191–97.

14. Benjamin A. Elman, "Ch'ing Dynasty 'Schools' of Scholarship," pp. 7–22; Steven B. Miles, "The New Face of *Kaozheng*: The *Huang Qing jingjie xubian* and Classical Studies After 1820," pp. 175–92.

15. Guy, *The Emperor's Four Treasuries*, pp. 155–56.

16. Philip A. Kuhn and Susan Mann Jones, "Dynastic Decline and the Rise of Rebellion," p. 159.

17. As Benjamin Elman notes, the scholarly traditions that emerged in Guangdong, Hunan, and other regions in the nineteenth century "were in many ways tributaries of or reactions against the dominant scholarly trends that developed in Kiangnan (Jiangnan) urban centers." Elman, *From Philosophy to Philology*, p. 12.

18. "Xuehaitang scholars" is an etic term that I use to describe an emic category. As we shall see in Chapter 3, by 1830 a group of urban Cantonese literati referred to themselves as "our like-minded associates at the Xuehaitang" or "the various gentlemen of the Xuehaitang." Whereas many Cantonese literati at one time or another sat for Xuehaitang examinations, a smaller set of some 30 to 40 men were more closely linked to the academy at any given time. I include in this category important patrons, academy co-directors, authors whose writings are prominently featured in the four editions of collected Xuehaitang examination essays and poems, and literati who identify themselves with the academy in their writings or who are identified with the academy in their biographies. Although most Xuehaitang scholars did not take as strong of an oppositional stance as Neo-Confucians in the Song and therefore lacked some of their cohesion, I would argue that the core group of Xuehaitang scholars would meet Hoyt

Tillman's definition of a "fellowship" in that they "had a network of social relations and a sense of community with a shared tradition that distinguished them from other Confucians." Hoyt Cleveland Tillman, *Confucian Discourse and Chu Hsi's Ascendancy*, p. 3.

19. The studies that I have relied on most heavily include James L. Watson, "Chinese Kinship Reconsidered: Anthropological Perspectives on Historical Research"; Rubie S. Watson, *Inequality Among Brothers: Class and Kinship in South China*; David Faure, *The Structure of Chinese Rural Society: Lineage and Village in the Eastern New Territories, Hong Kong* (all based on research conducted in the New Territories), and David Faure, "What Made Foshan a Town? The Evolution of Rural-Urban Identities in Ming-Qing China"; Helen F. Siu, *Agents and Victims in South China: Accomplices in Rural Revolution*; Liu Zhiwei, "Lineage of the Sands: The Case of Shawan"; Katayama Tsuyoshi, "Shindai Kantonshō Shukō deruta no tokōsei ni tsuite"; and Janice Stockard, *Daughters of the Canton Delta: Marriage Patterns and Economic Strategies in South China* (addressing areas in Nanhai, Xinhui, Panyu, and Shunde counties).

20. One important exception to this is Baker's study of clan halls in Guangzhou. Hugh D. R. Baker, "Extended Kinship in the Traditional City," pp. 499–518. On Guangzhou during the last decade of the Qing and the early Republican era, see Edward J. M. Rhoads, "Merchant Associations in Canton, 1895–1911"; and Michael Tsin, *Nation, Governance, and Modernity in China: Canton, 1900–1927*. Foshan, the second largest city in the delta, has been the subject of two recent studies in English: Faure, "What Made Foshan a Town?"; and Mary Backus Rankin, "Managed by the People: Officials, Gentry, and the Foshan Charitable Granary, 1795–1845."

21. Liang Xuyong was a native of Yanbu 鹽步 township, whereas Gui was the grandson of a Zhejiang native who had come to Guangzhou only in the late eighteenth century. *Nanhai xianzhi*, 1872 edition, 13.38b; Gui Hong, *Jianzhai shichao*, biography, 1a–b.

22. On urban sojourners in other cities, see William T. Rowe, *Hankow: Commerce and Society in a Chinese City*; and Antonia Finnane, *Speaking of Yangzhou: A Chinese City, 1550–1850*.

23. Recent studies of urban institutions include Rowe, *Hankow* (on *huiguan* [native-place associations] in nineteenth-century Hankou), and Richard Belsky, "The Urban Ecology of Late Imperial Beijing Reconsidered: The Transformation of Social Space in China's Late Imperial Capital City" (on *huiguan* in Beijing); Timothy Brook, *Praying for Power: Buddhism and the Formation of Gentry Society in Late-Ming China*, and Susan Naquin, *Peking: Temples and City Life, 1400–1900* (both on monasteries and temples

in the Ming and Qing); Craig Clunas, *Fruitful Sites: Garden Culture in Ming Dynasty China* (on Suzhou gardens during the Ming); Mark C. Elliott, *The Manchu Way: The Eight Banners and Ethnic Identity in Late Imperial China* (on banner garrisons during the Qing); and Meyer-Fong, *Building Culture in Early Qing Yangzhou* (on a variety of sites in seventeenth-century Yangzhou). Whereas these studies are largely focused on central and northern China, Mary Backus Rankin, "Managed by the People," examines the formation and operation of a granary by the local elite of Foshan.

24. I am here drawing on Michel de Certeau's distinction between place and space. See his *Practice of Everyday Life*, pp. 117–18.

25. The differences between the Xuehaitang and other Cantonese academies, which will receive fuller treatment in Chapters 2 and 3, as well as the unique name that Ruan Yuan self-consciously gave to his new academy, leave one with the impression that the Xuehaitang should perhaps not even be considered an academy (*shuyuan*). Nevertheless, the Xuehaitang is invariably categorized as an academy in local gazetteers. Moreover, though much of the literature celebrating the Xuehaitang and introduced in Chapter 3 stresses the differences between the Xuehaitang and "department and prefectural academies," it just as often describes the Xuehaitang as an exemplary "academy" (*shuyuan*). The passage in Gui Wencan's *Jingxue bocai lu* referred to at the outset of this chapter is one example. Therefore, I will refer to the Xuehaitang as an academy throughout the present work.

26. In analyzing rural society in North China in the late Qing and early Republican periods, Prasenjit Duara has employed the concept of a "cultural nexus," which he describes as being "composed of hierarchical organizations and networks of informal relations that constantly intersected and interacted with one another." Adopting this form of analysis, one could say that the Xuehaitang was situated in a nexus of interrelated hierarchical institutions and informal relationships. Prasenjit Duara, *Culture, Power, and the State: Rural North China, 1900–1942*, p. 5.

27. As employed in the present work, the term "literati" may be conceived of as a subset of the larger category of the "cultural elite." Drawing on Benjamin Elman's notion of "classical literacy," Philip Kuhn defines the cultural elite as those who were "trained to read, explicate, and indeed memorize the canonical texts used in the civil-service examination system." Philip A. Kuhn, *Origins of the Modern Chinese State*, pp. 14–15; Elman, *A Cultural History of Civil Examinations in Late Imperial China*, pp. xxx–xxxi.

28. Elman, *From Philosophy to Philology*, pp. 92–94. Antonia Finnane has recently questioned the notion of the "blurring" of the social categories

of merchant (*shang* 商) and scholar-official, or gentry (*shen* 紳), in eighteenth-century Yangzhou. Finnane, *Speaking of Yangzhou*, pp. 253-64.

29. Hilary J. Beattie, *Land and Lineage in China: A Study of T'ung-ch'eng County, Anhwei, in the Ming and Ch'ing Dynasties*, pp. 88, 129-30; Esherick and Rankin, *Chinese Local Elites and Patterns of Dominance*, p. 306.

30. Angela Zito has argued that evidential research on obscure ancient ritual practice effectively raised the bar for attaining literati status. Zito, *Of Body and Brush*, pp. 70-76.

31. Pierre Bourdieu, *The Logic of Practice*, pp. 112-21, 124-25. Elman suggests that the term "cultural resources" is more applicable to late imperial China than Bourdieu's "cultural capital" because the latter assumes the existence of economic capitalism. See his *Classicism, Politics, and Kinship: The Ch'ang-chou School of New Text Confucianism in Late Imperial China*, p. xix.

32. Michael Szonyi takes this approach in his analysis of genealogies produced in Fujian during the Ming and Qing dynasties. See his *Practicing Kinship: Lineage and Descent in Late Imperial China*, p. 27.

33. See, for example, chapter 13 of Qian Mu, *Zhongguo jin sanbainian xueshushi*; Hamaguchi Fujio, *Shindai kōkyogaku no shisōshi*, pp. 544-47; and Elman, "The Hsueh-hai t'ang and the Rise of New Text Scholarship in Canton," *passim*.

34. Guy, *The Emperor's Four Treasuries*, pp. 154-56.

35. On Han-Song syncretism in Beijing and Jiangnan during the mid- and late nineteenth century, see Han-yin Chan Shen, "Tseng Kuo-fan in Peking, 1840-1852: His Ideas on Statecraft and Reform," pp. 63-64; and Barry Keenan, *Imperial China's Last Classical Academies: Social Change in the Lower Yangzi, 1864-1911*, pp. 84-86. Chen Li has not received much attention in Western scholarship, but Chinese scholars ranging from Qian Mu to Hu Chusheng have devoted articles or chapters to him; yet they tend to portray him as a solitary voice of criticism against the excesses of Han Learning and in favor of Han-Song syncretism in Guangzhou. Qian Mu, *Zhongguo jin sanbainian xueshu shi*, pp. 601-2; Hu Chusheng, *Qingdai xueshu shi yanjiu*, p. 273. Though Elman does not focus on Chen Li, he suggests that Han-Song syncretism was a widespread discourse among Xuehaitang scholars. See Elman, *From Philosophy to Philology*, p. 246.

36. Arthur W. Hummel, *Eminent Chinese of the Ch'ing Period, 1644-1912*, pp. 399-400.

37. Bol, "Neo-Confucianism and Local Society," p. 281. See also Peter K. Bol, "The 'Localist Turn' and 'Local Identity' in Later Imperial China," pp. 9-12.

38. Bryna Goodman, *Native Place, City, and Nation: Regional Networks and Identities in Shanghai, 1853-1937*, p. 46. Also focusing on late nineteenth- and early twentieth-century Shanghai, Emily Honig shows that the native-place identity of "Subei people" emerged as a label that the local elite applied to despised in-migrating laborers from northern Jiangsu and Shandong. Honig, *Creating Chinese Ethnicity: Subei People in Shanghai, 1850-1980*, pp. 4, 36; Honig, "Native Place and the Making of Chinese Ethnicity," p. 151.

39. Prasenjit Duara, *Sovereignty and Authenticity: Manchukuo and the East Asian Modern*, p. 235.

40. In his study of elites in Zhejiang during the late Qing and early Republican periods, Keith Schoppa observes that established lineages often led natives' criticisms of in-migrating elites in "inner cores" of the province. R. Keith Schoppa, *Chinese Elites and Political Change: Zhejiang Province in the Early Twentieth Century*, pp. 89-90.

41. May-bo Ching, "Literary, Ethnic or Territorial? Definitions of Guangdong Culture in the Late Qing and the Early Republic," p. 52.

42. This is the first full-length study of the Xuehaitang in any language; I do not, however, pretend to offer a comprehensive narrative history of the academy. Due to limitations of space and my own capabilities, I have chosen not to address some aspects of cultural production by Xuehaitang scholars—such as mathematics or calligraphy and painting—that deserve specialized studies. Nor have I explored the role of the Xuehaitang as a conduit for cultural interactions between Guangzhou and Southeast Asia, Japan, and Korea, or Europe and America. Nevertheless, based on the types of texts produced by Xuehaitang scholars, I do feel that the narrative I have constructed addresses the issues that were most salient to the authors.

CHAPTER I

1. The phrase "singing 'Water Melody'" (歌水調) in this line evokes images of the city of Yangzhou. The Tang poet Du Mu 杜牧 (803-52) begins one of his three poems on "Yangzhou" with a reference to the Sui Emperor Yangdi's (r. 605-18) activities in Jiangdu 江都 (Yangzhou). In the second couplet, Du asks who is singing the water melody (誰家唱水調) and explains in a note that the Sui emperor composed this melody upon the completion of a part of what would later become the Grand Canal. Du Mu, *Du Mu shixuan*, pp. 41-42. Also see Guo Maoqian, *Yuefu shiji*, pp. 1114-15. This Yangzhou reference conceivably also points to the "Yangzhou group" of courtesans on the Pearl River. *Guangzhou chengfang zhi*, p. 636.

2. *Yangcheng zhuzhi ci*, 1.18a. "Guangzhou" in the song's title is written as "City of Rams," another name for Guangzhou. What I have rendered here as "outsiders" in the Chinese is literally "people from outside the river" (外江人). This was a common reference in Qing-era Cantonese for natives of the Jiangnan region and points further north.

3. *Jiujiang Rulin xiang zhi*, 21.18b.

4. On the role of sojourning salt merchants in the cultural life of various Qing cities, see Ho Ping-ti, "The Salt Merchants of Yang-chou: A Study of Commercial Capitalism in Eighteenth-Century China"; William T. Rowe, *Hankow*; Man Bun Kwan, *The Salt Merchants of Tianjin: State-Making and Civil Society in Late Imperial China*; and Finnane, *Speaking of Yangzhou*. Harriet Zurndorfer examines Huizhou prefecture, which exported many of the sojourning salt merchants. Harriet T. Zurndorfer, *Change and Continuity in Chinese Local History: The Development of Hui-chou Prefecture, 800 to 1800*.

5. The emergence of Cantonese literati of Fujianese origin is best exemplified by Zhuang Yougong 莊有恭 (1713–67). The son of a Fujian native who had relocated to Guangzhou, Zhuang was enrolled as a local resident and eventually won top honors in the 1739 metropolitan examination, the first Guangdong "native" to receive this honor during the Qing. Zhuang Yougong's family claimed a distant agnatic relationship with the Zhuang lineage of Changzhou in Jiangsu. *Panyu xian zhi*, 44.9b; Elman, *Classicism, Politics, and Kinship*, p. 51.

6. The biographical section of the 1871 Panyu county gazetteer reveals that literati from older delta-based families were prominent in the sixteenth and seventeenth centuries, were joined by a few families of Fujianese origin in the eighteenth century, and began to be displaced by extraprovincials, especially northern Zhejiangese, in the nineteenth century. The prominence of migrants from Zhejiang is even more marked in the 1931 edition. *Panyu xian zhi*, juan 43–46; *Panyu xian xu zhi*, especially juan 19–21.

7. Though the "New City" technically designated only the neighborhoods located within the southern extension of the city walls, in common usage this term usually included the stretch of land lying between the southern wall of the New City and the shore of the Pearl River.

8. The Qing-era Huaai Street corresponds to sections four through six of present-day Zhongshan Road.

9. Wang Shizhen, *Guangzhou youlan xiao zhi*, 2a–3a.

10. Like Ruan Yuan a century later, Hui Shiqi imagined himself a modern-day Wen Weng 文翁, who during the Han dynasty had introduced Confucian learning to civilize the region corresponding to Sichuan. Qian Daxin, *Qianyantang wenji*, 38.23b–24a; *Han shu*, pp. 3625–26.

11. On Weng Fanggang, see Hummel, *Eminent Chinese*, pp. 856–57.

12. *Guangzhou chengfang zhi*, p. 304; Elliott, *The Manchu Way*, pp. 108–10, 126; John Henry Gray, *Walks in the City of Canton*, p. 30.

13. Mark Elliott stresses the extent to which banner garrisons altered the landscapes of the cities in which they were located. See Elliott, *The Manchu Way*, p. 89.

14. B. C. Henry, *Ling-nam, or Interior Views of Southern China: Including Explorations in the Hitherto Untraversed Island of Hainan*, p. 46.

15. *Guangdong shengli xinzuan*, 8.8a.

16. *Zhu Yue baqi zhi*, 24.10a.

17. Ibid., 24.6b.

18. The critic, Li Kefan 李可蕃 (1802 *jinshi*), was a native of the delta town of Foshan and a censor in the Qing bureaucracy. *Qing shilu Guangdong shiliao*, 3: 417.

19. Elliott, *The Manchu Way*, pp. 336, 339.

20. What might be called the "Cantonization" of Chinese bannermen in the Guangzhou garrison seems to be an exception to the general trend, identified by Mark Elliott, of Chinese bannermen "becoming Manchu." This might be attributed both to Guangzhou's remote location and to the lack of a wall separating the Banner Quarter from the rest of the population. Elliott, *The Manchu Way*, pp. 340–43.

21. *Zhu Yue baqi zhi*, 12.2a.

22. In his recent study of subcounty officials in Guangdong, Robert Antony points out that most of these "assistant and miscellaneous" (*zuoza* 佐雜) officials were ranked and received salaries. In the present study, I use James Cole's term "subofficials," rather than Antony's "subcounty officials," in order to include subordinate officials at all levels of administration within Guangdong province. Robert J. Antony, "Subcounty Officials, the State, and Local Communities in Guangdong Province, 1644–1860," pp. 30–31; James H. Cole, *Shaohsing: Competition and Cooperation in Nineteenth-Century China*, pp. 86–105.

23. Cole, *Shaohsing*, pp. 75, 118.

24. Guiji ("Kuei-chi," according to Wade-Giles romanization) is sometimes pronounced and written "Kuaiji." Some sources hint at a burgeoning northern Zhejiang presence in Guangzhou during the early Qing. For example, in poems composed between 1660 and 1676, the renowned Cantonese poet Chen Gongyin 陳恭尹 (1631–1700) mentions two brothers from Shanyin, Zhang Ti 張梯 and Zhang Shan 張杉, who sojourned in Guangzhou while visiting a nephew serving as salt inspector. Zhang Shan later died in Guangzhou. Chen Jinghong, *Dulutang shijian*, Zengjiang houji, pp. 71–72.

25. *Panyu xian zhi*, 33.23a; *Guangzhou chengfang zhi*, p. 121; Chen Li, *Dongshu ji*, 5.11a–12a.

26. The Xu genealogy employs the language of Confucian scholarly discourse to describe this incident. Thus, the *muyou* in Guangdong are portrayed as emphasizing transmissions of teachers (*shicheng*) and as maintaining the biases of scholarly cliques (*menhu zhi jian* 門戶之見). *Zhe Hang qian Yue Gaoyang Xushi jiapu*, preface 3a, biographies 11b.

27. Xiangshan county has been known as Zhongshan county since 1924.

28. *Zhe Hang qian Yue Gaoyang Xushi jiapu*, preface 3a, biographies 9a–19b; *Gaoyang Xushi jiapu*, 1.15a–b.

29. *Zhe Hang qian Yue Gaoyang Xushi jiapu*, biographies 13b, 19b.

30. Some members of the Xu family who stayed in Hangzhou were listed as residents of Qiantang, the county that shared jurisdiction of urban Hangzhou with Renhe. *Hangzhou fu zhi*, 137.6a–b.

31. *Zhe Hang qian Yue Gaoyang Xushi jiapu*, biographies 13b, 19b, postscript 4b; *Gaoyang Xushi jiapu*, preface 6a–7a, tables 1b–2a, 1.15b, 17a–b, 2.2a, 4a–7a; *Shunde xian zhi*, 1853 edition, 9.10a; *Xiangshan xian zhi*, 1827 edition, 3.72b; *Yuexiu shuyuan zhi*, 9.25b; Huang Zhi, *Yue xiaoji*, 3b. Xu Naiji was also associated with Ruan Yuan's Hangzhou academy, the Gujing jingshe, although none of his writings were included in the 1801 collection of the academy's papers. *Gujing jingshe wenji*, stele record and list of names, 6a.

32. There in fact seems to have been some overlap among families from northern Zhejiang that specialized in administrative service and those that focused on commerce. As Bradly Reed asserts in his study of clerks in Sichuan's Ba county, because similar sets of skills were required for commercial tasks and for service in the county salt office, it made sense for families to combine these two career strategies. Bradly W. Reed, *Talons and Teeth: County Clerks and Runners in the Qing Dynasty*, p. 83.

33. Ho Ping-ti points out that Yangzhou's salt merchants included many who had migrated from Shanxi and Shaanxi, and others from Huizhou, Anhui. Ho, "The Salt Merchants of Yang-chou," pp. 143–44. For a fuller treatment of this, see Finnane, *Speaking of Yangzhou*, pp. 49–62.

34. William C. Hunter, *Bits of Old China*, p. 21.

35. *Liang-Guang yanfa zhi*, 1836 edition, 33.20a–21a. An eighteenth-century source, *Yuetai zhengya lu*, provides some details about two early merchant families from Shanyin. Liu Huan 劉煥 was a Shanyin native who sojourned in Guangzhou and amassed a large library collection. His son, Liu Bangxian 劉邦憲, won a *juren* degree as a merchant-registered Guangzhou prefectural student in 1752. Another Shanyin native, Hu Zongyu

胡宗裕, was a merchant-registered student in Guangzhou who eventually became a Senior Licentiate through purchase. His son, Hu Guolin 胡國林, also earned a *juren* degree in 1752, but as a student registered in Heshan county. Unfortunately, the source does not explain how this son of a Shanyin sojourner managed to register as a student in Heshan. Hu Guolin appears as Guocai 國材 in the 1822 Guangdong provincial gazetteer, but in the 1833 Zhaoqing prefectural gazetteer as "Guolin, a Nanhai native and Heshan student." The *Yuetai zhengya lu* also has his name as Guolin. Luo Yuanhuan, *Yuetai zhengya lu*, 15b, 25b; *Guangdong tongzhi*, 79.37a, 80.16b, 17a; *Zhaoqing fu zhi*, 15.12a.

36. This Xu 徐 family should not be confused with the Xu 許 family discussed above, which specialized in the *muyou* profession.

37. *Panyu xian zhi*, 45.13b. As a further example, Ni Shihua's family hailed from Shangyu county in Shaoxing; he later became a Panyu resident and eventually earned a *jinshi* degree. His two uncles had both been in the salt trade. *Panyu xian zhi*, 46.2a.

38. Zhang Weiping, *Yitan lu*, *xia*.30a.

39. *Guangzhou chengfang zhi*, p. 42.

40. The fact that the chapel's establishment by Shaoxing merchants is described in a salt gabelle gazetteer strongly suggests that they were salt merchants. *Liang-Guang yanfa zhi*, 1884 edition, 53.48a; Gray, *Walks in the City of Canton*, pp. 545–46.

41. *Shenlou zhi*, pp. 12, 66.

42. The large number of migrants from Zhejiang who migrated to Guangzhou was not lost on the late eighteenth-century Panyu literatus Lü Jian: "Many people from Wu [southern Jiangsu] and Gui [northern Zhejiang] travel to Linghai [Guangdong]. In general, calculating over the past century, only four or five out of ten of those who come as administrators (*huan* 宦) are able to return, and six or seven of those who come as merchants (*gu* 賈) can return. And who knows how many are able to return of those who travel here, rely on others for a living, and become unsettled?" See Lü Jian, "Preface to Mr. Chen Hongqiao's Family Genealogy," in *Chenshi jiacheng juanmo*.

43. Wu and his son, Wu Chongyao (1810–63), were known to Westerners in Guangzhou as "Howqua." *Anhai Wushi ru Yue zupu*, preface, 3a, tables; Sucheta Mazumdar, *Sugar and Society in China: Peasants, Technology, and the World Market*, p. 117; Wolfram Eberhard, *Social Mobility in Traditional China*, pp. 82–84. Wu Guoying appears in Eberhard's text as "Wu Kuo-jung."

44. Wu Rongguang's surname, Wu 吳, should not be confused with the identically romanized surname of the Wu 伍 merchant family. Though an

official, Wu Rongguang was from a powerful merchant family in Foshan. Hummel, *Eminent Chinese*, p. 872.

45. *Anhai Wushi ru Yue zupu*, preface, 3b, "Commemoration of Myriad Pines Garden."

46. Pan Zhencheng is known in Western sources by his trading name, Puankhequa I. Weng Eang Cheong, *The Hong Merchants of Canton: Chinese Merchants in Sino-Western Trade*, pp. 159–60.

47. *Heyang shixi*, unpaginated.

48. Succeeding his father, Pan Youdu appears in Western sources as Puankhequa II.

49. *Heyang shixi*, unpaginated.

50. Like the maritime merchant Wu family, the Pan also cultivated marriage alliances with Wu Rongguang in Foshan. Pan Zhengchang 潘正常 (1787–1812) married Wu Rongguang's sister. Wu Rongguang, *Shiyun shanren wenji*, 3.52b.

51. The other maritime firms operated by Fujianese were the Cai Yifeng 蔡義豐 firm and the Ye Yicheng 葉義成 firm. Liang Jiabin, *Guangdong shisanhang kao*, pp. 216–17, 243–44, 267; Zhang Weiping, *Yitan lu*, xia.43b.

52. Mazumdar, *Sugar and Society in China*, p. 301.

53. Cheong, *The Hong Merchants of Canton*, p. 162.

54. *Guangzhou chengfang zhi*, p. 699.

55. Yun Jing, *Dayun shanfang wengao*, 4.13a–14a; *Nanhai xian zhi*, 1910 edition, 20.6b; Wu Rongguang, *Shiyun shanren wenji*, 4.16b.

56. Sow-theng Leong, *Migration and Ethnicity in Chinese History: Hakkas, Pengmin, and Their Neighbors*, p. 23.

57. As conceived by G. William Skinner, the Southeast Coast macroregion consists of southern Zhejiang, Fujian, and northeastern Guangdong, including Jiaying and the port city of Chaozhou. The neighboring Lingnan macroregion, in Skinner's definition, is made up of central and western Guangdong, along with most of neighboring Guangxi province. In other words, the latter macroregion is largely composed of the tributaries of the East, North, and West rivers, which converge on the Pearl River delta. G. William Skinner, "Regional Urbanization in Nineteenth-Century China," in Skinner, ed., *The City in Late Imperial China*, pp. 212, 214. In his recent study of the economic and environmental history of the region, Robert Marks further lends weight to the Skinnerian separation of Jiaying from the Pearl River delta by demonstrating that the Hakka homeland centered in Jiaying was not integrated into the Lingnan market in late imperial times. According to Marks, whereas rice was imported into the Pearl River delta from Guangxi along the West River, in easternmost Guangdong rice

was transported from Chaozhou to Jiaying. In fact, the price of rice in Chaozhou and Jiaying was generally higher than in the delta. Robert B. Marks, *Tigers, Rice, Silk, and Silt: Environment and Economy in Late Imperial South China*, pp. 259, 262.

58. Weng Xincun, "Ru Yue jicheng," 10/20 and 10/21/DG5. In the citations, diary dates are given in lunar calendar months and days, and reign eras—"DG" stands for Daoguang. Weng did note a great amount of merchandise being transported by male and female porters across the mountain path connecting the Han and East river systems.

59. Leong, *Migration and Ethnicity in Chinese History*, pp. 57, 60, 62, 70; Mazumdar, *Sugar and Society in China*, p. 213.

60. Leong, *Migration and Ethnicity in Chinese History*, p. 76.

61. Guangzhou's academies may also have drawn Jiaying literati to the provincial city. Though a few academies were established in Jiaying during the eighteenth century, along with two in the 1870s, they do not seem to have commanded a great deal of prestige. Liu Boji, *Guangdong shuyuan zhidu*, pp. 50, 67; Ōkubo Eiko, *Min-Shin jidai shoin no kenkyū*, p. 76. Tileman Grimm stresses the urbanization of Guangdong's academies during the Qing, with Guangzhou academies maintaining a dominant presence. See Grimm, "Academies and Urban Systems in Kwangtung," pp. 496–97.

62. Xie Lansheng, *Xingxingzhai wengao*, 31a.

63. The Qiu ancestors had migrated to Jiaying from Tingzhou prefecture in Fujian, also part of the Hakka homeland. *Panyu xian zhi*, 45.6a.

64. Ibid.; *Yuexiu shuyuan zhi*, 16.1a; *Guangzhoushi Qiushizongci tekan*, pp. 11–13.

65. Meizhou 梅州 was another term for Jiaying. Chen Tan, *Kuangzhai shiyou ji*, juan 66.

66. In-migrants who had not yet settled in Guangzhou might be termed "careerists." Rowe, *Hankow*, pp. 220–21.

67. Rowe, *Hankow*, p. 217.

68. Western contemporaries of Liang Jinguo referred to him as Kinqua I. Liang Jiabin, *Panyu Huangpu Liangshi wushi zhuanlue*, p. 76.

69. Lu Guanheng was known to Westerners as Mowqua I. Liang Jiabin, *Guangdong shisanhang kao*, pp. 238–40.

70. Heshan was a relatively new county, created in 1732 by combining a portion of Xinhui and a neighboring county. Yi Rongzhi's ancestors had settled in the section of Xinhui out of which Heshan was later formed. Yi Rongzhi also went by the name Yi Yuanchang 易元昌. *Xinhui xian zhi*, 1840 edition, 2.4b; Liang Jiabin, *Guangdong shisanhang kao*, p. 336.

71. *Yi Xiulitang jiapu*, 17a–19b.

72. Rowe, *Hankow*, pp. 214, 243.

73. Rhoads, "Merchant Associations in Canton," p. 101.

74. Skinner, *The City in Late Imperial China*, p. 535.

75. *Guangzhou chengfang zhi*, p. 520; Hunter, *Bits of Old China*, p. 172; Gray, *Walks in the City of Canton*, p. 185.

76. Kwan, *The Salt Merchants of Tianjin*, pp. 10, 26. Like those in Guangzhou, several of the Tianjin salt merchants had Shaoxing roots or connections. See Kwan, *The Salt Merchants of Tianjin*, pp. 53, 80.

77. William T. Rowe, "Success Stories: Lineage and Elite Status in Hanyang County, Hubei, c. 1368-1949," pp. 67-68.

78. Finnane, *Speaking of Yangzhou*, p. 238.

79. Marks, *Tigers, Rice, Silk, and Silt*, pp. 76, 105.

80. Siu, *Agents and Victims in South China*, pp. 23-24.

81. I want to thank Sucheta Mazumdar for first drawing my attention to this.

82. Tan Dihua, *Qingdai Zhujiang sanjiaozhou de shatian*, p. 2.

83. Marks, *Tigers, Rice, Silk, and Silt*, p. 77. Though Marks and other scholars refer to the existence of the Mulberry Garden Enclosure from the Song, I have not found any reference to this name until the Qing, when a series of gazetteers entitled *Sangyuanwei zhi* were produced beginning in 1794. On this issue, see Katayama Tsuyoshi, "Shukō deruta Sōeni no kōzō to chisui soshiki," p. 147.

84. See Fig. 9.

85. A *qing* is equal to about fourteen acres. Tan Dihua, *Qingdai Zhujiang sanjiaozhou de shatian*, pp. 204, 230.

86. Henry, *Ling-nam*, p. 69.

87. Huang Peifang, *Yunquan suizha*, 1.14b.

88. Faure, "What Made Foshan a Town?," pp. 13-15; Marks, *Tigers, Rice, Silk, and Silt*, p. 192.

89. Rent derived from the sands supported many of the Long lineage halls. *Longshi jiapu*, 14.24b.

90. Janice Stockard, *Daughters of the Canton Delta: Marriage Patterns and Economic Strategies in South China, 1860-1930*, pp. 10-11, 102-3. Stockard notes that delayed transfer marriage was rare for informants from the immediate vicinity of Guangzhou. This may in part be explained by the large number of in-migrants and sojourners from other regions who settled in the city. See also Helen F. Siu, "Where Were the Women? Rethinking Marriage Resistance and Regional Culture in South China," pp. 35-36.

91. In using the term "lineage" here, I am following the definition proposed by James L. Watson, as modified by David Faure. Watson defines the lineage as "a corporate group which celebrates *ritual unity* based on *demonstrated descent* from a common ancestor" (italics added). Faure sug-

gests that for a set of agnatic kin to function as a corporate group "it was only necessary that common descent was *acknowledged. Demonstration* of common descent was not a prerequisite" (italics added). In his study of kinship practice in late imperial Fuzhou, Michael Szonyi uses the term to refer to "a self-professed patrilineal descent group," as the maintenance of corporate property was not an essential criterion for indigenous Chinese concepts of zong 宗 or zu 族. Though Szonyi's point is well taken, in this study I follow Watson's and Faure's definitions in order to highlight the corporate nature of lineages in Jiujiang and the Pearl River delta hinterland in contrast to urban-based descent groups in Guangzhou. See James L. Watson, "Chinese Kinship Reconsidered," pp. 589–622; David Faure, "The Lineage as a Cultural Invention: The Case of the Pearl River Delta," p. 22; and Szonyi, *Practicing Kinship*, p. 4.

92. Marks, *Tigers, Rice, Silk, and Silt*, pp. 183, 194.

93. Mazumdar, *Sugar and Society in China*, pp. 316–17.

94. Ibid., pp. 225, 230–31. The difficulty experienced by in-migrating elites in establishing themselves in the Pearl River delta hinterland should lead us to qualify, at least for older parts of the delta, William Rowe's assertion that "Chinese gentry-merchants by Qing times could easily buy into the rural elite." See Rowe, "Success Stories," p. 58. Nevertheless, Thomas Buoye shows that some customary rights restricting the sale of land were increasingly being curtailed from the eighteenth century, which would have facilitated urban elites' penetration of the rural land market. Buoye, "From Patrimony to Commodity: Changing Concepts of Land and Social Conflict in Guangdong Province During the Qianlong Reign (1736–1995)," p. 52.

95. The Luo and Long lineages in Daliang claimed descent from Zhujixiang ancestors who relocated to Daliang in the Southern Song dynasty. There was both a Northgate Luo and a Southgate Luo lineage in Daliang. Luo Dunyan, *Luo Wenke gong yiji*, chronological biography, 1a; *Shunde Beimen Luoshi zupu*, 5.1a; *Longshi zupu*, 1.40a; Tan Dihua, *Guangdong lishi wenti lunwen ji*, p. 313. Other foundation legends in delta lineage genealogies include those of the Deng of Dongguan, who asserted that one of their ancestors married a sister of a Song emperor, and the Cui of Shatou, who claimed to be related to the noted Cantonese native and Southern Song official Cui Yuzhi (1158–1239). Faure, "The Lineage as a Cultural Invention," pp. 9, 11–12.

96. The Long lineage of Daliang, for example, had an eleventh-century ancestor buried at Huangpu 黃圃 township, in Xiangshan county to the south of Shunde. Tan Dihua, *Qingdai Zhujiang sanjiaozhou de shatian*, p. 14.

97. *Shunde xian zhi*, 1929 edition, 17.3b, 6a, 18.4a, 11b.
98. *Guangzhou chengfang zhi*, p. 281; *Yangcheng Lujiang shuyuan quanpu*, ce 1:3a, 22a; Baker, "Extended Kinship in the Traditional City," pp. 512–17.
99. Mazumdar, *Sugar and Society in China*, p. 243.
100. *Guangzhou chengfang zhi*, pp. 235–36, 452–53; *Nanhai Luogefang Kongshi jiapu*, passim.
101. The Du residence was in the Huilong neighborhood 迴龍社 in the New City. *Chengnan Dushi jiapu*, Du You preface 1a–b.
102. *Chengnan Dushi jiapu*, ce 1: 16a–b.
103. Ibid., *ce* 1: 22a, 28a–31a, 55a–58a; *ce* 2: 23a; Henry, *Ling-nam*, p. 29.
104. These marriages were to daughters of Pan Zhengchen 潘正琛 (1786–1847), Pan Youke 潘有科 (1808–30), Wu Bingjun 伍秉鈞 (d. 1801), and Lu Guanheng. *Xiguan Yangshi zhipu*, *passim* (unpaginated).
105. Ibid.
106. Ibid.; Tan Zongjun, "Preface to the City-West Yang Genealogy," in *Yangshi jiapu*. Both the *Xiguan Yangshi zhipu* and the *Yangshi jiapu* describe the same family of Yang Dalin. The former work is undated but records events through 1878. The latter work includes Tan Zongjun's 1882 preface.
107. Rowe, "Success Stories," p. 68.
108. Siu, *Agents and Victims in South China*, p. 39.
109. Tan Dihua, *Qingdai Zhujiang sanjiaozhou de shatian*, p. 17.
110. Long Tinghuai, *Jingxuexuan wenji*, Zhu Changyi 朱昌頤 preface 3a–b.
111. Siu, *Agents and Victims in South China*, pp. 25, 39; Robert Y. Eng, "Institutional and Secondary Landlordism in the Pearl River Delta, 1600–1949," p. 5.
112. Siu, "Where Were the Women?" p. 52. For a detailed study of one lineage bordering on the sands, see Liu Zhiwei, "Lineage on the Sands."
113. Tan Dihua, *Qingdai Zhujiang sanjiaozhou de shatian*, p. 39.
114. *Panyu xian xu zhi*, 21.5a.

CHAPTER 2

EPIGRAPH: Liu Binhua, *Lingnan qunya*, second series, Xie Lansheng chapter, 16b.
1. Zhang Weiping, *Songxin shiji*, in *Zhang Nanshan quanji*, 2: 103–4. Zhang does not indicate the year in which this gathering occurred, but

judging from the placement of the poem in his chronologically arranged collection of poetry, it must have been either 1812 or 1813.

2. Xie Jingqing, *Xuji Hanyin fenyun*, and Yuan Rixing, *Xuanji Hanyin fenyun*, Xie Jingqing prefaces and Song Baochun postscript; *Panyu xian zhi*, 44.4b; Wen Runeng, *Yuedong shihai*, pp. 2018-19; *Yuexiu shuyuan zhi*, 15.48a-b; *Nanhai xian zhi*, 1835 edition, 39.37b-39a; Chen Li, *Dongshu ji*, 3.24a; Xian Yuqing, *Xian Yuqing wenji*, pp. 91-93. On the sojourning literatus who had introduced the book to Xie Jingqing, Song Baochun 宋葆淳, see Jiang Fan, *Hanxue shicheng ji*, p. 27. The art historian Yeewan Koon points out that Xie Jingqing was Li Jian's art dealer. Yeewan Koon, personal communication, October 16, 2003.

3. Xie Lansheng's Studio of Constant Awareness appears to have derived its name from a passage in Zhu Xi's *Conversations of Master Zhu, Arranged Topically. Zhuzi yulei*, 12.1b. Daniel Gardner translates this passage as follows: "To keep the mind constantly alert, then to regulate it with rules as well, is the way to nurture the mind both from within and without." Gardner, *Learning To Be a Sage*, p. 164.

4. These visits to Mashe coincided with the Double Ninth (*Chongyang* 重陽) festival on the ninth day of the ninth lunar month, when many Cantonese visited their ancestors' tombs. Xie Lansheng, *Changxingxingzhai riji*, 9/8 and 9/9/DG1, 9/7 and 9/8/DG2. (In the citations, diary dates are given in lunar calendar months and days, and reign eras—"JQ" stands for Jiaqing and "DG" for Daoguang. Intercalary [*run* 潤] months are indicated with an "r.") The mountain that Xie Lansheng and his sons visited on their trips to the countryside was Sunwubian 孫屋邊, located in the hills of Taozi 桃子 township just north of Mashe. See the maps in *Nanhai xian zhi*, 1872 edition, 1.28a, 2.6b.

5. Xie Lansheng, *Changxingxingzhai riji*, 9/8 and 9/10/DG3, 9/9 and 9/10/DG6. Wu Chongyao, *Chuting qijiu yishi, xuji*, 20.4b; *Yuexiu shuyuan zhi*, 15.48a-49a, 52a; *Guan Shudetang jiapu*, 15.48a, 18.12b-13a, 19.33b.

6. The Huata 花塔, or Flowery Pagoda, at Liurong Monastery was a major landmark in Guangzhou.

7. Henry, *Ling-nam*, p. 53; *Chinese Repository*, 2.6 (October 1833), p. 259; S. Wells Williams, *The Middle Kingdom*, p. 165; Hunter, *Bits of Old China*, pp. 176-77; Gray, *Walks in the City of Canton*, pp. 51, 58. Susan Mann notes the popularity of visits to Buddhist monasteries among women from elite families. Susan Mann, *Precious Records: Women in China's Long Eighteenth Century*, pp. 179-80, 187.

8. Most of the popular monasteries that Brook describes were further removed from urban centers than was Haichuang. See chap. 3 of Brook, *Praying for Power*, especially p. 114.

9. Pan Zhengwei, *Tingfanlou shuhua ji*, pp. 464-65.

10. Xie Lansheng, *Xingxingzhai wengao*, 19a; Xie Lansheng, *Changxingxingzhai riji*, 6/10/JQ24, 1/12/JQ25, 4/9/JQ25, 4/17/JQ25, 9/18/JQ25, 10/5/DG1, 12/7/DG5, 1/14/DG9.

11. Yun Jing, *Dayun shanfang wengao*, second collection, 3.34a-35a; Pan Feisheng, *Shuojiantang ji, Laojian wengao*, 86b. The "Six Gentlemen" (六君子) almost certainly refers to a painting attributed to the great Yuan-era painter, Ni Zan (1301-74). Dated 1345, Ni's painting depicts six tall and thin trees. Osvald Sirén, *Chinese Painting: Leading Masters and Principles*, 4: 80-81, and 6: pl. 94; James Cahill, *Hills Beyond a River: Chinese Painting of the Yüan Dynasty, 1279-1368*, p. 118. Although Yun Jing does not explain the allusion to this particular painting, Ni Zan was an extremely popular painter among nineteenth-century Cantonese literati. One Xuehaitang codirector in the late 1850s, Shen Shiliang (1823-60), compiled a chronological biography of Ni Zan. Shen, *Ni Gaoshi nianpu*.

12. Xie Lansheng, *Changxingxingzhai riji*, 5/4/JQ25, 5/5/JQ25, 5/5/DG4.

13. Ibid., 5/24/DG4, 5/2/DG5, 5/27/DG6. Ruan Yuan noted that Cantonese "litchi societies" held contests to see who could eat the most litchis in a single sitting, the losers being punished with drinks. Ruan Yuan, *Yanjingshi ji*, vol. 3, *Yanjingshi xuji*, pp. 195-96.

14. Xie Lansheng, *Changxingxingzhai riji*, 5/11/DG2, 5/14/DG5.

15. On a similar annual cycle of events for Beijing, see Naquin, *Peking*, pp. 272-80.

16. Dorothy Ko borrows the notion of a "floating world" from Japanese *ukiyoe* (prints of the floating world) of the Tokugawa period to describe the fluidity of boundaries in late-Ming Jiangnan. Ko, *Teachers of the Inner Chambers: Women and Culture in Seventeenth-Century China*, p. 30. This term is especially apt for nineteenth-century Guangzhou, as it was employed in a poem on the Pearl River by Zhang Weiping, written in the 1840s but reminiscent of his youth in the Jiaqing era. Zhang describes "scholars and maidens" who express their sentiments to one another "in this floating world." Zhang Weiping, *Songxin shiji*, in *Zhang Nanshan quanji*, 2: 507.

17. This stands in contrast to the Yangzi River, separating Hankou and Wuchang, which was more of an impediment than a conduit. See Rowe, *Hankow*, p. 21.

18. Osmond Tiffany, Jr., *The Canton Chinese, or the American's Sojourn in the Celestial Empire*, pp. 24-25; *Chinese Repository*, 2.7 (November 1833), p. 306.

19. *Chinese Repository*, 2.7 (November 1833), pp. 306-7.

20. Tiffany, *The Canton Chinese*, p. 24.

21. Li Jun, *Shi Yue riji*, xia.25b.
22. Shen Fu, *Fusheng liuji*, 4.11a. For a translation, see Shen Fu, *Six Records of a Floating Life*, translated by Leonard Pratt and Chiang Su-hui, p. 121.
23. Xie Lansheng, *Changxingxingzhai riji*, 7/25/JQ25.
24. Ibid., 9/14/JQ24, 4/22/JQ25.
25. Ibid., 9/8/DG2.
26. Ibid., 5/27/DG4. On the distinction between the elegant and vulgar as drawn by Jiangnan literati in the late Ming, see Craig Clunas, *Superfluous Things: Material Culture and Social Status in Early Modern China*, pp. 82–83.
27. Hunter, *Bits of Old China*, p. 31.
28. Zhang Weiping, *Huajia xiantan*, 1.3a. Zhang Weiping married a Jin woman. Jin Jingmao, *Zhang Nanshan xiansheng nianpu cuolue*, 1b.
29. Pan Yizeng, *Panyu Panshi shilue*, Pan Youwei chapter, 2a, Pan Zhenggang chapter, 1a; Xie Lansheng, *Changxingxingzhai riji*, 11/4/DG2. The child who began his formal education under Xie was Pan Zhengyu 潘正裕 (1818–91).
30. *Guangzhou chengfang zhi*, p. 698; Gray, *Walks in the City of Canton*, p. 79.
31. *Panyu Henan xiao zhi*, 9.4b, 6a–8a.
32. Chen Qikun, *Chen Libu shigao*, Xungai chapter, 2.2a, 7.7a. Chen Qikun and his cousin, Qirui, were grandsons of a Shanyin man who accumulated three thousand taels working as a *muyou* in Guangzhou during the eighteenth century. After spending his savings to help a friend in a legal case, he was unable to return and his grandsons thus were later born as Panyu natives. Qirui also served as a *muyou* in Guangdong. Chen Li, *Dongshu ji*, 6.15b; *Panyu xian xu zhi*, 19.9a–b; Zhang Weiping, *Yitan lu*, xia.25a.
33. Zhang Weiping, *Yitan lu*, xia.28b; He Ruoyao, *He Gongzan yishu*, prose collection, 9b.
34. *Xinhui xian zhi xu*, 6.15b.
35. *Panyu xian zhi*, 46.11b; Zhang Weiping, *Yitan lu*, xia.42b.
36. *Guangzhou chengfang zhi*, pp. 452–53; *Nanhai Luogefang Kongshi jiapu*, 14.33a. During Jixun's time, the Kong family was in the process of accumulating a large collection of painting and calligraphy. The collection was later catalogued by Jixun's third son, Guangtao (b. 1832), in *Yuexuelou shuhua lu*.
37. Feng Shilü and Feng Shibiao, *Xian junzi taishi gong nianpu*, 51a; Zhang Weiping, *Yitan lu*, xia.14b.
38. Chen Zaiqian, comp., *Guochao Lingnan wenchao*, 6.7a.

39. Rhoads, "Merchant Associations in Canton," p. 101; Skinner, *The City in Late Imperial China*, p. 535.

40. *Guangzhou chengfang zhi*, pp. 71, 80.

41. Ibid., pp. 439-40. Xu Xiangguang's grandfather was a petty merchant who relocated from Chaozhou prefecture to Guangzhou; there he took a second wife who would become Xiangguang's grandmother. Xiangguang's father and uncle managed to break into the salt trade. Examination degrees soon followed: Xiangguang was a *jinshi* and his brother a *juren*; Xiangguang's sons included two *juren* and a *jinshi*. Gong Zizhen, *Dingan xuji*, 4.17a-b; *Guangzhou Gaodijie Xushi jiazu*, pp. 103-4.

42. Xiong Jingxing, *Jiyang xiguan shichai*, 2.37a.

43. *Guangzhou chengfang zhi*, pp. 643-44. One Western visitor to the garden described it as "a very small landscape garden" but nonetheless decorated with colored stones in "exquisite taste." Gray, *Walks in the City of Canton*, p. 647. Deng Dalin's father was a Xiangshan pharmacist who owned a shop in the New City named the Hall of Assisting Longevity (*Zuoshoutang* 佐壽堂). Deng Dalin, *Xingzhuang tiyong, Xinglinzhuang xinghua shi*, 4.8b, prefaces.

44. Jin Jingmao, *Zhang Nanshan xiansheng nianpu cuolue*, 7b.

45. *Guangzhou chengfang zhi*, pp. 608-9.

46. Xie Lansheng, *Changxingxingzhai riji*, 2/6/JQ25, 4/5/DG2, 8/6/DG2.

47. Ibid., 10/20/JQ24, 2/6/JQ25, 11/8/JQ25.

48. Ibid., 6/28/DG4. The "Lu brothers" were some or all of the four sons of Lu Guanheng, including Lu Wenjin. See *Chaolian xiang zhi*, p. 75. Originally a native of Jiangdu county in Yangzhou, Wang Pu registered as a Panyu resident after long sojourning in Guangzhou. Wang Zhaoyong, *Lingnan hua zhenglue*, 10.3.

49. Xie Lansheng, *Changxingxingzhai riji*, 12/11-12/17/DG1. The Shitou Lu claimed descent from a collateral branch of the more prominent Lu of Chaolian township in Xinhui. See *Chaolian xiang zhi*, pp. 46, 74-75.

50. Xie Lansheng, *Changxingxingzhai riji*, 6/19/DG1.

51. Ibid., 7/10/DG4.

52. Ibid., 2/23/DG2.

53. Pan Zhengwei, *Tingfeng lou shuhua ji*, pp. 17-22, 76, 353, 464; Yeewan Koon, "Windblown Whispers: A Cohong Merchant's Art Collection and Its Impact on Early Nineteenth-Century Guangzhou Painting."

54. *Yuexiu shuyuan zhi*, 15.51a; Xie Lansheng, *Changxingxingzhai riji*, 6/24/DG1, 6/10/DG3.

55. Xie Lansheng, *Changxingxingzhai riji*, 5/3/DG6.

56. Ibid., 12/8/JQ25, 5/5/DG5.
57. Ibid., 12/3 and 12/4/JQ24, 4/25/JQ25, 10/6/JQ25, 11/6/JQ25, 1/21/DG6. Xie Jiawu, introduced in Chapter 1, was not related to Xie Lansheng.
58. Clunas, *Superfluous Things*, p. 163; Yü Ying-shih, "Shi-shang hudong yu Ruxue zhuanxiang: Ming-Qing shehuishi yu sixiangshi zhi yi mianxiang," pp. 11, 14–15.
59. Zhang Weiping, *Yitan lu*, xia.44a.
60. Zhang Weiping, *Songxin shiji*, in *Zhang Nanshan quanji*, 2: 99–100.
61. *Liang-Guang yanfa zhi*, 1884 edition, 47.14b–15a.
62. Liu Binhua, *Lingnan qunya*, Xie Lansheng chapter, 12a-b.
63. *Shenlou zhi*, p. 22.
64. *Chengnan Dushi jiapu*, 19b–20a.
65. Lin Botong, *Gongji xiaoyan*, 21b.
66. Tan Zongjun, *Licun suibi*, 9a-b; *Yuedong cheng'an chubian*, 29.56a–59b; *Xinhui xian zhi*, 14.6a; *Panyu xian zhi*, 44.3b–4a.
67. Tan Zongjun, *Licun suibi*, 9b–10a; *Yuedong cheng'an chubian*, 29.61b; Zhang Biao, *Modizhai wencun*, 51a–52b.
68. Zhang Biao, *Modizhai wencun*, 53a.
69. Tan Zongjun, *Licun suibi*, 10a.
70. Chen Tan, *Ganyutang wen/wai ji*, 2.7a, 11.1a; Zhang Biao, *Modizhai wencun*, 51a.
71. *Panyu Henan xiao zhi*, 3.32b–33a.
72. In a recent paper on the Lu Guanheng case, Zhou Xiang largely confirms this impression. She further suggests that the case may be analyzed in terms of competing alliances of merchants and literati. That is, the Pan family was perhaps using the literati that it sponsored to undermine the position of the rival Wu family, which maintained marriage ties to Lu Guanheng. Zhou Xiang, "A Sketch on the Local Worthy Worshipping of Lu Guanheng," p. 28.
73. *Yuexiu shuyuan zhi*, 9.24b.
74. Ibid., 1.2b, 5.1a-b, 9.21b–22a, 9.24a–28a.
75. Ibid., 2.15b, 4.19b–21b, 5.13b–17b. Yuexiu's 100 "formal students" included 80 licentiates/state students and 20 apprentice students, and its 50 "outer students" included 40 licentiates/state students and 10 apprentice students. Five of the bannermen students were "formal students" and four were "outer students." Typically, "outer students" did not reside at academies and they received lower stipends, if any at all. It should also be noted that Luo Hanzhang 羅含章 later changed his surname back to the original surname of Cheng 程.
76. Ibid., 15.49a.

77. In his classic study of the Yangzhou salt merchants, Ho Ping-ti points out that the merchant quota for provincial examinations was exclusively for salt merchants. He notes that two academies in Yangzhou exclusively served the sons of salt merchant families. See Ho, "The Salt Merchants of Yang-chou," p. 155, note 68, p. 165. *Guangzhou chengfang zhi*, 66.17; *Yuehua jilue*, 1.12a.

78. Ōkubo Eiko emphasizes the connections linking Yuexiu Academy, as well as Yuehua, with the salt merchants and administration. Ōkubo Eiko, *Min-Shin jidai shoin no kenkyū*, pp. 329–30.

79. Yuehua's 118 "formal students" included 89 licentiates/state students and 20 apprentice students, plus 5 banner licentiates/state students and 4 banner apprentice students; the 67 "outer students" included 36 licentiates/state students and 24 apprentice students, plus 4 banner licentiates/state students and 3 banner apprentice students. *Guangzhou fu zhi*, 66.17, 79.12b; *Yuehua jilue*, 1.4a, 21b, 2.8a–b, 13b, 4.31a, 33b.

80. *Yuexiu shuyuan zhi*, 1.8b, 2.6a, 13a, 7.1a–b; *Yuehua jilue*, 3.1a.

81. Here I follow Thomas Wilson in defining Cheng-Zhu Learning as the "doctrinally narrow conception of Confucianism promulgated by the throne" and most often taken as a standard in the civil service examinations. I use *lixue*, as did most Qing Confucians, to refer to Song and Ming philosophical Confucianism in general; this is what is often referred to as "Neo-Confucianism" in Western scholarship on China. Finally, "Song Learning," as used by Qing scholars, is one half of a dichotomy with Han Learning. Song Learning is supposed to be most concerned with "meaning and principle," whereas Han Learning focuses primarily upon "glossing" the Classics. See Thomas A. Wilson, *Genealogy of the Way: The Construction and Uses of the Confucian Tradition in Late Imperial China*, p. 19.

82. The "Cheng brothers of Luo" refers to Cheng Yi and his older brother, Cheng Hao. *Yuexiu shuyuan zhi*, 14.7a.

83. Ibid., 4.33b; Lao Tong, *Feng Qianzhai xiansheng nianpu*, 1a, 36a. The nineteenth-century Cantonese literatus Chen Tan described Feng in his role as academy director "consistently taking as his standard the notions of heart-mind and nature in Cheng-Zhu learning." Chen Tan, *Kuangzhai zaji*, 5.13b.

84. *Yuexiu shuyuan zhi*, 15.31a.

85. *Yuehua jilue*, 3.1a, 4.11a, 12b–13a, 15a–b.

86. Ibid., 4.15b–16a.

87. *Yuexiu shuyuan zhi*, 2.15b–16b, 3.15a–b, 5.16a, 14.18b–19a, 24a–b; Luo Hanzhang, *Lingnan ji*, 7.54a–b. On Chen Changqi's role in the compilation of the *Siku quanshu*, see Guy, *The Emperor's Four Treasuries*, p. 84.

88. An impression of how significant Xie Lansheng's Yangcheng salary was in relation to his total annual income is produced when we consider that for the year 1824 Xie recorded in the margin above 12/1/DG4 in his diary having earned "a total of 1,562 da yuan 大元." Unfortunately, it is not clear whether or not he includes the Yangcheng salary in this figure. Yangcheng's annual class of 110 "formal students" comprised 70 licentiates/state students and 40 apprentice students; the 60 "outer students" included 40 licentiates/state students and 20 apprentice students. *Guangzhou fu zhi*, 66.20, 72.14b; Luo Hanzhang, *Lingnan ji*, 7.63a–b; *Guangdong shengli xinzuan*, 4.5a.

89. Luo Hanzhang, *Lingnan ji*, 7.63b–64b.

90. Chen Zaiqian, comp., *Guochao Lingnan wenchao*, 5.6a.

91. *Nanhai xian zhi*, 1835 edition, 19.13a, 39.38a–b; *Panyu xian zhi*, 9.14a; *Yuexiu shuyuan zhi*, 15.49b–50a; Xie Lansheng, *Changxingxingzhai riji*, 10/20/JQ25, 4/21/DG1, 9/28/DG2. On the selection of academy students for advancement in the civil service examination system, see Sheng, *Zhongguo shuyuan zhidu*, p. 138.

92. Xie Lansheng, *Changxingxingzhai riji*, 1/22/DG4, 1/18/DG6, 1/21/DG9, and margin above 1/18/DG1.

93. Ibid., 3/26/DG3, 3/28/DG3, 4/1/DG3.

94. Ibid., 6/1/JQ25, 11/12/DG1. I have not found the Tongdong firm listed in any studies of the Cohong merchants. Liang Jiabin, *Guangdong shisanhang kao*, *passim*; Kuo-tung Anthony Chen, *The Insolvency of the Chinese Hong Merchants, 1760–1843*, *passim*.

95. Cai Zhaofu 蔡昭復 (Seunqua III) was the unfortunate merchant whose property was confiscated. See Cheong, *The Hong Merchants of Canton*, p. 264, Kuo-tung Anthony Ch'en, *The Insolvency of the Chinese Hong Merchants*, pp. 267–68; *Guangzhou fu zhi*, 66.24a; *Wenlan zhongshen lu, beiji* 7b; Xie Lansheng, *Changxingxingzhai wenji*, unpaginated.

96. *Wenlan zhongshen lu, beiji* 9a–10a, 13b.

97. *Nanhai xian zhi*, 1835 edition, 11.50b–51a.

98. *Wenlan zhongshen lu, beiji* 2a, 4a, 7b–8a, 13a–b. Cui Bi records Wenlan Academy as having been constructed in 1811. Cui Bi, *Baiyun Yuexiu er shan hezhi*, 17.7a. Also see Ōkubo, *Min-Shin jidai shoin no kenkyū*, pp. 332–33.

99. *Nanhai xian zhi*, 1910 edition, 15.6b; *Shunde xian zhi*, 1853 edition, 26.6a–7a; *Zhu Yue baqi zhi*, 23.14a; *Wenlan zhongshen lu, beiji* 13b–14b; Xie Lansheng, *Changxingxingzhai riji*, 6/22/JQ25, 8/5DG3, 8/28/DG3, 11/17/DG3, 11/19/DG3, 11/20/DG3, 11/22/DG3, 1/28/DG4, 3/5/DG5. For an interesting account of the role of Wenlan Academy in local

politics during the last decade of the Qing, see Tsin, *Nation, Governance, and Modernity in China*, pp. 35, 44–46.

100. On the transition from Ming to Qing academies in Guangdong, see Grimm, "Academies and Urban Systems in Kwangtung"; and Liu Boji, *Guangdong shuyuan zhidu*, pp. 45–46.

101. Huang Peifang, *Yueyue caotang shihua*, p. 103; *Laoshi zupu*, 3.32b; *Guan Shudetang jiapu*, 20.33b; *Nanhai xian zhi*, 1835 edition, 39.28b–29a; Tan Zongjun, *Licun suibi*, 10a, 13b–14a.

102. Aofeng Academy is described as a place where the local elite "held poetry and wine gatherings" on the double-ninth (ninth day of the ninth lunar month). Autumn trips by Xie Lansheng and his sons to Mashe coincided with this event. Xie Lansheng wrote an essay for a commemorative stele marking the academy's founding in 1815. *Nanhai xian zhi* 1835 edition, 4.14a. Xie Lansheng, *Changxingxingzhai riji*, 3/22/DG2, r3/28/DG2, 4/24/DG2, 7/18/DG2, 8/11/DG2.

103. Tan Zongjun, *Licun suibi*, 16b. Tan renders Qiu Xi as Qiu Xing (性) in his text.

104. *Sanguo zhi*, pp. 1317–21; *Guangzhou chengfang zhi*, pp. 377–87. As late as the Tang and Song, Guangdong was still essentially considered to be beyond civilization's reach, which made it a common destination for exiles. See Edward H. Schafer, *The Vermilion Bird: T'ang Images of the South*, pp. 37–44.

105. Yi Bingshou, *Liuchun caotang shichao*, 5.21a–b; Huang Peifang, *Yueyue caotang shihua*, p. 75; Chen Tan, *Ganyutang wen/waiji*, 1.12a–13a; Chen Tan, *Kuangzhai shiyou ji*, 9.1a, 13.1b, 48.3b; Zeng Yu, *Shangyu maowu waiji*, 49a–50b; *Panyu xian xu zhi*, 19.25a; Yan Ming, *Qingdai Guangdong shige yanjiu*, pp. 39–42. Zeng Yu was both a noted anthologist and an expert composer of parallel prose, a literary genre that would become an important component of the Xuehaitang curriculum. Zhang Weiping, *Guochao shiren zhenglue*, 2: 41.1a–4a. For a more detailed history of Guangxu Monastery and the Yu Fan Shrine, see Steven B. Miles, "Celebrating the Yu Fan Shrine: Literati Networks and Local Identity in Early Nineteenth-Century Guangzhou."

106. The lodge was named after two sites between which it was situated—White Cloud Mountain and Cascading Springs. Huang Peifang, "Commemoration of Additional Construction at Cloud and Springs Mountain Lodge," in Tan Dihua, Cao Tengfei, and Xian Jianmin, comp., *Guangdong beike ji*, p. 17.

107. *Panyu xian zhi*, 16.5b; Huang Peifang, *Yueyue caotang shihua*, p. 68; Huang Peifang, *Linghailou shichao*, 4.1a–b; *Nanhai Luogefang Kongshi*

jiapu, 14.28b; "Commemoration of Cloud and Springs Mountain Lodge," in *Guangdong beike ji*, p. 16.

108. Referring to this group as the "White Cloud Mountain school," James Polachek suggests that these poets represented a "rival academic influence" to the Xuehaitang during the 1830s. James M. Polachek, *The Inner Opium War*, p. 145. Nevertheless, in 1832 Ruan Yuan's most devoted followers among the early Xuehaitang co-directors, Wu Lanxiu and Zeng Zhao, would host Cheng Enze (1785–1837) at Cloud and Springs Mountain Lodge. In Guangzhou to oversee the provincial examinations, Cheng was closely associated with Ruan Yuan and passed several Cantonese literati associated with the Xuehaitang, including Yi Kezhong and Chen Li. Ju Huang, *Ju Shaonan xiansheng yigao*, 1.16a. The second collection of Xuehaitang writings, printed in 1838, even contains poems by Lin Botong and others on the theme of "'Cloud and Springs Mountain Lodge' in Imitation of Wang Wei's 'Stonegate Monastery on Indigo Fields Mountain.'" *Xuehaitang erji*, juan 18.

109. Zhang Weiping, *Yitan lu*, xia.43a; Zhang Biao, *Modizhai wencun*, 55a–b.

110. *Nanhai xian zhi*, 1910 edition, 19.2a; Zeng Zhao, "Preface to Longing for the Ancient Hall Literary Tests," in Chen Zaiqian, comp., *Guochao Lingnan wenchao*, 17.6b–7a. I have not been able to identify one member of the group, Yang "Qiuheng" (楊"秋衡"), since he is listed by an alternative name. I suspect that he is Yang Maojian 楊懋建, a Jiaying literatus who took Xuehaitang examinations in the 1820s.

111. Zeng Zhao, "Preface to Longing for the Ancient Hall Literary Tests," in Chen Zaiqian, comp., *Guochao Lingnan wenchao*, 17.6b. The chronology in the editor's comments is somewhat confusing, as the Xigutang meetings do not seem to have predated the first Xuehaitang examinations. Presumably, he refers to the construction of the Xuehaitang academy grounds in 1824.

112. Rong Zhaozu, "Xuehaitang kao, fu Jupo jingshe kaolue," p. 33.

113. Zeng Zhao, "Preface to Longing for the Ancient Hall Literary Tests," in Chen Zaiqian, comp., *Guochao Lingnan wenchao*, 17.6a–b.

114. Zeng Zhao, *Mianchenglou jichao*, 4.17a–20b; Ma Fu'an, *Zhizhai wenchao*, Luo Dunyan preface 2a, *xia*.23a–b.

CHAPTER 3

EPIGRAPH: Wu Lanxiu, *Licun yincao*, 1.3b.

1. Ruan Yuan, *Yanjingshi ji*, p. 505.

2. *Guangdong tongzhi*, prefatory material; Xie Lansheng, *Changxingxingzhai riji*, 11/2/JQ24.

3. *Guangdong tongzhi*, prefatory material.

4. Xie Lansheng, *Changxingxingzhai riji*, 3/29/JQ25. The Xie Lansheng diary provides some insight into the process of compiling a gazetteer. As one of four chief editors, throughout much of 1819 and 1820 Xie reported receiving various sections delivered to him by the section editors. Among his recorded assessments of those sections, for example, was his praise of both Zheng Haoruo's tables of officials and Wu Lanxiu's tables of administrative vicissitudes. He also noted meetings with Ruan Yuan, the overall sponsor and organizer of the project. See ibid., 5/1/JQ25, 6/28/JQ25.

5. Zhang Weiping, *Songxin shilu*, 3.11b. The anthology, presumably, was the *Huang Qing jingjie*.

6. On Ruan Yuan's role in addressing security issues at his posts in Zhejiang and Guangdong, see Wei Peh T'i, "Juan Yuan: A Biographical Study with Special Reference to Mid-Ch'ing Security and Control in Southern China, 1799–1835."

7. Xie Lansheng, *Changxingxingzhai riji*, 1/27/DG1, 3/12/DG1. Zhang Jian et al., in *Ruan Yuan nianpu* (under the original title *Leitang'an zhu dizi ji*), p. 132, state that tests began on April 14 (second day of the third month by the lunar calendar), 1820. Li Xubai, *Qingdai Guangdong puxue yanjiu*, p. 27, and Hummel, *Eminent Chinese*, p. 401, follow this. In contrast, most primary sources date the commencement of Xuehaitang examinations in 1821, for example the *Nanhai xian zhi*, 1872 edition, 4.12b, and *Xuehaitang ji*, 16.4a. A piece of anecdotal evidence further suggesting that Xuehaitang examinations began in 1821 is that Xie Lansheng records in his diary on 1/27/DG1, the same day that he first noted that the governor-general tested scholars, that he "borrowed Qian Daxin's *Yangxin lu*." We know from Gui Wencan that the *Yangxin lu* was one of the topics of the first examination. It seems likely that Xie's interest in the *Yangxin lu* was stimulated by this first Xuehaitang examination topic in 1821. Therefore, I follow most local sources and the Xie Lansheng diary by taking 1821 as the beginning of Xuehaitang examinations. Gui Wencan, *Jingxue bocai lu*, 4.1a–b; Xie Lansheng, *Changxingxingzhai riji*, 1/27/DG1.

8. Gui Wencan, *Jingxue bocai lu*, 4.1a–b.

9. *Xuehaitang ji*, 6.6a–27a; Elman, *From Philosophy to Philology*, pp. 174–76.

10. This refers to a passage from the *Lunyu* (6.25). See James Legge, *The Chinese Classics*, 1: 193.

11. This refers to a passage from the *Zhongyong* (20.19). See Legge, *The Chinese Classics*, 1: 413.

12. Ruan Yuan, "Preface to *Xuehaitang ji*," in *Nanhai xian zhi*, 1872 edition, 12.23b.

13. *Xuehaitang ji*, juan 2.

14. Ruan Yuan, *Yanjingshi ji*, juan 10. In an 1821 letter to the Fujianese scholar Chen Shouqi 陳壽祺 (1771-1834), Ruan described this as a recently completed essay about issues that had been on his mind for decades. Chen Shouqi, *Zuohai wenji*, prefatory material, 1a.

15. Lin Botong, *Xiubentang gao*, 1.7a-11b. See also *Xuehaitang ji*, juan 2. On Lin Botong and Han-Song syncretism, see Elman, *From Philosophy to Philology*, p. 246.

16. Zeng Zhao, *Mianchenglou jichao*, 1.23b-31a.

17. This refers to one of the Southern Dynasties, the Song (420-79), not the later Song dynasty (960-1279) that produced the masters of Neo-Confucianism. On Ruan's somewhat idiosyncratic appreciation of the Southern Dynasties' classical scholarship, see his "Xuehaitang cewen" (Xuehaitang test questions) in *Yanjingshi ji*, *Yanjingshi xuji*, p. 129.

18. This refers to the *Sancang* 三倉 and *Erya* 爾雅.

19. That is, Xiao Tong's *Wenxuan*, or *Selections of Refined Literature*.

20. *Nanhai xian zhi*, 1872 edition, 12.24a.

21. Elman, *From Philosophy to Philology*, p. 246; Elman, "Ch'ing Dynasty 'Schools' of Scholarship," pp. 31-33; He Yousen, "Chen Lanfu de xueshu ji qi yuanyuan," p. 2.

22. Min Erchang, *Jiang Ziping xiansheng nianpu*, 12b-17a; Yi Kezhong, *Jianguanglou ji*, lyric poetry prefatory material, *beixing cao* chapter.

23. Jiang Fan, *Guochao Hanxue shicheng ji*, pp. 12-13.

24. Ibid., p. 4. On the ways in which the status of *kaozheng* scholarship was transformed through imperial sponsorship, see Guy, *The Emperor's Four Treasuries*, pp. 155-56.

25. For an example of his critique of Jiang Fan, see Fang Dongshu, *Hanxue shangdui*, 1.21a-22a. On Fang's critique, also see Elman, *From Philosophy to Philology*, pp. 242-45; Hamaguchi Fujio, *Shindai kōkyogaku no shisōshi*, esp. pp. 172-73. Elman sees Fang Dongshu's defense of Song Learning as stemming from the fact that Song Learning supporters like Fang "were under considerable attack by their Han-Learning contemporaries." Elman, *From Philosophy to Philology*, p. 244. Yet Fang's posture as the isolated, embattled critic may also be seen as a common stance taken by literati who identified themselves as Neo-Confucians throughout late imperial Chinese history. It is reminiscent of the "oppositional stance" and "sense of distinctiveness" that Peter Bol argues shaped Neo-Confucian identities and propelled Neo-Confucian movements in the Song, Yuan, and Ming. See Bol, "Neo-Confucianism and Local Society," pp. 260, 267.

26. Fang Dongshu, *Shulin yangzhi*, 1.1a.

27. Rong Zhaozu, "Xuehaitang kao," p. 112; Chen Li, *Dongshu zazu*, 11.30a; Fang Dongshu, *Yiweixuan wenji*, nianpu, 5b-9a. If this speculation is correct, then Fang was being somewhat disingenuous in a letter to Ruan explaining that he had written the *Hanxue shangdui* but "did not yet dare to show it to anyone." See Fang Dongshu, *Yiweixuan wenji*, 7.1b.

28. Elman, *Classicism, Politics, and Kinship*, pp. xxvi-xxx.

29. Ruan Yuan, *Yanjingshi ji*, vol. 3, *Yanjingshi xuji*, p. 199.

30. Wang Jia, *Shiyi ji*, p. 155.

31. *Xuehaitang ji*, 16.22b-23a.

32. *Nanhai xian zhi*, 1872 edition, 12.24a.

33. Scholarly lineage is also implied here. *Xuehaitang ji*, 16.23a.

34. The relevant lines read, "The hundred rivers mimic [literally, "study" (*xue* 學)] the sea, and indeed reach (至) the sea; hills and mounds mimic the mountains, but do not reach the mountains." Wang Rongbao, *Fayan yishu*, 2.6a-b. A pavilion further up the hill on the academy grounds, the Reach Mountain Pavilion, further added to the connection between the academy and this passage from Yang Xiong's *Fayan*. *Xuehaitang zhi*, tushuo, 3a. In his commemorative writings, Cui Bi emphatically denies that the name "Xuehai" has anything to do with Yang Xiong; in contrast, Xie Niangong makes specific reference to Yang Xiong. *Xuehaitang ji*, 16.16a.

35. Xie Lansheng, "Yuexiushan Xuehaitang ji," in *Changxingxingzhai wenji*, second CE.

36. *Xuehaitang zhi*, 39a.

37. James Polachek describes the Xuehaitang as the center of a Han Learning clique. See *The Inner Opium War*, pp. 119-20. Benjamin Elman emphasizes New Text Confucianism at the academy. See his "The Hsüeh-hai t'ang [Xuehaitang] and the Rise of New Text Scholarship in Canton," pp. 51-82.

38. This includes *juan* 16, comprising accounts, in various genres, of the establishment of the Xuehaitang.

39. On Ruan Yuan's fondness for *Wenxuan* scholarship, see Kondō Mitsuo, *Shinchō kōshōgaku no kenkyū*, pp. 412-23; Meyer-Fong, *Building Culture in Early Qing Yangzhou*, p. 117.

40. Ruan Yuan, *Yanjingshi ji*, pp. 657-63; Wang Yunxi and Yang Ming, *Wei-Jin-Nanbeichao wenxue piping shi*, pp. 192-94, 205; Theodore Huters, "From Writing to Literature: The Development of Late Qing Theories of Prose," pp. 85-89; Man-kam Leung, "Juan Yuan (1764-1849): The Life, Works, and Career of a Chinese Scholar-Bureaucrat," pp. 109-11, 117.

41. Luo Hanzhang, *Lingnan ji*, 7.81b.

42. *Panyu xian xu zhi*, 19.21b, 25b.

43. The portion of this phrase referring to literature, *shi guwen ci* 詩古文詞, was not entirely unprecedented in early nineteenth-century Guangzhou. Writing in 1796 about his older contemporary Luo Yuanhuan, Lao Tong claimed that people near and far praised Luo's *shi guwen ci*. Luo Yuanhuan, *Yuetai zhengya lu*, Lao preface, 1a. Similarly, the 1822 Guangdong provincial gazetteer biography of the 1768 Panyu *juren* Hong Ruiyuan 洪瑞元 describes Hong's *shi guwen ci* as the best of his time. Hong, incidentally, is also said to have favored Han Learning in his classical studies. *Guangdong tongzhi*, 287.28a. In the context of the civil service examinations, *lüshi guwen ci* 律詩古文詞 referred to regulated verse, ancient-style prose, and lyric poetry. Elman, *A Cultural History of Civil Examinations in Late Imperial China*, p. 548.

44. In his 1821 letter to Chen Shouqi, Ruan Yuan remarked that, though Cantonese scholarship could not match that of Fujian (Chen was a Fujian native), he "had found roughly three or four fine scholars." One imagines that Ruan would have found more literati whom he judged to be "fine scholars" in his native Yangzhou. Chen Shouqi, *Zuohai wenji*, prefatory material, 1b. Li Xubai points this out in his book, *Guangdong puxue yanjiu*, p. 29.

45. *Nanhai xian zhi*, 1872 edition, 18.9b.

46. Emphasis added. *Panyu xian zhi*, 46.6a. As Benjamin Elman has noted, poetry had become an increasingly important component of the civil service examinations in the 60 years before the founding of the Xuehaitang. Elman, *A Cultural History of Civil Examinations in Late Imperial China*, pp. 546–52.

47. Xie Lansheng, *Changxingxingzhai riji*, 10/24/DG2. This translation is from Stephen Owen, *Readings in Chinese Literary Thought*, p. 311. Yang Hsien-yi and Gladys Yang translate the phrase as "the moon is bright over the bank at night." Yang and Yang, "The Twenty-Four Modes of Poetry," p. 67.

48. *Xuehaitang ji*, 14.2a–b. The line that Xie Lansheng used in the Yangcheng examination was from the fourth of Sikong Tu's twenty-four poems. See Sikong Tu, *Ershisi shipin*, 1b; Owen, *Readings in Chinese Literary Thought*, pp. 299–303.

49. The examination topics were "Imitate Yuan-Era Poets' Poems on Ten Terraces to Chant on Ten Terraces in Guangdong," and "Imitate Zhang Jiuling's 'Observing the Moon While Longing for the Remote.'" Both exercises were incorporated into the *Xuehaitang ji*. Xie Lansheng, *Changxingxingzhai riji*, 6/9/DG3, 9/9/DG3; *Xuehaitang ji*, 14.8a–14b, 25a–b.

50. *Xuehaitang ji*, table of contents. A very useful source for understanding the range of students at the Xuehaitang is Rong Zhaozu, "Xuehaitang

kao," which lists the students in each of four collections of Xuehaitang examinations papers, as well as the co-directors and "specialized students."

51. Weng Xincun, *Xuehaitang dinghai keshi lu*, unpaginated; Weng Tongshu, *Weng Wenduan gong nianpu*, p. 54. For both the spring and winter tests, students' papers were ranked separately in two categories: classical exegesis and history essays, on the one hand, and *shi* poems and rhapsodies, on the other. In the Classics and Histories category of the spring examination, for example, Weng listed 4 students in the top rank, 8 in the second, and 26 in the third, noting that an additional 12 were initially considered for ranking and 126 were left unranked altogether. For poetry, Weng listed 6, 10, and 106 in the top three ranks, and noted an additional 150 for initial consideration and 40 that were not ranked. This means that a total of 176 scholars submitted essays and 312 submitted poems, with some who submitted both essays and poems—far fewer than the number of students competing for positions at Yangcheng Academy. Of these, Weng only listed the name and registered residence of students who were ranked in the three top tiers in each category (38 essayists and 122 poets).

52. Chen Li, *Dongshu ji*, 3.29b; Chen Pu, *Chigang caotang yiwen, yishi*, 4.25b; Pan Yizeng, *Panyu Panshi shilue*, Pan Zhenggang chapter, 1a; Yun Jing, *Dayun shanfang wengao*, first series, 4.39a–b; Zhang Weiping, *Yitan lu*, xia.6b. Zhang Bingwen's salt merchant father-in-law, Geng Guofan 耿國藩, hosted and exchanged poems with the likes of Hang Shijun 杭世駿 (1696–1773) during his term as Yuexiu Academy director in the 1750s. Hang Shijun, *Lingnan ji*, 2.7b–8a, 4.15b.

53. The Zhang family claimed that its ancestors—descendants of Jiuling's brother—had moved to Sichuan during the Song and then to Zhejiang in the Ming. Lin Botong, *Xiubentang ji*, 4.4a.

54. Gui Wencan, *Jingxue bocai lu*, 11.15a; *Panyu xian xu zhi*, 19.24b–25b.

55. The sources do not agree on Zhang Biao's native place. The 1871 Panyu gazetteer and the source it draws upon, Zeng Zhao's family biography, indicate Shaoxing prefecture; Chen Li's biography designates Zhang's native place as Shanyin county, which is in Shaoxing. But Zheng Xianfu's funerary inscription and Zhang Qizeng's epitaph indicate Renhe county. This confusion does not clarify Zhang Biao's particular native place, but it nevertheless reveals the extent to which both Shaoxing and Hangzhou prefectures were recognized as common native-place origins of many Panyu residents during the nineteenth century. *Panyu xian zhi*, 46.10a–b; Zeng Zhao, *Mianchenglou jichao*, 4.15b–16b; Chen Li, *Dongshu ji*, 5.4b–6b; Zheng Xianfu, *Buxuexuan wenji xuke*, 4.19a; Zhang Qizeng, *Bianzhen liangshi wenchao*, 2.6b.

56. *Panyu xian zhi*, 46.3a-b; Jin Xiling, *Qushushi yiji*, 16.16a. In light of Charlotte Furth's observation that literate physicians in late Ming Jiangnan cities were not far removed socially from urban degree-holding gentry, Lin Botong's emergence from a family of physicians does not seem surprising. Furth, *A Flourishing Yin: Gender in China's Medical History, 960–1665*, p. 156.

57. Lin Botong, *Xiubentang gao*, 4.6a-7a; *Panyu xian zhi*, 44.4b-5b. Another prominent member of the Wu family, Wu Han 吳函, was a rare eighteenth-century Cantonese literati noted for mastery of parallel prose. Luo Yuanhuan, *Yuetai zhengya lu*, 14a.

58. *Nanhai xian zhi*, 1910 edition, 20.6b; Weng Xincun, *Xuehaitang dinghai keshi lu*, unpaginated.

59. Chen Li, *Dongshu ji*, 5.12b-13a.

60. *Panyu xian zhi*, 48.2b; *Nanhai Luoge Kongshi jiapu*, 14.32a; Yi Kezhong, *Jianguanglou ji*, Jiang Yuan preface, 1a. Yi Kezhong's father, Yi Yu 儀堉, is described in the Liang-Guang salt gazetteer as a "clerk from Shanxi" 山西吏員 and served as a deputy and salt receiver in Lufeng county (in eastern coastal Guangdong) and Yangjiang county (on the coast southwest of Guangzhou), from 1778 to 1784. *Liang-Guang yanfa zhi*, 1884 edition, 50.35b, 38a, 51.37a; *Panyu xian zhi*, 48.2b. Meng Hongguang 孟鴻光, another son of a Shanxi man, was born in Guangzhou, registered as a Panyu resident, and was included in the second collection of Xuehaitang writings, the *Xuehaitang erji*. Chen Li, *Dongshu ji*, 5.19b-20a.

61. *Panyu xian zhi*, 33.18a-b, 46.1b.

62. *Zhu Yue baqi zhi*, 21.2a, 23.4b-5a, 11a; Chen Pu, *Chigang caotang yiwen*, 1.1a; Li Changrong, *Liutang shiyou shilu*, Xu Rong chapter, 7b.

63. Elliott, *The Manchu Way*, pp. 340-43; Zhang Weiping, *Yitan lu*, *shang*.107b. In his *Yitan lu*, a collection of biographical information on Qing poets, as well as excerpts from and assessments of their poetry, Zhang Weiping includes Xiukun in the first chapter, which contains poets from outside Guangdong. The second chapter is composed exclusively of poets registered in Guangdong counties. Thus, despite the fact that Xiukun spent his childhood in Guangzhou, Zhang Weiping classified him as an outsider. On Yinglian, father of the notorious Heshen's mother, see Hummel, *Eminent Chinese*, p. 288.

64. Only 39 out of the 240 scholars who were ranked in the 1827 spring or winter examinations were Jiaying natives, but they formed the only significant contingent of scholars outside the Pearl River delta prefectures of Guangzhou and Zhaoqing. *Xuehaitang dinghai keshi lu*, unpaginated.

65. *Yuexiu shuyuan zhi*, 10.15b, 17a; *Jiaying zhou zhi*, 23.48b-49a.

66. *Jiaying zhou zhi*, 23.49a-b, 63a-b; Zhang Qizeng, *Bianzhen liangwu wenchao*, 2.1a-3b.

67. Tan Zongjun, *Licun caotang shichao*, 6.12b-13b; *Yangshi jiapu*, Tan Zongjun preface, 1a; Tang Wenzhi, *Rujingtang wenji*, 6.33a. A same-generation relative of Tan Ying, Tan Xinyi 譚心翼, was ranked in the 1827 spring and winter examinations at the Xuehaitang. See Weng Xincun, *Xuehaitang dinghai keshi lu*.

68. *Shunde xian zhi*, 1929 edition, 20.14b-15a; Tan Zongjun, *Licun caotang shichao*, 6.14a.

69. *Nanhai xian zhi* 1872 edition, 18.9b-10a; Chen Chunrong 陳春榮, *Xiangmeng chunhanguan shichao* 香夢春寒館詩鈔, quoted in *Guangzhou chengfang zhi*, pp. 643-44. The edition of *Guangzhou chengfang zhi* that I have used writes Xiong Jingxing's lodge as Jixiang 吉祥 (Auspicious Fortune) rather than Jiyang 吉羊 (Auspicious Rams). I am following Xiong Jingxing's poetry collection in choosing the latter. Xiong, *Jiyang xiguan shichao*, 2.37a. "Auspicious Rams" most likely refers to the five rams that carried five immortals in the foundation legend of Guangzhou. See *Guangzhou chengfang zhi*, p. 2.

70. *Nanhai xian zhi*, 1872 edition, 19.22a.

71. Wu Yingkui, *Yanshan wenji fu pulixuan biji*, 3.26a-29a; *Heshan xian zhi*, 9.13a; *Xuehaitang ji*, 11.21a.

72. *Panyu xian xu zhi*, 19.21b-23a.

73. Wu Rongguang, *Shiyun shanren wenji*, 3.47a, 4.37b.

74. Zhou Yinqing sometimes appears by the name Zhou Yiqing 周以清.

75. Ma Fuan, *Zhizhai wenchao*, xia.18b, 22a-b; Zeng Zhao, *Mianchenglou jichao*, 4.17a-20b.

76. One exception was Chen Tong, from Longjiang township, one of only two members of the old elite ensconced in the Enclosure district townships of Longshan, Longjiang, and Jiujiang included in the *Xuehaitang ji*. Hu Tiaode, a Xigutang member and a native of Jiujiang township, would have several works included in the second collection of Xuehaitang writings.

77. Ren Zhaolin's lineage cousin, Ren Dachun (1738-89), was an eminent *kaozheng* scholar. Jiang Fan, *Hanxue shicheng ji*, p. 158.

78. *Nanhai xian zhi*, 1872 edition, 18.8a.

79. *Panyu xian zhi*, 46.6a, 45.7b. On the powerful He lineage of Shawan, see Liu Zhiwei, "Lineage on the Sands," pp. 21-43.

80. *Nanhai xian zhi*, 1872 edition, 4.12b, 12.15b-16b.

81. *Xuehaitang zhi*, 6b.

82. Gui Wencan, *Jingxue bocai lu*, 4.1a; *Chinese Repository*, May 1835, pp. 34-36; Huang Zhi, *Yue xiaoji*, 2.24b; Wen Xun, *Dengyun shanfang wengao*, 2.36a-b.

83. *Xuehaitang zhi*, 6b.

84. Ibid.

85. Henry, *Ling-nam*, p. 53.

86. Both Tilemann Grimm and Benjamin Elman locate the Xuehaitang just outside the city wall. Yet contemporary accounts place the academy inside the city wall, as do the city map drawn for the 1835 Nanhai gazetteer (see Fig. 1) and the map drawn by Chen Li for the 1879 Guangzhou prefectural gazetteer (see Fig. 7). Grimm, "Academies and Urban Systems in Kwangtung," p. 490; Elman, "The Hsüeh-hai t'ang," p. 52; *Nanhai xian zhi*, 1835 edition, 3.2b-3a; *Guangzhou fu zhi*, 8.3b-4a; *Xuehaitang ji*, 16.4a. According to Xie Lansheng's diary, he attended a meeting at Haichuang on September 20, 1824, to discuss construction of the Xuehaitang. Xie Lansheng, *Changxingxingzhai riji*, R7/28/DG4.

87. *Xuehaitang ji*, 16.4a, 12a, 18b; Xie Lansheng, *Changxingxingzhai riji*, 12/3/DG4, 12/6/DG4.

88. Ruan Yuan, *Yanjingshi ji*, vol. 3, *Yanjingshi xuji*, p. 199; Xie Lansheng, *Changxingxongzhai riji*, 1/22/DG5.

89. Further exemplifying the ties between the Xuehaitang and other Guangzhou academies, in September 1826 Xie Lansheng asked Yangcheng students to write a poem on the theme, "Completion of the Wenlan Pavilion." Xie Lansheng, *Changxingxingzhai riji*, 9/17/DG5, 11/7/DG5, 12/21/DG5, 8/24/DG6. The name of the Wenlan Pavilion evoked memories both of Wenlan Academy, where the early Xuehaitang examinations had been administered, and the Wenlan Pavilion in Hangzhou, where one set of the *Siku quanshu* collectanea was housed. Hummel, *Eminent Chinese*, p. 122.

90. *Nanhai xian zhi*, 1872 edition, 12.24a.

91. I am drawing this notion of "visual hierarchy" from Rowe, *Hankow*, p. 25.

92. The academy gazetteer, for example, describes the scene looking south from the front of the Xuehaitang as taking in "kitchen smoke from myriad households, like fish scales springing up in layers, with [Liurong Monastery's] Flowery Pagoda standing erect in the west, and the Pipa Islet Pagoda standing erect in the east." *Xuehaitang zhi*, *tushuo*, 2b.

93. Ruan Yuan wrote a poem on the 1824 renovation of the city wall and Zhenhai Tower. See his *Yanjingshi ji*, vol. 3, *Yanjingshi xuji*, p. 197.

94. Linda Walton describes Southern Sung academies as appropriating contested spaces from sites originally dominated by Buddhist and Daoist institutions. Linda Walton, *Academies and Society in Southern Sung China*, p. 96.

95. *Yuexiu shuyuan zhi*, 15.43b.

96. This theme was repeated frequently in poetry about the Xuehaitang. *Xuehaitang ji*, 16.21a.

97. Clunas, *Fruitful Sites*, p. 152.

98. *Xuehaitang zhi*, 44a; *Guangzhou fu zhi*, 81.30b. One exception to the noticeable exclusion of women from Xuehaitang academy grounds can be found in a Chen Li essay mourning the death of his daughter, Chen Lü 陳律 (1857-75/76). In this essay, Chen recalls frequently taking his young daughter to the academy; as he met with other co-directors or students, she romped through the bamboo and flowers. In this intimate portrait of his daughter, Chen Li mentions that she later had no memory of this, which suggests that a girl's presence at the Xuehaitang was not thought exceptional if she had not yet reached the age at which such gendered practices as binding the feet and tying the hair in tufts required that she be separated from male playmates. Chen Li, *Dongshu ji*, 6.29a-31a; Wang Zongyan, "Chen Dongshu xiansheng nianpu," pp. 85, 110; Susan Mann, *Precious Records*, pp. 55-56. One woman who joined in celebrating the opening of the Xuehaitang was Ruan Yuan's wife, Kong Luhua 孔璐華 (1777-1833). Her poem "From the Guangdong Yamen on the Newly Established Xuehaitang" is vivid enough in some places to give the impression that the author personally visited the site: "[My husband] added a few buildings, with hall and terrace / Seas expansive and skies vast suddenly open one's eyes." Given the title "From the Guangdong Yamen" (廣東節署), it is just as likely that Kong is responding to poems written by her husband or the writings in various genres generated by Cantonese literati to mark the opening of the academy grounds. Kong Luhua, *Tang-Song jiujinglou gao*, 3a-b; Hummel, *Eminent Chinese*, p. 402. I thank Li Xiaorong for bringing this poem to my attention.

99. *Xuehaitang ji*, 16.1b-2a.

100. Ibid., 16.4b.

101. Ibid., 16.12a.

102. Schafer, *The Vermilion Bird*, pp. 125-29.

103. *Xuehaitang zhi*, 40a-42a; *Xuehaitang ji*, 16.21a.

104. Chen Li, *Dongshu yigao*, 39.3.

105. Walton, *Academies and Society in Southern Sung China*, p. 105.

106. I avoid the term "natural" in describing the physical environment of the Xuehaitang, as Ruan Yuan ordered many trees chopped down and

the other elements of the landscape altered. Ruan Yuan, *Yanjingshi ji*, vol. 3, *Yanjingshi xuji*, p. 200.

107. *Xuehaitang ji*, 16.21a; Michael Loewe, ed., *Early Chinese Texts: A Bibliographical Guide*, p. 94-95.

108. As noted earlier, in writings ranging from local gazetteers to Gui Wencan's *Jingxue bocai lu*, the Xuehaitang was still classified as a *shuyuan*.

109. *Gujing jingshe wen xuji*, preface, 1a; *Hangzhou fu zhi*, 10.3b.

110. *Xuehaitang ji*, 16.21a-b.

111. *Xuehaitang zhi*, 14b. An income of 1,607.982 taels was reported for 1846. *Guangdong shengli xinzuan*, 4.5a.

112. Wang Quan, *Suishanguan conggao*, 4.6a.

113. Later, when the maritime merchants were unable to make annual interest payments, the money was withdrawn and redeposited with pawn merchants in Guangzhou and Foshan. *Guangdong shengli xinzuan*, 4.5b; *Xuehaitang zhi*, 13b-15a.

114. *Xuehaitang ji*, 16.18b.

115. Ibid., 16.12b.

116. Gui Wencan, *Jingxue bocai lu*, 4.4b. Ruan Yuan depicted Cantonese learning as still suffering from a neglect of written scholarship stemming from the influence of Chen Xianzhang and Zhan Ruoshui. He Yousen, "Ruan Yuan de jingxue ji qi zhixue fangfa," p. 22. Modern intellectual historians have often taken for granted the prevalence of the Chen Xianzhang and Zhan Ruoshui school of learning in Guangdong throughout the late imperial era. For an example of an intellectual historian taking Chen-Zhan learning as the essence of Cantonese intellectual discourse, see Yang Nianqun, *Ruxue diyuhua de jindai xingtai*, pp. 131-43. My perusal of biographies in Pearl River delta gazetteers and genealogies only turned up a few advocates of Chen-Zhan Confucianism in early nineteenth-century Guangzhou. Deng Chun, a native of Dongguan county, east of Guangzhou, is a rare example of a Cantonese literatus active during Ruan Yuan's term as governor-general who at least at one time had been an avid follower of Chen Xianzhang. In his biography of Deng, Zeng Zhao claims that as a youth Deng had been enamored with Chen Xianzhang and Wang Yangming learning, but later realized his "faults" after reading the works of Cheng Yi and Zhu Xi. Zeng Zhao, *Mianchenglou jichao*, 4.14b-15a; *Dongguan xian zhi*, 71.1b. One Xuehaitang examinee after Ruan Yuan left Guangzhou, Ruan Rongling, was a scholar from Xinhui who celebrated the life and scholarship of Chen Xiangzhang. In 1851, Rongling compiled a chronological biography of the Xinhui philosopher as well as a list of his disciples during the Ming. Ruan Rongling, *Baisha menren kao*.

117. Walton, *Academies and Society in Southern Sung China*, p. 13. John Meskill argues that social critics dissatisfied with the moral tone of officialdom led the academy movement in the sixteenth century. See John Meskill, *Academies in Ming China: A Historical Essay*, pp. 66, 84.

118. Xie Lansheng, *Changxingxingzhai riji*, 3/9/DG1, 5/16/DG2. The passages are drawn from *Lunyu* 13.2 and 19.10, and the translations, with changes in romanization, follow James Legge, *The Chinese Classics*, 1: 262, 243.

119. Weng Xincun, *Xuehaitang dinghai keshi lu*, unpaginated.

120. *Huang Qing jingjie*, prefatory material; Steven B. Miles, "The New Face of *Kaozheng*: The *Huang Qing jingjie xubian* and Classical Studies After 1820," pp. 175–92.

121. Gui Wencan, *Jingxue bocai lu*, 8.10a.

122. *Nanhai xian zhi*, 1872 edition, 12.24a. Ruan Yuan here employs the language of the "Tribute of Yu" section of the *Shujing*. See Legge, *The Chinese Classics*, 3: 150.

123. *Xuehaitang ji*, 16.10a. For Ruan Yuan's commemoration of the Gujing jingshu, see Ruan Yuan, *Yanjingshi ji*, pp. 505–6. Part of Ruan's essay is translated in Elman, *From Philosophy to Philology*, p. 58.

124. *Yuexiu shuyuan zhi*, 7.19.

125. *Yuehua jilue*, 4.16b.

126. *Yuexiu shuyuan zhi*, 10.15b–17a, 12.2a–4a, 13.13b–14a; Wang Zongyan, "Chen Dongshu xiansheng nianpu," pp. 60–66.

127. *Nanhai xian zhi*, 1835 edition, 11.50a.

128. *Xuehaitang zhi*, 44a.

129. Xie Lansheng, *Changxingxingzhai riji*, 6/13/DG5, 8/15/DG5, 9/23/DG5, 5/15/DG5, 8/15/DG6; Wu Lanxiu, *Licun yincao*, 1.4a. A similar outing at the Xuehaitang, hosted by Xu Naiji, is described in Xie Lansheng, *Changxingxingzhai shuhua tiba*, shang.40a.

130. Kong Luhua, *Tang-Song jiujinglou gao*, 3b. Thanks to Li Xiaorong for bringing this poem to my attention.

131. Tan Ying, *Lezhitang shiji*, 2.23b.

132. The first phrase appears in a poem written by Wu Lanxiu in the mid-1830s, on the occasion of Xu Rong's departure for official service in Zhejiang; the second is found in an 1837 poem by Huang Weiqing 黃位清, one of the scholars included in the *Xuehaitang ji*. Wu Chongyao, *Chuting qijiu yishi*, houji, 1.15b; Huang Weiqing, *Songfengge shichao*, 9b.

133. Elman, *Classicism, Politics, and Kinship*, pp. xxiii, xxxiii, 7–8.

CHAPTER 4

EPIGRAPH: *Xuehaitang ji*, 14.20a–23a.

1. "Man" is a general name referring to "southern barbarians"; "Dan" refers to the Boat People.
2. *Nanhai xian zhi*, 1872 edition, 18.15b.
3. Xu Shaoqi, *Guangdong cangshu jishi shi*, pp. 150–53, 162–66, 178–80.
4. Ibid., pp. 174–75; Xu Shaoqi, "Guangzhou banpian jilue," 57b; Tan Zongjun, *Licun caotang shichao*, 6.14a. Liang's mother's sacrifices for her son's education seem modeled after the dowry donations celebrated by Neo-Confucians since the Southern Song. Bettine Birge, *Women, Property, and Confucian Reaction in Sung and Yüan China (960–1368)*, pp. 158–59.
5. The revival of interest in the Southern Han among nineteenth-century Cantonese scholars and poets is treated more fully in Steven B. Miles, "Rewriting the Southern Han (917–971): The Production of Local Culture in Nineteenth-Century Guangzhou."
6. Qu Dajun, *Guangdong xinyu*, 11.11a, 11.18a–19b, 19.5a–6b.
7. Ibid., 19.6b.
8. Loewe, *Early Chinese Texts*, p. 113.
9. Wu Lanxiu, *Nan-Han ji*, Jiang Fan postscript, 1a.
10. Ibid., Tan Ying postscript, 1b.
11. In addition to his studies of the Southern Han, Liang compiled two works on the earlier Southern Yue kingdom: *Nan-Yue conglu* 南越叢錄 (Assembled notes on the Southern Yue) and *Nan-Yue wuzhu zhuan* 南越五主傳 (Biographies of the five rulers of the Southern Yue). Rong Zhaozu, "Xuehaitang kao," p. 39.
12. Liang Tingnan, *Nan-Han shu*, p. 5.
13. Ibid., p. 23.
14. Elman, *Cultural History*, pp. 546–58.
15. See Appendix B.
16. In the Gujing jingshe collected writings, only the last two of fourteen *juan* are devoted to poetry. See *Gujing jingshe wenji*, *passim*. See also the second collection, *Gujing jingshe wen xuji*.
17. *Guangzhou fu zhi*, 48.2b; Yi Kezhong, *Jianguanglou ji*, Zheng Xianfu preface, 1a.
18. The text contained a prior postscript from 1719, by a native of Henan province who had acquired it from a Shaoxing merchant, who in turn had managed to get hold of a copy that once belonged to the famous Jiangnan poet Qian Qianyi 錢謙益 (1582–1664).
19. Fang Xinru, *Nanhai baiyong*, 35a–37b.

20. That is, *Yu* 禺 (the hill's name) and *yu* 隅 (corner) are interchangeable.

21. *Xuehaitang ji*, 11.3a.

22. Ibid., 11.22a.

23. Xie Lansheng, *Changxingxingzhai riji*, 11/23/DG1. See Appendix B.

24. Fan Feng, *Nanhai baiyong xubian*, passim.

25. Cai Xiang wrote a single-*juan Lizhi pu* 荔枝譜 in the eleventh century. Xu Bo in the late Ming composed a supplement to Cai's handbook. Deng Qingcai wrote a further supplement, prefaced in 1628, and printed it together with the Cai and Xu handbooks under the title *Minzhong lizhi tongpu* 閩中荔支通譜 during the Chongzhen era (1628–44). In a preface to the comprehensive handbook, one editor noted criticisms of Fujianese parochialism in Cai Xiang's original work but was confident that the supplements by Xu and Deng would suffice to compel "children of Wu 吳 [southern Jiangsu] to hold their tongues and guests from Yue 粵 [Guangdong] to search their souls." Deng Qingcai, *Minzhong lizhi tongpu*, Huang preface, 4a.

26. Zhu Yizun 朱彝尊 (1629–1709), a classical scholar and bibliophile from Zhejiang, traveled to Guangdong in 1692.

27. *Xuehaitang ji*, 15.7b. Tan Ying composed 100 poems, but only 60 were included in the *Xuehaitang ji*. The same 60 poems were incorporated into Tan's collected writings. See *Nanhai xian zhi*, 1872 edition, 18.14b; Tan Ying, *Lezhitang shiji*, 1.5b–12b.

28. *Xuehaitang ji*, 15.7b. "Guangnan" here essentially corresponds to Guangdong.

29. Ibid., 15.8b.

30. Wen Rugua (1784 *jinshi*) belonged to the Wen lineage from the Enclosure district township of Longshan.

31. *Xuehaitang ji*, 15.8b.

32. Zhang Jiuling, *Qujiang ji*, 1.13a–b.

33. See Su Shi, *Su Dongpo quanji*, 1: 455.

34. The Tang poet Bai Juyi 白居易 (722–846) wrote an "Essay on a Painting of Litchis" 荔枝圖序 after having an artist do a painting of Sichuan litchis.

35. *Xuehiatang ji*, 15.7b.

36. The Baiyue 百越, or Hundred Yue Tribes, could refer broadly to the indigenous peoples of south China from modern-day Zhejiang along the coast through Fujian and Guangdong, and into Guangxi. Here, Tan takes the term as a referent to Guangdong.

37. Su Shi was a native of Emei shan 峨眉山 in Sichuan and once served as a supervisor (*tiju* 提舉) of the Yuju [Daoist] Temple (玉局觀) north of Chengdu.

38. This is taken from the second of Su Shi's "Eating Litchis." The last two lines of Su's poem read, "Daily eating three hundred litchis, / no harm in long being a Lingnan resident" (日啖荔支三百顆, 不妨長作嶺南人). See *Su Dongpo quanji*, 1: 455.

39. *Xuehaitang ji*, 15.12b.

40. The pass through the Great Yu Range (Dayuling 大庾嶺) separating Jiangxi and Guangdong was known as Plum Pass 梅關.

41. "South of the Heavens" (Tiannan 天南) is another name for Guangdong or Lingnan. *Xuehaitang ji*, 15.15b.

42. Ibid., 15.16a. Lin referred to a passage in Li Zhao, *Tang guoshi bu*, *xia*.12b.

43. Yi Kezhong, *Jianguanglou ji*, lyrics, 8b.

44. Ruan Yuan points out in a prefatory note that the "five-corner peach" is another name for the *yangtao*.

45. Ruan Yuan, *Yanjingshi ji*, vol. 3, *Yanjing shi xuji*, p. 185. Professor Cai Hongsheng 蔡鴻生 of Zhongshan University drew attention to this poem at the Conference on Nineteenth-Century Lingnan, held at Zhongshan University, Guangzhou, on December 26, 1998.

46. David Faure, "Becoming Cantonese, the Ming Dynasty Transition," pp. 37, 40. In fact, the delta had been quite peripheral to the elite of northern Guangdong during the Tang. See Marks, *Tigers, Rice, Silk, and Silt*, pp. 62–63.

47. *Guangdong tongzhi*, 198.26a.

48. Ibid., 198.20a.

49. One noteworthy exception to the dearth of anthology projects in eighteenth-century Guangzhou was the *Guangdong shichao* 廣東詩鈔 (Transcribed poetry from Guangdong). Three doyens of Cantonese high culture, Che Tengfang 車騰芳 (1720 *juren*), Luo Tianchi, and He Mengyao, initiated this project in 1764, but all died before half of the poems had been collected. The project quickly lost momentum and was never completed. This false start stands in marked contrast to the numerous Guangdong anthologies successfully produced a half century later. Luo Yuanhuan, *Yuetai zhengya lu*, 22a.

50. *Guangdong tongzhi*, 198.22b–24b; *Panyu xian zhi*, 1872 edition, 27.41a–44a; Xu Shaoqi, "Guangzhou banpian jilue," 60a–b; Huang Yinpu, *Guangdong wenxian shumu zhijian lu*, p. 199. In the early 1840s, the Foshan merchant Liang Jiutu 梁九圖 (1816–80) and the Shunde poet Wu Bing-

nan 吳炳南 cooperated in producing an anthology of Cantonese poetry entitled *Lingbiao shizhuan* 嶺表詩傳.

51. *Guangzhou fu zhi*, 132.9b.

52. On Zhang Bao and the gentry-led defense against him, see Frederic Wakeman, Jr., *Strangers at the Gate: Social Disorder in South China, 1839–1861*, p. 24; Dian Murray, *Pirates of the South China Coast, 1790–1810*, especially pp. 73–76, 124–31.

53. *Shunde xian zhi*, 1853 edition, 27.9b; Luo Xuepeng, *Guangdong wenxian*, Tang Qingchuan 唐晴川 preface, 4a; and Feng Longguan, "Eulogy for Imperial Academy of Learning Collegian and Fellow [Shunde] County Native Luo Xuepeng," 1a.

54. In his study of late Ming Jiangnan, Chow Kai-wing argues that publishing was not prohibitively expensive. Chow, *Publishing, Culture, and Power in Early Modern China*, pp. 61–62.

55. Luo Xuepeng, *Guangdong wenxian*. *Nan-Han shu* author and future Xuehaitang co-director Liang Tingnan was listed as a proofreader.

56. *Guangdong tongzhi*, 198.23a–b. A four-installment edition was in circulation in the spring of 1826, when Xie Lansheng received a copy from a Shunde literatus and forwarded it to the lieutenant-governor. Additional four-installment editions were reprinted in 1863 and 1872 by the "Chunhui tang." Xie Lansheng, *Changxingxingzhai riji*, 3/28/DG6.

57. Luo Xuepeng, *Guangdong wenxian*, Tang preface, 2b.

58. Gui Wencan, *Jingxue bocai lu*, 11.20a; Xu Shaoqi, *Guangdong cangshu jishi shi*, p. 176.

59. The banner on the title pages of the second and third installments reads, "The most important books from Lingnan." Luo Xuepeng, *Guangdong wenxian*; Roger Chartier, *The Order of Books: Readers, Authors, and Libraries in Europe Between the Fourteenth and Eighteenth Centuries*, p. 22; Lucille Chia, *Printing for Profit: The Commercial Publishers of Jianyang, Fujian (11th–17th Centuries)*, pp. 39–44; Chow, *Publishing, Culture, and Power*, pp. 119, 126–27, 167.

60. Guy, *The Emperor's Four Treasuries*, p. 104; Cheuk-woon Taam, *The Development of Chinese Libraries Under the Ch'ing Dynasty, 1644–1911*, pp. 36–37.

61. Luo Xuepeng, *Guangdong wenxian*, Luo Xuepeng preface, 2a.

62. Ibid., editorial principles, 8a.

63. John Meskill describes Hai Rui's efforts to contain the power of landed elites in Jiangnan's Songjiang prefecture, when he served as governor of Nan Zhili. Meskill, *Gentlemanly Interests and Wealth on the Yangtze Delta*, pp. 132–35.

64. Luo Xuepeng, *Guangdong wenxian*, editorial principles, 8a–b.
65. See Legge, *The Chinese Classics*, 5: 507.
66. See the biography of Hai Rui in *Guangdong tongzhi*, 302.11a.
67. Luo Xuepeng, *Guangdong wenxian*, editorial principles, 6b.
68. Ibid., editorial principles, 5b.
69. Ibid., second installment, preface, 1a.
70. *Guangdong tongzhi*, 285.17a–18a, 4a–b, 27a–b, 284.3a.
71. Luo Xuepeng, *Guangdong wenxian*, second installment, editorial principles, 6a–b. In her study of academies during the Song dynasty, Linda Walton points out how the connections between beautiful landscapes and talented men are emphasized in inscriptions commemorating the establishment of academies. But in these inscriptions this relationship does not seem to be tied to a *particular* local context. Walton, *Academies and Society in Southern Sung China*, pp. 108–11.
72. Luo Xuepeng, *Guangdong wenxian*, fourth installment, 20.1b.
73. The *Yueyatang congshu* deserves further analysis, as it contains some interesting works, including, for example, Wen Zhenheng's 文震亨 (1585–1645) *Zhang wu zhi* 長物志. See Clunas, *Superfluous Things*.
74. Pan Shicheng, *Haishan xianguan congshu*.
75. In his eulogy of Wu Chongyao, Tan Ying states that Wu was the fifth son of Wu Bingjian. Wu Ziwei's 1956 genealogy shows Chongyao as the fourth son. This discrepancy suggests that an original third son listed in eulogies of Wu Bingjian, Wu Yuane 伍元菼, died prematurely. See Tan Ying, *Lezhitang wenji*, 4.19a; *Lingnan Wushi hezu zongpu*, 4 *xia*.6b.
76. Sucheta Mazumdar documents a foreign trust fund, belonging to the Wu family and managed by Russell and Company, that provided substantial income between 1878 and 1891. See Mazumdar, *Sugar and Society in China*, p. 117.
77. Chen Tan, *Kuangzhai shiyou ji*, Zhong Qishao chapter; Xu Yubin, *Dongrongguan yigao*, Wu Yanliu postscript.
78. Chen Li, *Dongshu yigao*, 29.7.
79. *Nanhai xian zhi*, 1872 edition, 18.14a.
80. Tan Ying, *Lezhitang wenji*, 11.12a.
81. Jiang Fan and Jiang Yuan were not related, although Jiang Fan had studied under Jiang Yuan's grandfather, Jiang Sheng. Hummel, *Eminent Chinese*, pp. 140–41.
82. Li Guangting later compiled his own collectanea. Li Guangting, *Rongyuan congshu*; *Guangdong tongzhi*, prefatory material, 6b–7a; Min Erchang, *Jiang Ziping xiansheng nianpu*, 15b–17a; Yi Kezhong, *Jianguanglou ji*, Jiang Yuan preface, 1b; Li Guangting, *Wanmei shuwu wenchao*, 1.30b. Other examples of Tan Ying's key role in the Guangzhou printing

world can be found throughout the letters in Chen Li's literary collections, *Dongshu ji* and *Dongshu xuji*.

83. The *Lingnan yishu* writes Chen Lian as 陳槤, whereas other texts write his name as 陳璉. See Huang Zuo, *Guangzhou renwu zhuan*, pp. 332-33; and Wen Runeng, *Yuedong shihai*, p. 194.

84. Zeng Zhao, *Mianchenglou jichao*, 2.25b; Wu Chongyao, *Lingnan yishu*, first installment, postscript to *Chunqiu biedian*; second installment, postscripts to *Guo jilian shugao* and *Suandi*; third installment, postscript to *Xiaoxue guxun*.

85. Tan Ying, *Lezhitang wenji*, 11.12b-13a.

86. Wu Chongyao, *Lingnan yishu*, preface, 1a.

87. Duo Jiao 鐸椒 was Grand Mentor of the state of Chu during the Han dynasty and author of *Duoshi wei* 鐸氏微. During the earlier period of the Warring States, the local rulers of the area corresponding to modern Guangdong paid tribute to the Chu court. *Shiji*, p. 510.

88. Zhang Mai 張買 was a native of the Southern Yue kingdom who served under Han Huidi (r. 194 BCE-188 BCE). He was adept at composing "Yueou"—Yue, or Cantonese, songs. *Guangdong tongzhi*, 268.4a. In the following notes to the *Lingnan yishu* preface, I largely refer to the 1822 *Guangdong tongzhi*, because this source was compiled by scholars who frequently interacted with Tan Ying and closely approximates the understanding that Tan would have had about these historical figures and texts.

89. Chen Qin 陳欽 was a native of the area corresponding to present-day Zhaoqing prefecture, which, according to the *Guangdong tongzhi* editors, belonged to Cangwu during the Han. He taught the Zuo Commentary to Wang Mang. See *Guangdong tongzhi*, 296.b.

90. Yang Fu was a Nanhai native during the reign of the Later Han Zhangdi (r. 76-88). His *Yiwu zhi* 異物志 appeared in some sources as *Nanyi yiwu zhi* 南裔異物志.

91. Shi Xie 士燮 (137?-226) was a regional leader who controlled Guangzhou from his base in Jiaozhi in northern Vietnam. In his youth, he had studied the Zuo Commentary of the *Chunqiu* in the Han capital of Luoyang. *Guangdong tongzhi*, 296.5b.

92. Wang Fan 王範 was a Nanhai native under the Han. His *Jiao-Guang chunqiu* 交廣春秋 recorded the institutions of his native region. *Guangdong tongzhi*, 268.15a.

93. I am not certain about this reference. Chapter 48 of the *Liang History* is devoted to biographies of the "forest of scholars." The first biography in this chapter is that of Fu Manrong 伏曼容, a native of Shandong who sojourned with his maternal uncle in Nanhai. Fu lectured on the *Yijing*

in the court of Song Mingdi (r. 465-72) and later compiled a collection of commentaries on this Classic. See *Liang shu*, pp. 662-63.

94. Huang Zheng 黃整 was a native of Nanhai during the Jin dynasty (265-419). His literary collection was listed in the annotations to the bibliographical treatise of the official history of the Sui dynasty (581-618). *Sui shu*, p. 1065; *Guangdong tongzhi*, 195.1a, 268.17a.

95. Qujiang in northern Guangdong was the native place of Zhang Jiuling. Tan Ying's text actually reads Quhong 曲紅, rather than Qujiang 曲江. The *Zhongwen da cidian* cites a passage from *Yijueliao zaji* 猗覺寮雜記, by Zhu Yi 朱翌 of the Song dynasty, explaining that Quhong was used interchangeably with Qujiang. Another example of Tan Ying's use of Quhong for Qujiang may be found in his postscript to Wu Yingkui's *Lingnan lizhi pu*. See Wu Chongyao, *Lingnan yishu*, fifth installment, *Lingnan lizhi pu*, Tan postscript, 1a-b.

96. *Shijian* 事鑒 refers to Zhang Jiuling's *Jinjianlu*. According to the *Tang shu* biography of Zhang, "Earlier, during the thousand autumns festival (the emperor's birthday celebration), dukes and princes all presented precious mirrors. But Jiuling offered up a 'mirror of affairs' in ten chapters, called *Qianqiu jinjian lu* 千秋金鑑錄, as an indirect remonstration." See *Tang shu*, p. 4429.

97. The 1822 provincial gazetteer listed a *Tang nianli* 唐年歷, authored by Liu Ke, but notes that it was no longer extant. Liu was a Qujiang native who served as an attendant censor under the Tang. *Guangdong tongzhi*, 189.1a.

98. Wu Chongyao, *Lingnan yishu*, preface, 1a.

99. *Xuehaitang erji*, 14.13a-24a. The 1822 provincial gazetteer had also judged currently circulating editions of the *Jinjian lu* to be spurious. *Guangdong tongzhi*, 194.1a-b.

100. Zhou Yinqing, *Diansan shenggao*, 7.8a. See Luo Xuepeng, *Guangdong wenxian*, editorial principles, 6b.

101. This refers to Hu Binwang's *Liushi xingwang lu*. See *Guangdong tongzhi*, 288.12a-b.

102. Li Daxing 李大性 was a native of Sihui west of Guangzhou during the Song dynasty. He presented to the throne his study of Song institutions, *Diangu bianyi* 典故辯疑. See *Guangdong tongzhi*, 296.14a.

103. Gu Chengzhi 古成之 (*zi* Yashi 亞奭) was a native of Heyuan, in Huizhou prefecture, who later moved to Zengcheng, in Guangzhou prefecture. The first *jinshi* that Guangzhou produced during the Song, Gu also authored a work on the *Yijing* entitled *Shan Yi zhushu* 刪易注疏. See *Guangdong tongzhi*, 290.4a-5b.

104. This refers to Yu Jing 余靖 (zi Andao 安道), a Qujiang native during the Song. See *Guangdong tongzhi*, 288.14a.

105. Chen Zhuo 陳拙 (zi Yongzhuo 用拙) was a Lianzhou native who earned the *jinshi* degree in 904. He later served under the Southern Han and wrote the *Da Tang zhengsheng qinji* 大唐正聲琴籍. See *Guangdong tongzhi*, 303.21a.

106. This refers to Huang Sun 黃損 (zi Yizhi 益之), like Chen Zhuo a native of Lianzhou during the Southern Han. Huang authored a book entitled *Shefa* 射法 (Archery method). Liang Tingnan, *Nan-Han shu*, pp. 53–54.

107. Liu Zhen 劉鎮 (hao Suiru 隨如) was a native of Nanhai during the Song. The anthologist of Qing poetry, Li E 厲鶚 (hao Fanxie 樊榭), noted in his biographical sketch of Liu Zhen that he had once printed a collection of poetry entitled *Suiru baiyong* 隨如百詠 (Suiru's hundred odes). See Li E, *Songshi jishi*, 59.30b; Tan Zongjun, *Licun caotang shichao*, 6.12b.

108. Yuzi 與子 refers to the Song statesman Cui Yuzhi, whose literary collection is recorded in the *Ji Cangwei cangshu mu* 季滄葦藏書目, a bibliographical record by the early Qing bibliophile Ji Zhenyi 季振宜 (hao Cangwei 滄葦). See Ji Zhenyi, *Ji Cangwei cangshu mu*, 28a.

109. This refers to a scholar from Boluo county named Zhang Xuan 張萱 (zi Mengqi 孟奇, 1558–1641). In 1608, he showed an unfinished 27-*juan* manuscript of his *Yiyao* 疑耀 to scholars in Nanjing. Years later he came across a printed version of his work in 7 *juan*, which had been attributed to Li Zhi 李贄 (1527–1602, hao Zhuoru 卓吾). See L. Carrington Goodrich and Chaoying Fang, eds., *Dictionary of Ming Biography, 1368–1644*, p. 78.

110. This refers to Ou Huairui's (zi Qitu 啟圖) unfinished anthology of Cantonese poetry, *Jiaoya*. Kuang Lu (hao Haixue 海雪), the eccentric poet from Panyu so admired by Chen Tan, had a collection of his own poetry under the same title.

111. That is, there are questions about the proper arrangement of some texts.

112. Wu Chongyao, *Lingnan yishu*, preface, 1a–b.

113. Qiu Jun (canonized as Wenzhuang 文莊) wrote a supplement to the *Daxue yanyi* 大學衍義 by Zhen Dexiu 真德秀 (1178–1235).

114. Zhan Ruoshui (hao Ganquan 甘泉) in 1528 presented to the emperor his 100-*juan* study of statecraft, entitled *Shengxue gewu tong* 聖學格物通.

115. Mt. Song 嵩 in Henan province was one of the Five Sacred Mountains; "Hua" 華 refers to the three peaks of the westernmost of the Five Sacred Mountains.

116. Wu Chongyao, *Lingnan yishu*, preface, 2a.

117. Ibid., preface, 2a.
118. *Guangdong tongzhi*, 193.11b, 15b; Wu Chongyao, *Lingnan yishu*, fifth installment.
119. Wu Chongyao, *Lingnan yishu*, fifth installment, Huang Zigao, *Yueshi souyi*, preface.
120. Liu Shinan, *Qing shi liupai shi*, pp. 19–20.
121. Qu Dajun, *Guangdong xinyu*, 11.9b–11a.
122. Wu Chongyao, *Lingnan yishu*, second installment, Jiang Fan, "Preface to Collected Writings of Liu Xiren," 1a.
123. The *Suandi* is composed of only eight *juan*, but each of these is large enough to require an entire *ce* 冊, and together they occupy almost an entire *han* 函, or case (or the whole case, in some versions I have seen).
124. Wu Chongyao, *Lingnan yishu*, second installment, *Suandi*, postscript, 1b.
125. Ibid., fifth installment, *Cetian yueshu* 測天約術, postscript, 1a. Although not quoted in full in the *Lingnan yishu*, Wen's biography relates one instance in which Dai Zhen sought advice from Chen, and another in which Chen humbled Wang Niansun's learned but conceited son, Wang Yinzhi. For the full biography, see Wen Xun, *Dengyun shanfang wengao*, 2.29b–30a.
126. Xinning county has been known since the 1930s as Taishan county. Chen Yufu had placed first in the 1690 Guangdong provincial examinations but was not particularly familiar to Cantonese literati in the early nineteenth century. When Chen's descendants decided to publish his collected writings in the early 1840s, however, they asked Xuehaitang co-director Lin Botong to write a preface. Yang Rongxu and a few other Xuehaitang scholars were listed as proofreaders. Chen Yufu, *Shexutang ji*, prefatory material.
127. Wu Chongyao, *Lingnan yishu*, third installment, *Zhengxue xu* 正學續, preface, 7b–8a.
128. *Zhengxue xu*, 2.25b.
129. Wu Chongyao, *Lingnan yishu*, fourth installment, *Zhouyi benyi zhu* 周易本義註, postscript, 1b.
130. Ibid., fifth installment, *Lingnan lizhi pu*, preface, 1a.
131. Ibid., fifth installment, *Lingnan lizhi pu*, Tan Ying postscript, 1a.
132. Elman, *From Philosophy to Philology*, pp. 143–56.
133. Though it is beyond the scope of this study, a related question worth exploring is the extent to which trends in calligraphy and painting, such as the creation of a "Lingnan school" of painting, were also largely dominated by Xuehaitang scholars or descendants of recent immigrants to Guangdong. Yeewan Koon will shed light on some of these questions in

her forthcoming dissertation, "Literati Iconoclasm: Violence and Estrangement in the Arts of Su Renshan," Institute of Fine Arts, New York University.

CHAPTER 5

EPIGRAPH: Chen Pu, *Chigang caotang yishi*, 6.7b. A photograph of Chen Pu's painting is included at the beginning of Rong Zhaozu's "Xuehaitang kao," but I have not been able to locate the original painting.

1. Marks, *Rice, Tigers, Silk, and Silt*, p. 219; *Guangzhou chengfang zhi*, p. 82.

2. Marks, *Rice, Tigers, Silk, and Silt*, p. 333; Leong, *Migration and Ethnicity in Chinese History*, pp. 62, 74; Wakeman, *Strangers at the Gate*, pp. 109–25.

3. For example, the second half of Qian Mu's classic study of Qing intellectual history largely seeks to document the mounting criticism and growing irrelevance of Qianlong- and Jiaqing-era evidential research in the nineteenth century. See his *Zhongguo jin sanbai nian xueshu shi*, especially chaps. 9, 11, 12, and 13. Describing the social context of the eighteenth-century evidential research movement in Jiangnan, Benjamin Elman argues that, as a result of the devastation of the Taiping Rebellion, the Jiangnan academic community "was not adequately rehabilitated." Elman, *From Philosophy to Philology*, p. 252.

4. See Appendix A. High turnover was also the case between 1857 and 1863, when eight new appointments were made. Polachek's attention is drawn to the Xuehaitang because one of the Xuehaitang co-directors close to Ruan Yuan, Wu Lanxiu, wrote an essay advocating the legalization of opium as a strategy for arresting the outflow of silver. Polachek, *Inner Opium War*, p. 120. Polachek's main concern is to explain the internal dynamics that led the Qing empire into the Opium War; his narrative does not, however, address Guangzhou's academies during the post-crisis reconstruction and hence misses a fundamental continuity. He describes a "revolution in academic fashion" carried out by provincial officials in Guangzhou, who fervently opposed the scholarly-literary ideals and the political policies of Ruan Yuan, and who were supported by local literati disgruntled with the dominance of the Xuehaitang. Thus, according to Polachek, the stubbornly anti-opium imperial commissioner Lin Zexu (1785–1850) and his sympathizer, Governor-General Deng Tingzhen (1776–1846), initiated a "frantic juggling" of Guangzhou academy directorships over the months preceding and during the war, in which they sought to refurbish the Xuehaitang by appointing likeminded scholars as co-directors. Polachek, *Inner*

Opium War, pp. 144–49. Deng Tingzhen in fact seems to have sponsored both supporters and critics of the Xuehaitang. For example, he sponsored the printing of the second edition of Xuehaitang student writings in 1838 but was also a consistent patron of the vociferous critic Fang Dongshu. Deng Bangkang, *Deng shangshu nianpu*, 9b–10a, 12b, 13b.

5. Li Changrong, *Liutang shiyou shilu*, Xu Rong chapter, 9b; *Hangzhou fu zhi*, 101.3b.

6. Another early co-director, Zhang Biao, withdrew from the co-directorate due to his encroaching blindness.

7. According to Chen Pu, he was descended from a general who served the Jin dynasty (265–419), and whose descendants were Panyu natives. An ancestor during the Song is supposed to have resided in the southern part of the county, on the border of what were sands in the Qing. A sixth-generation descendant of this Song ancestor was believed to have moved to Chigang, presumably sometime during the Ming. Chen Pu, *Chigang caotang yiwen*, 3.2a.

8. Ibid., 3.2a.

9. Li Guangting was a native of Shimen 石門 township. *Panyu xian xu zhi*, 20.16b. Chen Pu wrote Li Guangting's funerary inscription. See *Chigang caotang yiwen*, 3.10a.

10. The Bichong Zou claimed descent from an ancestor who relocated from Nanxiong during the Song dynasty. Zou Boqi, *Zou zhengjun yishu*, *Zou Zhengjun cungao*, 38a.

11. Chen Pu, *Chigang caotang yiwen*, 1.18a.

12. *Heyang shixi*, 9b–10a. The *Xuehaitang sanji* contains one poem by Pan Dinggui, and the *Xuehaitang siji* has five poems by Pan Shu.

13. In contrast to the numerous Jiaying scholars whose works were incorporated in the *Xuehaitang ji*, only nine were included in the 1838 *Xuehaitang erji*, three in the 1859 *Xuehaitang sanji*, and just one in the 1886 *Xuehaitang siji*.

14. Chen Li, *Dongshu ji*, 6.20b–21a; Shen Shiliang, *Lenghuashi cichao*, 1.3b. Li Xubai praises Xu Hao as the first legal secretary in Guangdong to study the Classics and Histories and produce significant scholarship. In fact, many Xuehaitang scholars—at least those with northern Zhejiang roots—certainly belonged to such families. Li Xubai, *Qingdai Guangdong puxue yanjiu*, p. 71. For another *muyou*, who found time for scholarship on numerology, *Shuowen* studies, and the Zhu Xi exegesis of the *Lunyu*, see the 1931 Panyu gazetteer biography of Chen Qirui. *Panyu xian xu zhi*, 19.12b.

15. Jin Xiling was the son of Jin Jinghua 金菁華. His uncles included Jing'e, the resident teacher at the Wu family estate in Henan, and

Jingmao, the *juren* turned salt merchant. Lin Botong, *Xiubentang gao*, 4.8a.

16. Wang Zhaoyong, "Biography of Sub-Director of Shaozhou Prefectural School Shen," 1a, in Shen Shiliang, *Xiao Qituo an shichao*. Other Xuehaitang scholars with Shaoxing roots who registered as Panyu natives included Wu Feng (d. 1867), Liu Changling 劉昌齡 (1825–89), and Tao Fuxiang. Wu was from Shanyin and had writings in both the third and fourth collections of Xuehaitang writings. Liu, a co-director, was also from a Shanyin family. His grandfather was a *muyou* in Guangdong, and so the family later registered as Panyu residents. Also a co-director, Tao was a seventh-generation descendant of a sojourner from Guiji. I suspect that one of the scholars in the *Xuehaitang ji*, Tao Kechang 陶克昌, also a Panyu native, was a member of the same descent group. Wu Feng, *Qiushixuan yigao, shang*.11b; Rong Zhaozu, "Xuehaitang kao," p. 57; *Panyu xian xu zhi*, 23.1b.

17. The Shanyin Wangs claimed descent from a migrant from Huizhou, Anhui, at the end of the Yuan dynasty. *Shanyin Wangshi pu*, pp. 1–3.

18. Unlike many gazetteer biographies, the Wang genealogy does not obscure ancestors' specialization as legal secretaries. One of Lunzhi's sons, Wang Kai, served under Zeng Yu when the latter was Hunan governor in 1807–1809. *Shanyin Wangshi pu*, p. 53.

19. The Wang genealogy reports that Wang Quan earned as much as "one thousand taels" every year, suggesting that claims of family members being "too poor" to return indicate that they were unwilling to forgo the profits that must have drawn them to pursue careers in Guangdong in the first place. *Shanyin Wangshi pu*, pp. 57–58; Wang Quan, *Suishanguan conggao*, 8.6b. Suggesting the existence of a network of Zhejiang sojourners in Guangzhou, another source notes that Wang Quan taught the legal trade to his nephew Tao Erkun 陶爾琨, a native of Shanyin. Zhang Xintai, *Yueyou xiaoji*, 6.10a.

20. According to Rong Zhaozu, Zhaoquan was selected as a specialized student in 1881, and Zhaoyong in 1884. The Wang genealogy claims that Zhaohong was also a specialized student. Rong Zhaozu, "Xuehaitang kao," pp. 4–5; *Shanyin Wangshi pu*, pp. 77–82, 101.

21. *Shanyin Wangshi pu*, pp. 75, 79. Zhu Qilian had several essays and poems included in the *Xuehaitang siji*. In the Wang genealogy, one can also find evidence of a strategy of cultivating marriage alliances among the in-migrating Zhejiang cohort. For instance, in an epitaph for Wang Quan contained in the Wang genealogy, his student, and fellow Shaoxing native and Panyu resident, Tao Shaoxue (1863–1908) remarks, "Over the generations those with whom my descent group have arranged marriages have all come from lineages relocated from Zhejiang," and explains that he

writes this epitaph "to expound on virtues of the maintenance [of the practice] . . . and to admonish against the baseness of Cantonese customs." *Shanyin Wangshi pu*, p. 82.

22. *Shanyin Wangshi pu*, p. 87. Liao Zhen and Liao Tingxiang belonged to a rural Nanhai lineage that claimed descent from ancestors who had settled the delta during the Song dynasty. Nevertheless, Liao Tingxiang, his father (Liao Zhen), his grandfather, and his great-grandfather were all buried at Guangzhou. This suggests that Zhen and Tingxiang represent an urbanized segment of a rural Nanhai lineage. Liao Zhen appears in the genealogy as Liao Zhenfa 廖震發. *Liao Weize tang jiapu*, 4.54b–57b.

23. Another in-migrating Zhejiang family that sent its sons to the Xuehaitang was the Gui family of Nanhai. After his ancestors resided in Ningbo prefecture's Cixi/Ciqi 慈溪 county since the Song, Gui Hong's 桂鴻 (1746–1807) grandfather served as a prefectural jail warden in Hunan for over thirty years. "Too poor" to return to Cixi, he perished in Hunan while his son worked his way down to Guangzhou, where he served as a yamen secretary and then registered as a Nanhai resident. This son in turn had three sons, two of whom were educated at Yuexiu Academy. One of these, Gui Hong, "accompanied [officials'] administrations and became skilled at clerking services" (隨幕諳習吏事) before passing the 1786 provincial examinations and thereby winning a place among the city's literati elite. Hong's grandsons Gui Wenxuan 桂文烜, Gui Wencan (whose *Jingxue bocai lu* is quoted in the Introduction), and Gui Wenchi were all Xuehaitang students. Two of Gui Wencan's sons in turn were Xuehaitang specialized students in 1872 and 1891. These Nanhai Guis seem to have intermarried with the Panyu Taos described in note 16, above. Gui Wencan's older brother was married to the daughter of Panyu resident Tao Kexie 陶克諧. Gui Hong, *Jianzhai shichao*, epitaph, 1a–7a; Gui Tan, *Huimuxuan gao*, Gui Hong biography, 1b, 4a; Zheng Xianfu, *Buxuexuan wenji*, 4.26a; Gui Wencan, *Qianxintang ji*, unpaginated.

24. Zhang Qizeng, *Bianzhen liangshi wenchai*, 2.3a–b. Based on the common features of his name, I suspect that Zhang Qixuan 張其翽, a Jiaying native who took the 1827 spring examination at the Xuehaitang, was also related to Qizeng and Qihan. Weng Xincun, *Xuehaitang dinghai keshi lu*, unpaginated. The *Xuehaitang sanji* contains an essay by Huang Zigao's son, Huang Jiantai 黃漸泰, and four poems by Zigao's son-in-law, Liu Xizhang 劉錫章 (1840 *juren*) of Panyu.

25. Ye Renlan's original name was Ye Mengzhen 葉夢鎮. Weng Xincun, *Xuehaitang dinghai keshi lu*, unpaginated.

26. Another possible example of family connections is suggested by the fact that Tan Zongjun's older sister married a Liang of Shunde's Lunjiao

township, native place of Liang Tingnan. Tan Zongjun, *Licun caotang shichao*, 6.15b–16a; Tan Zongjun, *Xigutang ji*, 2.33a–b.

27. Deng, Chen, Liao, Zheng, and Liang, as well as Tan, all had their writings included in the *Xuehaitang siji*. This collection also contains the writings of Liang's father and Xiong Jingxing's son-in-law, Liang Shugong 梁樹功 (ca. 1820–72). Tan Zongjun, *Licun caotang shichao*, 6.16a; Chen Li, *Dongshu ji*, 6.18a.

28. Elman, *Classicism, Politics, and Kinship*, pp. xxiii, xxxiii, 7–8.

29. *Guangzhou fu zhi*, 82.3b–29b. For a summary of these events, see Wakeman, *Strangers at the Gate*, pp. 139–48.

30. Chen Pu, *Chigang caotang yiwen*, 3.10b.

31. George Wingrove Cooke, *China: Being "The Times" Special Correspondent from China for the Years 1857–1858*, pp. 50, 291–94.

32. Cooke, *China*, pp. 285, 315–19.

33. Cooke, a British correspondent observing the "Arrow War," described "a collegiate quadrangle" where "the dons of the ecclesiastical institution once clustered," but which had now "become a British headquarters." This conceivably could refer either to the Xuehaitang and the adjacent Wenlan Pavilion, or perhaps to the several temples nearby. Ibid., pp. 321, 342; J. Y. Wong, *Yeh Ming-ch'en: Viceroy of Liang Kuang, 1852–8*, pp. 36, 178–85.

34. *Nanhai xian zhi*, 1872 edition, 26.10a–b; Cooke, *China*, p. 353; Shi Cheng, *Quting suoyu*, 8.6b–7a; Yi Kezhong, *Jianguanglou ji*, Chen Pu postscript, 1a; Chen Pu, *Chigang caotang yishi*, 4.13b; Li Changrong, *Liutang shiyou shilu*, Jin Jingmao chapter, 1a; Zhang Weiping, *Xiantan lu, xia*.30a.

35. Chen Li, *Dongshu xuji*, p. 71; *Xuehaitang zhi*, 30b–31a; *Guangzhou chengfang zhi*, p. 156. The map of Bichong township in the Tongzhi edition of the Nanhai gazetteer shows a Zou ancestral hall. See *Nanhai xian zhi*, 1872 edition, 1.42b. Like the Xuehaitang examinations, the 1860 supplementary *suike* (licensing and qualifying) examinations for Nanhai and Panyu counties temporarily used the Haichuang Monastery grounds due to the destruction of the examination grounds. See Tan Zongjun, *Licun caotang shichao*, 6.14b.

36. Huang Peifang's younger admirer, Li Changrong—who did abandon the city, returning only in the fall of 1858—noted that Huang had not left the Old City for four years prior to visiting his New City Willow Hall in February 1859. Li Changrong, *Liutang shiyou shilu*, Huang Peifang chapter, 1a.

37. Chen Pu, *Chigang caotang yishi*, 4.13a. Chen's use of wild deer (*milu* 麋鹿) alludes to imagery found in Zuo Si's "Wei Capital Rhapsody" in the *Wenxuan*, and to the *Shiji* biography of Liu Chang. See Knechtges, vol. 1,

p. 433 (he translates *milu* as "elaphures"), and Watson, *Records of the Grand Historian*, vol. 2, p. 334.

38. Chen Pu, *Chigang caotang yishi*, 1.7a, 4.14b. Chen Pu was close to Zhao Zhongyang 招仲敭, a frequent Xuehaitang examinee, whom he had visited previously. The Zhao ancestral shrine and Hengsha village were located in Caochang 草場 township. See *Nanhai xian zhi*, 1872 edition, 1.19b. The most famous member of the Hengsha Zhao was Zhao Ziyong 招子庸 (1789-1847), a renowned composer of popular Cantonese songs (*Yueou* 粵謳) and a close friend of Xie Lansheng. Xian Yuqing, *Xian Yuqing wenji*, p. 120.

39. Tan Zongjun, *Licun caotang shichao*, 6.14a. The title of one Tan Ying poem mentions by their sobriquets two He brothers (Zaotang 藻堂 and Xingpu 星浦), but I have not been able to identify them or ascertain their connection to the Tans. Nevertheless, a He shrine is indicated in the village of Heshun in the Nanhai gazetteer map of Lower Baishi 下白石 township. Tan Ying, *Lezhitang shiji*, 12.19b; *Nanhai xian zhi*, 1872 edition, 1.27a.

40. Tan Ying, *Lezhitang shiji*, 12.19b; Tan Zongjun, *Licun caotang shichao*, 1.9b-10a. The *she*, or altar to the soil and grains, often defined the ritual focus of rural communities. See Szonyi, *Practicing Kinship*, pp. 174-82.

41. Li Ruwei had twenty poems in the *Xuehaitang sanji*. Wang Zhaoyong biography of Shen Shiliang, 1a-2b, and Zheng Xianfu preface, 1a, both in Shen Shiliang, *Xiao Qituo an shichao*.

42. Shen Shiliang, *Xiao Qituo an shichao*, 4.5b-9a; *Shunde xian zhi*, 1853 edition, 2.9b-10a.

43. *Huang Shenzhi shourong jigong lu*, unpaginated. Some excerpts of this can be found in *Guangzhou chengfang zhi*, pp. 430-32.

44. Derk Bodde, *Festivals in Classical China: New Year and Other Annual Observances During the Han Dynasty, 206 BC-AD 220*, pp. 273-81.

45. On Wang Shizhen and the Red Bridge lustration festival ceremonies, see Meyer-Fong, *Building Culture in Early Qing China*, p. 59. The lustration festival was also the ritual focus of what James Polachek calls the Spring Purification circle in the capital, though he suggests that members of this circle adhered to the ceremony primarily for the purpose of maintaining an appearance of continuity with "northern-clique courtiers" such as Weng Fanggang, Zeng Yu, and Ruan Yuan. Polachek, *Inner Opium War*, pp. 84-85.

46. Huang Zhi, *Yue xiaoji*, 2.20b; *Guangzhou chengfang zhi*, p. 132. This festival had added local significance because the third day of the third month was also the birthday of the very popular Beidi deity worshiped in temples in Foshan and Xiguan. Gray, *Walks in the City of Canton*, p. 122,

Nanhai xian zhi, 1835 edition, 8.14b. Also see Liu Zhiwei, "Lineage on the Sands," p. 40.

47. Both Zhang Weiping and the poet Chen Tan participated in the 1815 lustration ceremony. In 1836 Chen and Pan Dinggui observed the occasion once again at the same site. Chen Tan, *Ganyutang wen/waiji*, 3.11a–b.

48. *Xuehaitang ji*, 10.38a–40a.

49. Zhang Weiping, *Tingsonglu pianti wenchao*, 4.11a–12a. The "Immortal City" (Xiancheng 仙城) refers to Guangzhou, which was said to have been founded by five immortals astride five rams. Among those in attendance were Ding Xi 丁熙 (ca. 1808–50), Huang Yujie, Li Yingtian, Wen Xun, and Tao Keqin (on the Panyu Taos, see note 16, above). Zhang Shen 張深, a native of Dantu county in Jiangsu and an acting magistrate of Dapu county in far eastern Guangdong during the mid-1830s, seems to have been the only member of the Jiangnan contingent that Zhang Weiping mentions in his essay. Three invited guests who were unable to attend were Xu Yubin, Li Changrong, and Duan Peilan. Dou Zhen, *Guochao shuhuajia bilu*, 3.16b–17a; *Dapu xian zhi*, 17.3b.

50. Li Changrong, *Liutang shiyou shilu*, Su Liupeng chapter, Tan Ying chapter, Du You chapter.

51. Xu Yubin, *Dongrongguan yigao*, 4.14a, 5.13a–b. A Shunde native, Li Yingtian had an essay and four poems in the *Xuehaitang sanji*; his father, Li Qinghua 李清華, had an essay and a poem in the *Xuehaitang ji*. Another lustration celebration, probably held in the 1850s at Haichuang Monastery, was attended by Zhang Weiping, Huang Peifang, Tan Ying, and the Xuehaitang co-director Yang Rong(xu), among others. Yang Rongxu, *Yang Fuxiang xiansheng yigao bubian*, unpaginated.

52. *Gengshen xiuxi ji*, Tan Ying general preface, 2a, *passim*. On autumn lustration celebrations, see Bodde, *Festivals in Classical China*, pp. 285–88. These celebrations were not unprecedented in nineteenth-century Guangzhou. For example, in 1832, the provincial examiner, Cheng Enze (1785–1837), and Tan Ying had hosted an autumn lustration ceremony at Cloud and Springs Mountain Lodge. Chen Liangyu, *Meiwo shichao*, 2.20a.

53. *Gengshen xiuxi ji*, Willow Hall Spring Lustration Poems, 5b; *Guangzhou chengfang zhi*, pp. 120–21.

54. *Gengshen xiuxi ji*, Willow Hall Spring Lustration Poems, 3a.

55. Ibid., 3b. Not all of the *Gengshen xiuxi ji* poems are so somber. The collection of poems on the Willow Hall ceremony includes a poem sent by Liang Chen 梁琛 (a painter from Shunde) to Li Changrong in response to a letter in which Li had told him of the event. In the title of his poem, Liang also invites Su Liupeng to rent a boat on the Pearl River and bring some

"famous flowers" (i.e., renowned courtesans) to conduct a supplementary lustration ceremony, and wondered whether the Willow Hall group would see Liang and Su as two crazy old men. In the text of his poem, Liang fears that the others would "laugh at my many sentiments like a young man." In a note at the end of his poem, Liang speculates that "there should still be some famous flowers of the Pearl River" who survived the recent disorders. Ibid., 6b.

56. Mary Wright uses the example of the Tongzhi Restoration to argue that a modern state cannot be grafted onto a Confucian society. See Wright, *The Last Stand of Chinese Conservatism: The T'ung-chih Restoration, 1862–1874*, pp. 9–10, 299–300. Taking a local approach, Mary Rankin suggests that reconstruction in the Tongzhi era "fostered a rapid and permanent expansion of elite-managed, quasi-governmental activities." Rankin, *Elite Activism and Political Transformation in China: Zhejiang Province, 1865–1911*, p. 3.

57. *Shunde xian zhi*, 1829 edition, 18.2a–4a, 19b–23a, 18.14b; Wakeman, *Strangers at the Gate*, pp. 152–56; Tan Dihua, *Qingdai Zhujiang sanjiaozhou de shatian*, p. 245; Eng, "Institutional and Secondary Landlordism in the Pearl River Delta," p. 13; Sasaki Masaya, "Juntoku-ken kyōshin to Tōkai jūrokusa," esp. pp. 209–19. One of the eighteen Shunde gentry managers of the bureau, Li Chaomin 黎超民, whom Sasaki does not identify, was an uncle of Li Rumei, who hosted Shen Shiliang at Changjiao township in 1858. Sasaki, "Juntoku-ken kyōshin to Tōkai jūrokusa," p. 216; Shen Shiliang, *Xiao Qituo an shichao*, 4.7a.

58. Tan Dihua, *Qingdai Zhujiang sanjiaozhou de shatian*, p. 39.

59. Fan Feng, *Yinan shimo*, 11a.

60. Chen Li, *Dongshu yigao*, 53.5. As early as 1846, a sojourning literatus from Hunan identified demobilized braves as a source of banditry and disorder in Guangdong. Zhou Shouchang, *Siyitang rizha*, 27a.

61. In an early example of this during the Opium War, Zeng Zhao and Fan Feng proposed to Qi Gong that sands accumulated by wealthy families be confiscated by the state. Liang Tingnan, *Yifen jiwen*, p. 52.

62. Guo Songtao, *Guo Songtao riji*, p. 161. In addition to providing strategic information for military defense, this mapping project must also have provided knowledge useful for further exploitation of the sands. James Polachek documents the efforts, in 1841 and 1842, of the urban Cantonese gentry to put together a militia force to patrol sands owned by urban corporations, and to collect rents from land there in exchange for fees paid to the bureau. He suggests that provincial officials acquiesced to, or even encouraged, this scheme. See Polachek, *Inner Opium War*, pp. 172–73.

63. Chen Qikun's father, as a *muyou* on Ruan Yuan's staff, had advocated importing foreign rice to supply the rice-deficient Pearl River delta. *Panyu xian xu zhi*, 19.10a–b.

64. *Guangdong shengli xinzuan*, 2.28a–b; *Panyu xian xu zhi*, 19.10a–b; *Nanhai xian zhi*, 1872 edition, 12.32b–33b, 13.32a; *Nanhai xian zhi*, 1910 edition, 15.6a; Jin Xiling, *Qushushi yiji*, 16.16; *Huangshi jiacheng*, 3.45a; Liang Jiabin, *Guangdong shisanhang kao*, pp. 323–24; *Zhu Ciqi xiansheng shishi kao*. Mary Rankin describes a similar gentry-managed granary in Foshan, created on the initiative of the local elite in the 1790s. The Foshan gentry increasingly asserted their independence from official oversight during the first half of the nineteenth century. Rankin, "Managed by the People," pp. 20–23, 38–39. On urban charitable granaries in the early nineteenth century, see Pierre-Étienne Will and R. Bin Wong, *Nourish the People: The State Civilian Granary System in China, 1650–1850*, p. 89.

65. *Xuehaitang zhi*, 18b; Shi Cheng, *Quting suoyu*, 8.9a, 15b.

66. Lu Duanfu, *Minsu xiankao Houshan fujun nianpu*, 7a, 62a; Qian Yiji, *Kanshizhai jishi xugao*, 3.25a; Chen Li, *Dongshu ji*, 2.28a; *Xuehaitang zhuanke zhangcheng*, 3b.

67. *Xuehaitang zhi*, 35a–b.

68. *Nanhai xian zhi*, 1872 edition, 12.24a. The relevant passage is quoted on p. 141.

69. *Xuehaitang zhuanke zhangcheng*, 3a–b; *Xuehaitang zhi*, 25b–26a.

70. Chen Li, *Dongshu xuji*, p. 71; *Xuehaitang zhi*, 23b, 30b–31a; *Gengshen xiuxi ji*, Tan Ying preface, 3b; Tan Zongjun, *Licun caotang shichao*, 6.14b.

71. *Xuehaitang zhuanke zhangcheng*, 9a–10b; Chen Li, *Dongshu zazu*, 11.22a.

72. By the late 1880s, Xuehaitang examinations evidently were held monthly from the second through the eleventh lunar months, a more frequent rate than the quarterly schedule in the early years of the academy.

73. Chen Li, *Dongshu xuji*, pp. 41–42.

74. Wen Tingshi, *Wen Tingshi ji*, p. 1070; Rong Zhaozu, "Xuehaitang kao," p. 73.

75. Liu Boji, *Guangdong shuyuan zhidu*, pp. 78–79.

76. Keenan, *Imperial China's Last Classical Academies*, pp. 11–19; Rankin, *Elite Activism*, pp. 97, 316–318 (Appendix B). Ōkubo Eiko provides tables listing instances of academy construction and renovation for all of the provinces, as well as for the empire as a whole, but does not give annual rates of construction and renovation. When annual rates are considered, the Tongzhi reign appears to have been the most active period during the Qing. See Ōkubo, *Min-Shin jidai shoin no kenkyū*, pp. 78–85, 123.

77. He Wenqi was a native of Zhenyong 鎮涌 township, along the West River in the Enclosure district upstream from Jiujiang. Like most lineages in the Enclosure district, the He lineage of Yanqiao village in Zhenyong claimed descent from Zhujixiang ancestors. He Wenqi was actively involved in the construction of lineage genealogical and ritual practices. He was appointed to Yuexiu in 1842, and was still the director when the 1847 *Yuexiu shuyuan zhi* was compiled. He edited a collection of Yuexiu student examinations in 1848, which included essays by Luo Jiaqin and Long Yuanbu 龍元佈, scions of the powerful Daliang Luo and Long lineages. In the autumn of 1851, he prefaced a collection of his own reading notes, but soon left the academy after a dispute with the governor-general. *Xuxiu Nanhai Yanqiao Heshi jiapu*, 2.1a–b, 5.2b–3a, 9.7b; *Yuexiu shuyuan keyi*; He Wenqi, *Keyu huichao*; He Wenqi, *Sishu jiangyi*, Lü Hong preface; Jian Chaoliang, *Dushutang ji*, prose, 6.13a–14a.

78. Shi Cheng, *Quting suoyu*, 8.13a, 16b.

79. *Yuehua jilue*, preface, 4b, 1.4b.

80. *Yuehua keyi, passim.*

81. Deng Shixian was a native of Shatou 沙頭, just northwest of Jiujiang. On Luo Jiaqin, see *Shunde xian zhi*, 1929 edition, 17.16a.

82. James Polachek portrays the Yuexiu and Yuehua as "rival" academies to the Xuehaitang and suggests that between 1838 and 1840 Lin Zexu sought to downgrade the status of the Xuehaitang relative to other academies in the city. His claim is based on Lin's decision to set up office at Yuehua Academy and his exclusion of Xuehaitang students from a series of special examinations that he held in Guangzhou. Polachek, *Inner Opium War*, pp. 123, 145, 147. The first point rests on the expectation that an imperial commissioner on special assignment to Guangzhou would have resided at the Xuehaitang, which, if true, would impart great symbolic significance to Lin's decision to reside instead at Yuehua. Yet, though officials who wished to patronize the Xuehaitang might host banquets on academy grounds, even perhaps staying the night, there is no record of any official using academy grounds as an official yamen. Moreover, due to the academy's design and its location away from the center of town, it may not have been a very suitable place for an imperial commissioner and his coterie to conduct affairs of state. In contrast, Yuehua Academy was located in the heart of the Old City, near other official yamen, and its student dormitories would have provided sufficient space to house secretaries and other functionaries. Polachek cites Arthur Waley's description of Lin's residence at Yuehua Academy but does not quote the passage, which helps to contextualize Lin's selection: "This Academy had in recent years been constantly requisitioned for official purposes, and it had been

selected on the present occasion because it was at a conveniently short distance from the premises of the Chinese guild-merchants and the adjacent factories of the foreign traders." Waley, *The Opium War Through Chinese Eyes*, p. 20. It is also worth noting that one of the Xuehaitang scholars closest to Ruan Yuan, Wu Lanxiu, resided at the "rival" Yuexiu Academy. *Nanhai xian zhi*, 1872 edition, 26.10b. The second point supporting Polachek's notion of a readjustment of the Xuehaitang's status vis-à-vis the other academies is that when, in July 1839, Lin Zexu held examinations to "fathom the local scholarly climate" (*guanfeng* 觀風), he "excluded" Xuehaitang students from the competition. Polachek, *Inner Opium War*, p. 148. For Lin Zexu's exclusion of Xuehaitang students, Polachek cites Lin Zexu, *Lin Wenzhong gong riji*, pp. 347, 349, and Liang Tingnan's *Yifen jiwen* (in *Yapian zhanzheng*, 6: 13). The latter source notes only that Lin "selected and gathered several hundred students from the three academies (*shuyuan*) in the provincial city—Yuexiu, Yuehua, and Yangcheng—for an examination to fathom local scholarly trends." But I am not convinced that excluding Xuehaitang students from a *guanfeng* examination was unusual, as the format of these examinations closely matched regular examinations in conventional academies but was entirely different from those routinely conducted by the Xuehaitang. It may have been the case that Xuehaitang students were never asked by any official to take a *guanfeng* examination.

83. Shi Cheng, *Quting suoyu*, 8.12a, 16b; *Yuexiu shuyuan keyi*.

84. Wu Feng, *Qiushixuan yigao*, shang.1b; Tan Zongjun, *Licun caotang shichao*, 1.1a, 2.22a, 6.15a; Rong Zhaozu, "Xuehaitang kao," p. 52.

85. *Yuehua jilue*, 4.28a–b, *Yuexiu shuyuan zhi*, 6.10a–35a; Fu Weisen, *Duanxi shuyuan zhi*, 7.1a–57b.

86. Gray, *Walks in the City of Canton*, p. 412.

87. *Guangzhou fu zhi*, 72.13; Chen Li, *Dongshu ji*, 2.29a; *Xuehaitang siji*, 22.38b–39a; *Zhu Yue baqi zhi*, 24.9a. Visiting Guangzhou again in 1870, Fang Junyi perhaps exerted pressure on his successor to support the academy that he had established. Fang Junyi, *Erzhixuan wencun*, 18.2a.

88. Chen Li, *Dongshu ji*, 2.29a; Chen Li, *Dongshu xuji*, p. 26; Rong Zhaozu, "Xuehaitang kao," pp. 146–47. Another factor explaining Jupo's similarity to the Xuehaitang is that Fang Junyi was close to several Xuehaitang scholars and, during his tenure in Guangzhou, even wrote a set of poems on the "Hundred Chants on the South Sea Region" theme. Fang Junyi, *Erzhixuan shichao*, 13.7a, 9a–b, 14.11a–27a.

89. The 100 Yingyuan students included 30 "inner students," 20 "outer students," and 50 "attached students." *Yingyuan shuyuan zhilue*, 3a–b, 20a–23b.

90. Wang Kaitai's ancestor was Wang Shidan 王式丹 (1645–1718).

91. *Yingyuan shuyuan zhilue*, 3a–b, 28a.

92. Under the Yuan dynasty, Fujian was divided into eight routes 路, and during the Ming and Qing Dynasties it was divided into eight prefectures and departments.

93. *Xuehaitang siji*, 22.41a. In Zhejiang, Hangzhou's Fuwen Academy 敷文書院 in 1836 created monthly classes for *juren*. See *Fuwen shuyuan zhilue*, 7a–b. Fuzhou's Zhengyi shuyuan 正誼書院 was established as an academy exclusively for *juren* just when Wang was creating the Yingyuan Academy. See Li Xiaofeng, *Zhongguo shuyuan cidian*, p. 95.

94. Mo Xuanqing 莫宣卿 was a *zhuangyuan* during the Tang, and a native of Fengzhou, which in the Qing belonged to Zhaoqing prefecture. Zhaoqing was referred to as Duan 端. See *Guangdong tongzhi*, 296.9a–10b.

95. Lun Wenxu 倫文敘 (Yugang 淤岡), a Nanhai native, was the 1499 *zhuangyuan*. His eldest son, Lun Yiliang 倫以諒, was the Guangdong *jieyuan* (that is, first place in the provincial examinations) in 1516. The second son, Lun Yixun 倫以訓, was the *huiyuan*—first in the metropolitan examination prior to the palace examination—in the following year. Finally, a third son, Lun Yishen 倫以詵, according to his biography in the Guangdong provincial gazetteer, was slated to be placed among the top three candidates in the palace examination of 1538; however, due to the enmity of an opponent at court he was relegated to the second class of *jinshi*. See *Guangdong tongzhi*, 276.15b–18a.

96. *Xuehaitang siji*, 22.41a–b.

97. Ibid., 22.42a.

98. *Yingyuan shuyuan zhilue*, 6b, 12a.

99. Wang Kaitai was a native of Baoying county in the northern hinterland of Yanghzou prefecture. *Yingyuan shuyuan zhilue*, 7b.

100. Established in 1887, Guangya shuyuan was formally opened in 1888. The name of the academy suggested its mission of selecting refined scholars from both "Guang" provinces: Guangdong and Guangxi. Thus, it could also be translated as "Academy for the Refinement of the Guang Provinces." William Ayers, *Chang Chih-tung and Educational Reform in China*, pp. 58–59; Zhou Hanguang, *Zhang Zhidong yu Guangya shuyuan*, pp. 306–11.

CHAPTER 6

EPIGRAPH: Chen Li, *Chen Dongshu xiansheng shici*, "Moved by My Old Teachers," second poem, p. 49.

1. The Jianzhang Palace 建章宮 was a palace in the western suburbs of the Former Han dynasty capital of Changan. See *Han shu*, p. 1245.

2. Chen Li, *Dongshu dushuji*, "Self-Narration," pp. 1–2.

3. Li Xubai, "Qingdai Guangdong wenhua de jiejingti: Dongshu xuepai," p. 96.

4. Extant segments of a manuscript genealogy maintained by Chen Li contain contrasting claims regarding the Chen family's native place in Shaoxing. Prefaces to eighteenth-century versions of the Jiangning Chen genealogy claim that the ancestor had moved from Guiji, whereas an 1806 preface to the Guangzhou branch of the Chen genealogy states that the native place was Shanyin. *Chenshi jiacheng juanmo*, unpaginated.

5. Chen Li, *Dongshuji*, 5.19a.

6. Ibid., 5.17a; *Chenshi jiacheng juanmo*. The Chen residence in the New City was not far from Xie Lansheng's Studio of Constant Awareness. Wang Zongyan, "Chen Dongshu xiansheng nianpu," p. 57; *Guangzhou chengfang zhi*, pp. 485–86.

7. Chen Li's birth mother was a concubine of Chen Dajing. Chen Li, *Dongshu ji*, 5.18b–19a.

8. Ibid., 16.12a.

9. Wang Zongyan, "Chen Dongshu xiansheng nianpu," p. 59.

10. One of these private teachers was Wang Hejun 王和鈞, a Panyu resident who studied at Yuexiu Academy under He Nanyu in the 1820s. *Yuexiu shuyuan zhi*, 12.5a.

11. Chen Li, *Dongshu ji*, 5.27b; Weng Xincun, *Xuehaitang dinghai keshi lu*; Deng Youtong, *Qingdai Guangdong cilin biao*, note on Yang Rongxu. On the Nanhai Gui family, see Chapter 5, note 23.

12. Wang Zongyan, "Chen Dongshu xiansheng nianpu," pp. 60–62; Chen Li, *Dongshu ji*, 5.14b.

13. Gui Wencan, *Jingxue bocai lu*, 5.7a–b. On Ruan Yuan's patronage of Ling Tingkan, see Zhang Shouan, *Yi li dai li*, pp. 6, 79.

14. *Xuehaitang ji*, juan 3–4.

15. Wang Zongyan, "Chen Dongshu xiansheng nianpu," pp. 62–63; Gui Wencan, *Jingxue bocai lu*, 4.4a, 5.7b, 12.10a; Yi Kezhong, *Jianguanglou ji*, ci chapter, 39b–40a; Benjamin A. Elman, "Changes in Confucian Civil Service Examinations from the Ming to the Ch'ing Dynasty," pp. 116–23.

16. Wang Zongyan, "Chen Dongshu xiansheng nianpu," pp. 66, 83–84.

17. Chen Li's *Qieyun kao* had a great impact on Chinese philological studies well into the twentieth century. Wang Zongyan, "Chen Dongshu xiansheng nianpu," p. 65; Chen Li, *Qieyun kao*, 1.1b, 6.1a–b, 2b, 5b ff; Jerry Norman, *Chinese*, pp. 24–28.

18. Zhang Weiping, *Zhang Nanshan quanji*, vol. 2, *Songxin shiji*, p. 582; Wang Zongyan, "Chen Dongshu xiansheng nianpu," p. 52.

19. Wang Zongyan, "Chen Dongshu xiansheng nianpu," pp. 72–75.

20. Over the course of two years, Chen Li took students at the New City's Gongdelin 功德林 Monastery, where Shen Shiliang had studied under Li Ruwei. *Panyu xian zhi*, 24.20a.

21. Wang Zongyan, "Chen Dongshu xiansheng nianpu," pp. 65–66; *Xuehaitang zhi*, 23.a.

22. Rain Flower Terrace (Yuhuatai 雨花臺) was located on Jubao Mountain, south of Nanjing, where it commanded a view of Nanjing and the Yangzi River.

23. Wang Zongyan, "Chen Dongshu xiansheng nianpu," pp. 70, 76, 78; Chen Li, *Dongshu xuji*, p. 128; *Chenshi jiacheng juanmo*. This practice of re-establishing or maintaining ties to ancestral graves in the broader Jiangnan region may have been common among the community of sojourners who resided in Guangzhou, registered as Panyu students, and had the opportunity to travel through Jiangnan. For example, the brothers Ding Xi and Ding Zhao 丁照, both Xuehaitang examinees, were Panyu residents whose ancestors were from Zhuji county in Shaoxing. In 1849, both Ding Xi and Chen Li were returning from a failed attempt at the metropolitan examinations. Once they reached the Huai River, they parted so that Ding could visit his ancestors' graves in Zhuji. As Chen Li explains in an epitaph for Ding, he visited Zhuji on five separate occasions and purchased land to support a family to look after the ancestral tombs. Chen Li, *Dongshu xuji*, p. 136.

24. Chen Li's descendants preserved his copy of Ruan Yuan's entire literary collection, punctuated by Chen Li, which is now stored in the Zhongshan University Library Rare Books Room. Ruan Yuan, *Yanjingshi ji*, punctuation and comments by Chen Li, *passim*.

25. Wang Zongyan, "Chen Dongshu xiansheng nianpu," pp. 69, 78; Chen Li, *Dongshu yigao*, 15.6; Shen Shiliang, *Xiao Qituo an shichao*, 1.10b.

26. In an original intertextual note, Chen explained that he and Fang viewed a newly acquired copy of the Song loyalist general Yue Fei's 岳飛 (1103–41) manuscript memorials.

27. Pines and catalpas were trees that typically surrounded graves.

28. Jinling was an alternative name for Nanjing.

29. Shushi 朱提 is a mountain in southwestern China that was known for producing silver and can thus be taken to represent "silver." *Han shu*, pp. 1178, 1599–600.

30. Chen Li, *Chen Dongshu xiansheng shici*, p. 98. Chen Li and Fang Junyi maintained a correspondence after Fang's departure from Guangzhou. Fang Junyi, *Erzhixuan wencun*, 18.1a–4a.

31. Chen Li, *Dongshu ji*, 1.27b–29a.

32. Chen Li, *Dongshu zazu*, 10.12a.

33. Chen Li, *Dongshu xuji*, p. 156. Such cases of what might be termed "Jiangnan envy" were not limited to in-migrants: Tan Zongjun recounted a dream in 1884 in which he met an old man who showed him a poem, saying Tan had written it in his former life. When Tan asked the old man who he had been in this former life, the man said that Tan had been Deng Hanyi of Jiangdu. Tan Zongjun, *Licun suibi*, 7b. Jiangdu was one of the two counties that shared jurisdiction of Yangzhou. Deng Hanyi 鄧漢儀 (1617–89) was actually a native of Taizhou but lived in Yangzhou while editing part of his *Shiguan* 詩觀 anthology. See Meyer-Fong, *Building Culture in Early Qing Yangzhou*, pp. 99–102.

34. Chen Li, *Dongshu xuji*, p. 156.

35. Chen Li, *Dongshu ji*, 4.20b. Wang Zongyan, in his chronological biography of Chen, judges this letter to have been written in 1873. See Wang Zongyan, "Chen Dongshu xiansheng nianpu," p. 108.

36. See Qian Mu, *Zhongguo jin sanbainian xueshu shi*, pp. 601 ff.

37. Hu Chusheng, *Qingdai xueshushi yanjiu*, p. 265.

38. He Yousen, "Chen Lanfu de xueshu ji qi yuanyuan," pp. 1–19; Wang Zongyan, "Chen Dongshu xiansheng nianpu," p. 69.

39. The Zhong household was located in Shuixi 水西 village in Luogang 蘿岡; the Zhong claimed descent from an ancestor who had settled Luogang in the twelfth century. Chen Li, *Dongshu ji*, 2.29b–30a; Chen Qikun, "Chishou Wenlinlang renchen ke juren Hanlinyuan dianbu qinjia Neige zhongshu xian Zhong jun jiazhuan."

40. Chen Li, *Dongshu ji*, 2.29b, 3.28b, 4.32a; Wang Zongyan, "Chen Dongshu xiansheng nianpu," pp. 76–92; *Dongguan xian zhi*, 53.20a.

41. Chen Li, *Zhuzi yulei richao*, preface, 1a. On the original work by Zhu Xi, see Daniel Gardner, *Learning to Be a Sage*, passim.

42. Chen Li, *Dongshu zazu*, 12.13a–b, quoting Cheng Enze, "Preface for Di Shuying's *Mengzi biannian*." For similar critiques by Zhu Xi, see Zhu Xi, *Zhuzi yulei*, 10.8b; and Gardner, *Learning to Be a Sage*, p. 139.

43. The 1872 Nanhai gazetteer notes of the book market that it had really flourished a half century earlier, in Ruan Yuan's time as governor-general, thus implying that the market by 1872 had lost some of its previous luster. See *Nanhai xian zhi*, 1872 edition, 5.20a.

44. Chen Li, *Dongshu zazu*, 12.14a.

45. Chen Li, *Dongshu yigao*, 7.1. The *Bencao gangmu* 本草綱目, compiled by Li Shizhen 李時珍 (1518–93), was a pioneering comprehensive pharmacopoeia. Goodrich and Fang, *Dictionary of Ming Biography*, p. 859.

46. Chen Li, *Dongshu zazu*, 2.33a. I have revised my original translation of this passage in light of John Makeham's recently published translation of the *Zhonglun*. Xu Gan, *Balanced Discourses*, pp. 12–15.

47. Chen Li, *Dongshu zazu*, 2.33a.

48. For Dai Junheng's 戴鈞衡 (1814–55) similar lament about contemporary reading practices, see Alexander Woodside, "State, Scholars, and Orthodoxy: The Ch'ing Academies, 1736–1839," p. 173. A similar distinction in reading practices can be found in recent scholarship on the history of reading in Europe. See Chartier, *The Order of Books*, p. 17.

49. Chen Li, *Dongshu zazu*, 12.16b.

50. Chen Li, "Chen Lanfu xiansheng Li yigao," part 2, p. 189. For examples of Zhu Xi's use of "masticating" and "flavor," see Zhu Xi, *Zhuzi yulei*, 10.8a, 11.13a; these are translated in Gardner, *Learning to Be a Sage*, pp. 137, 155. On a similar use of the compound *jujue*, see Stephen Owen, *Remembrances: The Experience of the Past in Classical Chinese Literature*, p. 83.

51. For examples, see Chen's critique of Wang interpretations of the *Shijing* in *Dongshu zazu*, 11.12a. These can also be found in the Chen Li manuscripts. Chen Li, *Dongshu yigao*, 10.1.

52. Chen Li, *Dongshu zazu*, 11.11b–12a.

53. Chen Li, *Dongshu yigao*, 33.3. This seems to have been more a rhetorical strategy than an "accurate" self-representation.

54. Ibid., 26.9, 51.1.

55. Ibid., 38.3.

56. *Liji*, 36.9a. James Legge translates this excerpt as follows: "According to the system of teaching now-a-days, . . . in what they (the masters) lay on their learners they are not sincere." Legge, *Li Chi*, 2: 86.

57. Chen Li, *Dongshu yigao*, 26.6.

58. See Yu Ying-shih, "Some Preliminary Observations on the Rise of Ch'ing Confucian Intellectualism," pp. 105–46.

59. See, for example, Chen Li, *Dongshu yigao*, 16.13.

60. Chen Li, *Dongshu zazu*, 11.15a-b.

61. On *Daotong*, see Wilson, *Genealogy of the Way*, pp. 82–97.

62. Chen Li, *Dongshu yigao*, 17.15, 35.3, 50.5; Chen Li, *Dongshu zazu*, 7.12b–13a, 25a; John B. Henderson, *Scripture, Canon, and Commentary: A Comparison of Confucian and Western Exegesis*, pp. 208–9.

63. Shi Gexin argues that strong critiques of Han Learning persisted until mid-century and that attempts to mediate between the schools of Han

and Song Learning did not really dominate until the late nineteenth century. Shi, *Wan Qing lixue yanjiu*, pp. 100–101.

64. *Shunde xian zhi*, 1929 edition, 17.12b, 23a.

65. *Nanhai xian zhi*, 1872 edition, 14.18a–b. According to the Xian genealogy, Ruan Yuan had wanted to hire Xian Yi to help compile classical exegeses, presumably referring to the *Huang-Qing jingjie*, but Xian refused in protest against Ruan's preference for Han Learning over Song Learning. Significantly, genealogy editors link Xian Yi's stance with the fact that a lineage ancestor had studied under the great Cantonese Neo-Confucian during the Ming, Zhan Ruoshui. *Nanhai Heyuan Xianshi jiapu*, 6.2.17a–b.

66. Xu Hao, *Tongjietang jingshuo*, preface.

67. Huang Bingkun, *Xigutang wencun*, 5.4a.

68. Wen Xun, *Dengyun shanfang wengao*, 2.29b–30a; Guy, *The Emperor's Four Treasuries*, p. 84.

69. Chen Zaiqian, comp., *Guochao Lingnan wenchao*, 13.1a–2a.

70. Jin Xiling, *Qushushi yiji*, 16.18a.

71. Lin Botong, *Xiubentang gao*, 2.19a–22a.

72. Li Zhongpei, *Zhuzi bufei guxun shuo*, preface 1a–b, 1.7b, 16.20b.

73. Jin Xiling, *Qushushi yiji*, 11.1a–2a.

74. Jin Xiling, *Lixue yongyan* (appended to *Qushushi yiji*), passim. Gui Wencan, a younger cousin of Chen Li's close friend, Gui Wenyao, as well as a onetime student of Chen himself and author of the *Jingxue bocai lu*, wrote a work entitled *Zhuzi shu Zheng lu* 朱子述鄭錄 (Record of cases in which Master Zhu follows Zheng), specifically in response to Ruan Yuan's desire to avoid partisan disputes. *Qingshi liezhuan*, 69.67a.

75. Xu Hao, *Tongjietang wenji*, 5b.

76. Wen Xun, *Dengyun shanfang wengao*, 1.20b–21a.

77. Hu Chusheng, *Qingdai xueshushi yanjiu*, p. 273.

78. Chen Li, *Dongshu ji*, 3.27a.

79. Chen Li, *Hanru tongyi*, preface.

80. Chen Li, *Dongshu zazu*, 2.20a–b. Another motif common in Han-Song syncretic discourse was to suggest that, in contrast to the practice of dynastic histories since the Song, historians should desist from separately classifying biographies of Confucians into "Daoxue" (Learning of the Way—associated with Song Learning) and "Rulin" (Forest of Scholars—associated with Han Learning) sections. Xuehaitang co-director Zhou Yinqing, in a colophon to the "Daoxue" biographical section of the *Song shi*, regards this artificial separation as a root cause of the current discord between Han and Song Learning. Zhou Yinqing, *Diansan shenggao*, 7.3a–5a.

81. Chen Li, *Hanru tongyi*, passim.

82. The work has survived in various stages of production: (1) *Dongshu dushuji*, a published work consisting of the chapters on the Classics plus one chapter each on Zheng Xuan and Zhu Xi; (2) *Dongshu zazu*, essentially the chapters on classical studies in each dynasty, hastily printed by Chen Li's students after his death; and (3) *Dongshu yigao*, 53 volumes of manuscript notes transcribed by Chen's students and currently housed in the Zhongshan University Library. Manuscript notes that are dated range from 1853 to 1872, mostly clustered in the mid-1860s. The 53 volumes are arranged by topic, although these are not always entirely accurate. Portions of the manuscript notes were published in two issues of the *Lingnan xuebao*: 2.2 (1931) and 2.3 (1932). The *Dongshu dushuji*, minus the Zheng Xuan and Zhu Xi chapters, is included in the *Huang Qing jingjie xubian*, *juan* 945–54.

83. Legge, *The Chinese Classics*, 1: 150, translates the passage as "Learning without thought is labour lost; thought without learning is perilous."

84. Chen Li, *Dongshu ji*, 4.17a.

85. Chen Li, *Dongshu zazu*, 8.12b–13b.

86. Chen Li, *Dongshu yigao*, 51.1.

87. It was not unusual for nineteenth-century Cantonese poets to articulate Han-Song syncretic discourse in verse. In a poem written during the 1820s, Zhang Weiping described his views on classical scholarship and added in interlinear text, "Han Learning and Song Learning both have advantages and disadvantages; one must look at each individual person in judging them." Zhang Weiping, "Miscellaneous Poems from the Eastern Garden," number 5, in *Zhang Nanshan quanji*, vol. 2, *Songxin shiji*, p. 409. John Henderson asserts that "parallel modes of discourse were highly developed by Neo-Confucian commentators." Henderson, *Scripture, Canon, and Commentary*, p. 167. In this sense, Chen Li's use of parallelism may also be seen as a Neo-Confucian influence.

88. Chen Li, *Dongshu dushuji*, *juan* 15, p. 2.

89. Ibid., *juan* 15; Chen Li, *Dongshu zazu*, 6.16a.

90. Chen Li, *Dongshu zazu*, 11.10a.

91. Chen Li, *Dongshu yigao*, 29.3.

92. Chen Li, *Dongshu dushuji*, *juan* 21, p. 9.

93. Wang Zongyan, "Chen Dongshu xiansheng nianpu," p. 88.

94. Chen Li, *Qieyun kao*, *Qieyun kao waipian*, preface 1a.

95. Chen Li, "Chen Lanfu xiansheng Li yigao," part 1, p. 158.

96. Ibid., part 1, p. 163.

97. In his manuscript notes on the opening passage of the *Lunyu*, Chen Li remarks on how difficult it can be to avoid resenting the fact that one's talents are not recognized. He then notes: "Now there is one who recognizes my talents, Governor Guo." See Chen Li, *Dongshu yigao*, 16.2.

98. See, for example, Guo Songtao, *Guo Songtao riji*, 2: 310. The Academia Sinica's Fu Sinian Library holds a printed edition of the *Dongshu dushuji* thoroughly punctuated by Guo Songtao.

99. Guo Songtao, *Guo Songtao riji*, pp. 147, 161, 167, 338, 349, 372, 374.

100. Chen Li, *Dongshu ji*, 2.28a–29a.

101. Gu Yanwu created this motto by piecing together two separate quotations from the *Lunyu*, 12.15 and 13.20. See Legge, *The Chinese Classics*, 1: 257, 271; Qian Mu, *Zhongguo jin sanbainian xueshushi*, pp. 122–24. The second half of the motto literally reads something like, "extensively study in regard to writing (*wen*)." But Chen clearly identifies *wenxue* 文學 as the study of classical texts. Chen Li, *Dongshu ji*, 2.29a–b.

102. Chen Li, *Dongshu xuji*, p. 27.

103. This largely follows James Hightower's translation. In the context of Chen Li's views on scholarship, I am altering Hightower's rendering of *jing* as "essence" to "precision." See James Robert Hightower, trans., *Han Shih Wai Chuan: Han Ying's Illustrations of the Didactic Application of the Classic of Songs*, p. 72.

104. *Jupo jingshe ji*, 1–2.

105. Ibid., 75, 152.

106. Zhang Yu 張禹 (d. 5 BCE) produced the first syncretic version of the *Lunyu*, basing his section and sentence commentary (*zhangju*) on the Lu 魯 version but incorporating elements of the Qi 齊 version. Zhang's became the standard version of the *Lunyu*. See Loewe, *Early Chinese Texts*, p. 316. The *Jingdian shiwen* 經典釋文 was a seventh-century text seen as an essential tool in evidential research of the Classics. The *Jiaokanji* 校勘記 was an exhaustive set of collation notes for the Thirteen Classics with Han and Tang commentaries and subcommentaries produced by Ruan Yuan and included in the *Huang Qing jingjie*. *Jupo jingshe ji*, 106.

107. Wang Zongyan, "Chen Dongshu xiansheng nianpu," pp. 92, 96, 98.

108. Guo Songtao, *Guo Songtao riji*, p. 161; Chen Li, *Dongshu xuji*, pp. 17–20.

109. See Chen's 1872 letter to Zheng Xianfu, in Chen Li, *Dongshu xuji*, p. 203.

110. Chen Li, *Dongshu yigao*, 39.1.

111. According to Chen Li's student Gui Wencan, Zeng might have been prompted to write this letter when Gui called on the eminent scholar-official at Nanjing in the summer of 1871. Gui Wencan, *Qianxintang ji*, unpaginated. See also Chen Li, *Dongshu xuji*, p. 201.

112. Wang Zongyan, "Chen Dongshu xiansheng nianpu," pp. 107–8. This does not exhaust the list of texts printed by Chen Li in this period. For example, during the 1870s at the Xuehaitang he organized the printing of three collections of dynastic institutions: *Tongdian*, *Xu Tongdian*, and *Huangchao tongdian*. Chen Li, *Dongshu ji*, 4.20b.

113. Chen Li, *Dongshu zazu*, 11.22a.

114. Chen Li, *Dongshu xuji*, p. 157.

115. Attributed to the Former Han Confucian Fu Sheng 伏勝, the *Shangshu dazhuan* 尚書大傳 was an early commentary on the *Shangshu*, or *Shujing*. Zheng Xuan wrote annotations to the *Shangshu dazhuan*. The *Zheng zhi* 鄭志 was a record of Zheng Xuan compiled by his students. Feng Zuoxun 馮佐勳 was a Shunde native who had one essay in the *Xuehaitang siji*. Chen Li, *Dongshu yigao*, 17.11.

116. Chen Li, "Chen Lanfu xiansheng Li yigao," p. 158.

117. Elman, *From Philosophy to Philology*, p. 67.

118. Chen Huan's definitive work on the Mao recension is the *Maoshi zhuanshu* 毛詩傳疏.

119. Chen Li, *Dongshu ji*, 4.19b–20b; Wang Zongyan, "Chen Dongshu xiansheng nianpu," p. 107.

120. Liu Wenqi's major work on the Zuo commentary is entitled *Zuozhuan jiushu kaozheng* 左傳舊疏考證. Chen Li, *Dongshu yigao*, 29.7.

CHAPTER 7

EPIGRAPH: Zhu Ciqi, *Zhu Jiujiang xiansheng ji*, 3.7b.

1. Jian Chaoliang, "Chronological Biography," 41a, in Zhu Ciqi, *Zhu Jiujiang xiansheng ji*; *Jiujiang Rulin xiang zhi*, 14.39b.

2. In his chapter on the early thought of Kang Youwei, Richard C. Howard briefly addresses Zhu Ciqi. See his "K'ang Yu-wei (1858–1927): His Intellectual Background and Early Thought," pp. 294–316.

3. Tan Dihua, *Qingdai Zhujiang sanjiaozhou de shatian*, pp. 204, 230; Kenneth Ruddle and Zhong Gongfu, *Integrated Agriculture-Aquaculture in South China: The Dike-Pond System of the Zhujiang Delta*, pp. 9–11, 30; *Jiujiang Rulin xiang zhi*, 3.8b, 4.3a.

4. *Nanhai xian zhi*, 1872 edition, maps 3b–15a. Robert Antony observes that the Qing state increased the number of subcounty officials in Guangdong, typically locating them in major markets. Antony, "Subcounty Officials," p. 28.

5. *Jiujiang Rulin xiang zhi*, 4.76a.

6. Henry, *Ling-nam*, p. 69.

7. *Jiujiang xiang zhi*, 1.1a.

8. *Sangyuanwei zhi*, 7.16b, 8.2a; *Jiujiang Rulin xiang zhi*, 7.7b-8b; Katayama, "Shukō deruta Sōeni no kōzō to chisui soshiki," p. 147.

9. Lin Shuyan, *Xijiang yuhua diaocha baogao shu*, pp. 3, 7, 14, 17–21; Ruddle and Zhong, *Integrated Agriculture-Aquaculture in South China*, p. 33; *Jiujiang Rulin xiang zhi*, 5.22b.

10. *Jiujiang Rulin xiang zhi*, 5.22b-24b; Tan Dihua, *Qingdai Zhujiang sanjiaozhou de shatian*, p. 230. A genealogy of the He lineage in Zhenyong township notes that "the people of Jiujiang bring fish sprouts to our township for sale." *Xuxiu Nanhai Yanqiao Heshi jiapu*, 10.42a.

11. Qu Dajun, *Guangdong xinyu*, 22.22a-b; *Jiujiang xiang zhi*, 2.18a; Ruddle and Zhong, pp. 33, 45.

12. *Jiujiang xiang zhi*, 2.20a-b. I have not found any reference to the 1501 transference of fishing rights to Jiujiang natives in the *Ming shilu* for the Hongzhi reign (1488–1505) of Emperor Xiaozong. A chronological biography of Liu Daxia compiled by his great-grandson suggests that, rather than granting fishing rights from Dan to Jiujiang natives, Liu in fact made efforts to keep Dan fishermen from absconding by reducing the taxes levied on them and preventing interference by the "influential and powerful." Thus, it appears that Jiujiang fishermen had learned Dan techniques for harvesting West River fish fry and then used Jiujiang's status as a settled community of registered landowners and taxpayers, as well as the township's growing literati connections, to wrest control of the trade from the Dan. Liu Daxia, *Liu Zhongxuan gong yiji, nianpu*, 2.3a.

13. *Jiujiang xiang zhi*, 2.18a; Lin, *Xijiang yuhua*, p. 21.

14. Several examples can be found in Zhu Ciqi's extant writings. One Jiujiang resident, surnamed Cen 岑, was orphaned as a boy and taken care of by Zhu Ciqi. The young Cen later made a fortune in Vietnam. See Zhu Ciqi, *Zhu Jiujiang xiansheng ji, Lishan jiwen*, 16b. Elsewhere, Zhu has a poem written on the occasion of receiving a letter from Vietnam by an old friend, Chen Ruchen 陳如琛, presumably a Jiujiang native. Zhu Ciqi, *Zhu Jiujiang xiansheng ji*, 2.6a.

15. *Jiujiang Rulin xiang zhi*, 3.8a-b; Qu Dajun, *Guangdong xinyu*, 22.15a.

16. *Jiujiang xiang zhi*, 2.28a.

17. Ibid., 2.5b.

18. *Guan Shudetang jiapu*, 3.1b-2a. There is some evidence that at least the Guan were residing in Jiujiang prior to the late Song. In the early nineteenth century, a Zhu unearthed a devotional stele dated 1086 and inscribed with the names of a certain Guan Cong 關聰 and his wife, neé Fan 范. *Jiujiang Rulin xiang zhi*, 7.6a-7a.

19. *Jiujiang Rulin xiang zhi*, 6.30a–b.

20. A good example of this can be found in the genealogy of one branch of the Jiujiang Guan. Guan Xinda 關信大, of the eighteenth generation, had a son, Guan Ruiyun 關瑞雲, of the nineteenth generation, who was buried in Guangxi when he died. Ruiyun's grandson, Guan Shenqi 關莘奇, was a Cangwu county student. The genealogy notes the names of his two sons but contains no further information on their heirs, suggesting loss of contact. *Guan Shude tang jiapu*, 9.92a, 11.37a, 14.6a. See also *Jiujiang Rulin xiang zhi*, juan 14.

21. *Jiujiang Rulin xiang zhi*, 4.76a. For the importance of controlling markets in the rise of powerful localized lineages in the Pearl River delta during the Qing, see Rubie Watson, *Inequality Among Brothers*, pp. 12, 73.

22. *Jiujiang xiang zhi*, 2.5b, 4.21a; *Jiujiang Rulin xiang zhi*, 6.36a, 10.39b, 12.37a, 14.12a–13a, 43a–44a.

23. *Cangwu xian zhi*, 4.31a, 35a.

24. *Jiujiang Rulin xiang zhi*, 14.18a, 15.1b–2a. On the tight loyalties between the Feng and Ming, see the account of Feng Bingxin 馮炳新 saving Ming Zhigang's mother (also a Feng?) from the Red Turbans in 1854, at 15.9a.

25. *Nanhai Jiujiang Zhushi jiapu*, 11.2b.

26. Ibid., 11.2b–3a.

27. This aspect of the foundation legend further suggests that the Guan may have been settled in Jiujiang longer than other descent-groups and that the Zhu indeed moved into the area at a later date. In his study of settlement and lineage building in the eastern New Territories, David Faure notes that marriage was one of the means by which settlement rights could be attained by in-migrating descent groups. Faure, *The Structure of Chinese Rural Society*, p. 31. Descendants of Zhu Ziyi expressed their close relationship to the Guan by annually offering sacrifices at the tomb of Guan and his wife, neé Mai 麥.

28. *Nanhai Jiujiang Zhushi jiapu*, 2.1a, 9.91a–b, 11.2b.

29. Ibid., 6.44a, 7.2a, 10.7b–8b; *Jiujiang xiang zhi*, 4.27a–b.

30. For example, an examination of the principal wives of fourteenth-generation (the generation of Zhu Ciqi's father) Yisi Hall Zhu reveals that a total of 163 Zhu men took Guan wives. The next largest numbers were: 53 Huang wives, 33 Chen, and 30 Zeng. Yisi Hall Zhu of this generation took 11 Feng women as wives. Though native places of wives are not indicated in the genealogical tables, the overwhelming numbers of Guan and the large numbers of Huang, Chen, and Zeng suggest that the Jiujiang Zhu most often married women from within the township. From biographies

of notable Zhu lineage members, one can see as well that most wives mentioned are taken from Jiujiang or nearby townships such as Datong. See *Nanhai Jiujiang Zhushi jiapu, juan* 5.

31. *Jiujiang xiang zhi*, 5.17b; *Jiujiang Rulin xiang zhi*, 14.2a. For other examples of Zhu-Guan teacher-student relationships, see *Nanhai Jiujiang Zhushi jiapu*, 11.73b, 76b.

32. *Nanhai Jiujiang Zhushi jiapu*, 7.35a, 39a, 11.16a; *Jiujiang xiang zhi*, 4.41–42b; *Jiujiang Rulin xiang zhi*, 13.10a.

33. *Huangshi jiacheng*, passim.

34. *Nanhai Jiujiang Zhushi jiapu*, 7.35a.

35. The name of the academy, Huian shuyuan 晦菴書院, referred to the name of Zhu Xi and his "secluded cottage" in Fujian. *Nanhai Jiujiang Zhushi jiapu*, 11.65b; Wing-Tsit Chan, *Chu Hsi: New Studies*, p. 72.

36. *Longshan xiang zhi*, 10.18a–29b; *Longjiang xiang zhi, juan* 2.

37. *Jiujiang Rulin xiang zhi*, 14.18b. Aside from Wen Runeng, the other participants were Zeng Wenjin 曾文錦, Feng Cheng 馮城 (1770 *juren*), Guan Shangmou 關上謀 (1771 *juren*), and Cai Chaoqun 蔡超群 (1794 *juren*).

38. *Jiujiang xiang zhi*, 2.18a–b. This is quoted in Qu Dajun, *Guangdong xinyu*, 22.24a–b.

39. *Jiujiang Rulin xiang zhi*, 5.26b–27a.

40. One of these inscriptions, issued by the Cangwu county magistrate in 1780, is partially preserved in the Zhongshan Park in Wuzhou, Guangxi. *Jiujiang Rulin xiang zhi*, 5.28a–32b.

41. *Jiujiang Rulin xiang zhi*, 2.35a.

42. *Chongji Sangyuanwei zhi*, 1.8a, 7a–b; *Jiujiang Rulin xiang zhi*, 2.37b, 1.17b–18a.

43. *Jiujiang Rulin xiang zhi*, 2.37b, 38a, 39b.

44. *Sangyuanwei zhi*, 8.16a–b; *Jiujiang Rulin xiang zhi*, 14.30a.

45. *Jiujiang Rulin xiang zhi*, 2.42a.

46. Ibid., 14.40a.

47. Some passages in the Enclosure gazetteers reveal that the interests of Jiujiang and other areas of the Enclosure did not always coincide. The 1833 gazetteer records an incident in the first decade of the eighteenth century in which two Jiujiang gentry, a Guan and a Zhu, in an apparent land reclamation effort, bribed county yamen functionaries to allow construction of a section of dike that would have benefited Jiujiang but increased the risk of flooding upstream. Their scheme was eventually blocked by the protests of gentry from neighboring townships. *Sangyuanwei zhi*, 8.6a–b.

48. Hu Ting's teacher was Zhu Daonan 朱道南 (1756 *juren*). *Jiujiang Rulin xiang zhi*, 2.32a–b, 14.14a; *Nanhai Jiujiang Zhushi jiapu*, 11.63a. Also

see *Qingshilu* entries for Qianlong 45 (1780): 8/16, 8/18, 8/25, 9/18. *Qing shilu Guangdong shiliao*, 2: 446–51.

49. *Jiujiang Rulin xiang zhi*, 2.36a–b; *Nanhai Jiujiang Zhushi jiapu*, 11.67b. On Zhang Bao's activities in the delta, see Murray, *Pirates of the South China Coast*, pp. 123–30.

50. *Jiujiang Rulin xiang zhi*, 4.36a–37b.

51. The academy's name is not even noted in the 1883 gazetteer section on academies. *Jiujiang Rulin xiang zhi*, 2.34a, 4.6a–9b; also see *Qingshilu* entry for Qianlong 51 (1786): 3/25. *Qing shilu Guangdong shiliao*, 3: 44.

52. *Jiujiang Rulin xiang zhi*, 3.12a.

53. Ibid., 2.48b, 4.27a–29a.

54. Ibid., 4.76b–78a, 14.13b–14a, 15b.

55. Ibid., 2.32a–b, 35a, 4.6a–7b, 14.21b–23a.

56. Ibid., 4.7a–b; Zhang Jian et al., comps., *Ruan Yuan nianpu*, p. 153. On Ruan Yuan's promotion of seal and clerical script, see Elman, *From Philosophy to Philology*, pp. 191–97.

57. *Jiujiang Rulin xiang zhi*, 14.21b–23a.

58. *Nanhai Jiujiang Zhushi jiapu*, 11.73a–b, 12.6a; *Jiujiang Rulin xiang zhi*, 15.3b–4a.

59. *Nanhai Jiujiang Zhushi jiapu*, 2.99b–100a.

60. Ibid., 10.9b–10b, 11.80a–85b; Zhu Ciqi, *Zhushi chuanfang ji*, 1.9a, 13a–b.

61. Zhu Ciqi, *Zhushi chuanfang ji*, 4.24a, records two poems by Zhu Shiqi entitled "Sending Second Brother Off to Vietnam." See also *Zhu Jiujiang xiansheng ji*, "Chronological Biography," 1b.

62. *Jiujiang Rulin xiang zhi*, 14.33a–b. One other Zhu of the fifteenth generation, Zhu Yaoxun 朱堯勳 (ca. 1791–1854), of the Cunzhu Branch, was apparently quite close to Zhu Chengfa's family; Yaoxun is said to have served Chengfa's wife, née Zhang, as his own mother. Yaoxun took Xuehaitang examinations in the Daoguang era, and had one poem printed in the *Xuehaitang erji*. *Nanhai Jiujiang Zhushi jiapu*, 2.100b, 11.78b.

63. Ruan had Zhu write a poem entitled "Observing the Sea at Huangmu Gulf." A few years later, Ruan would incorporate this theme in a Xuehaitang poetry exercise in which students were required to use the method of Jiang Yan's 江淹 (444–505) "Poems in Assorted Styles" to imitate Song, Yuan, and Ming poems. The third poem in this exercise is "'Observing the Sea at Huangmu Cove,' Imitating Meng Haoran's 'Looking out at Dongting Lake.'" This exercise also includes two poems on a Jiujiang theme: "'On a Painting of a Rulin Township Fishing Station,' Imitating Yu Ji's 'Poem on a Painting of a Fishing Village.'" One of the poems on this theme, by Jiujiang native Hu Tiaode, includes extensive annotations describing the

harvesting of West River fish fry by Jiujiang fishermen. *Xuehaitang erji*, 18.4b, 18a–20a.

64. "Chronological Biography," 2b–4b; *Jiujiang Rulin xiang zhi*, 15.15b.

65. Zhu Ciqi, *Zhu Jiujiang ji*, Qian Yiji preface.

66. Zhu Wenbin is another excellent example of the extent of Jiujiang interests in Cangwu, Guangxi. He not only earned *shengyuan* and *juren* degrees as a Cangwu registered student but chose as his sobriquet "Wusheng" 梧生, which could either mean "born in [Cang]wu" or "[Cang]wu student."

67. "Chronological Biography," 6b; *Jiujiang Rulin xiang zhi*, 21.18a.

68. The Jiujiang gazetteer places this event in 1834; however, the editors include a poem by Zhu Ciqi commemorating the event addressed to "the two *juren* Ming Lun and Feng Rutang." As Ming Lun did not earn the *juren* degree until 1835, the editors of Zhu Ciqi's chronological biography seem correct in placing the event after 1835, in 1839. See "Chronological Biography," 8a; *Jiujiang Rulin xiang zhi*, 2.40a–b. See also *Zhu Ciqi xiansheng shishi kao*, which also describes the event as occurring in 1839. The 1910 Nanhai gazetteer likewise places the event in 1839. *Nanhai xian zhi*, 1910 edition, 15.1a.

69. *Jiujiang Rulin xiang zhi*, 2.42a, 4.79a–81a, 14.30b, 45a–b; *Nanhai xian zhi*, 1910 edition, 15.1a; "Chronological Biography," 6a.

70. *Jiujiang Rulin xiang zhi*, 5.36a–b.

71. Ibid., 2.41a, 3.9b, 14.23a–b, 29a–b; "Chronological Biography," 7a; *Zhu Ciqi xiansheng shishi kao*.

72. *Jiujiang Rulin xiang zhi*, 3.8b.

73. Ibid., 2.40a, 42a; *Nanhai xian zhi*, 1910 edition, 15.1a. Hsiao Kung-chuan cites Jiujiang in several instances, and Feng's actions in particular, as evidence of gentry taking a lead in enforcing "ideological control" in rural China. See his *Rural China: Imperial Control in the Nineteenth Century*, p. 293. Janice Stockard points to Feng's crusade as an example of Qing portrayals of delayed-transfer marriage as marriage resistance and its consequent repression. See Stockard, *Daughters of the Canton Delta*, pp. 108–9. Considering the fact that Feng emerged from the very culture he was repressing, I think his actions might also be read as an attempt to redefine what it meant to be a native of the Enclosure district and Jiujiang in particular. In place of such practices as delayed-transfer marriage, Feng projects an alternative identity centered around the type of morality promoted by Feng and his associates at Rulin Academy.

74. *Nanhai xian zhi*, 1910 edition, 6.23b.

75. Henry, *Ling-nam*, p. 70.

76. Ibid.
77. *Jiujiang Rulin xiang zhi*, 2.44a–b.
78. Ibid., 2.45a, 14.33a–b; "Petition by the Jiujiang *Bao* Gentry," 1855, in *Guangdong Hongbing qiyi shiliao*, pp. 249–50.
79. *Jiujiang Rulin xiang zhi*, 2.44a–b, 14.27b–28a, 41b, 44a–b.
80. "Chronological Biography," 35b, 36a–b; *Jiujiang Rulin xiang zhi*, 15.6a.
81. "Chronological Biography," 24a–b.
82. Guanghua was the next township beyond Ganzhu in Shunde county, on the southeastern outskirts of the Enclosure area.
83. *Jiujiang Rulin xiang zhi*, 14.49a; "Chronological Biography," 35b; Kang Youwei, *Kang Nanhai xiansheng zibian nianpu*, pp. 7–10; *Shunde xianzhi*, 1929 edition, 20.3a.
84. *Yuedong Jianshi datong pu*, 2.13a, 9.15a; *Shunde Jian'an Jianshi jiapu*, preface 1a; Zhao Fengtian, *Kang Changsu (Nanhai) xiansheng nianpu*, p. 2. Ōkubo Eiko provides a short list of Zhu Ciqi's students, culled from the 1910 Nanhai gazetteer. See Ōkubo, *Min-Shin jidai shoin no kenkyū*, pp. 402–4.
85. Jian Chaoliang, *Dushutang ji*, prose 6.13a–14a.
86. The village of Baisha was located in Xinhui county; Ganquan was east of Guangzhou, in Zengcheng county.
87. "Chronological Biography," pp. 12–13, 16, 54–55; *Jiujiang Rulin xiang zhi*, 14.39a.
88. Zhu Ciqi, *Zhu Jiujiang xiansheng ji*, 7.18a–19b; Guo Songtao, *Guo Songtao riji*, pp. 137, 138, 146–47, 161, 167, 349, 372, 374.
89. Chen Pu, *Chigang caotang yiwen*, 1.31a.
90. *Zhu Ciqi xiansheng shishi kao*.
91. *Jiujiang Rulin xiang zhi*, 14.16b–7a, 15.4b. In contrast to the Qing, during the late Ming, Jiujiang had several adherents of Chen-Zhan Confucianism.
92. Ibid., 14.25b.
93. *Nanhai xian zhi*, 1910 edition, 19.9b. Pan Jili's father, Pan Zhiyuan 潘志元, had earned his money in the salt trade in Guangxi before establishing a medicine shop in Guangzhou. There, inspired by Ruan Yuan's learning, he purchased rare books at the market inside the South Gate. When he heard that Ruan's most devoted follower in Guangzhou, Zeng Zhao, was teaching at the city's West Lake Academy, Pan ordered his son Jili to study at the academy. There, Zeng introduced Pan Jili to the "schools method" of the Han Confucians. *Pan Shidian tang zupu*, 6.31a–32b.
94. *Zhu Ciqi xiansheng shishi kao*.
95. "Chronological Biography," 22b.

96. Zhu Ciqi, *Zhu Jiujiang xiansheng ji*, 7.14a.

97. Zhang Qihuang, *Zhu Jiujiang xiansheng ji zhu*, "Chronological Biography," annotations 8a.

98. "Chronological Biography," 25a–26a; Kang Youwei, *Kang Nanhai xiansheng zibian nianpu*, p. 8.

99. "Chronological Biography," 28a. Fang Bao was looked up to as a model by advocates of *guwen* and Song Learning in the nineteenth century.

100. "Chronological Biography," 27b–28a.

101. "Chronological Biography," 28b.

102. Zhang Qihuang, *Zhu Jiujiang xiansheng ji zhu*, "Chronological Biography" annotations, 9a.

103. In taking this stance, Zhu Ciqi was following a common Neo-Confucian strategy. "Being different," Peter Bol argues, "had an important transformative function: it made the Neo-Confucian identity a conscious choice, one that required an act of conversion." Bol, "Neo-Confucianism and Local Society, Twelfth to Sixteenth Century: A Case Study," pp. 254–55.

104. Zhu Ciqi, *Zhushi chuanfang ji*, editorial principles 3b.

105. Ibid., 1.5a–6a; Wu Shanjia, *Fushe xingshi zhuanlue*, 9.3a.

106. Zhu Ciqi, *Zhushi chuanfang ji*, 1.9a.

107. *Jiujiang Rulin xiang zhi*, 14.39b, 15.6a; *Zhu Jiujiang xiansheng shishi kao*. The Zhu were not alone among Jiujiang lineages in printing genealogies in the latter decades of the nineteenth century. The 1883 gazetteer notes one other, the *Lishi jiapu* 黎氏家譜, compiled in the 1870s by Li Guochen's son. At least one other Jiujiang genealogy was compiled before the turn of the century, for the Shude branch of the Guan lineage in 1897. *Guan Shudetang jiapu*.

108. *Nanhai Jiujiang Zhushu jiapu*, 7.10a, 11.44a–45a.

109. Chow, *The Rise of Confucian Ritualism in Late Imperial China*, pp. 215–17.

110. *Nanhai Jiujiang Zhushi jiapu*, preface and editorial principles 5b, 7a.

111. *Jiujiang Rulin xiang zhi*, 14.25b.

112. For an analysis of the 1657 gazetteer and Jiujiang during the Ming, see Steven B. Miles, "From Small Fry to Big Fish: Representing the Rise of Jiujiang Township, Nanhai County, 1395–1657."

113. *Jiujiang Rulin xiang zhi*, preface.

114. Ibid., 3.1a.

115. Ibid., 3.8a.

116. In his study of lineage building in late imperial Fuzhou, Michael Szonyi suggests that the genealogy should be seen as a "strategic text, which

is intended to produce and does produce certain effects" as part of the "practice of kinship." Szonyi, *Practicing Kinship*, p. 27.

117. Peter Bol argues that local histories of Wuzhou (Jinhua) produced during the Song and Yuan showed that the lineage and the community had contributed to a larger, empire-wide culture. Peter K. Bol, "The Rise of Local History: History, Geography, and Culture in Southern Song and Yuan Wuzhou," p. 75.

118. See, for example, Zhu Ciqi's editorial principles for the genealogy and the *Chuanfang ji* in *Zhu Jiujiang xiansheng ji*, pp. 305–30.

119. *Nanhai xian zhi*, 1835 edition, 39.38b. Two years before he died, Xie Lansheng wrote in his diary: "I read through my old letters, picking out the ones worth preserving and burning the rest." Xie Lansheng, *Changxingxingzhai riji*, 2/7/DG9. Zhu Ciqi may also have had a precedent from Jiujiang, as the 1657 gazetteer biography of Zeng Chenshi 曾陳詩 (1630 *juren*) records a collection of his prose—or more likely, poetry—entitled *Fenyu cao* 焚餘草 (Drafts remaining from the fire), though the precise circumstances of this text's production are unclear. *Jiujiang xiang zhi*, 3.13b. Dorothy Ko suggests that similar names for collections of women's writings in seventeenth-century Jiangnan may often have been tropes. Ko, *Teachers of the Inner Chambers*, p. 99.

CHAPTER 8

EPIGRAPH: Wang Quan, *Suishanguan conggao, Suishanguan weigao*, "Six Miscellaneous Poems Written on a Summer Day," fourth poem, 8.12b.

1. Skinner, "Mobility Strategies in Late Imperial China: A Regional Systems Analysis," p. 335.

2. Zurndorfer, *Change and Continuity*. For Huizhou merchants and elite culture, see pp. 225–30.

3. Cole, *Shaohsing, passim*.

4. Finnane, *Speaking of Yangzhou*, pp. 99, 239.

5. Jerry Dennerline, *The Chia-ting Loyalists: Confucian Leadership and Social Change in Seventeenth-Century China*, p. 117. Peter Perdue describes successful Jiangxi merchants sojourning in Xiangtan, Hunan. Peter C. Perdue, "Insiders and Outsiders: The Xiangtan Riot of 1819 and Collective Action in Hunan," pp. 173–75.

6. Rowe, *Hankou*, p. 90.

7. Finnane, *Speaking of Yangzhou*, pp. 199–203.

8. Naquin, *Peking*, p. 128.

9. Rowe, *Hankow*, especially pp. 259–67.

10. Wang Zhaoyong, *Weishangzhai zawen*, 2.8a.

11. Though the precise background of Wang Quan's wife, neé Zhang 張, is not stated, an epitaph makes clear that she was the most virtuous of the many virtuous daughters of families relocated from Zhejiang. Wang Chu's wife, neé Lu 盧, a Shanyin native, gives a good picture of marriage strategies among in-migrating families. Her mother was the daughter of Wang Jinjian 汪金鑑 (1762–1822), the younger brother of Wang Quan's and Wang Chu's grandfather. In his later years, Jinjian served in the Guangdong Nan-Shao-Lian circuit yamen. *Shanyin Wangshi pu*, pp. 10–19, 54, 81; Wang Zhaoyong, *Weishangzhai zawen*, 5.12a.

12. Wang Quan, *Suishanguan conggao*, 6.3a, 8.6b, epitaph 1a.

13. Timothy Brook uses this notion to describe two contrasting sets of commitments among the late Ming gentry: one Neo-Confucian, state-oriented, and public, and the other Buddhist, local, and largely private. Brook, *Praying for Power*, p. 311.

14. Faure, "Becoming Cantonese, the Ming Dynasty Transition," p. 37.

15. Peter Bol addresses these different types of localisms in his article "The 'Localist Turn' and 'Local Identity' in Later Imperial China."

16. Robert Hymes, *Statesmen and Gentlemen: The Elite of Fu-Chou, Chiang-Hsi, in Northern and Southern Sung*, especially pp. 124–35; Bol, "The Rise of Local History," 41.

17. Wakeman, *Strangers at the Gate*, pp. 115–16; Philip A. Kuhn, *Rebellion and Its Enemies in Late Imperial China: Militarization and Social Structure, 1796–1864*, pp. 215–16; Rankin, *Elite Activism*, pp. 15–21; Esherick and Rankin, *Chinese Local Elites*. Two recent studies of localist texts in the early nineteenth century are Tobie Meyer-Fong's and Antonia Finnane's books on Yangzhou. Meyer-Fong, *Building Culture*, pp. 114–27; Finnane, *Speaking of Yangzhou*, pp. 283–92.

18. Duara, *Sovereignty and Authenticity*, see chap. 6; Tim Oakes, "China's Provincial Identities: Reviving Regionalism and Reinventing 'Chineseness,'" especially pp. 674–83.

19. One important source produced during the Republican era is the *Guangzhou chengfang zhi* by Huang Foyi, whose father, Huang Yingkui 黃映奎, was an 1875 specialized student at the Xuehaitang and a grandnephew of Huang Peifang. "Xuehaitang kao," p. 74.

20. Examples of important sources reprinted in Guangdong during the 1990s include new editions of Huang Foyi's *Guangzhou chengfang zhi*, in the "Lingnan Library" series of the Guangdong People's Press, and Zhang Weiping's collected poems, by Guangdong Higher Educational Publishers in their "Lingnan Collectanea" series.

21. Field trip to Jiujiang, May 1997. The anthropologist Jakob Klein accompanied me on this trip.

22. Rowe, *Hankow*, pp. 247–51.

23. Finnane, *Speaking of Yangzhou*, pp. 284–92.

24. Goodman, *Native Place, City, and Nation*, p. 312.

25. Duara, *Sovereignty and Authenticity*, pp. 209–10. Scholars working on other countries have drawn similar conclusions about the relationship between the local and the national. Jennifer Jenkins, for example, asserts that in early twentieth-century Hamburg, Germany, "study of the local place," or *Heimatkunde*, "articulated an ideal of the self that was brought into focus through its connection to larger communities" such as the nation. Jenkins, *Provincial Modernity: Local Culture and Liberal Politics in Fin-de-Siècle Hamburg*, p. 149.

26. Meyer-Fong, *Building Culture in Early Qing Yangzhou*, pp. 90–91.

27. John Dardess, *A Ming Society: T'ai-ho County, Kiangsi, in the Fourteenth to Seventeenth Centuries*, pp. 247–49.

28. In his dissertation on Ruan Yuan, Man-kam Leung sees the Gujing jingshe and Xuehaitang as examples of, and motors driving, the "growing independence of the provinces from the central government in matters dealing with literary and cultural fields." He points out that "this change shifted the control over education from the central government to the provincial authorities. From 1800 onwards new *shu-yuan* were created, catering to the demands and interests of the local communities." Leung, "Juan Yuan (1764–1849)," p. 265. I would largely concur with this, but further suggest that the local communities, upon closer inspection, may have been composed of both local—even insular—and cosmopolitan elements.

29. Wang Quan, *Suishanguan conggao, Suishanguan weigao*, 8.22b. Wang Quan's companion on this occasion was a certain Wang Yunlin 王蘊璘. In a poem written in a similar tone, Wang Quan's friend Chen Liangyu records an 1881 gathering of old Cantonese literati, including the Xuehaitang luminaries Chen Pu and Jin Xiling, at Haichuang Monastery. He lists all of the participants and their ages, ranging from 59 to 86 *sui*. Chen Liangyu, *Meiwo shichao / Meiwo cichao, Meiwo yigao*, poems 12a.

30. *Panyu xian xu zhi*, 10.23a.

31. Wang Zhaoyong, *Weishang laoren ziding nianpu*, pp. 3–4; Leong, *Migration and Ethnicity in Chinese History*, pp. 74–75. Based on (in some cases incomplete) records from Maoming, Kaiping, and Chixi, it does not appear that Wang Chu followed a single magistrate from one post to another, although it is clear that he left some positions when the

magistrate he was working under left his post. In some cases, such as in Chixi in the late 1860s, Wang Chu's employment may have been facilitated by fellow Shanyin natives serving as subofficials in the same jurisdiction. *Maoming xian zhi*, 4.16b–17a; *Kaiping xian zhi*, 24.10b–11a; *Chixi xian zhi*, 5.2a–b.

32. Wang Zhaoyong, *Weishang laoren ziding nianpu*, pp. 5–7.

33. Mann, *Precious Records*, pp. 102–5; Wang Zhaoyong, *Weishangzhai zawen*, 5.12b–13a.

34. In 1877, Shilin moved to Shaozhou prefecture, where his son was learning the *muyou* trade under a distant cousin. Wang Shilin's son, Dayuan 汪達元 (1851–1906), was eventually buried in Guangzhou. Wang Zhaoyong, *Weishang laoren ziding nianpu*, pp. 4–7; *Shanyin Wangshi pu*, p. 86.

35. Wang Zhaoyong, *Weishang laoren ziding nianpu*, p. 7. Tao Shaoxue's father, Tao Wending 陶文鼎, was a Guiji native who long sojourned in Guangdong and eventually registered as a Panyu resident. Wending was almost certainly a *muyou* like Wang Chu; his biographers explain that, until his mother's illness prevented it, Wending had "sojourned in the four directions" (*ke sifang* 客四方). *Panyu xian xu zhi*, 24.5a. In 1880, Wang Zhaoyong studied under another Panyu Tao, the 1867 *juren* Tao Jichang 陶繼昌. Wang Zhaoyong, *Weishang laoren ziding nianpu*, p. 8; *Panyu xian zhi*, 12.40b.

36. Wang Zhaoyong, *Weishang laoren ziding nianpu*, pp. 7–13; Wang Zhaoyong, *Weishangzhai zawen*, 6.8b; "Xuehaitang kao," p. 145.

37. Wang Zhaoyong, *Weishang laoren ziding nianpu*, pp. 8, 10–11, 13–14. Wang Zhaoyong headed the Longshan shuyuan 龍山書院 in Lufeng county.

38. Wang Zhaoyong, *Weishang laoren ziding nianpu*, pp. 22–28.

39. Wang Chu worked and resided in Sanshui for two years, Qujiang for a year, Yingde for four years, Sihui for a year, and Lufeng for a year.

40. Zhang Cixi, *Wang Jingwei xiansheng xingshi lu*, "Wang Jingwei xiansheng nianpu," 1a–3b; Wang Zhaoyong, *Weishang laoren ziding nianpu*, p. 13; *Panyu xian xu zhi*, 25.24b. Wang studied at the Yushan shuyuan 禺山書院 in the Panyu section of Guangzhou. Tao Fuxiang taught at this academy beginning in 1887, but it is unclear how long he remained there. Liu Boji, *Guangdong shuyuan zhidu*, p. 250.

41. Another family member, Zhaoyong's son Wang Zuze 汪祖澤, also studied at Tokyo College of Law and Administration, graduating in 1910. *Panyu xian xu zhi*, 17.2b; Wang Zhaoyong, *Weishang laoren ziding nianpu*, pp. 26, 34; Edward J. M. Rhoads, *China's Republican Revolution: The Case of Kwangtung, 1895–1913*, pp. 102–3.

42. *Shanyin Wangshi pu*, pp. 13, 17, 104; Wang Zhaoyong, *Weishang laoren ziding nianpu*, p. 27; Howard L. Boorman, *Biographical Dictionary of Republican China*, 3: 369–70; Zhang Cixi, *Wang Jingwei xiansheng xingshi lu*, "Wang Jingwei xiansheng nianpu," 3b–6b. Wang Jingwei appears only by his original name, Wang Zhaoming 汪兆銘, in the Wang genealogy. Thanks to Du Yongtao for bringing this to my attention.

43. Wang Zhaoyong, *Weishang laoren ziding nianpu*, pp. 35–38, 40, 42–46, 48, 51, 56; Zhang Cixi, *Wang Jingwei xiansheng xingshi lu*, "Wang Jingwei xiansheng nianpu," 4b, 5b–6a; Rhoads, *China's Republican Revolution*, p. 235.

44. Wang Zhaoyong's work was entitled *Yuan Guangdong yimin lu* 元廣東遺民錄. Wang Zhaoyong, *Weishang laoren ziding nianpu*, pp. 34, 36, 39–40, 43, 47–48, 51; Wang Zhaoyong, *Lingnan hua zhenglue*.

45. Wang Zhaoyong, *Weishang laoren ziding nianpu*, pp. 36, 52.

46. The Panyu magistrate was Wang Zhaoyong's fourth son, Wang Zongzhun 汪宗準 (b. 1889). The stele with the engraved image of Chen Li is now at the Guangzhou Museum in Yuexiu Park. Wang Zhaoyong, *Weishang laoren ziding nianpu*, pp. 43, 49. Wang Zhaoyong's youngest son, Zongyan 宗衍 (b. 1908), inherited his father's passion, compiling the chronological biography of Chen Li, an indispensable source for Chapter 6. He also supplemented the collection of Chen Li's poetry edited by his father and published it in Hong Kong in 1972. Chen Li, *Chen Dongshu xiansheng shici*.

47. Wang Zhaoyong, *Weishang laoren ziding nianpu*, pp. 40, 53–54; Wang Zhaoyong, *Guangzhou cheng canzhuan lu*.

48. Wang Zhaoyong's chronological autobiography states that Guangdong civil governor Zhang Jinfang 張錦芳 sponsored the renewal of Xuehaitang examinations in 1920. Yet the standard table of Republican-era officials notes that Zhang Jinfang was only briefly assigned by the military government to serve as civil governor in the previous year. Conceivably, Zhang Jinfang made the decision to sponsor the examinations in 1919, and the first round of examinations was not held until 1920. Wang Zhaoyong, *Weishang laoren ziding nianpu*, p. 41; Yang Jialuo, *Zhonghua minguo zhiguan nianbiao*, pp. 415–16; Tsin, *Nation, Governance, and Modernity in China*, pp. 55–56.

49. Other co-directors included the Shunde literatus Zhou Chaohuai 周朝槐, 1901 Panyu *juren* Pan Yingqi 潘應祺, 1874 Panyu *juren* and former Xuehaitang and Jupo jingshe co-director Yao Yun 姚筠, and Maoming native and former Guangya shuyuan student Lin Henian 林鶴年 (1859–1938). When some of these co-directors resigned, their replacements included the 1881 Xuehaitang specialized student and 1885 Shunde *juren* Lu

Naitong 盧乃潼; and Xu Shaoqi 徐紹棨 (1879–1948), nephew of the legal secretary and Confucian scholar from Qiantang, Xu Hao. Wang Zhaoyong, *Weishang laoren ziding nianpu*, p. 41, *Panyu xian xu zhi*, 16.8a, 15a; "Xuehaitang kao," pp. 59, 80; Wu Daorong, *Guangdong wenzheng zuozhe kao*, p. 276; Xu Youchun, *Minguo renwu da cidian*, p. 718.

50. Wang Zhaoyong, *Weishang laoren ziding nianpu*, pp. 41–42. Zhang Jinfang was replaced as civil governor by Yang Yongtai 楊永泰 (1880–1936) in May 1920, and Yang in turn was displaced by Chen Jiongming in October of that year. Both Yang and Chen apparently continued to finance the Xuehaitang examinations through the end of 1921. Boorman, *Biographical Dictionary of Republican China*, 1: 176, 4: 18.

51. Wang Zhaoyong, *Weishang laoren ziding nianpu*, p. 44.

52. *Xuehaitang keyi*, 2.25b–26a, 38a–39a.

53. Ibid., 3.3b.

54. *Guangzhou chengfang zhi*, p. 132.

55. *Xuehaitang keyi*, 3.1b.

WORKS CITED

Anhai Wushi ru Yue zupu 安海伍氏入粵族譜 (Genealogy of the Anhai Wu surname in Guangdong). Ed. Wu Ziwei 伍子偉. 1956.

Antony, Robert J. "Subcounty Officials, the State, and Local Communities in Guangdong Province, 1644–1860." In Robert J. Antony and Jane Kate Leonard, eds., *Dragons, Tigers, and Dogs: Qing Crisis Management and the Boundaries of State Power in Late Imperial China*. Ithaca: East Asia Program, Cornell University, 2002, pp. 27–59.

Ayers, William. *Chang Chih-tung and Educational Reform in China*. Cambridge: Harvard University Press, 1971.

Bai Qianshan. *Fu Shan's World: The Transformation of Chinese Calligraphy in the Seventeenth Century*. Cambridge: Harvard University Asia Center, 2003.

Baker, Hugh D. R. "Extended Kinship in the Traditional City." In G. William Skinner, ed., *The City in Late Imperial China*. Stanford: Stanford University Press, 1977, pp. 499–518.

Beattie, Hilary. *Land and Lineage in China: A Study of T'ung-ch'eng County, Anhwei, in the Ming and Ch'ing Dynasties*. Cambridge: Cambridge University Press, 1979.

Belsky, Richard. "The Urban Ecology of Late Imperial China Reconsidered: The Transformation of Social Space in China's Late Imperial Capital City." *Journal of Urban History* 27.1 (November 2000): 54–74.

Birge, Bettine. *Women, Property, and Confucian Reaction in Sung and Yüan China (960–1368)*. New York: Cambridge University Press, 2002.

Birrell, Anne. *Popular Songs and Ballads of Han China*. London: Unwin Hyman, 1988.

Bodde, Derk. *Festivals in Classical China: New Year and Other Annual Observances During the Han Dynasty, 206 BC–AD 220*. Princeton: Princeton University Press, 1975.
Bol, Peter K. "The 'Localist Turn' and 'Local Identity' in Later Imperial China." *Late Imperial China* 24.2 (December 2003): 1–50.
———. "Neo-Confucianism and Local Society, Twelfth to Sixteenth Century: A Case Study." In Paul Jakov Smith and Richard von Glahn, eds., *The Song-Yuan-Ming Transition in Chinese History*. Cambridge: Harvard University Press, 2003, pp. 241–83.
———. "The Rise of Local History: History, Geography, and Culture in Southern Song and Yuan Wuzhou." *Harvard Journal of Asiatic Studies* 61.1 (June 2001): 37–76.
Boorman, Howard L., ed. *Biographical Dictionary of Republican China*. 4 vols. New York: Columbia University Press, 1967–71.
Bourdieu, Pierre. *The Logic of Practice*. Trans. Richard Nice. Stanford: Stanford University Press, 1990.
Brook, Timothy. *Praying for Power: Buddhism and the Formation of Gentry Society in Late-Ming China*. Cambridge: Council on East Asian Studies, Harvard University, 1993.
Buoye, Thomas. "From Patrimony to Commodity: Changing Concepts of Land and Social Conflict in Guangdong Province During the Qianlong Reign (1736–1795)." *Late Imperial China* 14.2 (December 1993): 33–59.
Cahill, James. *Hills Beyond a River: Painting of the Yüan Dynasty, 1279–1368*. New York: Weatherhill, 1976.
Cangwu xian zhi 蒼梧縣志 (Cangwu county gazetteer). 1871.
Certeau, Michel de. *The Practice of Everyday Life*. Trans. Steven Rendall. Berkeley: University of California Press, 1984.
Chan Wing-Tsit. *Chu Hsi: New Studies*. Honolulu: University of Hawaii Press, 1989.
Changle xian zhi 長樂縣志 (Changle county gazetteer). Daoguang era.
Chaolian xiang zhi 潮連鄉志 (Chaolian township gazetteer). 1946. *Zhongguo difang zhi jicheng*, vol. 32. Nanjing: Jiangsu guji chubanshe, 1992.
Chartier, Roger. *The Order of Books: Readers, Authors, and Libraries in Europe Between the Fourteenth and Eighteenth Centuries*. Trans. Lydia G. Cochrane. Stanford: Stanford University Press, 1994.
Chen Dongyuan 陳東原. "Qingdai shuyuan fengqi zhi bianqian" 清代書院風氣之變遷 (The transformation of Qing dynasty academies). *Xuefeng* 學風 (June 1933): 15–20.
———. *Zhongguo jiaoyu shi* 中國教育史 (A history of education in China). Shanghai: Shangwu yinshuguan, 1936.

Chen Jinghong 陳荊鴻, annot. *Dulutang shijian* 獨漉堂詩箋. Hong Kong: Zhonghua shuju, no date.

Ch'en, Kuo-tung Anthony. *The Insolvency of the Chinese Hong Merchants, 1760–1843*. Taipei: Institute of Economics, Academia Sinica, 1990.

Chen Li 陳澧. *Chen Dongshu xiansheng shici* 陳東塾先生詩詞 (*Shi* and *ci* poetry of Chen Li). Hong Kong: Chongwen shudian, 1972.

———. "Chen Lanfu xiansheng Li yigao" 陳蘭甫先生澧遺稿 (Bequeathed manuscripts of Chen Li). Part I, *Lingnan xuebao* 2.2 (1931): 149–83, ed. Chen Shouyi 陳受頤, and Part II, 2.3 (1932): 174–214, ed. Yang Shouchang 楊壽昌.

———. *Dongshu dushuji* 東塾讀書記 (Reading notes from the Eastern Study). Shanghai: Shangwu yinshuguan, 1930.

———. *Dongshu ji* 東塾集 (Collection from the Eastern Study). *Jindai Zhongguo shiliao congkan*, vol. 461. Taipei: Wenhai chubanshe, 1970.

———. *Dongshu xiansheng shichao bieben* 東塾先生詩鈔別本 (Transcribed manuscript poems of Chen Li). Ed. Zhu Zifan 朱子範. Wanjuanshu lou ben.

———. *Dongshu xuji* 東塾續集 (Continuation of collection from the Eastern Study). *Jindai Zhongguo shiliao congkan*, vol. 762. Taipei: Wenhai chubanshe, 1970.

———. *Dongshu yigao* 東塾遺稿 (Transcribed reading notes of Chen Li). Manuscript copies, 53 vols. Zhongshan University Library.

———. *Dongshu zazu* 東塾雜俎 (Miscellanies from the Eastern Study). Guxueyuan edition, 1883. *Jingjitang congshu* 敬躋堂叢書. Beijing: Zhongguo shudian, no date.

———. *Hanru tongyi* 漢儒通義 (Comprehensive meanings among Han Confucians). *Dongshu congshu* edition, 1870.

———. *Qieyun kao* 切韻考 (An investigation of the *qieyun* method). *Dongshu congshu* edition, 1870. Taipei: Xuesheng shuju, 1977.

———. *Zhuzi yulei richao* 朱子語類日鈔 (Daily transcriptions from the *Zhuzi yulei*). Guangya shuju edition, 1900.

Chen Liangyu 陳良玉. *Meiwo shichao / Meiwo cichao* 梅窩詩鈔/梅窩詞鈔 (Transcribed *shi* poems from Plum Den / Transcribed lyric poems from Plum Den). Reprinted, together with *Meiwo yigao* 梅窩遺稿 (Bequeathed manuscripts from Plum Den). 1898.

Chen Pu 陳璞. *Chigang caotang yiwen, yishi* 尺岡草堂遺文遺詩 (Bequeathed prose and poetry from the Foot-ridge Thatched Hall). 1889.

Chen Qikun 陳其錕. *Chen Libu shigao* 陳禮部詩稿 (Manuscript poems of Chen Qikun). 1852.

———. "Chishou Wenlinlang renchen ke juren Hanlinyuan dianbu qinjia Neige zhongshu xian Zhong jun jiazhuan" 敕授文林郎壬辰科舉人

翰林院典簿欽加內閣中書銜鍾君家傳 (Family biography of Zhong Fengqing). Stele inscription, Shuixi village, Luogang town, Baiyun district, Guangzhou city.

Chen Shouqi 陳壽祺. *Zuohai wenji* 左海文集 (Prose collection from the Eastern Sea). *Xuxiu Siku quanshu*, vol. 1496. Shanghai: Shanghai guji chubanshe, 1995–99.

Chen Tan 陳曇. *Ganyutang wen/waiji* 感遇堂文外集 (Prose collection with appended works from the Hall of Being Moved by Circumstances). 1852.

———. *Kuangzhai shiyou ji* 鄺齋師友集 (Collected writings of teachers and friends of the Kuang Studio). Manuscript copy. Held in the Zhongshan wenxianguan.

———. *Kuangzhai zaji* 鄺齋雜記 (Miscellaneous notes from the Kuang Studio). 1828.

Chen Yufu 陳遇夫. *Shexutang ji* 涉需堂集 (Collection from the Hall of Crossing and Waiting). Held in the Zhongshan wenxianguan.

Chen Zaiqian 陳在謙, ed. *Guochao Lingnan wenchao* 國朝嶺南文鈔 (Lingnan prose manuscripts from the present dynasty). Xuehaitang edition, Daoguang reign.

Chengnan Dushi jiapu 城南杜氏家譜 (Genealogy of the City-south Du). Ed. Du You 杜游. 1848, 1896. Held in the Zhongshan wenxianguan.

Chenshi jiacheng, juanmo 陳氏家乘, 卷末 (Chen surname family records, with postscript chapter). Ed. Chen Li 陳澧. Manuscript copy. Zhongshan Library.

Cheong, Weng Eang. *The Hong Merchants of Canton: Chinese Merchants in Sino-Western Trade*. Richmond, Surrey: Curzon Press, 1997.

Chia, Lucille. *Printing for Profit: The Commerical Publishers of Jianyang, Fujian (11th–17th Centuries)*. Cambridge: Harvard University Asia Center, 2002.

Chinese Repository. Vols. 1–20. 1832–51.

Ching, May-bo. "Literary, Ethnic or Territorial? Definitions of Guangdong Culture in the Late Qing and the Early Republic." In David Faure and Tao Tao Liu, eds., *Unity and Diversity: Local Cultures and Identities in China*. Hong Kong: Hong Kong University Press, 1996, pp. 51–67.

Chixi xian zhi 赤溪縣志 (Chixi county gazetteer). 1920.

Chongji Sangyuanwei zhi 崇輯桑園圍志 (The recompiled gazetteer of the Mulberry Garden Embankment). Ed. He Ruquan 何如銓. 1889.

Chow Kai-wing. *Publishing, Culture, and Power in Early Modern China*. Stanford: Stanford University Pres, 2004.

———. *The Rise of Confucian Ritualism in Late Imperial China: Ethics, Classics, and Lineage Discourse*. Stanford: Stanford University Press, 1994.

Clunas, Craig. *Fruitful Sites: Garden Culture in Ming Dynasty China*. Durham: Duke University Press, 1996.

———. *Superfluous Things: Material Culture and Social Status in Early Modern China*. Cambridge, Eng.: Polity Press, 1991.

Cole, James H. *Shaohsing: Competition and Cooperation in Nineteenth-Century China*. Tucson: University of Arizona Press, 1986.

Cooke, George Wingrove. *China: Being "The Times" Special Correspondent from China in the Years 1857–1858*. Reprinted—Wilmington, Delaware: Scholarly Resources, 1972.

Cui Bi 崔弼. *Baiyun Yuexiu er shan hezhi* 白雲越秀二山合志 (A combined gazetteer of the Baiyun and Yuexiu mountains). 1849.

Dapu xian zhi 大埔縣志 (Dapu county gazetteer). 1943. Reprinted—Taipei: Dapu tongxianghui, 1971.

Dardess, John W. *A Ming Society: T'ai-ho County, Kiangsi, in the Fourteenth to Seventeenth Centuries*. Berkeley: University of California Press, 1996.

Deng Bangkang 鄧邦康, ed. *Deng shangshu nianpu* 鄧尚書年譜 (Chronological biography of Deng Tingzhen). 1910. East China Normal University Library.

Deng Dalin 鄧大林, ed. *Xingzhuang tiyong* 杏莊題詠 (Poems composed at Almond Villa), 1846, with *Xinglinzhuang xinghua shi* 杏林莊杏花詩 (Poems on almond flowers from the Almond Grove Villa). 1851.

Deng Qingcai 鄧慶宷. *Minzhong lizhi tongpu* 閩中荔支通譜 (Comprehensive handbook of Fujian litchis). Chongzhen era. *Xuxiu Siku quanshu*, vol. 1116. Shanghai: Shanghai guji chubanshe, 1995–99.

Deng Youtong 鄧又同, ed. *Qingdai Guangdong cilin biao* 清代廣東詞林表 (Table of Hanlin academicians from Guangdong in the Qing). 1946. Manuscript copy. Held in the Zhongshan wenxianguan.

Dennerline, Jerry. *The Chia-ting Loyalists: Confucian Leadership and Social Change in Seventeenth-Century China*. New Haven: Yale University Press, 1981.

Dongguan xian zhi 東莞縣志 (Dongguan county gazetteer). Compiled 1911. Printed 1921.

Dou Zhen 竇鎮. *Guochao shuhuajia bilu* 國朝書畫家筆錄 (Notes on calligraphers and painters of the present dynasty). 1911.

Du Mu 杜牧. *Du Mu shixuan* 杜牧詩選 (Selected poems of Du Mu). Ed. and annot. Zhou Xifu. Taipei: Yuanliu chuban gongsi, 1988.

Duanxi shuyuan zhi 端溪書院志 (Duanxi academy gazetteer). Comp. Fu Weisen 傅維森. 1900.

Duara, Prasenjit. *Culture, Power, and the State: Rural North China, 1900–1942*. Stanford: Stanford University Press, 1988.

———. *Sovereignty and Authenticity: Manchukuo and the East Asian Modern*. Lanham: Rowman and Littlefield, 2003.

Eberhard, Wolfram. *Social Mobility in Traditional China*. Leiden: E. J. Brill, 1962.

Elliott, Mark C. *The Manchu Way: The Eight Banners and Ethnic Identity in Late Imperial China*. Stanford: Stanford University Press, 2001.

Elman, Benjamin A. "Changes in Confucian Civil Service Examinations from the Ming to the Ch'ing Dynasty." In Benjamin A. Elman and Alexander Woodside, eds., *Education and Society in Late Imperial China, 1600–1900*. Berkeley: University of California Press, 1994, pp. 111–49.

———. "Ch'ing Dynasty 'Schools' of Scholarship." *Ch'ing-shih wen-t'i* 4 (December 1981): 1–44.

———. *Classicism, Politics, and Kinship: The Ch'ang-chou School of New Text Confucianism in Late Imperial China*. Reprinted—Taipei: SMC Publishing, 1990.

———. *A Cultural History of Civil Examinations in Late Imperial China*. Berkeley: University of California Press, 2000.

———. *From Philosophy to Philology: Intellectual and Social Aspects of Change in Late Imperial China*. Cambridge: Council on East Asian Studies, Harvard University, 1984.

———. "The Hsueh-hai t'ang and the Rise of New Text Scholarship in Canton." *Ch'ing-shih wen-t'i* 4 (December 1979): 51–82.

Eng, Robert Y. "Institutional and Secondary Landlordism in the Pearl River Delta, 1600–1949." *Modern China* 12.1 (January 1986): 3–37.

Esherik, Joseph W., and Mary Backus Rankin, eds. *Chinese Local Elites and Patterns of Dominance*. Berkeley: University of California Press, 1990.

Fan Feng 樊封. *Nanhai baiyong xubian* 南海百詠續編 (Continuation of the "Hundred Chants of the South Sea Region"). *Congshu jicheng xubian, shibu, dililei, zazhi zhi shu*, vol. 54. Shanghai: Shanghai shudian, 1994.

———. *Yi'nan shimo* 夷難始末 (The foreign difficulties from beginning to end). No date. Held in the Tōyō Bunko.

Fang Dongshu 方東樹. *Hanxue shangdui* 漢學商兌 (An exchange on Han Learning). Taipei: Guangwen shuju, 1977.

———. *Shulin yangzhi* 書林揚觶 (Vessel raised amid a jungle of books). *Yiweixuan quanji*. 1889.

———. *Yiweixuan wenji* 儀衛軒文集 (Collected writings from the Ceremony Guardian Studio). 1868. East China Normal University Library.

Fang Junyi 方濬頤. *Erzhixuan shichao* 二知軒詩鈔 (Transcribed poems from the Doubling Knowledge Studio). 1866.

———. *Erzhixuan wencun* 二知軒文存 (Preserved prose from the Doubling Knowledge Studio). 1878. *Jindai Zhongguo shiliao congkan*, vol. 481. Taipei: Wenhai chubanshe, 1970.
Fang Xinru 方信孺. *Nanhai baiyong* 南海百咏 (Hundred chants on the South Sea region). 1821.
Faure, David. "Becoming Cantonese, the Ming Dynasty Transition." In Tao Tao Liu and David Faure, eds., *Unity and Diversity: Local Cultures and Identities in China*. Hong Kong: Hong Kong University Press, 1996, pp. 37-50.
———. "The Lineage as a Cultural Invention: The Case of the Pearl River Delta." *Modern China* 15.1 (January 1989): 4-36.
———. *The Structure of Chinese Rural Society: Lineage and Village in the Eastern New Territories, Hong Kong*. Hong Kong: Oxford University Press, 1986.
———. "What Made Foshan a Town? The Evolution of Rural-Urban Identities in Ming-Qing China." *Late Imperial China* 11.2 (December 1990): 1-31.
Faure, David, and Helen F. Siu, eds. *Down to Earth: The Territorial Bond in South China*. Stanford: Stanford University Press, 1995.
Feng Shilü 馮士履 and Feng Shibiao 馮士鑣. *Xian junzi taishi gong nianpu* 先君子太史公年譜 (Chronological biography of our deceased father). *Beijing tushuguan cang zhenben nianpu congke*, vol. 117. Beijing: Beijing tushuguan chubanshe, 1999.
Finnane, Antonia. *Speaking of Yangzhou: A Chinese City, 1550-1850*. Cambridge: Harvard University Asia Center, 2004.
Furth, Charlotte. *A Flourishing Yin: Gender in China's Medical History, 960-1665*. Berkeley: University of California Press, 1999.
Fuwen shuyuan zhilue 敷文書院志略 (Concise Fuwen academy gazetteer). Ed. Wei Songtang 魏頌唐. *Zhongguo lidai shuyuan zhi*, vol. 8. Nanjing: Jiangsu jiaoyu chubanshe, 1995.
Gaoyang Xushi jiapu 高陽許氏家譜 (Genealogy of the Gaoyang Xu). Ed. Xu Yinzhi 許引之 et al. 1920.
Gardner, Daniel. *Learning to Be a Sage: Selections from the Conversations of Master Chu, Arranged Topically*. Berkeley: University of California Press, 1990.
Gengshen xiuxi ji 庚申修禊集 (Literary collection from the 1860 lustration celebrations). Comp. Li Changrong 李長榮 and Tan Shouqu 譚壽衢. 1860.
Gong Zizhen 龔自珍. *Dingan xuji* 定盦續集 (Continued collected writings of Dingan). In *Gong Dingan quanji* 龔定盦全集 (Complete works of

Gong Dingan). *Xuxiu Siku quanshu*, vol. 1520. Shanghai: Shanghai guji chubanshe, 1995–1999.

Goodman, Bryna. *Native Place, City, and Nation: Regional Networks and Identities in Shanghai, 1853–1937*. Berkeley: University of California Press, 1995.

Goodrich, L. Carrington, and Chaoying Fang, eds. *Dictionary of Ming Biography, 1368–1644*. New York: Columbia University Press, 1976.

Gray, John Henry. *Walks in the City of Canton*. Hongkong: De Souza, 1875.

Grimm, Tilemann. "Academies and Urban Systems in Kwangtung." In G. William Skinner, ed., *The City in Late imperial China*. Stanford: Stanford University Press, 1977, pp. 475–98.

Guan Shudetang jiapu 關樹德堂家譜 (Genealogy of the Shude branch of the Guan lineage). Ed. Guan Zhaoxi 關兆熙. 1897. Held in the Zhongshan wenxianguan.

Guangdong Hongbing qiyi shiliao 廣東洪兵起義史料 (Historical materials on the uprising of the Torrential Army in Guangdong). Guangzhou: Guangdong renmin chubanshe, 1996.

Guangdong shengli xinzuan 廣東省例新纂 (Updated edition of legal precedents from Guangdong province). Ed. Huang Entong 黃恩彤. 1846.

Guangdong tongzhi 廣東通志 (Guangdong provincial gazetteer). 1822.

Guangdong tu 廣東圖 (Guangdong maps). Shejieyuan, 1866. Copy in Taiwan University Library.

Guangzhou chengfang zhi 廣州城坊志 (Gazetteer of Guangzhou city neighborhoods). Ed. Huang Foyi 黃佛頤. *Guangdong congshu* 廣東叢書 edition, 1948. Reprinted—Guangzhou: Guangdong renmin chubanshe, 1994.

Guangzhou fu zhi 廣州府志 (Guangzhou prefectural gazetteer). 1879. Reprinted—Taipei: Chengwen chubanshe, 1968.

Guangzhou Gaodijie Xushi jiazu 廣州高第街許氏家族 (The Xu lineage of Gaodi Street in Guangzhou). Comp. Li Tingxian 李廷賢 et al. Guangzhou: Guangdong renmin chubanshe, 1992.

Guangzhoushi Qiushi zongci tekan 廣州市丘氏宗祠特刊 (Special edition handbook of the Guangzhou city Qiu Ancestral Hall). Ed. Qiu Xiuqiang 丘秀強. Taipei: Henantang wenxianshe, 1973.

Gui Hong 桂鴻. *Jianzhai shichao* 漸齋詩鈔 (Transcribed poetry from the Permeating Study). 1857.

Gui Tan 桂壇. *Huimuxuan gao* 晦木軒稿 (Manuscripts from the Obscure Woods Study). 1898.

Gui Wencan 桂文燦. *Jingxue bocai lu* 經學博采錄 (Broadly selected record of classical scholarship). *Jingjitang congshu* edition. Taipei: Mingwen shuju, 1992.

———. *Qianxintang ji* 潛心堂集 (Collected writings from the Hall of the Concentrated Mind). Guangxu era. Held in the Zhongshan wenxianguan.

Gujing jingshe wenji 詁經精舍文集 (Collected writings of the Gujing jingshe). Ed. Ruan Yuan 阮元, 1801. *Zhongguo lidai shuyuan zhi*, vol. 15. Nanjing: Jiangsu jiaoyu chubanshe, 1995.

Gujing jingshe wen xuji 詁經精舍文續集 (Continuation of *Collected Writings of the Gujing jingshe*). Ed. Luo Wenjun 羅文俊. *Zhongguo lidai shuyuan zhi*, vol. 15. Nanjing: Jiangsu jiaoyu chubanshe, 1995.

Guo Maoqian 郭茂倩. *Yuefu shiji* 樂府詩集 (Collected Music Bureau poems). Beijing: Zhonghua shuju, 1979.

Guo Songtao 郭嵩燾. *Guo Songtao riji* 郭嵩燾日記 (Diary of Guo Songtao). Vol. 2, Tongzhi era. Reprinted—Changsha: Hunan renmin chubanshe, 1981.

Guy, R. Kent. *The Emperor's Four Treasuries: Scholars and the State in the Late Ch'ien-lung Era*. Cambridge: Council on East Asian Studies, Harvard University, 1987.

Hamaguchi Fujio 濱口富士雄. *Shindai kōkyogaku no shisōshi* 清代考拠学の思想史 (Intellectual history of Qing evidential research). Tokyo: Kokusho kankōkai, 1994.

Han shu 漢書 (History of the Han dynasty). Ban Gu 班固. Beijing: Zhonghua shuju, 1975.

Hang Shijun 杭世駿. *Lingnan ji* 嶺南集 (Lingnan collection). Xuehaitang edition. 1881.

Hangzhou fu zhi 杭州府志 (Hangzhou prefectural gazetteer). 1922.

He Ruoyao 何若瑤. *He Gongzan yishu* 何宮贊遺書 (Bequeathed works of He Ruoyao). 1882.

He Wenqi 何文綺. *Keyu huichao* 課餘彙鈔 (Extracurricular categorized transcriptions). 1865. Held in the Zhongshan wenxianguan.

———. *Sishu jiangyi* 四書講義 (Lectures on the *Four Books*). Guangxu era. Held in the Zhongshan wenxianguan.

He Yousen 何佑森. "Chen Lanfu de xueshu ji qi yuanyuan" 陳蘭甫的學術及其淵源 (Chen Li's scholarship and its origins). *Gugong wenxian* 2.4 (1971): 1-19.

———. "Ruan Yuan de jingxue ji qi zhixue fangfa" 阮元的經學及其治學方法 (Ruan Yuan's classical studies and his method of scholarship). *Gugong wenxian* 2.1 (December 1970): 19-34.

Henderson, John B. *Scripture, Canon, and Commentary: A Comparison of Confucian and Western Exegesis*. Princeton: Princeton University Press, 1991.

Henry, B. C. *Ling-nam, or Interior Views of Southern China: Including Explorations in the Hitherto Untraversed Island of Hainan*. London: S. W. Partridge, 1886.

Heshan xian zhi 鶴山縣志 (Heshan county gazetteer). 1826.

Heyang shixi 河陽世系 (Heyang [Pan clan] genealogy by generation). Ed. Pan Fushen 潘福燊. 1920. Manuscript copy. Held in the Zhongshan wenxianguan.

Hightower, James Robert, trans. *Han Shih Wai Chuan: Han Ying's Illustrations of the Didactic Application of the Classic of Songs*. Cambridge: Harvard University Press, 1952.

Ho, Ping-ti. "The Salt Merchants of Yang-chou: A Study of Commercial Capitalism in Eighteenth-Century China." *Harvard Journal of Asiatic Studies* 17.1–2 (June 1954): 130–68.

Honig, Emily. *Creating Chinese Ethnicity: Subei People in Shanghai, 1850–1980*. New Haven: Yale University Press, 1992.

———. "Native Place and the Making of Chinese Ethnicity." In Gail Hershatter,

Emily Honig, Jonathan N. Lipman, and Randall Stross, eds., *Remapping China: Fissures in Historical Terrain*. Stanford: Stanford University Press, 1996, pp. 143–55.

Howard, Richard C. "K'ang Yu-wei (1858–1927): His Intellectual Background and Early Thought." In Arthur F. Wright and Denis Twitchett, eds., *Confucian Personalities*. Stanford: Stanford University Press, 1962, pp. 294–316.

Hsiao Kung-ch'üan. *Rural China: Imperial Control in the Nineteenth Century*. Seattle: University of Washington, 1960.

Hu Chusheng 胡楚生. *Qingdai xueshushi yanjiu* 清代學術史研究 (A study of the history of Qing dynasty scholarship). Taipei: Xuesheng shuju, 1988.

Huang Bingkun 黃炳堃. *Xigutang wencun* 希古堂文存 (Preserved prose from the Longing for the Ancient Hall). 1921.

Huang Peifang 黃培芳. *Linghailou shichao* 嶺海樓詩鈔 (Transcribed poems from the Linghai Tower). 1841.

———. *Xiangshi shihua* 香石詩話 (Fragrant Stone reflections on poetry). Linghailou edition, 1810. Reprinted—Shanghai: Shanghai shudian, 1985.

———. *Yueyue caotang shihua* 粵岳草堂詩話 (Reflections on poetry from the Yue Peak Thatched Hall). In *Huang Peifang shihua sanzhong*. Guangzhou: Guangdong gaodeng jiaoyu chubanshe, 1995.

———. *Yunquan suizha* 雲泉隨札 (Rambling notes from Cloud and Springs). 1813.

Huang Weiqing 黃位清. *Songfengge shichao* 松風閣詩鈔 (Transcribed poetry from the Pine Breeze Belvedere). 1839.

Huang Yinpu 黃蔭普. *Guangdong wenxian shumu zhijian lu* 廣東文獻書目知見錄 (Bibliographical guide to Guangdong writings). Hong Kong: Chongwen shudian, 1972.

Huang Zhi 黃芝. *Yue xiaoji* 粵小記 (A concise record of Guangdong). 1832. Reprinted—Zhongshan Library, 1960.

Huang Zigao 黃子高. *Zhijiaxuan shichao* 知稼軒詩鈔 (Transcribed poems from the Knowing [the Painful Toil of] Sowing Studio). 1847.

Huang Zuo 黃佐. *Guangzhou renwu zhuan* 廣州人物傳 (Cantonese biographies). Preface, 1526. Reprinted—Guangzhou: Guangdong gaodeng jiaoyu chubanshe, 1991.

Huang Qing jingjie 皇清經解 (Qing dynasty exegeses of the Classics). Ed. Ruan Yuan. 1826. Reprinted—Taipei: Fuxing shuju, 1972.

Huang Qing jingjie xubian 皇清經解續編 (Continuation of *Qing Dynasty Exegeses of the Classics*). Ed. Wang Xianqian 王先謙. 1888. Reprinted—Taipei: Fuxing shuju, 1972.

Huang Shenzhi shourong jigong lu 黃慎之守戎記功錄 (A record of the merits of Lieutenant Huang Shenzhi). Ed. Huang Peifang 黃培芳 et al. 1855. Held in the Zhongshan wenxianguan.

Huangshi jiacheng 黃氏家乘 (Huang lineage genealogy). Ed. Huang Peifang 黃培芳. With *Huangshi jiacheng xubian* 續編 (Continuation of Huang lineage genealogy). Ed. Huang Jingwen 黃鯨文. 1905. Held in the Zhongshan wenxianguan.

Hummel, Arthur W. *Eminent Chinese of the Ch'ing Period, 1644–1912*. Reprinted—Taipei: SMC Publishing, 1991.

Hunter, William C. *Bits of Old China*. 2d edition. Shanghai: Kelly and Walsh, 1911.

Huters, Theodore. "From Writing to Literature: The Development of Late Qing Theories of Prose." *Harvard Journal of Asiatic Studies* 47.1 (June 1987): 51–96.

Hymes, Robert. *Statesmen and Gentlemen: The Elite of Fu-Chou, Chiang-Hsi, in Northern and Southern Sung*. Cambridge: Cambridge University Press, 1996.

Jenkins, Jennifer. *Provincial Modernity: Local Culture and Liberal Politics in Fin-de-Siècle Hamburg*. Ithaca: Cornell University Press, 2003.

Ji Zhenyi 季振宜. *Ji Cangwei cangshu mu* 季滄葦藏書目 (Bibliography of Ji Cangwei's book collection). 1805. *Xuxiu Siku quanshu*, vol. 920. Shanghai: Shanghai guji chubanshe, 1995–99.

Jian Chaoliang 簡朝亮. *Dushutang ji* 讀書堂集 (Collection from the Hall of Study). 1903.

Jiang Fan 江藩. *Guochao Hanxue shicheng ji* 國朝漢學師承記 (Record of the transmissions of teachers of Han Learning in the present dynasty). *Qingdai zhuanji congkan*, vol. 1. Taipei: Mingwen shuju, 1985.

Jiaying zhou zhi 嘉應州志 (Jiaying department gazetteer). 1898.

Jin Jingmao 金菁茅, comp. *Zhang Nanshan xiansheng nianpu cuolue* 張南山先生年譜撮略 (Concise chronological biography of Zhang Weiping). *Beijing tushuguan cang zhenben nianpu congke*, vol. 136. Beijing: Beijing tushuguan chubanshe, 1999.

Jin Xiling 金錫齡. *Qushushi yiji, fu Lixue yongyan* 劬書室遺集附理學庸言 (Bequeathed writings from the Toiling Over Books Study, with Common *lixue* terms). 1895.

Jiujiang Rulin xiang zhi 九江儒林鄉志 (Jiujiang Rulin township gazetteer). 1883. *Zhongguo difangzhi jicheng* 中國地方志集成, vol. 31. Nanjing: Jiangsu guji chubanshe, 1992.

Jiujiang xiang zhi 九江鄉志 (Jiujiang township gazetteer), 1657. Printed, 1874. *Zhongguo difangzhi jicheng*, vol. 31. Nanjing: Jiangsu guji chubanshe, 1992.

Ju Huang 居鍠. *Ju Shaonan xiansheng yigao* 居少楠先生遺稿 (Bequeathed manuscripts of Ju Huang). *Xiushilou congshu* edition. No date.

Jupo jingshe ji 菊坡精舍集 (Collected writings of the Jupo jingshe). Ed. Chen Li 陳澧. Guangxu era.

Kaiping xian zhi 開平縣志 (Kaiping county gazetteer). 1933.

Kang Youwei 康有爲. *Kang Nanhai xiansheng zibian nianpu* 康南海先生自編年譜 (Self-edited chronological biography of Kang Youwei). In Jiang Guilin, ed., *Kang Nanhai xiansheng yizhu huikan*, vol. 22. Taipei: Hongye shuju, 1976.

Katayama Tsuyoshi 片山剛. "Shindai Kantonshō Shukō deruta no tokōsei ni tsuite: zeiryō, koseki, dōzoku" 清代広東省珠江デルタの図甲制について: 税量, 戸籍, 同族 (On the *tujia* system in Guangdong's Pearl River Delta during the Qing dynasty: tax, household, and lineage). *Tōyō Gakuhō* 63.3-4 (1982): 1-34.

———. "Shukō deruta Sōeni no kōzō to chisui soshiki: Shindai Kenryū nenkan—Minkokuki 珠江デルタ桑園囲の構造と治水組織: 清代乾隆年間-民國期 (Structure and water control organization of the Mulberry Garden Enclosure in the Pearl River Delta: Qianlong reign to Republican period). *Tōyō bunka kenkyūjo kiyō* 121 (March 1993): 137-209.

Keenan, Barry C. *Imperial China's Last Classical Academies: Social Change in the Lower Yangzi, 1864-1911*. Berkeley: University of California Press, 1994.

Knechtges, David R., trans. Xiao Tong. *Wen xuan, or, Selections of Refined Literature*. Vol. 1. Princeton: Princeton University Press, 1982.
Ko, Dorothy. *Teachers of the Inner Chambers: Women and Culture in Seventeenth-Century China*. Stanford: Stanford University Press, 1994.
Kondō Mitsuo 近藤光男. *Shinchō kōshōgaku no kenkyū* 清朝考証学の研究 (A study of Qing dynasty evidential research). Tokyo: Kenbun shuppan, 1987.
Kong Guangtao 孔廣陶. *Yuexuelou shuhua li* 嶽雪樓書畫錄 (Record of calligraphy and paintings in the Peak Snow Tower). 1889.
Kong Luhua 孔璐華. *Tang-Song jiujinglou gao* 唐宋舊經樓稿 (Manuscripts from the Tower of Old Tang and Song Classics). In Cai Dianqi 蔡殿齊, comp., *Guochao guige shichao* 國朝閨閣詩鈔 (Transcribed women's poetry from the present dynasty). *Xuxiu Siku quanshu*, vol. 1626. Shanghai: Shanghai guji chubanshe, 1995–99.
Koon, Yeewan. "Windblown Whispers: A Cohong Merchant's Art Collection and Its Impact on Early Nineteenth-Century Guangzhou." Unpublished paper presented at the Workshop on Guangzhou's Cohong Merchants in Local and International Society, Fairbank Center for East Asian Research, Harvard University, October 18, 2003.
Kuhn, Philip A. *Origins of the Modern Chinese State*. Stanford: Stanford University Press, 2002.
———. *Rebellion and Its Enemies in Late Imperial China: Militarization and Social Structure*. Cambridge: Harvard University Press, 1970.
Kuhn, Philip A., and Susan Mann Jones. "Dynastic Decline and the Rise of Rebellion." In John K. Fairbank et al., eds., *The Cambridge History of China*, vol. 10. New York: Cambridge University Press, 1978, pp. 107-62.
Kwan, Man Bun. *The Salt Merchants of Tianjin: State-Making and Civil Society in Late Imperial China*. Honolulu: University of Hawai'i Press, 2001.
Lao Tong 勞潼 et al. *Feng Qianzhai xiansheng nianpu* 馮潛齋先生年譜 (Chronological biography of Feng Chengxiu). Reprinted—1911. Held in the Toyō Bunko.
Laoshi zupu 勞氏族譜 (Lao genealogy). Ed. Lao Hongxun 勞鴻勛. 1868. Held in the Zhongshan wenxianguan.
Legge, James, trans. *The Chinese Classics*. Five volumes. Reprinted—Taipei: SMC, 1985.
———. *Li Chi, Book of Rites*. Vol. 2. New Hyde Park, NY: University Books, 1967.
Leong, Sow-theng, *Migration and Ethnicity in Chinese History: Hakkas, Pengmin, and Their Neighbors*. Ed. Tim Wright. Stanford: Stanford University Press, 1997.

Leung, Man-kam. "Juan Yuan (1764–1849): The Life, Works, and Career of a Chinese Scholar-Bureaucrat." Ph.D. diss., University of Hawai'i, 1977.

Li Changrong 李長榮, ed. *Liutang shiyou shilu* 柳堂師友詩錄 (Recorded poetry of teachers and friends of the Willow Hall). 1863.

Li E 厲鶚. *Songshi jishi* 宋詩紀事 (Recorded affairs in Song poetry). *Qinding Siku quanshu*, vol. 1485. Taipei: Taiwan shangwu yinshuguan, 1983.

Li Guangting 李光廷. *Rongyuan congshu* 榕園叢書 (Banyan Garden collectanea). Alternative title: *Shouyuepian congshu* 守約篇叢書. 1874.

———. *Wanmei shuwu wenchao* 宛湄書屋文鈔 (Transcribed prose from the Winding Shore Library). 1879.

Li Jun 李鈞. *Shi Yue riji* 使粵日記 (Diary of my service in Guangdong). 1834.

Li Xiaofeng 李嘯風, ed. *Zhongguo shuyuan cidian* 中國書院辭典 (A dictionary of academies in China). Hangzhou: Zhejiang jiaoyu chubanshe, 1996.

Li Xubai 李續柏. *Qingdai Guangdong puxue yanjiu* 清代廣東樸學研究 (Research on unadorned learning in Guangdong during the Qing dynasty). Guangzhou: Guangdong sheng ditu chubanshe, 2001.

———. "Qingdai Guangdong wenhua de jiejingti: Dongshu xuepai" 清代廣東文化的結晶體：東塾學派 (The crystallization of Guangdong culture in the Qing: the Dongshu school of learning). *Guangdong shehui kexue* 59 (1996): 94–101.

Li Zhao 李肇. *Tang guoshi bu* 唐國史補 (Supplements to the history of the Tang dynasty). *Yingyin Wenyuange Siku quanshu*, vol. 1035. Taipei: Taiwan shangwu yinshuguan, 1983.

Li Zhongpei 李中培. *Zhuzi bufei guxun shuo* 朱子不廢古訓說 (Master Zhu did not reject the ancient glosses). 1843. Held in the Zhongshan wenxianguan.

Liang Jiabin 梁嘉彬. *Guangdong shisanhang kao* 廣東十三行考 (A study of the Thirteen Firms of Guangdong). Taipei: Donghai University, 1960.

———. *Panyu Huangpu Liangshi wushi zhuanlue* 番禺黃埔梁氏五世傳略 (Brief biographies of five generations of the Panyu Huangpu Liang lineage). *Shixue huikan* 史學彙刊 7 (1976). Held in the Tōyō Bunko.

Liang Jiutu 梁九圖 and Wu Bingnan 吳炳南, eds. *Lingbiao shizhuan* 嶺表詩傳 (Biographies of Lingbiao poets). 1840–43.

Liang Qichao 梁啓超. *Qingdai xueshu gailun* 清代學術概論 (Intellectual trends in the Qing period). Taipei: Taiwan shangwu yinshuguan, 1985.

Liang shu 梁書 (History of the Liang dynasty). Beijing: Zhonghua shuju, 1973.

Liang Tingnan 梁廷楠. *Nan-Han shu* 南漢書 (History of the Southern Han). Reprinted—Guangzhou: Guangdong renmin chubanshe, 1981.

———. *Yifen jiwen* 夷氛記聞 (Record of things heard about the foreign disturbances). Shanghai: Guoli Beiping yanjiuyuan shixue yanjiuhui, 1937.

Liang-Guang yanfa zhi 兩廣鹽法志 (Gazetteer of the Liang-Guang region salt gabelle). Ed. Deng Tingzhen et al. 1836.

Liang-Guang yanfa zhi 兩廣鹽法志 (Gazetteer of the Liang-Guang region salt gabelle). Ed. He Zhaoying et al. 1884.

Liao Weize tang jiapu 廖維則堂家譜 (Genealogy of the Liao Weize Hall). Ed. Liao Xingzhao 廖星照 and Liao Jingzong 廖景總. 1930. Held in the Zhongshan wenxianguan.

Liji 禮記 (Record of rites). In *Shisanjing zhushu*. 1815. Reprinted—Taipei: Xin wenfeng, 1988.

Lin Botong 林伯桐. *Gongji xiaoyan* 供冀小言 (Brief comments on respectful reverence). In *Qixiushan congshu* 啓秀山叢書. Alternative title: *Xuehaitang congke* 學海堂叢刻. 1877, 1886.

———. *Xiubentang gao* 修本堂稿 (Manuscripts from the Hall of Cultivating Fundamentals). In *Xiuben tang congshu*. 1844.

Lin Shuyan 林書顔, ed. *Xijiang yuhua diaocha baogao shu* 西江魚花調查報告書 (Report on investigation of West River fish flowers). Guangzhou: Jiansheting nonglinju, 1933.

Lin Zexu 林則徐. *Lin Wenzhong gong riji* 林文忠公日記 (Diary of Lin Zexu). *Jindai Zhongguo shiliao congkan xuji*, vol. 41. Taipei: Wenhai chubanshe, 1974.

Lingnan Wushi hezu zongpu 嶺南伍氏合族總譜 (Main genealogy of the entire Wu clan of Guangdong). Ed. Wu Quancui 伍詮萃. 1934.

Liu Binhua 劉彬華, ed. *Lingnan qunya* 嶺南群雅 (Collected refined writings from Guangdong). 1813.

Liu Boji 劉伯驥. *Guangdong shuyuan zhidu* 廣東書院制度 (The institution of academies in Guangdong). Taipei: Zhonghua congshu weiyuanhui, 1958.

Liu Daxia 劉大夏. *Liu Zhongxuan gong yiji, fu nianpu* 劉忠宣公遺集附年譜 (Bequeathed works of Liu Daxia, with chronological biography). *Siku weishoushu jikan*, sixth series, vol. 29. Beijing: Beijing chubanshe, 1997.

Liu Shinan 劉世南. *Qingshi liupai shi* 清詩流派史 (A history of schools of poetry in the Qing). Taipei: Wenjin chubanshe, 1995.

Liu Zhiwei. "Lineage on the Sands: The Case of Shawan." In David Faure and Helen F. Siu, eds., *Down to Earth: The Territorial Bond in South China*. Stanford: Stanford University Press, 1995, pp. 21–43.

Loewe, Michael. *Crisis and Conflict in Han China, 104 BC to AD 9*. London: Allen & Unwin, 1974.

———, ed. *Early Chinese Texts: A Bibliographical Guide*. Berkeley: University of California Press, 1993.

Long Tinghuai 龍廷槐. *Jingxuexuan wenji* 敬學軒文集 (Collected prose from the Studio of Revering Studies). 1834.

Longjiang xiang zhi 龍江鄉志 (Longjiang township gazetteer). 1926.

Longmen xian zhi 龍門縣志 (Longmen county gazetteer). 1851.

Longshan xiang zhi 龍山鄉志 (Longshan township gazetteer). 1930.

Longshi zupu 龍氏族譜 (Long lineage genealogy). Ed. Long Jingkai 龍景愷 et al. 1922. Held in the Zhongshan wenxianguan.

Lu Duanfu 盧端黼. *Minsu xiankao Houshan fujun nianpu* 敏肅顯考厚山府君年譜 (Chronological biography of my deceased father, Lu Kun). 1836. Held in the Tōyō Bunko.

Luo Dunyan 羅惇衍. *Luo Wenke gong yiji* 羅文恪公遺集 (Bequeathed writings of Luo Dunyan). Guangxu era. Held in the Zhongshan wenxianguan.

Luo Hanzhang 羅含章. *Lingnan ji* 嶺南集 (The Lingnan collection). 1821. Held in the Zhongshan wenxianguan.

Luo Xuepeng 羅學鵬. *Guangdong wenxian* 廣東文獻 (A collection of literature and records in Guangdong). Chunhuitang edition, 1863.

Luo Yuanhuan 羅元煥 and Chen Zhonghong 陳仲鴻. *Yuetai zhengya lu* 粵臺徵雅錄 (A record of refinement summoned from the Yue Terrace). In Wu Chongyao, *Lingnan yishu*.

Ma Fuan 馬福安. *Zhizhai wenchao* 止齋文鈔 (Prose from the Resting [in Perfect Goodness] Studio). In *Qixiushan congshu*, 2d series.

Ma Jigao 馬積高. *Qingdai xueshu sixiang de bianqian yu wenxue* 清代學術思想之變遷與文學 (Literature and the transformation of approaches to learning during the Qing). Changsha: Hunan chubanshe, 1996.

Mann, Susan. *Precious Records: Women in China's Long Eighteenth Century*. Stanford: Stanford University Press, 1997.

Maoming xian zhi 茂名縣志 (Maoming county gazetteer). 1888.

Marks, Robert B. *Tigers, Rice, Silk, and Silt: Environment and Economy in Late Imperial South China*. New York: Cambridge University Press, 1998.

Mazumdar, Sucheta. *Sugar and Society in China: Peasants, Technology, and the World Market*. Cambridge: Harvard University Asia Center, 1998.

Meskill, John. *Academies in Ming China: A Historical Essay*. Tucson: University of Arizona Press, 1982.

———. *Gentlemanly Interests and Wealth on the Yangtze Delta*. Ann Arbor: Association for Asian Studies, 1994.

Meyer-Fong, Tobie. *Building Culture in Early Qing Yangzhou*. Stanford: Stanford University Press, 2003.

Miles, Steven B. "Celebrating the Yu Fan Shrine: Literati Networks and Local Identity in Early Nineteenth-Century Guangzhou." *Late Imperial China* 25.2 (December 2004): 33–73.

———. "From Small Fry to Big Fish: Representing the Rise of Jiujiang Township, Nanhai County, 1395–1657." *Ming Studies* 48 (Fall 2003): 65–99.

———. "The New Face of *Kaozheng*: The *Huang Qing jingjie xubian* and Classical Studies After 1820." *Zhongguo wenxue yanjiu* 11 (May 1997): 175–92.

———. "Rewriting the Southern Han (917–971): The Production of Local Culture in Nineteenth-Century Guangzhou." *Harvard Journal of Asiatic Studies* 62.1 (June 2002): 39–75.

Min Erchang 閔爾昌, comp. *Jiang Ziping xiansheng nianpu* 江子屏先生年譜 (Chronological biography of Jiang Fan). 1927. Copy in East China Normal University Library.

Ming Xiaozong shilu 明孝宗實錄. (Veritable records of the reign of the Ming Xiaozong emperor). Taipei: Academia Sinica, 1963.

Murray, Dian. *Pirates of the South China Coast, 1790–1810*. Stanford: Stanford University Press, 1987.

Nanhai Heyuan Xianshi jiapu 南海鶴園冼氏家譜 (Heyuan, Nanhai Xian genealogy). Ed. Xian Baogan 冼寶榦. 1910. Held in the Zhongshan wenxianguan.

Nanhai Jiujiang Zhushi jiapu 南海九江朱氏家譜 (Jiujiang, Nanhai Zhu lineage genealogy). Ed. Zhu Zongqi 朱宗琦. 1869.

Nanhai Luogefang Kongshi jiapu 南海羅格房孔氏家譜 (Genealogy of the Luoge Kong of Nanhai). Ed. Kong Guangyong 孔廣鏞 and Kong Guangtao 孔廣陶. 1929. Held in the Zhongshan wenxianguan.

Nanhai xian zhi 南海縣志 (Nanhai county gazetteer). 1835.

Nanhai xian zhi 南海縣志 (Nanhai county gazetteer). 1872.

Nanhai xian zhi 南海縣志 (Nanhai county gazetteer). 1910.

Naquin, Susan. *Peking: Temples and City Life, 1400–1900*. Berkeley: University of California Press, 2000.

Norman, Jerry. *Chinese*. New York: Cambridge University Press, 1988.

Oakes, Tim. "China's Provincial Identities: Reviving Regionalism and Reinventing 'Chineseness.'" *Journal of Asian Studies* 59.3 (August 2000): 667–92.

Ōkubo Eiko 大久保英子. *Min-Shin jidai shoin no kenkyū* 明清時代書院の研究 (Research on academies in the Ming-Qing period). Tokyo: Kokusho kankōkai, 1976.

Owen, Stephen. *Readings in Chinese Literary Thought*. Cambridge: Council on East Asian Studies, Harvard University, 1992.

———. *Remembrances: The Experience of the Past in Classical Chinese Literature*. Cambridge: Harvard University Press, 1986.

Pan Feisheng 潘飛聲. *Shuojiantang ji* 說劍堂集 (Collection from the Hall of Speaking of the Sword). 1897.

Pan Shicheng 潘仕成. *Haishan xianguan congshu* 海山仙館叢書 (Sea Mountain Immortals' Lodge collectanea). Haishan xianguan, 1849.

Pan Shidian tang zupu 潘式典堂族譜 (Pan Shidian Hall genealogy). Ed. Pan Jili 潘繼李 and Pan Guisen 潘桂森. 1867 and 1924. Held in the Zhongshan wenxianguan.

Pan Yizeng 潘儀增, ed. *Panyu Panshi shilue* 番禺潘氏詩略 (Concise collection of poetry of the Pan family of Panyu). 1894.

Pan Zhengwei 潘正煒. *Tingfanlou shuhua ji* 聽颿樓書畫記 (Record of calligraphy and painting at the Listening to the Whispering Wind Tower). Taipei: Shijie shuju, 1980.

Panyu Henan xiao zhi 番禺河南小志 (Concise gazetteer of Henan in Panyu). Ed. Huang Renheng 黃任恒. 1945. Reprinted—*Zhongguo difang zhi jicheng*, vol. 32. Nanjing: Jiangsu guji chubanshe, 1992.

Panyu xian xu zhi 番禺縣續志 (Continuation of the Panyu county gazetteer). 1931.

Panyu xian zhi 番禺縣志 (Panyu county gazetteer). 1871. Reprinted—Taipei: Chengwen chubanshe, 1967.

Perdue, Peter C. "Insiders and Outsiders: The Xiangtan Riot of 1819 and Collective Action in Hunan." *Modern China* 12.2 (April 1986): 166–201.

Pi Xirui 皮錫瑞. *Jingxue lishi* 經學歷史 (History of classical studies). Banqiao: Yiwen yinshuguan, 1987.

Polachek, James M. *The Inner Opium War*. Cambridge: Council on East Asian Studies, Harvard University, 1992.

Qian Daxin 錢大昕. *Qianyantang wenji* 潛研堂文集 (Collected Prose from the Hall of Subtle Research). 1806.

Qian Mu 錢穆. *Zhongguo jin sanbainian xueshushi* 中國近三百年學術史 (A history of Chinese scholarship in the past three hundred years). Taipei: Taiwan Shangwu yinshuguan, 1987.

Qian Yiji 錢儀吉. *Kanshizhai jishi gao, xugao* 衎石齋記事稿續稿 (Manuscript records from the Stable Stone Study, with continuation). 1808, 1880.

Qing shilu Guangdong shiliao 清實錄廣東史料 (Historical materials on Guangdong from the Veritable Records of the Qing). Ed. Guangdong sheng difang shizhi bianweihui bangongshi and Guangzhou shi difang zhi bianweihui bangongshi. Guangzhou: Guangdong sheng ditu chubanshe, 1995.

Qingshi liezhuan 清?史列傳 (Arranged biographies from Qing history). Taipei: Zhonghua shuju, 1983.

Qu Dajun 屈大均. *Guangdong xinyu* 廣東新語 (New comments on Guangdong). *Xuxiu Siku quanshu*, vol. 734. Shanghai: Shanghai guji chubanshe, 1995–99.

Rankin, Mary Backus. *Elite Activism and Political Transformation in China: Zhejiang Province, 1865–1911.* Stanford: Stanford University Press, 1986.

———. "Managed by the People: Officials, Gentry, and the Foshan Charitable Granary, 1795–1845." *Late Imperial China* 15.2 (December 1994): 1–52.

Reed, Bradly W. *Talons and Teeth: County Clerks and Runners in the Qing Dynasty.* Stanford: Stanford University Press, 2000.

Rhoads, Edward J. M. *China's Republican Revolution: The Case of Kwangtung, 1895–1913.* Cambridge: Harvard University Press, 1975.

———. "Merchant Associations in Canton, 1895–1911." In Mark Elvin and G. William Skinner, eds., *The Chinese City Between Two Worlds.* Stanford: Stanford University Press, 1974, pp. 97–117.

Rong Zhaozu 容肇祖. "Xuehaitang kao, fu Jupo jingshe kaolue" 學海堂考附菊坡精舍考略 (A study of the Xuehaitang, with a supplemental brief study of the Jupo jingshe). *Lingnan xuebao* 3.3 (1934): 1–147.

Rowe, William T. *Hankow: Commerce and Society in a Chinese City, 1798–1889.* Stanford: Stanford University Press, 1984.

———. "Success Stories: Lineage and Elite Status in Hanyang County, Hubei, c. 1368–1949." In Joseph W. Esherik and Mary Backus Rankin, eds., *Chinese Local Elites and Patterns of Dominance.* Berkeley: University of California Press, 1990, pp. 51–81.

Ruan Rongling 阮榕齡. *Baisha menren kao* 白沙門人考 (Examination of the students of Chen Xianzhang). 1851.

Ruan Rongling 阮榕齡, ed. *Chen Baisha xiansheng nianpu* 陳白沙先生年譜 (Chronological biography of Chen Xianzhang). 1851.

Ruan Yuan 阮元. *Yanjingshiji* 揅經室集 (Collected writings from the Classics Research Study). Taipei: Shijie shuju, 1982.

———. *Yanjingshiji* 揅經室集 (Collected writings from the Classics Research Study). Wenxuanlou edition. Red ink punctuation and comments by Chen Li 陳澧. Held in the Zhongshan University Library.

Ruddle, Kenneth, and Gongfu Zhong. *Integrated Agriculture-Aquaculture in South China: The Dike-pond System of the Zhujiang Delta.* New York: Cambridge University Press, 1988.

Sanguo zhi 三國志 (History of the Three Kingdoms). Beijing: Zhonghua shuju, 1973.

Sangyuanwei zhi 桑園圍志 (Mulberry Garden Enclosure gazetteer). Ed. Ming Zhigang 明之綱. 1870.

Sasaki Masaya 佐々木正哉. "Juntoku-ken kyōshin to Tōkai jūrokusa" 順德縣鄉民と東海十六沙 (The gentry of Shunde county and the Donghai district). In *Kindai Chūgoku kenkyū*, vol. 3. Tokyo: Tokyo University Press, 1959, pp. 162–232.

Schafer, Edward H. *The Vermilion Bird: T'ang Images of the South*. Berkeley: University of California Press, 1967.

Schoppa, R. Keith. *Chinese Elites and Political Change: Zhejiang Province in the Early Twentieth Century*. Cambridge: Harvard University Press, 1982.

Shanyin Wangshi pu 山陰汪氏譜 (Shanyin Wang genealogy). Ed. Wang Zhaoyong 汪兆鏞. Wang Jingde tang, 1947.

Shen Fu 沈復. *Fusheng liuji* 浮生六記 (Six records of a floating life). In *Duwu'an congchao*. 1878.

———. *Six Records of a Floating Life*. Trans. Leonard Pratt and Chiang Su-hui. New York: Penguin Books, 1983.

Shen, Han-yin Chan. "Tseng Kuo-fan in Peking, 1840–1852: His Ideas on Statecraft and Reform." *Journal of Asian Studies* 27.1 (November 1967): 61–80.

Shen Shiliang 沈世良. *Lenghuashi cichao* 楞華室詞鈔 (Transcribed lyric poems from the Surangama and Avatamsaka Studio). 1854.

———. *Ni Gaoshi nianpu* 倪高士年譜 (Chronological biography of Ni Zan). Reprinted—1909.

———. *Xiao Qituo an shichao* 小祇陀盦詩鈔 (Transcribed poems from the Little Jeta Chapel). 1909.

Sheng Langxi 盛郎西. *Zhongguo shuyuan zhidu* 中國書院制度 (The institution of academies in China). Shanghai: Zhonghua shuju yinhang, 1934.

Shenlou zhi 蜃樓志 (An account of mirages). Yuling laoren 瘐嶺勞人. Jiaqing era. Reprinted—Gudian xiuxiang jinhui yanqing xiaoshuo zhenpin. Changchun: Jilin wenshi chubanshe, 1999.

Shi Cheng 史澄. *Quting suoyu* 趨庭瑣語 (Detailed admonishments of a father). 1885.

Shi Gexin 史革新. *Wan Qing lixue yanjiu* 晚清理學研究 (A study of *lixue* in the late Qing). Taipei: Wenjin chubanshe, 1994.

Shi ji 史記 (Records of the Grand Historian). Beijing: Zhonghua shuju, 1972.

Shunde Beimen Luoshi zupu 順德北門羅氏族譜 (Genealogy of the Northgate Luo in Shunde). 1882. Held in the Tōyō Bunko.

Shunde Jian'an Jianshi jiapu 順德簡岸簡氏家譜 (Genealogy of the Jian lineage of Jian'an, Shunde county). 1928.
Shunde xian zhi 順德縣志 (Shunde county gazetteer). 1853.
Shunde xian zhi 順德縣志 (Shunde county gazetteer). 1929.
Sikong Tu 司空圖. *Ershisi shi pin* 二十四詩品 (The twenty-four categories of poetry). In *Yiyuan junhua*, vol. 5. 1868.
Sirén, Osvald. *Chinese Painting: Leading Masters and Principles*. Seven volumes. New York: Ronald Press, 1956.
Siu, Helen F. *Agents and Victims in South China: Accomplices in Rural Revolution*. New Haven: Yale University Press, 1989.
———. "Where Were the Women? Rethinking Marriage Resistance and Regional Culture in South China." *Late Imperial China* 11.2 (December 1990): 32–62.
Skinner, G. William, ed. *The City in Late Imperial China*. Stanford: Stanford University Press, 1977.
Stockard, Janice. *Daughters of the Canton Delta: Marriage Patterns and Economic Strategies in South China, 1860–1930*. Stanford: Stanford University Press, 1989.
Su Shi 蘇軾. *Su Dongpo quanji* 蘇東坡全集 (The complete works of Su Shi). Hefei: Huangshan shushe, 1997.
Sui shu 隋書 (History of the Sui dynasty). Beijing: Zhonghua shuju, 1973.
Szonyi, Michael. *Practicing Kinship: Lineage and Descent in Late Imperial China*. Stanford: Stanford University Press, 2002.
Taam, Cheuk-woon. *The Development of Chinese Libraries Under the Ch'ing Dynasty, 1644–1911*. Private edition. University of Chicago Libraries, 1935.
Tan Dihua 譚棣華. *Guangdong lishi wenti lunwen ji* 廣東歷史問題論文集 (Collected essays on problems in Guangdong history). Taipei: Daohe chubanshe, 1993.
———. *Qingdai Zhujiang sanjiaozhou de shatian* 清代珠江三角洲的沙田 (The Pearl River delta sands in the Qing dynasty). Guangzhou: Guangdong renmin chubanshe, 1993.
Tan Dihua 譚棣華, Cao Tengfei 曹騰騑, and Xian Jianmin 洗劍民, eds. *Guangdong beike ji* 廣東碑刻集 (Collected Guangdong inscriptions). Guangzhou: Guangdong gaodeng jiaoyu chubanshe, 2001.
Tan Ying 譚瑩. *Lezhitang shiji* 樂志堂詩集 (Poetry collected from the Hall of Joyous Determination). Liyinyuan, 1860.
———. *Lezhitang wenji* 樂志堂文集 (Prose collected from the Hall of Joyous Determination). 1859.
Tan Zongjun 譚宗浚. *Licun caotang shichao* 荔村草堂詩鈔 (Transcribed poems from the Litchi Village Thatched Hall). 1892.

———. *Licun suibi* 荔村隨筆 (Random Jottings from Litchi Village). *Congshu jicheng xubian*, shi bu, zashi lei, suoji zhi shu, vol. 26. Shanghai: Shanghai shudian, 1994.

———. *Xigutang ji* 希古堂集 (Collected writings from Longing for the Ancient Hall). 1890.

Tang shu 唐書 ([Old] history of the Tang dynasty). Beijing: Zhonghua shuju, 1974.

Tang Wenzhi 唐文治. *Rujingtang wenji* 茹經堂文集 (Prose collection from the Contemplating Classics Hall). *Jindai Zhongguo shiliao congkan xuji*, vol. 31. Taibei: Wenhai chubanshe, 1974.

Tiffany, Osmond, Jr. *The Canton Chinese, or the American's Sojourn in the Celestial Empire*. Boston: James Munroe and Company, 1849.

Tillman, Hoyt Cleveland. *Confucian Discourse and Chu Hsi's Ascendancy*. Honolulu: University of Hawai'i Press, 1992.

Tsin, Michael. *Nation, Governance, and Modernity in China: Canton, 1900–1927*. Stanford: Stanford University Press, 1999.

Wakeman, Frederic, Jr. *Strangers at the Gate: Social Disorder in South China, 1839–1861*. Berkeley: University of California Press, 1966.

Waley, Arthur. *The Opium War through Chinese Eyes*. London: Allen & Unwin, 1958.

Walton, Linda. *Academies and Society in Southern Sung China*. Honolulu: University of Hawai'i Press, 1999.

Wang Jia 王嘉. *Shiyi ji* 拾遺記 (Record of collected anecdotes). Beijing: Zhonghua shuju, 1981.

Wang Quan 汪瑔. *Suishanguan conggao* 隨山館叢稿 (Manuscript collection from the Follow Mountain Lodge). 1881.

Wang Rongbao 汪榮寶. *Fayan yishu* 法言義疏 (Exegesis of the *Model Sayings*). 1933. *Xuxiu Siku quanshu*, vol. 933. Shanghai: Shanghai guji chubanshe, 1995.

Wang Shizhen 王士禛. *Guangzhou youlan xiao zhi* 廣州遊覽小志 (Concise account of my tours in Guangzhou). *Shiliao congbian*, vol. 41. Taipei: Guangwen shuju, 1968.

Wang Yunxi 王運熙 and Yang Ming 楊明. *Wei-Jin-Nanbeichao wenxue piping shi* 魏晉南北朝文學批評史 (A history of literary criticism in the Wei, Jin, and Northern and Southern Dynasties). Shanghai: Shanghai guji chubanshe, 1989.

Wang Zhaoyong 汪兆鏞. *Guangzhou cheng canzhuan lu* 廣州城殘塼錄 (A record of remnant bricks from the Guangzhou wall). Hong Kong: Suji shuzhuang, 1932.

———. *Lingnan hua zhenglue* 嶺南畫徵略 (Brief notes on Lingnan painters). *Qingdai zhuanji congkan*, vol. 80. Taipei: Mingwen shuju, 1985.

———. *Weishang laoren ziding nianpu* 微尚老人自訂年譜 (Chronological autobiography of Wang Zhaoyong). Wang Jingdetang, 1949.

———. *Weishangzhai zawen* 微尚齋雜文 (Miscellaneous writings from the Studio of Humble Nobility). *Jindai Zhongguo shiliao congkan xuji*, vol. 823. Taipei: Wenhai chubanshe, 1981.

Wang Zongyan 汪宗衍. "Chen Dongshu xiansheng nianpu" 陳東塾先生年譜 (Chronological biography of Chen Li). *Lingnan xuebao* 4:1 (April 1935): 55–118.

Watson, Burton, trans. Sima Qian. *Records of the Grand Historian*. New York: Columbia University Press, 1993.

Watson, James L. "Chinese Kinship Reconsidered: Anthropological Perspectives on Historical Research." *China Quarterly* 92 (December 1982): 589–622.

Watson, Rubie S. *Inequality Among Brothers: Class and Kinship in South China*. Cambridge: Cambridge University Press, 1985.

Wei, Peh T'i. "Juan Yuan: A Biographical Study with Special Reference to Mid-Ch'ing Security and Control in Southern China, 1799–1835." Ph.D. diss., University of Hong Kong, 1981.

Wen Runeng 溫汝能. *Yuedong shihai* 粵東詩海 (A sea of poetry from Guangdong). 1813. Reprinted—Guangzhou: Zhongshan daxue, 1999.

Wen Tingshi 文廷式. *Wen Tingshi ji* 文廷式集 (Collected works of Wen Tingshi). Beijing: Zhonghua shuju, 1993.

Wen Xun 溫訓. *Dengyun shanfang wengao* 登雲山房文稿 (Prose manuscripts from the Ascending Clouds Mountain Study). 1823.

Weng Tongshu 翁同書. *Weng Wenduan gong nianpu* 翁文端公年譜 (Chronological biography of Weng Xincun). *Beijing tushuguan cang zhenben nianpu congkan*, vol. 145. Beijing: Beijing tushuguan chubanshe, 1999.

Weng Xincun 翁心存. "Ru Yue jicheng" 入粵紀程 (Annals of travel into Guangdong). Appended to Weng Xincun, *Zhizhizhai riji*. Manuscript, 1825–62. Held in the Beijing Library.

———, ed. *Xuehaitang dinghai keshi lu* 學海堂丁亥課士錄 (Record of testing scholars at the Xuehaitang in 1827). Manuscript, 1827. Held in the Beijing Library.

Wenlan zhongshen lu 文瀾眾紳錄 (Record of the Wenlan Academy gentry). Ed. Lü Jianhuang 呂鑑煌. 1892.

Will, Pierre-Étienne, and R. Bin Wong. *Nourish the People: The State Civilian Granary System in China, 1650–1850*. Ann Arbor: Center for Chinese Studies, University of Michigan, 1991.

Williams, S. Wells. *The Middle Kingdom*. New York: Charles Scribner's Sons, 1883.

Wilson, Thomas A. *Genealogy of the Way: The Construction and Uses of the Confucian Tradition in Late Imperial China.* Stanford: Stanford University Press, 1995.

Wong, J. Y. *Yeh Ming-ch'en: Viceroy of Liang Kuang, 1852–8.* Cambridge: Cambridge University Press, 1976.

Woodside, Alexander. "State, Scholars, and Orthodoxy: The Ch'ing Academies, 1736–1839." In Kwang-ching Liu, ed., *Orthodoxy in Late Imperial China.* Berkeley: University of California Press, 1990, pp. 158–84.

Wright, Mary Clabaugh. *The Last Stand of Chinese Conservatism: The T'ung-chih Restoration, 1862–1874.* Stanford: Stanford University Press, 1957.

Wu Chongyao 伍崇曜, ed. *Chuting qijiu yishi* 楚庭耆舊遺詩 (Bequeathed poems of past scholars of the Chu Court). 1843.

———. *Lingnan yishu* 嶺南遺書 (Surviving works from Lingnan). Yueyatang. Daoguang to Tongzhi reigns.

Wu Daorong 吳道鎔, ed. *Guangdong wenzheng zuozhe kao* 廣東文徵作者考 (Examination of authors in the *Summoned Prose from Guangdong*). 1941.

Wu Feng 吳灃. *Qiushixuan yigao* 求是軒遺稿 (Manuscripts bequeathed from the Seeking Facts Studio). 1867.

Wu Lanxiu 吳蘭修. *Licun yincao* 荔村吟草 (Manuscript verse from Litchi Village). 1934.

———. *Nan-Han ji* 南漢紀 (Annals of the Southern Han). In Wu Chongyao, ed., *Lingnan yishu*, fifth series.

Wu Rongguang 吳榮光. *Shiyun shanren wenji* 石雲山人文集 (Collected prose of the Stones and Clouds Mountain Man). 1841. *Xuxiu Siku qianshu*, vol. 1498. Shanghai: Shuanghai guji chubanshe, 1995–99.

Wu Shanjia 吳山嘉. *Fushe xingshi zhuanlue* 復社姓氏傳略 (Lists and concise biographies of Restoration Society members). Preface, 1832. In *Haiwangcun guji congkan*. Reprinted—Beijing: Zhongguo shudian, 1990.

Wu Yingkui 吳應逵. *Yanshan wenji, fu pulixuan biji* 雁山文集附譜荔軒筆記 (Collected prose from Goose Hill, with notes from the Compiling Litchi Handbook Studio). 1830. Reprinted—1936.

Xian Yuqing 洗玉清. *Xian Yuqing wenji* (Collected works of Xian Yuqing). Guangzhou: Zhongshan daxue chubanshe, 1995.

Xiangshan xianzhi 香山縣志 (Xiangshan county gazetteer). 1827.

Xiangshan xianzhi 香山縣志 (Xiangshan county gazetteer). 1873 and 1880.

Xiao Tong 蕭統, ed. *Wenxuan* 文選. Taipei: Yiwen yinshuguan, 1983.

Xie Guozhen 謝國楨. *Jindai shuyuan xuexiao zhidu bianqian kao* 近代書院學校制度變遷考 (An examination of institutional transformations in academies and schools in the modern era). 1936. *Jindai Zhongguo shiliao congkan xuji*, vol. 651. Taipei: Wenhai chubanshe, 1979.

Xie Jingqing 謝景卿. *Xuji Hanyin fenyun* 續集漢印分韻 (Continued collection of Han-style seal imprints, categorized by rhyme). 1803. With Yuan Rixing 袁日省. *Xuanji Hanyin fenyun* 選集漢印分韻 (Collection of Han-style seal imprints, categorized by rhyme). Transcribed by Xie Yunsheng 謝雲生. 1797.

Xie Lansheng 謝蘭生. *Changxingxingzhai riji* 常惺惺齋日記 (Diary from the Studio of Constant Awareness). Manuscript, 1819–29. Held in the Beijing Library.

———. *Changxingxingzhai shi* 常惺惺齋詩 (Poems from the Studio of Constant Awareness). Manuscript. Beijing Library.

———. *Changxingxingzhai shuhua tiba* 常惺惺齋書畫題跋 (Calligraphy and painting colophons from the Studio of Constant Awareness). Macau: Wenji tushu gongsi, no date.

———. *Changxingxingzhai wenji* 常惺惺齋文集 (Collected prose from the Studio of Constant Awareness). Manuscript. Held in the Zhongshan wenxianguan.

———. *Xingxingzhai wengao* 惺惺齋文稿 (Manuscript prose from the Studio of [Constant] Awareness). Manuscript. Held in the Zhongshan wenxianguan.

Xiguan Yangshi zhipu 西關楊氏支譜 (Branch genealogy of the Xiguan Yang). Guangxu era. Held in the Zhongshan wenxianguan.

Xinhui xian zhi 新會縣志 (Xinhui county gazetteer). 1841.

Xinhui xian zhi xu 新會縣志續 (Continuation of the Xinhui county gazetteer). 1871.

Xinning xian zhi 新寧縣志 (Xinning county gazetteer). 1891.

Xiong Jingxing 熊景星. *Jiyang xiguan shichao* 吉羊溪館詩鈔 (Transcribed poems from the Auspicious Rams Streamside Lodge). Preface, 1864. Held in the Zhongshan wenxianguan.

Xu Gan. *Balanced Discourses*. Trans. John Makeham. New Haven: Yale University Press, 2002.

Xu Hao 徐灝. *Tongjietang jingshuo* 通介堂經說 (Classical exegesis from the Comprehensive and Upright Hall). 1854.

———. *Tongjietang wenji* 通介堂文集 (Collected prose from the Comprehensive and Upright Hall). 1924.

Xu Qi 徐琪. *Yuedong qisheng ji* 粵東葺勝記 (A record of repairing sites in Yuedong). 1899.

Xu Shaoqi 徐紹棨. *Guangdong cangshu jishi shi* 廣東藏書紀事詩 (Poems chronicling book collectors in Guangdong). *Jindai Zhongguo shiliao congkan xubian*, vols. 199–200. Taipei: Wenhai chubanshe, 1975.

———. "Guangzhou banpian jilue" 廣州版片紀略 (A concise record of printing in Guangzhou). In Ye Gongchuo 葉恭綽, ed., *Juyuan yumo*, 195?, 57a–62b.

Xu Youchun 徐友春, ed. *Minguo renwu da cidian* 民國人物大辭典 (Comprehensive biographical dictionary of Republican China). Shijiazhuang: Hebei renmin chubanshe, 1991.

Xu Yubin 許玉彬. *Dongrongguan yigao* 冬榮館遺稿 (Bequeathed manuscripts from the Winter Luxuriance Lodge). 1861.

Xuehaitang erji 學海堂二集 (Second series of Xuehaitang collected writings). Ed. Wu Lanxiu 吳蘭修. 1838. *Zhongguo lidai shuyuan zhi*, vol. 13. Nanjing: Jiangsu jiaoyu chubanshe, 1995.

Xuehaitang ji 學海堂集 (Xuehaitang collected writings). Ed. Ruan Yuan 阮元. 1826. *Zhongguo lidai shuyuan zhi*, vol. 13. Nanjing: Jiangsu jiaoyu chubanshe, 1995.

Xuehaitang keti 學海堂課題 (Xuehaitang examination questions). Guangxu era. Held in the Zhongshan wenxianguan.

Xuehaitang keyi 學海堂課藝 (Xuehaitang examination papers). 1924. Held in the Zhongshan wenxianguan.

Xuehaitang sanji 學海堂三集 (Third series of Xuehaitang collected writings). Ed. Zhang Weiping 張維屏. 1859. *Zhongguo lidai shuyuan zhi*, vol. 14. Nanjing: Jiangsu jiaoyu chubanshe, 1995.

Xuehaitang siji 學海堂四集 (Fourth series of Xuehaitang collected writings). Ed. Chen Li 陳澧 and Jin Xiling 金錫齡. 1886. *Zhongguo lidai shuyuan zhi*, vol. 14. Nanjing: Jiangsu jiaoyu chubanshe, 1995.

Xuehaitang zhi 學海堂志 (Xuehaitang academy gazetteer). Ed. Lin Botong 林伯桐. Reprint of Taiwan Normal University Library manuscript edition. Taipei: Guangwen shuju, 1971.

Xuehaitang zhuanke zhangcheng 學海堂專課章程 (Regulations for Xuehaitang specialized classes). Guangxu era. Held in the Zhongshan wenxianguan.

Xuxiu Nanhai Yanqiao Heshi jiapu 續修南海煙橋何氏家譜 (Revised genealogy of the Yanqiao He of Nanhai county). Ed. He Shaozhuang 何紹莊 et al. Hong Kong: Renji yinwuguan, 1954. Held in the Zhongshan wenxianguan.

Yan Ming 嚴明. *Qingdai Guangdong shige yanjiu* 清代廣東詩歌研究 (A study of poetry in Guangdong during the Qing). Taipei: Wenjin chubanshe, 1991.

Yang Hsien-yi and Gladys Yang. "The Twenty-four Modes of Poetry." *Chinese Literature* 7 (1963): 65–77.

Yang Jialuo 楊家駱. *Zhonghua minguo zhiguan nianbiao* 中華民國職官年表 (Chronological tables of officials of the Republic of China). Taipei: Dingwen shuju, 1978.

Yang Nianqun 楊念群. *Ruxue diyuhua de jindai xingtai: san da zhishi qunti hudong de bijiao yanjiu* 儒學地域化的近代形態：三大知識群體互動的比較研究 (The modern models of regional Confucianism: a comparative research into the interaction of three intellectual group). Beijing: Sanlian shudian, 1997.

Yang Rongxu 楊榮緒. *Yang Fuxiang xiansheng yigao bubian* 楊黼香先生遺稿補編 (Supplement to the bequeathed manuscripts of Yang Rongxu). Ed. Wu Daorong. Republican-era manuscript. Held in the Zhongshan wenxianguan.

Yangcheng Lujiang shuyuan quanpu 羊城廬江書院全譜 (Complete chronicle of Guangzhou's Lujiang Academy). Ed. He Zetang 何澤棠 et al. 1894.

Yangcheng zhuzhi ci 羊城竹枝詞 (City of Rams bamboo branch songs). 1875. Held in the Zhongshan University Library.

Yangshi jiapu 楊氏家譜 (Yang genealogy). 1919. Held in the Zhongshan wenxianguan.

Yapian zhancheng 鴉片戰爭 (The Opium War). Shanghai: Shenzhou guoguangshe, 1954.

Ye Gongchuo 葉恭綽. *Xiaan huigao* 遐菴彙稿 (Collected manuscripts of Ye Gongchuo). *Jindai Zhongguo shiliao congkan*, vol. 158. Taipei: Wenhai chubanshe, 1968.

Ye Yanlan 葉衍蘭 and Ye Gongchuo 葉恭綽. *Qingdai xuezhe xiangzhuan* 清代學者象傳 (Images and biographies of Qing dynasty scholars). Taipei: Wenhai chubanshe, 1969.

Yi Bingshou 伊秉綬. *Liuchun caotang shichao* 留春草堂詩鈔 (Transcribed poetry from the Retaining Spring Thatched Hall). 1814.

Yi Kezhong 儀克中. *Jianguanglou ji* 劍光樓集 (Collected writings from the Sword's Radiance Building). 1835, 1882.

Yi Xiuli tang jiapu 易修禮堂家譜 (Genealogy of the Xiuli branch of the Yi lineage). Ed. Yi Xuehui 易學洄. No date. Held in the Tōyō Bunko.

Yingyuan shuyuan zhilue 應元書院志略 (Concise Yingyuan academy gazetteer). Ed. Wang Kaitai 王凱泰. 1870. *Zhongguo lidai shuyuan zhi*, vol. 3. Nanjing: Jiangsu jiaoyu chubanshe, 1995.

Yü Ying-shih 余英時. "Shi-shang hudong yu Ruxue zhuanxiang: Ming-Qing shehuishi yu sixiangshi zhi yi mianxiang" 士商互動與儒學轉向：明清社會史與思想史之一面向 (Gentry-merchant interaction and the transformation of Confuciansim: one facet of Ming-Qing social and intellectual history). In Hao Yanping and Wei Xiumei, eds., *Jinshi Zhongguo zhi chuantong yu tuibian: Liu Guangjing yuanshi qishiwu sui zhushou lunwenji*, vol. 1. Taipei: Institute of Modern History, Academia Sinica, 1998, pp. 3–52.

———. "Some Preliminary Observations on the Rise of Ch'ing Confucian Intellectualism." *Tsing Hua Journal of Chinese Studies* 11 (December 1975): 105–46.

Yuedong cheng'an chubian 粵東成案初編 (Established cases from Guangdong, first edition). Ed. Zhu Yun 朱橒. 1832. Beijing University Library.

Yuedong Jianshi da tongpu 粵東簡氏大同譜 (Comprehensive genealogy of the Jian surname in Guangdong). Ed. Jian Binhou 簡賓侯. *Beijing tushuguan cang jiapu congkan*, Min-Yue series, vols. 42–44. Beijing: Beijing tushuguan chubanshe, 2000.

Yuehua jilue 越華紀略 (Concise account of Yuehua Academy). Ed. Liang Tingnan 梁廷楠. 1843. Held in the Zhongshan wenxianguan.

Yuehua keyi 越華課藝 (Yuehua examination papers). Ed. Liang Zhaohuang 梁肇煌. 1884. Held in the Zhongshan wenxianguan.

Yuexiu shuyuan keyi 粵秀書院課藝 (Yuexiu Academy examination papers). Ed. He Wenqi 何文綺. 1848. Held in the Zhongshan wenxianguan.

Yuexiu shuyuan zhi 粵秀書院志 (Yuexiu academy gazetteer). Ed. Liang Tingnan 梁廷楠. 1847. *Zhongguo lidai shuyuan zhi*, vol. 3. Nanjing: Jiangsu jiaoyu chubanshe, 1995.

Yun Jing 惲敬. *Dayun shanfang wengao* 大雲山房文稿 (Prose manuscripts from the Great Cloud Mountain Study). 1817.

Zeng Yu 曾燠. *Shangyu maowu waiji* 賞雨茅屋外集 (Collected writings from the Appreciating Rain Thatched Hut). Preface, 1810.

Zeng Zhao 曾釗. *Mianchenglou jichao* 面城樓集鈔 (Collected transcriptions from the Building Facing the City). In *Qixiushan congshu*, 2d series.

Zhang Biao 張杓. *Modizhai wencun* 磨甋齋文存 (Prose preserved from the Polishing Tiles Studio). 1884.

Zhang Cixi 張次溪. *Wang Jingwei xiansheng xingshilu* 汪精衛先生行實錄 (A factual record of Wang Jingwei's activities). Dongguan: Zhangshi baiyuantang, 1943.

Zhang Jian 張鑑 et al., eds. *Ruan Yuan nianpu* 阮元年譜 (Chronological biography of Ruan Yuan). Original title: *Leitang'an zhu dizi ji* 雷塘庵主弟子記 (Disciples' record of the Master of Thunder Embankment Chapel). Daoguang-Xianfeng era. Reprinted—Beijing: Zhonghua shuju, 1995.

Zhang Jiuling 張九齡. *Qujiang ji* 曲江集 (Collected writings of Zhang Jiuling). In *Yingyin Wenyuange Siku quanshu*, vol. 1066. Taipei: Taiwan Shangwu yinshuguan, 1983.

Zhang Qihuang 張啓煌. *Zhu Jiujiang xiansheng ji zhu* 朱九江先生集注 (Annotation of the collected writings of Zhu Ciqi). 1930. Held in the Zhongshan wenxianguan.

Zhang Qizeng 張其曾 (with a 羽 radical on the right). *Bianzhen liangshi wenchao* 辮貞亮室文鈔 (Transcribed prose from the Weaving Uprightness and Clarity Studio). 1903.

Zhang Shouan 張壽安. *Yi li dai li: Ling Tingkan yu Qing zhongye ruxue sixiang zhi zhuanbian* 以禮代理: 凌廷堪與清中葉儒學思想之轉變 (Replacing principle with ritual: Ling Tingkan and the transformation of Confucian thought in the mid-Qing). Taipei: Institute of Modern History, Academia Sinica, 1994.

Zhang Weiping 張維屏. *Guochao shiren zhenglue chubian* 國朝詩人徵略初編 (Brief notes on poets of our dynasty, first edition). *Qingdai zhuanji congkan*, vols. 21–22. Taipei: Mingwen shuju, 1985.

———. *Huajia xiantan* 花甲閒談 (Leisurely talks at age sixty). 1839.

———. *Songxin shilu* 松心詩錄 (Recorded poetry from Pine Heart). 1854. Harvard-Yenching Library.

———. *Tingsonglu pianti wenchao* 聽松廬駢體文鈔 (Transcribed parallel prose from the Hut for Listening to the Pines). 1850.

———. *Yitan lu* 藝談錄 (Record of talks on the literati arts).

———. *Zhang Nanshan quanji* 張南山全集 (Complete works of Zhang Weiping). Reprinted—Guangzhou: Guangdong gaodeng jiaoyu chubanshe, 1993.

Zhang Xintai 張心泰. *Yueyou xiaoji* 粵遊小記 (Concise record of my tours in Guangdong). 1884.

Zhang Zhengfan 張正藩. *Zhongguo shuyuan zhidu kaolue* 中國書院制度考略 (Concise examination of the institution of academies in China). Jiangsu: Jiangsu jiaoyu chubanshe, 1985.

Zhao Fengtian 趙豐田, ed. *Kang Changsu (Youwei) xiansheng nianpu* 康長素(有爲)先生年譜 (Chronological biography of Kang Youwei). Hong Kong: Chongwen shudian, 1975.

Zhaoqing fu zhi 肇慶府志 (Zhaoqing prefectural gazetteer). 1833.

Zhe-Hang qian Yue Gaoyang Xushi jiapu 浙杭遷粵高陽許氏家譜 (Genealogy of the Gaoyang Xu relocated from Hangzhou, Zhejiang to Guangdong). Ed. Xu Zhihua 許之華. 1947.

Zheng Xianfu 鄭獻甫. *Buxuexuan wenji* 補學軒文集 (Collected prose from the Replenishment of Learning Studio). 1855. *Jindai Zhongguo shiliao congkan xuji*, vol. 212. Taipei: Wenhai chubanshe, 1975.

———. *Buxuexuan wenji xuke* 補學軒文集續刻 (More collected prose from the Replenishment of Learning Studio). 1872. *Jindai Zhongguo shiliao congkan xuji*, vol. 213. Taipei: Wenhai chubanshe, 1975.
Zhongwen da cidian 中文大辭典. 1985.
Zhou Hanguang 周漢光. *Zhang Zhidong yu Guangya shuyuan* 張之洞與廣雅書院 (Zhang Zhidong and Guangya Academy). Taipei: Zhongguo wenhua daxue, 1983.
Zhou Shouchang 周壽昌. *Siyitang rizha* 思益堂日札 (Daily notes from the Hall of Contemplating Increase). Appended to Zhou Shouchang, *Siyitang shichao* 思益堂詩鈔 (Transcribed poems from the Hall of Contemplating Increase). 1888.
Zhou Xiang. "A Sketch on the Case of Local Worthy Worshipping of Lu Guanheng." Unpublished paper presented at the Workshop on Guangzhou's Cohong Merchants in Local and International Society, Fairbank Center for East Asian Research, Harvard University, October 18, 2003.
Zhou Yinqing 周寅清. *Diansan shenggao* 典三賸稿 (Remaining manuscripts of Zhou Yinqing).
Zhu Ciqi 朱次琦. *Zhu Jiujiang xiansheng ji* 朱九江先生集 (Collected writings of Zhu Ciqi). *Jindai Zhongguo shiliao congkan*, vol. 127, Taipei: Wenhai chubanshe, 1967.
———. *Zhushi chuanfang ji* 朱氏傳芳集 (Collection of famous transmitted Zhu lineage writings). 1861.
Zhu Ciqi xiansheng shishi kao 朱次琦先生實事考 (Investigation of facts about Zhu Ciqi). Library title for a collection of several manuscripts by and about Zhu Ciqi, including *Caifang ce* 采訪冊, *Shuili bei* 水利碑, and *Huaxiang ji* 畫像記. Held in the Zhongshan wenxianguan.
Zhu Xi 朱熹. *Zhuzi yulei* 朱子語類 (Conversations of Master Zhu, topically arranged). Taipei: Zhengzhong shuju, 1962.
Zhu Yue baqi zhi 駐粵八旗志 (Gazetteer of Eight Banners units garrisoned in Guangzhou). Ed. Fan Feng 樊封 et al. 1889 edition.
Zito, Angela. *Of Body & Brush: Grand Sacrifice as Text/Performance in Eighteenth-Century China*. Chicago: University of Chicago Press, 1997.
Zou Boqi 鄒伯奇. *Zou Zhengjun yishu* 鄒徵君遺書 (Bequeathed works of Zou Boqi). 1873.
Zurndorfer, Harriet T. *Change and Continuity in Chinese Local History: The Development of Hui-chou Prefecture, 800 to 1800*. Leiden: E. J. Brill, 1989.

CHARACTER LIST

Aofeng shuyuan　鰲峯書院

Bailudong　白鹿洞
Baisha　白沙
Ban Gu　班固
bao　堡
Beidi　北帝
benji　本紀
bi　筆
bianhua qizhi　變化氣質
Bichong　泌沖
bo　博
Bogui　柏貴
Boshan　伯山
boxue　博學
bu　埠

Cai Jinquan　蔡錦泉
Cai Xiang　蔡襄
Caishen　財神
Chan (Zen)　禪
Changjiao　昌教
Changshousi　長壽寺
Changzhou　長洲
Chaolian　潮連
Chen Bangyan　陳邦彥

Chen Bomin　陳博民
Chen Changqi　陳昌齊
Chen Dajing　陳大經
Chen Hongchi　陳鴻墀
Chen Huan　陳奐
Chen Huang　陳滉
Chen Jiongming　陳炯明
Chen Li　陳澧
Chen Lian　陳槤
Chen Liangyu　陳良玉
Chen Lüheng　陳履恆
Chen Pu　陳璞
Chen Qikun　陳其錕
Chen Qinghe　陳慶龢
Chen Qingxiu　陳慶修
Chen Qirong　陳起榮
Chen Shiqi　陳士奇
Chen Shoutong　陳受同
Chen Tan　陳曇
Chen Xianzhang　陳獻章
Chen Xinmin　陳信民
Chen Yanxu　陳衍緒
Chen Yufu　陳遇夫
Chen Zaiqian　陳在謙
Chen Zisheng　陳子升
Chen Zizhuang　陳子壯

Chen Zongkan　陳宗侃
Chen Zongyi　陳宗誼
Cheng Enze　程恩澤
Cheng Hao　程顥
Cheng Yi　程頤
Cheng-Zhu　程朱
Chengnan　城南
Chigang　赤岡
chongshang mingjie　崇尚名節
Chunhui caotang　春暉草堂
Chunhui caotang shiji　春暉草堂詩集
Chunqiu fanlu　春秋繁露
Chunqiu sanzhuan yitong ping　春秋三傳異同評
ci　詞
cu　粗
Cui　崔
Cui Bi　崔弼
Cui Dinglai　崔鼎來
Cui Yanwen　崔顏問
Cui Yuzhi　崔與之
Cunzhu　存著

Daguo　大果
Dai Wang　戴望
Dai Zhen　戴震
Daliang　大良
Dan　蜑
Daotong　道統
Datong　大桐
dayi　大義
dayi weiyan　大義微言
Deng Chun　鄧淳
Deng Dalin　鄧大林
Deng Qingcai　鄧慶寀
Deng Shixian　鄧士憲
Deng Tingzhen　鄧廷楨
Deng Weisen　鄧維森
dengyun tu　等韻圖
Deyuelou　得月樓

Dicang'an　地藏菴
Ding Richang　丁日昌
Ding Xi　丁熙
Dingxing shu　定性書
Dong Zhongshu　董仲舒
Donghai shiliu sha　東海十六沙
Dongsheng　東生
Dongshu leigao　東塾類稿
Dongyu　東裕
Du Fu　杜甫
Du Mian　杜冕
Du Renfeng　杜仁鳳
Du Song　杜崧
Du Xian　杜憲
Du Yong　杜用
Du You　杜游
Duan Peilan　段佩蘭
Duan Yucai　段玉裁
Duanwu　端午
Duanxi shuyuan　端溪書院
Duanxi yanshi　端溪硯史
dujing　讀經
dunxing xiaodi　敦行孝弟

Erhai　洱海
Erya　爾雅

Fan Feng　樊封
Fan Mengjiao　樊夢蛟
Fan Zhongyan　范仲淹
Fang Bao　方苞
Fang Dongshu　方東樹
Fang Junyi　方濬頤
Fang Xinru　方信孺
fayu　法語
Feng　馮
Feng Chengxiu　馮成修
Feng Fengchu　馮奉初
Feng Jinglue　馮景略
Feng Longguan　馮龍官
Feng Minchang　馮敏昌

Feng Rutang 馮汝棠
Feng Shizong 馮拭宗
Feng Xiyong 馮錫鏞
Feng Yunzheng 馮雲蒸
Feng Yushun 馮毓舜
fenjiao 分校
Fenyu ji 焚餘集
fenzuan 分纂
fu 賦
Fushe 復社
Futai 孚泰

Ganquan 甘泉
Ganzhu 甘竹
Gao Shizhao 高士釗
Gao Xueyao 高學燿
gaofeng 高風
Geng Weiyou 耿維祐
gongsuo 公所
Gongyang 公羊
Gu jingjie huihan 古經解彙函
Gu Yanwu 顧炎武
Guan 關
Guan Jiaju 關家駒
Guan Shangjin 關上進
Guan Shiang 關士昂
Guan Shilong 關仕龍
Guan Zhongyang 關仲瑒
Guangdong wenxuan 廣東文選
Guanghua 光華
Guangli 廣利
Guangxiaosi 光孝寺
Guangyun 廣韻
"Guangzhou yin shuo" 廣州音說
Guanshan 官山
Gui Wencan 桂文燦
Gui Wenchi 桂文熾
Gui Wenyao 桂文燿
Gujing jingshe 詁經精舍
Guo Shangbin 郭尚賓

Guo Songtao 郭嵩燾
Guochao Linghai shichao 國朝嶺海詩鈔
Guochao mingchen yanxing lu 國朝名臣言行錄
Guochao yimin zhuan 國朝遺民傳
Guoshi bu 國史補
guti shi 古體詩
guwen ci 古文詞
guxue 古學

Hai Rui 海瑞
Haichuangsi 海幢寺
Haiyu 海語
Han ji 漢紀
Han Shanggui 韓上桂
Han shu 漢書
Han Yu 韓愈
Han zhu 漢主
Hanshi waizhuan 韓詩外傳
Han-Song tiaohe 漢宋調和
hao yi ze bo, bo ze jing 好一則博博則精
Hao Yixing 郝懿行
Haoshang Guanyuxuan 濠上觀魚軒
He Mengyao 何夢瑤
He Nanyu 何南鈺
He Qijie 何其杰
He Taiqing 何太青
He Wenqi 何文綺
He Xiu 何休
He Yan 何晏
Henan 河南
Hengsha 橫沙
Heqing 河清
Heshun 和順
Hong Xiuquan 洪秀全
Hong Yixuan 洪頤煊
Hongsheng 洪聖

Hou Du　侯度
Hou Jinxuan　侯金鉉
Hou Kang　侯康
Hu Binwang　胡賓王
Hu Fang　胡方
Hu Hanmin　胡漢民
Hu Tiaode　胡調德
Hu Ting　胡挺
Hu Wei　胡渭
hua　華
Huadi　花地
Hualinsi　華林寺
Huang Jing　黃經
Huang Kan　黃侃
Huang Peifang　黃培芳
Huang Qiaosong　黃喬松
Huang Rongkang　黃榮康
Huang Shixian　黃世顯
Huang Xianbiao　黃賢彪
Huang Zhen　黃震
Huang Zhong　黃衷
Huang Zigao　黃子高
Huang Zongxi　黃宗羲
Huang Zuo　黃佐
Huangchao tongdian　皇朝通典
Huangpu　黃埔
Huangshi richao　黃氏日抄
Hui Dong　惠棟
Hui Shiqi　惠士奇
Huiai　惠愛
huiguan　會館
Huijicang　惠濟倉
huiwen　會文
Husanjiao pingshi fa　弧三角平視法

ji　記
Ji Huijia　秸會嘉
jiafa　家法
jiajie　假借
Jian Chaoliang　簡朝亮

Jiang Fan　江藩
Jiang Sheng　江聲
Jiang Yili　蔣益澧
Jiang Yuan　江沅
jianshe weiyi　檢攝威儀
Jiangyue　江月
jianxin　見心
jianyuan　監院
Jiaoya　嶠雅
Jiaozhou ji　交州記
jie　解
jiejing　解經
Jin Jing'e　金菁莪
Jin Jingmao　金菁茅
Jin Xiling　金錫齡
jing　精
Jin'gangjing　金剛經
Jingji zuangu　經籍纂詁
Jingshen　經神
Jingshi shi guwen ci　經史詩古文詞
Jingyi shuwen　經義述聞
Jinjian lu　金鑑錄
Jinsi lu　近思錄
jinwen　今文
jin zhi xue　今之學
Jiqing　吉慶
Jiujiang　九江
jiwen　祭文
Jiyuan　寄園
ju　咀
jue　嚼
jueju　絕句
Jupo jingshe　菊坡精舍

Kang Youwei　康有爲
kao　考
kaozheng　考證
Kaozheng Hushi Yugong tu　考正胡氏禹貢圖
"*Kaozheng lun*"　考證論

Kong 孔
Kong Anguo 孔安國
Kong Jifan 孔繼藩
Kong Jixun 孔繼勳
kongshu 空疏
kongtan xingli 空談性理
Kuang Lu 鄺露
Kuiwen hui 魁文會
Kunxue jiwen 困學紀聞

Laba 臘八
Lai 賴
Lao Chongguang 勞崇光
Lao Tong 勞潼
laosha weitian 老沙圍田
Laoxuean biji 老學菴筆記
Lelou 勒樓
li (unit of distance) 里
li (principle) 理
li (clerk) 吏
Li Changrong 李長榮
li cuo wu 理蹉務
Li Daoyuan 酈道元
Li Fuping 李黼平
Li Futai 李福泰
Li Guangting 李光廷
Li Guangzhao 李光昭
Li Guochen 黎國琛
Li Hongzhang 李鴻章
Li Hu 李湖
Li Jian 黎簡
Li Jun 李鈞
Li Maoying 李昴英
Li Nengding 李能定
Li Rumei 李如梅
Li Ruwei 黎如瑋
Li Shan 李善
Li Suiqiu 黎遂球
Li Xun 黎璿
Li Yingtian 李應田
Li Yingzhong 李應中

Li Zhengwei 李徵霨
Li Zhifang 李直方
Li Zhongpei 李中培
Lian 濂
Liang Chu 梁儲
Liang Guozhen 梁國珍
Liang Jingguo 梁經國
Liang Lunshu 梁綸樞
Liang Mei 梁梅
Liang Qi 梁起
Liang Tingnan 梁廷枏
Liang Xuyong 梁序鏞
Liang Yaochen 梁燿宸
Liang Yaoshu 梁燿樞
Liang Yusen 梁玉森
Liang Zhaohuang 梁肇煌
liangzhi 良知
Liao Ji 廖紀
Liao Tingxiang 廖廷相
Liao Xiongguang 廖熊光
Liao Zhen 廖震
liezhuan 列傳
Lijing bianzhi zhai 離經辨志齋
Lijingwen 隸經文
Lin Botong 林伯桐
Lin Shixian 林事賢
Lin Zexu 林則徐
Ling Tingkan 凌廷堪
Ling Yangzao 凌揚藻
Lingnan 嶺南
Lingnan lizhi pu 嶺南荔枝普
Lingnan wenxian 嶺南文獻
Liu Binhua 劉彬華
Liu Chang 劉錩
Liu Daxia 劉大夏
Liu Gongmian 劉恭冕
Liu Huadong 劉華東
Liu Ke 劉軻
Liu Qixiong 劉起雄
Liu Shan 劉冊

Liu Tianhui　劉天惠
Liu Wenqi　劉文淇
Liu Xing'en　柳興恩
Liu Xinqi　劉欣期
Liu Yan　劉巘
Liu Yusong　劉毓崧
Liu Zechang　劉澤長
Liurongsi　六榕寺
Liushi xingwang lu　劉氏興亡錄
liwen　理問
lixue　理學
Lixue jianyan　理學簡言
Lizhiwan　荔枝灣
Long Tinghuai　龍廷槐
Long Yuanxi　龍元僖
Longjiang　龍江
Longshan　龍山
Longxi shuyuan　龍溪書院
Lu Fayan　陸法言
Lu Guanheng　盧觀恆
Lu Kun　盧坤
Lu Wenjin　盧文錦
Lujiang　廬江
lun　論
Lunyu yishu　論語義疏
Luo　洛
Luo Chuanqiu　羅傳球
Luo Dunyan　羅惇衍
Luo Hanzhang　羅含章
Luo Jiabao　羅家保
Luo Jiaqin　羅家勤
Luo Lianghui　羅良會
Luo Tianchi (Shunde)　羅天尺
Luo Tianchi (Xinhui)　羅天池
Luo Xuepeng　羅學鵬
Luo Yuliang　羅遇良
Luo Zhaocang　羅照滄
Luoge　羅格
Lushan zhi　廬山志
Lü Hong　呂洪
Lü Jian　呂堅

Lü Xiang　呂翔
lüshi　律詩

Ma Fuan　馬福安
Man　蠻
Mao Qiling　毛奇齡
Maoshi guxun zhuan　毛詩故訓傳
Maoshi tongkao　毛詩通攷
Maoshi Zheng-Zhu hechao　毛詩鄭朱合鈔
Mashe　麻奢
Mengzhan　孟瞻
Ming Bingzhang　明秉璋
Ming Jingran　明景然
Ming Lizhao　明離照
Ming Lun　明倫
Ming Yong　明永
Ming Zhigang　明之綱
Mingluntang　明倫堂
Mingru xuean　明儒學案
mumian　木棉
muyou　幕友

Nan-Han dili zhi　南漢地理志
Nan-Han jinshi zhi　南漢金石志
Nan-Han shu kaoyi　南漢書攷異
Neifu ditu　內俯地圖
Ni Shihua　倪世華
Ni Zan　倪瓚
nianpu　年譜

Ou Huairui　區懷瑞
Ou Shiheng　區仕衡
Ou Yuzhang　區玉章

Pan Dinggui　潘定桂
Pan Feisheng　潘飛聲
Pan Jili　潘繼李
Pan Naicheng　潘乃成
Pan Shichang　潘士昌

Pan Shicheng 潘仕成
Pan Shu 潘恕
Pan Wenyin 潘文因
Pan Youdu 潘有度
Pan Youwei 潘有為
Pan Zhaokeng 潘兆鏗
Pan Zhencheng 潘振承
Pan Zhengheng 潘正亨
Pan Zhengheng 潘正衡
Pan Zhengwei 潘正煒
Penglai 蓬萊
picheng 批呈
Punti (Bendi) 本地
puxue 樸學

Qi Gong 祁貢 (with a 土 radical on the left)
Qi Lin 漆璘
Qi Shaonan 齊召南
Qian Daxin 錢大昕
Qian Yiji 錢儀吉
qi di shishen 其地士紳
qie kao ji you genju 切考極有根據
Qieyun kao waipian 切韻考外篇
Qin Huitian 秦蕙田
qing 頃
qingjin feishen 青襟廢紳
Qiu Jun 邱濬
Qiu Xi 邱熙
Qiu Xiande 邱先德
qixi 氣習
Qu Dajun 屈大均
Quan Tang wen 全唐文
Qujiang 曲江

Ren Dachun 任大椿
Ren Zhaolin 任兆麟
Rizhi lu 日知錄
Ruan Fu 阮福

Ruan Rongling 阮榕齡
Ruan Yuan 阮元
Ruilin 瑞麟
Rulin gumiao 儒林古廟
Rulin shuyuan 儒林書院
Rulin wenshe sixu 儒林文社絲墟
Rulin zhuan 儒林傳

Sangyuanwei 桑園圍
Santongshu xiangshuo 三統術詳說
sanwen 散文
Sanzhu 三祝
Shajiao 沙窖
shangji 商籍
Shangsha 上沙
Shanhai jing 山海經
shantang 山堂
shatan 沙坦
shatian 沙田
Shatian zongju 沙田總局
Shatou 沙頭
Shawan 沙灣
she 社
Shen Fu 沈復
Shen Shiliang 沈世良
Shen Zetang 沈澤棠
shendong 紳董
shengjian 生監
Shenglü tongkao 聲律通考
shengyuan 生員
shi (poetry) 詩
shi (literatus) 士
shi (explications) 釋
Shi Cheng 史澄
Shi Duan 史端
Shi Shanchang 史善長
shicheng 師承
shidaifu 士大夫
shifa 師法
Shiguo chunqiu 十國春秋
shihui 詩會

Shimei 世美
shiqianzu 始遷祖
shiren 市人
Shisanjing zhushu 十三經注疏
Shitao 石濤
Shitou 石頭
shiwen 時文
Shixing ji 始興記
shixue 實學
shizi 士子
shizu 始祖
shuhou 書後
Shuijing zhu 水經注
shuju 書局
Shulin yangzhi 書林揚觶
Shunde tuanlian zongju 順德團練總局
shuo 說
Shuowen 說文
Shuowen shengbiao 說文聲表
Shuowen shengtong 說文聲統
shuyuan 書院
si 巳
si da zhen 四大鎮
Sikong Tu 司空圖
Siku quanshu 四庫全書
Siku quanshu zongmu tiyao 四庫全書總目提要
song 頌
Songya 松崖
Su Liupeng 蘇六朋
Su Shi 蘇軾
Suandi 算迪
Sun Fen 孫蕡
Sushu 蘇書

Taiji tushuo 太極圖說
Taiping yulan 太平御覽
Taiquan 泰泉
Tan Dajing 譚大經
Tan Jianlong 譚見龍

Tan Jingzhao 譚敬昭
Tan Ying 譚瑩
Tan Zongjun 譚宗浚
Tan Zuqiang 譚祖鏘
Tao Fuxiang 陶福祥
Tao Shaoxue 陶邵學
Tang 湯
tang 堂
Tao Yuanming 陶淵明
Tianbao 天寶
tici 題詞
Tiejiao 鐵窖
tong 同
Tongan 同安
Tongdian 通典
Tongdong 同東
Tongfu 同孚
tongru 通儒
tongsheng 童生
Tongzhitang jingjie 通志堂經解

waikesheng 外課生
waisheng ren 外省人
Wang Chu 汪琡
Wang Ding 汪鼎
Wang Guorui 王國瑞
Wang Jia 王嘉
Wang Jianxin 王鑑心
Wang Jingwei 汪精衛
Wang Kaitai 王凱泰
Wang Lunzhi 汪倫秩
Wang Niansun 王念孫
Wang Pu 汪浦
Wang Quan 汪琼
Wang Shaozhi 王韶之
Wang Shilin 汪士林
Wang Shizhen 王士禎
Wang Su 王肅
Wang Xizhi 王羲之
Wang Yangming 王陽明
Wang Yinglin 王應麟

Wang Yinzhi   王引之
Wang Yun   王筠
Wang Zhaohong   汪兆鋐
Wang Zhaoming   汪兆銘
Wang Zhaoquan   汪兆銓
Wang Zhaoyong   汪兆鏞
Wang Zhi   王植
Wansongyuan   萬松園
wei   味
Wei Jilian   尉繼蓮
Wei Xi   魏禧
wei yi   威儀
Wei Zhongxian   魏忠賢
weifa   未發
weinei ren   圍內人
weishen   圍紳
weitian   圍田
wen   文
Wen   溫
Wen Rugua   溫汝适
Wen Runeng   溫汝能
Wen Tingshi   文廷式
Wen Xun   溫訓
Wen Zhongweng   溫仲翁
Wenchang   文昌
Weng Fanggang   翁方綱
Weng Xincun   翁心存
wenji   文集
wenke   文課
Wenlange   文瀾閣
Wenlan shuyuan   文瀾書院
Wenpu   文圃
Wu Bingjian   伍秉鑑
Wu Bingyong   伍秉墉
Wu Bingzhen   伍秉珍
Wu Chaofeng   伍朝鳳
Wu Chongyao   伍崇曜
Wu Dianbei   伍典備
Wu Feng   吳灃
Wu Guoying   伍國瑩
Wu Jiashu   吳家樹

Wu Kuiguang   吳奎光
Wu Lanxiu   吳蘭修
Wu Linguang   吳林光
Wu Miguang   吳彌光
Wu Ping   吳俜 (聘)
Wu Renchen   吳任臣
Wu Rongguang   吳榮光
Wu Shaotang   伍紹棠
Wu Wenqi   吳文起
Wu Xuezao   伍學藻
Wu Yingchang   吳應昌
Wu Yingkui   吳應逵
Wu Yuanhua   伍元華
Wu Yuansong   伍元崧
Wu Yue   吳岳
Wuli tongkao   五禮通考
Wushi shizheng lu   五史實徵錄

xi   禊
xian jin shi   嫌近市
Xian Yi   洗沂
xiang   鄉
xianggui   鄉規
xiangmiao   詳妙
xianshi Zheren huan Yue   先世浙人宦粵
Xiaoxue   小學
Xiaoxue huihan   小學彙函
Xicheng   西成
Xie Guangfu   謝光輔
Xie Guansheng   謝觀生
Xie Jiawu   謝嘉梧
Xie Jingqing   謝景卿
Xie Lansheng   謝蘭生
Xie Niandian   謝念典
Xie Niangong   謝念功
Xie Youren   謝有仁
Xie Youwen   謝有文
Xie Yunsheng   謝雲生
Xiguan   西關
Xigutang   希古堂

Xijiang 西江
Xijiang dahai tu 西江達海圖
xin 心
xing 性
xingming guxun 性命古訓
Xingwang 興王
Xingxue yuanliu 性學源流
Xiong Jingxing 熊景星
Xiqiao 西樵
Xiukun 秀琨
Xiuyi 繡衣
Xu Benyi 徐本義
Xu Bo 徐勃 (with a 火 radical on the left)
Xu Gan 徐幹
Xu Hao 徐灝
Xu Jun 許鈞
Xu Naiji 許乃濟
Xu Nailai 許乃來
Xu Naizhao 許乃釗
Xu Qiguang 許其光
Xu Qikang 許其康
Xu Qiyang 許其颺
Xu Qing 徐青
Xu Rong 徐榮
Xu Shen 許慎
Xu tongdian 續通典
Xu Xiangguang 許祥光
Xu Xuecheng 許學程
Xu Xuefan 許學范
Xu Xuezhou 許學周
Xu Xuezhu 許學朱
Xu Yong 許鏞
Xu Yubin 許玉彬
Xu Yue 許鉞
Xuehai 學海
Xuehaitang 學海堂
Xuehaitang *shi* 學海堂士
Xuehaitang *tongren* 學海堂同人
Xuehaitang *zhuren* 學海堂諸人
Xueji 學記
Xuejin taoyuan 學津討原
xueshu 學術
Xuesi lu 學思錄
xuetang 學堂
xuezhang 學長
Xun Yue 荀悅
xungu 訓詁

Yan Xun 顏薰
Yang Dalin 楊大霖
Yang Fu 楊孚
Yang Rongxu 楊榮緒
Yang Shiji 楊時濟
Yang Xiong 揚雄
Yang Yuanfu 楊元富
Yangcheng shuyuan 羊城書院
yangshang 洋商
yangtao 楊桃
Yangxin lu 養新錄
Yanjingshi zai xuji 揅經室再續集
Ye Menglin 葉夢麟
Ye Menglong 葉夢龍
Ye Mingchen 葉名琛
Ye Renlan 葉紉蘭
Ye Tingxun 葉廷勳
Ye Tingying 葉廷瑛
Yi Jiangnan guan 憶江南館
Yi Kezhong 儀克中
Yi Rongzhi 易容之
yi you butong 亦有不同
yifa 已發
Yihe 怡和
yili 義理
Yili sanjia hechao 儀禮三家合鈔
yili zhi xue 義理之學
yimin 遺民
Yinglian 英廉
Yingyuan shuyuan 應元書院

Yisi 繹思
Yisongyuan 義松園
Yiwen leiju 藝文類聚
Yiwu zhi 異物志
Yongguan 顒觀
Yongqing 永清
you zongzhu 有宗主
Yu Bifang 虞必芳
Yu Binggang 余秉剛
Yu Fan 虞翻
Yu Jing 余靖
Yu Shen 余深
Yu Shimei 于式枚
Yu Yabao 余亞保
Yu Yue 俞樾
Yuan Mei 袁枚
yuanzhang 院長
Yue 粵
Yue shisanjia ji 粵十三家集
Yuedong jinshi lue 粵東金石略
Yuedong wenhai 粵東文海
Yuehua shuyuan 越華書院
Yueshi souyi 粵詩蒐逸
Yuexiu shuyuan 粵秀書院
Yueyatang congshu 粵雅堂叢書
Yugong zhuizhi 禹貢錐指
yuhua 魚花
yulu 語錄
yumiao 魚苗
Yun Jing 惲敬
Yunquan shanguan 雲泉山館
yuxiang 魚餉

zan 贊
Zeng Guofan 曾國藩
Zeng Yu 曾燠
Zeng Zhao 曾釗
Zeng Zhongli 曾中立
Zhan Ruoshui 湛若水
Zhang Bao 張保
Zhang Biao 張杓
Zhang Bingwen 張炳文
Zhang Fenghua 張鳳華
Zhang Haipeng 張海鵬
Zhang Jinfang 張錦芳
Zhang Jiuling 張九齡
Zhang Le 張樂
Zhang Qihan 張其翰
Zhang Qizeng 張其翼
Zhang Ruzhi 張如芝
Zhang Tingjin 張廷錦
Zhang Weiping 張維屏
Zhang Yanji 張衍基
Zhang Yuan 張元
Zhang Zai 張載
Zhang Zhidong 張之洞
zhangju 章句
Zhao 招
Zhao Jun 趙均
Zhao Qi 趙岐
Zhao Qiying 趙齊嬰
Zhao Tuo 趙佗
Zheng Fen 鄭棻
Zheng Haoruo 鄭灝若
Zheng Quan 鄭權
Zheng Xianfu 鄭獻甫
Zheng Xuan 鄭玄
Zhengjuesi 正覺寺
zhengkesheng 正課生
Zhengxue xu 正學續
Zhenhai 鎮海
Zhenyong 鎮涌
zhi 質
zhijie 直介
zhiyi zhi shi 志義之士
Zhong Fengqing 鍾逢慶
Zhong lun 中論
Zhong Qishao 鍾啓韶
Zhongshan 鍾山
Zhongshan ji 鍾山集

Zhou Dunyi 周敦頤
Zhou Guo 周果
Zhou Yinqing 周寅清
Zhouyi benyi zhu 周易本義註
zhu 主
Zhu Bingqi 朱炳琦
Zhu Bolian 朱伯蓮
Zhu Chengfa 朱成發
Zhu Chengwan 朱程萬
Zhu Ciqi 朱次琦
Zhu Guangyun 朱光允
Zhu Guocai 朱國材
Zhu Jizhao 朱吉兆
Zhu Lingxiao 朱淩霄
Zhu Mo 朱謨
Zhu Qilian 朱啟連
Zhu Rang 朱讓
Zhu Shilian 朱實蓮
Zhu Shiqi 朱士琦
Zhu Shuida 朱稅達
Zhu Tinggui 朱廷貴
Zhu Wenbin 朱文彬
Zhu Wenjin 朱文錦
Zhu Xi 朱熹
Zhu Yuanlong 朱元龍
Zhu Yun 朱筠
Zhu Ziyi 朱子議
Zhu Zongqi 朱宗琦
zhuan 專
zhuangshi 壯士
zhuanke 專課
zhuanke sheng 專課生
zhubu 主簿
zhujing 主敬
Zhujixiang 珠璣巷
zhuniang 珠娘
Zhuolun 卓輪
zhuzhi ci 竹枝詞
Zhuzi shu Zheng lu 朱子述鄭錄
Zhuzi xuedi 朱子學的
Zhuzi yulei 朱子語類
Zilin 字林
zimu 字母
zishu 自述
Ziyang shanren 紫陽山人
zong 宗
zongzuan 總纂
Zuo Zongtang 左宗棠

INDEX

Academies, see Shuyuan
Almond Grove Villa, 67, 178–79
Anthologies, 141–162
Auspicious Rams Streamside Lodge, 67, 109, 348n69

Bailudong (White Deer Grotto Academy), 76
Ban Gu, 132–33, 207
Bannermen, 27–29, 106–7, 167
Bichong, 167, 173–74
Bogui, 176
Bol, Peter, 17, 282
Brook, Timothy, 60, 281

Cai Jinquan, 59, 65
Cai lineage (Longjiang), 247
Cai Xiang, 138
Cangwu, 245, 249
Changjiao, 185
Changshou Monastery, 59, 177–80 passim, 188
Chen Bangyan, 148, 271
Chen Bomin, 241–44 passim, 251
Chen Changqi, 78, 92, 158, 220
Chen Dajing, 203–4
Chen Hongchi, 205
Chen Huan, 233
Chen Huang, 65
Chen Jiongming, 292, 295
Chen Li, 123–24, 178, 182–84, 187–91 passim, 197, 281, 294; Han-Song syncretism, 15–16, 201–2, 213, 219–27, 235; and Zhu Ciqi, 20–21, 269; and *Dongshu dushuji*, 195, 224–26, 379n82; and Jupo jingshe, 195–96, 229–31; *kaozheng* studies by, 205–8, 227–28, 231–32; *Qieyun kao*, 206–7; and Jiangnan, 208–10, 233–34; critique of *kaozheng*, 211–19, 234–35; *Zhuzi yulei richao*, 213, 219; *Hanru tongyi*, 223–24, 226; *Shenglü tongkao*, 227–28
Chen Lian, 151
Chen Liangyu, 167, 169–70, 178, 281
Chen lineage (Jiujiang), 243, 254
Chen Lüheng, 252, 255
Chen Pu, 167, 170, 174, 176, 194, 197, 264–65, 281, 296

Chen Qikun, 65, 178, 180, 183, 193
Chen Qinghe, 170
Chen Qirong, 178–79
Chen Shiqi, 203
Chen Shoutong, 170
Chen Tan, 64, 66, 72–74, 85, 105
Chen Xianzhang, 72–73, 120, 125, 146–48, 263–65, 296, 351*n*116
Chen Xinmin, 255, 259–60
Chen Yanxu, 170
Chen Yufu, 158–59
Chen Zaiqian, 142
Chen Zizhuang, 269–71
Chen Zongkan, 169–170, 191
Chen Zongyi, 213
Cheng Enze, 205–6, 214
Cheng Hao, 76, 80
Cheng Yi, 5–6, 15, 76, 147, 219, 296
Ching May-bo, 18
Chow, Kai-wing, 271
Chuting qijiu yishi, 149
Cloud and Springs Mountain Lodge, *see* Yunquan shanguan
Clunas, Craig, 70, 115
Cohong merchants, *see* Maritime merchants
Cole, James, 29, 278
Confucianism: Han, 6, 122; Song, 5–6, 96
Crises, mid-century, 164–65, 171–73, 199
Cui Bi, 92, 103, 110, 119
Cui Yuzhi, 85, 146, 147, 195
Cultural geography, 124, 163
Cultural symbols, 117, 163, 180

Dai Wang, 233
Dai Zhen, 158, 210, 220, 222
Daliang, 40, 45–46, 142, 148, 181, 248, 285
Dan (Boat People), 62–63, 249–50
Daotong, 218–19
Dardess, John, 285
Deng Chun, 86, 92
Deng Dalin, 67, 178
Deng Qingcai, 138
Deng Shixian, 193
Deng Tingzhen, 183
Deng Weisen, 170
Dennerline, Jerry, 278
Ding Xi, 67, 375*n*23
Dongguan, 44, 46, 182
Dongsheng firm, 69
Dongyu firm, 69, 82
Du family, 49, 66
Du Fu, 186, 190
Du Mian, 49, 66
Du Renfeng, 49
Du Song, 49
Du Xian, 49
Du Yong, 49, 66, 71
Du You, 50, 66–67, 178, 180
Duan Peilan, 85–86
Duan Yucai, 218, 221
Duanwu Festival, 61
Duanxi shuyuan, 76, 194–95
Duara, Prasenjit, 284

Elliott, Mark, 107
Elman, Benjamin, 8, 161, 233
Enclosure district, 24, 44–48, 110, 181, 239–43, 251, 274–75, 285
Epigraphy, 27
Ershisi shipin, 103
Evidential research, *see Kaozheng*

Fan Feng, 107, 119–20, 166–67, 177–79, 182
Fan Mengjiao, 107

Fan Zhongyan, 262
Fang Bao, 87, 268
Fang Dongshu, 97-99, 102, 104, 222
Fang Junyi, 195, 209, 229, 232
Fang Xinru, 135, 136
Faure, David, 141, 281, 330-31*n*91
Feng Chengxiu, 76-77
Feng Fengchu, 251
Feng Jinglue, 255
Feng lineage (Jiujiang), 244, 248, 255
Feng Longguan, 144
Feng Minchang, 66, 77, 115
Feng Rutang, 251, 258-60, 272
Feng Shizong, 255, 272
Feng Xiyong, 255, 261, 272
Feng Yunzheng, 254-55
Feng Yushun, 244
Finnane, Antonia, 42, 278, 284
Flood of 1833, 164
Flower boats, 56, 61-62
Foshan, 45-46, 108-9, 248, 254, 259, 274, 280, 285
Fujian, 34-36
Fushe, *see* Restoration Society

Ganzhu, 44-45
Garden of the Righteous Pines, *see* Yisongyuan
Geng Weiyou, 76
Gengshen xiuxi ji, 179-80
Gentry, 13, 41, 74
Goodman, Bryna, 18, 284
Gu Yanwu, 7, 94-95, 230
Guan Jiaju, 260
Guan lineage (Jiujiang), 83, 243, 246, 248, 255, 258, 262, 383*n*27
Guan Nanxiong, 243
Guan Shangjin, 244, 246
Guan Shiang, 252

Guan Shilong, 83, 265
Guan Zhongyang, 261
Guangdong, 1-2, 18, 24-25
Guangdong provincial gazetteer, 27, 92, 97, 130, 184, 231, 342*n*4
Guangdong wenxian, 142-49, 153-54, 161, 274
Guangdong wenxuan, 141
Guangdong xinyu, 130, 157, 242, 283
Guangli firm, 39, 68-71 *passim*, 81, 82
Guangxi, 242-45 *passim*
Guangxiao Monastery, 59, 85, 133, 179
Guangya shuyuan, 199
Guangzhou, 1-4, 23, 25; and Pearl River delta, 9-13 *passim*, 18, 53-54, 110, 16-175 *passim*, 180-84, 263265; Huiai Street, 25, 28, 33, 47, 74, 173, 324*n*8; British and French occupation, 172-73, 176-78, 181, 212; reconstruction, 180-84, 227-32
Gui family, 365*n*23
Gui Wencan, 1-2, 10-11, 183, 210, 231, 233, 264, 365*n*23
Gui Wenchi, 197
Gui Wenyao, 204, 208
Guiji, 32
Gujing jingshe, 8, 92, 96, 118, 122, 135, 194
Guo Shangbin, 152
Guo Songtao, 182, 188189, 228-29, 264
Guochao Linghai shichao, 142
Guochao Lingnan wenchao, 142
Guwen (ancient prose), 7-8, 102

Hai Rui, 146

Haichuang (Sea Banner) Monastery, 59–69 *passim*, 80
Haishan xianguan congshu, 149
Hakkas, 36–39, 107–8, 165, 167, 280
Han ji, 132
Han Learning, 6, 15–16, 77–78, 97, 110, 159; at Xuehaitang, 92, 101, 126; critique of, 211, 218–27, 268
Han Shanggui, 148
Hanshi waizhuan, 230
Han shu, 132–33, 207
Han-Song syncretism, 15–16, 97, 159–60, 378n80, 379n87; Chen Li and, 202, 213, 219–27, 235–36; Zhu Ciqi and, 202, 266–67
Han Yu, 147, 157, 186, 219
Hangzhou, 8, 32, 168
Hankou, 40, 42, 284
Hanxue shangdui, 98–99
Hanxue shicheng ji, 98, 267
Hao Yixing, 122
He Mengyao, 26, 77–78, 151, 158
He Nanyu, 123
He Qijie, 108
He Taiqing, 81
He Wenqi, 83, 193–94, 263, 371n77
He Xiu, 99, 100, 226, 231
He Yan, 217, 231
He Yousen, 212
Henan (Guangzhou), 34–35, 40–42, 61, 63, 66–68, 112
Hengsha, 174, 212
Henry, B. C., 240
Heshan, 40, 44, 65, 109
Heshun, 174
Heyuan, 212
History: local, 129–34, 162
Hong Yixuan, 152

Hou Du, 204–5
Hou Jinxuan, 106
Hou Kang, 106, 121, 160, 166, 173, 204–5, 222, 267
Howqua, *see* Wu Bingjian; Wu Chongyao
Hu Binwang, 130, 154
Hu Chusheng, 211
Hu Fang, 72–73, 159–60
Hu Hanmin, 292
Hu Tiaode, 86–87, 251, 254, 266
Hu Ting, 252–53
Hu Wei, 205, 207
Huadi, 55, 67
Huang Jing, 220
Huang Kan, 217
Huang Peifang, 45, 48, 66, 174, 183, 220, 283; in literary gatherings, 60, 67, 85–87, 174, 177–80 *passim*; and the Xuehaitang, 113, 123, 166
Huang Qiaosong, 60, 65, 85–86
Huang-Qing jingjie, 2, 194–95, 268; compilation and printing of, 2, 5, 97, 121–22; storage of 113, 122, 173–74; reprinting of 187, 231
Huang Rongkang, 296
Huang Shenzhi shourong jigong lu, 176–77
Huang Xianbiao, 176–77
Huang Zhen, 224
Huang Zhong, 151
Huang Zigao, 86, 151, 154, 156, 166
Huang Zongxi, 267
Huang Zuo, 48, 85, 151–52, 155, 174, 247, 283
Huangshi richao, 224
Hui Dong, 6, 26, 97, 216
Hui Shiqi, 26, 57, 77, 158, 160

Huiguan, 40–41, 279
Huiwen, 82–84
"Hundred Chants on the South Sea Region," 135–37
Hymes, Robert, 282

Identity: elite, 12, 126, 279, 287; local, 17–18, 282–86
In-migration, 11, 14, 29–39, 73, 104–6, 125, 170–71, 279, 285

Ji Huijia, 250
Jian Chaoliang, 238, 263, 268
Jiang Fan, 92, 97–98, 132, 136, 151, 157–58, 226
Jiang Sheng, 97
Jiang Yili, 195, 229
Jiang Yong, 210
Jiang Yuan, 151–52
Jiangnan, 5, 18–19, 29, 122, 318n6; Chen Li and, 203, 233–34
Jiangnan literati, 27, 128, 151–52, 157, 207, 285
Jiaozhou ji, 156
Jiaying, 36–39, 167
Jin family, 33, 64, 168
Jin Jing'e, 64
Jin Jingmao, 33, 64, 68
Jin Xiling, 168–69, 187, 210, 221–22, 229
Jingji zuangu, 92
Jinjian lu, 146–47, 153–54
Jingxue bocai lu, 1–2
Jingyi shuwen, 216, 230–31
Jiqing, 203
Jiujiang, 44–45, 110, 237, 239–55, 260–61, 284; Great Market, 240, 244, 253; 1657 gazetteer, 240, 249, 272; fish industry, 241–43, 249–50, 255, 259, 382n12; flooding, 250–51, 258, 270; Silk Market, 253, 255; Grain Wharf, 258–59
Jupo jingshe, 195–99 passim, 229–32, 289, 294

Kang Youwei, 84, 263, 267
Kaozheng, 5–8, 95, 162, 205, 227, 233, 266, 271; and local studies, 16, 153
Keenan, Barry, 192
Kind Relief Granary (Huiji cang), 183–84, 191–93, 266
Kinqua, *see* Liang Jingguo
Kong Anguo, 76
Kong family, 48, 65–66, 86, 280
Kong Jixun, 65–66, 85–86
Kong Luhua, 125, 350n98
Kuang Lu, 66, 148
Kuhn, Philip, 8
Kwan, Man Bun, 42

Lao Chongguang, 184, 187, 231
Lao Tong, 83, 106, 110
Leong, Sow-theng, 37
Li Changrong, 67, 177–80
Li Fuping, 38, 77–78, 123, 257
Li Futai, 189
Li Guangting, 151, 167, 172
Li Guangzhao, 65, 92, 107, 136
Li Guochen, 258, 272
Li Hongzhang, 260
Li Hu, 251–54 passim
Li Jian, 58, 60, 69, 74
Li Jun, 62
Li lineage (Changjiao), 175
Li Maoying, 146–47
Li Nengding, 187, 210, 212
Li Rumei, 139
Li Ruwei, 175
Li Suiqiu, 148
Li Xun, 272

Li Yingtian, 178
Li Zhongpei, 221
Liang Chu, 146
Liang-Guang yanfa zhi, 32
Liang Guozhen, 102, 109, 206
Liang Jingguo, 39, 203
Liang Lunshu, 177, 193
Liang Mei, 65, 108-9, 121, 128, 139, 166, 170, 204
Liang Qi, 170
Liang Tingnan, 129-30, 133-34, 167, 177, 193
Liang Xuyong, 1, 10-11, 83, 317n2, 320n21
Liang Yaochen, 263
Liang Yaoshu, 263, 269
Liang Yusen, 179
Liang Zhaohuang, 193
Liao Ji, 107-8
Liao Tingxiang, 169-70, 194
Liao Xiongguang, 258
Liao Zhen, 169
Library collections, 127-28, 152, 161-62, 194-95
Lin Botong, 71, 85-87, 122, 140, 163, 173, 183; scholarship of, 96, 110, 160, 210, 221-22; background and family, 105-6, 166, 169; as Xuehaitang co-director, 118, 185, 204
Lin Shixian, 169
Lin Zexu, 193, 371-72n82
Lineages, 43, 46, 330-31n91
Ling Tingkan, 205
Ling Yangzao, 142, 160
Lingnan, 5
Lingnan hua zhenglue, 292-93, 296
"Lingnan Litchi Songs," 137-41, 277, 282
Lingnan qunya, 142
Lingnan wenxian, 141

Lingnan yishu, 149-61
Litchi, 137-41, 160-61, 277, 282
Litchi Cove (Lizhiwan), 50, 61, 63, 89, 121, 140, 160, 174
Literati, 13, 321n27
Literati culture, 176-80
Liu Binhua, 55-58 *passim*, 76-77, 80, 92, 94, 142
Liu Boji, 192
Liu Chang, 130, 132, 136
Liu Changling, 364n16
Liu Daxia, 242
Liu Gongmian, 211, 233
Liu Huadong, 72-73, 92, 105, 159
Liu Ke, 151, 157
Liu Qixiong, 28
Liu Tianhui, 50, 86, 110
Liu Wenqi, 234
Liu Xing'en, 233
Liu Xinqi, 156
Liu Yan, 129-32 *passim*
Liu Yusong, 234
Liu Zechang, 121
Liurong Monastery, 59, 109, 113, 258
Liushi xingwang lu, 130
Lixue, 5, 76-77, 97, 147-49, 160, 190, 338n81
Local culture, 162-63
Localist texts, 16-19
Local Worthies Shrine, 71-72
Long lineage (Daliang), 45-47, 51, 109-10, 181-82, 331n96
Long Tinghuai, 51
Long Yuanxi, 181
Longjiang, 44-45, 59, 247, 261
Longshan, 44-45, 247-48, 274
Longxi shuyuan, 212, 231
Lu Fanyan, 206
Lu Guanheng, 39-40, 71-74, 159
Lu Kun, 185, 187, 190, 257

Lu Wenjin, 35, 71–73, 159
Lü Jian, 203, 327*n*42
Lujiang academy, 47
Lunyu (Analects), 77, 95, 121, 224
Luo Chuanqiu, 40
Luo Dunyan, 143, 181, 220
Luo Hanzhang, 75, 78–80, 102
Luo Jiabao, 40
Luo Jiaqin, 193
Luo Lianghui, 143, 148
Luo lineage (Daliang), 40, 45, 51, 142–43, 181–82, 193, 220, 331*n*95; contrast to urban elite, 47, 109–10, 220
Luo Tianchi (Shunde), 26
Luo Tianchi (Xinhui), 178
Luo Xuepeng, 142–49, 152, 154, 157, 161–63
Luo Yuliang, 40
Luoge, 48
Lustration festival, 177–80

Ma Fuan, 86–87, 102, 109, 118
Macao, 292, 295
Manchukuo, 284
Mann, Susan, 8
Mao Qiling, 157
Maritime merchants, 34–36, 39–40, 63–65, 68–74, 81, 163, 251, 280
Marks, Robert, 43, 328–29*n*57
Mashe, 57–58
Mazumdar, Sucheta, 46, 48
Merchant registration, *see Shangji*
Meyer-Fong, Tobie, 7
Militias, 172, 181–82, 261
Ming Bingzhang, 253
Ming Jingran, 245
Ming lineage (Jiujiang), 245
Ming Lizhao, 245, 254–55
Ming Lun, 251, 259

Ming Yong, 265
Ming Zhigang, 251, 258–58, 261, 270, 272
Mingru xuean, 267
Mobility, social, 12–14, 18, 52, 276–82, 286–87
Mowqua, *see* Lu Guanheng; Lu Wenjin
Myrobalan Grove, 84, 179
Mulberry Garden Enclosure (Sangyuanwei), 24, 35, 44, 239–42, 251, 258, 330*n*83
Mumian, 61
Muyou, 27, 30, 105, 168–69, 183, 280, 288–91
Myriad Pines Garden, *see* Wansongyuan

Nan-Han ji, 132
Nan-Han shu, 133
Nanhai, 10–11, 25, 42, 44
Nanxiong, 47–49, 243–45, 248, 273
Naquin, Susan, 279
Neo-Confucianism, 77, 80, 265, 338*n*81, 343*n*25
New City, 40–42, 67, 324*n*7
New Text Confucianism, 99–100, 226
Ni Zan, 69

Old City, 40–42, 66–67, 114–15
Opium War, First, 165, 182, 193
Opium War, Second, 172
Ou Huairui, 141
Ou Shiheng, 151
Ou Yuzhang, 183, 192

Pan Dinggui, 167
Pan family, 35, 50, 63, 68–70, 74, 82

Pan Jili, 266
Pan Shichang, 143, 148
Pan Shicheng, 52–53, 63, 67, 149
Pan Shu, 167, 179
Pan Wenyin, 148
Pan Youdu, 35, 64, 206
Pan Youwei, 35, 64, 71
Pan Zhencheng, 35
Pan Zhengheng (1779–1837), 49, 73, 85, 166
Pan Zhengheng (1787–1830), 74, 167
Pan Zhengwei, 69
Panyu, 25, 46, 110, 167; and in-migration, 29, 32–33, 42, 104–5, 203
Parallel prose, 7–8, 102, 190
Pawn merchants, 49, 71
Pearl River, 62
Pearl River delta, 3–4, 10, 42–53, 281–82; and Guangzhou, 9–13 passim, 18, 53–54, 171–75 passim, 180–84, 246–47, 263–65, 272–75, 285
Poetry, local, 134–41, 162
Polachek, James, 166, 362n4, 371–72n82
Printing, 127–28, 161–62, 227–28, 231–32, 269–75
Puankhequa, see Pan Zhencheng; Pan Youdu
Punti, 37, 165
Puxue, 6, 115–16

Qi Gong, 183, 259, 266
Qi Lin, 106
Qi Shaonan, 207
Qian Daxin, 94–95, 158, 206, 220
Qian Mu, 211, 218
Qian Yiji, 185, 190, 257, 267
Qieyun, 206–7, 210

Qin Huitian, 271
Qiu Jun, 77, 146–47
Qiu Xi, 50, 61, 63, 84
Qiu Xiande, 38, 70, 74–75
Qu Dajun, 130, 141, 157, 242, 283

Rankin, Mary, 192
Reading practices, 214–16
Red Turban uprising, 171, 176–77, 212, 261
Ren Dachun, 158
Ren Zhaolin, 110
Renhe, 30
Restoration Society, 270–71
Rhapsodies (*fu*), 7–8, 190
Rhoads, Edward, 40–41
Rowe, William, 39–40, 42, 278, 284
Ruan Fu, 61, 99, 104, 157
Ruan Rongling, 65
Ruan Yuan, 2, 61, 84, 130, 140, 162, 221, 250–51, 254–55; and *Huang Qing jingjie*, 2, 5, 99, 121–22; and local studies, 7, 16–17; literary agenda of, 7, 87–88, 101–3, 134–35, 152, 157; legacy, 27, 199, 296; and the Xuehaitang, 91–105, 110–25 passim, 127, 285; preface to *Xuehaitang ji* preface, 185, 190; Chen Li and, 208, 212; Zhu Ciqi and, 257, 266–68
Ruilin, 232
Rulin shuyuan, 249, 252–55, 258–62, 272
Rulin zhuan, 159, 271, 378n80

Salt merchants, 32–34, 63–66 passim, 70, 75, 106, 204, 280, 326–27n35

Sands (*shatian, shatan*), 24, 51–53, 119, 182–83
Schools method (*jiafa*), 126, 225–26, 231
Sea Mountain Immortals' Lodge, 63, 67, 229
Sea of Learning Hall, *see* Xuehaitang
Shanghai, 284
Shangji, 32–33, 105
Shanyin, 32–33, 168, 179, 280
Shaoxing, 32–34, 168–69, 278
Shaozhou, 141
Shawan, 251–52
Shen Fu, 62
Shen Shiliang, 168–69, 175, 178, 281, 290
Shen Zetang, 169, 290
Shenlou zhi, 34, 71
Shi family, 29–30, 194
Shi Cheng, 30, 184, 193–94
Shi Duan, 194
Shi Shanchang, 29–30
Shiguo chunqiu, 130–33 *passim*
Shijian, see *Jinjian lu*
Shisanjing zhushi, 92, 186, 194, 232
Shitao, 69
Shixing ji, 156
Shixue, 6, 205–6
Shuijing zhu, 207
Shulin yangzhi, 98–99
Shunde, 26, 37, 44, 109, 143
Shuyuan, 2, 117, 192–93, 198–99, 321*n*25
Siku quanshu, 8, 15, 78, 144–45, 158, 160, 204, 211, 232
Six Records of a Floating Life, 62
Skinner, G. William, 40–41, 277, 328*n*57
Song Learning, 15–16, 76, 78, 95, 218–27, 338*n*81

Song shi, 267
Southern Garden, 112, 146
Southern Han (Nan-Han), 117, 129–37, *passim*
Southern Yue (Nan-Yue), 84, 116, 136, 177
Specialized courses (*zhuanke*), 185–90
Specialized students (*zhuanke sheng*), 185–90, 228–29, 258
Stockard, Janice, 45, 330*n*90
Su Liupeng, 178
Su Shi, 85, 139
Suandi, 151–52, 158
Sun Fen, 146, 147
Sun Yat-sen, 291
Szonyi, Michael, 331*n*91

Taihe, 285
Tan Dajing, 71, 159
Tan Jianlong, 108
Tan Jingzhao, 65, 85
Tan Ying, 102–3, 124, 128, 132, 166, 174–80 *passim*, 205; as anthologist, 97, 142, 149–63, 188, 277; social background, 108, 280; "Lingnan Litchi Songs," 138–39, 282
Tan Zongjun, 170, 174–75, 194
Tan Zuqiang, 296
Tang Litchi Garden, 61, 63, 84
Tao Fuxiang, 289, 364*n*16
Tao Shaoxue, 289
Tao Yuanming, 228
Tianbao firm, 39, 81
Tianjin, 42
Tongwen firm, 35
Tongzhi Restoration, 180–81
Transregional networks, 9, 18

Unadorned learning, *see Puxue*

Urban sojourning, 11
Urban space, 11
Urban elite, 13–14
Urbanization, 39–40, 48–51, 108

Vietnam, 243, 257, 262

Walton, Linda, 117
Wang Chu, 168–69, 280, 288–91
Wang Ding, 168
Wang family, 21, 168–69, 276, 280–85 *passim*
Wang Jia, 100
Wang Jianxin, 82, 184
Wang Jingwei, *see* Wang Zhaoming
Wang Kaitai, 196, 199
Wang Lunzhi, 168
Wang Niansun, 216, 220, 226
Wang Pu, 68
Wang Quan, 21, 168–69, 179, 191, 276–89 *passim*, 292, 296
Wang Shaozhi, 156
Wang Shilin, 189
Wang Shizhen, 26, 177, 180
Wang Su, 226
Wang Xizhi, 177, 179–80
Wang Yangming, 100, 120, 268
Wang Yinglin, 94–95
Wang Yinzhi, 216, 226, 230–31
Wang Yun, 267
Wang Zhaohong, 169
Wang Zhaoming, 290–92
Wang Zhaoquan, 169, 287, 289, 295
Wang Zhaoyong, 169, 287–96 *passim*
Wang Zhi, 76
Wansongyuan, 65, 150
Watson, James L., 330–31*n*91

Wei Jilian, 203–4
Wei Xi, 87
Wei Zhongxian, 270
Wen lineage (Longshan), 47, 63, 142, 247
Wen Rugua, 138
Wen Runeng, 142, 152, 156, 162, 248
Wen Tingshi, 191
Wen Xun, 86, 108, 158, 206, 220, 222
Weng Fanggang, 26–27, 93
Weng Xincun, 37, 104, 121, 204, 222–23, 257
Wenlan Pavilion, 113, 122, 173, 197
Wenlan shuyuan, 81–82, 94, 111–12, 119
Wenxuan, 7, 101, 102, 155, 186, 194
West River (Xijiang), 10, 42–48 *passim*, 242, 259
Willow Hall, 67, 178, 180
Wu Bingjian, 35, 60, 68–69, 119
Wu Bingyong, 60, 68–69
Wu Bingzhen, 68–69
Wu Chaofeng, 34
Wu Chongyao, 142, 149–52, 177, 231, 327*n*43
Wu Dianbei, 34–35
Wu family, 34–35, 50, 63, 65, 68, 82, 149
Wu Feng, 194, 364*n*16
Wu Guoying, 34–35
Wu Jiashu, 106
Wu Kuiguang, 109
Wu Lanxiu, 86, 92, 97, 107–8, 140, 151–52, 166, 292; and Xie Lansheng, 59, 80; and the Xuehaitang, 102, 113–19 *passim*, 123–24, 185; studies

of the Southern Han, 128-37 *passim*, 160
Wu Linguang, 109
Wu Miguang, 109
Wu Renchen, 130-33 *passim*
Wu Rongguang, 35, 109
Wu Shaotang, 150, 151
Wu Wenqi, 220
Wu Yingchang, 106
Wu Yingkui, 66, 86-87, 92, 110, 151, 157, 160-61, 166; and the Xuehaitang, 109, 118, 124
Wu Yuanhua, 68-69, 150
Wu Yuankui, 150
Wu Yuansong, 35, 149
Wu Yue, 116

Xian Yi, 220, 378n65
Xiangshan, 30
Xicheng firm, 39, 68, 82
Xie family, 36
Xie Guangfu, 110
Xie Guansheng, 58, 65, 68
Xie Jiawu, 36, 69
Xie Jingqing, 57-58
Xie Lansheng, 19, 37, 55-71 *passim*, 74-86 *passim*, 92-94, 275; diary, 56, 81, 94; at Yangcheng Academy, 78-81, 103, 121, 123, 137, 204, 257; and the Xuehaitang, 100, 113, 123-24
Xie Niandian, 166
Xie Niangong, 59, 68, 86, 94, 109, 123, 166
Xie Youren, 36, 65, 67, 177
Xie Youwen, 36
Xie Yunsheng, 58
Xiguan, 34, 40-41, 63, 66-68, 81-82, 108, 112, 176
Xigutang, 86-88

Xinhui, 44, 65, 68, 72-73, 120, 125
Xiong Jingxing, 59, 65-67, 70, 86, 92, 166, 170, 177; and the Xuehaitang, 102, 109, 118, 123
Xiukun, 104, 107, 116, 118
Xu Benyi, 33
Xu Bo, 138
Xu family (Qiantang), 168
Xu family (Renhe), 30-31, 168
Xu Gan, 214-15
Xu Hao, 168, 178-79, 220, 222, 283
Xu Jun, 31
Xu Naiji, 31, 94
Xu Nailai, 31
Xu Naizhao, 31
Xu Qiguang, 30-31, 168
Xu Qikang, 30
Xu Qing, 38
Xu Qiyang, 30
Xu Rong, 29, 86, 100, 102, 106, 118, 166
Xu Shen, 15, 226
Xu Xiangguang, 67, 336n41
Xu Xuefan, 31
Xu Xuezhou, 30
Xu Xuezhu, 31
Xu Yong, 30-31
Xu Yubin, 150, 178
Xu Yue, 31
Xue Xuecheng, 30
Xuehaitang, 2; scholars at, 9, 103-11, 125, 162, 165-71, 319n18; organization and activities, 11-12, 117-19; curriculum, 88, 94-103, 116, 121, 125, 128, 185-91, 217, 221, 346n51; founding, 89, 99-100, 111-19, 342n7; as cultural resource, 111, 169, 199, 278-79; reconstruction, 173, 184-91, 197; relation to

448   INDEX

other academies, 199–200; Republican-era revival, 295–97, 393n48
Xuehaitang ji, 99–110, 119–23 passim, 134–37, 154, 188, 206, 282; Ruan Yuan preface to, 95–97, 113, 185–86
Xuehaitang keyi, 296–97
Xuehaitang sanji, 169, 194
Xuehaitang siji, 169–70, 197, 229
Xun Yue, 132

Yan Xun, 178–79
Yang Dalin, 50, 82, 108
Yang family, 50
Yang Fu, 112, 153, 155, 156
Yang Rongxu, 31, 66, 204, 224
Yang Shiji, 86
Yang Xiong, 100
Yang Yuanfu, 50
Yangcheng shuyuan, 78–80, 114–15, 191, 193
Yangzhou, 5, 16, 42, 177, 284
Ye family, 36, 66, 69, 106
Ye Gongchuo, 293 (fig. 10)
Ye Menglin, 56, 60, 66
Ye Menglong, 56, 60, 66, 70, 92
Ye Mingchen, 171, 195
Ye Renlan, 170
Ye Tingxun, 36, 50, 56, 66, 92, 106, 170
Ye Tingying, 106, 170
Ye Yanlan, 293 (fig. 10)
Yi Kezhong, 73, 92–93, 97, 140, 166, 173, 206; and the Xuehaitang, 103, 106, 135; and the Kind Relief Granary, 183, 266
Yi Rongzhi, 39, 65
Yi Yuanchang, *see* Yi Rongzhi
Yihe firm, 35, 68, 82, 149

Yili (meaning and principle), 6, 223
Yinglian, 107
Yingyuan Temple, 178, 195–96
Yingyuan shuyuan, 195–98
Yisongyuan, 64
Yiwu zhi, 155–56
Yu Bifang, 102
Yu Binggang, 259
Yu Fan, 84–85
Yu Jing, 141
Yu Shimei, 191
Yu Yabao, 259
Yu Yue, 233
Yü Ying-shih, 70
Yuan Mei, 65
Yue shisanjia ji, 149
Yuedong shihai, 142, 156
Yuedong wenhai, 142
Yuehua shuyuan, 75–78, 114–15, 134, 191–94 passim, 279, 371–72n82
Yueshi souyi, 156
Yuexiu Hill, 112–17, 124, 173, 176–77, 192–97 passim, 296
Yuexiu shuyuan, 74–78, 114–15, 123, 134, 191–94
Yueyatang congshu, 149
Yugong zhuizhi, 205, 207
Yun Jing, 36, 60
Yunquan shanguan, 85–86, 341n108

Zeng Guofan, 232
Zeng lineage (Jiujiang), 243, 261
Zeng Yu, 81, 84–85, 130, 177, 180
Zeng Zhao, 86–87, 92–93, 96–99 passim, 128, 151–52, 155–60 passim, 166; and the Xuehaitang, 110, 118, 122–23, 185, 195, 205–6; and

Han Learning, 217, 266; and Jiujiang, 251, 254, 257
Zeng Zhongli, 272
Zhan Ruoshui, 146–47, 263–65
Zhang Bao, 143, 252
Zhang Biao, 38, 86, 105, 346n55
Zhang Bingwen, 64, 105
Zhang Fenghua, 53
Zhang Haipeng, 151
Zhang Jinfang, 65, 69
Zhang Jiuling, 105, 135, 139, 141, 146–47, 153, 156–57
Zhang Qihan, 108, 170
Zhang Qizeng, 167, 170, 187
Zhang Ruzhi, 60, 82
Zhang Tingjin, 31
Zhang Weiping, 33, 50, 60, 64–71 *passim*, 85–87, 128; and the Xuehaitang, 104–5, 123; in reconstruction era, 166, 169, 177–80 *passim*; and Chen Li, 204, 207, 211
Zhang Yanji, 73, 83
Zhang Yuan, 104
Zhang Zai, 76, 80
Zhang Zhidong, 182, 190
Zhao lineage (Hengsha), 174, 212
Zhao Jun, 109, 113, 116, 118
Zhao Qi, 209, 223
Zhao Qiying, 231, 233
Zhao Tuo, 177
Zhaoqing, 44, 76
Zheng Fen, 65, 100
Zheng Haoruo, 85, 92, 102, 105
Zheng Quan, 170, 189
Zheng Xianfu, 193
Zheng Xuan, 6, 15, 76, 91, 99–101, 159, 207; Chen Li's assessment of, 201, 211, 217, 222–27, 231–32
Zhengjue Monastery, 252–53, 258

Zhengxue xu, 158–59
Zhenhai Tower, 114, 171, 173, 176
Zhenyong, 253, 263, 371n77
Zhong Fengqing, 212
Zhong Qishao, 60, 65, 69, 82, 109, 150
Zhonglun, 214–15
Zhou Dunyi, 76, 80, 219
Zhou Yinqing, 109, 154, 167, 189–90, 229
Zhouyi benyi zhu, 72
Zhu Bingqi, 257
Zhu Bolian, 252
Zhu Chengfa, 256
Zhu Chengwan, 252
Zhu Ciqi, 84, 255, 257–60, 274–75, 283–84; and Chen Li compared, 21, 237–38, 257, 266–68, 275; and Xuehaitang, 187, 256, 266–69 *passim*; *Zhushi chuanfang ji*, 238, 269–70; Zhu lineage genealogy, 238, 245, 270–71; *Jiujiang Rulin xiang zhi*, 238, 272–74; and Jiujiang, 256, 259, 262–66
Zhu Guangyun, 244
Zhu Guocai, 246
Zhu Jizhao, 247
Zhu lineage (Jiujiang), 243–47 *passim*, 256, 269–70
Zhu Lingxiao, 246
Zhu Mo, 246–47, 269
Zhu Qilian, 169
Zhu Rang, 246, 270
Zhu Shilian, 252, 269–71
Zhu Shiqi, 256–59, 270
Zhu Shuida, 245
Zhu Tinggui, 262, 270
Zhu Wenbin, 258
Zhu Wenjin, 246

Zhu Xi, 5–6, 15, 76, 117, 147, 265; in the Xuehaitang curriculum, 95, 97, 186; Chen Li's assessment of, 201, 211, 213, 214, 219, 221–27, 231
Zhu Yizun, 138
Zhu Yuanlong, 245
Zhu Yun, 158
Zhu Ziyi, 245–46
Zhu Zongqi, 257, 270, 272
Zhuang Yougong, 324n5
Zhujixiang, 47–49, 282
Zhuzi xuedi, 77, 146–47
Zou Boqi, 150, 158, 167, 173–74, 183, 217, 231, 233
Zuo Zongtang, 268
Zurndorfer, Harriet, 277

Harvard East Asian Monographs
(* out-of-print)

- *1. Liang Fang-chung, *The Single-Whip Method of Taxation in China*
- *2. Harold C. Hinton, *The Grain Tribute System of China, 1845–1911*
- 3. Ellsworth C. Carlson, *The Kaiping Mines, 1877–1912*
- *4. Chao Kuo-chün, *Agrarian Policies of Mainland China: A Documentary Study, 1949–1956*
- *5. Edgar Snow, *Random Notes on Red China, 1936–1945*
- *6. Edwin George Beal, Jr., *The Origin of Likin, 1835–1864*
- 7. Chao Kuo-chün, *Economic Planning and Organization in Mainland China: A Documentary Study, 1949–1957*
- *8. John K. Fairbank, *Ching Documents: An Introductory Syllabus*
- *9. Helen Yin and Yi-chang Yin, *Economic Statistics of Mainland China, 1949–1957*
- 10. Wolfgang Franke, *The Reform and Abolition of the Traditional Chinese Examination System*
- 11. Albert Feuerwerker and S. Cheng, *Chinese Communist Studies of Modern Chinese History*
- 12. C. John Stanley, *Late Ching Finance: Hu Kuang-yung as an Innovator*
- 13. S. M. Meng, *The Tsungli Yamen: Its Organization and Functions*
- *14. Ssu-yü Teng, *Historiography of the Taiping Rebellion*
- 15. Chun-Jo Liu, *Controversies in Modern Chinese Intellectual History: An Analytic Bibliography of Periodical Articles, Mainly of the May Fourth and Post-May Fourth Era*
- *16. Edward J. M. Rhoads, *The Chinese Red Army, 1927–1963: An Annotated Bibliography*
- *17. Andrew J. Nathan, *A History of the China International Famine Relief Commission*
- *18. Frank H. H. King (ed.) and Prescott Clarke, *A Research Guide to China-Coast Newspapers, 1822–1911*
- *19. Ellis Joffe, *Party and Army: Professionalism and Political Control in the Chinese Officer Corps, 1949–1964*

*20. Toshio G. Tsukahira, *Feudal Control in Tokugawa Japan: The Sankin Kōtai System*

*21. Kwang-Ching Liu, ed., *American Missionaries in China: Papers from Harvard Seminars*

*22. George Moseley, *A Sino-Soviet Cultural Frontier: The Ili Kazakh Autonomous Chou*

23. Carl F. Nathan, *Plague Prevention and Politics in Manchuria, 1910–1931*

*24. Adrian Arthur Bennett, *John Fryer: The Introduction of Western Science and Technology into Nineteenth-Century China*

*25. Donald J. Friedman, *The Road from Isolation: The Campaign of the American Committee for Non-Participation in Japanese Aggression, 1938–1941*

*26. Edward LeFevour, *Western Enterprise in Late Ching China: A Selective Survey of Jardine, Matheson and Company's Operations, 1842–1895*

27. Charles Neuhauser, *Third World Politics: China and the Afro-Asian People's Solidarity Organization, 1957–1967*

*28. Kungtu C. Sun, assisted by Ralph W. Huenemann, *The Economic Development of Manchuria in the First Half of the Twentieth Century*

*29. Shahid Javed Burki, *A Study of Chinese Communes, 1965*

30. John Carter Vincent, *The Extraterritorial System in China: Final Phase*

31. Madeleine Chi, *China Diplomacy, 1914–1918*

*32. Clifton Jackson Phillips, *Protestant America and the Pagan World: The First Half Century of the American Board of Commissioners for Foreign Missions, 1810–1860*

*33. James Pusey, *Wu Han: Attacking the Present Through the Past*

*34. Ying-wan Cheng, *Postal Communication in China and Its Modernization, 1860–1896*

35. Tuvia Blumenthal, *Saving in Postwar Japan*

36. Peter Frost, *The Bakumatsu Currency Crisis*

37. Stephen C. Lockwood, *Augustine Heard and Company, 1858–1862*

38. Robert R. Campbell, *James Duncan Campbell: A Memoir by His Son*

39. Jerome Alan Cohen, ed., *The Dynamics of China's Foreign Relations*

40. V. V. Vishnyakova-Akimova, *Two Years in Revolutionary China, 1925–1927*, tr. Steven L. Levine

41. Meron Medzini, *French Policy in Japan During the Closing Years of the Tokugawa Regime*

42. Ezra Vogel, Margie Sargent, Vivienne B. Shue, Thomas Jay Mathews, and Deborah S. Davis, *The Cultural Revolution in the Provinces*

43. Sidney A. Forsythe, *An American Missionary Community in China, 1895–1905*

*44. Benjamin I. Schwartz, ed., *Reflections on the May Fourth Movement.: A Symposium*
*45. Ching Young Choe, *The Rule of the Taewŏngun, 1864–1873: Restoration in Yi Korea*
46. W. P. J. Hall, *A Bibliographical Guide to Japanese Research on the Chinese Economy, 1958–1970*
47. Jack J. Gerson, *Horatio Nelson Lay and Sino-British Relations, 1854–1864*
48. Paul Richard Bohr, *Famine and the Missionary: Timothy Richard as Relief Administrator and Advocate of National Reform*
49. Endymion Wilkinson, *The History of Imperial China: A Research Guide*
50. Britten Dean, *China and Great Britain: The Diplomacy of Commercial Relations, 1860–1864*
51. Ellsworth C. Carlson, *The Foochow Missionaries, 1847–1880*
52. Yeh-chien Wang, *An Estimate of the Land-Tax Collection in China, 1753 and 1908*
53. Richard M. Pfeffer, *Understanding Business Contracts in China, 1949–1963*
*54. Han-sheng Chuan and Richard Kraus, *Mid-Ching Rice Markets and Trade: An Essay in Price History*
55. Ranbir Vohra, *Lao She and the Chinese Revolution*
56. Liang-lin Hsiao, *China's Foreign Trade Statistics, 1864–1949*
*57. Lee-hsia Hsu Ting, *Government Control of the Press in Modern China, 1900–1949*
*58. Edward W. Wagner, *The Literati Purges: Political Conflict in Early Yi Korea*
*59. Joungwon A. Kim, *Divided Korea: The Politics of Development, 1945–1972*
60. Noriko Kamachi, John K. Fairbank, and Chūzō Ichiko, *Japanese Studies of Modern China Since 1953: A Bibliographical Guide to Historical and Social-Science Research on the Nineteenth and Twentieth Centuries, Supplementary Volume for 1953–1969*
61. Donald A. Gibbs and Yun-chen Li, *A Bibliography of Studies and Translations of Modern Chinese Literature, 1918–1942*
62. Robert H. Silin, *Leadership and Values: The Organization of Large-Scale Taiwanese Enterprises*
63. David Pong, *A Critical Guide to the Kwangtung Provincial Archives Deposited at the Public Record Office of London*
*64. Fred W. Drake, *China Charts the World: Hsu Chi-yü and His Geography of 1848*
*65. William A. Brown and Urgrunge Onon, translators and annotators, *History of the Mongolian People's Republic*
66. Edward L. Farmer, *Early Ming Government: The Evolution of Dual Capitals*
*67. Ralph C. Croizier, *Koxinga and Chinese Nationalism: History, Myth, and the Hero*

*68. William J. Tyler, tr., *The Psychological World of Natsume Sōseki*, by Doi Takeo

69. Eric Widmer, *The Russian Ecclesiastical Mission in Peking During the Eighteenth Century*

*70. Charlton M. Lewis, *Prologue to the Chinese Revolution: The Transformation of Ideas and Institutions in Hunan Province, 1891–1907*

71. Preston Torbert, *The Ching Imperial Household Department: A Study of Its Organization and Principal Functions, 1662–1796*

72. Paul A. Cohen and John E. Schrecker, eds., *Reform in Nineteenth-Century China*

73. Jon Sigurdson, *Rural Industrialism in China*

74. Kang Chao, *The Development of Cotton Textile Production in China*

75. Valentin Rabe, *The Home Base of American China Missions, 1880–1920*

*76. Sarasin Viraphol, *Tribute and Profit: Sino-Siamese Trade, 1652–1853*

77. Ch'i-ch'ing Hsiao, *The Military Establishment of the Yuan Dynasty*

78. Meishi Tsai, *Contemporary Chinese Novels and Short Stories, 1949–1974: An Annotated Bibliography*

*79. Wellington K. K. Chan, *Merchants, Mandarins and Modern Enterprise in Late Ching China*

80. Endymion Wilkinson, *Landlord and Labor in Late Imperial China: Case Studies from Shandong by Jing Su and Luo Lun*

*81. Barry Keenan, *The Dewey Experiment in China: Educational Reform and Political Power in the Early Republic*

*82. George A. Hayden, *Crime and Punishment in Medieval Chinese Drama: Three Judge Pao Plays*

*83. Sang-Chul Suh, *Growth and Structural Changes in the Korean Economy, 1910–1940*

84. J. W. Dower, *Empire and Aftermath: Yoshida Shigeru and the Japanese Experience, 1878–1954*

85. Martin Collcutt, *Five Mountains: The Rinzai Zen Monastic Institution in Medieval Japan*

86. Kwang Suk Kim and Michael Roemer, *Growth and Structural Transformation*

87. Anne O. Krueger, *The Developmental Role of the Foreign Sector and Aid*

*88. Edwin S. Mills and Byung-Nak Song, *Urbanization and Urban Problems*

89. Sung Hwan Ban, Pal Yong Moon, and Dwight H. Perkins, *Rural Development*

*90. Noel F. McGinn, Donald R. Snodgrass, Yung Bong Kim, Shin-Bok Kim, and Quee-Young Kim, *Education and Development in Korea*

*91. Leroy P. Jones and Il SaKong, *Government, Business, and Entrepreneurship in Economic Development: The Korean Case*

92. Edward S. Mason, Dwight H. Perkins, Kwang Suk Kim, David C. Cole, Mahn Je Kim et al., *The Economic and Social Modernization of the Republic of Korea*

93. Robert Repetto, Tai Hwan Kwon, Son-Ung Kim, Dae Young Kim, John E. Sloboda, and Peter J. Donaldson, *Economic Development, Population Policy, and Demographic Transition in the Republic of Korea*

94. Parks M. Coble, Jr., *The Shanghai Capitalists and the Nationalist Government, 1927–1937*

95. Noriko Kamachi, *Reform in China: Huang Tsun-hsien and the Japanese Model*

96. Richard Wich, *Sino-Soviet Crisis Politics: A Study of Political Change and Communication*

97. Lillian M. Li, *China's Silk Trade: Traditional Industry in the Modern World, 1842–1937*

98. R. David Arkush, *Fei Xiaotong and Sociology in Revolutionary China*

*99. Kenneth Alan Grossberg, *Japan's Renaissance: The Politics of the Muromachi Bakufu*

100. James Reeve Pusey, *China and Charles Darwin*

101. Hoyt Cleveland Tillman, *Utilitarian Confucianism: Chen Liang's Challenge to Chu Hsi*

102. Thomas A. Stanley, *Ōsugi Sakae, Anarchist in Taishō Japan: The Creativity of the Ego*

103. Jonathan K. Ocko, *Bureaucratic Reform in Provincial China: Ting Jih-ch'ang in Restoration Kiangsu, 1867–1870*

104. James Reed, *The Missionary Mind and American East Asia Policy, 1911–1915*

105. Neil L. Waters, *Japan's Local Pragmatists: The Transition from Bakumatsu to Meiji in the Kawasaki Region*

106. David C. Cole and Yung Chul Park, *Financial Development in Korea, 1945–1978*

107. Roy Bahl, Chuk Kyo Kim, and Chong Kee Park, *Public Finances During the Korean Modernization Process*

108. William D. Wray, *Mitsubishi and the N.Y.K, 1870–1914: Business Strategy in the Japanese Shipping Industry*

109. Ralph William Huenemann, *The Dragon and the Iron Horse: The Economics of Railroads in China, 1876–1937*

*110. Benjamin A. Elman, *From Philosophy to Philology: Intellectual and Social Aspects of Change in Late Imperial China*

111. Jane Kate Leonard, *Wei Yüan and China's Rediscovery of the Maritime World*

112. Luke S. K. Kwong, *A Mosaic of the Hundred Days:. Personalities, Politics, and Ideas of 1898*
*113. John E. Wills, Jr., *Embassies and Illusions: Dutch and Portuguese Envoys to K'ang-hsi, 1666–1687*
114. Joshua A. Fogel, *Politics and Sinology: The Case of Naitō Konan (1866–1934)*
*115. Jeffrey C. Kinkley, ed., *After Mao: Chinese Literature and Society, 1978–1981*
116. C. Andrew Gerstle, *Circles of Fantasy: Convention in the Plays of Chikamatsu*
117. Andrew Gordon, *The Evolution of Labor Relations in Japan: Heavy Industry, 1853–1955*
*118. Daniel K. Gardner, *Chu Hsi and the "Ta Hsueh": Neo-Confucian Reflection on the Confucian Canon*
119. Christine Guth Kanda, *Shinzō: Hachiman Imagery and Its Development*
*120. Robert Borgen, *Sugawara no Michizane and the Early Heian Court*
121. Chang-tai Hung, *Going to the People: Chinese Intellectual and Folk Literature, 1918–1937*
*122. Michael A. Cusumano, *The Japanese Automobile Industry: Technology and Management at Nissan and Toyota*
123. Richard von Glahn, *The Country of Streams and Grottoes: Expansion, Settlement, and the Civilizing of the Sichuan Frontier in Song Times*
124. Steven D. Carter, *The Road to Komatsubara: A Classical Reading of the Renga Hyakuin*
125. Katherine F. Bruner, John K. Fairbank, and Richard T. Smith, *Entering China's Service: Robert Hart's Journals, 1854–1863*
126. Bob Tadashi Wakabayashi, *Anti-Foreignism and Western Learning in Early-Modern Japan: The "New Theses" of 1825*
127. Atsuko Hirai, *Individualism and Socialism: The Life and Thought of Kawai Eijirō (1891–1944)*
128. Ellen Widmer, *The Margins of Utopia: "Shui-hu hou-chuan" and the Literature of Ming Loyalism*
129. R. Kent Guy, *The Emperor's Four Treasuries: Scholars and the State in the Late Chien-lung Era*
130. Peter C. Perdue, *Exhausting the Earth: State and Peasant in Hunan, 1500–1850*
131. Susan Chan Egan, *A Latterday Confucian: Reminiscences of William Hung (1893–1980)*
132. James T. C. Liu, *China Turning Inward: Intellectual-Political Changes in the Early Twelfth Century*
*133. Paul A. Cohen, *Between Tradition and Modernity: Wang T'ao and Reform in Late Ching China*

134. Kate Wildman Nakai, *Shogunal Politics: Arai Hakuseki and the Premises of Tokugawa Rule*
*135. Parks M. Coble, *Facing Japan: Chinese Politics and Japanese Imperialism, 1931–1937*
136. Jon L. Saari, *Legacies of Childhood: Growing Up Chinese in a Time of Crisis, 1890–1920*
137. Susan Downing Videen, *Tales of Heichū*
138. Heinz Morioka and Miyoko Sasaki, *Rakugo: The Popular Narrative Art of Japan*
139. Joshua A. Fogel, *Nakae Ushikichi in China: The Mourning of Spirit*
140. Alexander Barton Woodside, *Vietnam and the Chinese Model.: A Comparative Study of Vietnamese and Chinese Government in the First Half of the Nineteenth Century*
*141. George Elison, *Deus Destroyed: The Image of Christianity in Early Modern Japan*
142. William D. Wray, ed., *Managing Industrial Enterprise: Cases from Japan's Prewar Experience*
*143. T'ung-tsu Ch'ü, *Local Government in China Under the Ching*
144. Marie Anchordoguy, *Computers, Inc.: Japan's Challenge to IBM*
145. Barbara Molony, *Technology and Investment: The Prewar Japanese Chemical Industry*
146. Mary Elizabeth Berry, *Hideyoshi*
147. Laura E. Hein, *Fueling Growth: The Energy Revolution and Economic Policy in Postwar Japan*
148. Wen-hsin Yeh, *The Alienated Academy: Culture and Politics in Republican China, 1919–1937*
149. Dru C. Gladney, *Muslim Chinese: Ethnic Nationalism in the People's Republic*
150. Merle Goldman and Paul A. Cohen, eds., *Ideas Across Cultures: Essays on Chinese Thought in Honor of Benjamin L Schwartz*
151. James M. Polachek, *The Inner Opium War*
152. Gail Lee Bernstein, *Japanese Marxist: A Portrait of Kawakami Hajime, 1879–1946*
*153. Lloyd E. Eastman, *The Abortive Revolution: China Under Nationalist Rule, 1927–1937*
154. Mark Mason, *American Multinationals and Japan: The Political Economy of Japanese Capital Controls, 1899–1980*
155. Richard J. Smith, John K. Fairbank, and Katherine F. Bruner, *Robert Hart and China's Early Modernization: His Journals, 1863–1866*
156. George J. Tanabe, Jr., *Myōe the Dreamkeeper: Fantasy and Knowledge in Kamakura Buddhism*

157. William Wayne Farris, *Heavenly Warriors: The Evolution of Japan's Military, 500–1300*
158. Yu-ming Shaw, *An American Missionary in China: John Leighton Stuart and Chinese-American Relations*
159. James B. Palais, *Politics and Policy in Traditional Korea*
*160. Douglas Reynolds, *China, 1898–1912: The Xinzheng Revolution and Japan*
161. Roger R. Thompson, *China's Local Councils in the Age of Constitutional Reform, 1898–1911*
162. William Johnston, *The Modern Epidemic: History of Tuberculosis in Japan*
163. Constantine Nomikos Vaporis, *Breaking Barriers: Travel and the State in Early Modern Japan*
164. Irmela Hijiya-Kirschnereit, *Rituals of Self-Revelation: Shishōsetsu as Literary Genre and Socio-Cultural Phenomenon*
165. James C. Baxter, *The Meiji Unification Through the Lens of Ishikawa Prefecture*
166. Thomas R. H. Havens, *Architects of Affluence: The Tsutsumi Family and the Seibu-Saison Enterprises in Twentieth-Century Japan*
167. Anthony Hood Chambers, *The Secret Window: Ideal Worlds in Tanizaki's Fiction*
168. Steven J. Ericson, *The Sound of the Whistle: Railroads and the State in Meiji Japan*
169. Andrew Edmund Goble, *Kenmu: Go-Daigo's Revolution*
170. Denise Potrzeba Lett, *In Pursuit of Status: The Making of South Korea's "New" Urban Middle Class*
171. Mimi Hall Yiengpruksawan, *Hiraizumi: Buddhist Art and Regional Politics in Twelfth-Century Japan*
172. Charles Shirō Inouye, *The Similitude of Blossoms: A Critical Biography of Izumi Kyōka (1873-1939), Japanese Novelist and Playwright*
173. Aviad E. Raz, *Riding the Black Ship: Japan and Tokyo Disneyland*
174. Deborah J. Milly, *Poverty, Equality, and Growth: The Politics of Economic Need in Postwar Japan*
175. See Heng Teow, *Japan's Cultural Policy Toward China, 1918-1931: A Comparative Perspective*
176. Michael A. Fuller, *An Introduction to Literary Chinese*
177. Frederick R. Dickinson, *War and National Reinvention: Japan in the Great War, 1914-1919*
178. John Solt, *Shredding the Tapestry of Meaning: The Poetry and Poetics of Kitasono Katue (1902-1978)*
179. Edward Pratt, *Japan's Protoindustrial Elite: The Economic Foundations of the Gōnō*
180. Atsuko Sakaki, *Recontextualizing Texts: Narrative Performance in Modern Japanese Fiction*

181. Soon-Won Park, *Colonial Industrialization and Labor in Korea: The Onoda Cement Factory*
182. JaHyun Kim Haboush and Martina Deuchler, *Culture and the State in Late Chosŏn Korea*
183. John W. Chaffee, *Branches of Heaven: A History of the Imperial Clan of Sung China*
184. Gi-Wook Shin and Michael Robinson, eds., *Colonial Modernity in Korea*
185. Nam-lin Hur, *Prayer and Play in Late Tokugawa Japan: Asakusa Sensōji and Edo Society*
186. Kristin Stapleton, *Civilizing Chengdu: Chinese Urban Reform, 1895–1937*
187. Hyung Il Pai, *Constructing "Korean" Origins: A Critical Review of Archaeology, Historiography, and Racial Myth in Korean State-Formation Theories*
188. Brian D. Ruppert, *Jewel in the Ashes: Buddha Relics and Power in Early Medieval Japan*
189. Susan Daruvala, *Zhou Zuoren and an Alternative Chinese Response to Modernity*
*190. James Z. Lee, *The Political Economy of a Frontier: Southwest China, 1250–1850*
191. Kerry Smith, *A Time of Crisis: Japan, the Great Depression, and Rural Revitalization*
192. Michael Lewis, *Becoming Apart: National Power and Local Politics in Toyama, 1868–1945*
193. William C. Kirby, Man-houng Lin, James Chin Shih, and David A. Pietz, eds., *State and Economy in Republican China: A Handbook for Scholars*
194. Timothy S. George, *Minamata: Pollution and the Struggle for Democracy in Postwar Japan*
195. Billy K. L. So, *Prosperity, Region, and Institutions in Maritime China: The South Fukien Pattern, 946–1368*
196. Yoshihisa Tak Matsusaka, *The Making of Japanese Manchuria, 1904–1932*
197. Maram Epstein, *Competing Discourses: Orthodoxy, Authenticity, and Engendered Meanings in Late Imperial Chinese Fiction*
198. Curtis J. Milhaupt, J. Mark Ramseyer, and Michael K. Young, eds. and comps., *Japanese Law in Context: Readings in Society, the Economy, and Politics*
199. Haruo Iguchi, *Unfinished Business: Ayukawa Yoshisuke and U.S.-Japan Relations, 1937–1952*
200. Scott Pearce, Audrey Spiro, and Patricia Ebrey, *Culture and Power in the Reconstitution of the Chinese Realm, 200–600*
201. Terry Kawashima, *Writing Margins: The Textual Construction of Gender in Heian and Kamakura Japan*
202. Martin W. Huang, *Desire and Fictional Narrative in Late Imperial China*

203. Robert S. Ross and Jiang Changbin, eds., *Re-examining the Cold War: U.S.-China Diplomacy, 1954–1973*
204. Guanhua Wang, *In Search of Justice: The 1905–1906 Chinese Anti-American Boycott*
205. David Schaberg, *A Patterned Past: Form and Thought in Early Chinese Historiography*
206. Christine Yano, *Tears of Longing: Nostalgia and the Nation in Japanese Popular Song*
207. Milena Doleželová-Velingerová and Oldřich Král, with Graham Sanders, eds., *The Appropriation of Cultural Capital: China's May Fourth Project*
208. Robert N. Huey, *The Making of 'Shinkokinshū'*
209. Lee Butler, *Emperor and Aristocracy in Japan, 1467–1680: Resilience and Renewal*
210. Suzanne Ogden, *Inklings of Democracy in China*
211. Kenneth J. Ruoff, *The People's Emperor: Democracy and the Japanese Monarchy, 1945–1995*
212. Haun Saussy, *Great Walls of Discourse and Other Adventures in Cultural China*
213. Aviad E. Raz, *Emotions at Work: Normative Control, Organizations, and Culture in Japan and America*
214. Rebecca E. Karl and Peter Zarrow, eds., *Rethinking the 1898 Reform Period: Political and Cultural Change in Late Qing China*
215. Kevin O'Rourke, *The Book of Korean Shijo*
216. Ezra F. Vogel, ed., *The Golden Age of the U.S.-China-Japan Triangle, 1972–1989*
217. Thomas A Wilson, ed., *On Sacred Grounds: Culture, Society, Politics, and the Formation of the Cult of Confucius*
218. Donald S. Sutton, *Steps of Perfection: Exorcistic Performers and Chinese Religion in Twentieth-Century Taiwan*
219. Daqing Yang, *Technology of Empire: Telecommunications and Japanese Expansionism, 1895–1945*
220. Qianshen Bai, *Fu Shan's World: The Transformation of Chinese Calligraphy in the Seventeenth Century*
221. Paul Jakov Smith and Richard von Glahn, eds., *The Song-Yuan-Ming Transition in Chinese History*
222. Rania Huntington, *Alien Kind: Foxes and Late Imperial Chinese Narrative*
223. Jordan Sand, *House and Home in Modern Japan: Architecture, Domestic Space, and Bourgeois Culture, 1880–1930*
224. Karl Gerth, *China Made: Consumer Culture and the Creation of the Nation*

225. Xiaoshan Yang, *Metamorphosis of the Private Sphere: Gardens and Objects in Tang-Song Poetry*
226. Barbara Mittler, *A Newspaper for China? Power, Identity, and Change in Shanghai's News Media, 1872–1912*
227. Joyce A. Madancy, *The Troublesome Legacy of Commissioner Lin: The Opium Trade and Opium Suppression in Fujian Province, 1820s to 1920s*
228. John Makeham, *Transmitters and Creators: Chinese Commentators and Commentaries on the Analects*
229. Elisabeth Köll, *From Cotton Mill to Business Empire: The Emergence of Regional Enterprises in Modern China*
230. Emma Teng, *Taiwan's Imagined Geography: Chinese Colonial Travel Writing and Pictures, 1683–1895*
231. Wilt Idema and Beata Grant, *The Red Brush: Writing Women of Imperial China*
232. Eric C. Rath, *The Ethos of Noh: Actors and Their Art*
233. Elizabeth Remick, *Building Local States: China During the Republican and Post-Mao Eras*
234. Lynn Struve, ed., *The Qing Formation in World-Historical Time*
235. D. Max Moerman, *Localizing Paradise: Kumano Pilgrimage and the Religious Landscape of Premodern Japan*
236. Antonia Finnane, *Speaking of Yangzhou: A Chinese City, 1550–1850*
237. Brian Platt, *Burning and Building: Schooling and State Formation in Japan, 1750–1890*
238. Gail Bernstein, Andrew Gordon, and Kate Wildman Nakai, eds., *Public Spheres, Private Lives in Modern Japan, 1600–1950: Essays in Honor of Albert Craig*
239. Wu Hung and Katherine R. Tsiang, *Body and Face in Chinese Visual Culture*
240. Stephen Dodd, *Writing Home: Representations of the Native Place in Modern Japanese Literature*
241. David Anthony Bello, *Opium and the Limits of Empire: Drug Prohibition in the Chinese Interior, 1729–1850*
242. Hosea Hirata, *Discourses of Seduction: History, Evil, Desire, and Modern Japanese Literature*
243. Kyung Moon Hwang, *Beyond Birth: Social Status in the Emergence of Modern Korea*
244. Brian R. Dott, *Identity Reflections: Pilgrimages to Mount Tai in Late Imperial China*
245. Mark McNally, *Proving the Way: Conflict and Practice in the History of Japanese Nativism*

246. Yongping Wu, *A Political Explanation of Economic Growth: State Survival, Bureaucratic Politics, and Private Enterprises in the Making of Taiwan's Economy, 1950–1985*
247. Kyu Hyun Kim, *The Age of Visions and Arguments: Parliamentarianism and the National Public Sphere in Early Meiji Japan*
248. Zvi Ben-Dor Benite, *The Dao of Muhammad: A Cultural History of Muslims in Late Imperial China*
249. David Der-wei Wang and Shang Wei, eds., *Dynastic Crisis and Cultural Innovation: From the Late Ming to the Late Qing and Beyond*
250. Wilt L. Idema, Wai-yee Li, and Ellen Widmer, eds., *Trauma and Transcendence in Early Qing Literature*
251. Barbara Molony and Kathleen Uno, eds., *Gendering Modern Japanese History*
252. Hiroshi Aoyagi, *Islands of Eight Million Smiles: Idol Performance and Symbolic Production in Contemporary Japan*
253. Wai-yee Li, *The Readability of the Past in Early Chinese Historiography*
254. William C. Kirby, Robert S. Ross, and Gong Li, eds., *Normalization of U.S.-China Relations: An International History*
255. Ellen Gardner Nakamura, *Practical Pursuits: Takano Chōei, Takahashi Keisaku, and Western Medicine in Nineteenth-Century Japan*
256. Jonathan W. Best, *A History of the Early Korean Kingdom of Paekche, together with an annotated translation of* The Paekche Annals *of the* Samguk sagi
257. Liang Pan, *The United Nations in Japan's Foreign and Security Policymaking, 1945–1992: National Security, Party Politics, and International Status*
258. Richard Belsky, *Localities at the Center: Native Place, Space, and Power in Late Imperial Beijing*
259. Zwia Lipkin, *"Useless to the State": "Social Problems" and Social Engineering in Nationalist Nanjing, 1927–1937*
260. William O. Gardner, *Advertising Tower: Japanese Modernism and Modernity in the 1920s*
261. Stephen Owen, *The Making of Early Chinese Classical Poetry*
262. Martin J. Powers, *Pattern and Person: Ornament, Society, and Self in Classical China*
263. Anna M. Shields, *Crafting a Collection: The Cultural Contexts and Poetic Practice of the* Huajian ji 花間集 *(Collection from Among the Flowers)*
264. Stephen Owen, *The Late Tang: Chinese Poetry of the Mid-Ninth Century (827–860)*
265. Sara L. Friedman, *Intimate Politics: Marriage, the Market, and State Power in Southeastern China*

266. Patricia Buckley Ebrey and Maggie Bickford, *Emperor Huizong and Late Northern Song China: The Politics of Culture and the Culture of Politics*
267. Sophie Volpp, *Worldly Stage: Theatricality in Seventeenth-Century China*
268. Ellen Widmer, *The Beauty and the Book: Women and Fiction in Nineteenth-Century China*
269. Steven B. Miles, *The Sea of Learning: Mobility and Identity in Nineteenth-Century Guangzhou*